INTERNATIONAL CRIMINAL LAW
AND HUMAN RIGHTS

AUSTRALIA
Law Book Co.
Sydney

CANADA and USA
Carswell
Toronto

HONG KONG
Sweet & Maxwell Asia

NEW ZEALAND
Brookers
Wellington

SINGAPORE and MALAYSIA
Sweet & Maxwell Asia
Singapore and Kuala Lumpur

INTERNATIONAL CRIMINAL LAW AND HUMAN RIGHTS

FIRST EDITION

by

CLAIRE de THAN, B.A. (HONS) LL.M.
Senior Lecturer in Law, City University

and

EDWIN SHORTS, M.A.
Barrister-at-Law.
Senior Lecturer in Law,
London Metropolitan University

LONDON
SWEET & MAXWELL
2003

Published in 2003 by
Sweet & Maxwell Limited
100 Avenue Road
Swiss Cottage
London NW3 3PF
(http://www.sweetandmaxwell.co.uk)

Typeset by *J&L Composition*
Printed in Great Britain by *Ashford Colour Press Ltd*

A CIP catalogue record
for this book is available
from the British Library

ISBN 0 421 72250 9

Dedication (by Claire de Than)

For Wilma and Lawrence

Dedication (by Edwin Shorts)

This book is dedicated to Moshe and Gina Klein

ACKNOWLEDGMENTS

The authors and publishers would like to thank the following for permission to reproduce materials from publications in which they have copyright.

The European Convention for the Prevention of Torture and Inhuman or Degrading Treatment and extracts reproduced from the European Convention of Human Rights, © *Council of Europe; All rights reserved.*

Extracts reproduced with permission from 29 AJIL Supp. 443 (1935); 41 AJIL 145–51 (1947), © The American Society of International Law.

Extracts reproduced with permission of Oxford University Press from the European Journal of International Law: Vol.8 (638), 1998; Vol.5 (326), 1994.

© (2002) By the President and Fellows of Harvard College and the Harvard International Law Journal.

Extracts reproduced from Vol. 2, Women & International Human Rights Law, © Transnational Publishers, Inc.

Extracts reproduced from the All England Law Reports, reproduced by permission of Reed Elsevier (UK) Limited trading as LexisNexis UK.

Extracts reproduced with permission from McGill Law Journal: (2000) 46 McGill L.J. 217.

Material used with the kind permission of Copyright © United Nations. All rights reserved.

Extracts reproduced courtesy of © James R. McHenry III.

The Hague Convention courtesy of UNESCO.

Extracts from "Shattered Lives: Sexual Violence during the Rwandan Genocide and its Aftermath" by Binaifer Nowrojee reproduced courtesy of Human Rights Watch.

Extracts from "From the Furies of Nanking to the Eumenides of the International Criminal Court; the Evolution of Sexual Assaults as International Crimes" reproduced courtesy of PACE International Law Review.

Extracts reproduced with kind permission of ©AMS Press, Inc.

Copyright © 2003 The New York Times Co. Reprinted with permission.

PREFACE

In comparison with national legal systems, international criminal law is still in its infancy. Until fairly recently, its growth had been somewhat stunted due to the lack of an international judicial forum and the reluctance of nations to put on trial perpetrators of international crimes. At last, international criminal law is rapidly developing via empirical means and not merely through the differing theoretical concepts expounded by various legal academics and commentators.

The publication of this book emerges at a time when international criminal law and human rights are at the forefront of global legal and political interest. The main purpose of this text is to provide students, academics and other interested persons with an accessible, thorough and in-depth analysis of this complex and challenging field. In addition to using a wide variety of sources to explain the new law and the role and operation of the future court, it analyses and interprets the various challenges confronting it and assesses its future role in public international law. Even though each of the chapter headings merits an individual book in its own right, the constraints of the written material permitted for this work has meant that analyses of certain residual matters have had to be omitted in preference to the more substantive issues. However, some issues will be considered in online chapters. Each international crime is examined in a separate chapter, *e.g.* genocide, war crimes, torture, crimes against humanity. Of particular note is the up-to-date chapter on terrorism as an international crime, which has hitherto received very limited treatment in texts on international criminal law. Further, a series of chapters address the boundaries of, and relationship between, international criminal law and human rights; for example human rights violations of women as international crime, and the uneasy position of human rights in extradition and immigration law. International Criminal Law and Human Rights serves admirably as a textbook on international criminal law and the new Court, but it ranges much further than that and also provides the reader with an important and often-missed context.

Contents include: Key Concepts and Basic Definitions. Criminal jurisdiction and state immunity. State immunity. Genocide. Crimes against Humanity. War crimes. Torture. Terrorism. "Uncommon crimes". International Criminal Court for the indictment of Individuals. Women, sexual violence and international crime: a unifying example. Finally, there are a number of Appendices dealing with the more important Articles of International Conventions and Statutes.

The authors would especially like to express their profound gratitude and thanks to Professor Douwe Korff for his contribution to this book by writing the chapter on War Crimes. He successfully undertook this task on very short notice with great enthusiasm and professionalism.

In conclusion, we hope that the reader finds this particular book both beneficial and enlightening.

CONTENTS

PART ONE: GENERAL ISSUES

CONTENTS

PART 4: INDIVIDUAL HUMAN RIGHTS IN INTERNATIONAL CRIMINAL LAW

CONTENTS

APPENDICES

TABLE OF CASES

TABLE OF UK CASES

TABLE OF INTERNATIONAL CASES

TABLE OF STATUTES

TABLE OF INTERNATIONAL TREATIES
AND CONVENTIONS

PART ONE: GENERAL ISSUES

Chapter 1

KEY CONCEPTS AND BASIC DEFINITIONS

INTRODUCTION

This introductory section is part glossary, part introduction to some of the   **1–001**
issues which affect international criminal law and human rights. It may be of
particular use to readers who have little or no prior knowledge of international
law concepts. Each issue will be dealt with at various points in the book, and
there is no special significance to the order used. The second part of this chapter deals with the issue of state responsibility, with particular reference to international criminal law. The third part highlights some of the issues relating to
asylum, which will be developed further in an online chapter. There will also
be further online materials for the first section of this chapter.

"*MENS REA*" AND "*ACTUS REUS*": THE BUILDING BLOCKS OF INTERNATIONAL CRIMES

All current international crimes can be split, as in the domestic criminal law of   **1–002**
common law systems, into *actus reus* (the prohibited act or conduct) and *mens
rea* (the state of mind which must be established to have existed at the time of
the offence). At present there are no crimes of strict liability (*i.e.* crimes for
which no *mens rea* need be proved) within international criminal law. Most
relevant conventions specify the required *mens rea*, which is usually phrased in
terms of "intention" or "wilfulness". Lack of *mens rea* will also formulate a
defence, including mistake, duress or insanity; this is examined below.

Pre-ICC, the use of standards of mens rea was somewhat idiosyncratic, but
the Rome Statute has attempted to clarify and consolidate the definitions of the
crimes within its purview. It should be noted that as a consequence there are differences in the definitions of some international crimes depending on where
they are to be prosecuted, since the ICC has not always adopted any prior crime
definition, whether Convention or customary law-based, without amendment.

It should be remembered that consensus-led drafting, as evidenced in the
Rome Statute of the ICC and in the Elements of Crimes as well as in treaties
and conventions, can create uneasy compromises and difficulties of definition. The parties to the ICC Statute have hugely different domestic criminal
laws, and even within either the civil or common law tradition there is considerable variance as to the definitional elements of crimes and the meanings
of the latter concepts. Except for anecdotal evidence, we cannot know with
precision which states influenced which pieces of drafting.

Mens rea for the ICC under the Rome Statute

1–003   Article 30 of the Rome Statute provides:

> "1.   Unless otherwise provided, a person shall be criminally responsible and liable for punishment for a crime within the jurisdiction of the Court only if the material elements are committed with intent and knowledge.
>
> 2.   For the purposes of this Article, a person has intent where:
>
>> (a)   In relation to conduct, that person means to engage in the conduct;
>>
>> (b)   In relation to a consequence, that person means to cause that consequence or is aware that it will occur in the ordinary course of events.
>
> 3.   For the purposes of this Article, "knowledge" means awareness that a circumstance exists or a consequence will occur in the ordinary course of events. 'Know' and 'knowingly' shall be construed accordingly."

- Thus, awareness that a consequence will occur in the ordinary course of events, is *both* intent and knowledge.

- There is no definition of knowledge in relation to conduct.

- during PrepCom debates there was much discussion of whether the phrasing should be "intent and knowledge" or whether, for some crimes and in some circumstances, knowledge alone might be enough. Both are required in Art. 30, but it should be noted that there is a discrepancy in para.2 of the Elements of Crimes, which provides:

"As stated in Article 30, unless otherwise provided, a person shall be criminally responsible and liable for punishment for a crime within the jurisdiction of the Court only if the material elements are committed with intent and knowledge. Where no reference is made in the Elements of Crimes to a mental element for any particular conduct, consequence or circumstance listed, it is understood that the relevant mental element, *i.e.* intent, knowledge, *or both*, set out in Article 30 applies . . ."

It is hoped that such discrepancies will be corrected or explained in the early decisions of the ICC.

- Article 30 appears to use "intent" in two quite different senses: in 30(2)(a) it is close to voluntariness or volition, and in 30(2)(b) it is closer to "purpose". Thus, if this analysis is agreed by the court in future cases, conduct must be voluntary and its consequences must be sought by the defendant. According to para. 3 of the Elements of Crimes. "Existence of intent and knowledge may be inferred from the relevant facts and circumstances."

- It should be noted that in some of the Statute's provisions, the word "intentionally" appears, in addition to the general base-line Art. 30 requirement for "intent and knowledge". For examples, see Chapter

6. There are also various other mental state-related words in this chapter, *e.g.* "calculated", "wanton", and "wilful": these are not defined in the General Part of the Statute, which could have caused considerable problems for the court. However, many of them were dealt with in the Elements of Crimes, and some of these terms do additionally have relatively undisputed definitions and case law elsewhere in international criminal law (treaties, conventions, ICTY and ICTR, for example) which may minimise the difficulty.

- Negligence is not enough *mens rea* for liability under the Statute, although some parts of the Elements of Crimes seem to be capable of interpretation in that sense.

- Although recklessness as a mental state was dropped at the Rome Conference for the ICC crimes, it does in fact make an appearance in Art. 28 in the context of military responsibility.

AGE OF CRIMINAL RESPONSIBILITY

Article 26 provides that the court shall have no jurisdiction over any person **1–004** who was under the age of eighteen at the time of the alleged commission of the offence.

This rule can be compared to the huge variance of ages in national legal systems and the difference between those countries which require more evidence of blameworthiness when the defendant is child, and those which (including the UK) do not.

OMISSIONS AND CONDUCT

The Rome Conference failed to draft an Article concerning "the physical **1–005** element" of crimes, although there was majority agreement that there could be liability for omissions in some situations. The problem related to the level of culpability which should be required before an omission could trigger liability. It was therefore decided that the ICC should develop case law to deal with this issue; at present there is in general nothing to prevent a person being liable for failing to act, with a prohibited consequence falling within one of the crimes.

CAUSATION

Before the Rome Conference, the 1996 Compilation of Proposals contained **1–006** a draft paragraph on causation which hinted that accountability for an international crime was more than a simple question of factual causation of the prohibited harm, committed with the appropriate mental element. This proposal was dropped before the Rome Conference and so this another issue which will be determined by case law.

DOUBLE JEOPARDY/*NE BIS IN IDEM*

1–007 It is a basic legal principle that a person should not be tried twice for the same crime or, more accurately, that a person should not be submitted to repeated prosecution in relation to the same conduct, whether in the same jurisdiction or different ones. Both ICTY and ICTR prohibit the trial of a person before either of those tribunals if he has previously stood trial in a national court.

However there are exceptions for cases where the national court proceedings were not independent or impartial; where the national court trial was for a non-international crime, *i.e.* a minor offence rather than one such as murder; where the original trial was an artifice for the prevention of an international crime trial; or where the case was not prosecuted diligently. Further, if a person being sentenced by ICTY or ICTR has stood trial in a national court for the same conduct, then this shall be taken into account in the sentence he receives. Once tried by an international tribunal or court, a person cannot be tried in a national court in relation to the same conduct. However, both ICTY and ICTR allow prosecution appeals against acquittal, which common law orthodoxy would consider to be a violation of double jeopardy principles. For example, in *Tadic* the Trial Chamber's decision to acquit was reversed by the Appeals Chamber.

1–008 The ICC Statute also provides in Art. 20 that:

> "1. Except as provided by this Statute, no person shall be tried before the Court with respect to conduct which formed the basis of crimes for which the person has been convicted or acquitted by the Court.
> 2. No person shall be tried by another court for a crime referred to in Article 5 for which that person has already been convicted or acquitted by the Court.
> 3. No person who has been tried by another court for conduct also proscribed under Articles 6, 7 or 8 shall be tried by the Court with respect to the same conduct unless the proceedings in the other court:
>
>   (a) were for the purpose of shielding the person concerned from criminal responsibility for crimes within the jurisdiction of the Court; or
>   (b) otherwise were not conducted independently or impartially in accordance with the norms of due process recognised by international law and were conducted in a manner which, in the circumstances, was inconsistent with an intent to bring the person concerned to justice."

A related issue is that of cumulative charging; *i.e.* that a person may be charged with several international criminal offences in relation to the same conduct when this is possible on the facts. In *Akayesu*, ICTR held that this was justifiable in three situations:

> "(1) where the offences have different elements; or
> (2) where the provisions creating the offences protect different interests; or
> (3) where it is necessary to record a conviction for both offences in order fully to describe what the accused did."

"However, . . . it is not justifiable to convict an accused of two offences in relation to the same set of facts where

(a) one offence is a lesser included offence of the other, for example, murder and grievous bodily harm, robbery and theft, or rape and indecent assault; or

(b) where one offence charges accomplice liability and the other offence charges liability as a principal, *e.g.* genocide and complicity in genocide." (para. 468)

This issue and its implications are discussed in detail in later chapters in relation to specific offences.

ACCOMPLICES/JOINT ENTERPRISE

Most international crimes involve the actions or consent of more than one **1–009** person; the scale and circumstances of most dictate this. Similar rules have developed in relation to accessory liability in international criminal law to those in existence in most national legal systems. A person who becomes involved in any respect in a crime committed by another may be held responsible for the actions of the other, regardless of whether the principal offender is caught or punished. If a person takes an active part in a crime with another, he may also be charged as a co-perpetrator, on a basis similar to that of joint enterprise in common law criminal justice systems.

Using the example of accomplice to torture: to distinguish a co-perpetrator from an aider or abettor, "it is crucial to ascertain whether the individual who takes part in the torture process also partakes of the purpose behind torture (that is, acts with the intention of obtaining information or a confession, of punishing, intimidating, humiliating or coercing the victim or a third person, or of discriminating, on any ground, against the victim or a third person." (Trial Chamber, *Furundzija*) To be convicted as a co-perpetrator, the accused "must participate in an integral part of the torture and partake of the purpose behind the torture, that is the intent to obtain information or a confession, to punish or intimidate, humiliate, coerce or discriminate against the victim or a third person." There is no requirement for the "common purpose" or plan to have been previously arranged or formulated: it may have arisen spontaneously "and may be inferred from the fact that a plurality of persons acts in unison to put into effect a joint criminal enterprise." (*Tadic* Appeal judgment, para. 227)

"Where the act of one accused contributes to the purpose of the other, and both acted simultaneously, in the same place and within full view of each other, over a prolonged period of time, the argument that there was no common purpose is plainly unsustainable." (*Furundzija* Appeal judgment, para. 120).

An accomplice, usually an aider (who renders assistance to the principal offender) or abettor (who encourages the principal and is present at the scene of the crime), need not have such a common purpose. According to the Appeal Chamber in *Tadic*:

> "... (ii) In the case of aiding and abetting no proof is required of the existence of a common concerted plan, let alone of the pre-existence of such a plan. No plan or agreement is required: indeed, the principal may not even know about the accomplice's contribution.
>
> (iii) The aider and abettor carries out acts specifically directed to assist, encourage or lend moral support to the perpetration of a certain specific crime ... and this support has a substantial effect upon the perpetration of the crime. By contrast, in the case of acting in pursuance of a common purpose or design, it is sufficient for the participant to perform acts that in some way are directed to the furthering of the common plan or purpose.
>
> (iv) In the case of aiding and abetting, the requisite mental element is knowledge that the acts performed by the aider and abettor assist the commission of a specific crime by the principal."

1–010   Article 25 of the ICC Statute provides for the criminal responsibility of both the above forms of accessory liability:

> "3.   In accordance with this Statute, a person shall be criminally responsible and liable for punishment for a crime within the jurisdiction of the Court if that person:
>
> (a)   Commits such a crime, whether as an individual, jointly with another or through another person, regardless of whether that other person is criminally responsible;
>
> (b)   Orders, solicits or induces the commission of such a crime which in fact occurs or is attempted; [this encompasses procuring and counselling as forms of accessory liability]
>
> (c)   For the purpose of facilitating the commission of such a crime. Aids, abets or otherwise assists in its commission or its attempted commission, including providing the means for its commission;
>
> (d)   In any other way contributes to the commission or attempted commission of such a crime by a group of persons acting with a common purpose. Such contribution shall be intentional and shall either:
>
> > (i)   Be made with the aim of furthering the criminal activity or criminal purpose of the group, where such activity or purpose involves the commission of a crime within the jurisdiction of the Court; or
> >
> > (ii) Be made in the knowledge of the intention of the group to commit the crime. . . ."

This Article has been applied by the ad hoc tribunals already, as in the case of *Blaskic*.

INCHOATES

1–011 Inchoate offences are a form of liability designed to cover situations where a full criminal offence has not yet been committed but was suggested (incitement), agreed to (conspiracy) or begun but not completed (attempt). Generally it does not matter for inchoate liability whether a full offence was possible on the facts of the case. Article 25(3) of the ICC Statute provides for criminal responsibility of a person who:

> "(e) In respect of the crime of genocide, directly and publicly incites others to commits genocide;
> (f) Attempts to commit such a crime by taking action that commences its execution by means of a substantial step, but the crime does not occur because of circumstances independent of the person's intentions. However, a person who abandons the effort to commit the crime or otherwise prevents the completion of the crime shall not be liable for punishment under this Statute for the attempt to commit that crime if that person completely and voluntarily gave up the criminal purpose."

Thus the ICC does not have jurisdiction over conspiracy to commit genocide, unlike ICTY and ICTR. This difference is due to disagreements at Rome about whether conspiracy should be viewed as an inchoate offence of a form of accessory liability. A conspiracy could be made to fit within accessory liability under Art. 25(3)(d).

The scope of liability for inchoate offences is thus limited under the ICC Statute, and far narrower than in national criminal laws. Only incitement to genocide and not to other offences is punishable under international criminal law. Conspiracy to commit offences other than genocide existed under the Nuremberg and Tokyo Charters but has not been on the agenda at ICTY or ICTR. It may well be the case that Art. 25(3)(d) of the ICC will be interpreted to provide a more expansive set of inchoate offences since there is in principle no reason why conspiracy to commit other international crimes should only attract liability in national courts. A notable departure from previous tribunals is to be found in respect of Art. 25(3)(f) of the ICC, which provides for criminal responsibility for those who attempt to commit any of the crimes within the court's jurisdiction. ICTY and ICTR only have liability for attempted genocide. These discrepancies are largely due to the fact that the *ad hoc* tribunals' Statutes were based on existing customary international law and Conventions, and then the only specific relevant reference to attempt as an offence was in the Genocide Convention.

IUS COGENS

Not all international crimes are equal; some have a higher status through recognition that they form part of the *"ius cogens"*, *i.e.* the "compelling law". Basically, *ius cogens* rules or norms of international law are those viewed as the most important of all, from which no derogation is possible, and which are binding on all states and/or persons regardless of their consent:

1–012

"that is, a norm that enjoys a higher rank in the international hierarchy than treaty law and even 'ordinary' customary rules. The most conspicuous consequence of this higher rank is that the principle at issue cannot be derogated from by States through international treaties or local or special customs or even general customary rules not endowed with the same normative force." (*Furundzija* judgment at 153)

Further, the status gives rise to the obligation for a state to either punish or extradite (*aut punire aut dedere*) a person who violates that norm; and on that basis universal jurisdiction for such violations is justified.

Sadly, there is no agreement as to which rules of international law reach the level of *ius cogens*, nor as to the precise consequences of attaining that standard. The following crimes are generally agreed to be ius cogens: genocide, crimes against humanity, war crimes, piracy, slavery, torture, and aggression. They have attained their *ius cogens* status because they threaten the security, peace or essential values of society as a whole and thus stand to be redressed by the international community as a matter of urgency. As a consequence of their *ius cogens* status, they constitute obligations *erga omnes* and thus create non-derogable duties. If a crime does not have that status, it will merely give states the power or right to proceed against its perpetrators without any obligation to do so.

ERGA OMNES OBLIGATIONS

1–013   These are "obligations owed towards all other members of the international community, each of which then has a correlative right ... the violation of such an obligation simultaneously constitutes a breach of the correlative right of all members of the international community and gives rise to a claim for compliance accruing to each and every member, which then has the right to insist on fulfilment of the obligation or in any case to call for the breach to be discontinued." (*Furundzija* judgment, para. 151).

DEFENCES

1–014   There were no complete defences permitted under the Nuremberg Charter, nor the ICTY or ICTR Statutes. However, superior orders could be a factor which mitigates sentence in all three tribunals; and the Rules of Procedure and Evidence of ICTY and ICTR allow the raising of "any special defence, including that of diminished or lack of metal responsibility" (Art. 67(A)(ii)). The full range of the defences common to national criminal law may in practice be raised in the *ad hoc* tribunals. Articles 31 and 32 of the ICC Statute create the first list of available defences in an international criminal tribunal: mental disease or defect; intoxication; self-defence; duress; "other grounds deriving from applicable law as set forth in Article 21"; and mistake negating *mens rea*. Some detail on each of the defences recognised by the ICC is worthwhile.

Duress

According to Art. 31(1)(d), duress is a defence where: 1–015

> "the conduct which is alleged to constitute a crime within the jurisdiction of the court has been caused by duress resulting from a threat of imminent death or of continuing or imminent serious bodily harm against that person or another person, and the person acts necessarily and reasonably to avoid this threat, provided that the person does not intend to cause a greater harm than the one sought to be avoided. Such a threat may either be:
>
> (i)   made by other persons; or
> (ii) constituted by other circumstances beyond that person's control."

Necessity

It should be noted that the ICC definition of duress encompasses a necessity   1–016
defence, or so-called "duress of circumstances", although it is hard to see circumstances existing which required the commission of an international crime without threats being made by a person to the perpetrator.

Self defence/defence of another/property

Article 31(1)(c) allows self defence/prevention of crime to be argued where: 1–017

> "the person acts reasonably to defend himself or herself or another person or, in the case of war crimes, property which is essential for the survival of the person or another person or property which is essential for accomplishing a military mission, against an imminent and unlawful use of force in a manner proportionate to the degree of danger to the person or the other person or property protected. The fact that the person was involved in a defensive operation conducted by forces shall not in itself constitute a ground for excluding criminal responsibility . . ."

Consent

It should briefly be noted that, unlike in most national criminal laws, consent   1–018
or belief in consent does not form a defence to sexual offences under the ICC Statute or the rulings of ICTY and ICTR. See Chapter 12 for detailed consideration of this matter.

Incapacity/insanity

> ". . . a person shall not be criminally responsible if, at the time of that person's   1–019
> conduct:
>
> (a)   the person suffers from a mental disease or defect that destroys his or her capacity to appreciate the unlawfulness or nature of his or her conduct, or capacity to control his or her conduct to conform to the requirements of law." (Art. 31(1)(a) of the ICC).

11

Unusually for both national and international criminal law, this defence provides a complete defence for a person suffering from diminished responsibility, not just for those qualifying for the narrower defence of insanity.

Intoxication

1–020   Intoxication may form a defence to the extent that it destroys his "capacity to appreciate the unlawfulness or nature of his or her conduct, or capacity to control his or her conduct to conform to the requirements of law." (Art. 31(1)(b) of the ICC). However, it will be no defence where the perpetrator is intoxicated of his own volition and "knew, or disregarded the risk, that, as a result of the intoxication, he or she was likely to engage in conduct constituting a crime within the jurisdiction of the Court".

Mistake

1–021   Article 32 provides:

> "1.   A mistake of fact shall be a ground for excluding criminal liability only if it negatives the mental element required by the crime.
> 2.   A mistake of law as to whether a particular type of conduct is a crime within the jurisdiction of the Court shall not be a ground for excluding criminal responsibility. A mistake of law may, however, be a ground for excluding criminal responsibility if it negates the mental element required by such a crime, or as provided for in Article 33." (*i.e.* under the defence of superior orders where the defendant did not know that an order was unlawful and it was "manifestly unlawful".)

RELATIONSHIP BETWEEN INTERNATIONAL CRIMINAL LAW AND HUMAN RIGHTS

1–022   As will be seen throughout this book, there is clear, visible cross-pollination and cross-referencing between international criminal law, international humanitarian law and international human rights, the first and last of which are really different perspectives on the same problem. The ICTY and ICTR judgments expressly refer to human rights cases and Conventions. For example, in *Furundzija*'s appeal, both sides and the Appeal Chamber made repeated reference to the ECHR and in particular to the case law on the Art. 6 right to a fair hearing, with its entwined more specific obligations.

The ICC Statute implicitly recognises this in several places, including the requirement in Art. 36 that candidates to be judges should have established competence in criminal law and procedure, or in "relevant areas of international law and international humanitarian law and the law of human rights . . .", albeit with a higher proportion of judges drawn from the criminal law background. Thus, if a human rights treaty or humanitarian law treaty includes a penal provision directed at individual accountability, then obviously such treaty overlaps with international criminal law. But international criminal law does not incorporate most of international humanitarian law or international human rights law.

It must be noted that international humanitarian law is an amalgam of state responsibility and individual criminal liability. Most of international humanitarian law cannot be prosecuted against an individual in a court of law. Much of it focuses on state practice in armed conflicts, not on the criminalization of specific acts for individual perpetrators. The 1949 Geneva Conventions, which shield from the ravages of warfare four categories of protected persons — wounded and sick combatants on land, wounded and sick combatants at sea, prisoners of war, and civilians under the control of a foreign state, only criminalise "grave breaches."

INTERNATIONAL CRIME/INTERNATIONAL CRIMINAL LAW

An international crime is an act which the international community recog- **1–023** nises as not only a violation of ordinary State criminal law but one which is so serious that it must be regarded as a matter for international concern; further, for one of a variety of reasons, it cannot be left to the State which would normally have jurisdiction over it. Such reasons include efficiency, practicality, and fears about the likelihood of prosecution by the state with jurisdiction. Almost all international crimes also qualify as serious human rights violations and many as violations of international humanitarian law, a factor which has done little to assist the clarity of principles or boundaries of international criminal law.

The list of international crimes is fast expanding and this process has been gaining in speed since the 1940s, but there is still disagreement as to its precise contents. Many authors argue that a crime is not an international crime unless it may be prosecuted in an international criminal tribunal whether permanent or *ad hoc* (at the time of writing, ICTY, ICTR and the ICC) but that definition would exclude some of the oldest international crimes with the most accepted status, including piracy. It is submitted therefore that such a definition is only a helpful starting point. Each international crime has its source in an international treaty/convention, a rule of customary international law, or a combination of the two. The former tend to be very specific and a response to a particular perceived crisis (genocide, hijack, torture, etc.) whereas customary international law is amorphous and elusive, yet far more flexible.

The definition of international criminal law is still difficult to formulate; only recently has it become possible to identify an international criminal legal system, and it remains a somewhat primitive one. The existence of the International Criminal Court will in time add sophistication to that system but it still lacks comprehensive penal sanctions, a centralised law enforcement agency or strategy, and universal agreement as to the scope of its offences. Even once the ICC has been functioning for many years, international criminal law will still require a third party, states, to enforce it through their domestic courts. Further, the scope of international criminal law will always evolve to meet new needs and priorities of the international community, both through treaties and through the development of new rules of customary international law. Such future developments are understandably almost impossible to predict. However any legal system, whatever its size and scope, requires some basic rules, principles, concepts and procedures; these could be discerned within international criminal law even before the ICC existed, with great input from ICTY and ICTR. What is lacking is a comprehensive nature, consistency of approach and interpretation.

BURDEN OF PROOF

1–024　In *Furundzija*'s appeal of March 2000 he argued unsuccessfully that the burden of proof in international criminal law was that "the evidence must be so overwhelming that it excludes every fair or rational hypothesis except that of guilt"... "the Trial Chamber was unreasonable in concluding that the only fair or rational hypothesis that could be derived from the evidence is that Mr Furundzija is guilty." Under the ICC Statute AA67(1)(i) the burden of proof cannot be reversed. It is usually stated that the Prosecution must prove its case 'beyond all reasonable doubt'.

APPEALS

1–025　Article 25(1)(b) of the ICTY Statute states that not every error of fact will cause the Appeals Chamber to overturn a decision of the Trial Chamber, only one which has led to a miscarriage of justice. The Appeals Chamber in the *Tadic* case (July 15, 1999) stated authoritatively:

> "the task of hearing, assessing and weighing the evidence presented at trial is left to the judges sitting in a Trial Chamber. Therefore, the Appeals Chamber must give a margin of deference to a finding of fact reached by a Trial Chamber. It is only where the evidence relied upon by the Trial Chamber could not reasonably have been accepted by any reasonable person that the Appeals Chamber can substitute its own finding for that of the Trial Chamber. It is important to note that two judges, both acting reasonably, can come to different conclusions on the basis of the same evidence." (para. 64)

Since the Trial Chamber has the opportunity to examine witnesses first-hand, it is better placed to assess the credibility and reliability of the evidence.

ARMED CONFLICT

1–026　In *Tadic*, the tribunal found that "an armed conflict exists whenever there is a resort to armed force between States or protracted armed violence between governmental authorities and organised armed groups or between such groups within a State."

STATE RESPONSIBILITY

Since the earliest times of "modern" international law, states have accepted   **1–027**
to a greater, or sometimes lesser degree, their commitments made *via* treaties
with other States as well as their responsibilities under customary international law. Such obligations have, in the past, been adhered to from purely
self-interest motives or from fear of the possible peaceful or non-peaceful
consequences of the alternative. Nevertheless, it is universally accepted that
States have various non-derogable responsibilities not only to other States,
but in certain circumstances, to the world at large. This is especially true in
the areas of international criminal law and human rights.

The doctrine of State responsibility is in itself a very broad and vaguely
defined concept. In simple terms it can be said that State responsibility
concerns the violation, *via* a wrongful act or omission, by a State of an international obligation that is owed to another State or States. The use of the
word "obligation" in this sense refers to both treaty and customary international law. Breaches of such obligations by a State give rise to that State's
responsibility and the consequences that flow therefrom.

State responsibility emanates from the conduct of the individual. But, do
the wrongful acts of States include both civil and criminal acts? Whereas
individual criminal responsibility has made great strides in recent times in
international law with the creation of the ICTY, ICTR and the establishment of the ICC, the same, sadly, cannot be said in the area of State responsibility. The notion that a State can be criminally liable has never been
universally accepted. After all, how is it possible to "punish" a State collectively for its illegal conduct? It is one thing to impose different forms of
sanctions against a State, it is quite another to instigate some criminal
penalty against the offending State. At the Second Reading of the Draft
Articles in 2001 (discussed below) a loose compromise was reached whereby
the International Law Commission settled on the words "a serious breach
under a peremptory norm of general international law" to allow for international "core" crimes to be part of the responsibility of a State. The resulting consequences of such a breach remain the civil remedies as stated in the
draft Articles on responsibility of States for internationally wrongful acts
(adopted by the International Law Commission at its 53rd session in 2001).

In 1949, at the request of the General Assembly, the International Law   **1–028**
Commission ("ILC") set about the task of working on the codification of the
principles of international law in relation to State responsibility. The whole
process of working on the draft Articles has taken some 46 years, from the
first session in 1955 to the 53rd session in 2001, and is a continuing one. The following is a brief discussion on the proposed draft Articles, with the emphasis being placed on those Articles which are considered to be especially
relevant to the areas of international criminal law and human rights.

There are 59 draft Articles in total, containing the following four parts;
Part One — The Internationally Wrongful Act of a State; Part Two —

Content of the International Responsibility of a State; Part Three — The Implementation of the International Responsibility of a State; Part Four — General Provisions. The "Commentaries to the Draft Articles" neatly summarise the principles behind the said Articles in the following words:

> "These articles seek to formulate, by way of codification and progressive development, the basic rules of international law concerning the responsibility of States for their internationally wrongful acts. The emphasis is on the *secondary rules* of State responsibility: that is to say, the general conditions under international law for the State to be considered responsible for wrongful acts or omissions, and the legal consequences which flow therefrom. The articles do not attempt to define the content of the international obligations breach of which gives rise to responsibility. This is the function of the *primary rules*, whose codification would involve restating most of substantive international law, customary and conventional" (at p. 59 — italics added)

Thus, the draft Articles themselves are not concerned with restating or developing existing international customary or treaty law *per se*, but rather highlight the conditions whereby a wrongful act has been committed by a State, and the resulting consequences of such an act.

Part 1 — Wrongful acts of a State

1–029 Draft Arts 1–27 are sub-divided into five chapters, consisting of the following: general principles, attribution of conduct of a State, breach of an international obligation, responsibility of a State towards another State, and circumstances precluding wrongfulness.

1–030 *General principles* Article 1 of the Draft Articles states that "[E]very internationally wrongful act of a State entails the internationally responsibility of that State". The words "wrongful acts" include both civil and criminal acts. Nowhere in the present draft Articles is the word "crime" mentioned or any derivation of the word. This position differs from what had been previously agreed by the ILC in 1976 by former draft Art. 19 which differentiated between "international crimes" and "delicts" (for further discussion see draft Art. 40). After much debate in 1998, the ILC decided to abandon the distinction for the time being, and hence wrongful acts includes both categories. The words "internationally responsibility" refer not only to wrongful acts in breach of international obligations committed by one State against another, but also may encompass those wrongful acts committed by a State or States which effect the entire or, at least, a substantial section of the international community.

Draft Art. 2 sets out the conditions upon which a State *via* an act or omission may be held responsible. It must be shown that the wrongful conduct "(a) Is attributable to the State under international law; and (b) Constitutes a breach of an international obligation of the State". Where a specific act is designated wrong under international law it matters not that the internal law of a State considers such an act legal, *i.e.* international law takes precedent in these circumstances (see draft Art. 32).

Attribution of conduct to a State In draft Art. 2(a) above for the act or **1–031** omission to be "attributable to the State" it must be shown that those persons were acting on behalf of that State. Is it a prerequisite that only State officials or government personnel come within the remit of persons recognised as committing wrongful acts or may private individuals also fall with such a category?

Draft Arts 4–7 relate to those persons who, in some way, are attached to State officialdom and are "empowered to exercise elements of the governmental authority". For instance, draft Art. 4 states that any State organ, be it legislative, executive, judicial or any other person who exercises authority on behalf of that State comes within the "attributable" perimeters for the purposes of State responsibility. It makes no difference the level of office held by the particular individual. However, other persons who are not organs of the State, but who nevertheless are "empowered by the law of that State to exercise elements of the governmental authority shall be considered an act of the State under international law, provided the person or entity is acting in that capacity in the particular instance." (draft Art. 5).

For example, in the case of *United States Diplomatic and Consular Staff in Tehran* (ICJ Reports 1980, 3), Iranian militants in 1979 forcibly took control of the US Embassy in Tehran and held 52 US citizens hostage. The US complained and the International Court of Justice ("ICJ") declared that Iran had violated various international treaties, including the 1961 and 1963 Vienna Conventions on Diplomatic and Consular Relations. In relation to State responsibility, the ICJ ruled that there was insufficient evidence to prove that the attack was officially authorised by the Iranian government, despite the fact that the authorities did not take action against the perpetrators or persuade them to release the hostages. Indeed, it has been argued that through the Ayatollah Khomeini's anti-US speeches, he encouraged acts which might put pressure on the US into returning the Shah, who was at that time receiving medical treatment in the US. The ICJ declared that Iran had certain responsibilities and obligations under international law, and especially under the Vienna Conventions, to safeguard the protection of US Embassy officials. The ICJ found that with regard to the attack itself, the Iranian authorities did not: (a) take appropriate measures to protect the premises or staff; (b) did not take steps to prevent the attack; (c) once the attack commenced, did not stop it; or (d) were negligent in their conduct as to the above, or remained inactive regarding (a), (b) and (c), above. As a result, Iran was in violation of the 1961 and 1963 Vienna Conventions. In relation to the events after the attack, the ICJ found that the Iranian authorities failed to take proper steps to: (i) bring the siege to a speedy end; (ii) restore the Embassy to US control; (iii) re-establish the *status quo*; and (iv) offer reparation for the damage caused. Indeed, the Iranian government seemed not to opose the action taken by the militants, and the Ayatollah Khomeini stated that "those people who hatched plots against

17

our Islamic movement in that place (the Embassy) do not enjoy international diplomatic respect". He went on to say that the hostages would remain there until the Shah was returned and his property handed back to Iran. The ICJ declared that by their actions the militants became agents of the State for these purposes and for which the Iranian government was internationally responsible. Iran's decision not to participate in the proceedings was found to be a violation of the Vienna Conventions, as well as general international law. The ICJ decided that Iran must: (a) immediately redress the situation; (b) release all hostages; (c) return control of the Embassy to the US; and (d) make full reparation. Iran did not comply with the ICJ's judgment. The hostages were eventually released in 1981.

1–032   It is irrelevant how the act by the organ, person or entity was carried out; even if the authority was exceeded or the person involved contravened instructions the State will ultimately still be responsible (see draft Art. 7). Therefore, persons whose actions are outside of their official status would probably not be considered as imputable to the State. This is so, even where the State itself is not at fault, *i.e.* objective responsibility, as opposed to subjective responsibility where some kind of fault, be it recklessness or negligence is necessary. For example, in the *Caire Case* (*France v Mexico*) — (UNRIAA Reports of International Arbitral Awards (1929) Vol. 5 516 at para. 531) the claimant, a French national, was shot dead by two Mexican officers during a revolution which took place in that State. One of the main issues was whether the State still remained responsible for the conduct of those soldiers who acted independently, and in breach of their instructions and orders from their commanding officers. The Commission stated that the State was "responsible for all the acts committed by its officials or organs which constitute criminal acts from the point of view of the law of nations, no matter if the official or organ in question has acted within or exceeded the limits of his competence". Thus, once the soldiers appeared to have acted as competent officials and acted in their capacity as members of the armed forces, then their actions, legal or otherwise, were considered to be imputed to the State. Draft Art. 7 would appear to be narrower in its scope than certain cases involving individual criminal responsibility. For instance, under international humanitarian law, the crime of torture may be committed by private persons, thus not allowing the perpetrator to escape the legal net for such conduct.

An act of State may be committed by nationals of another State provided the latter State grants authority for those persons to be put at the disposal of the former State (see draft Art. 6). In which case the conduct of such persons is directly attributed to the former State. In other words, once those persons are no longer under the direction and control of the sending State, it is the receiving State which bears the burden of responsibility for any breach of their obligations under international law.

1–033   *Acts of private persons attributed to the State* As a general rule, State responsibility does not include acts committed by private persons or entities. How-

18

ever, draft Arts 8–11 do deal with persons who although not possessing any official status may nevertheless commit wrongful acts which are attributable to the State. For instance, being instructed by or under the direction or control of that State in carrying out certain acts (see draft Art. 8). Thus, although some classes of persons who are not directly affiliated in some way to a State organ may still commit acts contrary to international law, for which the relevant State is responsible, that State will not be responsible for the acts of a private person in the absence of some element of government authorisation.

The question then becomes how much direction or control must the State possess before it can be said that the particular conduct can be imputed to that State. In the case of *Nicaragua v United States, Merits* (ICJ Reports (1986) 14), the United States sent aid to the *Contras* to assist them to overthrow the Nicaraguan government. The Nicaraguan government alleged that the United States had planted mines in its territorial waters and damaged its ships, in violation of international law by using force in its domestic affairs. One of the major issues to be decided was whether the activities carried out by the *Contras* were attributable to the United States. Nicaragua maintained that "the *Contras* are no more than bands of mercenaries which have been recruited, paid and commanded by the Government of the United States. This would mean that they have no real autonomy in relation to that Government" (para. 114). Accordingly, any acts committed by them ought to be imputed to the US. However, the court took the view that "financing, organizing, training, supplying and equipping of the *Contras,* the selection of its military or paramilitary targets, and the planning of the whole of its operation, is still insufficient in itself, on the basis of the evidence in the possession of the court" (para. 115), do not by themselves attribute the acts of the *Contras* to the United States. The court went on to state that the above acts could have been committed without the control of the United States. For the United States to be held legally responsible, it must have had "effective control of the military or paramilitary operations". Accordingly, since the court found no such control existed in these circumstances, it could not be said that the acts of the *Contras* could be attributed to the US.

A similar issue arose in the *Tadic* case, in connection with the degree of control that the Yugoslav authorities must have over the Bosnian Serb forces in order for the particular hostilities to be classified as an international conflict. The test applied in that case was one of "overall control" which involved more than just financial support and the supply of armoury and other military equipment, but also required involvement in the planning and supervision of military operations in that territory. It has been suggested that the "effective control" in the *Nicaraguan* case remains relevant to State responsibility since the "overall control" test in *Tadic* is restricted to cases of individual criminal responsibility. Although the "overall control" test appears narrower, in practice, where the relevant court considers all the facts of a particular scenario, the difference between the two tests may, in practice, turn out to be negligible.

1–034   Draft Arts 4–8 deal with situations where the State itself is connected through government authorisation in some way with the wrongful acts of the individual, organ or entity. However, even where there is no nexus between the government and the person or persons committing the wrongful act, their conduct may, under certain circumstances, still be attributed to the State where such persons take on governmental tasks without the express or implied authority of the State to carry out such a role. Draft Art. 9 states that "[T]he conduct of a person or group of persons shall be considered an act of a State under international law if the person or group of persons is in fact exercising elements of the government authority in the absence or default of the official authorities and in circumstances such as to call for the exercise of those elements of authority". In these circumstances private individuals are in fact taking on some of the functions of a government authority, but without the permission of the State to do so. The Commentaries to the Draft Articles give examples of such rare cases, "such as during revolution, armed conflict or foreign occupation, where the regular authorities dissolve, are dis-intergrating, have been suppressed or are for the time being inoperative. They may also cover cases where lawful authority is being gradually restored, *e.g.* after foreign occupation" (at p. 109). Recent examples of the latter might include Afghanistan and Iraq in the early days of their occupation. Unlike draft Art. 4, the acts of these particular individuals are not part of any government or even any *de facto* government. They are acting in this role as private persons performing certain public functions for the benefit of the State and its people. Where wrongful acts are committed in these limited circumstances, such conduct which amounts to a breach of a State's obligations is nevertheless attributed to that specific State.

Under draft Art. 10(1) "[T]he conduct of an insurrectional movement which becomes the new government of a State shall be considered an act of that State under international law". Thus, where an insurrection is successful and is now the new government, then the acts of those persons during the rebellion will be imputed to the present State. If the insurrection has been put down, then the authorities are not responsible for the actions of those rebels during the struggle. The same conditions hold true for the establishing of a new State in draft Art. 10(2).

As a general rule, wrongful acts committed by private persons which were, at the time, not known to or not aware of by the State are not imputable to that State. However, according to draft Art. 11 "[C]onduct which is not attributable to a State under the preceding articles shall nevertheless be considered an act of that State under international law if and to the extent that the State acknowledges and adopts the conduct in question as its own". Thus if a State acknowledges *and* adopts the act as its own after the event, then that act becomes imputed to the State. Knowledge by itself is insufficient; the State must also adopt the conduct. Thus, in the *US Diplomatic and Consular Staff in Tehran* case, above, the initial attack on the Embassy by the militants was not attributed to the Iranian government; it was only later on when, far from attempting to end the siege, the government wholeheartedly gave its approval, and thus effectively adopting and taking responsibility for the whole situation.

Breach of an international obligation Draft Arts 12–15 deal with breach by **1–035** a State of an international obligation. Draft Art. 12 sets out in very general terms the circumstances of when such a breach occurs. *i.e.* "[T]here is a breach of an international obligation by a State when an act of that State is not in conformity with what is required of it by that obligation, regardless of its origin or character". Whether such a breach has in fact occurred will require analysis on a case-by-case basis and may be the result of some act or omission by the State, or a combination of both. States may also commit internationally wrongful acts by encouraging or assisting other States to do so. Thus, under draft Art. 16 "[A] State which aids or assists another State in the commission of an internationally wrongful act by the latter is internationally responsible for doing so if: (a) that State does so with knowledge of the circumstances of the internationally wrongful act; and (b) the act would be internationally wrongful if committed by that State". Similar consequences arise under draft Art. 17 in relation to the situation where a State "directs and controls" another State into committing an internationally wrongful act. The main difference between the two draft Articles is that under draft Art. 16 the State giving the aid will only be liable for wrongful acts up to the amount of aid or assistance supplied. Whereas, under draft Art. 17 a State which directs and controls wrongful activities of another State will be adjudged liable for that whole wrongful act.

Acts not considered wrongful Certain acts are recognised as not being **1–036** wrongful for the purposes of these draft Articles. These precluding circumstances are contained in draft Arts 20–27 and include such provisions as, consent, *e.g.* one State allows another State to carry out acts in the former State (draft Art. 20); self-defence (draft Art. 21); countermeasures (draft Art. 22); *force majeure* (draft Art. 23), the meaning of which is set out in that Article as "the occurrence of an irresistible force or of an unforeseen act, beyond the control of the State, making it materially impossible in the circumstances to perform the obligation". The Commentaries to the Draft Articles state that for this particular defence to be operative "three elements must be met: (a) the act in question must be brought about by an irresistible force or an unforseen event, (b) which is beyond the control of the State concerned, and (c) which makes it materially impossible in the circumstances to perform the obligation" (at p. 183). Accordingly, the grounds on which a plea of *force majeure* would be successful are very limited. Other defences include distress (draft Art. 24), necessity (draft Art. 25), and acts arising under a peremptory norm of general international law (draft Art. 26). The case of the *Rainbow Warrior* (*New Zealand v France*) 82 I.L.R. 499 provides a good illustration of the application of the defences of *force majeure* and distress. The facts of that case were that in 1985 Greenpeace sent a number of ships into New Zealand waters where the French were conducting nuclear tests. On July 10 of that year, the French military security service using explosives destroyed the Rainbow Warrior, and one crew member was killed. Two officers from the French Directorate General of External Security were prosecuted and convicted for the offences (manslaughter and criminal damage) and were each sentenced to serve a total of ten years imprisonment. In July 1986 a treaty was entered into between the French and the New Zealand governments whereby the prisoners were to serve a minimum of three of those years on the French military base on the island of Hao. However, for medical reasons, both officers were returned to France before the minimum period expired and without the proper consent of New Zealand. On a claim before the arbitration tribunal by the New Zealand authorities, France put forward the defences of *force majeure*, distress and necessary. The tribunal in deciding whether or not the defence of *force majeure* was relevant in this case, stated that "*force majeure* was in absolute terms and applied only where circumstances rendered compliance with an international impossibility. It did not apply where, as here, circumstances merely made compliance more difficult and burdensome" (at p. 503). Even where the situation makes it *very difficult* for the State to act in conformity with its obligations, such problems will still not reach the standard required to apply *force majeure.* Accordingly, repatriation of a French officer for health reasons which did not require an immediate operation did not constitute a *force majeure.*

In relation to distress, it is not considered a wrongful act ". . . if the author of the act in question has no other reasonable way, in a situation of distress, of saving the author's life or the lives of other persons entrusted to the author's care" (draft Art. 24(1)). In the *Rainbow Warrior* case, the tribunal declared that in order for France to justify their position for "distress", *i.e.* that the taking the officers off the island was "of extreme urgency involving elementary humanitarian considerations", three conditions must be fulfilled:

(1) the existence of very exceptional circumstances of extreme urgency involving medical or other considerations;

(2) the original situation is reverted to after the emergency has subsided; and

(3) obtaining the consent of New Zealand in terms of the 1986 agreement.

After substantial medical evidence and reports were admitted, the tribunal found that there was indeed sufficient reasons for one of the officers to be repatriated to France for treatment; accordingly, this was not in breach of their obligations. However, by failing to return the officer to the island to continue his sentence, the tribunal found this to be in violation of the agreement, and a material and continuing breach of its obligations under international law; in particular under Art. 60(3) of the Vienna Convention on the Law of

Treaties 1969 which defines "a material breach" as: (a) a repudiation of the treaty not sanctioned by the present Convention; or (b) the violation of a provision essential to the accomplishment of the object or purpose of the treaty.

As regards the other officer, she was pregnant and complications had set in whereby the French authorities deemed it necessary that she be returned home (added to this was the fact that her father was dying of cancer). Without the required consent under the agreement, the French decided to repatriate her. The tribunal declared that the French committed a material breach, as defined by Art. 60(3) of the Vienna Convention, by not obtaining in good faith the consent of the New Zealand authorities to leave the island. Consequently, France had committed a material and continuing breach by failing to order her to return to the island. Although there was no claim for material damage the tribunal recommended that France and New Zealand set up a fund to promote close and friendly relations, with France making an initial contribution of $US two million.

Part 2 — Content of the international responsibility of a State

Consequences of an international wrongful act The legal consequences of an   1–037
internationally wrongful act are stipulated in draft Arts 28 to 39 and include the responsible State ceasing the wrongful act and/or offering appropriate assurances and guarantees of non-repetition, if circumstances so require (draft Art. 30) and/or making full reparation for the injury (material or moral) caused (draft Art. 31) by, for instance: (i) restitution *i.e.* placing the State in the situation it was in prior to the wrongful act, unless it is not materially possible, or to do so would be disproportionate to the benefit deriving from restitution instead of compensation (draft Art. 35); (ii) compensation (draft Art. 36) *e.g.* reparations by the German government to those Jewish families who suffered at the hands of the Nazis during the Second World War; such compensation continues today; and (iii) satisfaction — by an "acknowledgement of the breach, an expression of regret, a formal apology or another appropriate modality". (draft Art. 37)

Serious breaches of obligations under peremptory norms of general   1–038
international law Part 1 concerns internationally wrongful acts under international law and the consequences which flow from any breach thereof. However, some breaches of a State's obligations are so fundamental that any violation may well result in the concern of the entire international community, *i.e.* they are obligations which are considered to be *ergo omnes*. This is so, even where the wrongful act only involved a dispute between two States or the act was committed within the borders of one State. In such circumstances, it has been said that the international community have a legal interest, and more positively, a legal duty, in the protection of such obligations. Draft Art. 40(1) deals with serious breaches of obligations under peremptory norms of general international law, and probably comes closest to

recognising types of "international crimes" for which a State may be held responsible. Article 53 of the Vienna Convention on the Law of Treaties 1969 states that "a peremptory norm of international law is a norm accepted and recognised by the international community of States as a whole as a norm from which no derogation is permitted and which can be modified only by a subsequent norm of general international law having the same character". For example, acts of aggression, grave breaches of the Geneva Conventions and acts in breach of the Genocide Convention are considered so serious that any State responsible for committing such violations should be held accountable for such actions to the international community. Other international crimes such as torture, apartheid and slavery would also probably fall within the category of a peremptory norm under existing international law. These types of wrongful acts are considered so grave that they are non-derogable, even in times of national emergency or war, and there are no exceptions. Further, whereas wrongful acts under draft Art. 1 do not necessarily entail the mental element of intention by the offending State, a serious breach of an obligation involving an international crime, by its very definition, requires intention under both treaty and customary law. Although the present draft Articles do not mention the words "international crimes" and make no distinction between those types of acts and wrongful acts, that was not always the case. In 1976 the ILC provisionally adopted "draft Art. 19" which set out, *inter alia*, what constituted an "international crime". For example, draft Art. 19(3)(a)–(d) stated that an international crime may result from a serious breach of an international obligation of essential importance, which included the following: the right of self-determination of peoples; prohibiting aggression; prohibiting slavery, genocide and apartheid; as well as prohibiting massive pollution of the atmosphere or of the seas. However, in 1998 the ILC decided to abandon draft Art. 19 due to the inherent difficulties with the actual wording of that provision. Some members felt that the Article related to primary rules as opposed to secondary rules, and that particular problems regarding terminology were going to be difficult to overcome. For instance, what constitutes a "serious breach" and what definitions were to be given to the individual offences listed? There was also the fear that some States themselves might in the future fall foul of the offences mentioned. After much debate it was felt that including a separate Article which stipulated a special category for serious breaches of international obligations was sufficient to surmount the possible future problems encountered by "Art. 19" — hence the now substituted draft Art. 40(1). By not specifically designating draft Art. 40 as an "international crimes" provision, it can be argued that the ILC has managed to retain the ideals of the former draft Art. 19 without having to undergo the very difficult task of defining the individual offences attributed to that Article. A breach of a peremptory norm is, in itself, a serious violation, and as such, at least as far as international criminal law is concerned, the international community has an interest in ensuring that all States abide by their responsibilities. Sadly, in practice, this is not necessarily the case.

Examples, such as the genocidal acts carried out in Cambodia and Rwanda are reminders that the international community itself is very often to blame for ignoring the atrocities committed by those States against their own nationals, much less condemning or taking immediate positive action to alleviate an already volitile situation.

What constitutes a "serious breach of an obligation" is stipulated in draft Art. 40(2) as being "if it involves a gross or systematic failure by the responsible State to fulfil the obligation". Although the words "gross or systematic" are seen as disjunctive, in practice any serious breach of a peremptory norm of the examples cited above will more than likely involve both elements. Accordingly, minor infringements of an international obligation would probably not come within the bounds of this specific draft Article.

The gravity of the breach not only calls upon the international community to condemn the wrongful acts of the offending State, but also requires that that State suffer the consequences in respect of that breach. Draft Art. 41(1) requires that "States shall co-operate to bring to an end through lawful means any serious breach within the meaning of draft Art. 40", and "[N]o State shall recognise as lawful a situation created by a serious breach within the meaning of draft Art. 40, nor render aid or assistance in maintaining that situation" (draft Art. 41(2)). Unlike States that commit international wrongful acts, under draft Art. 41(1) the international community is obligated to cooperate to bring to an end the serious breach irrespective of whether or not other States have been affected by the breach. Although draft Art. 41(1) does not specify how the cooperation should be achieved, in practice States do collaborate together either collectively *via* the United Nations or as individual States, against the offending State that has violated its obligations. Usually this is done through various means such as diplomatic negotiations or sanctions or severing complete ties with the offending State, or as a last resort, the threat of the use of force. Draft Art. 41(1) generally involves some form of positive action by the international community to change the status quo, whereas under draft Art. 41(2) the international community is under a negative duty not to recognise the offending State's action, *e.g.* not to recognise the unlawful invasion of one State by another, nor to assist that State in any manner whatsoever.

Part 3 — The implementation of the international responsibility of a State

Invocation of responsibility by an injured State This particular section of the draft Articles deals with, *inter alia*, the questions of: (1) under what circumstances are States entitled to invoke the responsibility of another State in breach of its obligations; and (2) what countermeasures may a State invoke against the offending State? In relation to question (1) above, the only States that are entitled to invoke the responsibility of another State may be described as an injured State and a non-injured State identified in draft Arts 42 and 48(1)(a) and (b) respectively.   1–039

Draft Art. 42 refers to *an injured State*, "if the obligation breached is owed to: (a) that State individually; or (b) a group of States including that State, or the international community as a whole, and the breach of the obligation: (i) specifically affects that State; or (ii) is such a character as radically to change the position of all the other States to which the obligation is owed with respect to the further performance of the obligation". It matters not whether the obligation entailed a breach of a treaty that was bilateral or multilateral, or whether the responsibility involved were either unilateral or reciprocal. Draft Art. 48(1) refers to *any State other than an injured State* provided "(a) the obligation breached is owed to a group of States including that State, and is established for the protection of a collective interest of the group; or (b) the obligation breached is owed to the international community as a whole". The difference between the two types of invoking States is that in draft Art. 42 the injured State must itself have been affected by the breach. In relation to damages, the draft Articles differentiate between an injured State and any State other than the injured State. In (a) the injured State must have suffered either material, moral or legal damage. For instance, in the *Rainbow Warrior* case New Zealand did not claim material damage but did maintain that it had suffered legal damage, by being a victim of a violation of its treaty rights, as well as moral damage, by France causing deep offence to the honour, dignity and prestige of the State (82 I.L.R. 499 at 569 para. 108). The injured State must itself have been affected by the breach, and it matters not whether, for instance, the treaty was bilateral or multilateral, or whether the responsibility was unilateral or reciprocal.

On the other hand, draft Art. 48(1) deals with the situation where the State, although not injured by the breach, is entitled to invoke the responsibility of the offending State simply because the innocent State is part of a group of States which are owed the specific obligation and which involves the protection of a collective interest of the group, or obligations *erga omnes, i.e.* owed to the entire international community.

Draft Art. 48(2) sets out the limited types of claims that a State might invoke against an offending State. Under draft Art. 48(2)(a), a claimant State may seek from the responsible State "(a) cessation of the internationally wrongful act, and assurances and guarantees of non-repetition in accordance with draft Art. 30; and (b) performance of the obligation of reparation in accordance with the preceding articles, in the interest of the injured State or of the beneficiaries of the obligation breached". "Reparation" takes the same form as that set out in draft Arts 35, 36 and 37, *i.e.* restitution, compensation and satisfaction. The available remedies against the offending State are not to be considered as a form of punishment, but rather a means of encouraging the specific State to adhere to its obligations under international law. It may appear odd that since there is no injured State there can, nevertheless, be a reparation claim against another State which has breached its responsibilities. In the Commentaries to the Draft Articles it is stated that "[I]n accordance with subparagraph 2 (b), such a claim must be made in the interest of the injured State, if any, or of the beneficiaries of the obligation breached. This aspect of draft Art. 48(2) involves a measure of progressive development, which is justified since it provides a means of protecting the community or collective interest at stake. In this context it may be noted that certain provisions, for example in various human rights treaties, allow invocation of responsibility by any State party. In those cases where they have been resorted to, a clear distinction has been drawn between the capacity of the applicant State to raise the matter and the interests of the beneficiaries of the obligation. Thus, a State invoking responsibility under draft Art. 48 and claiming anything more than a declaratory remedy and cessation may be called on to establish that it is acting in the interests of the injured party". (p. 323) Moreover, where a State has been directly affected by the breach, it is akin to being an injured State within draft Art. 42 and may therefore also claim to be compensated for the breach from the State responsible. Where a number of States have been so affected, each State is entitled to make a separate claim.

Countermeasures Where the injured State has made a claim for cessation   **1–040**
and/or reparation against the responsible State for an internationally wrongful act, which has proved unsuccessful, and further negotiations fail, the former State may take alternative action *via* draft Art. 49, *i.e.* countermeasures. Countermeasures includes all paths *via* peaceful means to bring about, as far as possible, "the resumption of performance of the obligations in question" (draft Art. 49(3). Such measures may involve sanctions of various types including; embargoes, boycotts, suspension of financial aid and withdrawal of scientific and/or economic assistance and so forth. But it excludes the threat or use of force. Countermeasures may only be applied where there is the "non-performance for the time being of international obligations of the State taking the measures towards the responsible State" (draft Art. 49(2)). Their use is restricted to existing obligations by the responsible State, for instance, where the responsible State is in breach of its treaty obligation, and the injured State deems it necessary to take such action in order to persuade the offending State to resume its commitments under the treaty. Any action in these circumstances is limited and must not be disproportionate to the seriousness of the breach. It should be noted that any countermeasures are temporary in nature and under draft Art. 52(3) "must be suspended without undue delay if: (a) the intentionally wrongful act has ceased; and (b) the dispute is pending before a court or tribunal which has the authority to make decisions binding on the parties. Once the offending State has complied with its obligations under Part 2, the countermeasures must be withdrawn (draft Art. 53). Countermeasures are not restricted to a State affected by the breach and under draft Art. 54 any State entitled by draft Art. 48(1) to invoke the responsibility of another State, may "take lawful measures against that State to ensure cessation of the breach and reparation in the interest of the injured State or of the beneficiaries of the obligation breached."

Any countermeasures eventually undertaken are not unencumbered and the injured State remains committed to respect certain existing international

27

obligations, considered to be so important, that irrespective of the breach, these particular obligations must not be interfered with. Thus, according to draft Art. 50(a)–(d) "[C]ountermeasures shall not affect: (a) The obligation to refrain from the threat or use of force as embodied in the Charter of the United Nations". This is in line with Member States' obligations under Art. 2(4) of the Charter; (b) obligations for the protection of fundamental human rights. For example, the injured State must take into account the resulting possible harm on a civilian population, whose safety and welfare take precedent over any action taken; (c) obligations of a humanitarian character prohibiting reprisals; and (d) other obligations under peremptory norms of general international law. The United Nations have, in recent years applied sanctions, notably against the former State of Southern Rhodesia in 1966, South Africa in 1986 and until fairly recently, against Libya and Iraq.

In addition to the above, countermeasures are prohibited where the injured State is obligated "(a) under any dispute settlement procedure applicable between it and the responsible State; (b) to respect the inviolability of diplomatic or consular agents, premises archives and documents" (draft Art. 50(2)(a) and (b)). In (a) above the dispute settlement must be connected to the internationally wrongful act. In (b) above the main purpose behind this particular proscription is to protect the health, safety and immunity of diplomatic personnel; thus attempting to avoid a repeat of the debacle situation which occurred in the *United States Diplomatic and Consular Staff in Tehran* case in 1979.

Part 4 — General provisions

1–041 Under draft Art. 55, known as the *"lex specialis"* rule, "[T]hese articles do not apply where and to the extent that the conditions for the existence of an internationally wrongful act or the content or implementation of the internationally responsibility of a State are governed by special rules of international law".

Finally, all the above draft articles "are without prejudice to the Charter of the United Nations" (draft Art. 59). Countermeasures in the draft articles prelude the threat or use of force unless authorised by the United Nations. Such action is already proscribed under customary international law as well as universally prohibited *via* Art. 2(4) of the United Nations Charter. Under international law the use of force is legitimate in very limited circumstances, *i.e.* self defence, under Art. 51 of the United Nations Charter and where authorised by the Security Council in line with Chapter VII, where there are threats to the peace, breaches of the peace or acts of aggression. However, as far as State obligations are concerned, in recent years certain States have deviated from the wording of the Charter. Examples include the NATO bombings in Serbia and Montenegro for humanitarian reasons, but in the absence of Security Council authorisation. In April 2003 a US and British-led force attacked Iraq on the questionable grounds of self-defence in order to pre-empt a strike by Saddam Hussein's "weapons of mass destruction".

ASYLUM: VICTIMS AND PERPETRATORS, RIGHTS AND CRIMES

This section will deal with the issues related to persecution and the international human rights of victims; perpetrators will be dealt with in an update on the linked website to this book. Besides examining their respective rights, the two elements of this chapter will examine whether they, as categories, possess equal rights and whether they should have them at all.

1–042

Victims

Victims of persecution generally have a number of international rights, especially in the form of political asylum and very rarely in some form of remedy in domestic or international courts against those responsible for that persecution. Their rights are set out in two general Conventions; the UN Universal Declaration of Human Rights and the Geneva Convention relating to the Status of Refugees of 1951.

1–043

The former, more honoured in the breach than in the observance, purported to give victims some form of redress and was signed in 1945 but the machinery for its enforcement did not come into operation until 1966 and it took another 10 years for its full enforcement.

The Geneva Convention however had a more immediate impact especially in Western Europe, especially as concerns the rights of asylum seekers. The crucial Art. 1A(2) gives the generally accepted definition of a refugee:

> (A person who) owing to a well-founded fear of being persecuted for reasons of race, religion, nationality, membership of a particular social group or political opinion is outside the country of his nationality and is unable, or, owing to such fear, is unwilling to avail himself of that protection of that country: or who, not having a nationality and being outside the country of his former habitual residence as a result of such events, is unable or, owing to such fear, is unwilling to return to it.

Given the situation, especially in post-war Europe, this definition was extremely wide and might encompass villains as well as victims. Article 1F exempts from refugee status those who have:

(a) committed a crime against peace, a war crime, or a crime against humanity, as defined in the international instruments drawn up to make provision in respect of such crimes;

(b) committed a serious non-political crime outside the country of refuge prior to his admission into that country as a refugee; or

(c) been guilty of acts contrary to the purposes and principles of the United Nations.

In all the above it is for the asylum seeker to prove his case. The standard of proof varies from country to country and from time to time, as will be seen in subsequent cases.

A well-founded fear

1–044   This has an objective and a subjective limb. The subjective element of fear is self-evident but the objective element is seen as requiring convincing objective evidence not just of the past rational existence of such a fear but its continuation and the likelihood of its continuing in the future. Further, the fear must be the result of membership of one or more of the designated group. It is not sufficient to be persecuted when that appears to be the norm in the home country as would occur in a civil war or a state of political unrest. The case of *Ward v The Secretary of State for the Home Department* [1997] Imm A.R. 236, demonstrates that forcibly. Here Ward had claimed in an unsuccessful appeal for asylum that she had been tortured by the Peruvian police on suspicion of being a member of the Shining Path terrorist group. The grounds for refusal are intriguing:

> The Secretary of State considered that the problems you have faced, even if true, amounted to nothing more than the sort of random difficulties faced by many thousands of people in Peru.

This scarcely tallies with the rights of persecutors where in a very real sense the random nature of their carrying out of a policy of victimisation assists their protestations of innocence or at least immunity (see the *Pinochet* case, described above).

Further, the fear must be of current or future persecution. The test here is of *reasonable likelihood* rather than the more demanding one of *balance of probabilities* as far as English law is concerned (Kanakakaran and Kaja). This standard of proof has been approved by the European Court of Human Rights. If there has been a change of regime favourable to the Applicant then asylum will almost certainly be refused. The decision of the House of Lords in *Adan v Secretary of State for the Home Department* [*The Times*, April 6, 1998] is a good illustration. Here the applicant had fled from Somalia in June 1988, at which time his fear of persecution was well-founded. He arrived in the UK in October 1990 when he was refused asylum but granted exceptional leave to stay. He wished to have his status as an asylum seeker confirmed, since this would grant him certain rights and privileges to which he was not entitled given his existing status. He was granted asylum but the Home Secretary appealed successfully to the House of Lords on the grounds that in the interim, the Somali Government had been overthrown and replaced by one to which Mr Adan was sympathetic. Again, like many an appeal court before, the Lords administered a pointed by-blow to the effect that the Convention was in their view not worded in such a way as to admit those fleeing from a civil war to take advantage of its protection.

The febrile atmosphere of the cold war at least established the USSR and it satellites as the *prima facie* enemy. On this logic, anyone fleeing such a regime was usually accepted as a victim and a legitimate asylum seeker, even when international law required the reception country to return asylum seekers. The highwatermark of this policy was the English case of *R v Governor of Brixton Prison Ex p. Kolczynski* [1955] 1 Q.B. 450. Here the crew of a Polish trawler mutinied and sought asylum in an English port. Treaty obligations and the International Law of the Sea required the UK authorities to return the crew to Poland. Lord Goddard, in the Court of Appeal, rejected these arguments and fell back on the Common Law. In essence he said that opposition to a One Party State, would practically indemnify those who rebelled agianst it, no matter what action was taken, even in breach of a treaty. Such a blanket indulgence no longer applies, and the English courts take a far more stringent view of what constitutes "well-founded" fear.

Persecution

The next limb is: what constitutes persecution? Can prosecution ever be so   **1–045** harsh as to constitute persecution? It appears so, especially if the prosecution is based on political reasons and a fair trial would be unlikely. The original ruling by Nolan J. in *R v IAT Ex p. Jonah* 1985 Imm A.R. 7, still carries weight. He adopted the ordinary dictionary definition; "to pursue with malignancy or injurious action, especially to oppress for holding a heretical opinion or belief." This looks more helpful than it is in reality since it does not provide an answer to whether discrimination can amount to persecution. English courts have generally seen discrimination which goes to the very heart of an appellant's life in the country he is fleeing from as constituting persecution such as a right to earn one's living or to practise a religion. The EU has attempted to formulate persecution in Draft Guidelines for the Application of the Criteria for Determining Refugee Status (November 1994).

> "In order to constitute 'persecution' within the meaning of Art 1A acts must . . . constitute by their nature and/or repetition an attack on some seriousness which would render normal life in the country of origin impossible ('normality' of life must be assessed having regard to the prevailing conditions in the country)".

Who is conducting the persecution? The general rule is that the State must   **1–046** either be a party to the persecution or that it is knowingly complicit in the persecution. In the later case, those conducting the persecution are seen in English law, but not in some other EU countries as agents of the State.

Problems have arisen when asylum seekers have arrived in the UK from another EU State which is seen as "a safe third country".

Appeals have been made, particularly by those sent to France. Before the 1996 Immigration and Asylum Act special adjudicators had often held that France was not a safe third country on the grounds that asylum seekers, especially Algerians, might not have a proper opportunity to have their claims determined in accordance with French law and the 1951 Convention. This was the claim made in *R v Secretary of State for the Home Department Ex p. Canbolat* [1997] 1 W.L.R. 1569, CA. Canbolat was a Turkish Kurd who arrived in Britain from France and sought asylum on the grounds that she feared persecution in Turkey. The Home Secretary issued a deportation certificate following s.2(2) of the AIA 1996 authorising her return to France as a safe third country. After an unsuccessful attempt for leave for judicial review, the Court of Appeal found that prior to the Secretary of State sending an asylum seeker to a safe third country, he should satisfy himself that there is no real risk to the applicant in being sent there as long as his decision is reasonable. In this case it was deemed reasonable to do so because normally the French immigration courts functioned fairly and:

> "The unpredictability of human behaviour or the remote possibility of changes in administrative law or procedures which there is no reason to anticipate would not be a real risk." (Woolf MR 577 at H)

On these grounds the application was refused.

However, the House of Lords took a principled stand in *R v Secretary of State for the Home Department, Ex p. Adan* [2001] 2 W.L.R. 143, HL, where they found that if safe third countries restrict the interpretation of the Convention in such a way as "persecution" only covered conduct attributable to a State, then asylum seekers threatened with violence from Non-State bodies should not be sent there. Similarly there is a line of authority which suggests that toleration of lack of protection is sufficient to amount to persecution. The French Conseil d"Etat suggested that the test was whether the State encouraged or voluntarily tolerated any ill treatment, but the US Supreme Court took a more restrictive line requiring complicity from the state rather than inaction. The English courts have taken a even stricter line exemplified in *Ouanes v Secretary of State for the Home Department* [1998] 1 W.L.R. 218, CA. The Court of Appeal were faced with the deportation of a midwife employed by the Algerian Ministry of Health. They claimed that by giving her clients contraceptive advice, she was in danger of attack from Muslim fundamentalists sided with the Home Secretary against her. The grounds were partly based on the fact that although the Government was her employer, it could not be expected to protect her whilst she practised as a midwife.

The Convention reasons

Persecution is not enough of a reason to appeal, it must be for a Convention **1–047** reason such as; race, religion, nationality, membership of a particular social group or political opinion.

Race

This is often taken as a fundamental basis for an appeal. Existance of racial **1–048** discrimination is often taken as the basis for persecution if it affects human dignity to the extent of making it incompatible with human rights. Draft EU Guidelines have suggested a working definition:

> "persecution should be deemed to be founded on racial grounds where the persecutor regards the victim of his persecution as belonging to a racial group other than is own, by reason of a real or supposed difference, and this forms the grounds for his action."

Religion

Persecution here can take the form of either a total ban or making it so **1–049** impossible for those of a particular religion to practise it. Proselytising religions are particularly problematic. The Universal Declaration of Human Rights allows for the right to manifest a religion publicly. However, States are granted a margin of appreciation if such behaviour would cause offence to others. A particularly egregious example of this arose with the persecution by the Chinese authorities of the Falung Gong cult. Although it has many of the trappings of a religion, it does not posit the existence of a god as such, being more of a mixture of folk worship such as; Confucianism and Buddhism. For that reason alone, most tribunals have not allowed it to be considered as a religion. Such a eurocentrist definition has probably caused a number of errors in determining the status of Falung Gong asylum seekers. This is exacerbated by the fact that the Chinese authorities see the movement as a religion and persecute it accordingly. Further because it is not recognised as a religion in European terms, the rights under the UDHR are not granted to it and the margin of appreciation favours the authorities.

Nationality

The Convention allows for a broad definition of nationality. Sikhs are seen **1–050** as a nationality, but Jews are not. Roma gypsies are so defined as are Kurds. In general any group which is defined as not having full citizenship are seen as comprisng a national group. For example, Croat citizens of Serbian ethnicity are so defined especially as their passports are all issued from one particular town in Croatia irrespective of where the were actually born or were living. Such a passport immediately identifes them in the eyes of the authorities and makes discrimination easier against them.

Political opinion

1–051 This section has two limbs. The first, the holding of actual opinion and with this the right to express it. Any restriction on peaceful demonstrations may be seen as persecution and form a basis for asylum. The second arises when the State infers that the asylum seeker has a political standpoint often only revealed when the asylum seeker flees the country.

Particular social group

1–052 This category has been the most difficult to define. The definition of a "particular social group" has also been made in a highly restrictive sense. The Court of Appeal when faced with the deportation of a midwife employed by the Algerian Ministry of Health, who claimed that by giving her clients contraceptive advice, she was in danger of attack from Muslim Fundamentalists, sided with the Home Secretary against her.

The grounds were that she was not a member of a "particular social group" liable to attack. (See *Ouares v Secretary of State for the Home Department* [1998] 1 W.L.R. 218, CA). The court held that Government employed midwives, although they had a common employer could not be such a group: "The expression 'particular social group' does not in my view cover a body linked only by the work they do." (*per* Pill L.J. at 224)

This exemption does, however apply to Pakistani women in real fear of the death penalty imposed for adultery by Sharia law. Two cases (*R v Immigration Appeals Tribunal Ex p. Shah; Islam v Secretary of State for the Home Department* [1998] 1 W.L.R. 74, CA) decided together by the Court of Appeal showed the reluctance of the courts to define new areas of this category on the grounds that "solitary individuals" did not exhibit "cohesiveness, co-operation or interdependence" (*Islam v SSHD* (1999) AC [1999] 2 W.L.R. 1015) which were seen as the prerequisites required to be defined as belonging to a particular social group. However the House of Lords reversed this judgment in a courageous decision.

> "Domestic abuse of women and violence towards women is prevalent in Pakistan. That is also true of many other countries and by itself it does not give rise to a claim to refugee status. The distinctive feature of this case is that in Pakistan women are unprotected by the state: discrimination against women in Pakistan is partly tolerated by the state and partly sanctioned by the state."

This brief introduction to the interface between immigration, asylum and human rights will be continued at various points throughout this book, but in particular in a separate section detailing the interplay between rights of perpetrators and international crime on the companion website.

Chapter 2

CRIMINAL JURISDICTION AND STATE IMMUNITY

INTRODUCTION

The relevance of jurisdiction to international criminal law may not be   **2–001**
immediately obvious, but it is something of a hot topic at present and there
are in fact three separate but inter-related issues. First, in which circumstances does international law have jurisdiction over a criminal dispute?
This issue will be dealt with in Chapter 10, where the adaptation of the
principles of jurisdiction for the ICC will also be examined. Secondly, when
may a State exercise its own criminal law if the facts or parties of the case
before it have an international or cross-jurisdictional dimension? Discussion
of this question will form the first part of the present chapter. Thirdly, in
which circumstances may a State or person refuse to submit to criminal
prosecution, whether under national or international law? This last question
of immunity will be covered by the second part of the present chapter. The
related issue of State responsibility in international criminal law will also be
dealt with in Chapter 3.

The boundary between a State's sovereign ability to prosecute individuals
according to its domestic criminal law and the realm of international law is
a difficult one, and has been the scene of many power struggles. However,
this is not the only jurisdictional issue in international criminal law, since
more than one State may believe that it has the right to regulate an event
according to its domestic law. Examples include cases where a crime has
arguably occurred in more than one State (as in drug trafficking), or where
a suspect flees his home State to avoid prosecution but is detected overseas.
The ICC is a new (if justifiable) complication. A State's jurisdiction is comprised of a bundle of abilities, both civil and criminal, and includes the right
to make and enforce laws within its geographical boundaries and regarding
its nationals and residents. Foreign nationals become subject to the laws of
any State they enter, and face its penalties rather than those of the State
they call home.

In the present context, conflicts have arisen where a State has attempted
to exercise its criminal law upon a person, thing or event which is physically
outside its boundaries, where two States have had conflicting views of
whether particular conduct should be classified as criminal, or where a State
has refused to comply with international opinion that a person should be
extradited in order to face prosecution in another State. The application of

the principle *"aut dedere aut judicare"* has not been without difficulties, although many international bilateral or multilateral agreements require a State either to try or extradite a suspect within its custody. The Pinochet litigation has shown that, in practice, exceptions have been carved out. The existing system of international criminal law relies to a great degree upon consent and co-operation of States if suspects are ever to reach trial. The ICC will not solve this problem entirely, since it has jurisdiction neither over all international crimes nor all territories. In many situations, recourse will still have to be made to the pre-existing jurisdictional principles of customary and international law, and of the regional criminal tribunals. Further, certain persons may be able to avoid prosecution in any State due to the principle of State immunity, which has become recognised in international law.

2–002   A State may make any laws it wishes, but it cannot guarantee their enforceability if they conflict with its international law, EU or human rights obligations. Neither can it generally expect to interfere with the corresponding and equal sovereign powers of other States. Thus, a basic rule is that a State's jurisdiction is co-extensive with its physical boundaries and may extend to affect its own nationals, whatever their physical location. In the *Lotus* case (1927) PCLJ, Series A, No.10, it was stated that:

> "a State may not exercise its power in any form in the territory of another State. In this sense jurisdiction is certainly territorial; it cannot be exercised by a State outside its territory except by virtue of a permissive rule derived from international custom or a convention."

Usually there is no problem, since States respect each other's boundaries or settle competing claims to jurisdiction over an event in a mutually satisfactory manner. Custody of the suspect will determine almost every case and so, unless extradition is sought by another State, the State having custody of an offender will generally be able to institute proceedings against him according to its national law. Situations such as terrorism, drug trafficking and sex tourism, which have been judged to pose a particular threat to international safety or human rights, have been met with mutual co-operation measures that redefine and extend the meaning of jurisdiction in those specific contexts. However, it will be seen that there are also instances where a State may unilaterally assert jurisdiction over persons, things or events outside its physical limits if it appears that there is a sufficiently strong connection between that State and the alleged crime or the person suspected of committing it.

> "Far from laying down a general prohibition to the effect that States may not extend the application of their laws and the jurisdiction of their courts to persons, property and acts outside their territory, it [international law] leaves them in this respect a wide measure of discretion which is only limited in certain cases by prohibitive rules . . ." (the *Lotus* case [1927], see below)

In order to assert such extra-territorial criminal jurisdiction, the State concerned will, of course, have to defeat any competing claim to jurisdiction from the State within whose territory the alleged offender is to be found, or the events in question occurred. However, once it has been settled that a particular State has jurisdiction over a crime or suspect, international law steps back and does not force the exercise of this jurisdiction. Thus, it is possible for a State to assert jurisdiction with the sole purpose of preventing any criminal action being taken in relation to an event. Dickinson, in his "Introductory Comment to the Harvard Draft Convention on Jurisdiction with Respect to Crime 1935" (1935) 29 AJIL Supp 443, stated that there were five basic principles upon which criminal jurisdiction could be asserted, and this classification remains the standard, if tired, explanation of jurisdiction. However, merely fitting the facts of a case within one of these five situations does not guarantee that a State will be able to justify and win jurisdiction, since the categories conflict and are of different levels of significance. In fact, the Draft Convention, which was never implemented, accepted the first four principles but rejected the fifth on the basis that it was not sufficiently supported by international law. However, in recent years the fifth principle has been argued more frequently, although the protracted power struggles surrounding such cases as the Lockerbie bombing have evidenced the practical and ethical problems of such arguments. As Dickinson argued:

"These five general principles are: first, the territorial principle, determining jurisdiction by reference to the place where the offence is committed; second, the nationality principle, determining jurisdiction by reference to the nationality or national character of the person committing the offence; third, the protective principle, determining jurisdiction by reference to the national interest injured by the offence; fourth, the universality principle, determining jurisdiction by reference to the custody of the person committing the offence; and fifth, the passive personality principle, determining jurisdiction by reference to the nationality or national character of the person injured by the offence. Of these five principles, the first is everywhere regarded as of primary importance and of fundamental character. The second is universally accepted, though there are striking differences in the extent to which it is used in the different national systems. The third is claimed by most States, regarded with misgivings by a few, and generally ranked as the basis of an auxiliary competence. The fourth is widely, though by no means universally accepted as the basis of an auxiliary competence, except for the offence of piracy, with respect to which it is a generally recognised principle of jurisdiction [*N.B.* the category of crimes of universal jurisdiction has greatly widened in the intervening years to include such offences as slavery and slave trading, hijacking and hostage taking; see Chapter 9]. The fifth, asserted in some form by a considerable number of States and contested by others, is admittedly auxiliary in character, and is probably not essential for any State if the ends served are adequately provided for by another principle."

The five justifications upon which a claim of jurisdiction may be made are the territorial principle, the nationality principle, the protective principle, the universality principle and the passive personality principle. Each of these will be examined in turn in relation to their comparative importance in recent cases.

The territorial principle

2–003   Territoriality is normally the strongest claim to criminal jurisdiction, particularly when combined with physical custody of the suspect. Without an ability to prosecute all crimes that occur within its borders, a State's sovereignty would be severely compromised, cases would be substantially delayed and witnesses would either be unavailable or would have to be shipped to the State with the strongest claim to jurisdiction over the event. Thus, a State governs all events and persons within its territory, even if the event is merely part of a criminal course of conduct, *e.g.* where pornography is downloaded from the internet and the host site is overseas, or where a person passes through the territory for only a brief period of time (or indeed is brought there involuntarily: see *Larsonneur* [1933] where a woman was convicted under the Aliens Order 1920 of a strict liability criminal immigration offence after being brought to the UK against her will and literally deposited on English soil).

When a crime has been committed totally inside the boundaries of one State there will be few practical problems in applying the territorial principle, and so most of the problem cases are those where it is difficult to pinpoint the exact place where the crime was committed. If, for example, a murder victim is poisoned on a train travelling through several countries, will it be the State in which the poisoning took place who can claim jurisdiction; or the State in which the death took place; or the State in which the body was discovered? Territorial jurisdiction has been viewed as either subjective or objective in different cases. Subjective territoriality gives jurisdiction to the State in which the offence began, which in this example would be the State in which the poisoning took place (note that the poisoning itself might be a criminal offence in many States" national laws, regardless of whether or not the victim died). Objective territoriality gives jurisdiction to the State where the offence ended or was completed, which in the example would be the State where the death took place. Since both subjective and objective viewpoints are recognised by international law, the two States have concurrent jurisdiction and either may prosecute, although the rules of double jeopardy will prevent two convictions for the same conduct (see discussion of double jeopardy, below).

The subjective reasoning was applied by the House of Lords in *Treacy v DPP* [1971] A.C. 537, a blackmail case, where the letter containing the demand and the corresponding threat was posted in the Isle of Wight and received by the victim in Germany. The victim did not inform her own police but those of the UK. The House of Lords upheld the defendant's conviction for blackmail since the physical act of posting the letter commenced the offence and occurred within the UK. In addition, of course, the defendant was within the territory and therefore the custody of the UK, thereby strengthening the case considerably.

Nowadays, English courts appear to be less keen upon the objective and **2–004** subjective approaches and avoid looking for a single location in which the crime can be said to have occurred. Rather, they are happy to allow prosecution and conviction whenever a substantial proportion of the conduct which constitutes the offence has occurred within the UK, unless to do so would be unfair to another State by compromising a claim of jurisdiction, which it could otherwise have sustained in international law (see Lord Griffiths" speech in *Somchai Liangsiriprasert v Government of the USA* [1990] 3 W.L.R. 606). This is broadly in line with the recommendations of Art. 3 of the Harvard Draft Convention, which would allow jurisdiction on the grounds of territoriality to a State whenever a crime is committed "in whole or in part" within its territory. It should be noted that, in practice, there is a tendency for States to negotiate agreements as to jurisdiction in situations where it is clear that the issue could arise. For example, before the completion of the Channel Tunnel, France and the UK reached an agreement that each could exercise its jurisdiction on the other's soil. Under the agreement, titled the Protocol Concerning Frontier Controls and Policing, Co-operation in Criminal Justice, Public Safety and Mutual Assistance relating to the Channel Fixed Link 1991, French officers work at Control Zones at the English end of the tunnel and vice versa. Similar provisions exist for Eurostar.

A difficult application of the objective principle by the PCIJ (now I.C.J.) can be seen in the *Lotus* case: *France v Turkey* (1927) PCIJ Reports Series A, No.10.

Facts. There had been a collision on the high seas between a French steamer, the Lotus, and a Turkish steamer, the Boz-Kourt, in which eight Turkish nationals died. After the Lotus docked in Turkey, criminal proceedings for involuntary manslaughter were brought in Turkey against the captain of the Turkish ship and the watch officer of the French ship. France argued that Turkey did not have jurisdiction over the French national, and Turkey countered with the (no longer justifiable) argument that ships at high seas are part of the territory whose flag they fly, so the deaths had occurred on Turkish "soil", which allowed prosecution through objective territoriality.

Decision. The court delivered a split decision, decided in favour of Turkey by the President's casting vote. It appears from the court's arguments that they considered that the State asserting jurisdiction did not have to prove its case and so it fell upon France, as the State disputing Turkey's claim, to prove that Turkey's claim flouted a rule of international law. Further, the majority of the court did not consider it necessary to discuss whether Turkey's claim would be better founded upon the passive personality principle, that is, by reference to the identity of the victim. More recent cases appear to expect the State asserting its own jurisdiction to prove a rule of international law supporting it, and even at the time the judgment was controversial: see *Brierly* (1928) 44 L.Q.R. 154.

The nationality principle

International law has interfered very little with the right of a State to regulate **2–005** the criminal behaviour of its citizens overseas. As to the question of the definition of "national", that falls squarely within the discretion of each State. Article 1 of the Hague Convention on the Conflict of Nationality Laws 1930 provides that:

> "It is for each State to determine under its own law who are its nationals. This law shall be recognised by other States in so far as it is consistent with international conventions, international custom and the principles of law generally recognised with regard to nationality."

In the case of *Nottebohm* [1955] I.C.J. Rep 4, the I.C.J. found that nationality "is a legal bond having as its basis a social fact of attachment, a genuine connection of reciprocal rights and duties." A person will be a national of a State if the State so holds and so long as there is a genuine link between him and that State; a reason why he is more closely related to that State than to any other. The two most obvious such links are birth and parental nationality. It is clear from the Hague Convention 1930 that a State may rely on the suspect's nationality either at the time of the offence or the time of commencement of proceedings.

Most States reserve the power to prosecute their nationals for acts committed overseas, particularly in relation to serious offences. The tendency is stronger in civil law systems than common law systems, and in relation to issues of perceived social concern such as terrorism and sex with children (see the Sexual Offences (Amendment) Act 2000). The suspect cannot, of course, be prosecuted unless and until he returns within his national jurisdiction except in those States which allow conviction in absentia. The UK allows prosecution of nationals for offences committed wholly overseas in relation to, amongst others, terrorism, sex tourism, homicide, bigamy and treason.

The protective principle

2–006   The protective principle seeks to safeguard a State's most fundamental interests by allowing criminal liability to be imposed upon a foreign national who commits an act overseas. Jurisdiction is imposed in order to protect the State's interest in national security, geographical integrity or vital economic interests. It is a firmly entrenched principle, but its narrowness and the potential conflict with claims of nationality and territoriality have made its application relatively rare. Despite this, many States have legislation which allows it. The principle is found in many treaties, *e.g.* in relation to aircraft hijacking (see para. 9–003) and in economic and immigration offences such as evading taxes and duties. Although not described as such by the court in question, *Joyce v DPP* [1946] A.C. 347 seems to be an application of the protective principle.

Facts. William Joyce ("Lord Haw-Haw") broadcast propaganda on behalf of the Nazis from Ireland during the Second World War. Although he claimed during radio broadcasts to be English, he was born in the United States. In 1933 he had fraudulently applied for, and acquired, a British passport by lying about his place of birth.

In 1940 he claimed to have been given German nationality. He was tried in England for treason.

Decision.   The main question for the House of Lords was whether they had jurisdiction to try Joyce, a foreign national, for events occurring wholly overseas. They found that they did, stating that:

> "The statute in question deals with treason committed within or 'without the realm'. No principle of comity demands that a State should ignore the crime of treason committed against it outside its own territory. On the contrary a proper regard for its own security requires that all those who commit that crime, whether or not they commit it within or without the realm, should be amenable to its laws."

> Since Joyce had succeeded in obtaining a British passport, he had undertaken to be loyal to the Crown, and so could be regarded as owing it allegiance as if he were a national. Hence he was duly convicted.

Eichmann (see, discussion below) can also be argued as an example of the protective principle, albeit a hidden one.

The universality principle

> "By their very nature [some matters] are the concern of all States. In view of the importance of the rights involved, all States can be held to have a legal interest in their protection, they are obligations *erga omnes*." (I.C.J., *Barcelona Traction Case*, ICJR [1970] 3, para. 3)

2–007

Although the ICJ was not dealing with the issue of jurisdiction but with that of diplomatic protection (which is a civil matter), it went on to state that some international crimes such as slavery and genocide fulfilled the above definition. Where an offence is so serious that it can be regarded as the concern of all States, with a corresponding pressure to avoid impunity for those suspected of committing it, then it may be either stated to be an offence of universal jurisdiction in a multilateral agreement (such as the Genocide Convention), or found to be such as a matter of customary international law. Thus, after the Second World War, the Nuremberg Tribunal exercised jurisdiction over war crimes, crimes against peace and wartime crimes against humanity. The extreme nature of these crimes led to their near-unanimous acceptance as being of universal jurisdiction.

An increasing number of international crimes are being declared to be of universal jurisdiction, so that there is no need for the State asserting jurisdiction to show that it has any connection to the crime whatsoever. This is a reflection of the belief that some crimes are so serious and threatening to international peace, human rights and security that they affect all States and all people. Hence, all States have an interest in, and perhaps a duty to ensure, trial of persons suspected of such offences. Most such crimes are discussed in detail elsewhere in this book. Piracy was the first to receive concrete recognition through its status in customary international law. Slavery followed shortly afterwards, along with torture, hostage-taking, hijacking, genocide and others in swift succession. War crimes are also usually stated to be crimes of universal jurisdiction. Of course, if the State in which the offence occurred (the territorial State) wishes to assert its jurisdiction and mount a just and effective trial, then normally all other States should defer to the primacy of its claim.

Much of this field will change when the new ICC comes fully into operation, but the latter does not have jurisdiction over all crimes previously found to be of universal jurisdiction. Its definition of the "most serious international crimes" has excluded some which are clearly of universal jurisdiction such as piracy, slavery and terrorism. Further, unless membership of the ICC ever becomes truly universal, the fallback position of customary jurisdictional principles will still have its place. Crimes of universal jurisdiction are generally those which are so abhorrent that they are viewed not only as criminal behaviour in the domestic-law sense, but as having the nature of an attack upon international safety or order. However, there is a note of warning; trials in national courts based on universal jurisdiction for international crimes have been rare until recently, and often fraught with difficulties. However, these trials may be fairer and more effective than those in territorial States or the State of the defendant's nationality (which may of course coincide). In Rwanda, for example, trials for crimes committed in 1994 began in 1996 and numbered over 3000 by 2001, resulting in hundreds of death sentences and several mass public executions. There have been serious concerns about the fairness of such trials and the conditions of pre-trial detention.

2–008   In *Eichmann* [1961] 36 I.L.R. 5:

Facts. Adolph Eichmann, the head of the Jewish Office of the Gestapo, had been primarily responsible for administering Hitler's "final solution". Israeli secret agents found him in Argentina in 1960 and abducted him, taking him to Israel to face charges of crimes against humanity, war crimes and crimes against the Jewish people. It was argued by his legal representatives that Israel did not have jurisdiction, since Eichmann was a German national at the time of the offences. Further, the crimes had occurred outside Israel and the victims were not Israeli nationals, thus none of the specific heads upon which jurisdiction could be claimed existed. Additionally, Israel had not existed as a State at the time of the offences, so was claiming jurisdiction over events before its "birth".

Decision. Eichmann was convicted and sentenced to death. The Jerusalem District Court found that it had jurisdiction since the charges "are not crimes under Israeli law alone. These crimes, which struck at the whole of mankind and shocked the conscience of nations, are grave offences against the law of nations itself (*delicta juris gentium*). Therefore, so far from international law negating or limiting the jurisdiction of countries with respect to such crimes, international law is, in the absence of an International Criminal Court, in need of the judicial and legislative organs of every country to give effect to its criminal interdictions and to bring the criminals to court."

The illegality of Eichmann's arrest should not make a difference to his conviction. It was a brave decision for Israel to try Eichmann, since, although there is no reason whatsoever to dispute the fairness of the trial, it could have been called into question far more easily than if the trial had occurred in a "neutral" country.

In *Demjanyuk* [1985] 603 F. Supp. 1468 (ND Ohio), while debating a request for extradition, the court agreed that Israel would have jurisdiction to try the defendant for offences committed in Eastern European concentration camps. The rationale for such universal jurisdiction was that offenders charged with such offences were "the common enemies of mankind and all nations have an equal interest in their apprehension and punishment."

But it should be noted that it is not enough for an offence to be accepted as being of universal jurisdiction in international law. Before a State with custody of a suspect may use universal jurisdiction as the basis of his trial, it must have an acceptance of such jurisdiction within its own national law. Thus, although the jurisdiction is universal and available to any State, legislation may be required to empower that State to use it. If the State wishing to commence a trial does not yet have custody of the suspect, then it will have to convince the State which does have custody to extradite the suspect. In order to determine whether extradition should be ordered, the courts of the custodian State will embark upon an examination of all competing claims to jurisdiction, whatever their basis. As will be discussed elsewhere in this book, the extradition process will only succeed where the international crimes alleged are also crimes in the States concerned. There is thus a great deal of uncertainty as to whether a claim on this jurisdictional basis will ever reach trial.

Many States have opposed universal criminal jurisdiction on the basis of **2–009** fears that it would remove diplomatic protection from their citizens; further fears have sprung up regarding its use by States whose legal systems are viewed with suspicion. But the ostensible reason usually given has been that of State sovereignty in criminal matters. The future of universal jurisdiction remains unclear and in need of new justifications, since the lack of an effective international criminal court was oft-cited in support of exercise of universal jurisdiction by States keen to exercise it, such as Spain, France and the Nordic States. But in any case it must not be forgotten that universal jurisdiction exists because all States have an interest in its existence; the most serious crimes require global solutions and international co-operation in order to address them. This does not mean that the exercise of universal criminal jurisdiction by States in their national courts is the only or even the best solution to crimes such as terrorism, but for the moment it is arguably the most practical one. The ICC and universal criminal jurisdiction are not alternatives but partners in the fight against international crimes; an ICC which had exclusive jurisdiction over its crimes is impossible to countenance at the present time.

An attempt to reduce the uncertainty and inconsistency created by differing State practice and interpretations of customary international law principles in relation to universal jurisdiction may be found in the Princeton Principles on Universal Jurisdiction. The Principles, if adopted widely by States, would endorse "Universal jurisdiction based solely on the nature of the crime, without regard to where the crime was committed, the nationality of the alleged perpetrator, the nationality of the victim, or any other connection to the state exercising such jurisdiction." Universal jurisdiction would exist for piracy, slavery, war crimes, crimes against peace, crimes against humanity, genocide and torture, and the list could of course be expanded to take account of changes in the perceived seriousness of international crimes such as terrorism and other transnational crime.

Specific universal crimes will receive further attention elsewhere in this book.

The passive personality principle

2–010   This principle argues that, although neither the crime nor the defendant are within the boundaries of the State asserting jurisdiction, the latter State should be able to host a trial because the actual or possible victims of the crime are among its nationals. It is the weakest claim to jurisdiction and has been used only rarely, and its unpopularity is evident both in the Harvard Draft Convention on Jurisdiction with Respect to Crime 1935 and the dissenting judgment in the *Lotus* case. It does appear to be somewhat arbitrary, since nationality of the victim may be a question of chance rather than of the suspect's choice. The ICC does not employ passive personality as a basis of its jurisdiction, although of course such cases may continue to be brought outside its sphere of operation. Recent world events, with the heightened awareness of, and impetus to address, acts of international terrorism, may well cause a fresh resurgence of passive personality cases. The principle does have its uses, particularly where the nationality State of the suspect is unwilling to try him.

In *Cutting* (1886) (reported in Moore's Digest Vol. II (1906)), the passive personality principle was among the grounds used to justify the conviction of the defendant for defamation by a Mexican court. He had made statements against a Mexican national which were published in Texas. This was a crime according to the Mexican law of defamation, even though the defendant was a US national who remained outside the jurisdiction. The US made representations to the Mexican Government that it would be a violation of international law to prosecute "a citizen of the United States for an offence committed and consummated in his own country, merely because the person offended happened to be a Mexican". In fact, the defendant was soon released, either due to an outcry from the US or the original complainant's withdrawal from the case, depending on the viewpoint taken.

However, it now appears that passive personality is losing its unpopularity as a basis of jurisdiction. In recent years, the United States has repeatedly sought jurisdiction over offences where the victims included US nationals.

This is in stark contrast to its earlier position in the *Cutting* case, as can be seen in three recent cases: *Achille Lauro* (1985); *Yunis* (1989); and *US v Alvarez-Marchain* (1992).

In the *Achille Lauro* affair, the US tried to gain jurisdiction over the hijack- **2–011** ing trials by seeking the extradition from Italy of the main hijacking suspect. There was no arguable link between the hijacking of the ship and the US except the nationality of one of the victims, who was killed by the hijackers. However, hijacking was and remains an international crime, and so the universality principle could have been argued in justification. In fact, in 1986 the US went on to further display its changed opinion of the passive personality principle by enacting the Omnibus Diplomatic Security and Anti-Terrorism Act, which allows them US to prosecute for offences of homicide or physical violence committed outside its physical jurisdiction, so long as a US national was a victim *and* the Attorney General certifies that the offence fits a definition of terrorism. The US Terrorist Prosecution Act of 1985 has similar impact in respect of terrorist offences.

In *United States v Yunis* (1989) 83 AJIL 94, a Lebanese national was convicted by a US court of piracy and hostage-taking for his involvement in the hijack of a Royal Jordanian Airline plane. His conviction was upheld on appeal on the basis that, since US nationals had been passengers on the plane, the passive personality principle allowed it. Universality was also used in the court's argument. Yunis argued that passive personality could be used only where the victims were chosen with their nationality as a criterion, but that argument was rejected by the appeal court.

In *United States v Alvarez-Marchain* [1992] I.L.R. 355:

Facts. The defendant, a Mexican national, was accused of being a party to the torture and murder in Mexico of a US Drug Enforcement agent. There was an extradition treaty between the US and Mexico, but instead of using that route, the defendant was kidnapped by US agents and taken to the US for trial.

Decision. The first two courts found that the US did not have jurisdiction, but on final appeal to the Supreme Court, the US Government succeeded in establishing jurisdiction. The Supreme Court held that the venue of the trial could be within the US, provided that the methods by which the defendant had been brought within the national boundaries did not breach any of US obligations under the treaties between the two States. Having studied the extradition treaty in question, the court held that there had been no such breach and hence the US had jurisdiction. The court did not base its decision expressly on grounds of passive personality, but again the link between the US and the crime was the nationality of the victim. Although the murder involved torture, no attempt was made to assert universality on that ground. The problem with this is that, regardless of the provisions of the specific extradition treaty, the kidnapping of the defendant appears at least dubious in customary international law.

In one of the many *Pinochet* cases worldwide, France based its claim for extradition and jurisdiction upon the passive personality principle, failing only due to the practical problem of not receiving physical custody of the defendant.

Double jeopardy

2–012 It remains to be seen whether two or more States could try a defendant for the same crime, each asserting jurisdiction on a separate basis. In English law, the double jeopardy rule would operate to prevent a defendant from facing a second trial after being convicted or acquitted in another State for the same actions. It should be noted, however, that there are exceptions to this complex rule. For example, it applies only where the defendant would otherwise stand at risk of punishment twice. So, if there were no realistic prospect of him serving a sentence imposed by a foreign court, he might be retried by a domestic court (see *R v Thomas* [1985] Q.B. 604). It is also uncertain to what extent the offences charged by the two jurisdictions need to be of similar type before the rule would operate in international law. The International Criminal Court attempts to resolve the problem; see Chapter 10.

EXTRADITION, ASYLUM AND ILLEGAL SEIZURE OF OFFENDERS

Extradition

2–013 The process of extradition, in theory at least, should operate as a facilitator of trial where the suspect is physically outside the boundaries of the State asserting criminal jurisdiction over him and his trial. Without the existence of this useful tool, persons suspected of involvement in serious offences might never face trial due to the unwillingness or lack of jurisdiction of their country of residence to prosecute, and the inability of the country wishing to try them to obtain their physical presence in the relevant jurisdiction. There is little acceptance of a notion of "sanctuary" in international law. There is the greatest level of acceptance of extradition where the State seeking it is the State on whose territory the offence occurred. It is far less likely to succeed where jurisdiction is being alleged on the basis of passive personality, for example. For such an important tool of the criminal prosecution of serious offenders, it is perhaps surprising that there is no one method of determining where and in which circumstances extradition will be available. Historically, it developed through bilateral and multilateral treaties in the nineteenth century and, whilst the world coverage of such treaties is now extensive, there are some notable gaps (see Chapter 11) Customary international law will neither force nor prevent extradition, and most States have domestic legislation that supplements the operation of the treaties they have signed.

Extradition relies upon the existence of a complex network of treaties and reciprocal agreements between States, and so there is potential for gaps and hard cases within its rules. As it is, in essence, a surrender of sovereignty by one State in favour of the State asserting jurisdiction, the process may be protracted and involve much negotiation. In order for a suspect to be extradited, a series of rules is followed:

- there must be an identified person whose surrender is sought;

- the offence of which the accused is suspected must be within the terms of an existing treaty or reciprocal agreement between the two States in question;

- some offences or types of offence are routinely excluded from the category of extraditable crimes (*e.g.* political, terrorist and religious offences), although there have been recent moves to combat international terrorism by limiting the operation of this exception: see Chapter 8; and

- the act or activity of which the suspect is accused should be a criminal offence in both the relevant jurisdictions, regardless of whether different labels are used.

Once extradition has been successful, the receiving State should only prosecute the suspect for the offence on the basis of which he was extradited. Thus a thorough criminal investigation and list of potential charges should be made before negotiations for surrender even start.

One remaining problem arises where more than one State can argue jurisdiction over a person by use of different justifications. If both the crime is committed and the suspect is found within State X, may State Y, of which he is a national, assert a supervening jurisdiction and use an existing extradition agreement to further this aim? Or, if the suspect for a universal crime is within State X, which wishes to host his trial, may another State use the nationality of the suspect or the victim in order to achieve his surrender? There is no clear answer to either of these questions at present, although it arose in the *Lockerbie* litigation and it is likely that other terrorist cases will eventually have to resolve such issues.

Asylum

Extradition cannot be discussed fully without considering the related and contradictory topic of asylum. Since ancient times, suspects have sought sanctuary of one form another from criminal prosecution forces or from sentencing. Asylum may still be granted by States, according to their own law and international obligations (known as territorial asylum), or on "foreign" soil within a State, such as consuls and diplomatic premises (known as extraterritorial asylum). While this is a complex and quickly developing field of law and practice, some general observations will be made here briefly.   **2–014**

Territorial asylum

A State, due to its intrinsic sovereignty, *may* grant asylum to any person within its territory, so long as it does not breach the obligations it has freely   **2–015** incurred under any relevant extradition treaty. Over and above this sovereign ability, in both regional and international human rights law there is a *duty* upon each signatory State to grant asylum to persons who are escaping from persecution, rather than from legitimate prosecution. For example, Art. 14 of the Universal Declaration of Human Rights provides that:

> "(1) Every person has the right to seek and enjoy in other countries asylum from persecution.
> (2) This right may not be invoked in the case of prosecutions genuinely arising from non-political crimes or from acts contrary to the purposes and principle of the United Nations."

Further, the United Nations Declaration on Territorial Asylum of 1967 provides detailed guidance on when and how asylum should be granted. A body of "refugee law" has developed in recent years as customary international law, with strength added by various international Conventions; see Chapter 11.

Extra-territorial asylum

2–016   This form of shelter and protection is still largely regulated by practice rather than by law. There is no right either to grant diplomatic asylum or to receive it, but when a person is in imminent physical danger, a relevant treaty has been signed, or local custom can be established to adopt the practice, then diplomatic asylum may be granted. In practice, temporary shelter or respite is often given by consuls and embassies, but complex wrangles are inevitable if an extended stay is sought. The I.C.J. has confirmed both the complexity of this area and its lack of clear rules in the *Asylum* case [1951] I.C.J. Rep 1.

Illegal seizure

2–017   It can be seen that, in several of the cases discussed so far on jurisdiction, the methods by which the defendants were brought within the territory of the State asserting jurisdiction were at least unorthodox and sometimes illegal.

However, the illegality of the seizure of the offender need not affect the legality of his subsequent trial. In *Eichmann* (see the discussion, above), the court approved the following statement from Moore's Digest of International Law, Vol. 4, p. 311:

> "Where a fugitive is brought back by kidnapping, or by other irregular means, and not under an extradition treaty, he cannot, although an extradition treaty exists between the two countries, set up in answer to the indictment the unlawful manner in which he was brought within the jurisdiction of the court. It belongs exclusively to the government from whose territory he was taken to complain of the violation of its rights."

In the commentary to the Harvard Draft Convention, it was suggested that a better rule would be:

"In exercising jurisdiction under this Convention, no State shall prosecute or punish any person who has been brought within its territory or a place subject to its authority by recourse to measures in violation of international law or international convention without first obtaining the consent of the State or States whose rights have been violated by such measures."

In *France v Great Britain* (the *Savarkar* case) Scott, Hague Court Reports (1911) p. 275, an Indian national who was being extradited to India from Great Britain escaped from the ship transporting him and swam ashore to France, where he was arrested and returned to British custody. The arresting officer was acting under a mistaken belief that Savarkar was a crew member of the ship and was wanted for offences committed on board the ship. Once the mistake was realised, France sought the return of Savarkar to its jurisdiction but failed. The Permanent Court found that, since there had been a genuine mistake by the French officer rather than deliberate fraud or coercion by any British representative, the suspect's custody was not illegal or a violation of France's sovereignty:

"While admitting that an irregularity was committed by the arrest of Savarkar and by his being handed over to the British police, there is no rule of international law imposing, in circumstances such as those which have been set out above, any obligation on the Power which has in its custody a prisoner, to restore him because of a mistake committed by the foreign agent who delivered him up to that Power." (*ibid.* at p. 279)

A recent elaboration of the principle can be seen in: *R v Horseferry Road* **2–018** *Magistrates Court, Ex p. Bennett* [1994] 1 A.C. 42.

Facts. The suspect was a national of New Zealand who had committed theft and fraud offences in England, but was presently situated in South Africa. The domestic prosecution agencies (the Crown Prosecution Service and the police force) decided that extradition would not be sought under the Extradition Act 1989, but meanwhile the suspect was arrested in South Africa and was being deported to New Zealand. En route he stopped in Taipei, where he was arrested by South African police officers, taken back to Johannesburg and then finally flown under arrest to England. Allegedly, this was carried out as part of a collusive plan between the South African and English police forces. On arrival at Heathrow, the suspect was arrested and stood trial in England.

Decision. The case reached the House of Lords on the question of whether the complicated, unorthodox and probably illegal method by which the suspect was brought into the British jurisdiction should affect the outcome of his trial. The House of Lords stated that, although the defendant's trial could be a fair one regardless of this factor, the courts should use their powers to declare that such executive action was a serious abuse of power, and should not go unchecked. Thus, courts should stop the trial of any defendant whose presence within the jurisdiction had been improperly obtained. Lord Griffiths stated that:

"Extradition procedures are designed not only to ensure that criminals are returned from one country to another but also to protect the rights of those who are accused of crimes by the requesting country. Thus sufficient evidence has to be produced to show a *prima facie* case against the accused and the rule of speciality protects the accused from being tried for any crime other than that for which he was extradited. If a practice developed in which the police or prosecuting authorities of this country ignored extradition procedures and secured the return of an accused by a mere request to police colleagues in another country they would be flouting the extradition procedures and depriving the accused of the safeguards built into the extradition process for his benefit. The courts, of course, have no power to apply direct discipline to the police or the prosecuting authorities, but they can refuse to allow them to take advantage of abuse of power by regarding their behaviour as an abuse of process and thus preventing a prosecution."

The minority of the court argued that, since the suspect had a civil remedy for his abduction, the wrongfulness of his arrival in Britain should not concern the criminal courts. It may be noticed that the *Bennett* case did not involve competing claims to jurisdiction, but rather a collaborative approach. It may not, therefore, be a solution to the former type of case.

Chapter 3

STATE IMMUNITY: WHETHER A STATE OR ITS REPRESENTATIVES CAN BE BROUGHT BEFORE ANOTHER STATE'S COURTS WITHOUT ITS CONSENT

INTRODUCTION

States generally have jurisdiction over persons, property and happenings   3–001
within their own boundaries under the clearest basis for jurisdiction of them
all, the territoriality principle. However, what we are concerned with here are
the exceptions to this principle. Certain persons, property and happenings are
exempt from national law's jurisdiction under international law. Immunity is
not the best term for this, since the exemption is from application of the
national law's remedies rather than from legal liability itself. Immunity has
traditionally applied to specific persons (such as foreign diplomats and consuls) and to foreign States themselves (including armed forces, Heads of State
and State vessels), but now some international organisations share its bene-
fits. The key area of debate in recent years, from the perspective of international criminal law, has been the extent to which a former Head of State
enjoys continuing immunity from indictment, extradition, prosecution and
punishment in relation to his actions committed while he still possessed his
official title. This issue will be discussed in detail below, with reference to the
Pinochet litigation.

An important distinction must be drawn between State immunity and
"non-justiciability". Non-justiciability is where a national court is incapable
of ever asserting any jurisdiction over a matter, and so no domestic proceedings can be brought at all, while immunity is the situation where a domestic
court does, in general, have jurisdiction over a matter, but in the circumstances in question the identity of one of the parties prevents that jurisdiction from being used. Thus, immunities are a concession and are open to
change or waiver, but non-justiciability is an absolute bar to proceedings in a
domestic court.

State immunity

States and their governments have long been granted civil and criminal   3–002
immunity from the jurisdiction of other States. Since each State is sovereign,
no one State can be expected to submit to the courts and verdicts of

another. That would be an affront to its dignity. Until the end of the nineteenth century, State immunity was absolute immunity: see *The Porto Alexandre* [1920] P30, CA. As soon as a defendant identified itself as a State or a State's government, any action against it was barred. However, international trade and the process of globalisation have led to the development of the doctrine of restrictive immunity, under which a foreign State has immunity only for decisions *iure imperii*.(*i.e.* public acts of States) not private acts of States (*iure gestionis*). There appeared to be little good reason why States should never have to face the consequences of their actions, whereas private individuals certainly did. Most cases have concerned civil actions against States or governments, but the principles have also been applied to potential criminal trials. The issue of immunity usually arises before national courts, and so it is necessary in each case to look at the domestic provisions for immunity and at regional agreements such as the European Convention on State Immunity 1972.

Most States now employ restrictive immunity, and this is backed up by two main treaties. First, the 1926 Brussels Convention for the Unification of Certain Rules Relating to the Immunity of State Owned Vessels puts State-owned ships on the same footing as private vessels, except "ships of war, government yachts, patrol vessels, hospital ships and other craft owned or operated by a State and used at the time a cause of action arises exclusively on governmental and non-commercial service": these vessels cannot be seized or detained by law or judicial proceedings). Second, the 1972 European Convention on State Immunity reverses this position by allowing immunity except in certain listed cases. Most bilateral treaties also allow restrictive immunity. Customary international law in general allows immunity for the administrative functions of government, but not regarding commercial functions. In the Uk the issue is dealt with by the State Immunity Act 1978, see discussion elsewhere.

Heads of State

3–003 While a State and its government may continue to enjoy immunity from civil and, in some cases, criminal law, the position in relation to Heads of State and government officials who commit serious human rights violations or international crimes has long been different. The Nuremberg Tribunal's Charter expressly and flatly rejected any such immunity argument, as do ICTY, ICTR and the ICC Statute. Many national courts have followed suit in affirming individual responsibility for international crimes, regardless of the identity of the suspect (see *Eichmann*, discussed above, and *Pinochet*, discussed below). However, what about those international crimes which fall outside either the territorial jurisdiction of such tribunals, or the list of crimes which they judge?

Where a potential defendant is *currently* a State official, particularly when he is still a Head of State, there is not only a great deal of practical difficulty in indicting him for an international crime, but also a legal barrier in the form of his technical identification with his State. It is not entirely clear whether the current position is that a *former* Head of State/government official may be prosecuted for international crimes committed at any time, since they cannot have formed part of his official duties, or whether there is simply no such concept as immunity from prosecution for international crimes. Arguably, the former is the more likely position. However, the latter contains much merit as a practical step in addressing the visible trend toward impunity for gross human rights violations and serious international crimes that pervaded the twentieth century, and shows no real sign of stopping. A denial of any individual immunity for such acts, whenever and in whatever capacity they were committed, would be a formidable improvement when coupled with the assertion of universal jurisdiction for all international crimes. Then, the only real obstacles would be practical ones, such as choice of forum for trial, the complexities of extradition law and procedure, and gaining physical custody of a suspect before age and infirmity made trial unlikely.

The House of Lords in the *Pinochet* case, [1999] 2 All ER 97 held that the effectiveness of the Torture Convention would be severely limited if Head of State immunity were to be a defence. However, the House of Lords was only considering that particular international crime (see below), and expressly stated that the defence would have applied to murder charges. Further, the decision was very much reliant on Pinochet's position as former, rather than current, Head of State. The existence of immunity (although in a limited form) was thereby legitimised. The uncertainty as to the extent of immunity will be ameliorated once the International Criminal Court is fully operational, since Art. 27(2) of the ICC Statute gives the court jurisdiction regardless of any official capacity of the suspect and regardless of whether any immunity would otherwise exist under either national or international law.

The *Pinochet* case was a "first" in many ways — the first time a former Head of State was arrested for crimes against humanity, the first time that the immunity of a Head of State for international crimes was removed by an English court (a show of great strength and enterprise by Spanish, French, Dutch and Belgian domestic courts), and the first time the House of Lords had to hold a re-hearing because of the forgetfulness of one of its members. **3–004**

The second House of Lords decision in UK *Pinochet* case found that a former Head of State was not entitled to immunity for violations of international criminal law/serious human rights violations. But previously a Head of State clearly did have such immunity, at least for his official acts, and torture has sometimes been held to be capable of classification as an "official act". What does this case tell us about the relationship between domestic law and international law? What are its implications for other former Heads of State? It remains difficult to answer these questions accurately, particularly since the decision in the *Congo* case (below).

The *Pinochet* cases around the world and their impact on jurisdiction and State immunity

3–005   As a case study, the *Pinochet* saga amply illustrates the problems of jurisdiction and immunity faced by national courts attempting to try suspects for international crimes. It also displays the creativity which national courts have employed in their construction of relevant Conventions, treaties and customary law principles.

In September 1973 a military coup was carried out in Chile, during which General Augusto Pinochet overthrew the Socialist government of President Allende. During the 1970s, Operation Condor allegedly resulted in a concerted campaign by the then military governments of Chile, Argentina, Paraguay, Bolivia, Uruguay (and possibly others), which led to kidnapping, torture, murder and terrorist acts. The victims included political activists, students and citizens of several countries. It was believed that Chile was the hub of Operation Condor.

A Chilean amnesty law of 1978 prohibited the prosecution of crimes committed before that date. Pinochet remained in power until 1990, when as part of the agreement relating to his replacement by a democratically elected president, he was given an amnesty, the terms of which were not made public at the time. Further, he had legal immunity through his position as "senator for Life", a title which he had arranged for himself to be given. In October 1998, Pinochet visited London on official business, stopping for medical treatment for a back injury. He was arrested on October 16, 1998 on a warrant issued by a Spanish Court, which alleged that he was involved in the murder of Spanish citizens in Chile, see below. A further Spanish warrant was issued on October 22, adding more charges of murder, plus hostage-taking and torture. Spain then requested extradition on the basis of genocide, terrorism and torture committed throughout Pinochet's time in power in Chile.

3–006   While the first *Pinochet* case was actually started in Netherlands in 1994, the first landmark one took place in the Spanish National Court on November 4, 1998.

In October 1998, when prosecutors heard that Pinochet was in the UK to have medical treatment, arrest warrants were issued in Spain for genocide, terrorism and torture during "operation Condor". In November the court issued orders confirming its jurisdiction to investigate acts of genocide in Argentina and Chile; it also unanimously found universal jurisdiction to exist in Spanish law for genocide and terrorism, including torture as part of genocide, and hence requested extradition by UK. The court also mentioned, but did not use, passive personality because 500 Spanish citizens disappeared in Argentina and 50 in Chile. The charges related to: pardons by President Menem of all person charged re Argentine military coup 1976–1983 and the amnesty which prevented all other prosecutions; and the disappearances of several thousand people in Chile between the 1973 coup and 1990.

Unlike the later UK courts, the Spanish courts found no problem regarding retroactivity (*i.e.* they had not signed the genocide and torture conventions at the time of the events charged). The court also gave a very wide reading of genocide to include destruction of political group — such as to now include elimination of the elderly or aids patients. This reading goes against all relevant Conventions and the definition used by the ICC; more properly the category of crimes against humanity should have been employed.

It is a shame that the Spanish court did not examine the potential torture charges in any detail, since this prevents meaningful comparison with the UK House of Lords, which ironically looked at little else. However the Spanish court held that the amnesty was void because it was contrary to international law. This is a courageous decision which, if adopted by the national courts of many other jurisdictions, would go a long way towards the recognition of the importance of exercising national criminal jurisdiction over people responsible for gross and systematic human rights violations, and of surmounting the complex legal problems involved in such a strategy.   3–007

French Tribunal de Grande instance, November 2, 1998. A few days before   3–008
the landmark Spanish case, the French courts took a different approach to a similar jurisdictional problem. Several French victims of the Pinochet regime had filed charges when they heard of his arrest in UK, alleging *inter alia* crimes against humanity, torture, and disappearances. This case was argued on a different basis to the Spanish case, using passive personality to assert jurisdiction regarding a priest, a student and various others who disappeared while in Chile. The prosecutor faced two main problems before could request extradition from UK. First, the case could not be argued *via* universal jurisdiction because previous French courts had held that it does not exist in the French legal system for crimes against humanity. A solution to this was found by the above-mentioned use of passive personality jurisdiction. Secondly, there was a problem of time prescription; the court found the charges to be of crimes against humanity and so time-barred under French law, but also found that disappearances were a separate international crime with no such problem. This was an innovation even in French law but one which, it is argued, should be adopted by other States since it solves major problems in international law and creates greater consistency between national laws.

Belgian case, November 8, 1999. This very important ruling is often over-   3–009
looked in accounts of the *Pinochet* litigation but is notable since it was unprecedented: the decision was handed down days after the High Court in the UK decided that Pinochet was entitled to Head of State immunity but before that decision was reversed. In early November 1998, six Chilean exiles living in Belgium brought charges against Pinochet for international crimes including murder, torture, and hostage taking. The investigating magistrate held that the alleged crimes could not possibly be official acts performed in the normal exercise of the function of the head of State, whose task consists of protecting his citizens not subjecting them to international crimes of the

most serious nature. Thus Pinochet could not claim any immunity. Further, the court allowed retroactive jurisdiction in respect of events which occurred before Belgian law itself endorsed universal jurisdiction for international crimes. The judgment also differed from the UK House of Lords regarding when the double criminality requirement must be satisfied for extradition. The Belgian court took what is submitted to be the preferable view, that the conduct must have been a crime in customary international law at time of the relevant events. It was also held that there is no limitation period for crimes against humanity.

3–010   ***The United Kingdom case: In re Pinochet: R v Bow St. magistrates Ex p. Pinochet Ugarte (No.3) 1999.*** Caution must be exercised when reading this case since the central issue was extradition and so the court's statements on international criminal jurisdiction and immunity are *obiter* strictly.

After his arrest on November 18, 1998, Pinochet sought judicial review and *habeas corpus* (*i.e.* release) in the High Court, which quashed both of the issued arrest warrants on the ground that a former head of State was entitled to immunity from prosecution. The alleged torture and hostage-taking formed part of Pinochet's functions as head of State because they were actions committed with ostensible government authority; it had not been alleged that he himself had tortured or kidnapped the victims, but rather that he had used State power to achieve that result. The Crown Prosecution Service appealed by the leapfrog method to the House of Lords; in the meantime Spain had formally requested extradition. The House of Lords exceptionally allowed non-governmental organisations, including Amnesty International and Human Rights Watch to make submissions as *amici curiae.*

The first House of Lords to hear the appeal found that, whilst a current Head of State does have immunity from criminal proceedings (unanimous), Pinochet had no immunity (by a majority of 3:2) under international law. Although a former Head of State does have some immunity, it is less extensive than while he is still in office, and cannot apply to charges of hostage-taking and torture. Actions illegal under international law could not be defended under immunity. For Lord Steyn, hostage-taking, genocide and torture were established crimes in international law long before the actions alleged against Pinochet occurred; thus it was unlikely that such actions could be referred to as "acts performed in the exercise of the functions of a head of State".

3–011   *Per* Lords Nicholls [1998] 4 All E.R. 897 at 939–40:

> "International law recognises, of course, that the functions of a Head of State might include activities which are wrongful, even illegal, by the law of his own State or by the law of other States. However, international law has made it plain that certain types of conduct, including torture and hostage-taking, are not acceptable conduct on the part of anyone. That applies as much to Heads of State, or even more so, as it does to everyone else; the contrary conclusion would make a mockery of international law. . . ."

The two dissenting judges, Lords Slynn and Lloyd, differed in their views as to why immunity should be granted. Lord Lloyd's view was that crimes were committed by almost all those who lead revolutions, and thus immunity should stand or fall for all of them. Further, by hearing the extradition case, an English court would be giving its opinion upon the validity of the Chilean amnesty, and hence interfering in the latter State's sovereignty. Lord Slynn, however, felt that immunity did apply to any case brought before an English court, but that the allegations should be tried by either a Chilean court or an international tribunal.

The Home Secretary authorised extradition, but then the House of Lords set aside its first decision because Lord Hoffman had failed to disclose he was a Director of Amnesty International. This was clearly a relevant consideration to the instant case, and hence there was a potential of either conflict of interest or bias.

Second House of Lords. On March 24, 1999, the new House, upheld the   **3–012** appeal in part (re murder, genocide, hostage-taking and other original charges) by a majority of 6:1, and held that extradition could proceed for the torture offences *but* only in relation to those committed after the UK signed the Convention Against Torture and Other Cruel, Inhuman or Degrading Treatment or Punishment. The issue of double criminality (a fundamental necessity for the extradition) meant that all the other charges could not be pursued, since they were not crimes under English law at the time when they were allegedly committed.

It should be pointed out that there was a notably large range of views and several important disagreements between the judges. The court stated that the immunity of a current Head of State is absolute, and that Pinochet was not charged with actually committing any of the alleged acts but with ordering them.

There were two key issues for the second House of Lords:

1.   Which of the charged offences were ones where extradition was possible. The 1989 Act requires double criminality *i.e.* the conduct charged must be an offence in both the extraditing and the receiving State: the problem for the court was when this had to be determined. It was held that it was at the time of the events to which the charges related, and therefore only torture committed after November 29, 1988 was an extraditable crime in UK.

2.   Pinochet's claim to immunity as Head of State.

The State Immunity Act 1978 gives a Head of State absolute immunity from all actions or prosecutions, but is silent as to the position of former Heads of State. The majority of the House of Lords held:

> "the immunity of a former Head of State persists only with respect to acts performed in the exercise of the functions of the Head of State, that is official acts,

whether at home or abroad. The determination of an official act must be made in accordance with international law. International crimes in the highest sense, such as torture, can never be deemed official acts of State."

Therefore, no immunity for Pinochet regarding the international crime of torture was possible. However, the court did not address why this was not so for the other charges because it only really discussed those which had survived the extradition stage of the case. This was a shame, because the court's reasoning would have been very useful in other cases, and the present case is now of limited authority.

3–013 Thus it was held that Pinochet could be extradited. On April 15, 1999, the Home Secretary announced his decision to extradite and that Pinochet was fit to stand trial, having rejected the argument that Chile should hold the trial under the nationality principle.

Pinochet was then re-arrested, but ultimately he succeeded in producing medical evidence that he was unfit to stand trial. He then went back to Chile in March 2000. The Supreme Court of Chile removed Pinochet's immunity in August 2000, but a "temporary" stay of proceedings was imposed and in fact no trial ever took place. Various countries still wish him to stand trial, including some courts in Chile.

Several points should be noted about this case. First, it is to most people a surprising decision, the first time a former Head of State has been refused immunity on the ground that such immunity is not possible regarding international crimes. Secondly, the decision was immediately welcomed by human rights groups, and seen as a significant step towards ending impunity for serious human rights violations and international crimes; a step towards making international treaties truly enforceable. Thirdly, both House of Lords panels appeared to be very willing to examine international law and its sources; this is unusual for an English court, but very encouraging. However, Lord Hope and other prominent judges did not like the result, so the decision was not uncontroversial.

3–014 The European Court of Human Rights and the Inter-American Court of Human Rights soon received applications from the victims for compensation for human rights violations.

The Home Secretary's non-extradition decision was refused judicial review when Spain asked for it on January 31, 2000. The ripples of the Pinochet case have been felt around the world, with doomed extradition requests or filed charges by victims from Switzerland, Italy, Germany and Sweden. Spurred on by the potential of the case, if not the final result, attempts have been made to seek redress for the actions of other former heads of State. Almost immediately after the second *Pinochet* case in the House of Lords, it was being used as an impetus towards other legal actions, if not technically as a precedent: for example Habre, former head of State of Chad, was indicted (on charges of murder and torture) in Senegal in February 2000, having lived there in exile since 1990.

In summary, the *Pinochet* case should make prosecutions of international crimes easier, but may make States more reluctant to undertake them in the first place due to the denial of immunity. But immunity is not always to be viewed negatively; it has been an important tool for making the transition to democratic government smooth after a revolution, and the extent to which this is now possible has greatly diminished. But, since there is no immunity from the ICC, surely it is sensible not to have it in domestic trials either.

Although later cases such as the *Congo* case, below, have thrown doubt upon the *Pinochet* decision, its impact has meant that very few abusive Heads or former Heads of State are contemplating foreign travel!   **3–015**

As an interesting side-point, Chile has established a doctrine that disappearance is a "continuing crime" of kidnapping, which continues until victim is found, and so no amnesty or limitation period is applicable.

However, before the international community had fully assimilated the Pinochet decision and decided whether it was a correct statement of current international law, doubt was thrown upon it by the International Court of Justice.

In the *Congo* case: *Democratic Republic of the Congo v Belgium*, I.C.J.,   **3–016** 2001, a warrant for arrest issued by Belgium against Abdoulaye Yerodia, the Congo's Minister for Foreign Affairs, for crimes against humanity was found to be unlawful by the majority of the ICJ. The ground for the decision was simply that current State officials are immune from criminal trial abroad regardless of the severity of the charges. Thus the ICJ refused to extend the "precedent" of Pinochet to serving officials. Since the purpose of State immunity as applied to Foreign Ministers is to "ensure the effective performance of their functions on behalf of their respective States", the threat of potential arrest while abroad would impede these functions and so was not to be permitted under customary international law. The logic of this argument held true regardless of whether the official was of current or former status, and even regardless of whether his alleged offence was committed in an official or private capacity. This last point runs contrary to some of the reasoning in the *Pinochet* judgment. Further, not only was there a lack of jurisdiction over the Minister for these reasons, but Belgium should also have been prevented from even issuing an arrest warrant. The only circumstances in which State officials would lose their "shield" against prosecution were:

1. when charged in their own State;

2. where their national State has waived immunity expressly;

3. for acts committed before or after serving as an official, or those committed in a private capacity while serving (although arrest abroad while serving would still not be possible); and

4. trial by a properly-constituted international tribunal such as the ICC.

This decision has been variously viewed as either a denial or an approval of the Pinochet ruling; the confusion stems from differing views of the significance of both decisions. Technically the *Congo* case dealt with a separate issue from that in *Pinochet*, since Yerodia was a serving State official at the time of the issue of the arrest warrant, rather than a former Head of State; however it is very difficult indeed to reconcile the reasoning behind the two judgments and, at the very least, the *Congo* case shows that optimistic views of the significance of the House of Lords decision in *Pinochet* for the death of State immunity were overblown.

However, a concurring minority of the ICJ led by Judge Higgins came to their conclusion by quite different and more Pinochet-friendly reasoning. While agreeing in a rich and well-referenced opinion that serving State officials could not be served with arrest warrants relating to prosecution overseas, they might not have complete immunity while themselves overseas on private visits; and, should it appear that a State was keeping a Minister in office artificially in order to maintain his immunity from suit, that immunity would be void. Finally, and most significantly, an ex-Minister or former holder of other State office might not have immunity for serious international crimes committed while in office, regardless of whether the crimes were committed as part of "official businesss" or in a private capacity. This last opinion sounds remarkably like statements from the House of Lords in *Pinochet*, that serious international crimes cannot possibly be part of normal State functions and so do not attract immunity. The concurring judges cited a variety of sources of customary international law and instances of State practice to support their opinion, including but by no means limited to the *Pinochet* litigation. Thus further cases are awaited in order to assign ranking to the differing views in, and within, the recent cases on criminal immunity form extra-territorial jurisdiction.

Of course a strong ICC would minimize the problem. One further potential solution may be found in the Princeton Principles on Universal Jurisdiction, which would all but eliminate amnesty as a defence, whenever it had been granted, and would only recognise criminal immunity for State officials during their term of office. Once they had the status of former officials, their crimes would be subject to universal jurisdiction regardless of when committed. However it comes and whatever its form, uniformity of approach in relation to both jurisdiction and State immunity would be a welcome development in international criminal law, plagued as it is by vagueness and uncertainty of principle.

Diplomatic immunity

3–017   While detailed discussion of diplomatic immunity is beyond the scope of this book, a brief explanation is helpful at this point. It has long been accepted that, in order to perform their functions, diplomats of foreign States require some privileges in the States they visit. Diplomatic missions overseas have existed since the fifteenth century and, along with their prevalence, there has developed (first as customary law and then in codified form) a broad diplomatic immunity from civil and criminal law of the host State. The aim of such immunity is not only to ease the job of a diplomat and demonstrate a measure of respect for the other State, but also to provide a tool to prevent harassment and blackmail of diplomats by host States. Diplomatic functions are extremely hampered if confidentiality and security are interfered with by local laws or officials. However, diplomatic immunity is not absolute. Should a member of diplomatic staff commit a serious violation of domestic or international criminal law or otherwise disgrace himself, then the host State is not entirely powerless and may require him to leave. The immunity is an exception from *the application of* territorial jurisdiction, but not from a State's other powers.

Under Art. 19 of the Vienna Convention on Diplomatic Relations of 1961, any diplomatic agent is immune from detention, arrest, and attack. Article 31 exempts him from criminal jurisdiction of the host State. The premises, archives and documents of the diplomatic mission are "inviolable" (Arts 22 and 24) and it appears that such archives and documents are protected regardless of where they may be at any given time. Diplomatic bags cannot be opened or detained (Art. 27(3)) and diplomatic communications cannot be intercepted or examined (Art. 27). Members of a diplomat's household have similar, if not entirely uncontroversial, protection (Art. 37).

A somewhat circular problem arises in connection to diplomatic immunity. If a protected person is suspected of involvement in a crime under national law or, for our purposes, in an international crime, then he cannot be arrested or questioned by the host State and, should he remain in the embassy, the building cannot be entered to ascertain his whereabouts. Potentially, serious harms may be committed with impunity. However, immunity cannot be a workable concept unless *all* criminal trials are impossible, and in any case to revoke immunity in order to allow a trial would arguably infringe the presumption of innocence. Any exception from diplomatic immunity would be easy prey for an unscrupulous State to pressurise foreign diplomats in order to obtain political advantage, since such an exception would require the making of value judgements as well as findings of fact concerning a diplomat's behaviour and whether his immunity had been abused. Article 44 of the Vienna Convention allows the host State to notify the sending State that a diplomat should be removed, without any requirement of justification or explanation and, although even that sanction is employed only very rarely, it is also possible to suspend or revoke diplomatic relations with a State that abuses its immunities. Of course, indirect methods of reducing impunity can be, and have been, employed, ranging from miraculous disappearances of diplomats, to the more orthodox Art. 44 request followed by an agreement as to sanctions or reparations to be provided by the diplomat's home State.

PART TWO: SPECIFIC CRIMES

Chapter 4

GENOCIDE

INTRODUCTION

In the hierarchy of international humanitarian crimes, genocide is widely per-   **4–001**
ceived as being the most barbaric, heinous and abominable of all the inhuman acts man is capable of committing against his fellow man. Despite
well-documented genocidal atrocities occurring throughout history, the
twentieth century was particularly horrific in the number of people from
many denominations who suffered and ultimately died at the hands of
various despots and rogue governments.

What makes a particular state embark upon such an extreme policy as
attempting to wipe-out an entire specific group or groups, usually comprising
of its own citizens? Past reasons have included: (i) a state attempting to purify
its own society, as in the case of the massacre and deportation of between one
and two million Armenians by the then Turkish government from 1915–1918;
(ii) a group being considered inferior and eventually used as a scapegoat for
the perceived troubles of a particular state, as in the case of the "Final Solution of the the Jewish Question" in Nazi Germany during the Second World
War; (iii) a state attempting to change the overall structure and ideology of a
society be it economic, social or political, as in the case of Cambodia between
1975 and 1979; (iv) a state preventing the right of self-determination of a
particular group, as in the case of East Timor in the 1990s; (v) a state promoting a specific culture within a state, as in the case of Kosovo in 1994; (vi)
eliminating groups which are perceived as a threat against the existing rulers,
as in the case of Rwanda in the 1990s; or (vii) a combination of the above.
Whatever the motives are, the international community has long since
recognised that genocide can never be a justifiable answer to any problem.

The word genocide (taken from the Greek *"genos"* meaning a race or
tribe, and the Latin *"cide"* meaning kill) is relatively modern and was first
penned in 1944 by the renowned jurist Raphael Lemkin in his book entitled
"Axis Rule in Occupied Europe". Lemkin was not only instrumental in focusing the conscience of the international community to take notice of the seriousness of genocide, but was also the principal proponent in formulating and
eventually persuading the United Nations to adopt the "UN Convention on
the Prevention and Punishment of the Crime of Genocide" ("the Convention") in 1948. What distinguishes genocide from other international crimes
is that with this particular crime the emphasis is placed on the treatment of

individuals because they form part of a group as opposed to individuals, *per se*. Genocide, Lemkin wrote, "is directed against the national group as an entity and the actions involved are directed against the individuals not in their capacity but as members of the national group".

4–002   Whilst the word "genocide" was not specifically used in the Nuremberg judgments, Art. 6(c) of the Charter, *i.e.* crimes against humanity, incorporated many of Lemkin's notions of the offence. Genocide was first legally drafted in count three of the indictments at Nuremberg against the accused where it was alleged that "they conducted deliberate and systematic genocide viz, the extermination of racial and national groups, against the civilian population of certain occupied territories in order to destroy particular races and classes of people and national, racial, or religious groups, particularly Jews, Poles, and Gypsies and others". The word was again used in subsequent military tribunals in the prosecution of German war criminals at that time. In the aftermath of these trials, genocide gained recognition as an international crime but without a precise definition being attached to it. In 1946 the General Assembly unanimously adopted resolution 96(I) which states that:

> "Genocide is a denial of the right of existence of an entire human group, as homicide is the denial of the right to life of individual human beings; such denial of the right of existence shocks the conscience of mankind, results in great losses to humanity in the form of cultural and other contribution represented by these human groups, and is contrary to moral law and to the spirit and aims of the United Nations. Many instances of such crimes of genocide have occurred when racial, religious, political and other groups have been destroyed, entirely or in part. The punishment of the crime of genocide is a matter of international concern."

The above resolution paved the way for the eventual adoption of the Convention on the Prevention and Punishment of the Crime of Genocide in 1948.

THE GENOCIDE CONVENTION

4–003   The plethora of publications by various academics in this area of international law over the past 57 years or so has highlighted the difficulties involved when attributing a particular situation as constituting genocide. A conservative and general meaning of genocide is "the intentional annihilation of a specific group or groups". But, this is neither a definitive nor demonstrably effective meaning. A more elaborate and refined definition is provided by the "UN Convention on the Prevention and Punishment of the Crime of Genocide 1948" ("the Convention"), the meaning of which is stated below. The following discussion will concentrate primarily on the legal aspects and difficulties surrounding the use and description of genocide at present under international law.

The Convention came into force on January 12, 1951 and under Art. I confirms the status of genocide as an international crime during war or peacetime. Nowadays it is generally accepted as having acquired the standing of *jus cogens* and applies *ergo omnes*. At present 133 States have ratified the Convention. The United States did not ratify the Convention until 1988. There are, however, some notable non-signatories, such as, Japan, Nigeria, Kenya, Indonesia and Trinidad and Tobago — it is ironic that the latter played a very important role in the establishing of the International Criminal Court and were one of the first states to have ratified the Statute which includes genocide as one of its core crimes. The definition of genocide is set out in Art. II and provides that:

"In the present Convention, genocide means any of the following acts committed with intent to destroy, in whole or in part, a national, ethnical, racial or religious group, as such:

    (a) killing members of the group;
    (b) causing serious bodily or mental harm to members of the group;
    (c) deliberately inflicting on the group conditions of life calculated to bring about its physical destruction in whole or in part;
    (d) imposing measures intended to prevent births within the group;
    (e) forcibly transferring children of the group to another group."

The above definition is stated in identical words in Art. 4(2) of the SITY, Art. 2(2) of the SICTR and Art. 6 of the SICC.

The treaty itself is a seriously flawed document. Apart from a somewhat loose definition of the word genocide, the absence of any detailed meanings of its provisions has led to serious problems of interpretation. Moveover, the lack of compulsory means of enforcement mechanisms to punish those responsible for such atrocities has until recently rendered this particular treaty, for all practical purposes, virtually redundant. It is therefore necessary to examine the court's decisions of present indictees by the ICTY and ICTR, as well as the genocide "Elements of Crimes" provisions of the ICC, in order to properly evaluate the progress made in recent years in this area of international criminal law.

The meaning of the word "group" Article II contains some major weak-   **4–004** nesses. First and foremost, the specific group targeted for extinction is restricted to those categories of people of national, ethnical, racial or religious origins and is therefore discriminatory. Omitted, intentionally, are social, cultural, political and other groups. Why? One reason is that genocide is supposedly a very specific and distinctive crime. At the time of the adoption of the Convention it was thought that including "other groups" whose characteristics did not possess the qualities of stability or permanency nor who were not easily identifiable, would create uncertainty and ambiguity within the meaning of the word genocide. However, by excluding some groups offending states may have a legitimate defence under the Convention. If, for instance, political groups were included in the definition, this may prove a disincentive for certain states to ratify the Convention for fear that their own internal political problems would become a matter for interference by the international community — a scenario which they would almost certainly wish to avoid. Further, even if genocidal action is taken against a recognised group, say a racial group, a state may argue that that specific group was targeted, not because of their race but because of their political opposition, as, for instance, being enemies of the state, and therefore their actions were outside the scope of Art. II. However, it is widely recognised that the motive, be it political or otherwise, behind the genocidal act is irrelevant if the consequences result in the elimination of a protected group. On the other hand, even if a particular state were to successfully argue the "political motive", circumstances permitting, those involved may still be prosecuted under other categories of internationally recognised crimes, *e.g.* crimes against humanity or war crimes.

It has been forcibly argued by notable academics that the bombings during the Second World War of Dresden against the German people, as well as the Hiroshima and Nagasaki bombings of the Japanese were tantamount to crimes of genocide. Proponents of this argument say that since these specific targets could not be described as "military objectives" during wartime, it was the intention of the Allies to destroy these protected groups within the meaning of genocide. Opponents of this interpretation suggest that those people were targeted not because of their identifiable group status but because they were the war time enemy. As evidence of this they proffer the argument that once these people were no longer viewed as the enemy, i.e. at the conclusion of the war, the targeting ceased. Therefore, it should not be classed as genocide. This "enemy motive" appears to be a parallel argument to that of the "political motive" debate, *i.e.* are the motives behind the killings really relevant? It matters not that the killings ended when the war was over, what is more important is the intention, and that was to cause the mass deaths of innocent civilians of a particular group or groups. It is suggested that once an act of genocide has been committed and the material and mental elements proved, then it does not matter that the acts had been discontinued merely because that group has surrendered or is no longer a threat. Whether or not those particular bombings are classed as genocide there is perhaps a much stronger case for arguing that those who committed such acts were guilty of other acts contrary to international humanitarian law, *e.g.* war crimes and/or crimes against humanity; an issue that was not fully debated at the time of the Nuremberg trials.

The Cambodian experience in the 1970s illustrates the difficulties in defining the circumstances surrounding genocide, and in particular the meaning of the word "group". After a protracted civil war, the Khmer Rouge seized power in Cambodia under the now infamous leadership of Pol Pot in April 1975. Between that period and 1979, the country was renamed the Democratic Republic of Kampuchea, and underwent what can only be described one of the most horrifying metamorphoses in recent times. It was a period of indiscriminate massacres, of enforced slavery, starvation, torture, wide-scale annihilation, of subjugation and the wholesale destruction of all groups, irrespective of their social, cultural, religious or national identity. To declare the Khmer Rouge as a legitimate ruling body is a misnomer. From the beginning they were bent on medieval practices and policies for the purpose of destroying all existing peaceful, racial and religious groups that did not correspond to their ideology of one people, one race. For example, the Cham people, which numbered approximately 250,000 were by 1979 cut by two thirds. Buddhist monks, which had hitherto numbered between some 60,000–70,000 were almost entirely exterminated and only around 1,000 survived the onslaught. Out of an estimated 20,000 Vietnamese, few, if any survived. The Chinese population of some 430,000 was reduced by 50 per cent. No proper judicial system existed and torture, murder, disappearances and summary killings were common place — the inmates were indeed running the asylum. Although, by far the greatest number of casualties during this period were the atrocities carried out against the Khmer people themselves; upwards of one million were killed. Were these particular deeds done for political reasons or was the objective the extermination of a national group? The available evidence points to the latter and the indiscriminate but targeted killing of these people. For example, whole villages in various areas were selected for annihilation and destruction because they contained Khmers, and not for their political affiliations. Although there remains some doubt as to whether the intention was to destroy this particular group, it is arguable, in light of the recent cases before the ICTY and ICTR that the actions of the Khmer Rouge amounted to genocide within the meaning of Art. II in relation to the destruction of that particular group, at least, in part. The atrocities inflicted against people of all nationalities and against all political, social, cultural and religious group can never be precisely calculated, but it is estimated that between 1972 and 1975, a conservative calculation puts the number of people eliminated at between two to three million out of a population of just below eight million (See *"Genocide — Conceptual and Historical Dimensions"*, George J. Andreopoulos ed. (University of Pennsylvania Press, 1997); and *"Contemporary Genocides: causes, cases, consequences"*, Albert J. Jongman ed. (PIOOM, Leiden, 1996)).

The restriction on the meaning of the word "group", highlights the deficiency that political and social groups, homosexuals, the aged, the mentally and physically disabled and so forth are *per se* excluded from the protection of Art. II. Indeed, many of the killings during the Second World War could not be characterised as genocide because the Nazis deliberately exterminated such groups as gay men, gypsies, the mentally ill and so forth, as well as some 150,000 of its own "pure" race. However, since State Parties are obliged to incorporate the crime of genocide into their national laws, there is nothing preventing a particular State legally declaring that such a crime may be committed against "all" groups, irrespective of their particular characteristics. What state parties are not permitted to do is narrow the definition. **4–005**

At the time of drafting the Convention it was decided that an essential element of a group included those groups that were both stable and permanent — another reason why political groups did not come within the perimeters of protected victims under the Convention. One difficulty with defining protected groups under Art. II is that some groups are not necessarily stable or permanent, since members of such groups may join or opt out of one group in favour of another. Indeed, it is often the case nowadays that individuals are members of more than one group, even from birth. As the law stands at present, there are no definitive objective criteria for determining the special features of each protected group. In Rwanda, the Tutsis were designated as an ethnic group — their identity cards referred to the ethnicity of the holder, in this case either a Hutu or a Tutsi. Also there was little doubt that such people came within the requirement for a stable and permanent group. In general terms, it was stated in *Akayesu* (at paras 512–515) that "a national group is defined as a people who are perceived to share a legal bond based on common citizenship, coupled with reciprocity of rights and duties. Ethnic group is a group whose members share a common language or culture (or a group which distinguishes itself as such; or a group identified as such by others, including perpetrators of the crimes (*Kayishema and Ruzindana* — judgment at para. 98)). Racial group is based on the hereditary physical traits often identified with a geographical region, irrespective of linguistic, cultural, national or religious factors. Religious group is one whose members share the same religion, denomination or mould of worship". All the above meanings possess their own inherent weaknesses and continue to cause problems of interpretation for the tribunals.

Who or what then determines whether a particular people are designated a racial, national, religious or ethnic group? Should it be the persecuted or persecutor who decides who belongs to what group, or does there exist a precise legal test for determining this issue? There are strong arguments to suggest that since it is the victims of a group who are being targeted, it is they who should decide into which category they belong. In the Jewish religion/race, the children of a Jewish mother are technically Jewish irrespective of the group identity of the father. But during the Hitler era no such distinction was made and Jews included those individuals whose grandparents or even great grand parents were Jews, irrespective of whether the children were even aware of their ancestry, and targeted all persons with a Jewish "connection". On the other hand, since it is the perpetrators who have singled out that group or groups for extermination, is it they who should declare the qualification of the group? The approach taken by the Trial Chamber in *Jelisic* in deciding this difficult issue was to look at how the perpetrator views his victims, *i.e.* a subjective determination. The Trial Chamber in this case stated that "(I)t is the stigmatisation of a group as a distinct national, ethnical or racial unit by the community which allows it to be determined whether a targeted population constitutes a national, ethnical or racial group in the eyes of the alleged perpetrators" (para. 70). How does a perpetrator select his chosen group victims? The Chamber further stated that a group may be stigmatised *via* two possibilities, *i.e.* by a positive or negative criterion. The positive approach consists of the perpetrators selecting a particular group or groups because of their special characteristics. The negative approach applies where the perpetrators target all the protected groups who do not belong to their own group. In relation to the events which occurred during the troubles in the Former Yugoslavia, in some instances the group specifically selected was Bosnian Muslim (the positive approach), whilst in Croatia, for instance, genocide was committed against all non-Serb groups (the negative approach). One of the difficulties with this subjective test is that the perpetrator may give the targeted group characteristics which do not conform to the true meaning of that particular group. Finally, the words "as such" in Art. II refer to the particular group being targeted, and not merely because some victims happen to include members of that group. Since genocide is a *mens rea* driven offence, it makes sense to look at the beliefs, purpose and bias of the accused on the issue of whether a group has been targeted — why should the perpetrator escape liability simply through ignorance or prejudice as to the beliefs, heritage or culture of his intended victims?

The meaning of the words "in whole or in part" It is not necessary for the **4–006** perpetrators to have eliminated the entire group for there to be an act of genocide; it will suffice if only a section of the targeted group is destroyed. It is important to always bear in mind that genocide is not committed against individuals, as individuals *per se*, but because the individual is a member of a particular group, *i.e.* the victim is selected as a result of his connection with that group. The question then becomes how many of that group must be destroyed in order for the words "in part" to constitute an element of genocide. As an adjunct to this, must the objective be to destroy the targeted group within the whole of that particular State or, would it still be considered a crime of genocide to eradicate a group within a specific, limited geographical area of the region?

In the case of *Prosecutor v Krstic* (Judgment August 2, 2001):

Facts. The accused was charged, *inter alia*, with genocide in relation to the massacres of Bosnian Muslim men of military age in Srebrenica between July 11, and November 1, 1995. One of the key issues in relation to genocide in this case was whether the accused intended to kill all the Bosnian Muslim men of military age at Srebrenica and whether those events constituted genocide within Art. 4 of the Statute of the ICTY (the equivalent of Art. II of the Convention). The population of the town of Srebrenica comprised of some 40,000 inhabitants, 73 per cent of which were Muslim and 25 per cent Serb. As part of the Yugoslav policy to force Bosnia and Herzegovina by military means from remaining independent, the town of Srebrenica represented an important strategic position in Eastern Bosnia. There existed overwhelming evidence that the Serb forces did indeed specifically target the Bosnian Muslim men irrespective of their status, *i.e.* civilian or military, and proceeded to kill those men *via* mass executions, murders, beatings and other acts which induced serious physical and mental harm on its victims. The accused denied that he intended to commit these crimes. Upwards of 7,000 men were eventually killed from the total population in that area. The defence submitted that the Bosnian Muslims of Srebrenica did not represent part of a protected group as set out in Art. 4(2) of the ICTY. Did the Bosnian Muslim men form at least part of a protected group? It will suffice for the crime of genocide if the acts committed by the perpetrator culminated in the destruction of a protected group which inhabited a particular area or region of a state; it is not necessary to eradicate that whole group of a particular state. Generally, the words "in part" refer in numerical terms to the intention to destroy a significant or substantial or considerable section of that group. However, the quantity of victims targeted does not necessarily form the ultimate test. "In part" may also involve the qualitative elements of the group, *e.g.* its leaders or influential representatives, if by eliminating them will result in the destruction of large numbers of the group (at para. 587). "such leadership includes political and administrative leaders, religious leaders, academics and intellectuals, business leaders and others — the totality *per se* may be a strong indication of genocide regardless of the actual numbers killed" (as stated in the Final Report of the Commission of Experts established pursuant to Security Council Resolution 782 (1992)). The Commission declared ". . . that the attack on the leadership must be viewed in the context of the fate of what happened to the rest of the group. If a group suffers extermination of its leadership and in the wake of that loss a large number of its members are killed or subjected to other heinous acts, for example deportation, the cluster of violations ought to be considered in its entirety in order to interpret the provisions of the Convention in a spirit consistent with its purpose" (para. 587). Thus, the crime of genocide may be activated by the destruction of even a numerically small part of a group if as a consequence the entire group is eliminated. The ultimate question will be what impact did the killing of, in this case, Bosnian-Muslim members have on the remainder of that same group.

Decision. In *Krstic*, the Prosecution argued that killing the Bosnian Muslim men in Srebrenica constituted not only a substantial part of that group, but also that those men represented a significant part of that group. "[I]t was common knowledge that the Bosnian Muslims of Eastern Bosnia constituted a patriarchal society in which men had more education, training and provided material support to their family. The Prosecution claimed that the VRS (the Bosnian Serb Army) troops were fully cognisant that by killing all the men of military age, they would profoundly disrupt the bedrock social and cultural foundations of the group" (para. 592). The survivors, women, children and the elderly were forcibly transported to Muslim held territory elsewhere with the object of permanently eliminating any prospects of the Bosnian Muslims ever returning to that area. The defence argued, *inter alia*, that had there been an intention to destroy the Bosnian Muslims, they would have murdered all its inhabitants, *i.e.* women and children, etc. as well as the men; instead the VRS merely wished to kill those men in order to eliminate a military threat (at para. 593). The Trial Chamber disagreed. They stated that: (1) the Bosnian Serb forces could not have failed to know by the time they decided to kill all the men, that this selective destruction of the group would have lasting impact upon the entire group; (2) the Bosnian forces had to be aware of the catastrophic impact that the disappearance of two or three generation of men would have on the survival of a traditional patriarchal society; (3) the killings and the forcible transfer of the women, children and elderly would inevitably result in the physical disappearance of the Bosnian Muslims of Srebrenica; and (4) intent by the Bosnian Serb forces to target the Bosnian Muslims as a group is further evidence by their destroying homes of Bosnian Muslims in Srebrenica and Potocari and the principal mosque in Srebrenica soon after the attack (para. 595). Accordingly, the Trial Chamber concluded that attempting to massacre all the Bosnian Muslim men of military age amounted to genocide for the purposes of Art. 4 of intending to destroy the Bosnian Muslim group of Srebrenica.

"Actus reus and mens rea" The *actus reus* of the offence comprises of any **4–007**
one of those acts committed by positive means or by acts of omission stated
in Art. II(a)–(e). This is an exhaustive list and thus not all acts protect a
group against the crime of genocide, although each of the sub-categories
may be carried out using varying methods of destruction, *e.g.* torture, rape,
persecution, starvation and so forth. Genocide is a unique crime — its aim
being the physical or biological destruction of the targeted group. However,
as was stated in *Krstic* the Trial Chamber noted that "attacking only the cultural or sociological characteristics of a human group in order to annihilate
these elements which give to that group its own identity distinct from the
rest of the community would not fall under the definition of genocide"
(para. 580). Nevertheless the Trial Chamber in that case pointed out that
the acts of destroying a particular group are often accompanied by the
deliberate detruction of the cultural and religious property of that group
also, and is relevant evidence when considering the mental element of the
offence.

The mental element of genocide differs from other international crimes
under the SITY, the ICTR and the ICC in that here the *mens rea* required for
genocide is one of specific intent (*dolus specialis*). In order for this special
intent to be established, it must be shown that the act was directed against a
national, ethnical, racial or religious group and was carried out with the clear
objective of destroying in whole or in part that particular group. Anything
different may constitute another offence, *e.g.* crimes against humanity, but it
will not be a crime of genocide. For instance:

(i)   acts which ultimately destroy in whole or in part a protected
group, but were not committed with the intent to destroy that
same group, will not constitute genocide;

(ii)   acts committed with any objective which is less than the destruction of a protected group, will not suffice for a prosecution of
genocide, even if the consequences of that action actually results
in the annihilation of that group;

(iii)   destroying one group when it was intended to destroy another will
also not amount to genocide; therefore, recklessness is not part of
the *mens rea* for this offence;

(iv)   the intention to destroy a particular group may take the form of a
plan or policy which may in fact not result in the extinction of that
group. But as long as the special intent exists which in reality does
not cause the destruction of the group, this may nevertheless
constitute attempted genocide;

(v)   it matters not that the acts were fully completed, what is relevant
only is that the perpetrator intended the genocidal events to come
to fruition; and

(vi) it is not necessary that the perpetrator intend every detail of the plan; it will suffice for the crime of genocide if he intended the end result.

Proof of specific intent may also be determined from the circumstances of the particular event. In determining whether special intent exists, the Trial Chamber in *The Prosecutor v Jean-Paul Akayesu* (Judgment September 2, 1998, para. 523) stated that the accused's intent "can be inferred from a certain number of presumptions of fact. The Chamber considers that it is possible to deduce the genocidal intent inherent in a particular act charged from the general context of the perpetration of other culpable acts systematically directed against that same group, whether these acts were committed by the same offender or by others. Other factors, such as the scale of atrocities committed, their general nature, in a region or a country, or futhermore, the fact of deliberately and systematically targeting victims on account of their membership of a particular group, while excluding the members of other groups, can enable the Chamber to infer the genocidal intent of a particular act." At first sight it would appear that the *mens rea* requirement for genocide is very narrow and strict. However, on closer inspection, and especially from the above statement, where the Trial Chamber will examine a broad range of inferences from various situations, the special intent element may be interpreted more liberally than the words suggest. But in what circumstances may inferences of intent be drawn? No court has, as yet, given any detailed guidelines on this particular issue. In *Kayishema and Ruzindana*, (Judgment May 21, 1999) the Chamber stated that " the specific intent can be inferred from words and deeds and may be demonstrated by a pattern of purposeful action" (para. 527). For example, in the instant case the accused Kayishema was the Prefect of Kibuya, where in specific "crime sites" tens of thousands of Tutsis were massacred. Overwhelming evidence existed to show that the accused was responsible for instigating, directing and leading attacks against that particular group, eventually culminating in their deaths. The Chamber found that the methodical manner in which those atrocities were carried out was further evidence of a specific intent. For example, in one of the crime sites, Bisesero, under the direction of both accused, Hutu attackers were taken by government buses and other vehicles to this supposedly safe area where they systematically shot, raped and hacked to death Tutsi men, women and children. As a result of this, the Chamber found that both accused (Ruzindana in respect of Bisesero only) were guilty of intending to destroy the Tutsi ethnic group.

In order for the prosecution to establish specific intent, it must be proved that the accused targeted a protected group, *i.e.* discriminatory intent is required. Merely attacking and killing members of a particular group is not sufficient to constitute genocide; it must be further proved that the perpetrator intended to destroy that group in whole or in part.

4–008   In the case of *Prosecutor v Jelisic*:

Facts. The accused was charged in the indictment with a total of 32 counts; one count of genocide and thirty one counts of violations of the laws or customs of war and crimes against humanity. He pleaded not guilty to genocide, but guilty to the other crimes. In relation to genocide, it was alleged that in May 1992 the accused intended to destroy a substantial part of the Bosnian Muslim detainees at the Laser Bus Company, the Brcko police station and the Luka camp, and of forcibly evacuating women, children and elderly men to other Muslim friendly regions. There was overwhelming evidence that hundreds of Muslims and some Croatian prisoners had been killed in the Luka camp by the accused and members of the Serb forces. There was also evidence to suggest that not only was he aware that Muslims were to be the main target, but also that he fully supported the actions of the Serb authorities.

Decision. It is not necessarily the case that the accused himself must have committed the offence. The accused was charged, *inter alia,* under Art. 7(1) of the SITY, as "a person who planned, instigated, ordered, committed or otherwise aided and abetted in the planning, preparation or execution of a crime", in this case genocide, and shall be deemed responsible for that crime. These inchoate and accessory liability offences are implicit within the framework of the crime and attract no lessor penalty than the full offence. Although the accused represented himself as the Luka camp commander, and referred to himself as the "Serb Adolf", there was no clear evidence produced which proved his actual *de jure* command status. Nevertheless, it was shown that he exercised a *de facto* authority over the other officials and detainees at the camp, and that during his command he discriminately targeted a specific group, *i.e.* Muslims, for execution and serious physical and mental harm. But what the Prosecutor failed to prove in this instance was that there existed a wider plan for the intentional destruction of the Muslim group in Brcko or elsewhere in that region during this period. On the evidence presented, it was most likely that the crimes that took place were more akin to random killings decided by the accused himself as he saw fit, and therefore the accused could only be found guilty, if at all, as a perpetrator in relation to genocide in these circumstances. Testimony proffered by witnesses showed that not only did the accused execute many detainees at the Luka camp, but also showed his extreme hatred for Muslims in general by his words and treatment of these people. However, his actions during this time appeared to the Trial Chamber to be carried out randomly, and indeed, there was evidence to suggest that he may have acted in excess of his authority. It had not been proved beyond reasonable doubt that the ultimate intention of the accused or of those others in authority that a policy or plan had been formulated, the purpose of which was to destroy the Muslim group in those places. Accordingly, since no specific intent had been proved, he was acquitted of the crime of genocide. Nevertheless, he was sentenced to 40 years imprisonment for war crimes and crimes against humanity.

Whether or not the crime of genocide requires the acts to be widespread and/or systematic is not entirely decided, although in reality such acts are not carried out spontaneously and require careful planning and execution. In *Jelisic*, the Trial Chamber noted that "it will be difficult in practice to provide proof of the genocidal intent of an individual if the crimes committed are not widespread and if the crime charged is not backed by an organisation or a system" (para. 101). However, although the existence of a specific plan for the crime of genocide may not be a necessary prerequisite, it nevertheless provides relevant evidence of the intention of the perpetrator to commit such an act. For example, in *Krstic* the Trial Chamber found as a matter of fact that a plan existed to kill all the Bosnian Muslim men of military age. Evidence of the plan included "the number and nature of the forces involved, the standardised coded language used by the units in communicating information about the killings, the scale of the executions, the invariability of the killing methods applied" (para. 572). All such actions constituted relevant evidence to show that a plan was in place to kill those men. Finally, the motives behind the acts of the perpetrator are immaterial.

Article II(a)–(e) — The prohibited acts of genocide under the Convention

4–009 The essence of genocide is the eradication by a state of a particular group. The prohibited acts for this crime comprise of an exhaustive list stated in Art. II (a)–(e). The multifarious methods and situations in which these crimes may be perpetrated include labour, prison and concentration camps which are set up to hold a particular group with the intention of bringing about their eventual destruction either through starvation, torture, experimentation, or a systematised means of extermination. The definitive example of the use of all these methods was the planned extermination of the European Jewish people and other groups during World War II and in more recent times the horrific acts committed in former Yugoslavia and the Tutsi/Hutu conflict in Rwanda.

Article II(a) — "Killing members of the group"

4–010 Killing members of the group refer to its members and not to individuals, *qua* individuals; the essence of genocide is to rid the particular state of the group *qua* group. Does the word "killing" refer to any act, howsoever caused, which ultimately leads to the death of another or must the act involve the intentional taking of the life of another? The French version uses the word "*meurtre*" which means an unlawful and intentional killing. Whereas the English word "killing" is broader and may include negligence or recklessness. Is even voluntariness necessary? Presumably so. But the ICTR has convicted where people had been threatened into killing others. If a doubt does arise then the accused should be given the benefit of that doubt. The Trial Chamber in *Kayishema* (para. 103) reiterated the words stated in Art. 17(5) of the International Law Commission Report 1996 that "the prohibited acts enumerated in sub-paragraphs (a)–(e) are by their very nature conscious, intentional or volitional acts which an individual could not usually commit without knowing that certain consequences are likely to result. They are not the type of acts which would normally occur by accident or event as a result of mere negligence. . . ." The Trial chamber concluded that since the word "killing" is linked to the intent to destroy in whole or in part, there is virtually no difference between the word "killing" in the English version and "*meurtre*" in the French version. However, there may be situations where the distinction is not so clear but since the essence of the crime is one of specific intent, it is arguable that it is more appropriate to adopt the "*meurtre*" expression as opposed to the broader meaning of "killing" in the English version. In the footnote of the elements of crimes provision of the ICC it is stated that the term "killed" is interchangeable with the term "caused death" — an expression which is in itself rather loose and ill-defined.

Article II(b) — "Causing serious bodily or mental harm to members of the group"

It may appear strange that since the substance of the offence is the intent to   **4–011** destroy a protected group, anything less will not constitute genocide. Thus, it should follow that causing serious physical or mental harm which does not induce death ought not to constitute genocide. Nevertheless, the destruction element may still be achieved, within the meaning of genocide, by acts which subsequently kill members of a group by means of causing serious bodily or mental harm. Under Art. II(b) the serious harm caused by the perpetrator must be so detrimental to the individual that that person can no longer function as a useful member of the targeted group, and in reality causes that group to no longer be able to continue as a group. The phrase "serious bodily harm" should be given its ordinary common sense meaning, *i.e.* "harm that seriously injures the health, causes disfigurement or causes any any serious injury to the external, internal organs or senses;" (*Kayishema*, para. 109). The phrase "serious mental harm" means any serious psychological damage to the victim by way of, for example, threats, intimidation, terror, fear, etc. Indeed, it is any action which seriously effects the mental well-being of the victim, accompanied by the specific intention to destroy the targeted group in whole or in part. Causing serious physical or mental harm without the requisite specific intent to destroy the protected group will not constitute genocide. The methods by which these acts may be committed include, but are not limited to, starvation, persecution, torture, and inhumane treatment or punishment, sexual violence and rape. In *Akayesu* the Trial Chamber were satisfied that on the facts of that particular case rape did indeed constitute genocide. They stated that these acts of rape and sexual violence "were committed solely against Tutsi women, may of whom were subjected to the worst public humiliation, mutilated, and raped several times, often in public, in the Bureau Communal premises or in other public places, and often by more than one assailant. These rapes resulted in physical and psychological destruction of Tutsi women, their families and their communities. Sexual violence was an integral part of the process of destruction, specifically targeting Tutsi women and specifically contributing to their destruction and to the destruction of the Tutsi group as a whole". (para. 731)

An offence under this particular category may also include the disfiguring and disabling of children, as in the Rwandan "hackings". In the *Eichmann* trial, the district court of Jerusalem in its judgment of December 12, 1961, stated that serious bodily or mental harm to members of the group included such acts "enslavement, starvation, deportation and persecution ... and by their detention in ghettos, transit camps and concentration camps in conditions which were designed to cause their degradation, deprivation of their rights as human beings, and to suppress them and cause their inhumane suffering and torture" (36 I.L.R. at 238). The physical and psychological harm need not necessarily be of a permanent nature but must be more than temporary and have the desired destructive element impact on the group in whole or in part.

Article II(c) — "Deliberately inflicting on the group conditions of life calculated to bring about its physical destruction in whole or in part"

4–012   This particular Article deals with the situation where a group undergoes severe inhuman treatment due to being placed in surroundings where the conditions ultimately cause, or are at least calculated to cause, the destruction of that group in whole or in part. Does the word "inflict" require a direct positive action by the accused, or does it mean "cause", which can be indirect or by omission? It was stated in *Akayesu* (para. 506) that the acts constituting deliberately inflicting on the group conditions of life include "subjecting a group of people to subsistence diet, systematic expulsion from homes and the reduction of essential medical services below minimum requirement". Similar words are used in the genocide elements of crimes provision Art. 6(c) of the ICC, where the footnote for this particular offence states that the words "conditions of life" may include "deprivation of resourses indispensible for survival, such as food or medical services, systematic expulsion from homes".

What differentiates this particular offence from others in this sub-category is the means by which the destruction is carried out. Here the methods used generally do not result in the immediate destruction of the group but rather inflict a slow torturous death on its victims. Under this Article, the particular conditions inflicted are generally viewed by the perpetrator as being systematically aimed at the group, as a group, as opposed to individuals being selected for destruction, although in the end the result is the same.

Article II(d) — "Imposing measure intended to prevent births within the group"

4–013   The destruction of a group not only means acts which subsequently eliminates that group but involves methods which prevent the future propagation of that group. Raphael Lemkin stated in 1946: "(T)he crime of genocide involves a wide range of actions, including not only the deprivation of life, but also the prevention of life (abortions, sterilisation) and also devices considerably endangering life and health (artificial infections, working to death in special camps, deliberate separation of families for depopulation purposes and so forth)" (*"Genocide as a Crime under International Law"* AJIL (1947) Vol. 41(1): 145–151.

In *Akayesu* (para. 507), the Trial Chamber held that the words "measures intended to prevent births within the group, should be construed as sexual mutilation, the practice of sterilisation, forced birth control, separation of the sexes and prohibition of marriages". Rape is also included in this category where the birth of the child is considered to be part of the father's group, although rape does not necessarily result in pregnancy. It is unsettled whether a live birth must result. Arguably not, since it is the intent and motivation which drives the liability of the defendant.

Article II(e) — "Forcibly transferring children of the group to another group"

It is not necessary for the actual forcible transfer of children from one group **4–014** to another to constitute this specific offence, other acts also when committed which have the same effect may come within this category of offence. For instance, in *Akayesu* (para. 509) the trial Chamber stated that acts of threats or trauma leading up to the transfer of children to another group may also fall within Art. II(e). "Children" means those persons who are under the age of 18. The problem with this specific Article is that forcibly transferring older children might not lead to the destruction of the targeted group and they may well revert back to their original roots some time in the future. It may only be temporary and not have any permanent effect.

Article III (b) — Conspiracy

The offence of conspiracy means where two or more persons agree to com- **4–015** mit a criminal act. The offence here concerns the conspiracy itself and not whether the eventual outcome of the conspiracy is achieved or not. Indeed, where the offence has been fully executed, the accused cannot be convicted of conspiracy, but can only be charged with the crime of genocide, *i.e.* the completed offence. In *Musema* (para. 189) the Trial Chamber declared that in order for the offence to be established, three elements were required: (i) an agreement to act; (ii) concerted wills; and (iii) the common goal to achieve the substantive offence. In relation to this offence, the *mens rea* consists of the special intent requirement, *i.e.* the intention to destroy in a whole or in part a national, ethnical, racial or religious group.

Article III (c) — Incitement

Under Article III(c), incitement comprises of enticing and motivating others **4–016** to commit an illegal act *via* such means as making prejudicial statements, written or verbal, in public; distributing offensive or provocative literature, including displaying posters; making public speeches, or *via* incitory statements made through the media. The primary concept of incitement is to put pressure on others to take action against, in the case of genocide, a group. It was stated in *Akayesu* (para. 557) that: "(T)he direct element of incitement implies that the incitement assume a direct form an specifically provoke another to engage in a criminal act, and that more than mere vague or indirect suggestion goes to constitute direct incitement". The *mens rea* of the offence consists of the intention of the inciter to motivate others to commit genocide. In *Akayesu* (para. 560), the Trial Chamber stated that incitement "implies a desire on the part of the perpetrator to create by his actions a particular state of mind necessary to commit such a crime in the minds of the person(s) he is so engaging. That is to say that the person who is inciting to commit genocide must have himself the specific intent to commit genocide". The Trial Chamber concluded that even where the inciter has been unsuccessful in his attempts to arouse others to commit genocide, since the foreseeable consequences of the crime are so serious, he may still be prosecuted for incitement irrespective of the end results (paras 561 and 562).

Article III (e) — Complicity in genocide

4–017   Complicity has long been recognised as an offence at the national level and under international humanitarian law since the time of the Nuremberg trials. Complicity in a crime involves assisting the principal offender in an illegal enterprise. Although it is a separate offence, it is inextricably linked to the main offence. Thus, it is necessary that the following elements exist: (a) an offence, in this case genocide; and (b) a principal offender. Further, it is not necessary for the accomplice to have actually committed any of the offences as set out in Art. II (a)–(e), above. The *actus reus* of his involvement may take the form of complicity by instigation, complicity by aiding and abetting, and complicity by procuring means. For example, supplying weapons or technical assistance to be used in a genocidal attack, knowing that this assistance was going to be used in the commission of the principal offence. What is an essential element for this particular offence is the commission of the act of genocide itself. In *Musema* the Trial Chamber noted that "complicity can only exist when there is a punishable, principal act committed by someone the commission of which the accomplice has associated himself with". (para. 171)

The *mens rea* for complicity in relation to genocide comprises of some positive endeavour by the accomplice to bring about the desired result knowing that the objective of the crime was to achieve the genocidal ends. However, if the accomplice is ignorant of the objective, then he cannot be guilty of complicity in genocide. (see *Akayesu* para. 541). However, that does not necessarily absolve the accomplice of culpability, he may still be prosecuted for some other offence related to that particular crime. It matters not that the accomplice did not himself intend to destroy the particular group. The mere fact that he knowingly acceded to the principal's policy or plan will be sufficient for him to be guilty of the offence, even if he himself did not have the intention to destroy the protected group. As a consequence, the special intent requirement applied to genocide itself, does not, as a prerequisite, feature in reference to complicity in genocide.

An accomplice is generally viewed as a person who is subordinate in the chain of command to the principal offender. It will depend on the facts of each individual case whether or not the accused was an accomplice in genocide or the principal offender. It may be the case that the accomplice was not involved in the planning or organising of the specific genocidal campaign, nevertheless if his actions are deemed to be of such overall importance and vital to the success of the campaign, he may still be found guilty as if a principal offender. Further, since an accomplice is not the original or principal protagonist in the crime he may not be prosecuted for being both complicit in the crime and as the principal offender. By its very nature, complicity concerns the crime itself as opposed to the actual prior planning and organising of the offence. Finally, it is not necessary for the principal offender to have been indicted for the offence, those who are complicit in the offence may be tried regardless of the main offender's involvement.

Articles IV–XII

The following is merely a brief overview of the more important remaining Articles of the Convention. Article IV makes no distinction or restriction as to the category of persons liable for prosecution for crimes of genocide. Such persons not only comprise of heads of state, public officials, as well as *de facto* public officials, but also include private individuals, irrespective of their occupation. In *Prosecutor v Ruzzio* ICTR-97-31-1, for instance, the accused was a broadcaster for the government radio station. He pleaded guilty, *inter alia*, to public incitement to genocide. He admitted that the purpose of his broadcasts was to "rally the people against the RPF", a term which was eventually expanded to mean the civilian Tutsi population and those Hutus politicians who were against the interim government. He further acknowledged that by broadcasting messages to the public using the word *"Inyenzi"* (meaning "persons to be killed"), in reality referred to the Tutsis. He was eventually sentenced to 12 years imprisonment for direct and public incitement to commit genocide, and for crimes against humanity.   **4–018**

Under Arts V and VI of the Genocide Convention, the State Parties agreed to introduce legislation to prosecute any persons accused of genocide offences either in the state in which the crime was committed or by an international tribunal which possesses the required jurisdiction. Unfortunately, prior to the Yugoslav and Rwandan Tribunals no such international court was ever established for this purpose.

Article V provides for State Parties to enact "the necessary legislation in Art. III". Sadly, the specific wording of this particular Article suffers from any enforceable implementation. A wide interpretation suggests merely voluntary measures to be undertaken by the respective State Party. This lack of compulsion to ensure proper enactment into national laws has no doubt hindered possible prosecutions, and in reality released State Parties from their obligations under the Convention.

Article VI sets out the jurisdictional element of the Convention and limits any prosecution for this particular crime to: (i) territorial jurisdiction; or (ii)   **4–019** *via* an international court. Although the idea of universal jurisdiction was initially proposed in the original draft of the Convention, it was eventually excluded as being a deterrent against states ratifying the Convention on those grounds. Notwithstanding this, it did not deter the Israeli government from successfully prosecuting Adolf Eichmann in 1961 for crimes amounting to genocide and considered such crimes as achieving universal jurisdiction status. Indeed, other States such as the United States, France, Spain, Belgium and Germany have introduced legislation which extends the territorial jurisdiction element beyond their borders to include nationality-based considerations. Fortunately, nowadays genocide is recognised as possessing universal jurisdiction and with the establishing of the ICC the second obstacle has been remedied.

Under Art. VII genocide shall not be considered as a political crime for the purposes of extradition. The Article goes on to state that the "Contracting Parties pledge themselves in such cases to grant extradition in accordance with their laws and treaties in force. This may have confusing results. Although under Art. VIII Contracting States may call upon the United Nations to prevent and suppress acts of genocide, in practice this has turned out to be a rather futile expectation. Three cases, Rwanda, Bosnia and Cambodia, serve as examples to show the lack of preventative measures taken by the international community initially in combating the atrocities carried out against the civilian population in these States. The United Nations either reacted half-heartedly to the situations in these territories or, despite well-documented evidence to the contrary, refused to recognise that genocidal acts were being committed in these areas. The tragic results of not taking positive immediate action in these cases only highlights the weaknesses of not only the Convention but also of the obligations of those powerful States who could have done much more to protect the lives of these innocent peoples.

Article IX establishes the jurisdiction of the International Court of Justice ("ICJ") to hear cases where there are allegations of genocide by one Contracting State against another. Such was the situation when Bosnia and Herzegovina complained to the ICJ (see ICJ Reports 1993) of alleged violations of the Genocide Convention against Yugoslavia (Serbia and Montenegro). Although there has been some headway, especially in relation to application and jurisdictional matters, no final decision has been made and the matter is still ongoing.

GENOCIDE AS A CRIME UNDER THE INTERNATIONAL CRIMINAL COURT

4–020   At the time of its inception, the Genocide Convention was to be for the prevention and punishment of this particular crime. The lack of compulsory implementation and total disregard for the spirit of the Convention by signatory States, has only highlighted its apparent weaknesses. Nowadays, unfortunately, the interpretation of the meaning of genocide shows no real signs of developing; the ICTY, ICTR and the even more recent ICC have pre-scribed to the exact same definition in their respective statutes. There has been a little progress *via* the introduction of the elements of crimes provi-sions (PCNICC/2000/1/Add.2), by the newly created International Criminal Court. In relation to the genocidal acts under the exhaustive list set out in Art. II(a)–(e) of the Convention, the ICC elements of crimes provision states, *e.g.* with regard to "deliberately inflicting conditions of life calculated to bring about physical destruction":

1   The perpetrator inflicted certain conditions of life upon one or more persons.

2   Such person or persons belong to a particular national, ethnical, racial or religious group.

3   The perpetrator intended to destroy, in whole or in part, that national, ethnical, racial or religious group, as such.

4   The conditions of life were calculated to bring about the physical destruction of that group, in whole or in part.

5   The conduct took place in the context of a manifest pattern of sim-ilar conduct directed against that group or was conduct that could itself effect such destruction.

Paragraph 1 above, is similar throughout, save substituting the respective offence after the words "the perpetrator". Paragraphs 2, 3 and 5 are common throughout the genocide element of crimes provisions. In reality, the actual wording of the elements shed little new light or progress on the understand-ing of the offence. Paragraph 5 is set out in confusing words and begs the question of whether the "specific intent" requirement in the ICTY and ICTR is similarly required under the ICC. In the introduction to the geno-cide elements of crime it is stated that "[N]otwithstanding the normal requirements for a mental element provided for in Art. 30, and recognising that knowledge of the circumstances will usually be addressed in proving genocidal intent, this circumstance will need to be decided by the court on a case-by-case basis". Article 30 of the ICC refers to the *mens rea* as "intent and knowledge". It would appear from the wording of the above that there may be a dilution, or at least widening, of the intent required for genocide. In the introduction to the genocide Elements of Crimes provisions the phrase "recognising that knowledge of the circumstances will *usually* be addressed in proving genocidal intent" may be interpreted to mean that lack of knowledge of the circumstances may unusually be sufficient to establish intent. Such an interpretation is particularly worrying. However, the final words of the above relating to the mental element being "decided by the court on a case-by-case basis" appears to leave the "specific intent" issue up to the judges, without any proper guidance laid out in the ICC. To doubt that the decisions of the ICTR and ICTY will provide the guidance on the meaning and importance of the words "specific intent" in preventing the "normal" intent being substituted for this particular offence.

The incohate offences, *i.e.* conspiracy, incitement, attempt and complicity, originally prescribed in Art. III of the Genocide Convention are not expressly set out in the ICC Statute. Nevertheless Art. 25 of the ICC does go some way to rectify this omission. For example, Art. 25(e) specifically states that a person who "in respect of the crime of genocide, directly or publicly incites others to commit genocide", shall be held criminally responsible. Furthermore, Art. 25(c) states that "[F]or the purposes of facilitating the commission of such a crime, aids, abets or otherwise assists in its commission or its attempted commission, including the means for its commission", shall be held criminally responsible for his action. Such a description is arguably wide enough to cover situations involving complicity. Under Art. 25(d) a person shall be responsible where "[I]n any other way contributes to the commission or attempted commission of such a crime by a group of persons acting with a common purpose. Such contribution shall be intentional and shall "be made in the knowledge of the intention of the group to commit the crime" (Art. 25(d)(ii)). It is arguable on one interpretation of this Article that the crime may, in certain circumstances, come within the confines of an act of conspiracy. The meaning of the word "attempt" is stated in Art. 25(e) as a person who "attempts to commit such a crime by taking action that commences its execution by means of a substantial step . . .". Thus it may be observed that even though the incohate offences are not expressly included under Art. 6 of the ICC, Art. 25 does, albeit not, un-problematically or totally, cater for such offences.

CONCLUSION

4–021 Because of its considered uniqueness, classifying and defining genocide in today's world has become one of the major stumbling blocks when attempting to pigeon-hole this particular crime. Genocide, in many cases, already overlaps with other international crimes such as war crimes and crimes against humanity. If any future definition is too wide, why have a separate classification of this crime at all? On the other hand, if any definition is too narrow, then it may become all too easy for defendants to raise a successful defence for what is regarded as the worst of all possible crimes.

The lack of implementation of the Convention Articles by Member States has been all too apparent in recent years. The international community and especially the United Nations must bear a high responsibility for not taking action earlier enough against known genocidal atrocities committed in the latter half of the last century. Not only could they have prevented genocide from occurring in already recognised troubled areas, had they taken swift political and/or military action, but also in certain cases where genocide was clearly occurring, the UN effectively turned a blind eye and even refused to acknowledge that acts of this magnitude were happening — Rwanda being a prime example of the latter. There is also the danger that by not taking some positive action in these circumstances may result in a form of passive encouragement to those perpetrators to believe that intervention will not be forthcoming if they pursue their policies of genocide. The ICC has done little to update and develop the Convention itself, although it was presented with the perfect opportunity to do so during the Rome Conference in 1998. Merely by incorporating Art. II into its statute has done nothing to advance the Convention itself. Finally, despite the highly emotive connotations associated with genocide, by constituting this offence as the most serious international crime, there is an inherent danger that other crimes, such as war crimes, crimes under the Geneva Conventions and crimes against humanity, will be treated less significantly, when in fact, they have just as far-reaching consequences as genocide.

Chapter 5

CRIMES AGAINST HUMANITY

INTRODUCTION

Crimes against humanity have been perpetrated against civilian groups since **5–001** the dawn of time. Indeed, empires were built on the subjugation, enslavement, massacres, and general overall ill-treatment of conquered peoples. Yet these horrific and inhumane acts meted out against innocent civilians has only in the last hundred years or so been recognised by the international community as morally unacceptable and reprehensible, and only less that sixty years ago became legally unsustainable.

Historically, some headway was made internationally for the introduction of laws against inhuman acts at the beginning of the last century *via* the Hague Convention IV of 1907 concerning the Laws and Customs of War on Land. Its Preamble includes the phrase that "the inhabitants and belligerents remain under the protection and governance of the principles of the law of nations, derived from the usages established among civilised people, from the laws of humanity, and from the dictates of the public conscience" (generally known as the "Martens Clause"). It was all very well stating that there existed laws of humanity which should be adhered to, it was quite another matter to prosecute those perpetrators for violations of those laws without the creation of an appropriate forum and in circumstances where no precise meaning or test of the law relating to humanity was yet established. Nevertheless, the international community was not totally blind to the dangers of not punishing those responsible for carrying out immense inhumane suffering against civilians. For example, in 1915 the major powers made statements condemning the massacres of the Armenians by the then Turkish government. During this period the Armenians were perceived as a threat by the Turkish government as a particular group whose historical and ethnic background did not fit in with the political ideology of that state. As a consequence, the authorities commenced a policy of systematic annihilation and deportation of the Armenians, resulting in the deaths of over one million people. The lack of any proper intervention by the international community did little to forward the legal development against such atrocities. There was also the problem of defining exactly what crimes had been perpetrated since any attempt at prosecuting those persons responsibility would surely be met with the defence that such a crime was retroactive. Unfortunately, at that time it was universally accepted that it remained principally a matter for the national authorities to decide whether or not legal action was to be taken against the perpetrators of such crimes. After the First World War, there was movement to make inhumane treatment against civilians an international criminal offence. There were even suggestions about creating a tribunal to deal with prosecutions of this nature. Although the Treaty of Versailles 1919 did contain provisions for war violations, no mention was made of individual prosecutions for atrocities committed against civilians. Even the later establishing of the League of Nations did nothing to further the protection of the civilian population against aggressive states, nor was it successful in preventing wars occurring in the first place.

Prior to the Second World War, the international community was more concerned with developing offences for the violations of the laws of war, rather than dealing with any "new" offences for atrocities committed against a civilian population. Questions relating to the serious mistreatment of civilians within a State's own borders were considered at that time to be the sole concern of that State, fundamentally under the sovereignty doctrine, and therefore outside the remit of international responsibility. After 1945 came the realisation that violations of the laws of war were not in the same category as inhumane acts carried out against a civilian population. According to the Nuremberg Charter crimes against humanity were to be treated as a separate offence under the then newly established International Military Tribunal. In the Nuremberg Charter of 1945 the definition of crimes against humanity was set out in Art. 6(c) as being:

> "murder, extermination enslavement, deportation, and other inhumane acts committed against any civilian population, before or during the war, or persecutions on political, racial or religious grounds in execution of or in connection with any crime within the jurisdiction of the Tribunal, whether or not in violation of the domestic law of the country where perpetrated".

At Nuremberg 16 of the accused were eventually found guilty of this offence. Later in that same year, the crimes against humanity provision of the Control Council Law No.10 ("CCL No.10") was set out in similar terms to the Nuremberg Charter save that the former extended the list of offences "to include but not limited to imprisonment, torture and rape" (Art. II(c)); thus, recognising the difficulties of restricting crimes against humanity offences to specific headings. Further, the absence of the words "in execution of or in connection with any crime within the jurisdiction of the tribunal" in the CCL No.10 showed that crimes against humanity were offences which may be committed in peacetime as well as war. In reality, it would have seriously diminished the gravity of such a crime if crimes against humanity were limited to armed conflicts alone. That this represents the present position is generally accepted under customary international law.

THE ELEMENTS FOR CRIMES AGAINST HUMANITY UNDER PRESENT INTERNATIONAL TRIBUNALS

Despite the universal condemnation of crimes against humanity, to this day, **5–002** no international convention exists which specifically deals with a State's actual responsibility in relation to this offence. The absence of any treaty has meant that states, until the recent establishment of the ICC, have largely been left to their own devices when considering under what circumstances perpetrators of this crime should be prosecuted. It is therefore necessary when considering the development and definition of this particular offence to have regard for the past decisions of the International Military Tribunals and the more recent judgments of the Yugoslav and Rwandan tribunals. For example, Art. 5 of the ICTY states that:

> The International Tribunal shall have the power to prosecute persons responsible for the following crimes when committed in armed conflict, whether international or internal in character, and directed against any civilian population:
>
> (a) murder; (b) extermination; (c) enslavment; (d) depotation: (e) imprisonment; (f) totuere; (g) rape; (h) persecutions on political, racial and religious grounds; (i) other inhumane acts.

The elements of crimes against humanity differ according to whether the accused is being prosecuted by the Yugoslav or Rwandan tribunal. Historically, the principles set out in Art. 5 of the ICTY are merely a continuation of the ideals already established by the Nuremberg trials. However, unlike the Nuremberg trials the proposition that crimes against humanity must be connected to an armed conflict was rejected by the Council Law No.10 and thereafter made redundant in general international law; thus such crimes may be committed in war or peacetime. However, Art. 5 of the ICTY (but not the ICTR or the ICC) has reverted back to the concept that the tribunal shall prosecute persons for crimes against humanity only "when committed in armed conflict". Is this a regressive step? Arguably not — crimes within Art. 5 must be considered in the circumstances which brought about the establishment of that particular *ad hoc* tribunal. The tribunal is, after all, limited to that period and those particular territories where the events took place. Further, the tribunal's decisions, although highly persuasive in national courts and the ICTR do not *per se* constitute customary international law, unless recognised or adopted as such. Therefore, under the ICTY and ICTR crimes against humanity should only be considered in light of their own special circumstances existing at that time and place.

The essential ingredient for crimes against humanity, common to both the ICTY and the ICTR, are the following:

(i) the perpetrator, through his actions, must have caused serious physical or mental suffering;

(ii)   the acts must be part of a widespread or systematic attack;

(iii) the attack must be against a civilian population;

(iv)   the act must be on discriminatory grounds (under the ICTR but not the ICTY); and

(v)   the perpetrator must possess intention and knowledge of the wider context in which the offence takes place (see *Akayesu* at para. 578).

The meaning of "committed in armed conflict"

5–003   Under customary international law the requirement of an armed conflict is not a necessary ingredient for crimes against humanity; the offence may also be committed in peacetime. However, as stated above, under Art. 5 of the ICTY (but not under the ICTR or the ICC) the presence of an armed conflict is still a jurisdictional pre-requisite. Armed conflict exists whenever "there is a resort to armed force between states or protracted armed violence between governmental authorities and organised armed groups or between such groups within a state" (*Tadic* judgment, para. 329). The Appeals Chamber in the *Tadic* case (judgment July 15, 1999, para. 249) stated that "the words 'committed in armed conflict' in Art. 5 of the Statute require nothing more than the *existence* of an armed conflict at the relevant time and place, and therefore the offences need only be committed during the period of the armed struggle". Moreover, they also declared that the Prosecution in that case was correct in asserting that the armed conflict requirement is a *jurisdictional* element, not a substantive element of the *mens rea* of crimes against humanity (*i.e.* not a legal ingredient of the subjective element of the crime). Thus the offence must be within the framework of an armed conflict, but the *mens rea* of the perpetrator does not necessarily have to encompass the conflict itself.

The meaning of "attack"

5–004   Apart from the necessary requirement of an armed conflict under the ICTY (but not the ICTR or the ICC), in relation to the "attack" element itself, it was stated in *Kunarac* (February 22, 2001 at para. 410) that; (i) there must be an attack; (ii) the acts of the perpetrator must be part of the attack; (iii) the attack must be directed against any civilian population; (iv) the attack must be widespread and systematic; and (v) the perpetrator must know of the wider context in which his acts occur and know that his acts are part of the attack. In the same case, the Trial Chamber described attack as "a course of conduct involving the commission of acts of violence" (para. 415). Attack is also similarly defined in Art. 7(2)(a) of the ICC as "a course of conduct involving the multiple commission of acts referred to in paragraph 1 against any civilian population, pursuant to or in furtherance of a State or organisational policy to commit such attack". The "attack" element is conceptually in line with the requirements of the ICTY and the ICTR. The words "course of conduct" suggest numerous acts over a period of time and not merely an isolated or random act carried out on the spur of the moment. However, where the attack is part of a widespread or systematic operation against a civilian population then even a single violent act upon an individual may amount to a crime against humanity. The "attack" need not necessarily take the form of an actual physical assault against civilians, but may also encompass non-violent conduct, such as policies of internment, apartheid, deportation, discrimination, etc.

Any such attack must be either state authorised or be part of some other organisational policy which seemingly means that the organisation in question need not necessarily be attached to the State, *i.e.* acts by ordinary businessmen, medical and training personnel, and so forth, would suffice. A similar issue was trounced out during the *Tadic* case (judgment of May 7, 1997) where the Tribunal referred to the Draft Code prepared by the International Law Commission in 1991, and especially the commentary which stated that ". . . the article does not rule out the possibility that private individuals with *de facto* power or organised in criminal gangs or groups might also commit the kind of systematic or mass violations of human rights covered (by crimes against humanity)".

The meaning of "widespread or systematic attack"

In order for the offence of crimes against humanity to be committed under the ICTY, ICTR and the ICC it is not necessary to actually destroy any group but only to carry out a policy of widespread or systematic violations. Despite the absence of the words "widespread or systematic" in Art. 5 of the ICTY (the words are explicitly mentioned in Art. 3 of the ICTR and Art. 7 of the ICC), they are nevertheless an essential element to be considered prior to any prosecution for crimes against humanity. The word widespread means "massive, frequent, large scale action, carried out collectively with considerable seriousness and directed against a multiplicity of victims. The concept of 'systematic' may be defined as thoroughly organised and following a regular pattern on the basis of a common policy involving substantive public or private resources". (*Prosecutor v Akayesu* — Judgment September 2, 1998, para. 579).   **5–005**

How "*widespread*" the attack must be is a question of enormity in relation to the scale of the atrocities and the number of victims involved. However, a common sense approach would suggest that if the primary purpose of the entire campaign was solely directed against a few civilians in a particular house, that that would not approach the scale required for it to constitute a crime against humanity. Normally, the very nature of crimes against humanity involves violations against civilians on a mass scale and not merely sporadic, isolated incidents. Mere private isolated acts against an individual will not suffice for crimes against humanity. However, an offence under this particular Article may be committed against even one person, provided it is connected with a systematic or widespread attack against any civilian population. It is the attack which must be widespread or systematic, not the acts of the perpetrator. This is so because in crimes against humanity the victim is not being targeted as an individual *per se* but because that person forms part of the civilian population. It is not always an easy task to determine whether the attack was widespread. Factors to be considered include the actual numerical size of the group, the area in which the population lives, and the grave consequences that resulted from the attack on a particular group.

The word *"systematic"* refers to the actual preparation, planning, strategy and the ultimate execution of those plans — in other words, the overall organisational skills attached to the particular operation. In *Prosecutor v Blaskic* (Judgment March 3, 2000) the Trial Chamber declared that systematic meant "the existence of a political objective, a plan pursuant to which the attach is perpetrated or an ideology, in the broad sense of the word, that is, to destroy, persecute or weaken a community; the perpetration of a criminal act on a very large scale against a group of civilians or the repeated and continuous commission of inhumane acts linked to one another; the preparation and use of significant public or private resources, whether military or other; the implication of high-level political and/or political and/or military authorities in the definition and establishment of the methodical plan" (para. 203). Either a widespread *or* systematic attack will suffice; it is not necessary for both types of action to be present.

Crimes against humanity are generally carried out pursuant to some preconceived policy by the State or other organisational group, although the policy need not be formal or precise. Therefore, any spontaneous action that does not include some form of prior government policy or plan would, it seems, not constitute a crime against humanity. However, it has not been finally settled that a policy is a definite requirement. In *Prosecutor v Kordic* (Judgment February 26, 2001) the Trial Chamber stated that "the existence of a plan or policy should better be regarded as indicative of the systematic character of offences charged as crimes against humanity" (para. 14). However, the Trial Chamber in *Prosecuter v Krnojelac* (Judgment March 15, 2002) stated that "there is no requirement under customary international law that the acts of the accused person (or of those persons for whose acts he is criminally responsible) be connected to a policy or plan"(para. 58). Although a State policy element will normally exist in situations where crimes against humanity are being carried out, for it to be a precondition seriously undermines the inhumane nature of the act itself and it is arguable that its inclusion is an unnecessary added complication for this specific offence. However, any such limitation could be remedied by a wider interpretation of the word "policy". If it could be considered sufficient for there to be a strong hatred or prejudice against a particular group, then that may be sufficient for the offence to be made out, in the absence of any policy to harm such a group. Further, although isolated and sporadic attacks do not *per se* constitute crimes against humanity, it is not unforeseeable that certain grave inhumane acts may occur in the absence of a preconceived policy. Attacks may take the form of an idea or notion to commit one or more of the enumerated offences for crimes against humanity, yet may not be part of a government or government sactioned policy or plan.

The meaning of "any civilian population"

It is now well established under customary international law that a distinction **5–006** must be made between targeting armed forces involved in a particular conflict and the civilian population caught up in the hostilities. In such circumstances all care must be taken by all sides to ensure that the civilian population and their property be protected from harm during the conflict. Article 48 of Additional Protocol I 1977 states that "in order to ensure respect for and protection of the civilian population and civilian objects, the Parties to the conflict shall at all times distinguish between the civilian population and combatants and between civilian objects and military objects and accordingly shall direct their operations only against military objectives". Indeed, under Art. 57 parties to the conflict are under a positive duty to take precautionary measures against attacks on civilians and civilian objects. Such is the importance attached to the protection of civilians that where there is doubt concerning the status of an individual within a civilian group the benefit of that doubt should be given in favour of that individual. (Art. 50(1) of the Additional Protocol I 1977)

Article 5 of the ICTY refers to crimes directed against *any* civilian population, irrespective of their race, nationality, religion or political status, and is therefore non-discriminatory, unlike Art. 3 of the ICTR, which cites that the attack against the civilian population must be on national, political, ethnic, racial or religious grounds, and is therefore discriminatory. Civilians include not only non-combatants, but also those who are *hors de combat* or persons no longer actively involved in the hostilities. In certain circumstances it may also comprise of those persons who were at one time members of an armed resistance movement, but have now abstained from such conduct. Further, in *Blaskic* (Judgment March 3, 2000) the Trial Chamber, reiterating the views of the Commission of Experts, pursuant to Security Council resolution 780 stated that "[A] head of family who under such circumstances tries to protect his family gun-in-hand does not thereby lose his status as a civilian. Maybe the same is the case for the sole policeman or local defence guard doing the same, even if they joined hands to try to prevent the cataclysm" (para. 213). Thus, the word civilian is given a much broader meaning than its normal common sense meaning. Indeed, even if there are a few members of an armed group intermingled with the targeted civilian population, once they remain predominantly civilian then that whole group will be considered civilian for the purposes of this particular offence.

Mens rea

5–007 The mental element for the offence of crimes against humanity is not expressly stated in the statutes of the Yugoslav or Rwandan tribunals, and thus its interpretation may only be adjudged from other sources such as existing international and domestic case law. The *mens rea* for the offence of crimes against humanity comprises of two essential elements — the intent to commit the underlying offence, combined with knowledge of the broader context in which the offence occurs (see *Prosecutor v Kupreskic et al* — Judgment January 14, 2000, para. 556). In relation to "knowledge" the Trial Chamber in *Prosecutor v Kayishema* (Judgment May 21, 1999) stated that:

> "the perpetrator must knowingly commit crimes against humanity in the sense that he must understand the overall context of his act. Part of what transforms an individual's act(s) into a crime against humanity is the inclusion of the act within a greater dimension of criminal conduct; therefore an accused should be aware of this greater dimension to be culpable thereof. Accordingly, actual or constructive knowledge of the broader context of the attack, meaning that the accused must know that his act(s) is part of a widespread or systematic attack on a civilian population and pursuant to some policy or plan, is necessary to satisfy the requisite *mens rea* of the accused" (paras 133 and 134).

Mere knowledge of a widespread or systematic attack is not enough; the perpetrator must also be aware that his actions formed part of the attack. In other words, he knew of the policy or plan, albeit not necessarily in specific terms, and accepted the risk by participating in that particular attack. It is not necessary that the perpetrator agreed with the particular policy or plan that was being put into execution or that he did not intend the result of his actions but nevertheless they would be achieved, or was reckless as to whether they would be achieved or not. In *Blaskic* the Trial Chamber stated that for the *mens rea* of a crime against humanity "it must be proved that the accused willingly agreed to carry out the functions he was performing; that these functions resulted in his collaboration with the political, military or civilian authorities defining the ideology, policy or plan at the root of the crimes; that he received order relating to the ideology, policy or plan; and lastly that he contributed to its commission through intentional acts or by simply refusing of his own accord to take the measures necessary to prevent their perpetration". (para. 257) Although under customary international law crimes against humanity may be committed against combatants and civilians alike under a strict interpretation of Art. 5 of the ICTY this particular offence is limited to civilians only. Accordingly, is it necessary for the prosecution to prove that the accused must have realised that his actions were against a civilian or at least that he was reckless to that fact? In *Kunarac et al* (Judgment February 22, 2201) it was stated that it was not necessary to show that the perpetrator specifically targeted civilians. However, it must be shown that "the perpetrator must have known or considered the possibility that the victim of his crime was a civilian.

The Trial Chamber stresses that, in case of doubt as to whether a person is a civilian, that person shall be considered a civilian. The prosecution must show that the perpetrator could not reasonably have believed that the victim was a member of the armed forces". (para. 435) Finally, once it has been established that the necessary conditions for a prosecution for crimes against humanity have been sustained, thereafter the motives, including personal reasons, behind the actions of the accused are immaterial.

Status of perpetrators for crimes against humanity

Do crimes against humanity necessarily have to be carried out by State officials, or is the status of the perpetrator irrelevant? It is not a precondition that crimes against humanity must be carried out by government officials only; a private group or organisation may well orchestrate policies amounting to crimes against humanity. Since crimes against humanity may include offences committed by a private individual, is it therefore necessary that his actions be authorised, sponsored or at least condoned by the government? The present position appears to be that even though it is not necessary for the perpetrator to have acquired State official status, their actions must at least be connected with a policy or plan by a government or any other organisation or group in order for there to be a crime against humanity. It is not unforeseeable that some private organised groups may have their own criminal agenda, in the absence of some government policy or plan, and consequently commit inhuman acts against a civilian population. Such a situation may arise where a specific group commit atrocities against other groups and for whatever reason are not prevented from discontinuing their actions by the state authorities or there is tacit approval of their actions by the state. Such people, it may be argued, should come within the boundaries of the jurisdiction for crime against humanity and be prosecuted for their actions. In *Kayishema* the Trial Chamber agreed with the views of the ILC in their Draft Codes of Crimes which explained that the meaning of the words "instigated or directed by a government or by any organisation or group" was "intended to exclude the situation in which an individual commits an inhumane act whilst acting on his own initiative pursuant to his own criminal plan in the absence of any encouragement or direction from either a government or a group or an organisation". (para. 125)

Limitation periods for crimes against humanity

Although most common law states do not set a limitation period for the prosecution of a criminal offence, many civil law jurisdictions do incorporate time periods after which prosecutions would effectively be barred. With respect to crimes against humanity, this time limitation factor may have prevented those perpetrators responsible for committing such crimes being brought to justice *via* the national courts. This discrepancy has somewhat been alleviated by

5–008

5–009

General Assembly Resolution 2391 adopting the Convention on the Non-Applicability of Statutory Limitations to War Crimes and Crimes Against Humanity 1968. Article 1 provides that no statutory limitation shall apply to war crimes or crimes against humanity, irrespective of the date of their commission, and even if such acts do not constitute a violation of the domestic law of the country in which they were committed (Art. 1(b)). Notwithstanding this, in practice, states remain reluctant to indict perpetrators for these crimes under national law.

CATEGORIES OF OFFENCES

5–010   Since crimes against humanity are inherently broad, there is always the danger that any exhaustive list provided by law will never be accurate or sufficiently competent enough to cover all variations of this offence. The sub-category headings for crimes against humanity in the ICTY and ICTR are identical, namely, murder, extermination, enslavement, deportation, imprisonment, torture, rape, persecutions on political, racial and religious grounds, and other inhumane acts. In Art. 7(1) of the ICC, the list is extended to include enforced disappearance of persons and the crime of apartheid (Art. 7(i) and (j). Further, under the ICC the sexual crimes have been broadened and are not limited to rape, but also comprise of "sexual slavery, enforced prostitution, forced pregnancy, enforced sterilization, or any other form of sexual violence of comparable gravity". (Art. 7(1)(g))

Murder

5–011   The principal question in relation to this offence is what precisely constitutes murder. The English version of Art. 3(a) of the ICTR uses the word "murder", whilst the French version uses the word "assassinat". Difficulties of translation in various national legal systems have created confusion and uncertainty in interpretation of the offence in international law. For instance, in numerous common law jurisdictions the *mens rea* of the offence does not necessarily include premeditation as a prerequisite, whereas in civil law states premeditation is generally a necessary ingredient of the offence. It was stated in *Kayishema and Ruzindana* (Judgment May 21, 1999) "murder and assassinat should be considered together in order to ascertain the standard of *mens rea* intended by the drafters and demanded by the ICTR statute. When murder is considered alongside with assassinat, the Chamber finds that the standard of *mens rea* required is intentional and premeditated killing" (para. 139). Thus, murder comprises of unlawful acts which: (i) causes the death of another; (ii) by a premeditated act or omission; (iii) intending to kill any person; or (iv) intending to cause grievous bodily harm to any person (para. 140). Accordingly, for murder to constitute an offence for crimes against humanity under Art. 3(a) of the ICTR, in addition to the above requirements, the victim must be a member of the civilian population and the act or omission must be part of a widespread or systematic attack against the civilian population on national, political, ethnical, racial or religious grounds. The words "civilian population" has a similar meaning to that of Art. 7(1) of the ICC and Art. 5 of the ICTY, save that in these latter Statutes the term is non-discriminatory.

In like manner to other crimes under the statute, where there is doubt as to their interpretation, the accused is to be given the benefit of that doubt. The level of doubt required is not stipulated. Is it based upon at least a reasonable doubt or will any doubt suffice? The Trial Chamber in *Kayishema* used the words "what is favourable to the accused". In that case the inclusion of premeditation as an essential element for murder was interpreted in favour of the accused.

Extermination

Extermination is primarily concerned with the mass destruction of a group   **5–012** of individuals; the emphasis in this category is placed on the scale of the destruction, unlike murder which may comprise of a singular incident. Under the ICTY, the necessary elements of the offence are that: "(i) the accused or his subordinate participated in the killing of certain named or described persons; (ii) the act or omission was unlawful and intentional; (iii) the unlawful act or omission must be part of a widespread attack; (iv) the attack must be against the civilian population. Under the ICTR, the attack must be on discriminatory grounds namely national, political, ethnical, racial or religious grounds" (*Blaskic*, para. 83). In *Kayishema et al*, the first accused, who was at the relevant time the Prefect of Kibuya, was charged with the massacres that took place in and around Kibuya between April 14, and June 30, 1994. By April 17, 1994, thousands of civilians sought refuge in the Catholic Church and Home St Jean complex in Kibuya; many of whom were ordered to go there by the accused. Soon after the accused ordered the Gendarmerie, communal police and armed civilians to attack the complex. As a result thousands of innocent people were killed and many others suffered serious injuries. Subsequently, the first accused was indicted for, *inter alia,* crimes against humanity, and specifically murder, extermination and other inhumane acts contrary to Art. 3 of the ICTR. The Trial Chamber in that case set out in precise language the essential elements of the particular crime of extermination, and which are as follows: "The actor participates in the mass killing of others or in the creation of conditions of life that lead to the mass killing of others, through his act(s) or omissions(s); having intended the killing, or being reckless, or grossly negligent as to whether the killing would result and; being aware that his act(s) or omissions(s) forms part of a mass killing event; where, his act(s) or omissions(s) forms part of a widespread or systematic attack against any civilian population on national, political, ethnic, racial or religious grounds" (para. 144). The elements of crimes provision of the ICC provides similar criteria, save that it does not state whether the offence may be committed negligently or recklessly. Paragraph 4 of the elements merely states that "the perpetrator knew that the conduct was part of or intended the conduct to be part of a widespread or systematic attack directed a civilian population".

As may be observed from the above definition, extermination of a group need not take immediate effect, nor is it necessary that positive actions were required. The offence may also be committed *via* omission, for instance by not providing sufficient food or medical treatment, provided the intention is ultimately to destroy those particular civilians (see Art. 7(2)(b) of the ICC for the definition of extermination). It cannot be stated with any real conviction that the definition of extermination in the ICC is a precise one. Although the definition clearly incorporates many of the other crimes set out in Art. 7(1)(a)–(b), *e.g.* murder, persecution, enforced disappearances of persons and so forth, their inclusion is more illustrative than exhaustive.

Historically, extermination was often associated with genocide, principally from its common usage when referring to the "extermination of the Jews" during the Second World War. However, extermination is not as restrictive as genocide. First, the specific intent *mens rea* requirement for genocide is not an essential element for this offence; the acts or omission may be committed either intentionally, or recklessly or by gross negligence. Secondly, the range of groups targeted is broader than that of genocide, especially under the ICTY or ICC where the crime may be committed against any group. Thirdly, it is not necessary for any entire or even part of a specific group to be destroyed; it will not detract from the offence if some individuals within that group are not specifically targeted. Fourthly, the group selected may be a mixture of different groups or not identifiable as a specific group or groups. Fifthly, extermination may also result where the targeted group is numerically small, for instance, in a small village or area. Finally, the killing of one person may suffice for this offence, provided that the perpetrator was aware that his actions were part of a mass destruction campaign.

Enslavement

5–013   The principles of the crime of slavery and enslavement under international law generally are dealt with in Chapter 9. The offence of slavery is universally accepted as not only constituting a crime against humanity but is also prohibited under treaty and international humanitarian law. Enslavement falls within the categories of those crimes which are considered *jus cogens* and as such entail individual criminal responsibility. Under customary international law, enslavement consists of "the exercise of any or all of the powers attaching to the right of ownership over a person. The *actus reus* of enslavement is the exercise of those powers and the *mens rea* is the intentional exercise of such powers" (*Kunarac* trial judgment, paras 539 and 540; see also Art. 1(1) of the Slavery Convention (1926)). There are two main components to this particular offence, ownership and control. In relation to the right of ownership, such power over another human being is not recognised in law and is in itself illegal. As regards control, the Trial Chamber in *Kunarac* (Judgment February 22, 2001) gave the following examples of the meaning of the word, *e.g.* "the control of victims being subjected to someone's movement, control of physical environment, psychological control, measures taken to prevent or deter escape, force, threat of force or coercion, duration, assertion of exclusivity, subjection to cruel treatment and abuse, control of sexuality and forced labour". (Trial judgment, para. 453)

Generally, enslavement during armed conflicts take the form of forced labour, i.e. involuntary and non-consensual work. Evidence of a lack of consent may also be adjudged by showing that the victim was not in a position to give his voluntary assent to undertake work. In other words, the victim had no real choice in the matter. In *Kunarac*, the Trial Chamber gave examples of where consent was impossible or irrelevant under the circumstances, *i.e.* "the threat or use of force or other forms or coercion; the fear of violence, deception or false promises; the victim's position of vulnerability; detention or captivity; psychological oppression or socio-economic conditions" (para. 542). This is not an exhaustive list but merely illustrative of the various indicators which may constitute enslavement.

In *Kunarac* (Appeals Chamber (June 12, 2002)), the Appeals Chamber did not accept that lack of consent was an element of the crime. Once it is proved that the accused exercised the right of ownership over the victim, it is irrelevant whether or not the victim objected. Nevertheless, despite not being an element of the crime itself, the Appeals Chamber went on to state that consent can be taken into account "from an evidential point of view as going to the question whether the prosecutor has established the element of the crime relating to the exercise by the accused of any or all of the powers attaching to the right of ownership". (para. 120)

Under Art. 7(2)(c) of the ICC enslavement "means the exercise of any or **5–014** all of the powers attaching to the right of ownership over a person and includes the exercise of such power in the course of trafficking in persons, in particular women and children". The elements for this particular offence under the ICC are set out as follows:

"1. The perpetrator exercised any or all of the powers attaching to the right of ownership over one or more persons, such as by purchasing, selling, lending or bartering such a person or persons, or by imposing on them a similar deprivation of liberty.
2. The conduct was committed as part of a widespread or systematic attack directed against a civilian population.
3. The perpetrator knew that the conduct was part of or intended the conduct to be part of a widespread or systematic attack directed against a civilian population".

Apart from the general essential elements for all crimes against humanity set out in paras 2 and 3, above, para. 1, in line with the meaning given by the ICTY and ICTR, re-emphasises the requirement for this specific offence of "the right of ownership". Lack of consent does not appear to the determining factor for enslavement under the ICC.

Deportation

5–015 In general terms, deportation is the forced evacuation of the whole or part of a civilian population from their homes to other areas. Under Art. 7(2)(d) of the ICC, the terms have been defined as the "forced displacement of the persons concerned by expulsion or other coercive acts from the area in which they are lawfully present, without grounds permitted under international law". In *Prosecutor v Krstic* (Judgment August 2, 2001) the accused was charged with three counts relating to deportations and forcible transfers. In two days (July 12 and 13, 1995) some 25,000 Bosnian Muslims women, children and elderly were forcibly removed from outside Srebenica and transported by buses to other areas within Bosnia, Herzegovina. It was stated in that case that "(B)oth deportation and forcible transfer relate to the involuntary and unlawful evacuation from the territory in which they reside. Yet, the two are not synonymous in customary international law. Deportation presumes transfer beyond state borders, whereas forcible transfer relates to displacements within a state" (para. 521). However, it is not the case that all deportations or forcible transfers are unlawful. There may arise situations which make it imperative, for the good and safety of the population, that they be uprooted and temporarily removed elsewhere. In times of peace, this may occur, for instance, where a natural or man-made disaster threatens the welfare of a population, the government may deem it necessary to evacuate these people to a safer place within or outside of their borders. But what makes their displacement illegal is that when the dangerous situation has subsided, they are not permitted to return to their homes. In times of war, Art. 49 of the Fourth Geneva Convention 1949 states that ". . . the Occupying Power may undertake total or partial evacuation of a given area if the security of the population or imperative military reasons so demand . . . Persons thus evacuated shall be transferred back to their homes as soon as the hostilities in question have ceased". The "imperative military reasons" element strongly suggests that the purpose of the evacuation should be linked to the protection of the population and then only as a last resort should those civilians be removed from their homes; anything less may well constitute an offence.

Generally, acts of forcible displacement involve a high degree of organisational planning and preparation by those carrying out such a policy. What degree of force is necessary? It is stated in the footnote of the relevant ICC's elements of crime provisions that the term "forcibly is not restricted to physical force, but may include threat of force or coercion, such as that caused by the fear of violence, duress, detention, psychological oppression or abuse of power against such persons or another person, or taking advantage of a coercive environment". In determining whether such events constitute forcible displacement it is suggested that the test is both objective and subjective, *i.e.* examining the surrounding circumstances that created the departure of the civilians — objective, and then determining whether those civilians perceived that had they remained they would have been in fear of their lives — subjective.

All too often, both historically and in recent times, civilians have been "forced" to depart from their homes, not due to some plan or policy on the part of an invading force, but for fear of the detrimental consequences if they were to remain. In many cases, the civilian population may decide it is better to leave "voluntarily" rather than remain and suffer serious ill-treatment by those who take over their particular area. Such events constitute a form of constructive removal. Whether it also amounts to an offence under the deportation and forcible transfer category is undecided. It is arguable that by pre-empting the intentions of an occupying force by leaving their homes, they do in reality come within the confines of persons who are being forcibly expelled.

Imprisonment

The general meaning of imprisonment is the deprivation of a person's liberty. **5–016** Although imprisonment *per se* is not illegal it is listed in the category of crimes against humanity as an offence in Art. 5 of the ICTY and Art. 3 of ICTR. No preceeding words indicate the scope of the imprisonment that is being referred to, *e.g.* arbitrary, unlawful, unwarranted, etc.

Torture

The crime of torture in international law is fully discussed in Chapter 7. **5–017** This particular section will concentrate specifically on the examination of the offence in relation to crimes against humanity and international humanitarian law.

The prohibition against torture is absolute; there are no exceptions under international humanitarian law or in international human rights law. Under international human rights law torture is defined by Art. 1 of the United Nations Convention against Torture (see Chapter 7) and in essence is the intentional infliction of severe physical or mental pain or suffering against a person or a third party for purposes such as of obtaining information or a confession or intimidation or coercion or punishing their victim, or for any reason based on discrimination of any kind. This list has subsequently been expanded to include humiliating the victim or a third person. Although it would appear that this is an exhaustive list, there would not seem to be any tangible reason why the torturer could not commit the offence for purely sadistic pleasures, without any real objective or motive. Even though rape constitutes a separate offence in international law, it may also amount to torture if it is part of the interrogation process. In *Prosecutor v Delalic et al —*

(Judgment November 16, 1998), the Trial Chamber stated that "... it is difficult to envisage circumstances in which rape, by, or at the instigation of a public official, or with the consent or acquiescence of an official, would be considered as occurring for a purpose that does not, in some way, involve punishment, coercion, discrimination or intimidation (para. 495). Although this statement was in reference to armed conflicts, the same notion would apply to torture during peacetime.

It is the seriousness and gravity of the act which will determine whether or not torture has been committed. Torture need not necessarily be conducted specifically against the victim. It may suffice if a person is being forced to watch others being treated inhumanely such that they are seriously affected by what they observe. For example, being forced to see a family member being raped or murdered may constitute torture.

5–018   Apart from the necessary ingredients required for all crimes against humanity, in *Akayesu*, the Trial Chamber defined the essential elements of torture as:

    (i)   The perpetrator must intentionally inflict severe physical or mental pain or suffering upon the victim for one or more of the following purposes:

        (a)   to obtain information or a confession from the victim or a third person;

        (b)   to punish the victim or a third person for an act committed or suspected of having been committed by either of them;

        (c)   for the purpose of intimidating or coercing the victim or the third person; and

        (d)   for any reason based on discrimination of any kind.

    (ii) The perpetrator was himself an official, or acted at the instigation of, or with the consent or acquiescence of, an official or person acting in an official capacity. (para. 594)

In *Kunarac* (Judgment February 22, 2001) the Trial Chamber stated that in international humanitarian law "the elements of the offence of torture, under customary international law are as follows:

    (i)   The infliction, by act or omission, of severe pain or suffering, whether physical or mental.

    (ii) The act or omission must be intentional.

    (iii) The act or omission must aim at obtaining information or a confession, or at punishing, intimidating or coercing the victim or a third person, or at discriminating, on any ground, against the victim or a third person". (para. 497)

Omitted from the above elements is any mention of the act of torture having to be carried out by a State official, *de facto* or otherwise. In international human rights law, and specifically under the UNCT, the offence may only be committed by State officials or their representatives; in international human-itarian law no such limitation is required and private individuals may also be prosecuted for the offence. The ICC also does not appear to restrict torture to government officials but only to such persons whose victims are "in the custody or under the control of the perpetrator". Although the perpetrator need not even possess *de facto* government status, this will be, at the very least, the case in many instances.

Under Art. 7(ii)(e) of the ICC, "[T]orture means the intentional infliction of severe pain or suffering, whether physical or mental, upon a person in the custody or under the control of the accused, except that torture shall not include pain or suffering arising only from, inherent in or incidental to lawful sanctions". In the elements of crimes provision for crimes against humanity under the ICC, torture means that:

- The perpetrator inflicted severe physical or mental pain or suffering upon one or more persons.

- Such person or persons were in the custody or under the control of the perpetrator.

- Such pain or suffering did not arise only from, and was not inherent in or identical to, lawful sanctions.

- The conduct was committed as part of a widespread or systematic attack directed against a civilian population.

- The perpetrator knew that the conduct was part of or intended the conduct to be part of a widespread or systematic attack directed against a civilian population.

Since torture is proscribed absolutely under international criminal law, it is difficult to envisage circumstances whereby it would be permitted (as high-lighted above), in relation to "lawful sanctions". It would appear that such an exception is axiomatic, since if the "pain and suffering arising from, inherent in or incidental to lawful sanctions" were permitted, it would not under such circumstances constitute torture. Thus, even where a State does not designate certain ill-treatment as torture, if the actions in fact come within the defini-tion, those persons responsible for committing such acts should nevertheless be prosecuted for torture.

Finally, although torture is expressly prohibited in war under Art. 8(2)(a)(ii), the accused may nevertheless be charged cumulatively for torture under crimes against humanity and as a war crime, since the elements of each specific provision differ. For instance, according to the elements of torture as a war crime the victims are limited to those persons who have "protected status" as opposed to "any civilian population" under the ICC, or indeed the ICTY, or the discriminatory grounds under Art. 3 of the ICTR.

Rape

5–019 In international law, rape has been recognised as a war crime since the Tokyo trials of the Second World War, and was at that time specifically incorporated as such within crimes against humanity in CCL (Control Council Law) No.10 of Art. II(c). Sadly, although in later Geneva Conventions (such as in 1977), and their additional protocols, rape is proscribed under international law, it was still regarded as a "secondary" crime by not specifically granting rape grave breach status in those conventions. However, it was stated in *Prosecutor v Furindizija*— (Judgment December 10, 1998) that "Rape may also amount to a grave breach of the Geneva Conventions, a violation of the laws or customs of war or an act of genocide, if the requisite elements are met" (para. 172). In most national legal systems the main elements of the crime of rape encompass the elements of lack of consent and sexual penetration. In international law, its definition is broader and continues to be developed (see Chapter 11 for further analysis).

Rape is a uniquely horrific crime. Whilst the purpose behind the act may possess certain characteristics of other crimes, such as torture, assault, physical and mental harm, the actual act itself which constitutes the *actus reus* of the offence is very specific in terms of the physical and psychological impact on the victim. More specifically, in *Kunarac* the Trial Chamber stated that "the crime of rape in international law is constituted by: the sexual penetration, however slight: (a) of the vagina or anus of the victim by the penis of the perpetrator or any other object used by the perpetrator; or (b) of the mouth of the victim by the penis of the perpetrator; where such sexual penetration occurs without the consent of the victim. Consent for this purpose must be given voluntarily, as a result of the victim's free will, assessed in the context of the surrounding circumstances. The *mens rea* is the intention to effect this sexual penetration, and the knowledge that it occurs without the consent of the victim". (para. 460)

In conjunction with the other necessary elements of crimes against humanity, rape was defined in *Akayesu* as "a physical invasion of a sexual nature, committed on a person under circumstances which are coercive. Sexual violence, which includes rape, is considered to be any act of a sexual nature which is committed on a person under circumstances which are coercive" (para. 598). In *Akayesu* the accused was bourgmestre of the Taba commune from April 1993 until June 1994. It was alleged that the accused was present during various sexual assaults and murders upon the Tutsi civilian population and failed to take any action to prevent those atrocities taking place. Some 2,000 Tutsis were subsequently killed during that period by local armed militia and communal police. The accused was eventually charged with, *inter alia*, seven counts of crimes against humanity including extermination, murder, torture, rape and other inhumane acts contrary to Art. 3 of the ICTR.

He was eventually found guilty on all counts of crimes against humanity and sentenced to between 10 and 15 years imprisonment for these specific crimes. He was also sentenced to life imprisonment for genocide and thereafter received a single sentence of life imprisonment for all his crimes.

Apart from the consequential extreme physical and mental torment and degradation, the resulting inhuman violation often leads to permanent harm, far worse than other physical injuries committed under other offences of crimes against humanity.   **5–020**

Rape within international law is not only restricted to penetration by the penis, but may also include acts such as oral sex, insertion of any object into the vagina or anus (*Furundzija* (Judgment December 10, 1998), para. 181). The perception of rape of international law continues to be expanded and is not limited to "normal" acts constituting the offence. Recent cases in both tribunals recognise that the crime of rape is to be determined from a conceptual perspective. Indeed, in *Prosecutor v Musema* (Judgment January 27, 2000), the Trial Chamber stated that "(I)n light of the dynamic ongoing evolution of the understanding of rape and the incorporation of this understanding into principles of international law, the Chamber considers that a conceptual definition is preferable to a mechanical definition of rape. The conceptual definition will better accommodate evolving norms of criminal justice". (para. 229)

Persecution

In an international setting, persecution has been historically associated with the ill treatment of various, usually, minority groups, such as the Jews, the Armenians, the Kurds, the Cambodians and so forth. What has been lacking in this particular crime in international law is a precise definition of the offence. During the Nuremberg trials, extermination, starvation, murder, torture, deportations, and enslavement, confiscating and plundering the homes and businesses of civilians, and the destruction of synagogues were all considered to be forms of persecution. It may be argued that any serious victimisation of a specific group constitutes the offence. However, it is not a catch-all crime. What sets this particular offence apart from other crimes against humanity is that persecution only constitutes a crime when committed on discriminatory grounds, *i.e.* political, racial or religious under Art. 5 of the ICTY; Art. 3 of the ICTR and Art. 6(c) of the Nuremberg Charter. However, the ICC has broadened the discriminatory aspect and under Art. 7(i)(h) states that persecution may be against any identifiable group or gender as defined by Art. 7(3) and "refers to the two sexes, male and female, within the context of society". Persecution specifically relates to any group, whether "on political, racial, religious, national, ethnic, cultural, religious, gender or other grounds that are universally recognised as impermissible under international law . . ." (Art. 7(1)(h)). There is no requirement that these crimes be related to or connected with any armed conflict, in compliance with CCL No.10 and present day customary international law, but differs from   **5–021** prosecutions under the ICTY where the existence of an armed conflict must be proved. "Any civilian population" includes ordinary civilians of any nationality as well as those persons who had previously been combatants but are now *hors de combat*, through being prisoners of war or debilitated through injury or sickness. "Gender", according to Art. 7(3), is given a restricted meaning and "refers to the two sexes, male and female, within the context of society". In *Crimes Against Humanity*, the author Geoffrey Robertson QC is appalled at this limited construction and calls it "the most ridiculous clause in any international treaty ever devised". He argues that persecution against such groups as transsexuals, homosexuals and lesbians would presumably be permissible "within the context of society, *i.e.* approved by a gay-bashing government or culture". It was inserted, seemingly to appease the Holy See, Islamic and States whose interventionist policies prevent certain minorities to live free from state interference. The last sentence in Art. 7(3) stating that the "term 'gender' does not indicate any meaning different from the above", only goes to enforce the restricted interpretation.

"*Persecution*" in the general sense of the term has a very broad meaning. It may be adjudged as any serious interference with the freedom and well-being of a civilian population by such means as physical and mental harm, deportation, inhumane treatment and punishment, unlawful arrest and imprisonment, enslavement, torture, eradication and other serious factors which affect their living conditions. One of the main purposes behind such persecutory acts is to induce such hardship on the victim group that they become alienated from the rest of society. Segregation by such means often leads to the actual destruction of an entire or at least a high proportion of such people. Although it is not a prerequisite that the specific targeted group must be destroyed, unlike genocide, nevertheless, in reality the consequences are that persecution often leads to the death of many members of the particular group.

In *Prosecutor v Kupreskic et al* (Judgment January 14, 2000) the Trial Chamber defined persecution as "the gross or blatant denial, on discriminatory grounds, of a fundamental right, laid down in international customary or treaty law, reaching the same level of gravity as the other acts prohibited in Art. 5" (para. 621). In that case all six accused were indicted for, *inter alia*, crimes against humanity, and specifically with persecution under Art. 5(h) of the ICTY. It was alleged that from October 1992 until April 1993 the accused persecuted the Bosnian-Muslim inhabitants of Ahmici-Santici and the surrounding areas by planning, organising and implementing an attack against those people which resulted in: (1) the deliberate and systematic killing of the people there; as well as (2) the destruction of their property; (3) their imprisonment; and (4) expulsion of the Bosnian-Muslims from the village and surrounding areas. The main question for the Tribunal was, could the above allegations amount to forms of persecution? In points (1), (3) and (4) above, the Trial Chamber found that such treatment could constitute persecution since those acts came within part of the enumerated offences of murder, imprisonment and deportation expressly set out in Art. 5. However, in point (2) above, not all destruction of property *per se* amounts to persecution. It must further be established that the destruction of the particular property will have a detrimental effect on the liberty and livelihood of those people in that area. As was stated by the Trial Chamber in *Kupreskic* (Judgment January 14, 2000) such destruction should be akin to "the same inhumane consequences as a forced transfer or deportation" (para. 631). In *Blaskic* (Judgment March 3, 2000), the accused was charged, *inter alia*, with the destruction and plunder of private property belonging to the Bosnian–Muslim civilian population. The Trial Chamber ruled that "the destruction of property must be construed to mean the destruction of towns, villages and other public or private property belonging to a given population or extensive devastation not justified by military necessity and carried unlawfully, wantonly and discriminatorily". (para. 234)

Apart from the basic elements of crimes against humanity and the discriminatory requirements relating to persecution set out in the various relevant provisions of the ICTY, ICTR and ICC, there is no exhaustive list of offences cited which constitutes this particular crime. There is no doubt that the subcategories listed in the other crimes against humanity provisions form, at least, a basis for persecutory offences. However, it may be the case that other offences cited in those same international tribunals should also be added to this list. However, does persecution include other conduct or laws not specifically mentioned in any of the Statutes of the existing tribunals? The trial Chamber in *Kupreskic* examined the historical effects of persecution, especially in relation to events before and during the Second World War in Germany. For example, laws were introduced by the Nazi regime that included preventing Jews from entering a profession, intermarrying and having sexual relationships with other Germans. Jews were also subjected to regular beatings, confiscation of their property and others were incited to persecute Jews. It served no purpose complaining to the authorities about their treatment; it was after all those same people who were carrying out the atrocities inflicted upon them (see *Kupreskic*, para. 612). **5–022**

Having examined the historical roots of persecution and specifically the judgments of the IMT the Trial Chamber in *Kupreskic* (para. 615) determined that the *actus reus* of the offence is the following:

(a) A narrow definition of persecution is not supported in customary international law. Persecution has been described by courts as a wide and particularly serious genus of crimes committed against the Jewish people and other groups by the Nazi regime.

(b) In their interpretation of persecution courts have included acts such as murder, extermination, torture, and other serious acts on the person such as those presently enumerated in Art. 5.

(c) Persecution can also involve a variety of other discriminatory acts, involving attacks on political, social, and economic rights.

(d)   Persecution is commonly used to describe a series of acts rather than a single act. Acts of persecution will usually form part of a policy or at least of a patterned practice, and must be regarded in their context. In reality, persecutory acts are often committed pursuant to a discriminatory policy or a widespread discriminatory practice.

(e)   As a corollary to (d), discriminatory acts charged as persecution must not be considered in isolation. Some of the acts mentioned above may not, in and of themselves, be so serious as to constitute a crime against humanity. For example, restrictions placed on a particular group to curtail their rights to participate in particular aspects of social life (such as visits to public parks, theatres or libraries) constitute discrimination, which is in itself a reprehensible act; however, they may not in and of themselves amount to persecution. These acts must not be considered in isolation but examined in their context and weighed for their cumulative effect.

Therefore, not only may there exist the conditions for the crime of persecution outside a particular international Statute, but also it is immaterial that the laws permitting these offences are legal under the national laws of the particular State.

The Trial Chamber in *Kupreskic* concluded that it was necessary that there be a link to other crimes stated in the SITY (para. 581). Nevertheless, the gravity of the offence must at least attain the same level as the other crimes against humanity enumerated in Art. 5 of the SICTY (para. 621).

5–023   In relation to other crimes against humanity offences, the *mens rea* for such crimes entail the specific intent to commit the underlying offence as well as possessing the knowledge of the context of a widespread or systematic attack on a civilian population, pursuant to some plan or policy. However, with regard to persecution the additional discriminatory (*i.e.* on political, racial or religious grounds) element is required. In *Kupreskic* the Trial Chamber noted that persecutory "acts were all aimed at singling out and attacking certain individuals on discriminatory grounds, by depriving them of the political, social or economic rights enjoyed by members of the wider society. The deprivation of these rights can be said to have as its aim the removal of those persons from the society in which they live alongside the perpetrators, or eventually even from humanity itself" (para. 634). Accordingly, as far as the mental element is concerned, must the accused also possess the discriminatory intent, *i.e.* have knowledge of the policy or plan that the attack was based on discriminatory grounds, or is it sufficient merely to have known of the context of the attack as in other crimes against humanity offences? The *mens rea* behind the crime of persecution is the specific intent to cause injury to an individual because of his membership of a particular group on religious, racial, or political grounds, *i.e.* discriminatory intent, and is distinguishable from the other offences for crimes against humanity under Art. 5 of the ICTY, which are non-discriminatory. In *Kordic* (Judgment February 26, 2001), the Prosecution whilst accepting that because of the discriminatory grounds factor a *"more particular mental state standard"* was required than other crimes against humanity, and rejected that the discriminatory *mens rea* for persecution amounts to a specific intent requirement. The Prosecution argued that "it is sufficient that the accused had knowledge of the discriminatory grounds on which the widespread or systematic attack against a civilian population was launched. Such knowledge does not relate to the subjective motives of the perpetrator, but to his objective knowledge that such acts fit into a widespread or systematic attack against a civilian population based on political, racial or religious grounds" (para. 216). This argument was rejected by the Trial Chamber. They stated that although it would be difficult to imagine a case where the perpetrator knew that his acts were committed in the context of a widespread or systematic attack and not be aware of the discriminatory grounds upon which they were being committed, nevertheless, because of the intense gravity of persecution and its distinctive discriminatory features, they found "that in order to possess the heightened *mens rea* for the crime of persecution, the accused must have shared the aim of the discriminatory policy". (para. 220)

In one respect, the *mens rea* for the crime of persecution is similar but not identical to genocide — similar in that the persons targeted are targeted because of their membership of that particular group. However, there are essential differences which were considered in *Kupreskic*, where the Trial Chamber stated that "[W]hile in the case of persecution the discriminatory intent can take multifarious inhumane forms and manifest itself in a plurality of actions including murder, in the case of genocide that intent must be accompanied by the intention to destroy, in whole or in part, the group to which the victims of the genocide belong. Thus, it can be said that, from the viewpoint of *mens rea,* genocide is an extreme and most inhuman form of persecution. To put it differently, when persecution escalates to the extreme form of wilful and deliberate acts designed to destroy a group or part of a group, it can be held that such persecution amounts to genocide". (para. 636)

Under Art. 7(2)(g) of the ICC, persecution "means the intentional and severe deprivation of fundamental rights contrary to international law by reason of the identity of the group". In this respect the offence also encompasses cultural and gender discrimination. Since the ICC is supposedly to form part of customary international law, does this mean that the crime of persecution has been further developed and extended from its historical meaning? Apparently not; it was stated by the Trial Chamber in *Kupreskic* that "although the Statute of the ICC may be indicative of the *opinio juris* of many States, Art. 7(1)(h) is not consonant with customary international law". As evidence of this the Trial Chamber went on to cite Art. 10 of the Statute which states that "Nothing in the Statute shall be interpreted as limiting or prejudicing in any way existing or developing rules of international law for purposes other than this Statute". This provision clearly conveys that the framers of the Statute did not intend to affect, amongst other things, *lex lata*, as regards such matters as the definition of war crimes, crimes against humanity and genocide". (para. 580)

Apartheid

5–024   In general terms, apartheid refers to the racial segregation and discrimination policies enacted by a government against a section of its own people. Historically, the term has been inextricably linked to the events that took place in South Africa, predominantly from the late 1940s until its prohibition there in 1994. The meaning of apartheid originates from the Afrikaans word for "apartness". After gaining independence in 1931, the minority white-controlled government set about instigating programmes of separation between whites and non-whites. However, it was not until 1946 that the international community intervened *via* a United Nations resolution which formally condemned the discriminatory practices of the South African government against the Indian minority living in that State. Sadly, the situation did not improve, and in 1948, after the National Party gained power, the policies of apartheid wholeheartedly began to take root. Legislation was introduced from 1949 onwards which intensified the whole situation. The racial separation policies enacted included the following:

- Racial groups were classified into four categories — white, black, coloured (persons of mixed race), and later on Indians and Asians.

- All black people had to carry "pass books" for identification purposes and when entering non-black areas.

- Legislation made it unlawful to intermarry and sexual relations between whites and other races were strictly prohibited.

- Black students were prohibited from attending most universities and black people in general received inferior education.

- Black people were relocated to other areas known as "homelands" in order to eventually rid black South Africans of their citizenship.

- Separate amenities were provided for blacks which were of a much lower standard.

- Many facilities and jobs were restricted to whites only, *e.g.* the police force and government positions.

- Protests and anti-apartheid organisations were prohibited.

- Arrest without trial.

- The right to vote was severely restricted for black people.

110

After numerous General Assembly resolutions calling for the end to such policies and practices, the United Nations in 1973 adopted *via* General Assembly Resolution 3068, the International Convention on the Suppression and Punishment of the Crime of Apartheid. Its Preamble states, *inter alia*, that in accordance with various existing international treaties and declarations (namely, the International Convention on the Elimination of All Forms of Racial Discrimination; the Genocide Convention; Universal Declaration of Human Rights; and the Declaration on the Granting of Independence to Colonial Countries and Peoples), ". . . States particularly condemn racial segregation and apartheid and undertake to prevent, prohibit and eradicate all practices of this nature in territories under their jurisdictions". (para. 4)

Article 1 of the Apartheid Convention states that apartheid ". . . are crimes violating the principles of international law (and) constitute a serious threat to international peace and security". Article 2 states that apartheid ". . . shall include similar policies and practices of racial segregation and discrimination as practised in southern Africa", and shall apply to the following inhuman acts committed for the purpose of establishing and maintaining domination by one racial group of persons over any other racial group of persons and systematically oppressing them. The inhuman acts under Art. II(a)–(f) include practices which deny a member of members of a racial group the basic right to life and liberty, *e.g.* murder, torture and cruel, inhuman or degrading treatment or punishment, arbitrary arrest and illegal imprisonment, and serious bodily or mental harm (Art. II(a)(i)–(iii)). Article II(b)–(f) further lists other acts which constitute crimes of apartheid. These include inflicting living conditions on a racial group calculated to cause its physical destruction in whole or in part; preventing a racial group from participation in the political, social, economic and cultural life of a State; denial of basic human rights, *e.g.* the right to work, the right to education, the right to a nationality, and so forth.

Under Art. IV of the Convention, state parties undertake "(T)o adopt any legislative or other measures necessary to suppress as well as to prevent any encouragement of the crime of apartheid and similar segregationist policies or their manifestations and to punish persons guilty of that crime". Unfortunately, these measures were not adhered to by the South African Government, and it was not until 1994, with the introduction of a new constitution, which gave the black population full voting rights and the subsequent elections, that the apartheid programme was finally made illegal and formally ended.

Although internationally recognised as a crime, apartheid has rarely been **5–025** used for prosecution purposes. However, it is by no means a "dead letter". This is reinforced by the ICC which includes the offence as part of its crimes against humanity provisions under Art. 7(i)(j). Paragraph 2 defines apartheid as "inhumane acts of a character similar to those referred to in paragraph 1, committed in the context of an institutionalised regime of systematic oppression and domination by one racial group over any other racial group or groups and committed with the intention of maintaining that regime". The elements of crimes within the ICC provides that apartheid exists where:

- The perpetrator committed an inhumane act against one or more persons.

- Such an act was an act referred to in Art. 7, para. 1, of the Statute, or was an act of a character similar to any of those acts.

- The perpetrator was aware of the factual circumstances that established the character of the act.

- The conduct was committed in the context of an institutionalised regime or systematic oppression and domination by one racial group over any other racial group or group.

- The perpetrator intended to maintain such regime by that conduct.

In the footnote of the apartheid element of crimes provisions, it is stated that the word "character" in 2 and 3 above, "refers to the nature and gravity of the act". Although "an inhumane act" is restricted to the sub-headings in Art. 7(1)(a)–(k), it is arguable that the words should be given a wider interpretation akin to violations of any of the rights stated in Art. II of the Apartheid Convention. The words "institutionalised regime" are not defined. However, since this offence is generally government-led and orchestrated, it is doubtful whether apartheid could be committed by perpetrators who have not been sanctioned by the state to instigate such policies. There is no doubt that apartheid programmes are in operation in many parts of the world, indeed where widespread racial discrimination by a State authority exists, it is difficult to envisage scenarios where a form of apartheid is also not present.

Enforced disappearance of persons

5–026　The State is under a duty to protect the freedom of its citizens. Any crime involving the enforced disappearance of a person directly derogates from a state's responsibility by taking away that freedom. Under Art. 7(2)(i) of the ICC elements of crimes provisions the words "enforced disappearance of persons" means "the arrest, detention or abduction of persons by, or with the authorization, support or acquiescence of, a State or a political organization, followed by a refusal to acknowledge that deprivation of freedom or to give information on the fate or whereabouts of those persons, with the intention of removing them from the protection of the law for a prolonged period of time". The above definition is set out in similar terms to Art. II of the Inter-American Convention on the Forced Disappearance of Persons 1994, and recognises that such a crime constitutes a crime against humanity. The prohibition against such practices is absolute and is not permitted under any circumstances. The essence of this crime is that in reality it amounts to a form of State kidnapping, of at least State sponsored or sanctioned. It is often the case that the victims of this crime never reappear alive again, or their bodies never discovered, or the victims" families never informed as to the reason or whereabouts of the person abducted. This particular crime against humanity has been incorporated as such by the ICC but is not included in the statutes of the ICTY or ICTR.

Other inhuman acts

The sub-category of *"other inhuman acts"* is not a catch-all offence. It does **5–027** possess its own individual meaning although arguably not as precise as other offences. Its use was included within Art. 6(c) of the Nuremberg Charter as a means of insurance to not only counteract any possible defence put forward by an accused that the indictment does not relate to any of the other categories of offences, but also to provide for any loophole left open by other offences not specifically mentioned.

Generally, other inhuman acts has been interpreted to mean any act committed which is of a similar nature to those acts which preceded it in the provisions of the particular Article, *e.g.* murder, extermination, deportation and so forth in Art. 3 of the ICTR and Art. 5 of the ICTY. The phrase "other inhumane acts" is primarily concerned with the seriousness and gravity of the offence. Thus, the crime is not limited to the enumerated acts set out in the statutes of the various international tribunals and may extend to *any* act or omission which causes the intentional physical or mental suffering of its victims. However, Art. 7 of the ICC states that other inhumane acts are acts "of a character similar to any other act referred to in Art. 7 paragraph of the Statute", thus limiting the offence to the crimes enumerated in Art. 7(1).

Whether the offence attains the level of serious physical or mental harm required is decided by the particular circumstances of each individual case, taking into account such factors as "the nature of the act or omission, the context in which it occurs, its duration and/or repetition, the physical, memtal and moral effects of the act on the victim and the personal circumstances of the victim, including age, sex and health" (*Delalic et al* (Judgment November 16, 1998), para. 536). In line with persecutory acts, it is not the name given to the particular act which is the determining factor, but rather the effect that that act or omission has on its victims, *i.e.* did the targeted civilians suffer serious bodily or psychological harm as a result of the intentional acts or omissions of the perpetrator? In *Kayishema* (Judgment May 21, 1999) the Trial Chamber concluded that for the accused to be convicted of this particular offence "he must commit an act of similar gravity and seriousness to the other enumerated crimes, with the intention to cause the other inhumane act, and with knowledge that the act is perpetrated within the overall context of the attack". (para. 154)

It may even be the case that third parties who have suffered as a result of, **5–028** for instance, witnessing acts committed by the perpetrator against others may constitute this as an offence. However, in *Kayishema* (para. 153) the Trial

Chamber stated that "an accused may be held liable under the circumstances only where, at the time of the act, the accused had the intention to inflict serious mental suffering on the third party, or where the accused knew that an act was likely to cause serious mental suffering and was reckless as to whether such suffering would result. Accordingly, if at the time of the act, the accused was unaware of the third party bearing witness to his act, then he cannot be held responsible for the mental suffering of the third party".

It is arguable that the emphasis for other inhumane acts lies not in the limited enumerated lists set out in the relevant crimes against humanity provisions of the international tribunals, but also encompasses other acts provided such conduct results in injuries of a serious or grave nature. Article 7(1)(a)–(k) of the ICC extends the sub-category list of crimes against humanity to include enforced disappearances of persons and the crime of apartheid. However, it would appear that any act which results in serious or grave harm to the health of civilians ought to constitute the offence.

Under the ICC the elements of crimes provision for "other inhumane acts" continues to state that: (1) The perpetrator inflicted great suffering, or serious injury to body or to mental or physical health, by means of an inhumane act; (2) such an act was of a character similar to any other act referred to in Art. 7 para. 1 of the Statute; (3) the perpetrator was aware of the factual circumstances that established the character of the act; (4) the conduct was committed as part of a widespread or systematic attack directed a civilian population; and (5) the perpetrator knew that the conduct was part of or intended the conduct to be part of a widespread or systematic attack against a civilian population. It does not include minor offences such as public order crimes or riots that are purely internal and are outside the perimeters of the jurisdiction of the court. The words stated in paras (4) and (5) above are common for each of the elements of the offences in Art. 7(1)(a)–(k).

CRIMES AGAINST HUMANITY UNDER THE INTERNATIONAL CRIMINAL COURT

5–029   One major problem facing the Rome Conference was constructing a definition for crimes against humanity since no previous meaning for those words had been formulated in existing treaties elsewhere. Eventually the following definition was agreed upon:

> "For the purpose of this Statute, crimes against humanity means any of the following acts when committed as part of a widespread or systematic attack against any civilian population, with knowledge of the attack". (Art. 7(1))

Article 7(1)(a)–(k) sets out the specific acts required to constitute a crime against humanity; namely, murder, extermination, enslavement, deportation, imprisonment, torture (includes acts of those other than state officials), rape, persecution, enforced disappearance, apartheid and other inhumane acts of a similar character intentionally causing great suffering, or serious injury to body or to mental or physical health. Thus, it not only includes conduct contrary to international law but also covers "other inhumane acts" within the jurisdiction of the court and refers to acts of a similar nature to those set out in Art. 7(1)(a)–(j), above. Moreover, Art. 7 appears to extend the category of offences already set out in the ICTY and ICTR. For example, under the ICC the list includes enforced disappearance of persons (Art. 7(1)(i)), apartheid (Art. 7(1)(j)), and sexual slavery, enforced pregnancy and sterilization (Art. 7(1)(g)). Further, the grounds for persecution are extended to include national, ethic, cultural or gender or other grounds that are universally recognised as impermissible under international law (Art. 7(1)(h)). After intense discussion by the Preparatory Commission, the elements of crimes for each enumerated offence for crimes against humanity were finalised by the PCNICC on June 29, 2000 (PCNICC/2000/INF/3/Add.2).

Mens rea

In order for a successful prosecution against an individual for crimes against humanity the perpetrator "must have knowledge of the attack". The attack itself need not necessarily form part of a positive act; acts of omission will also suffice. "Knowledge" need not only be actual, but also constructive knowledge would suffice in the circumstances. In the *Tadic* case (judgment — para. 638) the court said that "actual or constructive knowledge of the broader context of the attack, meaning that the accused must know that his act(s) is part of a widespread or systematic attack on a civilian population and pursuant to some kind of policy or plan, is necessary to satisfy the requisite *mens rea* element of the accused". Thus, inhumane acts by high-ranking officials will have difficulty in exculpating themselves from their responsibilities under this Article when organising and planning the attack, unless they are able to prove that the resulting atrocities were unforeseeable or that their subordinates disobeyed their orders and pursued their own agenda of mass violations under Art. 7(1)(a)–(k).

5–030

The words "pursuant to or in furtherance of" a State policy suggests that there may only be a violation of this particular Article where there is in existence a State policy or plan to carry out various acts within Art. 7(a)–(k). If no policy is *in situ*, then there is no crime. However, it may be the case that state acts are being perpetrated against the civilian population and those in authority condone or, at least, "turn a blind eye" to those illegal acts. On a narrow interpretation of the words "pursuant to or in furtherance of", it may be construed that there is no crime against humanity in these circumstances. For instance, officials who carry out torture against their victims may be able to argue that since no policy exists they cannot be held criminally liable for their actions, at least if indicted under Art. 7.

The elements of crimes provision, para. 3 when referring to the meaning of "attack", states that "[I]t is understood that 'policy to commit such attack' requires that the state or organization actively promote or encourage such an attack against a civilian population". Although these words would suggest that the policy itself must amount to some form of positive action taken by the state as opposed to some policy of omission, this is not necessary so. In footnote 6, relating to para. 3, it is stated that "such a policy may, in exceptional circumstances, be implemented by a deliberate failure to take action, which is consciously aimed at encouraging such attack. The existence of such a policy cannot be inferred solely from the absence of governmental or organizational action". If this is the case, then in the torture example, above, if it can be proved that the authorities were aware that torture was taking place, and failed to respond by taking some action to alleviate the situation, then despite there not being a state policy, it may be imputed, by association, that such a policy does, at least, *prima facie*, exist.

Chapter 6

WAR CRIMES

INTRODUCTION: WAR CRIMES AND INTERNATIONAL HUMANITARIAN LAW

War crimes are defined as "grave" or "serious" violations of the rules or customs of war — or, as it is now more commonly called, of international humanitarian law or IHL — for which individuals can be held individually responsible. This section will explain the development of the concept of war crimes, by reference to the development of IHL in general and through international criminal tribunals in particular. Since most of these matters are dealt with more specifically in Chapter 10, the discussion here is limited to some fairly brief overviews, intended merely to put the concept in its proper context. The elements of war crimes themselve are set out after a discussion of the relationship between IHL and international human rights law in this respect. Some broad conclusions are set out at the end of the chapter.   **6–001**

International Humanitarian Law (IHL)

The basic rules of modern IHL developed over a period of about a hundred   **6–002**
years: from the 1864 Geneva Convention "for the amelioration of the conditions of the wounded in armies in the field", inspired by Henri Dunant (the founder, in 1863, of the International Committee of the Red Cross, which is in many ways the custodian of IHL), *via* the Hague conferences of 1899 and 1907, the League of Nations 1925 Geneva Protocol prohibiting the use of poisonous gases and biological weapons, and the ICRC Conventions of 1929, to the current cornerstones of the IHL edifice, the four Geneva Conventions of 1949 and the two Additional Protocols to the Conventions of 1977. IHL continues to develop from this basis, with a large number of further Conventions, relating to or relevant to conduct in war having been adopted since then, such as the 1954 Hague Convention for the protection of cultural property in the event of armed conflict; the 1979 Hostages Convention; the 1980 Convention against non-detectable fragments, mines and booby-traps, and its 1985 Protocol concerning blinding laser weapons; the 1993 Chemical Weapons Convention; the 1997 Landmines Convention; and the 1999 Protocol to the 1954 Hague Convention.

   In its Advisory Opinion on the legality of the threat or use of nuclear weapons of 1996, (further referred to below under the heading "*using prohibited weapons*"), the International Court of Justice (ICJ) set out the basic principles of IHL in the following terms:

"The cardinal principles contained in the texts constituting the fabric of humanitarian law are the following. The first is aimed at the protection of the civilian population and civilian objects and establishes the distinction between combatants and non-combatants; States must never make civilians the objects of attack and must consequently never use weapons that are incapable of distinguishing between civilian and military targets. According to the second principle, it is prohibited to cause unnecessary suffering to combatants: it is accordingly prohibited to use weapons causing them such harm or uselessly aggravating their suffering . . .

In conformity with the aforementioned principles, humanitarian law, at a very early stage, prohibited certain types of weapons either because of their indiscriminate effect on combatants and civilians or because of the unnecessary suffering caused to combatants, that is to say, a harm greater than that unavoidable to achieve legitimate military objectives." (paras. 78ff)

The court also referred to the so-called "Martens Clause", which was first included in the 1899 Hague Convention with Respect to the Laws and Customs of War on Land. The clause is expressed in Art. 1(2) of the First Additional Protocol to the Geneva Conventions in the following terms:

"In cases not covered by this Protocol or by other international agreements, civilians and combatants remain under the protection and authority of the principles of international law derived from established custom, from the principles of humanity and from the dictates of public conscience."

The "cardinal principles" and the Martens Clause, set out by the ICJ, as well as many (though not all) of the rules in the four Geneva Conventions, and some rules in some specific treaties, have developed into customary law, and are thus binding on States, whether they are party to the conventions or treaties in question or not. The rules in other conventions have, however, not (yet) become customary law — and therefore only bind States that are party to them.

International criminal tribunals

6–003   The development of IHL has — intermittently — been accompanied by the establishment of international criminal tribunals. The first of these were the post-World War II Nuremberg and Tokyo tribunals, set up by the victorious Allies to try war criminals from the defeated Axis powers. However, the more important impetus towards the development of an effective, internationally-enforced law against war crimes came from the establishment, in the 1990s, of the International Criminal Tribunal for the former Yugoslavia (ICTY, 1993) and the International Criminal Tribunal for Rwanda (ICTR, 1994). Through their case-law, the latter *ad hoc* tribunals have helped to clarify IHL relating to war crimes in many respects. The development has culminated in the adoption, in 1998, of the Rome Statute of the (permanent) International Criminal Court (ICC), which entered into force on July 1, 2002. The ICC has its seat in The Hague in the Netherlands. The 18 judges were sworn in in March 2003, and the first prosecutor to the court, the Argentinian Luis Moreno Ocampo, was appointed in April and took up his work in June of that year.

The interplay between IHL and international criminal tribunals in the matter of war crimes

As far as war crimes are concerned, there is an interplay between the substantive rules, the violation of which constitute such crimes and the jurisdictions of the international tribunals, which has led to an expansion of international criminal responsibility and — jurisdiction.   **6–004**

Specifically, the traditional rules and customs of war were (as the term implies) concerned only with armed conflicts between States; and the Geneva Conventions (GC I, II, III and IV, hereafter jointly referred to as "the Conventions") and the first Additional Protocol (AP I) are also still almost entirely concerned with international armed conflict — although it must be noted that this includes military occupation even if the occupation meets with no armed resistance (or, one may add, if it occurs or continues after hostilities have ended): see Common Art. 2 of the Conventions.

The main exception is Art. 3 common to the Conventions, which prohibits certain serious violations of human rights and human dignity in "armed conflicts not of an international character". The second Additional Protocol to the Conventions (AP II) does deal specifically with such non-international conflicts — but it provides for less protection than the Conventions and AP I provide for with regard to international conflicts. None of the Conventions, and neither of the two Additional Protocols, moreover, apply to "situations of internal disturbances and tensions, such as riots, isolated and sporadic acts of violence or other acts of a similar nature" (see para. 6–010 below).

The Geneva Conventions oblige States to "provide effective penal sanctions for persons committing, or ordering to be committed" certain specified, "grave" violations of the Conventions (GC I, Arts 49 and 50; GC II, Arts 50 and 51; GC III, Arts 129 and 130; GC IV, Arts 146 and 147). Indeed, for such crimes, all States must assume power to prosecute and punish the perpetrators ("compulsory universal jurisdiction", further discussed in para. 6–073 below). However, in line with the traditional limitations of IHL, mentioned above, the provisions in question, and hence this duty, only applies if the violations were committed in international armed conflicts (see Art. 2 in each of the four Conventions).   **6–005**

More specifically, the four Geneva Conventions do not impose the same duty on States with regard to violations perpetrated in non-international armed conflicts. Violations of Common Art. 3 of the Conventions, or of AP II, therefore do not, *under the terms of the Conventions as they were understood in 1949*, incur compulsory universal penal jurisdiction — no matter how grave the acts concerned. However, Common Art. 3 has long been accepted as reflecting customary law, and it has also become a rule of customary international law that all States can pursue such violations, and such perpetrators, if they want to ("permissive universal jurisdiction", see para. 6–073, below).

In practice, it is not always easy to determine if a particular situation amounts to an "international" or "non-international" armed conflict. These days, States often involve themselves in conflicts in another State indirectly, through proxies or by support for insurgents or armed factions. In any case, the crimes are just as appalling, whether committed in an international or non-international conflict.

6–006   The Rwanda Tribunal was therefore given explicit jurisdiction over serious violations of Common Art. 3 and AP II (Art. 4 of the Statute of the ICTR) — but without it being made clear whether this meant that such violations now constituted "grave" violations of the Conventions or not. Article 2 of the Statute of the Yugoslav Tribunal gives the Tribunal power to prosecute "persons committing or ordering to be committed grave breaches of the Geneva Conventions of 12 August 1949", and lists the same crimes under this heading as are listed in the Conventions — but unlike the Conventions, the Statute of the ICTY does not explicitly limit the application of the provision listing these crimes to situations of international armed conflict. This allowed (and allows) for further development of the law — but to date the Tribunal has been cautious.

Specifically, the Appeals Chamber of the ICTY held, in the *Tadic* case, that Art. 2 of the ICTY Statute applies only when the conflict is international (see *Tadic* judgment, para. 80, confirming its view in the interlocutory decision on jurisdiction). However, the Trial Chamber in the subsequent *Celebici* case suggested that customary international law may have developed (or at least may be developing) beyond this:

"While Trial Chamber II in the *Tadic* case did not initially consider the nature of the armed conflict to be a relevant consideration in applying Article 2 of the Statute, the majority of the Appeals Chamber in the *Tadic* Jurisdiction Decision did find that grave breaches of the Geneva Conventions could only be committed in international armed conflicts and this requirement was thus an integral part of Article 2 of the Statute. In his Separate Opinion, however, Judge Abi-Saab opined that "a strong case can be made for the application of Article 2, even when the incriminated act takes place in an internal conflict". The majority of the Appeals Chamber did indeed recognise that a change in the customary law scope of the 'grave breaches regime' in this direction may be occuring. This Trial Chamber is also of the view that the possibility that customary law has developed the provisions of the Geneva Conventions since 1949 to constitute an extension of "grave breaches" to internal armed conflicts should be recognised." (*Delalic* judgment, para. 202)

The Trial Chamber recognised that applying Art. 2 of the ICTY Statute to non-international armed conflicts would entail an extension of the "grave breaches" regime on the basis of a teleological interpretation of the law, but clearly felt that that was justified as far as Common Art. 3 is concerned:

> "[I]t is the view of this Trial Chamber that violations of common article 3 of the Geneva Conventions may fall more logically within Article 2 of the Statute." (para. 317)

In the end, it nevertheless did not adopt this view "for the present purpose", *i.e.* as far as the specific *Delalic* case was concerned, preferring instead to follow "the more cautious approach" in that instance (*idem*). Nevertheless, the judgment clearly suggests that in future cases the Tribunal may consider (serious) violations of Common Art. 3 of the Conventions as *ipso facto* "grave violations" of the Geneva Conventions, if it deems this justified in the particular circumstances of the case.

War crimes in the Rome Statute of the ICC

The Rome Statute of the permanent International Criminal Court confirms this development, and indeed takes it one step further, by expressly including both "serious violations of Art. 3 common to the four Geneva Conventions of 12 August 1949" and "other serious violations of the laws and customs applicable in armed conflicts not of an international character" in the article concerning its juridiction over "war crimes", Art. 8: **6–007**

Article 8
War crimes

1. The Court shall have jurisdiction in respect of war crimes in particular when committed as part of a plan or policy or as part of a large-scale commission of such crimes.

2. For the purpose of this Statute, "war crimes" means:

(a) Grave breaches of the Geneva Conventions of 12 August 1949 . . .

(b) Other serious violations of the laws and customs applicable in international armed conflict . . .

(c) In the case of an armed conflict not of an international character, serious violations of article 3 common to the four Geneva Conventions of 12 August 1949 . . .

(d) . . .

(e) Other serious violations of the laws and customs applicable in armed conflicts not of an international character . . .

(f) ...

(emphasis added; the specific crimes listed in each of the paragraphs quoted above are discussed below)

In accordance with traditional IHL, the Statute still excludes crimes committed in "situations of internal disturbances and tensions, such as riots, isolated and sporadic acts of violence or other acts of a similar nature" from the concept of "war crimes" (Art. 8(2)(d) and (f)). However, in this respect too, there is some development, in that it adds that, at least as far as the "other serious violations of the laws and customs applicable in armed conflicts not of an international character" are concerned, the concept of "armed conflicts not of an international character" includes "armed conflicts that take place in the territory of a State when there is protracted armed conflict between governmental authorities and organized armed groups or between such groups." (Art. 8(2)(f)).

Elements of crime

6–008   When the Rome Statute was being drafted, some States felt that greater certainty and clarity should be provided on the meaning of the crimes over which the ICC was to have jurisdiction and asked that so-called "Elements of Crime" (EOC) be drafted to this end. This was done by a preparatory commission ("PrepCom"), which drew heavily on a study by the International Committee of the Red Cross (ICRC) of existing case-law and international humanitarian and human rights law instruments. The aim of the study was "to provide the government delegations taking part in PrepCom with the necessary legal background and to prepare a means of accurately interpreting war crimes as defined in the Rome Statute." (Knut Dörmann, *Elements of War Crimes under the Rome Statute of the International Criminal Court: sources and commentary*, ICRC and Cambridge University Press 2003, p. 3).

The Elements of Crimes, as adopted, play a formal role in the application of the Rome Statute: under Art. 9(1) of the Statute:

> "Elements of Crimes shall assist the Court in the interpretation and application of articles 6 [genocide], 7 [crimes against humanity] and 8 [war crimes]."

While not formally binding, the EOC are thus highly authoritative in the interpretation of the provisions in the Rome Statute relating to the crimes listed. The only formal limitation on their use is that they must be, and must be applied, consistent with the Statute (Art. 9(3)). They can help in the interpretation of the provisions relating to the crimes concerned, but they cannot stretch the meaning of those provisions beyond their proper meaning.

The EOC were adopted at the first session of the Assembly of States Parties to the Rome Staute, held from September 3–10, 2002 (see the Official

Record of the session in ICC-ASP/1/3 and Corr.1). It must be stressed, however, that they are not static: they can be amended by a two-thirds majority of the States Party to the Statute, voting in the so-called Assembly of States Parties (Art. 9(2)). Also, even in the absence of any formal amendment, relevant international law will of course continue to develop, and this too is likely to be reflected in the application of the provisions of the Statute. The above-mentioned publication by the ICRC thus provides what is essentially an updated version of the study submitted to PrepCom, taking into account important subsequent jurisprudence of the ICTY and ICTR. As such, it is the most authoritative commentary on the provisions in the Rome Statute relating to war crimes.

The war crimes listed in Art. 8 of the Rome Statute and over which the ICC therefore has jurisdiction will be discussed further below, with, reference to the Geneva Conventions, the case-law of the ICTY and the ICTR, and the Elements of War Crimes, as set out in, summarised and updated by, the ICRC Commentary will be discussed further, below. As such, the discussion will explain IHL relating to war crimes. However, as noted in the above quote from the introduction to the ICRC Commentary, and as will also become clear in the discussions of the various war crimes, there is an increasingly close relationship between international humanitarian law relating to war crimes and international human rights law. Before discussing these crimes as such, it is therefore useful to look at this relationship.

WAR CRIMES AND INTERNATIONAL HUMAN RIGHTS LAW

Introduction

Many of the war crimes we will be considering later also constitute violations   **6–009** of international human rights law: arbitrary killings, torture, inhuman or degrading treatment, rape, unfair trials, wanton destruction of property, etc. Indeed, the often highly-developed case-law under international human rights treaties (in particular, the International Covenant on Civil and Political Rights [ICCPR] and the European Convention on Human Rights [ECHR]) has informed the Elements of Crime which give guidance on the war crimes provisions in the Rome Statute.

However, there are also important differences, in particular as concerns the applicability of the different sets of rules; as concerns the persons who are subjects of these rules, the persons who benefit from their protection, and responsibility for breaches of the rules. In some respects, IHL has a wider application than human rights law; in others, the opposite. Sometimes, the two are formally linked and sometimes, they are converging. This is not the place to discuss these matters in detail; rather, a short overview of the differences and convergences will be given.

Applicability: (i) war and peace

6–010 As far as applicability is concerned, it is important first of all to stress again that IHL only applies in times of armed conflict — albeit that, as we have seen, this concept includes unresisted military occupation and/or occupation following hostilities, and albeit that IHL has also expanded from applying only in international armed conflicts to applying also in non-international armed conflicts (even if the rules differ for these different situations). The question of what does, and what does not, constitute an international armed conflict is further discussed below. Here, it will suffice to note that IHL does not apply in times of peace or indeed, as we have seen, in "situations of internal disturbances and tensions, such as riots, isolated and sporadic acts of violence or other acts of a similar nature".

International human rights law, by contrast, only applies in full in times of peace: the relevant treaties expressly allow for derogations from most of their requirements "in time of [war or other] public emergencies threatening the life of the nation" (Art. 4(1) of the ICCPR; Art. 15(1) of the ECHR). (The ICCPR does not include the word "war" — which is why it is placed it in brackets in this quote — but rather, includes war in the concept of public emergency. The reason is that the drafters did not want to give the impression that the United Nations had accepted war, even as a concept: M. Nowak, *UN Covenant on Civil and Political Rights: CCPR Commentary*, Art. 4, para. 12, Engel, 1993. The derogation provisions in both instruments undoubtedly apply to both international and non-international armed conflicts.)

The phrase in the human rights treaties, just quoted, also covers serious internal disturbances, which suggests that there may be a gap in protection between IHL and international human rights law with regard to such situations. However, States may only invoke the derogation clause in the human rights treaties if the internal disturbances are so serious as to "threaten the life of the nation", while (as we have seen) the Rome Statute makes clear that if there is a *protracted* [non-international] armed conflict between governmental authorities and *organized* armed groups or between such groups", IHL (and more in particular, the rules on war crimes) will apply. If there is a gap, that gap has been considerably narrowed because of this latter clarification.

6–011 More important is the fact that the derogation clauses in the human rights treaties may not be invoked to justify arbitrary killings, slavery, or torture, cruel, inhuman or degrading treatment or punishment (Art. 4(2) of the ICCPR; Art. 15(2) of the ECHR). As it is put in human rights parlance, the rights not to be subjected to such treatments are "non-derogable": States must continue to protect these rights, even in times of armed conflict. Under Art. 4(2) of the ICCPR, the right to freedom of thought, conscience and religion, too, is non-derogable — and since all the States that are Party to the ECHR are also party to the ICCPR, this must now be read into the ECHR also (see Arts 15(1) and 53 of the ECHR). Many war crimes will, by their nature, involve violations of non-derogable rights — and to that extent, both

IHL and international human rights law can apply to them (as long as the victims are "within the jurisdiction" of a Party to the ICCPR or ECHR, as discussed below).

As far as killing ("depravation of life") is concerned, the European Convention on Human Rights (like the ICCPR) declares the right to life to be "non-derogable" — but (unlike the ICCPR) adds "except in respects of deaths resulting from lawful acts of war". This means that in this respect the Convention formally defers to IHL, and to the Geneva Conventions in particular. Deprivation of life in the context of armed conflict, which is in accordance with the Geneva Conventions, is *ipso facto* also in conformity with the European Convention; and killings in armed conflict which violate the Geneva Conventions are *ipso facto* violations of the ECHR (again, provided the persons killed were "within the jurisdiction" of a Party to the ICCPR or ECHR, as discussed below).

Furthermore, even as concerns rights which are "derogable" under the human rights treaties — such as the right to property (the peaceful enjoyment of one's possessions) under Art. 1 of the First Protocol to the ECHR — the treaties stipulate that the abrogations or limitations of those rights in times of war or public emergency may not exceed what is "strictly required by the exigencies of the situation". The Geneva Conventions would again be relevant to the application of this test. Thus, wanton destruction of civilian property, in violation of the Geneva Conventions, would undoubtedly also be considered as a measure which "exceeds the exigencies of the situation" — although the reverse (that destruction of property which meets the test of the Geneva Conventions is *ipso facto* in accordance with the ECHR) may not be true.

A particularly complex question arises with regard to the "fair trial" requirements under IHL and international human rights law, respectively. On the one hand, the fair trial guarantees in the ICCPR and ECHR are not "non-derogable". On the other hand, the Geneva conventions (in particular GC III and IV) and the Rome Statute expressly make "wilfully depriving a prisoner of war or other protected person of the rights of fair and regular trial" and "the passing of sentences and the carrying out of executions without previous judgement pronounced by a regularly constituted court, affording all judicial guarantees which are generally recognized as indispensable" war crimes. This matter is further discussed in relation to the latter offence in particular, para. 6–063, below. Suffice it to note here that it is (at least) strongly arguable that while it is permissible under the human rights treaties in certain circumstances to either intern suspected insurgents, etc. (*i.e.* to detain them without trial), or to modify trial proceedings to meet the exigencies of an emergency, convicting people in manifestly *unfair* trials would constitute a violation of international human rights law, even if the trial is held in time of war or other emergency. The basic tests of whether a trial is "fair", established under the international human rights instruments, must therefore continue to be applied (at least as far as certain minima are concerned), even to special (emergency) courts. As we shall see those same tests are also relevant to the question of whether such special courts, — *e.g.* military tribunals — are in accordance with IHL.

Applicability: (ii) jurisdiction and territoriality

6–012   The second point that needs to be made about applicability is that IHL (and the Geneva Conventions in particular) applies to the actions of (in particular, the armed forces of) a State, irrespective where those actions take place. In terms of the Geneva Conventions and customary law, a person who commits a "grave" violation of the Conventions, or a serious violation of Common Art. 3, or other war crimes, is a war criminal, irrespective of where he committed his crime and irrespective of his nationality.

This principle is, as such, not affected by the fact that (in spite of efforts to have the universality of IHL in this respect reflected in the Rome Statute), the jurisdiction of the ICC is somewhat more circumscribed. As discussed in more detail elsewhere in this book, under the Rome Statute as finally adopted, the ICC has jurisdiction (subject to some important procedural requirements) over war crimes committed on the territory of a State Party to the treaty, and\or by a national of such a State-Party (see Art. 12 of the Statute). The latter means that, in theory at least, the court has jurisdiction over actions of armed forces of a State which is not party to the treaty, if those actions occur in the territory of a State which is a party to the treaty; and that in any case, the court has jurisdiction over the actions of any national of any State Party, wherever that national may have committed a war crime.

The latter falls short of the demand of many States who wanted the court to have universal jurisdiction, and reflects an unsuccesful attempt to mollify the United States in particular — even though, as just noted, actions by American (or any other) soldiers on the territory of a State that is party to the Statute could become subject to the jurisdiction of the court. In practice (as again discussed elsewhere in this book), the procedural hurdles to the effective exercise of jurisdiction in such a case are very considerable — but that is a different matter. Indeed, as further discussed in para. 6–073, even if there may be no compulsory universal jurisdiction in all cases, States can in any case claim permissive compulsory jurisdiction — irrespective of the jurisdiction of the ICC.

6–013   In spite of these jurisdictional complications relating to the ICC, IHL thus applies extremely widely, indeed universally, also to actions by States outside their own territory: nationals of States who have ratified the Rome Statute can be tried by the ICC for such actions irrespective of where they were committed; and nationals of other States may still be subject to the ICC if they commit their crimes on the territory of a State Party to the ICC, or to the jurisdiction of a State applying universal jurisdiction over war crimes, irrespective of where they committed their crimes.

126

By contrast, the ICCPR and the ECHR only require States Parties to "ensure" (ICCPR) or "secure" (ECHR) the rights and freedoms set out in those instruments to "all individuals within [their] territory and subject to [their] jurisdiction" (ICCPR), respectively to "everyone within their jurisdiction" (ECHR) (Art. 2(1) of the ICCPR; Art. 1 of the ECHR). In other words, they are only bound to conform to these treaties to the extent that their actions or omissions (or the actions or omissions of their agents: see below) affect individuals who are "within their territory" and/or "within their jurisdiction". This has raised questions about the applicability of the instruments with regard to military actions by States Parties outside of their own territory.

In the 1995 case of *Loizidou v Turkey* (15318/89) (1997) 23 E.H.R.R. 513, which concerned the Turkish occupation of Northern Cyprus, the European Court of Human Rights held that "in accordance with the concept of 'jurisdiction' in Art. 1 of the Convention, state responsibility may arise in respect of acts and events outside [a State Party's] frontiers" — and accordingly held Turkey responsible for its actions in the occupied part of the island. Indeed, in the subsequent case of *Cyprus v Turkey* (1997) 23 E.H.R.R. 244, the court added that since Turkey had "effective overall control" over the area, its responsibility was not confined to the acts of its own agents therein but was also engaged by the acts of the local administration which survived by virtue of Turkish support. Turkey's "jurisdiction" under Art. 1 was therefore considered to extend to securing the entire range of substantive Convention rights in Northern Cyprus.

The court reiterated this approach in its July 2001 admissibilty decision **6–014** in the case of *Ilaşcu et al. v Moldova and the Russian Federation*, which concerns acts which took place in the contested Transdniestrian region of Moldova:

> "The Court points out that the concept of 'jurisdiction' within the meaning of Article 1 of the Convention is not limited to the High Contracting Parties" national territory. For example, their responsibility can be involved because of acts of their authorities producing effects outside their own territory . . . Moreover, regard being had to the object and purpose of the Convention, the responsibility of a Contracting Party may also arise when as a consequence of military action — whether lawful or unlawful — it exercises effective control of an area outside its national territory. The obligation to secure, in such an area, the rights and freedoms set out in the Convention derives from the fact of such control whether it be exercised directly, through its armed forces, or through a subordinate local administration." (references omitted)

The court appeared to partially retract this view in its December 2001 admissibility decision in the *Bankovic* case concerning the NATO bombing of the Serbian radio and television station RTS during the Kosovo conflict in April 1999, in which it held that "the jurisdictional competence of a State is primarily territorial" (para. 59). The court then qualified that, by reference to the above Northern Cyprus cases, in two ways. First of all, the court did not disavow those judgments, but stressed that they were exceptional:

"In sum, the case-law of the Court demonstrates that its recognition of the exercise of extra-territorial jurisdiction by a Contracting State is exceptional: it has done so when the respondent State, through the effective control of the relevant territory and its inhabitants abroad as a consequence of military occupation or through the consent, invitation or acquiescence of the Government of that territory, exercises all or some of the public powers normally to be exercised by that Government." (para. 72)

That would suggest that if a party to the ECHR occupies foreign territory (whether lawfully or unlawfully — para. 70, confirming *Ilascu* in this respect) and exercises "effective overall control" in the area, the Convention applies to the actions of the occupying power. However, the court also said that:

"the Convention is a multi-lateral treaty operating . . . in an essentially regional context and notably in the legal space (*espace juridique*) of the Contracting States. The FRY [former Republic of Yugoslavia] clearly does not fall within this legal space. The Convention was not designed to be applied throughout the world, even in respect of the conduct of Contracting States. Accordingly, the desirability of avoiding a gap or vacuum in human rights" protection has so far been relied on by the Court in favour of establishing jurisdiction only when the territory in question was one that, but for the specific circumstances, would normally be covered by the Convention." (para. 80)

It is notable that the court did not say it would never apply the Convention to actions of a State Party in a territory which is not part of the territory of another State Party: it just said that "so far" it had not done so. Indeed, in its more recent (March 2003) judgment in the *Öcalan* case, it ruled that the arrest of this former leader of the Kurdistan Workers" Party (PKK) by Turkish security services in the international zone of Nairobi airport in Kenya was subject to the Convention — although in that case, it should be noted that the detainee was immediately taken to Turkey after his arrest.

In other words, if one Convention State invades and occupies part of the territory of another Convention State, and exercises "full overall control" in that area, the court *is* likely to rule that the Convention applies (in full!) to all the actions of the occupying State (although that State could invoke Art. 15 to derogate from some of its obligations, to the extent that the exigencies of the situation strictly justify the derogations). In such cases, in Europe, the Convention will apply, and the non-derogable rights guaranteed by the Convention in particular will have to be respected, concurrent with IHL. And the Convention may also apply (as it did in *Öcalan*) in cases involving the exercise of State power outside Europe, which is directly linked to (or, in this case, leads to) serious violations of the Convention on the Convention State's territory.

But the court is clearly reluctant to apply the Convention to activities by States Parties which take place entirely in areas occupied and controlled by a Convention State which are outside of the "legal space" of the Convention, *i.e.* to situations in which a Convention State occupies and controls part of the territory of a non-Council of Europe State. The court does not fully exclude the possibility of applying the Convention, but would seem to be prepared to do so in exceptional circumstances only. However, one of the matters which the court may take into account in this regard is the seriousness of the human rights violations in question. Given the willingness of the court to apply the Convention to cases in which actions by Convention States (in particular, extradition or expulsion) can lead to the death or torture of individuals in and by non-European States, one may speculate that the court would, perhaps, also be willing to apply the Convention to prevent or punish the use of extrajudicial killings or torture by the members of the armed forces of a Convention State in areas outside Europe occupied by such forces. To that extent, the Convention would again apply concurrently with IHL in such territories.

The situation under the ICCPR is not much clearer. On the one hand, the reference to "all individuals *within [their] territory and* subject to [their] jurisdiction" — inserted, against French and Chinese objections, at the behest of the USA — "was intended to avoid obligating States Parties to protect persons under their jurisdictional authority but outside their sovereign territory." (M. Nowak, *UN Covenant on Civil and Political Rights: CCPR Commentary*, Art. 2, para. 26). However, this can be said to mean no more than that "States are not responsible for violations [of the ICCPR] against persons over whom they have personal jurisdiction (in particular, nationals), when such violations take place on foreign territory *and are attributable to some other sovereign.*" (*idem*, para. 27, emphasis added). By contrast:

6–015

> "When States Parties, however, take *actions on foreign territory* that violate the rights of persons subject to their sovereign authority, it would be contrary to the purpose of the Covenant if they could not be held responsible. It is irrelevant whether these actions are permissible under general international law (*e.g.* . . . actions by occupation forces in accordance with the rules of the law of war) or constitute illegal interference, such as kidnapping of persons by secret service agents . . .

> [I]n the so-called *Passport cases* concerning Uruguay, [the Human Rights Committee] held that States Parties [to the ICCPR] are also responsible for violations of the Covenant (at least of Art. 12 [concerning freedom of movement — DK]) by foreign diplomatic representatives. [And it] considered communications by persons who had been kidnapped by Uruguayan agents in neighbouring States to be admissible, reasoning that States Parties are responsible for the actions of their agents on foreign territory." (*idem*, paras 28 & 29, original emphasis, footnotes omitted)

The Uruguay cases concerned actions by that State Party and its agents against its own nationals, on foreign soil, while the broader statement in the first paragraph quoted appears to be influenced, at least partly, by the European Court's judgments in the Northern Cyprus cases. It is also limited to actions against persons subject to a State Party's "sovereign authority", without clarifying what the situation is with regard to persons who are subject to a State Party's authority by virtue of occupation. Even so, the case-law suggests that, in spite of the express reference to individuals "within their territory" in Art. 2 of the ICCPR, the Human Rights Committee may be prepared to entertain complaints from victims in occupied territories about actions by States Parties occupying such territory — at least in serious case such as violations of non-derogable rights (the reference in the above paragraph to "actions which are permissible under general international law [such as] actions by occupation forces in accordance with the rules of war" should be read as referring to situations in which such actions come within the orbit of IHL, and not as limiting the general statement to actions which are lawful in terms of IHL). Specifically, the argument used by the European Court of Human Rights in *Bankovic*, that the ECHR is, by its nature, intended to apply only in Europe, cannot, of course, be used to limit the applicability of the ICCPR, which is global by its nature and design. If so, this would mean that the Covenant too can apply concurrantly with IHL in cases of occupation.

The subjects of IHL and of international human rights law

6–016   Both IHL and international human rights law are, as such, addressed to States; the main duty of compliance with the treaties in question rests on States. However, as explained above, under IHL it has long been a requirement that States prosecute individuals for war crimes, and where national courts have been unwilling or unable to do so, international tribunals have been charged with this task — initially *ad hoc* (as in the Nuremberg and Tokyo Tribunals, the ICTY and the ICTR) and now, by means of the ICC, in a general and permanent way. At least in respect of war crimes, individuals can therefore be said to be subjects — indeed, the main subjects — of IHL. As further discussed below, perpetrators of war crimes are individually responsible for their actions.

International human rights law, by contrast, has continued to be applied primarily to States only — with one, rather limited qualification and one, more important exception. In principle, if an agent of a State Party to an international human rights treaty — in particular, again, the ICCPR or the ECHR — violates any of the rights granted to an individual by the instrument in question, it is the State that is responsible for the violation, and not the individual. The State may be required to take action against the perpetrator of the act: if it fails to do so, that may show, or emphasise, the State's culpability. Conversely, if the State did take all reasonable measures to prevent the abuse, and/or to punish the perpetrator, it will generally be absolved of its international-legal responsibility. But in either case, the focus is on the actions or omissions of the State, rather than on the actions or omissions of the individual; or if the focus is on the latter, it is because he is acting for the State, and because his actions can be attributed to the State. Actions between private persons (persons not acting in an official capacity) are largely outside the scope of the international human rights instruments: the human rights treaties, by and large, do not have "horizontal effect"; they only relate to the "vertical" relationship between States and individuals.

This basic principle must first of all be qualified, in that, sometimes, States can be held responsible for actions of, and between, private individuals, if it is found that by their failure to regulate such behaviour they have deprived one of those individuals (or a particular category of individuals) of an essential aspect of a right which they are obliged to "secure" or "ensure". This is referred to as "indirect horizontal effect" or (to use the German term also often used in international discussions) *Drittwirkung*. Thus, in the case of *X and Y v the Netherlands* (A/91) (1986) 8 E.H.R.R. 235, the State was held to have violated the right to physical integrity and privacy of a young, mentally handicapped girl who had been sexually assaulted by a private individual in a private residential home, because its criminal law had failed to cover the rather unusual circumstances of the case. Although the "gap" in the criminal law had been unintentional, the State was liable for the fact that the perpetrator could not be prosecuted: in the circumstances of the case, the State had failed to adequately "secure" the girl's rights under the ECHR. That, however, is a highly unusual case. In any case, the judgment had no effect on the perpetrator of the crime as it did not bind him or indeed apply to him. He could not be prosecuted after the judgment any more than before it (because of the principle *nullum crimen sine lege*). The Convention did not touch him.

A more important exception to the principle that international human rights law has no "horizontal" effect applies, however, with regard to one particular right under international law: the right to be free from torture, inhuman or degrading treatment or punishment (the ICCPR adds "*cruel . . .* treatment or punishment" to the list, but this is elsewhere included in the other terms). **6–017**

The international law relating to torture *et al.* is discussed in detail in Chapter 7. Here, it will suffice to recall that torture, at least if committed by a State official, is now generally considered to be a crime unter international law, as well as, in appropriate circumstances (as discussed, below) a war crime, over which, under customary international law, States *may* claim universal jurisdiction ("permissive universal jurisdiction"). Whether customary international law extends compulsory universal jurisdiction to torture is more doubtful — although as noted below, Amnesty International argues that there is, at least, an emerging rule of customary law to this effect.

That there is a clear trend in that direction is indeed shown by the wide acceptance of the United Nations *Convention Against Torture*, which has been ratified by no less than 129 States. Briefly, apart from requiring that the carrying out or the condoning of torture be made a criminal offence in the State were the acts are committed (Art. 5(1)(a)), the Convention also stipulates that States must ('shall") give themselves extra-territorial jurisdiction to try the (alleged) perpetrators of such acts or omissions when the alleged offender is a national of the State in question (Art. 5(1)(b)). Any State Party may also ("if the State considers it appropriate") prosecute an offender (even in his absence) if the victim is a national of the State in question (Art. 5(1)(c)).

6–018 Most importantly, however, the Convention also requires all States that are Party to it to assume jurisdiction in cases of torture (or complicity or acquiescence in acts of torture), whenever the alleged offender is present in any territory under their jurisdiction, even if the offence was committed outside their territory and neither the perpetrator nor the victim were nationals of the State in question — except that the State in question can choose, alternatively, to extradite the alleged offender to another State Party, so that that other State Party may prosecute him or her (Art. 5(2): the principle *aut dedere aut punire*). As far as the alternative possibility is concerned, Art. 8 of the Convention ensures that the usual rules limiting extradition (existence of a treaty; specificity of the extraditable offences; and dual criminality, etc.) cannot be invoked to prevent extradition between States Parties of persons suspected of torture.

This means that, in principle, persons against whom there is *prima facie* evidence that they either actively participated in or condoned the carrying out of torture, or indeed that they were complicit in such acts by failing to act against the perpetrators (in particular, if they were in a position of authority over them) can — indeed, under the Convention must — be prosecuted whenever they find themselves in the territory of any of the 129 States Parties to the Convention. To that extent, therefore, the Convention can again be said to make torturers subjects of internal law.

This is subject to one important *caveat*: the Convention only applies to torture "inflicted by or at the instigation of a public official or other person acting in an official capacity." (Art. 1(1)). As far as torture committed by others is concerned, one must therefore revert to the position under customary law, which, as described above, has not yet been fully clarified. Or, if the offence occured in circumstances in which the Rome Statute applies, the perpetrator may be pursued under that treaty, as discussed below. In spite of the universal outlawing of torture, when it comes to effective remedial action, the differences in applicability of IHL and international human rights law remain important: the legal basis and nature of national and international steps against torturers may differ, depending on the context in which the offence took place and the status of the offender.

Protected persons and objects

6–019 There is a further crucial distinction between IHL and international human rights law. Different provisions of IHL protect different, specified categories of people or objects: so-called "protected persons" and "protected property". Although these categories can be quite broad, the restriction of the protection of IHL to such categories is crucially important, also, and in particular, as far as the perpetration of war crimes is concerned. Under IHL, if the rule, the violation of which constitutes a war crime, aims to protect only such special categories, the rule can only be violated, and a war crime can thus only be committed, against such categories.

International human rights law, by contrast, seeks to guarantee the rights enshrined in it to "all individuals" (ICCPR) or "everyone" (ECHR) — at least when such persons are "within" or "subject" to the jurisdiction of the State concerned, as discussed earlier. Under the human rights treaties, "all individuals"/"everyone" must be protected from arbitrary killings, torture, inhuman or degrading treatment or punishment, or slavery; "everyone" is entitled to a fair trial in the determination of (*inter alia*) a criminal charge against him. Indeed, under the ECHR "every natural or legal person" is entitled to the peaceful enjoyment of his possessions and to protection against arbitrary deprivation of property. In other words, companies, etc. too, can claim this latter protection.

The Four Categories of War Crimes listed in the Rome Statute of the ICC: General Issues and Elements Common to all these Crimes

Introduction

As mentioned above, Art. 8 of the Rome Statute lists four different categories of crimes as "war crimes", *i.e.*:   **6–020**

- grave breaches of the Geneva Conventions of August 12, 1949;

- other serious violations of the laws and customs applicable in international armed conflict;

- in the case of an armed conflict not of an international character, serious violations of Art. 3 common to the four Geneva Conventions of August 12, 1949; and

- other serious violations of the laws and customs applicable in armed conflicts not of an international character.

Under each of these headings, the Statute goes on to list a (for each category, exhaustive) series of specific crimes. As also already explained above, the stipulations in the Statute are expanded on and clarified in the so-called "Elements of Crime" (EOC), adopted in November 2002. While not binding on the ICC, the EOC must be taken into account in its decisions and judgments (Art. 9 of the Rome Statute). The Working Group which prepared the EOC realised that there were certain issues which were relevant to all crimes under Art. 8 of the Rome Statute, and which did not necessarily constitute elements of those crimes. It dealt with these in a General Introduction to the EOC. A number of other general issues are dealt with in the Statute but not further clarified in the EOC or the General Introduction to the EOC.

This section, will briefly discuss the following general issues and elements common to all the war crimes, with reference to the Rome Statute, to the EOC and the General Introduction to the EOC, and to the authoritative ICRC Commentary on the EOC: the question of "applicable law"; the principles *ne bis in idem, nullum crimen sine lege* and *nulla poena sine lege*; individual and joint criminal responsibility and "command responsibility"; *mens rea*; and exclusion of criminal responsibility. Several of these issues are addressed in more detail elsewhere in this book. In those cases, the discussions below are limited to very brief reminders of the relevant matters only.

The discussions below will focus on the elements common to the categories of crimes addressed under each of the above headings, with more selective analyses of (elements of) some individual crimes in each category. In the space of this book, the discussions of these matters too must, of necessity, be brief and limited to short summaries of the clarifications provided in the EOC and in the ICRC Commentary.

6–021   The final section will deal with the question (again already touched on, above) of sanctions against violations, *i.e.* with the rules concerning actions that States Parties to the treaty may, or are obliged, to take domestically. The rules concerning prosecution of war criminals before the ICC itself are dealt with in more detail in Chapter 10, and will therefore not be discussed here.

The question of "applicable law"

6–022   According to Art. 21(1) of the Rome Statute, the ICC must apply the following legal rules:

(a)   In the first place, this Statute, Elements of Crimes and its Rules of Procedure and Evidence;

(b)   In the second place, where appropriate, applicable treaties and the principles and rules of international law, including the established principles of the international law of armed conflict;

(c)   Failing that, general principles of law derived by the Court from national laws of legal systems of the world including, as appropriate, the national laws of States that would normally exercise jurisdiction over the crime, provided that those principles are not inconsistent with this Statute and with international law and internationally recognized norms and standards.

This means that, also and in particular in applying the law relating to the crimes over which the ICC has jurisdiction (including war crimes), the rules in the Statute can be developed in the light of wider rules and principles (such as treaty-based rules or rules of customary law, and indeed general principles of law derived from developed national legal systems), whenever the Statute leaves scope for this. An example can be found below, under the heading "*the required mental element*" with regard to the question of criminal intent and recklessness. This approach finds its limits, however, in the principle *nullem crimen sine lege*, further discussed below (together with the principle *nulla poena sine lege*), according to which "[t]he definition of a crime shall be strictly construed and shall not be extended by analogy."

Under Art. 21(2), the court *may* also apply principles and rules of law as interpreted in its previous decisions. In other words, while the court will of course generally be consistent in its application of the law and will follow its own previous decisions (and indeed is likely to build on decisions of the *ad hoc* tribunals), it is not bound by precedent.

Ne bis in idem

The Rome Statute deals with the principle that no-one shall be tried twice for the same offence (which is a rather complex issue for domestic courts, in particular in relation to crimes with an international aspect), in Art. 20 in the following terms: **6–023**

1. Except as provided in this Statute, no person shall be tried before the Court with respect to conduct which formed the basis of crimes for which the person has been convicted or acquitted by the Court.
2. No person shall be tried by another court for a crime [within the jurisdiction of the Court] for which that person has already been convicted or acquitted by the Court.
3. No person who has been tried by another court for conduct also proscribed under article 6 [genocide], 7 [crimes against humanity] or 8 [war crimes] shall be tried by the Court with respect to the same conduct unless the proceedings in the other court:

   (a) Were for the purpose of shielding the person concerned from criminal responsibility for crimes within the jurisdiction of the Court; or
   (b) Otherwise were not conducted independently or impartially in accordance with the norms of due process recognized by international law and were conducted in a manner which, in the circumstances, was inconsistent with an intent to bring the person concerned to justice.

This rightly limits the jurisdiction of the court to re-try a person to cases in which the first trial was either a deliberately facade, or otherwise calculated to avoid justice being done.

Nullum crimen, nulla poena sine lege

Article 22 of the Rome Statute stipulates: **6–024**

1. A person shall not be criminally responsible under this Statute unless the conduct in question constitutes, at the time it takes place, a crime within the jurisdiction of the Court.
2. The definition of a crime shall be strictly construed and shall not be extended by analogy. In case of ambiguity, the definition shall be interpreted in favour of the person being investigated, prosecuted or convicted.

3. This article shall not affect the characterization of any conduct as criminal under international law independently of this Statute.

To this, Art. 23 adds that "[a] person convicted by the Court may be punished only in accordance with this Statute."

These stipulations are of course reflections of general principles of criminal law, recognised by all developed (or, as they used to say, "civilised") nations. As already noted, it means, in particular, that the crimes in the Statute (including war crimes) may not be "stretched" to cover actions which are not clearly covered by the terms in which the crime is defined — although this does not stand in the way of interpreting some elements of the crimes widely, if this is justified by reference to relevant sources. Thus, the "mental element" of "intent" was interpreted by the ICTY in the *Blaskic* case as including recklessness, by reference to customary law.

In this context, it may also be noted that, as the General Introduction to the EOC confirms, particular conduct may constitute several crimes. The Working Group preparing the EOC felt it important to stress this point especially as regards sexual crimes, which can be part of crimes against humanity (Art. 7(1)(g) of the Rome Statute), of "other serious violations of the laws and customs applicable in international armed conflict" (Art. 8(2)(b)(xxii)), and of "other serious violations of the laws and customs applicable in armed conflicts not of an international character" (Art. 8(2)(e)(vi)), as well as amounting to torture, inhuman or degrading treatment, and other crimes. However, the clarification applies generally, to all crimes under the Statute.

Individual criminal responsibility

6–025   According to Art. 25(2) of the Rome Statute, any person who commits a crime within the jurisdiction of the court, including war crimes, "shall be individually responsible and liable for punishment in accordance with this Statute." A person is also individually criminally liable for attempting to commit such a crime (as long as this involves "taking action that commences [the crime's] execution by means of a substantial step") — unless he abandons the effort to commit the crime or otherwise prevents the completion of the crime, provided that he "completely and voluntarily gave up the criminal purpose" (Art. 25(3)(f)).

Crucially, the Statute stipulates, in Art. 27(1), that it is irrelevant if the perpetrator of the crime committed the crime in an "official capacity":

> "This Statute shall apply equally to all persons without any distinction based on official capacity. In particular, official capacity as a Head of State or Government, a member of a Government or parliament, an elected representative or a government official shall in no case exempt a person from criminal responsibility under this Statute, nor shall it, in and of itself, constitute a ground for reduction of sentence."

Furthermore, neither immunities nor special procedural rules which may attach to the official capacity of a person, whether under national or international law, will bar the court from exercising its jurisdiction over such a person (Art. 27(2)).

The required mental element (intent and knowledge)

On the question of the required *mens rea* (referred to in the Statute as "mental element") of (*inter alia*) war crimes, Art. 30 of the Rome Statute stipulates the following: **6–026**

Article 30
Mental element

1.   Unless otherwise provided, a person shall be criminally responsible and liable for punishment for a crime within the jurisdiction of the Court only if the material elements are committed with intent and knowledge.

2.   For the purposes of this article, a person has intent where:

(a) In relation to conduct, that person means to engage in the conduct;

(b) In relation to a consequence, that person means to cause that consequence or is aware that it will occur in the ordinary course of events.

3.   For the purposes of this article, "knowledge" means awareness that a circumstance exists or a consequence will occur in the ordinary course of events. "Know" and "knowingly" shall be construed accordingly.

In order to assist PrepCom, the ICRC prepared a paper on the mental element in the common law and in civil law systems and on the concepts of mistake of fact and mistake of law in national and international law, which is attached to the Commentary on the Rome Statute. Here, it must suffice to note that PrepCom drew on this paper in various respects.

In particular, the General Introduction to the EOC clarifies that "[e]xistence of intent and knowledge can be inferred from relevant facts and circumstances" and that (unless otherwise indicated in a particular crime) "[w]ith respect to mental elements associated with elements involving a value judgment, such as those using the term 'inhumane' or 'severe', it is not necessary that the perpetrator personally completed a particular value judgment". It is thus not a defence for the accused to say: "I knew I was going to cause harm, but I did not feel it would be severe," or to argue that he did not at the time of the commission of the offence believe it constituted "inhuman[e]" treatment.

As far as the phrase "[u]nless otherwise provided" in Art. 30(1) is concerned, the Working Group felt that a departure from the general "intent and knowledge" — rule could be based, not only on the Rome Statute itself, but **6–027** also on other sources of international law, such as applicable treaties and established principles of IHL. This allows for an extension of criminal liability for war crimes to crimes committed recklessly — as has been done already by the ICTY in the *Blaskic* case, already mentioned. (The issue is linked to the question of "wilful" killing as mentioned in Art. 8(2)(a), discussed below).

On the other hand, as discussed elsewhere in this book, it is difficult to see how one can have intent without knowledge. Where the Rome Statute therefore refers to "intent" or "intentional" in the context of a particular crime, this should not be read as meaning that intent, but not knowledge, is required. Rather, such references, by and large, serve to underline the importance of deliberateness on the part of the perpetrator in the particular context — which means that an extensive interpretation, on the lines of the *Blaskic* case, is therefore unlikely with regard to such offences.

The General Introduction also clarifies that where the definition of a crime uses the term "unlawful", this should be read as "in violation of international humanitatian law." Thus, for instance, the crime of deportation is not committed in evacuations carried out in accordance with the Geneva Conventions. Also, as noted below, in connection with exclusion of criminal responsibility, combatants can be said to aware of the "unlawfulness" of acts constituting war crimes, if they are aware that certain actions are contrary to IHL (irrespective of the position in national law).

Responsibility of accessories, commanders and superiors

6–028   According to the General Introduction, "[t]he elements [of crime], including the appropriate mental elements, apply *mutatis mutandis* to all those whose criminal responsibility may fall under articles 25 and 28 of the Statute."

Article 25 deals with such matters as individual and joint commissioning of war crimes (and other crimes within the jurisdiction of the ICC); ordering, soliciting or inducing such crimes; aiding, abetting or otherwise assisting in such crimes; contributing to the committing of war crimes by a group of persons acting with a common purpose; attempts; and indirect involvement in attempts. It must suffice to note that all such forms of involvement in a crime entail individual criminal responsibility for all those involved, irrespective of whether the other perpetrators are criminally responsible — except that contributing to the commission or attempted commission of a crime by a group of persons acting with a common purpose is only an offence under the Statute if the contribution is intentional *and* is either made with the aim of furthering the criminal activity or criminal purpose of the group, where such activity or purpose involves the commission of a crime within the jurisdiction of the court; *or* is made in the knowledge of the intention of the group to commit the crime (see Art. 25(3); as concerns a group acting with a common purpose, Art. 25(3)(d)).

Article 28 of the Rome Statute is of special importance. It deals with the individual criminal responsibility of commanders and other superiors:

Article 28
Responsibility of commanders and other superiors

In addition to other grounds of criminal responsibility under this Statute for crimes within the jurisdiction of the Court:

(a) A military commander or person effectively acting as a military commander shall be criminally responsible for crimes within the jurisdiction of the Court committed by forces under his or her effective command and control, or effective authority and control as the case may be, as a result of his or her failure to exercise control properly over such forces, where:

   (i)   That military commander or person either knew or, owing to the circumstances at the time, should have known that the forces were committing or about to commit such crimes; and

   (ii)   That military commander or person failed to take all necessary and reasonable measures within his or her power to prevent or repress their commission or to submit the matter to the competent authorities for investigation and prosecution.

(b) With respect to superior and subordinate relationships not described in paragraph (a), a superior shall be criminally responsible for crimes within the jurisdiction of the Court committed by subordinates under his or her effective authority and control, as a result of his or her failure to exercise control properly over such subordinates, where:

   (i)   The superior either knew, or consciously disregarded information which clearly indicated, that the subordinates were committing or about to commit such crimes;

   (ii)   The crimes concerned activities that were within the effective responsibility and control of the superior; and

   (iii) The superior failed to take all necessary and reasonable measures within his or her power to prevent or repress their commission or to submit the matter to the competent authorities for investigation and prosecution.

As is clear from the text, the criminal responsibility of commanders and superiors under this heading arises from omissions: from failure to take certain steps in relation to the perpetration of crimes within the jurisdiction of the ICC by others, *i.e.* by forces or subordinates under their effective command and control, or effective authority and control, as the case may be. (Of course, if the involvement of a commander or superior goes beyond this, to include some form of active involvement, he may be criminally liable, under Art. 25, as an accessory or even as a principal.)

A number of matters should be stressed. First, in all cases, responsibility **6–029** will only arise with regard to actions by forces or subordinates which are under the effective command and control, or under the effective authority, responsibility and control, of the commander or superior concerned.

Secondly, there is a question of knowledge — and here, the rules differ between commanders and superiors. A military commander is responsible if he "either knew or, owing to the circumstances at the time, *should have known* that the forces [under his command and control] were committing or about to commit such crimes" (para. (a)(i)). A superior other than a military commander (or than a person effectively acting as such a commander), by contrast, is liable if he "either knew, or *consciously disregarded information which clearly indicated*, that [his] subordinates were committing or about to commit such crimes" (para. (a)(iii)). Thirdly, the commander or superior must have had "reasonable measures" available to him to prevent or repress the crime. Lastly, he must have failed to take such measures.

With regard to these latter two points, it is useful to distinguish between preventive and repressive measures. Commanders and superiors are criminally liable if, when they knew (or, in the case of commanders, should have known) that war crimes (or other crimes within the jurisdiction of the ICC) were being, or were about to be, committed, they failed to implement measures which were available to them and which could have ended or prevented the crimes. If they either only learned of such crimes after the fact, or did not have the means available to stop or prevent them when they occured, they are still liable, if they failed to take repressive measures, *i.e.* if they failed to take steps to ensure that the perpetrators would be brought to justice. More specifically, they are liable, even with regard to crimes perpetrated by their forces or subordinates which took place without their knowledge or which they were unable to prevent, if they failed "to submit the matter to the competent authorities for investigation and prosecution", *i.e.* if they failed to at least report the events to the competent authorities.

How far up "command responsibility" extends is difficult to say. The post-World War II Tokyo Tribunal held Admiral Yamashita responsible for atrocities committed by his forces, even though he had lost almost all control, and could barely communicate with them. But these days, a more meaningful chain of command is usually required. In practice, Commanders-in-Chief are rarely called to account for failing to prevent or repress war crimes.

Exclusion of criminal responsibility

6–030 The Rome Statute contains a number of provisions on the question of when criminal responsibility can be excluded. Specifically, Art. 31(1) stipulates that (in addition to special grounds to be found in specific articles) a person shall not be criminally responsible if, at the time of that person's conduct:

(a) The person suffers from a mental disease or defect that destroys that person's capacity to appreciate the unlawfulness or nature of his or her conduct, or [his] capacity to control his or her conduct to conform to the requirements of law;

(b) The person is in a state of intoxication that destroys that person's capacity to appreciate the unlawfulness or nature of his or her conduct, or capacity to control his or her conduct to conform to the requirements of law, unless the person has become voluntarily intoxicated under such circumstances that the person knew, or disregarded the risk, that, as a result of the intoxication, he or she was likely to engage in conduct constituting a crime within the jurisdiction of the Court;

(c) The person acts reasonably to defend himself or herself or another person or, in the case of war crimes, property which is essential for the survival of the person or another person or property which is essential for accomplishing a military mission, against an imminent and unlawful use of force in a manner proportionate to the degree of danger to the person or the other person or property protected. The fact that the person was involved in a defensive operation conducted by forces shall not in itself constitute a ground for excluding criminal responsibility under this subparagraph;

(d) The conduct which is alleged to constitute a crime within the jurisdiction of the Court has been caused by duress resulting from a threat of imminent death or of continuing or imminent serious bodily harm against that person or another person, and the person acts necessarily and reasonably to avoid this threat, provided that the person does not intend to cause a greater harm than the one sought to be avoided. Such a threat may either be:

   (i) Made by other persons; or

   (ii) Constituted by other circumstances beyond that person's control.

According to Art. 32(1), "a mistake of fact shall be a ground for excluding criminal responsibility only if it negates the mental element required by the crime"; while under Art. 32(2), "a mistake of law as to whether a particular type of conduct is a crime within the jurisdiction of the Court shall not be a ground for excluding criminal responsibility. A mistake of law may, however, be a ground for excluding criminal responsibility if it negates the mental element required by such a crime, or as provided for in article 33."

The latter is a reference to the crucial question of whether, and if so when, "obeying superior orders" can be a defence. Of this, Art. 33 says the following:

Article 33
Superior orders and prescription of law

1. The fact that a crime within the jurisdiction of the Court has been committed by a person pursuant to an order of a Government or of a superior, whether military or civilian, shall not relieve that person of criminal responsibility unless:

(a) The person was under a legal obligation to obey orders of the Government or the superior in question;

(b) The person did not know that the order was unlawful; and

(c) The order was not manifestly unlawful.

2. For the purposes of this article, orders to commit genocide or crimes against humanity are manifestly unlawful.

It must be stressed that the conditions listed in para. (1), at (a)–(c) are cumulative; only if all three of these conditions have been met, will a person be able to avoid criminal responsibility for his actions. Given the sweeping terms in which the authority of commanders and superiors in armed forces is usually couched, and the corresponding, usually unconditional duty which this imposes on subordinates, the first condition will often be met, at least *in abstracto*. It is nevertheless important that the matter is specifically addressed in each case because, under Art. 25, a commander or superior giving an order to carry out acts which consitute war crimes (or other crimes within the jurisdiction of the ICC) will usually himself be responsible for those crimes (see, in particular, Art. 25(3)(b)).

The second and third conditions are more intricate. In particular, as already noted above, in connection with the issue of *mens rea*, the General Introduction to the EOC clarifies that where the definition of a crime uses the term "unlawful", this should be read as "in violation of international humanitarian law." Although this clarification specifically relates to elements of crime and not, as such, to exclusion of criminal liability (in respect of which the EOC and the General Introduction to the EOC are silent), it can also be applied to Art. 33.

6–031   It follows that it does not suffice that a subordinate who is ordered to carry out certain acts can show that the acts were "lawful" under his own law: in order to escape international criminal responsibility, he must show that he did not know that the acts were contrary to IHL, and more specifically that the order was not manifestly contrary to IHL. This applies in particular to officers and others who were trained in the rules and customs of law.

The point is reinforced by para. (2), which stipulates that "orders to commit genocide or crimes against humanity are [always] manifestly unlawful". Given that, as just noted, the conditions in para. (1) are cumulative, this means that the Statute here creates an irrebuttable presumption of culpability: subordinates are not absolved from these most serious offences, even if they can show that they were under a legal obligation to obey orders to carry out the acts constituting such offences, and did not know that their actions were unlawful: if they didn"t know this, they should have known as the unlawfulness was (legally and irrebuttably presumed to be) "manifest". It reinforces the point however, that with regard to war crimes (which is what we are concerned with), the defence of "obeying orders" can sometimes (even if only rarely) be invoked.

GRAVE BREACHES OF THE GENEVA CONVENTIONS

Crimes in this category

6–032   The first category of offences included in the concept of war crimes in the Rome Statute is "grave breaches of the Geneva Conventions of 12 August 1949", perpetrated against against persons or property protected under the Conventions. The relevant provision, Art. 8(2)(a) of the Rome Statute, lists the following specific crimes under this heading (note that this is an exhaustive list: only the crimes set out below constitute such "grave" breaches of the Conventions):

(i)   wilful killing;

(ii)   torture or inhuman treatment, including biological experiments;

(iii) wilfully causing great suffering, or serious injury to body or health;

(iv)   extensive destruction and appropriation of property, not justified by military necessity and carried out unlawfully and wantonly;

(v)   compelling a prisoner of war or other protected person to serve in the forces of a hostile Power;

(vi)   wilfully depriving a prisoner of war or other protected person of the rights of fair and regular trial;

(vii) unlawful deportation or transfer or unlawful confinement; and

(viii) taking of hostages.

Elements common to the crimes in this category

The PrepCom discerned two elements relating to the context in which the above-mentioned crimes occur, and two elements relating to the persons or property affected, common to those crimes.   **6–033**

Common elements relating to the context of the crimes

As far as the context is concerned, the EOC stress that for any of the above crimes to be regarded as war crimes, they must: (a) take place *in the context of*, and must have been *associated with*, an *international armed conflict*; and (b) the perpetrator must have been *aware* of *factual circumstances that established the existence of an armed conflict*. The first-mentioned requirements derive from the case-law of the *ad hoc* tribunals, and are further clarified in that case-law.   **6–034**

Thus, the ICTY has held that the words "*in the context of*" (rather than "in the course of") an armed conflict make clear that:

> "international humanitarian law applies from the initiation of . . . armed conflicts and extends beyond the cessation of hostilities until a general conclusion of peace is reached." (ICTY Appeals Chamber decision on interlocutory appeal on jurisdiction in the *Tadic* case, para. 70)

The ICTY has also held that while some of the provisions of the Geneva Conventions — in particular, those relating to the protection of prisoners of war and civilians — apply to the entire territory of the Parties to an international conflict, others may be limited to the vicinity of actual hostilities (but the latter has not yet been clarified more precisely).

The words *"associated with"* the armed conflict also reflect the jurisprudence of the *ad hoc* tribunals, which stresses that there must be sufficient *nexus* between the offences and the armed conflict. Thus, a murder committed for purely private reasons does not come within the scope of these war crimes, even if it happened to be perpetrated in an area and at a time of armed conflict. Indeed, it is clear from the case-law of the ICTY that the link with the conflict must be quite close.

6–035 An *"international armed conflict"* exists, first of all, whenever there is a difference between two or more States in which the armed forces of one or more of them intervene. In addition, an armed conflict within one State may become international if another State intervenes in the conflict through its troops, or if some of the participants in the internal conflict — or groups involved in the conflict — act on behalf of another State (ICTY Appeals Chamber judgment in the *Tadic* case, para. 84). The other State need not control such participants or groups in the same way, or to the same extent, as it controls its own armed forces: it will suffice if the other State:

> "has a role in organising, co-ordinating or planning the military actions of the military group, in addition to financing, training and equipping or providing operational support to the group. Acts performed by the group or members thereof may be regarded as acts of *de facto* State organs regardless of any specific instructions by the controlling State concerning the commission of each of those acts." (ICTY Appeals Chamber judgment in the *Tadic* case, para. 137)

As far as the mental element is concerned, the EOC are not entirely clear. They stress that there is no requirement that the perpetrator has carried out a legal evaluation of the question of whether there is an armed conflict, or of whether the conflict should be characterised as international or non-international, nor does the perpetrator have to be aware of the facts that establish the character of the conflict as international (*e.g.* as concerns the complications just discussed, of the extent of any control exercised by an other State over groups involved in an otherwise internal conflict). All that is required is confirmation that the perpetrator was aware of "factual circumstances that established the existence of an armed conflict that is implicit in the terms 'took place in the context of and was associated with'" such a conflict. He need not be aware of all the circumstances.

Common elements relating to the persons or property affected by the crimes (the question of "protected persons and — property")

6–036 The second general issue to be dealt with concerns the fact that the various rules in the different Geneva Conventions seek to protect specific categories of individuals or objects: in order to qualify as war crimes, the crimes listed in Art. 8(2)(a) must be perpetrated against such "protected persons" or "property".

As far as the objective aspect of this issue is concerned, it should be noted first of all that some rules in the Conventions seek to protect very broad categories of persons, *e.g.* all civilians in, or the entire civilian population of, the area concerned (Art. 51 of AP I); or all women, or all pregnant women, or all children in the area (Arts. 76–78 of AP I); or even the whole of the populations of the countries in conflict (Art. 13 of GC IV). However, most are more specific and seek to protect, *e.g.*:

- combatants; (Art. 44 of AP I)

- persons who take part in hostilities and fall into the power of an adverse Party; (Art. 45 of AP I)

- members of the armed forces of a Party to the conflict and associated militias, etc.;

- members of other militias or organised groups provided these fulfil certain conditions;

- certain persons who accompany armed forces but are not part of it, such as war correspondents or welfare officers;

- individuals involved in a *levée en masse*;

- crews of merchant ships and civil aircraft; (Art. 13 of GC I, Art. 13 of GC II)

- non-military medical personnel and members of the armed forces specially trained as hospital orderlies, nurses or auxiliary stretcher-bearers, when acting as such; and staff of the national Red Cross Societies; (Arts. 24, 25 and 26 of GC I)

- persons regularly and solely engaged in the operation and administration of civilian hospitals; (Art. 20 of GC IV)

- religious, medical and hospital personnel of hospital ships and their crews; (Arts 36, 37 of GC II)

- persons who find themselves in the hands of a Party to a conflict or of an Occupying Power of which they are not nationals; (Art. 4 of GC IV)

- prisoners of war (Art. 4 of GC III; Arts. 44 and 45 of AP I).

Clearly, many of these categories overlap; it is not always easy to distinguish between them (nor is that always necessary). The point to be made here is that violations of the rules in question will only constitute war crimes if they are perpetrated against the specific protected category of persons involved. If the same actions are taken against others, they may constitute human right violations or ordinary crimes — but they are not war crimes.

The same applies to "protected property". Some rules in the Conventions (in particular, in AP I) apply to all civilian objects — that is, to all objects which are not military objects (Art. 52 of AP I). Others (*e.g.* Art. 53 of AP I) apply to cultural or religious objects. The point again is that the crime listed in Art. 8(2)(a)(iv) — "*extensive destruction and appropriation of property, not justified by military necessity and carried out unlawfully and wantonly*" — is only a war crime if committed against a relevant category of "protected property".

6–037   As far as the subjective element of the crimes is concerned, the EOC clarify that it suffices that the perpetrator was aware of the factual circumstances that establish a particular protected status. In other words, the perpetrator need only have been aware that a particular person was a civilian, or a prisoner of war — he need not have known that the Conventions contained special rules protecting that person.

The case-law of the ICTY, and the discussion in PrepCom, have focussed on the scope of the category of "persons who find themselves in the hands of a Party to a conflict or of an Occupying Power of which they are not nationals" (Art. 4 of GC IV). In the *Tadic* case, the ICTY has held that, in the context of present-day inter-ethnic conflicts, the phrase — and in particular the reference to "nationals" — should be given a teleological rather than technical-literal meaning, so that a person may be accorded protected status even if he or she is of the same nationality as his captors:

> "not only the text and the drafting history of the Convention [GC IV] but also, and more importantly, the Convention's object and purpose suggest that allegiance to a Party to the conflict and correspondingly, control by this Party over persons in a given territory, may be regarded as the crucial test." (ICTY Appeals Chamber judgment in the *Tadic* case, para. 166).

According to the ICRC Commentary on the EOC, the PrepCom "decided [in this regard] that no more precision for the objective element should be included [in the EOC], so that the future ICC could be free to decide on whether to adopt the views expressed by the ICTY in relation to the protected status of persons under Art. 4 GC IV." However, as far as the subjective element is concerned, PrepCom was more explicit: it is not a precondition for criminal liability that the perpetrator knew that his victim(s) were foreign nationals. It specified, in a footnote to the EOC, that "the accused needs only to know that the victim belonged to an adverse party to the conflict."

A further matter not dealt with in the EOC may be noted in view of its contemporary importance. This is that, in the opinion of the ICTY:

> "there is no gap between the Third and Fourth Geneva Conventions. If an individual is not entitled to the protections of the Third Convention as a prisoner of war (or of the First or Second Conventions) he or she necessarily falls within the

ambit of Convention IV, provided that its article 4 requirements are satisfied. The [ICRC] Commentary to the Fourth Geneva Convention asserts that:

> "[e]very person in enemy hands must have some status under international law: he is either a prisoner of war and, as such, covered by the Third Convention, a civilian covered by the Fourth Convention, or again, a member of the medical personnel of the armed forces who is covered by the First Convention. There is no intermediate status; nobody in enemy hands can be outside the law . . ."

This position is confirmed by article 50 of Additional Protocol I which regards as civilians all person who are not combatants as defined in article 4(A)(1), (2), (3) and (6) of the Third Geneva Convention, and article 43 of the Protocol itself."

(ITCY judgment in the *Delalic* case, para. 271ff.)

The matter is closely related to the requirement under Art. 45(1) of AP I, that a person who takes part in hostilities and falls into the power of an adverse Party must be presumed to be a prisoner of war, and is therefore protected by the Third Convention, if he claims the status of prisoner of war, or if he appears to be entitled to such status, or if the Party on which he depends claims such status on his behalf. The Protocol adds, in the same provision, that if any doubt arises as to whether any such person is entitled to the status of prisoner of war:

> "he shall continue to have such status and, therefore, to be protected by the Third Convention and this Protocol until such time as his status has been determined by a competent tribunal."

The matter is related to the war crime listed in Art. 8(2)(a), at vi: "wilfilly depriving a prisoner of war or other protected person of the rights of fair and regular trial", as (briefly) discussed under the next heading in para. 6–043 (with reference to further discussion in para. 6–063ff).

Elements specific to some selected crimes

The next sections, will briefly mention a number of issues relating to a few, selected crimes (of the ones listed in Art. 8(2)(a) of the Rome Statute).   **6–038**

Wilful killing (Art. 8(2)(a)(i)) As concerns "wilful killing" (Art. 8(2)(a), at i), the EOC add little to the general elements, already discussed: that the crime is only a war crime if committed against a protected person; that it must have been perpetrated in the context of and have been associated with an international armed conflict; that the perpetrator must have been aware of relevant factual circumstances, but need not have made an appopriate legal evaluation of them, etc. PrepCom did clarify that the term "killed" is interchangeable with the term "caused death", and encompasses conduct such as the reduction of rations for prisoners of war resulting in their starvation and   **6–039** death. The ICRC Commentary adds, with reference to various national decisions and to the ICTY Prosecutor's pre-trial brief in the *Kovacevic* case, that:

> "the notion of 'wilful killing' must be limited to those acts or omissions which are contrary to existing treaty and customary law of armed conflict."

This usefully co-ordinates the law in this respect with the ECHR which, as we have seen, permits killings in time of war or national emergency which result from "lawful acts of war", but outlaws killings contrary to IHL.

A further link can be made between IHL and international human rights law in this respect, in that (as we have seen) a military commander or other superior may be liable for war crimes if he fails to report, *e.g.* the fact that killings were carried out by his forces or subordinates which may have violated IHL, so that these matters can be investigated and the perpetrators prosecuted if necessary. This requirement of IHL can be related to the so-called "procedural aspect" of the right to life under international human rights treaties, according to which States are required to carry out full and open investigations into killings by their police or armed forces which may have contravened the right to life, *i.e.* in times of war or other emergency, which may have contravened IHL.

As far as "wilfulness" is concerned, the discussions in PrepCom were not conclusive — but it may be recalled that the ICTY has held, in the *Blaskic* case, that the *mens rea* for all the "grave" breaches of the Geneva Conventions includes both guilty intent and "recklessness which may be likened to serious criminal negligence" (ICTY judgment in *Blaskic*, para. 152). More specifically, the ICTY was:

> "in no doubt that the necessary intent, meaning *mens rea*, required to establish the crimes of wilful killing and murder, as recognised in the Geneva Conventions, is present where there is demonstrated an intention on the part of the accused to kill, or inflict serious injury in reckless disregard of human life." (ICTY judgment in *Delalic*, para. 439)

Finally, it may be noted that (as the ICRC Commentary points out), in principle, proof of positive knowledge of the underlying facts is essential, but that in some post-Worl War II trials, accused were held liable on the ground that, due to their position, they must have known these facts. This applied, *e.g.* to the supplying of poison gas in the knowledge that the gas was to be used for the killing of interned civilians (the *Zyklon B* case), and to the handing over of POWs to an organisation which the accused must have known would kill them (the *von Leeb and Others* case). As the ICRC notes, this position is reflected in Arts 28(1)(a) and 30 of the Rome Statute.

6–040   ***Torture or inhuman treatment and wilfully causing great suffering, or serious injury to body or health (Art. 8(2)(a)(ii) and (iii))*** The prohibition of torture, inhuman or degrading treatment or punishment in international human rights law and the associated international crime of torture is discussed in some detail elsewhere in this book. Here, it may be noted that the second and third crimes listed in Art. 8(2)(a), at ii and iii — "torture or inhuman treatment, including biological experiments" and "wilfully causing great suffering, or serious injury to body or health" — will often cover treatment falling with the relevant international criminal — and human rights provisions, but that the demarcation lines between torture and inhuman or degrading treatment on the one hand, and between torture and inhuman treatment and great suffering and serious injury on the other, are not the same. However, these demarcation differences have become less important.

Specifically, PrepCom discussed the question of whether the term "torture", as used in Art. 8(2)(a) should be read in accordance with the definition of that term in Art. 7(2)(e), which relates to crimes against humanity, or whether it should be interpreted in line with the definition of torture in the United Nations Convention Against Torture, as has generally been done by the *ad hoc* tribunals.

Torture is defined in Art. 7(2)(e) as follows:

> " 'Torture' means the intentional infliction of severe pain or suffering, whether physical or mental, upon a person in the custody or under the control of the accused; except that torture shall not include pain or suffering arising only from, inherent in or incidental to, lawful sanctions."

The United Nations Convention Against Torture defines the term thus:

> "For the purposes of this Convention, the term 'torture' means any act by which severe pain and suffering, whether physical or mental, is intentionally inflicted on a person for such purposes as obtaining from him or a third person information or a confession, punishing him for an act he or a third person has committed or is suspected of having committed, or intimidating or coercing him or a third person, or for any reason based on discrimination of any kind, when such pain or suffering is inflicted by or at the instigation or with the consent or acquiescence of a public official or other person acting in an official capacity. It does not include pain or suffering arising from, inherent in or incidental to lawful sanctions."

The main differences between these definitions are: (i) that the United Nations Convention includes a list of purposes for which torture is typically used — although this list is clearly illustrative only, it does suggest that there must at least be some purpose to the acts concerned; (ii) that the definition in Art. 7(2)(e) refers to the victim being "in the custody or under the control" of the perpetrator; and (iii) that the United Nations Convention expressly limits the term to pain and suffering "inflicted by or at the instigation or with the consent or acquiescence of a public official or other person acting in an official capacity". However, the latter restriction in particular can be said to be a reflection of the specific, limited purpose of that Convention, as expressed by means of the introductory words "For the purposes of this Convention . . .".

In the case law of the *ad hoc* tribunals, the main distinction between tor- **6–041** ture and inhuman treatment on the one hand, and great suffering on the other, has been that (in line with the definition in the United Nations Convention) the tribunals have generally held that for torture to be committed, it must be shown that the pain and suffering inflicted on the victim served a purpose (such as listed in the Convention), while this need not be established for a conviction for wilfully causing great suffering. In the latter respect, it suffices that the perpetrator intended (or recklessly disregarded the likelihood) that such suffering would be caused; there is no need to show that the perpetrator was pursuing any particular aim in this. The PrepCom agreed, and a "purposive element" is therefore included in the EOC relating to the war crime of torture: it is an element of that crime that:

> "The perpetrator inflicted the pain or suffering for such purposes as obtaining information or a confession, punishment, intimidation or coercion or for any reason based on discrimination of any kind." (Element 2)

On the second issue, a proposal to include the "custody or control" requirement as an element was dropped, because PrepCom felt that it was better to include only the requirement that for the war crime of torture to take place, it is necessary that the victim is a "protected person" (Element 3, which of course merely repeats a general element, common to all the war crimes listed in Art. 8(2)(a), as discussed earlier).

On the question of whether to limit the concept of torture to acts committed by persons acting in an official capacity, the ICTY followed the UN Convention in principle, but with some flexibility:

> "In the context of international humanitarian law, this requirement must be interpreted to include officials of non-State parties to a conflict, in order for the prohibition to retain significance in situations of internal armed conflict or international armed conflict involving some non-State entities." (ICTY Judgment in the *Delalic* case, para. 473)

PrepCom went one step further. As it is put in the ICRC Commentary:

> "The vast majority of delegations to the PrepCom took the view that while war crimes necessarily take place in the context of an armed conflict and, in most cases, involve persons acting in an 'official capacity', the inclusion [of this requirement in the EOC] would create the unintended impression that non-State actors are not covered. This would greatly restrict the crime, particularly in non-international armed conflicts involving rebel groups."

Since PrepCom wanted the definition of torture to be identical for international and non-international armed conflicts, the requirement of the perpetrator acting in an "official capacity" was therefore deliberately not included in the elements of the crime of torture. This issues is further discussed in para. 6–061 below, under the heading *"mutilation, cruel treatment and torture"*.

6–042 As far as the grading of the concepts of "torture", "great suffering" and "serious injury", and "inhuman or degrading treatment or punishment" is concerned, it may suffice to note that acts of torture will, by their very nature, almost always also involve the inflicting of "great suffering" and/or "serious injury", and will always constitute "inhuman or degrading treatment or punishment" (as defined by the European Court of Human Rights, torture is an aggravated form of inhuman or degrading treatment or punishment). Acts which fulfil the elements of the war crime of "wilfully causing great suffering or serious injury to body or health" will usually also constitute inhuman or degrading treatment in terms of international human rights law. However, the ICTY held in the *Kordic* and *Cerkez* cases that:

> "the [war] crime is dinstinguished from that of inhuman treatment in that it requires a showing of serious mental or physical injury. Thus, acts where the resultant harm relates solely to an individual's human dignity are not included within this offence." (ICTY judgment in the *Kordic* and *Cerkez* cases, para. 245)

The other crimes listed in Art. 8(2)(a) The other crimes listed in Art. 8(2)(a) **6–043** will not be discussed here. In their broad meaning, they are reasonably clear in themselves; for further detail, the reader is referred to the ICRC Commentary. Suffice it to make just a few general comments. First, the crime of "extensive destruction and appropriation of property, not justified by military necessity and carried out unlawfully and wantonly" (Art. 8(2)(a), at iv) is, in many ways, linked to the crimes relating to attacks on civilian property (or disproportionately harming civilian property), discussed in para. 6–046 below: the brief comments made in that section are therefore also relevant here.

Secondly, the crime of "wilfully depriving a prisoner of war or other protected person of the rights of fair and regular trial" (Art. 8(2)(a), at vi) is closely linked to the crime of "The passing of sentences and the carrying out of executions without previous judgement pronounced by a regularly constituted court, affording all judicial guarantees which are generally recognized as indispensable." While the former crime can only be committed in international armed conflict, and the latter relates to non-international armed conflicts, the question of what are the essential guarantees in relation to both are basically the same, and may be answered by reference to estabished (detailed) international human rights (case) law. We will address these issues briefly in para. 6–063ff, below.

Here, one issue may however be noted. This is that if there is any doubt as to whether a person who takes part in hostilities and falls into the power of an adverse Party is entitled to the status of prisoner of war, he must be granted that status "until such time as his status as been determined by a competent tribunal" (Art. 45(1) of AP I). If one follows the ICTY ruling in the *Delalic* case and the ICRC view on the Fourth Geneva Convention to which the Tribunal referred, that there can be no gap in the system of protection under the Geneva Conventions, that "nobody in enemy hands can be outside the law" (as discussed above, in connection with the question of "protected persons"), it will be a war crime for any State to hold persons in detention without granting them at least the right to have their status determined in fair and regular trial proceedings.

OTHER SERIOUS VIOLATIONS OF THE LAWS AND CUSTOMS APPLICABLE IN INTERNATIONAL ARMED CONFLICT

Crimes in this category

6–044 Article 8(2)(b) of the Rome Statute of the ICC lists 26 "other serious violations of the laws and customs applicable in international armed conflict" (*i.e.* other than the "grave violations of the Geneva Conventions" listed in Art. 8(2)(a) and discussed above) as constituting war crimes, *i.e.*:

(i) Intentionally directing attacks against the civilian population as such or against individual civilians not taking direct part in hostilities;

(ii) Intentionally directing attacks against civilian objects, that is, objects which are not military objectives;

(iii) Intentionally directing attacks against personnel, installations, material, units or vehicles involved in a humanitarian assistance or peacekeeping mission in accordance with the Charter of the United Nations, as long as they are entitled to the protection given to civilians or civilian objects under the international law of armed conflict;

(iv) Intentionally launching an attack in the knowledge that such attack will cause incidental loss of life or injury to civilians or damage to civilian objects or widespread, long-term and severe damage to the natural environment which would be clearly excessive in relation to the concrete and direct overall military advantage anticipated;

(v) Attacking or bombarding, by whatever means, towns, villages, dwellings or buildings which are undefended and which are not military objectives;

(vi) Killing or wounding a combatant who, having laid down his arms or having no longer means of defence, has surrendered at discretion;

(vii) Making improper use of a flag of truce, of the flag or of the military insignia and uniform of the enemy or of the United Nations, as well as of the distinctive emblems of the Geneva Conventions, resulting in death or serious personal injury;

(viii) The transfer, directly or indirectly, by the Occupying Power of parts of its own civilian population into the territory it occupies, or the deportation or transfer of all or parts of the population of the occupied territory within or outside this territory;

(ix)   Intentionally directing attacks against buildings dedicated to religion, education, art, science or charitable purposes, historic monuments, hospitals and places where the sick and wounded are collected, provided they are not military objectives;

(x)   Subjecting persons who are in the power of an adverse party to physical mutilation or to medical or scientific experiments of any kind which are neither justified by the medical, dental or hospital treatment of the person concerned nor carried out in his or her interest, and which cause death to or seriously endanger the health of such person or persons;

(xi)   Killing or wounding treacherously individuals belonging to the hostile nation or army;

(xii)   Declaring that no quarter will be given;

(xiii)   Destroying or seizing the enemy's property unless such destruction or seizure be imperatively demanded by the necessities of war;

(xiv)   Declaring abolished, suspended or inadmissible in a court of law the rights and actions of the nationals of the hostile party;

(xv)   Compelling the nationals of the hostile party to take part in the operations of war directed against their own country, even if they were in the belligerent's service before the commencement of the war;

(xvi)   Pillaging a town or place, even when taken by assault;

(xvii)   Employing poison or poisoned weapons;

(xviii)   Employing asphyxiating, poisonous or other gases, and all analogous liquids, materials or devices;

(xix)   Employing bullets which expand or flatten easily in the human body, such as bullets with a hard envelope which does not entirely cover the core or is pierced with incisions;

(xx)   Employing weapons, projectiles and material and methods of warfare which are of a nature to cause superfluous injury or unnecessary suffering or which are inherently indiscriminate in violation of the international law of armed conflict, provided that such weapons, projectiles and material and methods of warfare are the subject of a comprehensive prohibition and are included in an annex to this Statute, by an amendment in accordance with the relevant provisions set forth in articles 121 and 123;

(xxi)   Committing outrages upon personal dignity, in particular humiliating and degrading treatment;

(xxii)   Committing rape, sexual slavery, enforced prostitution, forced pregnancy, as defined in article 7, paragraph 2 (f), enforced sterilization, or any other form of sexual violence also constituting a grave breach of the Geneva Conventions;

(xxiii)   Utilizing the presence of a civilian or other protected person to render certain points, areas or military forces immune from military operations;

(xxiv)   Intentionally directing attacks against buildings, material, medical units and transport, and personnel using the distinctive emblems of the Geneva Conventions in conformity with international law;

(xxv)   Intentionally using starvation of civilians as a method of warfare by depriving them of objects indispensable to their survival, including wilfully impeding relief supplies as provided for under the Geneva Conventions;

(xxvi)   Conscripting or enlisting children under the age of fifteen years into the national armed forces or using them to participate actively in hostilities.

Elements common to the crimes in this category

6–045   As the text of Art. 8(2)(b) itself makes clear, the crimes listed above (like the ones listed in Art. 8(2)(a)) only constitute war crimes if they are committed in situations of "international armed conflict" (However, as we shall see below, many of the crimes listed in Art. 8(2)(b) are also listed, in identical or nearly-identical terms, in Art. 8(2)(e), which relates to non-international armed conflict). To this, Art. 8(2)(b) — like Art. 8(2)(e) — adds the words "within the established framework of international law".

As far as the condition of an international armed conflict is concerned, the EOC are the same as those relating to "grave breaches of the Geneva Conventions", *i.e.*: the conduct must have taken place *in the context of* such an international conflict; it must have been *associated with* the armed conflict; and the perpetrator must have been *aware of the factual circumstances* that established the existence of an *armed conflict* (but need not have been aware of the precise, *i.e.* international or non-international — nature of the conflict). The comments on these elements, made in para. 6–033ff above, therefore equally apply to the crimes listed above.

Neither the EOC nor the ICRC Commentary comment on the meaning of the words "within the established framework of international law", used in Art. 8(2)(b) and (e), which both deal with "other crimes", beyond a primary category, listed in preceeding paragraphs. The phrase may be taken as reaffirmation that the "other crimes" listed must be strictly construed in accordance with customary and conventional IHL. Customary IHL however includes the two "cardinal principles" of IHL, mentioned above, to which most of the crimes listed in Art. 8(2)(b) relate. These crimes are discussed under the next two headings.

Unlawful attacks on civilians or civilian objects; indiscriminate attacks; and related crimes

Crimes number i, ii, iv, v, xiii, xvi, xxv As noted in para. 6–002 above, the first **6–046** "cardinal principle" of IHL is that (in the words of the ICJ):

> "states must never make civilians the objects of attack and must consequently never use weapons that are incapable of distinguishing between civilian and military targets."

As far as the first two crimes listed in Art. 8(2)(b) are concerned — attacking civilians or civilian objects — the EOC (apart from re-stating the general requirements that the offence must have been committed *"in the context of"* and must have been *"associated with"* an *international armed conflict,* and that the perpetrator must have been *aware* of the existence of an armed conflict) clarify that the perpetrator must have *directed* the attack; that the *object* of the attack must have been a *civilian population* as such or *individual civilians* not taking direct part in hostilities.

The EOC also generally say that the perpetrator must have *intended* such civilian populations or individual civilians to be the objects of the attack. However, the relevant intent here again encompasses both deliberate action and *recklesness* and, more in particular, *failure to take precautions.* As it is put in the ICRC Commentary on the related offence in Art. 85(3)(a) of AP I:

> "All precautions must be taken with a view to sparing civilians, both in planning and in carrying out an attack."

As the ICRC observes in the Commentary on the Rome Statute:

> "This offence [attacking civilians] is not limited to attacks against individual civilians. It essentially encompasses attacks that are not directed against a specific military objective or combatants or attacks employing indiscriminate weapons or attacks effectuated without taking necessary precautions to spare the civilian population or individual civilians, especially *failing to seek precise information* on the objects or persons to be attacked. The required *mens rea* may be inferred from the fact that the necessary precautions (in the sense of Art. 57 AP I, *e.g.* the use of available intelligence to identify the target) were not taken before and during an attack." (original emphasis)

In fact, although the statement above is made in connection with the crime of attacking civilians, it applies (as the Commentary itself acknowledges) "to all the war crimes relating to an unlawful attack against persons or objects protected against such attacks . . ." — whereby the word "unlawful" must as usual be read broadly as "contrary to IHL".

The comment therefore also applies to the crimes listed in Art. 8(2)(b) under numbers iv (causing excessive incidental death, injury or damage), v (attacking undefended places) and xiii (unjustified destruction or seizure of enemy property).

6–047   Also to be mentioned here is crime number xvi, pillaging — or "the appropriation of property for the private or personal use of the perpetrator", as it has been more specifically defined by PrepCom; and the crime of starvation of civilians as a method of warfare (crime number xv).

Using prohibited weapons

6–048   *Crimes number xvii–xx* The second "cardinal rule" identified by the ICJ — the prohibition of causing unnecessary suffering to combatants — is reflected in the Rome Statute in a number of specific crimes listed in Art. 8(2)(b), linked to specific kinds of prohibited weapons, and in a more general but, as we shall see, as yet empty crime.

As far as specific prohibited weapons are concerned, the crimes listed in numbers xvii (employing poison or poisoned weapons), xviii (employing prohibited gases, liquids, materials or devices) and xix (employing prohibited bullets) relate to the earliest international conventions on the rules of war, mentioned above: the prohibitions of the use of these weapons have, as the ICJ put it, become "intransgressible principles of international customary law".

However, the second "cardinal principle" is also more generally reflected in the Rome Statute, in the crime listed under number xx:

> "Employing weapons, projectiles and material and methods of warfare which are of a nature to cause superfluous injury or unnecessary suffering or which are inherently indiscriminate in violation of the international law of armed conflict . . ."

It should be noted however that, even though this phrase copies almost *verbatim* two rules of customary international law, contained in the Hague Regulations of 1907 and AP I, the drafters of the Rome Statute felt unable to leave the crime expressed in such general terms in that instrument. Rather, they decided that, as far as the jurisdiction of the ICC is concerned, this generally-worded crime should apply only to weapons, projectiles and material and methods of warfare listed in an annex to the Statute. In other words, although the rule quoted above as such constitutes customary law, the ICC will only have jurisdiction over violations of the rule which involve such later-to-be-listed weapons, projectiles, etc. To date, no such list has been adopted and the crime listed under number xx is therefore, for now, without substance as far as the ICC is concerned.

The issue must be seen in the light of the ruling of the ICJ in its *Advisory* **6–049** *Opinion on the Legality of the Threat or Use of Nuclear Weapons*, already referred to, and in which it confirmed the "cardinal rule". In this *Opinion*, the ICJ held that the threat or use of nuclear weapons would "generally" be contrary to IHL. However, the court also ruled, on the casting vote of the President of the Court, that:

> "in view of the current state of international law, and of the elements of fact at its disposal, the Court cannot conclude definitively whether the threat or use of nuclear weapons would be lawful or unlawful in an extreme circumstance of self-defence, in which the very survival of a State would be at stake." (final para., at E)

Clearly, the drafters of the Rome Statute did not want to enable to ICC to re-open this issue of its own motion: under the Statute, one cannot (yet) argue that the use of nuclear weapons would, always and invariably, constitute a war crime in terms of crime number xx.

However, nuclear weapons are, by their nature, indiscriminate; it is almost **6–050** unavoidable that they will kill or injure large numbers of civilians and cause widespread, long-term and severe damage to the natural environment. Their use will therefore, in all but the most unimaginable circumstances, still constitute the war crime of causing excessive incidental death, injury or damage, which is included in Art. 8(2)(b) of the Statute under number iv, as discussed under the previous heading.

Violations of the rights to life, to freedom from torture and inhuman or degrading treatment, and to respect for one's integrity and dignity

Crimes number vi, x, xii, xxi, xxii There is a considerable overlap between the **6–051** crime of "killing or wounding a combatant who is [*hors de combat*]" (crime number vi in Art. 8(2)(b)), actions relating to a declaration that "no quarter will be given" (which is a crime under Art. 8(2)(b) number xii), and "wilful killing" in Art. 8(2)(a), especially since (as we have noted above) the latter crime must be read as covering all killings contrary to IHL as applicable in international armed conflict.

The main point to note here is that there is again no gap in protection. Thus, the crime of killing or wounding a person who is *hors de combat* does not just apply to POWs, but rather, applies from the moment the individual:

> "ceases to fight, when his unit has surrendered, or when he is no longer capable of resistance either because he has been overpowered or is weaponless." (W. A. Solf, quoted in the ICRC Commentary on the Rome Statute)

Similarly, as it is put in the ICRC Commentary on Art. 41 of AP I, on which the crime is based (quoted in the Commentary on the Rome Statute):

"The rule [Art. 41 of AP I] protects both regular combatants and those combatants considered to be irregular, both those whose status seems unclear and ordinary civilians. There are no exceptions and respect for the rule is also imposed on the civilian population, who should, like the combatants, respect persons *hors de combat*."

Similarly seamless protection is also provided under the Rome Statute by the combined, overlapping application of Art. 8(2)(a), at i, Art. 8(2)(b), at vi and xii, and, as concerns ordinary civilians (i.e. civilians not in any way involved in hostilities), by the general prohibition of any attack on such civilians (and thus *a fortiori* of the killing of such individuals) under Art. 8(2)(b), at i.

There is a similar, close connection between the crimes listed in Art. 8(2)(b), numbers x (covering the crimes of mutilation and of medical or scientific experiments), xxi (outrages upon personal dignity) and xxii (rape and other sexual offences), on the one hand, and the crimes categorised as grave violations of the Geneva Conventions in Art. 8(2)(a), numbers ii (torture or inhuman treatment, including biological experiments) and iii (wilfully causing great suffering, or serious injury to body or health), on the other. In particular, there is (as explained elsewhere in this book) a broad spectrum in IHL, international criminal law and international human rights law, encompassing torture, inhuman treatment and degrading treatment — even if the delineations between these categories are not very clear. Here, it may suffice to note that in terms of human rights law mutilation and rape (in particular if carried out purposefully as an instrument of war) will almost always (in the opinion of the author, always) constitute torture, and that carrying out medical or scientific experiments on prisoners will also often amount to torture. "Outrages upon personal dignity" could, in some circumstances, amount to torture; in others they will constitute inhuman or degrading treatment. However, there is certain lower limit: it is an element of this latter crime that:

"[t]he severity of the humiliation, degradation or other violation [of the dignity of the person] was of such a degree as to be generally recognised as an outrage upon personal dignity." (2nd element of the crime)

In line with international human rights case-law (in particular, the case-law of the European Court of Human Rights), a footnote to the element includes the remark that:

". . . This element takes into account relevant aspects of the cultural background of the victim."

Examples given in the ICRC Commentary and drawn from post-World War II war crimes trials include forcing a person to eat something that is prohibited by his religion (such as forcing a Jew or a Muslim to eat pork), or cutting off the hair or beard of a person (such as a Sikh) whose religion forbids him to do so, or forcing a person (such as a Jehovah's Witness) to smoke when this is against his religion.

The same footnote also says that: **6–052**

> "For this crime [outrage upon personal dignity], 'persons' can include dead persons."

and adds:

> "It is understood that the victim need not personally be aware of the existence of the humiliation or degradation or other violation."

The latter means, for instance, that humiliating a mentally disabled or unconscious person is included in the crime. One may also think of the transmitting of televised humiliating images of prisoners or victims (dead or alive) without their knowledge.

Crucially, again, there is no gap in the protection accorded by the varying provisions: to the extent that treatments not constituting torture or mutilation, or sexual attacks or abuse, do not constitute a "grave" violation of the Geneva Conventions under Art. 8(2)(a), they will still constitute war crimes under the above-mentioned clauses in Art. 8(2)(b) (provided they don"t fall under the low threshold described in the second element of the crime of "outrage").

Violations of rules protecting special categories of persons or objects

Crimes number iii, ix, xxiv, xxvi A number of crimes listed in Art. 8(2)(b)   **6–053**
seek to penalise specific actions against specific, (protected) persons or objects: attacks on personnel or objects involved in a humanitarian assistance or peacekeeping mission (crime number iii) or using the Red Cross or Red Crescent symbols (crime number xxiv); attacks against religious buildings, educational institutions, museums, cultural or historical monuments, hospitals, etc. (crime number ix); and conscripting or enlisting children under the age of 15 into the national armed forces, or otherwise using them to participate actively in hostilities (crime number xxvi).

Suffice it to note that the crime of attack on religious, educational, etc. buildings (crime number ix) is only a war crime if the building is not a "military objective" (the same proviso is stipulated in crime number v, concerning attacks on undefended towns, noted in connection with protection of civilians). Article 52(2) of AP I clarifies that :

> ". . . military objectives are limited to those objects which by their nature, location, purpose or use make an effective contribution to military action and whose total or partial destruction, capture or neutralization, in the circumstances ruling at the time, offers a definite military advantage."

However, according to Art. 52(3) of AP I:

> "In case of doubt whether an object which is normally dedicated to civilian purposes, such as a place of worship, a house or other dwelling or a school, is being

used to make an effective contribution to military action, it shall be presumed not to be so used."

In relation to medical and cultural objects, the Hague Convention and its Second Protocol, and the First, Second and Fourth Geneva Conventions and AP I give further, precise indications as to when they loose their protection; and further conditions are stipulated in the Hague Convention and the Geneva Conventions before they may be attacked.

The other crimes listed in Article 8(2)(b)

6–054   *Crimes number vii, viii, xi, xiv, xv, xxiii* The rest of the crimes listed in Art. 8(2)(b) relate to violations of particular, miscellaneous rules of war. Crime number vii concerns improperly using a flag of truce, the enemy flag or enemy uniform or the Red Cross and the like, if this leads to death or serious personal injury of the victim. The EOC clarify that it suffices that "[t]he perpetrator knew that the conduct could result in death of serious personal injury." (element 5 in all the crimes covered). It is of a similar nature to crime number xi, concerning "treacherous" killing or wounding (also referred to as "perfidy"), which involves falsely creating, and then betraying, confidence.

It is also a crime for an occupying power to either: transfer parts of its own population into the territory it occupies, or to deport or transfer all or parts of the population of the occupied territory (crime number viii); to deprive nationals of an enemy State of their rights in a court of law (crime number xiv); to compel enemy nationals to take part in operations against their own country (crime number (xv); and to "utiliz[e] the presence of a civilian or other protected person [*e.g.* a POW] to render certain points, areas or military forces immune from military operations" (*e.g.* by using them as so-called "human shields") (crime number xxiii).

SERIOUS VIOLATIONS OF ARTICLE 3 COMMON TO THE FOUR GENEVA CONVENTIONS OF AUGUST 12, 1949, APPLICABLE IN ARMED CONFLICTS NOT OF AN INTERNATIONAL CHARACTER

Crimes in this category

6–055   As noted in para. 6–004 above, traditionally, IHL applied primarily to international armed conflicts; and the concept of war crimes was limited to violations of IHL that occured in international armed conflicts. However, the ICTR was given jurisdiction over serious violations of Common Art. 3 of the Geneva Conventions and AP II, which both apply specifically to non-international armed conflicts; the ICTY has interpreted its statute so as to give that tribunal, too, jurisdiction over serious violations of Common Art.

3 and other serious violations of IHL in non-international armed conflicts in the Former Yugoslavia; and this trend is confirmed in the Rome Statute of the ICC which formally includes such violations in the concept of war crimes (listed in Art. 8).

Article 8(2)(c) of the Rome Statute thus stipulates, first of all, that "[i]n the case of an armed conflict not of an international character", the following "serious violations of article 3 common to the four Geneva Conventions of 12 August 1949", if committed against certain specific (*protected*) categories of *persons*, constitute *war crimes* over which the ICC has jurisdiction. They are set out in almost identical terms to those used in Common Art. 3 (albeit in a slightly different order) as indicated:

(i)   violence to life and person, in particular murder of all kinds, mutilation, cruel treatment and torture (Common Art. 3, at (1)(a));

(ii) committing outrages upon personal dignity, in particular humiliating and degrading treatment (Common Art. 3, at (1)(c));

(iii) taking of hostages (Common Art. 3, at (1)(b)); and

(iv) the passing of sentences and the carrying out of executions without previous judgement pronounced by a regularly constituted court, affording all judicial guarantees which are generally recognised as indispensable (see Common Art. 3, at (1)(d) — however, in the GCs, the last words read ". . . *recognized as indispensable by civilized peoples.*").

Issues and elements common to the crimes in this category

There are two crucial pre-conditions which must be met before these crimes can be committed:

    6–056

- the crime must have been committed "in the case of an armed conflict not of an international character" — but some "internal disturbances" are not regarded as (internal) "armed conflicts"; and

- the crime must have been perpetrated against certain specific "protected" persons.

Certain EOC pertain to each of these issues.

Common issues and elements relating to the context of the crimes

The question of international and non-international armed conflicts was already touched upon above, where it was noted that Art. 8(2)(d) specifies with reference to Art. 8(2)(c) — just like Art. 8(2)(f) specifies with regard to Art. 8(2)(e), as noted below — that:

    6–057

"Paragraph 2(c) applies to armed conflicts not of an international character and thus does not apply to situations of internal disturbances and tensions, such as riots, isolated and sporadic acts of violence or other acts of a similar nature."

In other words, according to the Rome Statute, "internal disturbances" of the kinds indicated, by their nature, do not amount to an (internal) "armed conflict". Article 8(2)(d) does not expressly add the stipulation used in Art. 8(2)(f), that the concept of "armed conflicts not of an international character" include:

"armed conflicts that take place in the territory of a State when there is protracted armed conflict between governmental authorities and organized armed groups or between such groups." (Art. 8(2)(f), last sentence).

However, both the ICTR and the ICTY have clarified, quite generally, that the two elements mentioned in Art. 8(2)(f) are constituent elements of the concept of "armed conflict". For Common Art. 3 or other provisions of IHL to apply, there must be, as a minimum: (i) opposing, organised armed groups; (ii) a certain intensity of fighting; and (iii) a certain duration of the conflict. On the other hand, it is not essential that government forces are involved on one side or the other of the conflict, or that rebel forces exercise territorial control.

The ICTY has also excluded terrorist activity from the concept of "internal conflict", by mentioning it in the same breath as "civil unrest":

"[i]n order to distinguish [non-international armed conflicts] from cases of civil unrest or terrorist activities, the emphasis is on the protracted extent of the armed violence and the extent of organisation of the parties involved." (*Delalic* judgment, para. 184)

This is a regrettable over-simplification: terrorism can be both "protracted" and "organised" (and it can, of course, also be international). It would be a seriously retrogade step if this categorisation were to be used as a means of denying "suspected terrorists" the protection of IHL, or to limit the jurisdiction of the ICC over crimes committed against (or by) persons thus labelled.

These pre-conditions as to when a conflict falls within the scope of Art. 8(2)(c) do not (in the view of PrepCom) constitute elements of the crimes listed in Art. 8(2)(c); rather, they are seen as limitations to the jurisdiction of the ICC. However, it is (again) an element of the crime that it "*took place in the context of*" and "*was associated with*" the armed conflict (in this case, the non-international armed conflict) in question, and that the perpetrator was *aware* of the factual circumstances that established the *existence of an armed conflict* (but need not have been aware of the non-international nature of the conflict).

Common elements relating to the persons or property affected by the crimes (the question of "protected persons and — property")

The second main issue to be taken into account is that Art. 8(2)(c) protects **6–058** only certain specific categories of victims (certain "protected persons"), *i.e.*:

> "persons taking no active part in the hostilities, including members of armed forces who have laid down their arms and those placed *hors de combat* by sickness, wounds, detention or any other cause". (Introductory sentence to Art. 8(2)(c))

The word "including" makes clear that the category of "persons taking no active part in the hostilities" is a very wide one: it is not limited to combatants who are *hors de combat*, but includes, in the words of the ICTY:

> "civilians, prisoners of war, wounded and sick members of the armed forces in the field and wounded and shipwrecked members of the armed forces at sea." (*Tadic* judgment, para. 615).

It also includes the special protected categories of medical or religious personnel (whereby the latter term includes "non-confessional non-combatant military personnel carrying out similar functions"). The only question is whether the victim took a "direct" (or "active": the words are, in this regard, synonymous) part in the hostilities at the time of the offence — be this as a member of the armed forces who is not *hors de combat* or as a civilian taking part in a *levée en masse*, or as an irregular combatant: only if he did so take part, at that time, will the offence be outside the scope of the provision.

On the question of *mens rea*, it is an element of the crimes listed in Art. 8(2)(c) that the perpetrator was aware of "the factual circumstances that established" the status of the victim as falling within this description. In other words, the perpetrator need not have made the necessary legal assessment: it suffices if he knew that his victim did not take part in hostilties.

The crimes listed in Art. 8(2)(c) can, moreover, be perpetrated by both members of the armed forces and civilians. Although this was not spelled out by PrepCom, this has always been the position of the ICRC; and the ICTR expressly endorsed that view in its Appeals Chamber judgment in the *Akayesu* case (overturning the trial court's ruling on the issue).

Elements of Specific Crimes Listed in Article 8(2)(c)

The crimes listed under numbers (i) and (ii) in Art. 8(2)(c) — "violence to life and **6–059** person, in particular murder of all kinds, mutilation, cruel treatment and torture" and "committing outrages upon personal dignity, in particular humiliating and degrading treatment" — are very similar to the crimes listed as "grave violations" of the Conventions in Art. 8(2)(a), numbers (i)–(iii), discussed in para. 6–039ff above: *"wilful killing"*, *"torture or inhuman treatment, including* *biological experiments"*, and *"wilfully causing great suffering, or serious injury to body or health"*. In fact, in many respects they correspond.

Murder

6–060 PrepCom agreed with the view taken by the ICTY (and also adopted by the ICRC) that:

> "[there] can be no line drawn between 'wilful killing' and 'murder' which affects their content." (ICTY, *Delalic* judgment, para. 422).

The comments made in para. 6–039 above, with regard to "wilful killing" of protected persons in international armed conflicts, therefore equally apply to the "murder" of protected persons in non-international armed conflicts. Specifically, it may be assumed that the required *mens rea* includes both guilty intent and recklessness akin to serious criminal negligence. Also worth recalling is the liability of military commanders or other superiors for failing to report for further investigation murders allegedly committed by forces under their command or authority — which corresponds to the "procedural requirement" imposed on States under the "right to life" provisions in international human rights instruments.

Mutilation, cruel treatment and torture

6–061 PrepCom similarly held that there is no difference between the meaning of the word "torture" in Art. 8(2)(a), relating to international armed conflict, and the meaning of that word in Art. 8(2)(c), relating to non-international armed conflict; and indeed that there is no difference between the meaning of the term "inhuman treatment" in Art. 8(2)(a) and "cruel treatment" in Art. 8(2)(c). The comments made in respect of these terms in paras 6–040 and 6–061 above, therefore also apply with regard to Art. 8(2)(c).

Between them, the war crimes of mutilation, cruel treatment and torture, humiliating and degrading treatment, etc. can, in substance, be said to correspond to torture, inhuman or degrading treatment in international human rights law, but with the delineations being somewhat different. Suffice it to repeat that IHL has adopted the approach taken by the European Court of Human Rights and by the UN Convention against Torture, according to which, for treatment to amount to torture, it must serve a purpose (such as punishment or extracting confessions, or discrimination), while this is not a requirement for the other crimes. Also, that PrepCom decided not to limit the crime of torture to acts committed by State officials (as is done in the UN Convention), but extended this concept to include:

> "officials of non-State parties to a conflict, in order for the prohibition to retain significance in situations of internal armed conflicts or international armed conflicts involving some non-State entities." (ICTY, *Delalic* judgment, para. 473)

It is perhaps here, more than anywhere else, that my comment about terrorism has a particular resonance. There is always an increased risk of torture in connection with anti-terrorist measures. If terrorism is classified as, by its nature, no more than "civil unrest" rather than "armed conflict", this means that the torture of suspected terrorists cannot (ever) constitute a war crime under the Rome Statute (although it would of course remain an international crime under the UN Convention). However, if one classifies conflicts by reference to more objective criteria such as the level of organisation of the groups involved and the intensity and duration of the conflict, the torture of those suspected of involvement would be a war crime, irrespective of how the victims are classified. Furthermore, such an objective approach also allows for the prosecution for war crimes of terrorists involved in the torture of opponents or civilians.

Taking hostages

As far as the crime listed in Art. 8(2)(c) number iii is concerned — the taking of hostages — it may suffice to note that, yet again, PrepCom felt that there is no difference between this crime when committed in a non-international armed conflict, as compared to when it is committed in an international armed conflict, as proscribed by Art. 8(2)(a)(vii). **6–062**

Sentencing protected persons without due process

This brings us to the final crime listed in Art. 8(2)(c), set out under number iv: **6–063**

> "The passing of sentences and the carrying out of executions without previous judgement pronounced by a regularly constituted court, affording all judicial guarantees which are generally recognized as indispensable."

The provision encompasses two matters: the general question of the fairness of criminal proceedings against protected persons, and the more specific question of the imposition of the death penalty on such persons. Given that the latter raises a number of separate issues, and is subject to a number of special, additional constraints, it will be briefly discussed on its own under the next heading. The discussion here is therefore limited to the general questions of what constitutes a "regularly constituted court" and what are the "judicial guarantees which are generally recognised as indispensable"; and to the question of individual criminal responsibility for the crime; with a final comment on the impact of this provision on international human rights law.

The crime in Art. 8(2)(e) number iv can also be linked to a crime listed in Art. 8(2)(a) — *i.e.* the right to a "fair and regular trial" set out in number vi of that provision — which can be perpetrated in international armed conflicts. Indeed, on the question of what constitutes the essential elements of such a trial, these are referred to in more detailed discussion in this section. It may be noted that both crimes can be committed against a wide range of persons: the crime contained in Art. 8(2)(a) number vi relates to unfair trials of "prisoners of war and other protected persons", and the crimes set out in Art. 8(2)(c) number iv can be committed against anyone not involved in hostilities including, in particular, civilians.

The phrase "judicial guarantees which are generally recognized as indispensable" for a fair trial — which replaces the phrase "judicial guarantees which are recognized as indispensable by civilised peoples" in the Geneva Conventions — can be said to be a reference to "general principles of law" in this field: see Art. 38(1)(d) of the Statute of the ICJ, which lists the "general principles of law recognized by civilized nations" as a (tertiary) source of international law. The change of wording from "guarantees which are recognized as indispensable by civilised peoples" in the Geneva Conventions, to "generally recognized as indispensable" in the Rome Statute, can be seen as a reflection of the feeling that references to "civilised" and, by implication, not-civilised — nations are outdated.

6–064   Common Art. 3 does not itself clarify these guarantees. Furthermore, the *ad hoc* tribunals have, to date, not provided any clarification on the crime either. Some guidance on them can be found in Art. 6(2) of AP II, which specifies, with regard to the prosecution and punishment of criminal offences related to the armed conflict (para. (1)), that:

> (2)   No sentence shall be passed and no penalty shall be executed on a person found guilty of an offence except pursuant to a conviction pronounced by a court offering the essential guarantees of independence and impartiality.

In particular:

> (a)   the procedure shall provide for an accused to be informed without delay of the particulars of the offence alleged against him and shall afford the accused before and during his trial all necessary rights and means of defence;
>
> (b)   no one shall be convicted of an offence except on the basis of individual penal responsibility;
>
> (c)   no one shall be held guilty of any criminal offence on account of any act or omission which did not constitute a criminal offence, under the law, at the time when it was committed; nor shall a heavier penalty be imposed than that which was applicable at the time when the criminal offence was committed; if, after the commission of the offence, provision is made by law for the imposition of a lighter penalty, the offender shall benefit thereby;
>
> (d)   anyone charged with an offence is presumed innocent until proved guilty according to law;
>
> (e)   anyone charged with an offence shall have the right to be tried in his presence;
>
> (f)   no one shall be compelled to testify against himself or to confess guilt.

> (3)   A convicted person shall be advised on conviction of his judicial and other remedies and of the time-limits within which they may be exercised.

(4) . . .

(5) At the end of hostilities, the authorities in power shall endeavour to grant the broadest possible amnesty to persons who have participated in the armed conflict, or those deprived of their liberty for reasons related to the armed conflict, whether they are interned or detained.

The EOC adopted by PrepCom drew on the introductory sentence to Art. 6(2) of AP II, by clarifying, in Element 4, that a court is not "regularly constituted" if it does "not afford the essential guarantees of independence and impartiality". There was a debate in PrepCom on the desirability of listing the guarantees which are "indispensable" to ensure the independence and impartiality of the court and the "other judicial guarantees generally recognized as indispensable" for a fair trial. In fact, a joint Swiss/Hungarian/Costa Rican proposal to that effect was put forward. However, as the ICRC Commentary to the Rome Statute notes:

"While the judicial guarantees listed [in that proposal] were generally acceptable [to PrepCom], some States feared that even an illustrative list would suggest that rights omitted were not indispensable, others feared that there could be a discrepancy between this list of fair-trial guarantees and those contained in the Statute [i.e. as applicable to proceedings in the ICC itself], and a third group took the view that a violation of only one [fair-trial] right would not necessarily amount to a war crime. Instead of weakening the value of such a list of fair-trial guarantees by an introductory paragraph defining what was considered indispensable, States preferred not to include such a list. In addition, the concerns of the third group of States are reflected in footnote 59 [relating to element 4], which reads as follows:

'With respect to elements 4 and 5, the Court should consider whether, in the light of all the relevant circumstances, the cumulative effect of factors with respect to guarantees deprived the person or persons of a fair trial.'"

As the Commentary notes:

"This statement [the footnote] does not, however, mean that the denial of one guarantee might not amount to this crime. The Court must determine whether the denial of a particular guarantee deprived a person of a fair trial."

The ICRC comment is fully in line with international human rights law, in which it has also been held that the fairness of a trial must be judged by reference to all the elements of the trial, but that a single serious violation of a significant fair trial guarantee will in itself render a trial unfair. Indeed, the decision of the PrepCom not to list the "essential guarantees" for a fair trial allows IHL in this field to be linked to the continually-developing standards in international human rights law: as the latter develops, IHL can develop with it; and the jurisprudence of the ICC and the international human rights forums can draw on each other.

The ICRC Commentary adopts precisely this approach. In trying to clarify the "essential guarantees" mentioned in Art. 8(2)(c) of the Rome Statute, it refers to the detailed texts of and case law under the International Covenant on Civil and Political Rights (ICCPR), the European Convention on Human Rights (ECHR), the American Convention on Human Rights (ACHR), and the African Charter on Human and Peoples" Rights (ACHPR).

The extensive international human rights case law on the elements of a "fair trial" under these instruments (or at least under the ICCPR and the ECHR) are discussed elsewhere. Here, it may suffice to just list the broad elements set out in those instruments, listed by the ICRC, including the references to the Geneva Conventions and its Additional Protocols, and to the international human rights instruments provided in the ICRC Commentary. They are:

- The right to a fair (and public) hearing by an independent and impartial tribunal established by law, including the right of access to a court: (see Arts 6(2) AP II, 14(1) ICCPR, 6(1) ECHR, 8(1) ACHR).

- The right to be informed of the charges against one without delay: (see Arts 6(2)(a) AP II, 14(3) ICCPR, 6(3)(a) ECHR, 8(2)(b) ACHR).

- The right to be afforded before and during the trial all necessary rights and means of defence: (Art. 6(2)(a) AP II in general; see also Arts. 14(3) ICCPR. 6(3) ECHR, 8(2) ACHR)

which include the following pre-trial and trial minimum guarantees:

  - The right to be brought promptly before a judge or other officer authorised by law to exercise judicial power: (Arts 9(3) ICCPR, 5(3) ECHR, 7(5) ACHR).

  - The right to proceedings before a court, in order that the court may decide without delay on the lawfulness of one's detention and order one's release: (Arts 9(4) ICCPR, 5(4) ECHR, 7(6) ACHR).

  - The right to adequate time and facilities for the preparation of one's defence and to communicate with counsel of one's own choosing: (Arts 14(3)(b) ICCPR, 6(3)(b) ECHR, 8(2)(c), (d) ACHR).

  - The right to defend oneself in person or through legal assistance: (Arts 14(3)(d) ICCPR, 6(3)(c) ECHR, 8(2)(d), (e) ACHR, 7(1)(c) ACHPR).

  - The right to be tried without undue delay: (Arts 14(3)(c) ICCPR, 6(1) ECHR, 8(1) and 7(1)(d) ACHR ("within a reasonable time").

- – The right to present and examine witnesses: (Arts 14(3)(e) ICCPR, 6(3)(d) ECHR, 8(2)(f) ACHR; see also Art. 75(4)(g) AP I).

- – The right to an interpreter: (Arts 14(3)(f) ICCPR, 6(3)(e) ECHR, 8(2)(a) ACHR ('without charge').

- No one shall be convicted of an offence except on the basis of individual penal responsibility: (Art. 6(2)(b) AP II).

- The principle of *nullum crimen, nulla poena sine lege* and the prohibition of a heavier penalty than that provided at the time of the offence: (Arts 6(2)(c) AP II, 15 ICCPR, 7 ECHR, 9 ACHR, 7(2) ACHPR).

- The right to be presumed innocent: (Arts 6(2)(d) AP II, 14(2) ICCPR, 6(2) ECHR, 8(2) ACHR, 7(1)(b) ACHPR).

- The right to be tried in one's own presence: (Arts 6(2)(e) AP II, 14(3)(d) ICCPR, 8(2)(g) ACHR).

- The right not to be compelled to testify against oneself or to confess guilt: (Arts 6(2)(f) AP II, 14(3)(g) ICCPR, 8(2)(g), 8(3) ACHR).

- The right to be advised of one's judicial and other remedies and of the time-limits within which they may be exercised: (Art. 6(3) AP II).

- The right of the accused to have the judgment pronounced publicly: (Arts 75(4)(i) AP I, 14(1) ICCPR, 6(1) ECHR, 8(5) ACHR).

- The principle of *ne bis in idem*: (Arts 86 GC III, 117(3) GC IV, 75(4)(h) AP I, 14(7) ICCPR, 4 of the Seventh AP to the ECHR, 8(4) ACHR).

The first concerns the question of who is to be held liable for violations of the **6–065** crime set out in Art. 8(2)(c) under number iv. PrepCom, in this respect, set out five crucial elements (as well as the usual elements that the crime must have taken place *in the context of* and must have been *associated with* a *non-international armed conflict*; and that the perpetrator must have been *aware* of the *factual circumstances* that established the existence of an *armed conflict* — elements 6 and 7), *i.e.*:

(1) "the perpetrator passed sentence [on] one or more persons" (Element 1);

(2) that person was a protected person (*i.e.* a combatant who was *hors de combat*, or a civilian, or medical or religious personnel taking no part in the hostilities) (Element 2);

(3) the perpetrator was aware of "the factual circumstances that established this status", *i.e.* that the perpetrator knew that the person on trial belonged to such a category (Element 3);

(4) the court which passed sentence was not "regularly constituted", in that it did not afford the "essential guarantees of independence and impartiality", or in that the court did not afford all other "indispensable" judicial guarantees (Element 4); and

(5) the perpetrator was aware of the denial of the relevant guarantees and of the fact that those guarantees are essential or indispensable to a fair trial (Element 5).

As already noted, PrepCom added to this a footnote (footnote 59), clarifying that with respect to Elements 4 and 5, the question is not whether any single guarantee was absent or breached, but rather, whether taken as a whole, the trial was (un)fair.

The PrepCom also added, in a further footnote, that:

> "[t]he elements laid down in these documents do not address the different forms of individual criminal responsibility, as enunciated in articles 25 and 28 of the [Rome] Statute." (footnote 58, appended to the first element of this crime)

This is important, since otherwise the first element, set out above, could be interpreted as meaning that the crime can only be committed by trial judges (persons who "pass sentence"). While the precise scope of potential perpetrators remains unclear, one may therefore conclude that, at least, others involved in unfair procedures can also be guilty — although the stipulation in the 5th element, that the perpetrator must have been aware of the fact that certain guarantees, denied to the victim, were "essential or indispensable to a fair trial", suggests that the focus is on legal or otherwise qualified professionals involved in the system. Prosecutors participating in unfair trials and appeal court judges confirming a sentence, in particular, would appear to fall within the scope of the offence, as indeed may be court-appointed defence counsel in certain circumstances.

Indeed, one can argue (and the author would argue) that a Government or Occupying Power which adopted laws or regulations for the trial of protected persons, knowing those laws or regulations to be fundamentally lacking in "essential or indispensable" guarantees, are (at least) complicit in the passing of sentences by "courts" thus established and operated. This would, for once, provide for individual criminal responsibility of persons in the highest positions of authority.

6–066   Although the above-mentioned EOC specifically relate to the crime listed in Art. 8(2)(c) number iv, and are not set out with regard to the comparable crime in Art. 8(2)(a) number vi, there is no reason why they should not apply *mutatis mutandis* to the staging of unfair trials in international armed conflict.

The final point to be made in this sub-section concerns the effect, not of international human rights law on IHL, but *vice versa*.

Specifically, as noted in para. 6–010ff above, the application of international human rights standards is subject to derogation provisions, which allow for the suspension or limitation (to a degree otherwise not acceptable) of many of the rights protected, in time of war or other public emergencies. As also noted there, the right to a fair trial in the determination of any criminal charge against one is such a "derogable" right. However, any such derogations must be limited to what is "strictly required by the exigencies of the situation" — and they may not be inconsistent with the State Party's "other obligations under international law" (Arts 4(1) ICCPR, 15(1) ECHR).

The provisions in the Rome Statute which make it a war crime to deprive prisoners of war and civilians of a fair trial before an independent and impartial tribunal established by law, both in the context of international — and in non-international armed conflicts, therefore have a direct bearing on the application of the derogation provisions in the human rights treaties to the fair trial guarantee contained within those treaties. It means, first of all, that State Parties to the human rights treaties may not deprive defendants within these very broad categories of their right to a fair trial, in any circumstances covered by IHL. Neither captured enemy combatants in cases of war, captured rebels belonging to organised armed groups in non-international armed conflicts, nor civilians suspected of having colluded with such persons, may therefore be tried in improper proceedings before improperly constituted tribunals. They may be interned without trial (under both IHL and international human rights law, provided this is a measure which is "strictly required by" — and last no longer than strictly required by — the relevant emergency). But if they are put on trial, the court, and the proceedings, must be in accordance with minimum international standards which also apply in peacetime. This is not to say that the courts or the procedures need to be fully the same as in peacetime: special arrangements may be made to meet "the exigencies of the situation". However, such special arrangements may not fatally affect the most fundamental guarantees, or the fairness of the proceedings overall. **6–067**

Secondly, this has implications also for situations not covered by IHL but which may fall within the scope of the derogation clauses in the human rights treaties, *i.e.* to "situations of internal disturbances and tensions, such as riots, isolated and sporadic acts of violence or other acts of a similar nature," if and to the extent that such situations can be said to constitute "public emergencies threatening the life of the nation".

I already noted that, with IHL extending to situations of "protracted armed conflict between governmental authorities and organized armed groups or between such groups", the in-between category of low-level emergencies is becoming smaller. Here, it should be noted that it will be difficult (indeed, in the view of the author, impossible) to argue that States can establish courts, or introduce special procedures, for the trial of individuals in such situations which fall short of the internationally-recognised minimum standards, when they are not allowed to do so in the (by definition, worse) situations covered by IHL. If such departures from such minimum standards are not permitted in peacetime, and also not in times of full-scale war, nor in situations of serious, protracted internal disturbances, it cannot be the case that they are "strictly required" to meet the exigencies of lower-level insurgencies and upheavals.

6–068 The critical remarks made earlier, in paras 6–057 and 6–061 at the beginning of this section about mentioning terrorist activity in one breath with "civil unrest" outside the scope of IHL are relevant here. If the above is correct, a State may also not introduce improperly-constituted courts, or procedures which violate fundamental fair trial principles, to try "suspected terrorists". To the extent that the defendants are apprehended in the course of an international or non-international armed conflict subject to the Rome Statute, this is obvious: indeed, the judges, prosecutors, and perhaps even the governments or occuying powers establishing such unfair procedures, would be liable as war criminals. However, even if IHL did not apply, the State or occupying power would be in violation of its international human rights treaty obligations, and the persons convicted in such unfair proceedings could challenge their conviction on the basis of the above reasoning, to the extent that the State or occupying power in question allows for the bringing of individual complaints or petititons (*e.g.* under the Optional Protocol to the ICCPR or under the ECHR), or if such persons can invoke international human rights law in the relevant domestic courts.

Imposition of the death penalty

6–069 The crime listed in Art. 8(2)(c) under number iv, apart from prohibiting "the passing of sentences" by an improperly constituted court, or on the basis of improper (unfair) procedures (as discussed under the previous heading), also prohibits the carrying out of executions on the basis of such improper trials, and indeed, *a fortiori*, the carrying out of executions without (any) previous judgment (fair or unfair, by a properly constituted court or not). On the general issues of what does constitute a properly ("regularly") constituted court, and on the question of which guarantees are "indispensable" to such proceedings, the reader is referred to that discussion.

Here, it must be noted that the imposition of the death penalty is subject to a number of further constraints, under both IHL and international human rights law.

As far as IHL is concerned, the Geneva Conventions impose certain procedural requirements on the imposition of the death penalty on prisoners of war and civilians (including informing the prisoner's own country through a Protection Power or, and in practice more usually, through the Red Cross or Red Crescent, and respecting a period of six months between this and the actual execution: see Arts 100, 101 and 107 GC III regarding POWs; Arts 74 and 75 GC IV regarding civilians). To this, Art. 6(4) of AP II adds the stipulation that:

"The death penalty shall not be pronounced on persons who were under the age of eighteen years at the time of the offence and shall not be carried out on pregnant women or mothers of young children."

International human rights law adds to the constraints. Here, it must suffice to note that the fair trial guarantees must, under international human rights law, be rigourously adhered to in capital cases. More specifically, the European Court of Human Rights has held, in the recent *Öcalan* judgment, that deprivation of life following an unfair trial would *ipso facto* be a violation of the right to life. In the light of my observations under the previous heading on the applicability of the fair trial guarantees, also in times of emergency, this can be said to apply also to executions of POWs and civilians in times of international or non-international armed conflict, or of less intense conflicts or emergencies. Indeed, the court held in that case that:

"to impose a death sentence on a person after an unfair trial is to subject that person wrongfully to the fear that he would be executed. The fear and uncertainty as to the future generated by a sentence of death, in circumstances where there existed a real possibility that the sentence would be enforced . . . must give rise to a significant degree of human anguish. Such anguish cannot be dissociated from the unfairness of the proceedings underlying the sentence.

. . . the imposition of a capital sentence in such circumstances has to be considered, in itself, to amount to a form of inhuman treatment."

Admittedly, the court said that it reached this latter conclusion "having regard to the rejection by [the Member States of the Council of Europe] of capital punishment", a rejection which, the court felt, showed that the punishment "is no longer seen as having any legitimate place in a democratic society". However, the general sentiment and reasoning is clear.

OTHER SERIOUS VIOLATIONS OF THE LAWS AND CUSTOMS APPLICABLE IN ARMED CONFLICTS NOT OF AN INTERNATIONAL CHARACTER

Crimes in this category

The final list of war crimes which can be committed in situations of non-international armed conflict and which are subject to the jurisdiction of the ICC, is contained in Art. 8(2)(e) of the Rome Statute. It covers a range of offences which are identical, or very similar, to offences which, under Art. 8(2)(b) of the Statute, constitute war crimes when committed in times of international armed conflicts, as indicated below: **6–070**

(i)   Intentionally directing attacks against the civilian population as such or against individual civilians not taking direct part in hostilities (=Art. 8(2)(b), number i).

(ii)   Intentionally directing attacks against buildings, material, medical units and transport, and personnel using the distinctive emblems of the Geneva Conventions in conformity with international law (=Art. 8(2)(b), number xxiv).

(iii)   Intentionally directing attacks against personnel, installations, material, units or vehicles involved in a humanitarian assistance or peacekeeping mission in accordance with the Charter of the United Nations, as long as they are entitled to the protection given to civilians or civilian objects under the international law of armed conflict (=Art. 8(2)(b), number iii).

(iv)   Intentionally directing attacks against buildings dedicated to religion, education, art, science or charitable purposes, historic monuments, hospitals and places where the sick and wounded are collected, provided they are not military objectives (=Art. 8(2)(b), number ix).

(v)   Pillaging a town or place, even when taken by assault (=Art. 8(2)(b), number xvi).

(vi)   Committing rape, sexual slavery, enforced prostitution, forced pregnancy, as defined in Art. 7, para. 2(f), enforced sterilization, and any other form of sexual violence also constituting a serious violation of Art. 3 common to the four Geneva Conventions (=Art. 8(2)(b), number xii).

(vii)   Conscripting or enlisting children under the age of fifteen years into armed forces or groups or using them to participate actively in hostilities (=Art. 8(2)(b), number xxvi, except that the latter does not mention [other] "groups").

(viii)   Ordering the displacement of the civilian population for reasons related to the conflict, unless the security of the civilians involved or imperative military reasons so demand (=Art. 8(2)(b), number viii).

(ix)   Killing or wounding treacherously a combatant adversary (=Art. 8(2)(b), number xi, except that the latter refers to the treacherous killing or wounding of "individuals belonging to the hostile nation or army").

(x)   Declaring that no quarter will be given (=Art. 8(2)(b), number xii).

(xi)   Subjecting persons who are in the power of another party to the conflict to physical mutilation or to medical or scientific experiments of any kind which are neither justified by the medical, dental or hospital treatment of the person concerned nor carried out in his or her interest, and which cause death to or seriously endanger the health of such person or persons (=Art. 8(2)(b), number x).

(xii)   Destroying or seizing the property of an adversary unless such destruction or seizure be imperatively demanded by the necessities of the conflict (=Art. 8(2)(b), number xiii, except that the latter refers to "the enemy's property").

Issues and elements common to the crimes in this category; links with issues and elements of crimes listed in earlier provisions

Like Art. 8(2)(c), discussed in para. 6–055ff above, the crimes listed in Art.   **6–071**
8(2)(e) are war crimes if committed in "armed conflicts not of an international character" (as it is expressly stated in the introductory sentence to the above crimes). Article 8(2)(e) is also, like Art. 8(2)(c), followed by a further paragraph, limiting the concept of "non-international armed conflict" so as to exclude "situations of internal disturbances and tensions, such as riots, isolated and sporadic acts of violence or other acts of a similar nature" (Art. 8(2)(f), using the same words as Art. 8(2)(d)). Article 8(2)(f) adds that Art. 8(2)(e) applies to "armed conflicts that take place in the territory of a State when there is protracted armed conflict between governmental authorities and organized armed groups or between such groups" — but as was again already noted, the same applies with regard to Art. 8(2)(c).

On this issue, the EOC simply repeat the general elements, applicable to all war crimes, that the offence must have been committed "*in the context of*" and must have been "*associated with*" the relevant armed conflict (*i.e.* here, the relevant non-international armed conflict); and that the perpetrator must have been *aware* of "the factual circumstances that established the existence of an *armed conflict*" (but need not have been aware of the non-international nature of the conflict). On the question of what constitutes a "non-international armed conflict" for the purposes of these provisions, and on these elements, please refer to this earlier discussion.

The other general proviso placed on Art. 8(2)(e) by the text — that it applies "within the established framework of international law" — is the same as the one used in the other provision dealing with "other crimes", beyond a primary category listed in preceeding paras, Art. 8(2)(b), discussed above. Again, neither the EOC nor the ICRC Commentary comment on the meaning of the phrase; again, it may be taken as reaffirmation that the "other crimes" listed must be strictly construed in accordance with customary and conventional IHL. However, it may also again be noted that customary IHL includes the two "cardinal principles" of IHL, mentioned in para. 6–002 above, to which several of the crimes listed in Art. 8(2)(e) relate. This includes, in particular, unlawful attacks on civilians or civilian objects (crime numbers i and iv), pillaging (crime number v); and destroying or seizing property (crime number xii).

6–072   The PrepCom considered that with regard to all the crimes listed in Art. 8(2)(e) which correspond to crimes listed in Art. 8(2)(b), the elements of the crimes concerned were identical. In other words, the only difference between the war crimes discussed earlier, with reference to Art. 8(2)(b), and the war crimes addressed in this section is the context. If any of the crimes which are listed in (almost) identical terms in Arts. 8(2)(b) and (e) is committed in the context of an international armed conflict, it is a crime under the former provision; if it is committed in the context of a non-international armed conflict, it is a crime under the latter provision. That is the only difference. On the elements of all these crimes, please refer to para. 6–045.

The only crime, in respect of which there is a more substantial difference in wording (not inspired by the different context), is the crime listed in Art. 8(2)(e), number viii: displacing civilians. Even here, the crime is very similar to certain other crimes listed in the Statute, including, in particular, the crime included in Art. 8(2)(a), number vii, "unlawful deportation or transfer". The PrepCom adopted the following elements of this crime (apart from the general ones that the crime must have been committed in the *context* of a non-international armed conflict and must have been *associated* with that conflict; and that the perpetrator must have been *aware* of the existence of the conflict):

- the perpetrator ordered a displacement of a civilian population;

- such order was not justified by the security of the civilians involved or by military necessity; and

- the perpetrator was in a position to effect such displacement by giving such an order.

The ICRC Commentary further clarifies that while the term "civilian population" cannot be applied to a single, individual civilian, it also does not mean that the displacement was of the whole civilian population; and that the control required to satisfy the third element covers both *de jure* and *de facto* authority, so as to include individuals who have effective control of a situation by sheer strength of force.

SANCTIONS

6–073   As the ICRC pointed out in its statement welcoming the adoption of the Rome Statute of the ICC, the event clearly demonstrated the resolve of the great majority of States "to put an end to the impunity enjoyed by the perpetrators of the most heinous crimes, and hence to deter the commission of further violations." However, even prior to the adoption of the Statute (or indeed to the establishment of the *ad hoc* tribunals), States had important rights and obligations to act against such crimes, and these remain. The jurisdiction of the ICC does not replace, but is complementary to, national criminal jurisdiction.

Specifically, as already noted above, all States can already claim "universal jurisdiction" over such crimes — that is:

> "the ability of the prosecutor or investigating judge of any state to investigate or prosecute persons for crimes committed outside the state's territory which are not linked to that state by the nationality of the suspect or of the victim or by harm to the state's own national interests."

In most respect, such jurisdiction is optional: under customary international law, States *may* prosecute such crimes. The exercise of such "permissive universal jurisdiction" is deemed not to involve interference in the internal affairs of other States because the perpetration of such crimes is an affront to all humanity. States have (at least) permissive universal jurisdiction in respect of genocide, crimes against humanity — and in respect of all war crimes, that is, all the crimes listed in Art. 8 of the Rome Statute, as discussed earlier in this chapter.

In some respects, IHL goes further. Thus, as we already noted, the Geneva Conventions *oblige* States to "provide effective penal sanctions for persons committing, or ordering to be committed" certain specified, "grave" violations of the Conventions (Arts 49 and 50 of GC I; Arts 50 and 51 of GC II; Arts 129 and 130 of GC III; Arts 146 and 147 of GC IV). As we have seen, these crimes are reiterated in Art. 8(2)(a) of the Rome Statute, discussed above. For such crimes, all States *must*, under these Conventions, assume power to prosecute and punish the perpetrators, irrespective of whether the perpetrators or the victims of the crimes have a connection with the State Parties concerned: so-called "compulsory universal jurisdiction". At least, a State which is subject to this duty may not shelter the person: if it does not want to prosecute the person itself, it is obliged to extradite the person to another State which is willing to do so, or to hand over the person to an international tribunal (such as the ICTY or the ICTR or the ICC) which has jurisdiction over the matter: the principle of *aut dedere aut punire* ("hand over or punish").

We noted in para. 6–006 above, that the ICTY has suggested that the **6–074** "grave violations" regime has, under customary international law, developed to now include not just "grave" violations of the Geneva Conventions committed in international armed conflicts, but also serious violations of Common Art. 3 of the Geneva Conventions, which (in its own clear terms) applies in non-international armed conflicts: see Art. 8(2)(c) of the Rome Statute, discussed in para. 6–055ff above. If this is so, such violations too may have become subject to compulsory universal jurisdiction of States.

This is the more plausible since compulsory universal jurisdiction (subject to the principle of *aut dedere aut punire*) has also been adopted under various treaties including, most importantly, the 1984 UN Convention against Torture (as discussed in para. 6–016ff above, under the heading "subjects of IHL and international human rights law", and in more detail in Chapter 7). (The fact that the 1948 United Nations Genocide Convention does not create compulsory universal jurisdiction can be explained by the fact that it was adopted prior to the development of the trend.)

Indeed, Amnesty International argues that the principle should be applied, and increasingly is being applied, to all crimes under international law, and in particular to war crimes — that is, to all the crimes listed in Art. 8(2) of the Rome Statute, whether committed in international or in non-international armed conflict — to crimes against humanity and genocide, as well as to torture, extrajudicial executions and "disappearances":

> "To the extent that the *aut dedere aut judicare* principle may not yet be fully recognized as customary international law for all such crimes under international law, the evidence . . . indicates that it is an emerging general principle of law recognized by states. Moreover, Amnesty International believes that logic and morality dictate that this principle should be implemented by all states."

> (Amnesty International legal memorandum "*Universal Jurisdiction — the duty of States to enact and enforce legislation*. See there for a discussion of the differences between "crimes under international law", "crimes under national law of international concern", and "international crimes" [now more commonly referred to as "'serious breaches of obligations owed to the international community as a whole", so-called "*erga omnes* obligations"])

However, it is also clear that some States — and in particular the United States of America — oppose both the extension of universal jurisdiction in national practice and the extension of jurisdiction by international courts, and more in particular the ICC, at least when this would mean that their own nationals (and more in particular members of its armed forces) could be tried under such rules.

CONCLUSIONS

6–075   As this chapter has shown, international law relating to war crimes is complex. Whether certain crimes constitute such crimes itself is not always clear: the Rome Statute of the ICC (which we have taken as the basis for our discussions) lists a range of crimes under this heading which, until fairly recently, would not all have been so categorised. Furthermore, the rules relating to, and the elements of, the many crimes brought under that heading in the Statute still often differ, depending on the context in which the crimes are committed and the category of persons involved (be they perpetrators or victims). However, a number important developments and trends have been discerned.

First of all, the establishment of the recent *ad hoc* tribunals on the Former Yugoslavia and Rwanda has led to a substantial new *corpus* of case-law, which has helped to clarify IHL in this respect.

Secondly, there is a growing convergence between the rules of IHL which apply in international armed conflicts and those that apply in non-international armed conflicts. This can be seen most clearly from the fact (noted above) that PrepCom simply held that the elements of effectively all the "other serious violations" listed in Art. 8(2)(e) (concerning non-international armed conflicts) are "identical" to the corresponding "other serious violations" listed in Art. 8(2)(b) (concerning international armed conflicts). But the same is true with regard to the primary categories of war crimes set out in Art. 8(2)(a) and (c): the "grave violations" of the Geneva Conventions perpetrated in international armed conflict and the "serious violations" of Common Art. 3 of the Conventions perpetrated in non-international armed conflicts, as was shown in the relevant sections above.

Thirdly, there is a growing convergence — or at least, a strong cross-fertilisation — between the rules relating to and the elements of many war crimes and the rules and interpretations relating to closely related human rights guarantees including, in particular, the right to life, freedom from torture, inhuman and degrading treatment, and the right to a fair trial. **6–076**

These matters are interrelated, in particular in that the *ad hoc* tribunals, and PrepCom preparing the Elements of Crime relating to the crimes listed in the Rome Statute of ICC, have been able to draw on the extensive case law built up by the international human rights *fora* (in particular, the case law of the European Court of Human Rights under the ECHR and the views and general comments of the Human Rights Committee under the ICCPR) prior to the establishment of these tribunals. It is to be hoped and expected that the case-law of the international criminal tribunals will in turn inform the jurisprudence of the human rights bodies, and that the various bodies all will seek to minimise differences in legal interpretations of corresponding matters and to avoid gaps in protection between the various regimes for which they are responsible.

As a result, there is beginning to be a coherent body of rules, principles and interpretations which apply, across the board, to crimes such as "wilful killing" in international armed conflicts, "violence to life" and "murder" in non-international armed conflicts under IHL, and "arbitrary deprivation of life" under human rights law; to torture under IHL (whether committed in international or non-international armed conflicts) and torture in human rights law (although some qualification remains necessary in this respect with regard to the perpetrator); and which clarify what are the "essential guarantees" for an independent and impartial tribunal, and for a fair trial. Indeed, as far as the latter is concerned, we have seen in para. 6–066ff above, how the development of IHL relating to war crimes has helped to clarify the limitations on the rights of States to derogate from the "fair trial" provisions in human rights treaties in situations of national emergency or unrest.

Much still needs to be done, for instance when it comes to the question of universal jurisdiction. However, it has become clear that the fabric of international criminal law in respect of the crimes discussed in this chapter, which **6–077** is woven from the strands developed in each of these respects, IHL and human rights law, is becoming less coarse, more detailed (and more coherent in its details), and much less patchy. Holes which still existed in this fabric a few years ago are being filled in: perpetrators of these crimes are less likely to escape through them.

Chapter 7

TORURE

"Torture is not only one of the vilest acts that one human being can inflict on another, it is also among the most insidious of all human rights violations. All too often, it is veiled in secrecy — except from those who, cowering in nearby cells, might be its next victims. Victims are often too shamed or traumatised to speak out, or face further peril if they do; often, they die from their wounds. Perpetrators, meanwhile, are shielded by conspiracies of silence and by the legal and political machinery of states that resort to torture."(Statement made by Secretary-General Kofi Annan on the International Day in Support of Victims of Torture, June 26, 2000.)

INTRODUCTION

The above short statement neatly encapsulates the predicament facing victims   **7–001**
of torture and the ongoing problems of putting on trial those individuals
responsible for committing such atrocities.

Although torture is nowadays universally accepted as repugnant and
prohibited under customary international law and generally recognised as
achieving the status of *jus cogens,* in many parts of the world State-sponsored
torture continues to go unabated and those responsible remain in power
and unaccountable for their actions. Despite the multitude of regional and
international instruments condemning torture, its practice has not receded;
in fact the opposite is the true case. According to various international
NGOs, principally Amnesty International and Human Rights Watch,
nearly two-third's of the world's States still practice torture in some form
or other (see *Amnesty International Report 2000*, which puts the figure of
States at present using torture and ill-treatment techniques in 1999 at 132,
compared with 125 in 1998). Whilst some human rights abuses such as
summary executions and capital punishment appear to be on the decline,
official torture and ill-treatment remains on the increase. Publicly all States
now condemn the practice of torture or deny its existence within their own
territory. In reality, many States condone its use and in some cases it is
even encouraged and sanctioned by those in authority. Those State officials
who practice torture justify their actions as being legally authorised or at
the very least acceptable under the guise of "the ends justifying the
means".

Reasons behind torture

7–002   It would be naive to believe that when it comes to torture there exist boundaries beyond which no State using such methods would go to achieve its ends;
in many cases resulting in the death of the victim. The rationale behind the
persistent use of torture worldwide is manifold but generally there are five
main reasons for its continued practice: (1) to extract confessions; (2) to
gather information; (3) as a method of sadistic punishment; (4) to retain control by the state over its own citizens, by means of subjugation and intimidation; and (5) merely because the victim belongs to a particular group, be it
religious, racial, political or other. By its very nature the practice excludes any
form of refinement or limitation. It is rarely a one-off experience, but rather
generally forms part of a systematic and planned strategy calculated,
amongst other things, to undermine and sap the free will of the victim. The
methods used are inhumane, crude, and draconian, and generally carried out
under conditions intended to humiliate, debase and deprive victims of their
dignity, freedom and self-worth. The most common techniques applied
include severe beatings; use of electric shocks devices; "*falanga*" — thrashing
the soles of the feet; sexual abuse and rape; solitary confinement; medical
experimentation; asphyxiation ("*submarino*") through near-death suffocation
by excrement or contaminated water; ordering others to torture the victim;
denial of medical treatment; burning; the use of mind-altering drugs; extraditing the victim to another state which would use torture; and other barbaric
acts which result in physical and mental abuses. The severity of the interrogation techniques used will often depend on the character and demeanour of
the victim, *e.g.* has the victim been trained to endure intense bouts of pain
and suffering at the hands of state interrogators or is the intended victim
merely a child or old, timid, nervous or frightened? Moreover, despite some
States being openly condemned by the international community for using the
abuses mentioned above, other States, less widely acknowledged for outright
human rights violations still continue to employ more subtle indirect techniques which may nevertheless constitute a form of torture. For example: (a)
returning asylum seekers or illegal immigrants to their home State when there
is a real danger of such persons being subjected to torture; (b) where States
have retained the death penalty, the methods of execution administered; or
(c) prison conditions and the treatment of pre and post-trial prisoners in general and especially the "death row phenomenon". The above have all, in
recent years, come under international legal scrutiny as potentially amounting
to torture.

It is one thing, in principle, to achieve common agreement on the
universal prohibition of torture, it is quite another to implement such a prohibition and actively indict and severely punish those responsible for carrying
out such a crime. For example, Israel, has in the past not only shielded its own
police and security forces from prosecution in such cases, and from 1975 until
September 1999 effectively legalised some forms of torture by permitting, in

certain circumstances, "the application of a moderate degree of physical and psychological pressure" as part of the interrogation process of terrorist detainees; despite being a party to various international treaties which specifically condemned torture, such as the United Nations Convention Against Torture 1984 ("UNTC"), ratified in 1991, and the International Covenant on Civil and Political Rights 1966. Israeli authorities had long argued that their interrogation methods are: (a) legally permissible; (b) not in violation of their international responsibilities, since they do not constitute torture (despite substantial evidence to the contrary); and (c) that the existing national emergency justifies their irregular actions. Israel had defended its stance in this particular area on the grounds of its historical background and existing exceptional conditions in dealing with matters of defence. Historically, since the establishment of the State of Israel in 1948 terrorists activities against military and civilian targets have persisted until the present day. In order to combat this specific problem the General Security Service ("GSS") was created to fight and prevent terrorist hostilities, protect human life and to investigate such attacks against the state. As part of the GSS investigative process they have applied interrogation practices against detainees including "the application of non-violent psychological pressure" and "the application of a moderate degree of physical pressure". Such treatment of suspects was approved by the Report of the Commission of Inquiry Regarding the GSS" Interrogation Practices with Respect to Hostile Terrorist Activities (1987); ("The Landau Report" was published in 1995). The Landau Report justified this treatment on the grounds that: (1) it was very difficult to combat the danger by Arab groups on Israeli citizens using ordinary non-physical methods; (2) the GSS is different from ordinary police — their main objective being to gather information and intelligence. How this intelligence was received was not a vital factor; if disclosure outweighs the damage it would be admissible in evidence; and (3) the use of such methods must have been necessary and productive; effective interrogation, it was argued, would be impossible without some form of pressure. This appeared to be the Israeli position and policy until the landmark decision of the Supreme Court of Israel in September 1999 in the case discussed below.

The Public Committee Against Torture in Israel; The Association for Citizen's Rights in Israel and Others v The State of Israel: **7–003**

Facts.   The applicants argued before the Supreme Court, sitting as the High Court of Justice, that, *inter alia*, during the interrogation "physical pressure methods" employed by the respondents, the GSS, amounted to torture and thus under international law was illegal and should therefore be discontinued. These methods involved:

1.   Severe shaking. Although the state argued that its use would depend upon the severity of the danger that the interrogation was intending to prevent as well as considering the urgency of uncovering the information. The State further argued that "shaking is indispensable to fighting and winning the war on terrorism".

2. The "*shabach* position". This involved tying the suspect's hands through the gaps in the chair in which he was sitting, with the seat tilted forwards; placing a hood over the suspect's head and subjecting him to loud music over lengthy periods of time. The State argued that the hooding and loud music were used to prevent the suspect making contact with other suspects.

3. Other interrogation techniques included, excessive tightening of handcuffs, sleep deprivation and "frog crouching" (the suspect being made to crouch on the tips of his toes for long periods).

The State submitted that these methods did not amount to torture or inhuman or degrading treatment and did not cause pain and suffering. One of the main arguments put forward by the respondents was that under national law they were absolved from any criminal liability for their actions by virtue of the "defence of necessity" under s. 34(1) of the Penal Law 1977, and that this law includes, under certain circumstances, authorising the GSS to use physical methods to achieve their objectives. That Article provides that "a person will not bear criminal responsibility for committing any act immediately necessary for the purpose of saving the life, body or property, of either himself or his fellow person, from substantial danger of serious harm, imminent from the particular state of things, at the requisite timing and absent alternative means of avoiding the harm".

Decision. The court determined that every investigation must be conducted in a fair and reasonable manner. A reasonable investigation excludes the use of torture, for which there are no exceptions. Indeed, any form of violence is deemed unreasonable and constitutes a criminal offence. Thus, sleep deprivation, if the purpose of which is to "break" the suspect, and not merely a "side effect" of the investigation itself "shall not fall within the scope of a fair and reasonable investigation. Such means harm the rights and dignity of the suspect in a manner surpassing that which is required". Further, the court declared that apart from the ordinary handcuffing of a suspect, for the legitimate purposes of ensuring an officer's safety and to prevent escape, binding the suspect in the "*shabach*" position would in future be outlawed. The use of a hood, which covers the whole head, was also found to be illegal. The court said that such a method "degrades him (the suspect). It causes him to lose sight of time and place. It suffocates him. All these things are not included in the general authority to investigate". However, the court was still willing to permit the covering of the suspect's eyes, provided it did not cause pain or suffering. The court also prohibited the use of powerfully loud music as part of any interrogation process.

Despite no existing laws permitting the GSS to use physical interrogation methods, the respondents turned to the "necessity defence" as a justification for applying force. They submitted, in relation to this defence that it was not only legitimate to use physical methods in certain circumstances in order to combat terrorism, but that it was also their "moral duty". By way of justifying their actions the State put forward the example of the "ticking-time-bomb" scenario. For example, where the GSS believe that the suspect knows the whereabouts of a bomb that will undoubtedly explode, perhaps killing or at least injuring many people it is vital to obtain information on its location from the suspect and preferably as quickly as possible. In such a situation the respondents maintained that by virtue of the necessity defence set out in s.34(1) they were entitled to use physical means to extract the relevant information. The court rejected that the necessity defence should be applied in this manner. They stated that the defence should only be used by individuals reacting to a certain set of unforeseen circumstances at the specific time which warrants some immediate and spontaneous action; it is not to be used by the police or security services as part of the interrogation process in order to gather information of situations, however precarious, which will take place sometime in the future. The question for the court in this case was not one where an interrogator has been prosecuted for *having already* applied physical methods and thereafter argues the necessity defence. The issue here is whether a state official may invoke the necessity defence as a means of exculpating himself from any *future* criminal prosecution by arguing that he possesses the authority to use physical means. The court quoted from "The Use of Physical Force in Interrogations and the Necessity Defence" by Professor Enker which stated that "[N]ecessity is certainly not a basis for establishing a broad detailed code of behaviour such as how one should go about conducting intelligence interrogations in security matters, when one may or may not use force, how much force may be used and the like". Thereafter, the court held that the defence does not apply to actions taken during the interrogative process.

The above judgment not only changes the previous Landau Report's findings and is now arguably in line with existing international law but it also clarifies the situation in relation to the "necessity defence". The court's interpretation of this defence negates the legitimate use by the police or security forces of physical interrogation methods since such State powers can only be derived from legislation which specifically sanctions the use of physical means. Since no law, statute or otherwise, prescribes the use of physical methods as part of any interrogation procedures it follows that police and security forces have no authority to employ such methods and those responsible are now potentially criminally liable. Section 34(1) is limited to defences involving events which have already taken place, and not in order to elicit information from a suspect concerning some future occurrence. A member of the security forces may still attempt to use necessity as a defence, if indicted, but whether or not it will succeed will depend on all the circumstances of the case. It is unlikely that he will be permitted to invoke the s.34(1) defence in relation to physical interrogation practices since he will be presumed to have known that it is no longer available to a person in his position. Israel has, since 1991, ratified the UNCT, and it is about time that the legislature, in line with the State's responsibilities as a member, pass laws prohibiting the use of all forms of torture, which they are required to do under Art. 2(1) and 4 of the UNCT. It is not inconceivable that some forms of ill-treatment will continue, in spite of the 1999 decision. Legislation would be an enormous step in clarifying the situation as well as protecting the rights of those suspects held in custody.

Prohibition of torture under international law

Condemnation against torture practices are contained in various regional and international treaties, declarations and resolutions; most notably in Art. 1 of the United Nations Convention against Torture and other Cruel, Inhuman or Degrading Treatment or Punishment 1984 ("UNTC"); Arts 7 and 10(1) of the International Covenant on Civil and Political Rights 1966 ("ICCPR"); Art. 3 of the European Convention on Human Rights 1950; the

7–004

European Convention for the Prevention of Torture 1987; Art.5 of the African Charter on Human and Peoples" Rights 1981; the Inter-American Convention to Prevent and Punish Torture 1987; Art. 5 of the Universal Declaration of Human Rights ("UDHR") 1948; and the four Geneva Conventions 1949. However, torture is not treated in the same manner by all of these instruments and depending upon which treaty or declaration is cited in court or under consideration by the relevant committee, the results are far from foreseeable. It is therefore necessary to consider each treaty separately and to analyse the differences and similarities between some of the more common regional and international conventions. The following examination will focus primarily on the legal aspects of torture in human rights law and international humanitarian law, and the success and failure of relevant existing international and regional treaties in diminishing its practice, and in particular, various States' attitudes when it comes to bringing to justice the perpetrators of this particular crime. As an intricate and essential part of this examination, careful consideration will also be given to the various institutions such as courts, committees, commissions, working and monitoring groups, NGOs and the relevant Special Rapporteurs; all of which make a invaluable contribution in their efforts to ensure that State Parties uphold and adhere to their responsibilities under the corresponding treaties.

THE UNITED NATIONS CONVENTION AGAINST TORTURE AND OTHER CRUEL, INHUMAN OR DEGRADING TREATMENT OR PUNISHMENT 1984 ("UNCT")

7–005 After the Second World War, despite the plethora of international and regional instruments declaring torture illegal, no definition was ever properly or precisely formulated in these documents until 1975. In that year, the General Assembly (Resolution 3452 (XXX)) approved the United Nations Declaration on the Protection of all Persons from Torture and Other Cruel, Inhuman or Degrading Treatment or Punishment, and set out in Art. 1 a comprehensive definition of torture, which was eventually superseded by Art. 1 of the UNCT (see para. 7–007). Under Art. 3, the Declaration prohibited all forms of torture, and expounded no exceptions, even in times of war or national emergency. In 1984 the General Assembly adopted the UNCT, which finally came into force in June 1987 and has been ratified by some 120 States. The UNCT is divided into three distinguishing areas; Part I — Torture and its Implications (Art. 1–16); Part II — The Committee Against Torture (Art. 17–24); Part III — Responsibilities of State Parties (Articles 25–33). The whole ethos behind the UNCT is one of prevention and protection. The treaty is drafted in a manner which makes it incumbent on state parties to take positive measures through their national laws not only to prevent the practice of torture and other forms of maltreatment but also to punish those responsible for committing such offences.

PART I — TORTURE AND ITS IMPLICATIONS (ARTS 1–16)

The definition of torture is provided in Art. 1(1) and states that: 7–006

> *"For the purpose of this Convention the term "torture" means any act by which severe pain or suffering, whether physical or mental, is intentionally inflicted on a person for such purposes as obtaining from him or a third person information or a confession, punishing him for an act he or a third person has committed or is suspected of having committed, or intimidating or coercing him or a third person, or for any reason based on discrimination of any kind, when such pain or suffering is inflicted by or at the instigation of or with the consent or acquiescence of a public official or other person in an official capacity. It does not include pain or suffering arising only from, inherent in or incidental to lawful sanctions".*

Despite its apparent length and substance Art. 1 is couched in terms which create difficulties in interpretation and implementation. Art. 1 contains five essential ingredients: (i) the *actus reus* must result in severe physical or mental suffering; (ii) the *mens rea* is determined by intentionally inflicting harm upon the victim; (iii) the act must have been committed for certain purposes; (iv) the *rationae personae* is reserved for public officials, or at least those persons acting in a public capacity; and (v) torture excludes acts committed which are lawfully sanctioned. First and foremost, torture involves "severe mental pain or suffering". Thus, the harm inflicted must attain a high level of severity; (anything less will not amount to torture, but may nevertheless constitute cruel, inhuman and degrading treatment or punishment (see below)). In the United States the meaning applied to these words are stated in s.3(2) of the Torture Victim Protection Act 1991 as "prolonged mental harm caused by or resulting from", (a) the intentional infliction or threatened of severe physical pain or suffering; (b) the use of mind altering substances; (c) the threat of imminent death; or (d) the threat that another individual will imminently be subjected to either (a), (b) or (c), above. Secondly, there must be an intention to apply torture. Merely disregarding legal procedural interrogation methods will not, by itself, automatically constitute a violation of Art. 1. Thirdly, torture can only be established for the restricted purposes set out in an apparent exhaustive list in Art. 1, although the torturous acts themselves may be carried out in a variety of ways. Fourthly, in order for the UNCT to apply, torture practices must be carried out, or authorised, by public officials or those acting in an official capacity. Torture between private individuals or non-State groups or groups not acting with, at least, *de facto* State authority are exempt in human rights law under the UNCT. However, determining precisely who is a public official is not necessarily straightforward. In international humanitarian law, for example, The Trial Chamber in the *Celebici* case (Judgment November 16, 1998) stated that the word "official" "must be interpreted to include officials of non-state parties to a conflict, in order for the prohibition to retain significance in situations of internal conflicts or international conflicts involving non-state entities". (para. 473)

187

Some States nowadays lack a central government that is in total control over the whole of its own territory due, in most cases, to either existing civil wars or other armed conflicts between rival factions; recent examples have included the Democratic Republic of Congo (formerly Zaire), Rwanda, Sudan, Angola, Columbia, Afghanistan and Somalia. In such cases, does torture carried out by members of those warring groups, who do not legitimately represent a government authority, fall within the remit of Art. 1 of the UNCT, *i.e.* can such persons be considered as public officials for the purposes of torture? Part of the answer was given in the case of *Elmi v Australia (Com 120/1998)* where the author, a Somalian national, fled to Australia and sought asylum there. He alleged that because of the gross violations of human rights presently existing in his homeland, he would be in danger of being torture and possibly suffer death if he was forced to return. He claimed that he had been personally targeted by the Hawiya clan, a group that controlled most of Mogadishu, where he had previously lived. Both his father and brother had been executed; his sister raped and the remainder of his family forced to go into hiding. One of the questions for consideration by the Committee Against Torture was, in view of the absence of a legitimate government, could a member of the Hawyia clan be characterised as a public official? The Committee answered in the affirmative. They stated that certain factions took on the role of quasi-governmental institutions and provide various public services and "*de facto*, those factions exercise certain prerogatives that are comparable to those normally exercised by legitimate governments". Thus the members of these factions were considered public officials or at least acting in a public capacity for the purposes of Art. 1. However, it remains to be seen whether the meaning of "public official" can be extended to include persons belonging to warring groups which do not control any territory within a State. It is submitted that such individuals may come within Art. 1 if they are holding themselves out to be the *de facto* governing power of that state, or at least part of it. The fact that such groups may never achieve their ultimate goal of legitimacy should not detract from their legal obligations of upholding, even in times of a protracted civil war or other internal conflict, the rules of international law. Consequently, individual members of such groups should not be permitted to escape responsibility and those who commit acts of torture should be treated as public officials for the purposes of Art. 1.

7–007   The final wording of Art. 1 states that torture "does not include pain or suffering arising only from, inherent in or incidental to lawful sanctions". The inclusion of this phrase is somewhat unfortunate. It dilutes to some degree the absolute and non-derogable aspects of the crime, and may give defendants a defence in certain circumstances. However, such sanctions that are in place must themselves be reasonable and not contrary to international law. Accordingly, any national laws which legitimise torture or ill-treatment would constitute unreasonableness and be inconsistent with the principles and aims of the Convention and therefore be deemed illegal.

Although not specifically stated, Art. 1 is generally perceived of as relating to interrogations which occur in various "torture locations" such as detention centres, police stations, prisons, the victim's home or elsewhere, or indeed in any place provided the activity is carried out under the direct control, or with the authority, of public officials. However, it would probably not encompass a situation where the police applied ill-treatment to quell a riot or any civil disorder which resulted in an individual being seriously injured; this lack of liability would also probably come under the heading of acts "incidental to lawful sanctions". Thus, providing the law in question does not deflect from the spirit and purpose of Art. 1, the "lawful sanctions" defence may well be permissible. Nevertheless, where, for instance, the police use weapons such as stun guns, chemical sprays and the like against peaceful protestors, it is arguable that those responsible should be made subject to the provisions of the UNCT where there is proved to be the required intention to commit serious injury against innocent persons, in the absence of reasonable lawful authority.

Inter-American Convention to Prevent and Punish Torture 1985

Although torture is recognised as achieving the status of *jus cogens* and the responsibility of *erga omnes*, there is no universal definition of the offence. Indeed, many international and regional treaties do not provide a definition at all, but merely state in brief terms that torture is prohibited. Where a definition is proffered differences in width, scope and elements between the various treaties often lead to confusion and complications in interpretation. For example, Art. 2 of the Inter-American Convention to Prevent and Punish Torture 1985 ("Inter-American Torture Convention") states that: **7–008**

> "For the purpose of this Convention, torture shall be understood to be any act intentionally performed whereby physical or mental pain or suffering is inflicted on a person for purposes of criminal investigation, as a means of intimidation, as personal punishment, as a preventive measure, as a penalty, or for any other purpose. Torture shall also be understood to be the use of methods upon a person intended to obliterate the personality of the victim or to diminish his physical or mental capacities, even if they do not cause physical or mental anguish".

Unlike Art. 1 of the UNCT, under the Inter-American Torture Convention the word "severe" is omitted in Art. 2 when describing physical or mental pain to be inflicted on the victim. Therefore, it appears that the degree of intensity and cruelty required under the UNCT will need to be at a higher threshold before a violation of Art. 1 occurs. The UNCT also differs from the Inter-American Torture Convention by including in its examples of torture the words "or for any other purpose"; thereby seemingly expanding the situations under which the offence may occur. However, the words may also be interpreted to mean that the actions taken by the perpetrator will constitute a criminal act if they only take place for purposes which are linked to those already cited in Art. 2, *e.g.* criminal investigation, intimidation, penalty and so forth. The final sentence of Art. 2 above broadens the meaning of torture by including methods used to obliterate the victim's physical or mental capacities, even if they do not cause physical or mental anguish; thereby alleviating the necessity in this instance to prove that the victim endured physical or mental pain or suffering. However, in like manner to Art. 1 of the UNCT, the words "for the purpose of this convention" in Art. 2, above, restrict the application of the definition to that convention. Further, the category of persons liable for committing acts of torture under the Inter-American Torture Convention are limited to those individuals set out in Art. 3 and are as follows:

1) A public servant or employee who acting in that capacity orders, instigates or induces the use of torture, or who directly commits it or who, being able to prevent it, fails to do so (Art. 3(a));

2) A person who at the instigation of a public servant mentioned in subparagraph (a) orders, instigates or induces the use of torture, directly commits it or is an accomplish thereto (Art. 3(b)).

Thus, in line with the UNCT, Art. 3 above restricts those persons capable of committing torture to public officials or those acting as *de facto* officials, unlike other conventions, *e.g.* Art. 7 of the ICCPR, which may also include torture carried out by private individuals. The Human Rights Committee in its General Comment (April 3 1992) declared that "it is the duty of the state party to afford everyone protection through legislative and other measures as may be necessary against the acts prohibited by Art. 7, whether inflicted by acting in their official capacity, outside their official capacity or in a private capacity".

Legislating against torture under national law

7–009   Under Art. 4 of the UNCT State Parties must legislate to make torture a criminal offence. However, merely prohibiting torture is not enough. Torturers must be actively deterred from committing these crimes. An intricate part of this deterrence is *via* the judicial process by prosecuting those offenders who practice torture. For example, in the UK the relevant statute prohibiting torture is the Criminal Justice Act 1988 ("CJA"). The definition of torture in s.134 of the Act is similar to that of Art. 1 of the UNCT. Under s.134(6) any person found guilty of torture is liable to life imprisonment. Comparing the "lawful sanctions" defence in the UNCT, s.134(4) of the CJA states that "it shall be a defence for a person charged with an offence under this section in respect of any conduct of his to prove that he had lawful authority, justification or excuse for that conduct". At first sight this seems to grant a defendant a broader defence than the UNCT. The words "lawful authority" may be interpreted as permission being granted to a person by some authority or under the law, entitling that person to commit a certain act, *e.g.* an order given by a public official to a person to use torture upon another. In theory, the torturer may well have a legitimate defence, despite such a defence being contrary to Art. 2(3) of the UNCT which states "an order from a superior officer or a public authority may not be invoked as a justification of torture". No such expression is included within the CJA. The word "excuse" implies a set of circumstances whereby even though the act itself was illegal, there were, however, legitimate reasons why it should not constitute an unlawful act. This may well include a defence of necessity, permitting the defendant to prove that it was reasonable to use torture in the circumstances, *e.g.* a ticking-bomb scenario (but see above, *The Public Committee Against Torture in Israel et al. v The State of Israel at para.*). Similar arguments could be used for the defence of "justification". In practice, it is doubted whether the above defences would succeed. Under international law, from the time of the Second World War II trials until the present day Yugoslav and Rwandan tribunals, the "superior orders defence" has never been successful, having been expressly prohibited in the Articles of those tribunal statutes, including the newly established International Criminal Court. Moreover, since torture is an absolute and non-derogable crime it is difficult to envisage a factual situation which would permit a defendant to successfully prove a defence of torture. Once the offence of torture has been proved, even normal domestic defences, such as necessity, duress or in defence of another will not constitute sufficient grounds for exculpating the actions of a torturer, although they may well provide the accused with a defence for other serious crimes, such as murder. Although under UK law the ratification of an international treaty does not automatically become part of the national law until it is expressly incorporated by an Act of Parliament, the courts are still entitled to adhere to their responsibilities under international law and interpret the law accordingly. As yet no prosecutions have been brought in the UK under the CJA. The nearest the courts have come to hearing such a case was that of the former Chilean President, General Augusto Pinochet, who was detained in England for nearly two years, awaiting extradition to Spain on charges of torture. He was eventually permitted to return to Chile (for a full account see Chapter 2).

Application of Art.1 under International Humanitarian Law

The definition provided by Art. 1 of the UNCT is a part of human rights law, and is to that extent limited. Whilst torture is prohibited absolutely in peacetime as well as war, the lack of any definition of the offence in international humanitarian law has created interpretational problems for the existing international criminal tribunals. Recent ICTY decisions have examined the question of whether or not Art. 1 could be construed as the definition of torture under customary international law, irrespective of whether the acts were

7–010

committed in peacetime or as part of an armed conflict. For example, in the case of *Prosecutor v Kunarac* (Judgment February 22, 2001) the Trial Chamber stated that the definition in Art. 1 "was meant to apply at an inter-state level and was, for that reason directed at the states" obligations. The definition was also meant to apply only in the context of that Convention, and only to the extent that other international instruments or national laws did not give the individual a broader or better protection" (para. 404). They concluded that the definition could only be used, within the context of the Convention, as an interpretational aid in cases involving international humanitarian law. Nevertheless, in relation to armed conflicts, where torture constitutes an offence as part of a grave breach of the Geneva Conventions or a war crime or a crime against humanity, it may be the case that common elements exist which apply to both human rights law and international humanitarian law. For example the Trial Chamber in *Prosecutor v Furundzija* (Case No. IT-95–17/1–T (December 10, 1998 at para. 162) specified a number of elements required for torture in armed conflicts. They stated that torture under these circumstances:

(i)   consists of the infliction, by act of omission, of severe pain or suffering, whether physical or mental. In addition;

(ii)   this act or omission must be intentional;

(iii)   it must aim at obtaining information or a confession, or at punishing, intimidating, humiliating or coercing the victim or a third person, or at discriminating, on any ground, against the victim or a third person;

(iv)   it must be linked to an armed conflict; and

(v)   at least one of the persons involved in the torture process must be a public official or must at any rate act in a non-private capacity, *e.g.* as a *de facto* organ of a state or any other authority-wielding entity.

As is immediately apparent points (iii) and (iv) above differ in substance and content from Art. 1 of the UNCT. However, in *Kunarac* the Trial Chamber stated that three elements of the definition of torture within the UNCT are:

"uncontentious and are accepted as representing the status of customary international law on the subject:

(i)   Torture consists of the infliction, by act or omission, of severe pain or suffering, whether physical or mental.
(ii)   This act or omission must be intentional.
(iii)   The act must be instrumental to another purpose, in the sense that the infliction of pain must be aimed at reaching a certain goal." (para. 405)

In (i) above the words "severe pain or suffering" refers to the gravity of the ill-treatment against the victim. How severe must the ill-treatment be before it constitutes torture cannot be precisely calculated. In *Kvocka* (November

2, 2001) the Trial Chamber stated that "[I]n assessing the seriousness of any mistreatment, the Trial Chamber must first consider the objective severity of the harm inflicted. Subjective criteria, such as the physical or mental effect of the treatment upon the particular victim and, in some cases, factors such as the victim's age, sex, or state of health will also be relevant in assessing the gravity of the harm" (para. 143). The Trial Chamber examined various cases which came before the IMTFE, ECHR and the United Nations Human Rights Committee and set out in a non-exhaustive list actions which would constitute torture. Examples of existing torture methods include systematic beatings, electroshocks, burns, extended hanging from hand and/or legs chains, repeated immersion in a mixture of blood, urine, vomit and excrement ("submarino"), standing for great lengths of time, and simulated executions or amputations (para. 146).

The Trial Chamber in *Kunarac* declared that the following purposes in point (iii) above which form part of customary law are: (a) obtaining information or a confession; (b) punishing, intimidating or coercing the victim or a third person; (c) discriminating, on any ground, against the victim or a third person (para. 407). Added to the above list would also undoubtedly include acts of humiliation or discrimination, on any ground against the victim or third person. Further, whilst under the UNCT the offender must be either a public official or a person acting in that capacity, under international humanitarian law no such restriction is required; the status of the official is irrelevant and accountability may attach to any civilian. Accordingly, using Art. 1 of the UNCT as a template for a definition of torture under international humanitarian law would clearly not suffice. Although, as can be observed from the above examination, there are in existence elements which are common to both human rights law and international humanitarian law.

Jurisdiction over torture

Sadly, for whatever reasons, be it apathy or lack of political will or on national security grounds or because of foreign policy considerations, States, until fairly recently, have been reluctant to indict torture offenders. Such deficiencies in any legal system not only tend to encourage torture but are a form of derogation from a State's responsibilities under international law and may even be seen as a justification for torture, in contravention to Art. 2. Under Art. 2(1) there are no exceptions whatsoever justifying the use of torture. Nor is it a defence to argue that the particular official administering torture was only obeying the orders of a superior (Art. 2(2) and (3)). Further, by not prosecuting those responsible in the national courts, the universal jurisdictional principle becomes meaningless. However, Art. 5(1)(a)–(c) and 5(2) requires States, under certain jurisdictional circumstances, to take the appropriate legal action against would-be torture offenders, when:

7–011

(a) the offences are committed in any territory under its jurisdiction or on board a ship or aircraft registered in that State;

(b) the alleged offender is a national of that State;

(c) the victim is a national of that State if that State considers it appropriate; and

(d) the alleged offender is present in any territory under its jurisdiction and it does not extradite him pursuant to Art. 8 to any of the States mentioned in Art. 5(1), (see Art. 5(2)).

In the above circumstances a State Party is bound either to prosecute the offender or alternatively extradite him to the proper jurisdictional State for the purpose of prosecution (Art. 7). The basis upon which an offender may be extradited is contained in Art. 8(1)–(4). For instance, under Art. 8(1) existing extradition treaties between states shall presume to include extradition for torture offences, and undertake to incorporate the same provision in any future extradition treaty between them. Even where no extradition treaty exists between the requested and other state, Art. 8(2) states that "it may consider this Convention as the legal basis for extradition in respect of such offences. Extradition shall be subject to the other conditions provided by the law of the requested state".

Under customary international law States are required, not only to prohibit acts of torture and other forms of ill-treatment but also to prevent individuals from being placed in a situation where torture is liable to result. One such common occurrence involves potential asylum seekers and illegal immigrants. Ultimately the dilemma facing immigrant authorities remains the same in all cases, *i.e.* deciding the genuine from the bogus applicants. One important factor to be considered is whether by returning the individual to a State from which he fled, he would be personally at risk of being subjected to torture. The UNCT is principally concerned with the prevention of torture and ill-treatment. The predicament of each asylum seeker differs according to their particular background and circumstance, only one of which may be the possible danger of torture were the individual to be returned to his home State.

Refusal to extradite for fear of torture

7–012 Article 3(1) of the UNCT prohibits an individual being extradited to another State if there are "substantial grounds for believing that he would be in danger of being subjected to torture". Different meanings have been attributed to the words "substantial grounds for believing"; these include phrases such as "does there exist a real and foreseeable risk?" or "are there reasonable grounds for believing?" or "are there firm or sufficient grounds for believing that", if sent back that person may be subjected to torture? Moreover, problems may arise where a State Party's interpretation differs from that under the UNCT. For instance, the United States have construed the words "substantial grounds for believing" to mean "more likely than not"; a somewhat loose, and at first sight, a seemingly more favourable interpretation to any individual fighting extradition from that State. Under US law two categories exist under which an individual may temporarily resist expulsion to his home State. The first is "deferral of removal" and the second is "withholding of removal", within the meaning of s.241(b)(3) of the Immigration Nationality Act ("INA"). Under both the applicant must prove that if returned to his State of origin it is more likely than not that he will face torture. However, under the INA category certain individuals are not eligible under domestic law to avail themselves of this protection if they have persecuted others, have committed serious criminal offences, are a threat to national security or belong to certain terrorist groups (Art. 33 of the Convention Relating to the Status of Refugees 1951). Article 3 does not contain any such exceptions. Nevertheless, even though the individual may be ineligible under the INA, but has satisfied the burden of proof under the UNCT, the immigration judge may grant that person deferral of removal. This state of affairs does not bestow on the individual any rights to remain permanently in the US; it is a temporary protective measure until all the appropriate appeal procedures have been exhausted. Moreover, under either of the above categories the US government could legitimately send the individual concerned to a foreign State where he would not be subjected to torture. Thus, merely because an individual's application for asylum has been rejected does not automatically imply that he will not be successful in resisting extradition, at least temporarily, under the UNCT. Different approaches and considerations come into play.

Under Art. 3(2), whatever interpretation is adopted to the words "substantial ground for believing" the extraditing State must consider "all relevant considerations including, where applicable, the existence in the State concerned of a consistent pattern of gross, flagrant or mass violations of human rights". Such violations would include arbitrary detentions and executions, disappearances, torture and other ill-treatment of individuals. However, merely because such general violations under Art. 3(2) are shown to exist will not automatically entitle an individual to resist extradition. On the other hand, the absence of mass violations does not necessarily mean that an individual cannot be personally at risk of being tortured.

Where an individual has applied to the Committee Against Torture ("CAT") for consideration of his case against extradition, they will, when deciding the "substantial grounds" issue take into account such factors as his nationality, his ethnic group, his political status and association, his periods spent in detention, the credibility of allegations made by the individual, medical reports, corroborating and other evidence supporting claims of ill-treatment, and all other relevant circumstances which would put him in danger of being subjected to torture should he be returned to the State from which he fled. Where an individual asserts that he has already suffered torture, lack of any physical signs to that effect may well hinder his case against repatriation. On the other hand, evidence of physical injury will not automatically ensure his success, unless it can further be proved that his injuries were sustained at the hands of the State authorities from which he fled. But even where the applicant is successful in resisting extradition, it will not automatically follow that he will be granted asylum status. It only means that he will not be deported. If circumstances change whereby he is no longer in any danger then he may well be sent back to his homeland. Above all, each case must be considered on its own merits. As part of any proceedings before the Committee, the author must convince them that he himself is personally in danger of being exposed to torture, if returned. The test is overwhelmingly objective, although consideration must be given to the individual's subjective belief that if returned he would be subjected to torture. A good example of the yard-stick to be used by State Parties when deciding whether to extradite or not is the case of *Alan v Switzerland* (1997) 4 IHRR 66. The facts were that the author, a Turkish citizen of Kurdish extract, alleged that from 1981 through to 1989 the police had subjected him to torture at regular intervals. In 1990 he fled to Switzerland where he sought asylum. The Committee stated that merely because there continued to exist mass violations of human rights in Turkey did not of itself determine that the author was in danger of being tortured. It must further be shown that the author himself would be at risk, if he were to be returned. The Turkish authorities argued that the author was not in any danger. The Committee rejected this. There was sufficient evidence showing that the police were still investigating him; his family were under constant surveillance; his brother has been arrested and the author's village demolished. In light of this, if he were to be returned there was substantial evidence to suggest that he would undergo torture. Accordingly, the Committee found Turkey to have violated Art. 3 of the UNCT and requested that Switzerland should refrain from sending the author back to Turkey. Similar criteria were previously used by the Committee to prevent extradition in the case of *Mutombo v Switzerland* (UN Doc. A/49/44 1994). In that instance the Committee also considered the fact that the former state of Zaire, from which he was appealing extradition to, was not a party to the UNCT and therefore the author would not have the legal benefit of applying to the Committee for protection.

7–013   However, unlike the above two cases, in *HD v Switzerland* Com No.112/1998 IHRR Vol.7 No.2 2000, the Committee reached the opposite view on the issue of *refoulement*. In that case, the author, a Turkish citizen of Kurdish origin, was arrested at his home by the security forces on May 15, 1991. He was taken to a police station where he was interrogated regarding the whereabouts of his cousin who was an active member of the illegal PKK party. He alleged he was tortured through being beaten while blindfolded and suffered electric shock abuse by his interrogators; he was released finally on the May 28, 1991. He was re-arrested on June 5, 1991 and held in detention for one day, where, he alleged, death threats were made against him if he refused to turn informant. Eventually he and his family fled to Switzerland, arriving there on August 20, 1991. His requests and subsequent appeals for asylum were turned down by the Appeals Commission on Asylum Matters (CRA). The Federal Office for Refugees (the ODA) and the CRA declared that there were various inconsistencies in the author's story, including that: he could describe in detail the appliance used in his electric shock treatment, yet he was blindfolded throughout the relevant time; there were other inconsistencies regarding his length of period in detention; he had waited some two months before fleeing to Switzerland; and he and his wife had been issued with identity cards on July 9, 1991. At first he stated that these cards were obtained legally, but afterwards stated that they were obtained illegally through payment to an official at the identity card office. Despite forceful arguments put forward by the applicant's counsel against the above findings of the Swiss immigrant authorities, these were ultimately rejected. The CRA found that although the fighting between Turkish forces and the PKK existed, it was restricted to clearly defined areas within the country and persecution of Kurdish people was limited to certain villages and towns. Accordingly, the Swiss authorities found that if the author were to be returned to Turkey, he and his family could live in certain areas of the country where he would not personally be at risk of being tortured. In the proceedings before the Committee, they stated "that even in the presence of lingering doubts as to the truthfulness of the facts mentioned by the author of a communication, it must satisfy itself that the applicant's security will not be jeopardised. It is not necessary for the Committee to be so satisfied, that all the facts by the author should be proved: it is enough if the Committee considers them sufficiently well attested and credible" (pp. 391–392). The Committee noted that, although arrested and detained no charges were ever formulated against the author; there was no evidence of collaboration with the PKK since fleeing Turkey; neither he nor his family were being pursued by the Turkish authorities. Accordingly, the Committee declared that the author did not provide sufficient evidence to support his claim that if sent back to Turkey he would risk undergoing torture. Therefore, Switzerland was not in violation of Art. 3 by deciding that the author should be returned to his home State.

As stated above, the key determinant of the UNCT is one of prevention. It is the responsibility of each State Party to initiate safeguards against the use of torture *via* education, information, training and instructing its public officials (Art. 10). Where it is alleged that torture has taken place it is up to the relevant authorities to initiate a prompt and impartial investigation into the matter (Art. 12). This includes any investigation being carried out expeditiously, diligently, competently and independently. The reality is, however, that many State investigations are partisan, discriminate, ineffectual and indecisive, and merely end up protecting those public officials responsible for administering torture from proper scrutiny and prosecution. To combat this, an in-depth study by various human rights specialists and medical experts published a document entitled the "Manual on the Effective Investigation and Document of Torture and Other Cruel, Inhuman or Degrading Treatment or Punishment" ("The Istanbul Protocol" — August 1999). The manual is to be used by governments as a guideline for making more effective documentation when considering human rights abuses. Included in the manual is the recommendation that a separate commission of inquiry be set up to investigate torture allegations in cases where the State's investigation is found wanting. Its overall mandate would be to substantiate or disprove torture allegations. This would include clarifying the existing situation by interviewing and collecting statements from prisoners; gathering evidence of different types of torture methods used; their physical and psychological effects on torture victims; evidence of sexual abuse; existing interrogation procedures and amassing all other material essential to their inquiry. Such a commission would go a long way to ensuring a truly independent investigation, increase confidence of torture victims to speak out, and would assist overall in the consolidation of the purpose and object of the Convention itself.

Individual complaints of torture

7–014   Article 13 confers on an individual the right to complain to the authorities regarding allegations of torture "in any territory under its jurisdiction". In practice, the complaint procedures of many States have proved wholly inadequate. Investigations by many State authorities into allegations of torture have been, at best lax, at worst, biased against the complainant and generally result in an overall reluctance to bring those officials responsible to account for their actions. As a logical extension to Art. 13, under Art. 14 each State Party must ensure through its national laws that the complainant (either the victim or in the case of death, his family or dependants) has the legal right to bring a claim against those responsible, and if successful, be awarded compensation or other reparation, including, where appropriate punitive damages. In recent years there have been an increasing number of States recognising civil claims against those foreign state officials who have committed acts of torture and other human rights abuses abroad. In particular, in the past 20 years many private civil claims have been brought in the United States courts by victims, their dependants or family, against alleged torturers from other states, notably Bosnian-Serbs, Philippines, Guatemala, Haiti and China. Of special benefit to these litigants have been the Alien Tort Claims Act 1789 ("ATCA") and the Torture Victim Protection Act 1991 ("TVPA").

The ATCA (28 USC 1350) states that "The district courts shall have original jurisdiction of any civil action by (i) an alien (ii) for a tort only, (iii) committed in violation of the law of nations or a treaty of the United States" (numbers in brackets have been added). In order to bring such an action under the ATCA the would-be plaintiff must prove the three conditions set out above. In point (i) above, claims are restricted to non-US citizens. In point (ii) the claim must be for a tort action, *e.g.* genocide, crimes against humanity, war crimes, torture, disappearances and extrajudicial killings, although this is not an exhaustive list. In point (iii) the "law of nations" refers to international law, and not as it was in 1789 but as it has evolved in the world of today, and presumably the same notion will apply to future cases. However, it is not a prerequisite that there need be a link between the litigating state and the particular offence. Further, it is not a precondition that the defendant himself actually committed the offence; it is sufficient that he authorised or ordered the illegal act to be committed as a representative (be that person a State official or agent) of that foreign State. Although originally enacted to principally deal with various types of piracy cases, seizure of enemy vessels during wartime and the slavery business, it was successfully resurrected and effectively used in 1980 in the case of *Filartiga v Pena-Irala* [1980] 630 f (2nd Series) 876. US Court of Appeals, 2nd Circuit. In that case the plaintiffs, a father and daughter, applied for political asylum in the US. Whilst there they learnt of the presence of the former Inspector General of Police in Asuncion, Paraguay, who the plaintiffs claimed, was responsible for the death in 1976, through official torture, of the plaintiff's son and brother because of the father's political opposition to the Paraguayan government. The civil action was brought under the wrongful death statutes, *inter alia*; the ATCA, the UN Charter; the UDHR; the UN Declaration against Torture 1975 and practices contrary to the customary international law of human rights and the law of nations. The plaintiffs appealed against the District Court ruling that it did not have jurisdiction to hear the case. One of the substantive issues to be considered was whether in light of the ATCA the court possessed subject-matter jurisdiction in this case; in particular did torture violate the law of nations? It was held that it was universally accepted that State torture violates established norms of the international law of human rights and hence the law of nations (at p. 880). Thus, in contrast to the District Court's narrow construction of the ATCA, the Supreme Court declared that " in this modern age a state's treatment of its own citizens is a matter of international concern" (at p. 881) under the Preamble and Art. 55 and 56 of the UN Charter and as defined by the UDHR, *i.e.* "no one shall be subjected to torture" and is now part of customary international law. This remains so, irrespective of whether acts of torture are committed against foreigners or a State's own nationals. The court declared that "for purposes of civil liability, the torturer has become — like the pirate and slave trader before him — *hostis humani generis*, an enemy of all mankind" (at p. 890). Accordingly, it was decided that the District Court did possess the required jurisdiction to hear the case. Eventually, judgment was given for the plaintiffs and they were awarded in excess of $5 million each. However, before proper enforcement could be carried out the defendant was deported to Paraguay, and as yet the plaintiffs have not received any damages.

The importance of this decision lies in the fact that the family did have their day in court and judgment against the defendant publicly pronounced — the money seemingly not being the most important consideration. Also judgments of this kind may prevent future human rights violators from residing in the US, or having assets in the US which ultimately may be confiscated in order to enforce judgment damages. Further, despite the defendant being sent back to Paraguay, the judgment, albeit civil, may act as a deterrent against others who believe that their crimes will not follow them wherever they eventually decide to seek refuge.

7–015   As a means of strengthening, developing and clarifying the ATCA, the TVPA was introduced in 1991. Under the TVPA it must be proved that the offence was either one of torture or extrajudicial killing. The term "extrajudicial killing" is defined in s.3(a) as "a deliberate killing not authorized by a previous judgment pronounced by a regularly constituted court affording all the judicial guarantees which are recognized as indispensable by civilized peoples". The claimant must have exhausted all adequate and available domestic remedies in the State in which the offence occurred (s.2(b)); if indeed that State provided such a remedy in the first place. Other examples which may constitute "exhausting remedies" include instances where the proceedings were delayed unduly, or where it was impossible to receive a fair trial in the home State. Unlike the ATCA, the TVPA permits any US citizen to bring civil proceedings; it is not restricted to aliens. Under the TVPA any action must be commenced within 10 years of the offence being committed (s.2(c)), but the court does have a discretion to extend that period; under the ATCA no such limitation period exists. Although both statutes provide a cause of action, the TVPA is not itself a jurisdictional statute and any claim brought under the TVPA derive its jurisdiction *via* the ATCA. A fundamental distinction between the ATCA and the TVPA is that civil claims under the latter are restricted to individuals "who, under actual or apparent authority, or color of law, of any foreign nation" commits torture (s.2(a)), *i.e.* official torture or extrajudicial killings. Section 2(a)of the Act was particularly relevant in the case of *Kadic v Karadzic* (70 fr. 3d 232 (2nd cir. 1995)).

Facts.   The plaintiffs were citizens of Bosnia/Herzegovina. They were victims and representatives of victims who had suffered, *inter alia*, rape, forced prostitution, genocide, torture and summary execution at the hands of the Bosnian/Serb forces, under the command of the defendant Radovan Karadzic, the then president of the Bosnian — Serb Republic ("Srpska"). In the District Court the action was dismissed on the grounds of lack of subject-matter jurisdiction. The court there declared that Srpska was not an internationally recognised State and since ATCA did not apply to Non-State Actors, the plaintiffs' claims could not succeed. Further, the claim was also rejected under the TVPA since the defendant could not be said to have acted "under actual or apparent authority, or colour of law, of any foreign nation", as required by s.2(a) of that Act.

Decision.   The plaintiffs appealed to the US Court of Appeals against this decision. They based their appeal on, *inter alia*, the ATCA, the TVPA and the general federal-question jurisdictional statute. One of the main stumbling blocks for the appellants was the precondition under the ATCA that the particular acts must relate to torts committed in violation of the law of nations. The Court of Appeal stated that "If this inquiry discloses that the defendant's conduct violates well established universally recognised norms of international law then federal jurisdiction exists under the ATCA" (at p.239). The appellee maintained that international law applied only to persons acting under colour of a State's law, not private individuals. Since he was not a State actor of a recognised State, he could not have violated international law. This was rejected by the Appeal Court which declared that it has long been established that certain acts could be committed by private individuals which violated international law, *e.g.* piracy, slave trade, certain war crimes, genocide and aircraft highjacking (see the Restatement (Third) of the Foreign Relations Law of the United States, especially ss.702 and 404). Moreover, such acts are not to be restricted to the criminal law, but also include civil remedies (at pp. 239 and 240). The next question was whether the appellants' claims of genocide, war crimes, torture and degrading treatment and other instances of inflicting death, came within the ATCA. With regard to genocide, that crime has been recognised as existing under international law irrespective of whether the perpetrator was a State Actor or a private individual (see Art. 2 of the Genocide Act 1949; as well as under national law of the Genocide Convention Implementation Act 1987 for such crimes committed within the US). Accordingly, subject matter jurisdiction exists under the ATCA for this particular crime. In relation to war crimes, the appellants stated that "acts such as murder, rape, torture and arbitrary detention of civilians, committed in the course of hostilities violates the law of war" (at p. 242). Again, such acts have hitherto been established as contrary to international law since World War I and especially under the four Geneva Conventions and common Art.3 in relation to internal armed conflicts. Accordingly, the appellants had a legitimate claim under the ATCA. Claims for actions of torture and summary executions under the TVPA present a particular problem. Where such acts are not committed as part of genocide or war crimes they may only proceed in a court of law when committed by State officials or under colour of law. If, Srpska was not a State, then the appellants' action under the TVPA was unlikely to succeed. Was Srpska a State? The definition of a State under international law is as follows: "A State is an entity that has a defined territory and a permanent population, under the control of its own government and that engages in, or has the capacity to engage in, formal relations with other such entities". (*Klinghoffer v SNC Achillo Lauro* 937 f. 2d). Recognition by other States is not a precondition for the existence of a State. In this case, Srpska seems to have met the definitional requirements, *i.e.* "Srpska is alleged to control defined territory, control populations within its power, and to have entered into agreements with other governments (predominantly the former Yugoslavia). It has a president, a legislator, and its own currency. These circumstances readily appear to satisfy the criteria for a State in all aspects of international law" (at p. 245). Accordingly, the Appeal Court reversed the decision of the District Court and held, *inter alia*, that the plaintiffs sufficiently alleged violation of customary international law and law of war for purposes of the ATCA; that Srpska was a State and that the defendant acted under colour of law for purposes of international violations requiring official action (at p. 232).

Apart from pure acts of torture, other forms of less serious maltreatment methods are prohibited by public officials and contained in the full title of the UNCT, notably cruel, inhuman or degrading treatment or punishment ("CIDTP"). Under Art. 16 the safeguards against CIDTP and the redress actions stated in Arts 10 –14 also apply here. However, although "intention" is fundamental to the crime of torture, it is not a necessary ingredient in offences relating to CIDTP. What precisely constitutes CIDTP is not stated in the UNCT, nor is it defined properly elsewhere in other treaties, although it is universally proscribed under customary international law. Its meaning can only be explained from examples derived from established case law, which is more fully examined at para. 7–032.

PART II — THE COMMITTEE AGAINST TORTURE (ARTS 17–24)

7–016 The Committee Against Torture ("the Committee") was set up in January 1988 as a monitoring body to supervise the implementation and ensure adherence of State Parties under the Convention. The Committee comprises of 10 State Party members who are considered experts in the realm of human rights. They are elected by secret ballot and serve a term of four years, but are eligible for re-election (see Art. 17). The Committee meets twice annually but may meet in emergency session at the request of a majority of its members or a State Party. Decisions at each meeting are reached by a majority of those members present (according to Art. 18, a minimum of six members in attendance is required). Initially, within one year of ratification a State Party must present a report to the Committee, *via* the Secretary-General of the United Nations, detailing the action, if any, taken by them regarding their responsibilities under the UNCT. However, many States no not abide by the timescale and issue their reports many years later. The US, for instance, although ratified the UNCT in October 1994, did not publish its initial report until over five years later in November 1999. In the case of the initial report submitted by the US, the Committee in its observations and comments (CAT/C/24/6) stated its various concerns on a number of important matters, notably: (a) the failure of the US to make torture a federal crime in terms consistent with Art. 1; (b) the reservation to Art. 16 (see, above); (c) the continual ill-treatment by police and prison guards of civilians in prisons; (d) the restrictions on prisoners to take legal action against prison officials (physical injury must be proved before legal action is permitted); and (e) the continual use of electroshock devices and restraint chairs by officials. The Committee recommended that they take measures to rectify their concerns and in particular reconsider their standpoint against recognising the competence of the Committee to receive and consider communications from or on behalf of individuals under Art. 22. At present they only recognise the authority of the Committee on inter-state matters under Art. 21.

Further, some State reports are unclear, incomplete, biased and too general. There are guidelines set down by the Committee which declare that the initial report should contain certain specific data including, existing domestic laws relating to the prohibition of torture and CIDTP, and the preventative measures in place; legal remedies and compensation to torture victims, if any; extradition and asylum laws in force; detention, investigation and interrogation procedures; legislation relating to powers of arrest; admissibility of confessions and so forth. Thereafter, a progress report is to be submitted every four years. The Committee will examine these reports and make comments and recommendations to the State Party concerned on how matters may be improved or what important facts were omitted from the statement (Art. 19). The most common recommendations made by the Committee over the years include requesting the state party concerned to:

(a) introduce into their national laws a clear meaning of the word "torture" (Art. 1);

(b) initiate effective legislative, administrative, judicial or other measures which would prevent acts of torture (Art. 2(1));

(c) dispense with obeying orders of a superior as a justification or defence for using torture (Art. 2(3));

(d) ensure that there are no exceptions permitting torture (Art. 2(2));

(e) determine, in relation to matters concerning torture, under what circumstances extradition should be allowed or refused (Art. 3);

(f) ensure that torture is made a criminal offence and that those public officials responsible are properly indicted (Art. 4);

(g) educate public officials against the use of torture (Art. 10);

(h) ensure that acts of torture are fully and properly investigated (Art. 12);

(i) investigate complaints of torture by individuals (Art. 13);

(j) introduce laws guaranteeing torture victims receive compensation (Art. 14).

The Committee may request a particular State to report back stating what actions they have taken to improve conditions there. In cases where the Committee has learned, through reliable and credible sources, that a State Party is systematically practising torture, the latter shall be requested to examine and comment on these allegations. If necessary and pressing, a Committee member or members may engage in a confidential inquiry, which may include seeking permission from the offended State to visit their territory, in order to gather further information and hear testimony from witnesses. They will then, as soon as possible, report back their findings to the Committee. After examination of the report, which is also confidential, the Committee will consult with the state party concerned, making comments and suggestions on how to alleviate and improve the situation (Art. 20). However, before any such inquiry is undertaken, the Committee is under an obligation to seek co-operation from the State being investigated. That State Party is entitled to refuse assistance in any investigation. Under Art. 20 all reports and investigations are confidential. However, the Committee may include its findings in its annual report, which is public.

7–017   A good example of the workings of the Committee and problems of implementation under Art. 20 can be observed from the examination of Turkey. Turkey ratified the UNCT in August 1988. In 1990 the Committee examined various reports and allegations of systematic practices of torture in that State. The Committee were unconvinced by Turkey's response to these allegations and in 1991 undertook a confidential inquiry which included requesting permission to visit that State by two members of the Committee, which they duly did in 1992 (CAT A/48/44/Add.1). In 1993 the two members reported their findings to the Committee. Examination of the report was held at a closed meeting at which the Turkish representatives requested that the findings of the inquiry not be published in the Committee's annual report. This request was refused on the grounds that due to the extent and seriousness of the complaints of torture and ill-treatment, coupled with Turkey's complete denial of these allegations, it was necessary in this case to "name and shame" that State into taking some positive action to alleviate the existing problem. Although the Turkish authorities publicly denounced torture, the report by the Committee found that: (a) although few cases of torture could be proved with absolute certainty, its existence could not be denied; (b) torture was habitual, widespread and deliberate in many parts of the country; (c) there was inadequate legislation in place to prevent the practice of torture; and (d) although the systematic practise of torture may not be with the consent of the government, "its existence may indicate a discrepancy between policy as determined by the central government and its implementation by the local administration".

The Committee made a number of recommendations including: (i) the inspection by Ministry of the Interior officials of interrogation centres to ensure that the legal procedures for proper treatment of suspects in police custody are fully carried out; (ii) those responsible for torture or ill-treatment will be subject to legal penalties; (iii) train and educate public officials against the application of torture and other forms of ill-treatment; and (iv) set up an independent commission to combat torture; more specifically its role would be to visit and meet those persons held in detention centres and to investigate complaints of torture and ill-treatment and assist in the drafting of any legislation which concerns torture. The report further recommended that the Turkish authorities take the following urgent measures including: (i) eliminating the use of blindfolds during the questioning of a suspect; (ii) granting free legal assistance and access to lawyers to those persons in police custody; and (iii) destroying all solitary confinement cells known as "coffins". These cells lack light and ventilation and because of the cells" small dimensions prisoners could only either stand or crouch. The Committee stated that such places *per se* constituted torture a form of torture. In 1995, The Special Rapporteur against Torture, Mr. Nigel Rodley submitted his report to the Commission on Human Rights (Fiftieth Session), entitled "Question of the Human Rights of all Persons Subjected to any Form of Detention or Imprisonment, In Particular: Torture and Other

Cruel, Inhuman or Degrading Treatment or Punishment" (E/CN.4/1995/34). The report set out, with specific regard to Turkey, the purposes for which torture was used, *e.g.* to extract confessions, to force detainees to reveal the names of members of various illegal organisations and to intimidate detainees into becoming police informants. The types of torture applied included hosing with cold water, hanging victims by their arms which were tied behind their backs, using electro-shock devices, sexual assaults and food deprivation. The report also cited, in summary terms, many individual cases (paras 746 and 747). In cases where the government replied to these allegations, they either denied the findings of torture outright, or rejected the facts as stated, or initiated lack-lustre investigations which were biased and usually resulted in the public officials concerned being absolved from all liability. The Special Rapporteur concluded that "he finds most of them (government replies) contain unsubstantiated flat denials that evince a willingness to accept the version of events of the authorities or certain medical personnel, which patently lack credibility. Sadly, most such replies risk being taken as a signal by those responsible for the torture of the Government's willingness to protect them and to have them continue the practice" (para. 826).

The present-day conditions in Turkey have improved but remain far from satisfactory. Torture in that State remains endemic, systematic and widespread. Individuals and especially members of certain groups, *e.g.* the PKK (Kurdish Worker's Party) remain susceptible to arrest, detention and continue to be vulnerable to the dangers of ill-treatment by the authorities. A report in 1999 by Amnesty International, entitled Turkey. Torture A Major Concern (EUR 44/18/00) set out in detail the continual allegations of torture in that State, including severe beatings, electro-shock application, death threats, various degrees of sexual assault and so forth. Some of these torture victims eventually died in prison. In the past those officials responsible were rarely brought to trial, although in 1999, 10 police officers were prosecuted for torture offences. According to Amnesty's report, taken from official figures, between 1995 and 1999, of the 577 security officials indicted only 10 resulted in conviction and even then only very light sentences were imposed. However, in 1999 the Turkish Penal Code was amended and under Art. 243 the prison sentence for those convicted of torture and other abuses has been increased to eight years. Ever since Turkey's ratification of the UNCT in 1987 a constant and major concern has been the lack of efficient and independent investigations by the authorities into allegations of torture and ill-treatment. By way of recommendation, Amnesty has, in its report, proposed that Turkey take effective measures to improve the situation in line with their responsibilities under the UNCT including:

(i)   Ensuring that impartial, independent and prompt investigations be carried out to deal with allegations of torture and other human rights abuses (Art. 12).

(ii) Ensuring that those officials responsible for torture are properly indicted (Art. 4).

(iii) Determining that confessions made under torture should not be admissible as evidence in any hearing (Art. 15).

(iv) Entitling torture victims to bring legal actions for compensation and rehabilitation against the state (Art 14).

(v) Providing state officials with training, instruction and education on the evils of torture (Art. 10).

It remains to be seen whether all the above changes will be properly implemented in the foreseeable future, if at all. However, continued international pressure has seen some moderate changes materialising in recent years, albeit slow. Evidence that the newly-formed government in Turkey is seriously heeding the opinions of the international community can be gleaned from legislation going through at present to abolish capitol punishment in that State; they being the last State in Europe to retain the death penalty.

Inter-State Party complaints

7–018   Under Art. 21 State Parties may make complaints against each other *vis-à-vis* not adhering to their responsibilities as set out in the Convention. However, a State Party must first make a declaration recognising the competence of the Committee in such matters (although a State Party may later on withdraw its declaration — Art. 21(2)), as well as abiding by the following procedures set out in Art. 21(a)–(h). These procedures include the condition that any communication made by one State against another must be in writing. The receiving State must, within three months, reply explaining and clarifying the situation. If, within six months from receipt of the initial complaint, the problem is not satisfactorily resolved, either party may refer the matter to the Committee for consideration; such referrals are conducted by the Committee in closed meetings. The Committee will attempt to resolve the matter by friendly dialogue, which may include requesting the States involved to submit both oral and written statements; where necessary it may establish an *ad hoc* conciliation commission to further assist the parties. Within 12 months of the original referral, the Committee shall make a report stating a summary of the facts and any solution arrived at; otherwise, it will merely state an outline of the facts, attaching the various arguments submitted by the parties concerned.

Individual communications

7–019   Apart from inter-State communications it is possible, under certain conditions, for individuals of a State Party or their representatives to submit complaints of human rights violations to the Committee for consideration. The complainant, known as "the author" or other representatives shall not be entitled to have their communication admitted or examined by the Committee unless, as set out in Art. 22(1), (2) and (5):

(1) the State Party concerned has expressly declared the Committee's competence to receive such communications, and has not prior to the communication being transmitted to the Committee withdrew its declaration (Art. 23);

(2) the author has revealed his/her identity;

(3) the Committee has considered that the right of submission has been abused;

(4) the communication is compatible with the provisions of the Convention;

(5) the matter has not already been or is being considered *via* another international hearing or inquiry; and

(6) the author has exhausted all available domestic remedies.

However, even before the above criteria are satisfied and prior to any decision having been made, the Committee may request the alleged offending state to take certain provisional measures to protect the author from further harm. The communication, if deemed admissible, is then passed onto the alleged offending state which has six months to reply to the Committee setting out in its report information relating to, *inter alia*, explaining and clarifying the relevant issues, justification for its present policy, and any undertakings and remedies, where applicable, by the state in order to rectify the situation (Art. 22(3)). Although the matter under consideration must be examined in closed meetings, nevertheless both parties concerned may be requested to attend and participate when invited to do so by the Committee. After full consideration the Committee will then pronounce its views. If a State Party is found to be in violation of the Convention, the Committee will, in light of their findings and recommendations, request that State to report back on the action and remedies taken to rectify the situation. Whatever the outcome of the Committee's consideration, their views are not legally binding. Nevertheless, their decisions are very persuasive and State Parties generally accede to their findings. Finally, as part of its overall functions, the Committee shall publish its views on any specific communication in its annual report; thereafter to be circulated to all State Parties and to the General Assembly of the United Nations (Art. 24). At present, 40 State Parties have ratified both Arts 21 and 22; Japan, the US and the UK have only ratified Art. 21.

PART III — RESPONSIBILITIES OF STATE PARTIES (ARTS 25–33)

7–020 Part III of the Convention deals with the ratification, declarations, amendments, denunciations and reservation procedures. Under Art. 30(1) if a dispute arises between two or more States regarding the interpretation or application of the UNTC, which cannot be settled amicably, then the matter may be referred to arbitration at the request of at least one of the parties. If there is no agreement as to the organisation of the arbitration, then the matter may go before the International Court of Justice. However, a State may either prior to ratification, but after signing, reserve the right not to be bound by Art. 30(1), and in that case the other State Party or Parties shall also not be bound. For example, prior to its ratification of the UNCT, the US made certain reservations; one of which was to restrict its responsibilities under Art. 16 to only those abuses already prohibited by the Fifth, Eighth and/or Fourteenth Amendments of the Constitution.

The European Convention for the Prevention of Torture and Inhuman or Degrading Treatment or Punishment ("ECPT").

7–021 The ECPT came into force in February 1989. Its primary purpose is summarily set out in the Preamble of the Convention, *i.e.* "that the protection of persons deprived of their liberty against torture and inhuman or degrading treatment or punishment could be strengthened by non-judicial means of a preventive character based on visits". No definition of torture is cited in the Articles of the Convention, although Art. 3 of the European Convention on Human Rights is acknowledged as the basis upon which the ECPT operates. Further, the decisions of the present European Court or the recently defunct Commission of Human Rights do not possess any direct influence or authority over the workings of the ECPT. Nevertheless, some consideration may be given to the decisions of the above-mentioned judicial forums when determining whether or not torture or ill-treatment by public officials has been carried out.

The means by which individuals are protected against torture is achieved through the Committee of the ECPT, who, under Art. 1, through visiting States shall "examine the treatment of persons deprived of their liberty with a view to strengthening, if necessary, the protection of such persons from torture and from inhuman or degrading treatment or punishment". The Committee is made up of one member from each State Party (Art. 4); at present there are 44 such State Parties. Each member is elected by the Committee of Ministers of the Council of Europe and chosen because of their high moral character and expertise in the field of human rights (Art. 4(2)). They act independently of their own governments, are impartial and conscientious in all their undertakings (Art. 4(4)). Indeed under Rule 2 of the Rules of Procedure they make a declaration to that effect. They are elected for a period of four years and are eligible for re-election, but only once (but under Protocol 2, may be re-elected twice). All Committee meetings are held *in camera*, and their decisions are taken by a majority of those present (Art. 6) — a minimum of a majority of those members attending a meeting constitutes a quorum. The hierarchy of the Committee consists of a President and a first and second Vice-President (together they make up the Bureau of the Committee) and a Secretariat. Unlike the European Court of Human Rights, any decisions made by the Committee are not legally enforceable. Their primary function is to prepare reports after having visited a State where persons are deprived of their liberty by a public authority. The reports generally contain comments, observations and recommendations and usually request further information on the conditions relating to the practices of torture and other forms of ill-treatment in the specific state under investigation. Ultimately, whether their recommendations are complied with depends on the attitude and collaboration of the State visited. The purpose of the Committee is not to punish or condemn State Parties, but by constructive and friendly dialogue, persuade governments to implement their recommendations; thereby improving a State's treatment of its citizens deprived of their liberty. Therefore, it is essential, if the Convention is not to be considered a lame-duck, that State Parties abide by their responsibilities under Art. 3 which demand co-operation between the Committee and the State concerned.

First and foremost, in order for the Convention to bite, an individual must have been deprived of his liberty, whether legal or otherwise, by a State official. Once this pre-condition occurs, any investigation carried out by the Committee is not restricted to the actual mental and physical condition of the detainee *per se*, but includes all other surrounding circumstances material to his treatment whilst in detention. For instance, has the detainee been held incommunicado or in solitary confinement? Has he been refused access to legal advice or to a medical examination? Have the appropriate legal procedures for his detention been adhered to, *e.g.* reasons given for his arrest and detention, proper custody records made, correct interrogation practices followed, rest periods complied with, safeguards implemented with respect to maximum detention periods and so forth? In these respects the remit of the Committee is broad and far-reaching.

A pre-determinant to the feasibility and application of the Convention is the whole question of visits. There are four different types of visits; initial, periodic, *ad hoc* and follow-up. From the outset, it was envisaged that periodic visits would regularly take place every two years or so. In practice, the Committee has not been able to achieve this goal. This lapse has been partly due to the increased membership of the Convention over the years, and partly due to the Committee's commitments to re-visit certain states that require more frequent monitoring and scrutiny. Nowadays, *ad hoc* visits are more common, and concentration is focused on information received by the Committee that acts of torture and other forms of ill-treatment are frequently and systematically committed in a particular state, and immediate action needs to be taken. Follow-up visits take place, more often-than-not, in order to discover whether

7–022

recommendations made in previous reports have been implemented or, at least, been improved upon. Periodic visits normally take between 10–14 days; *ad hoc* visits are usually much shorter, normally between 2–5 days, but exceptionally may be much longer according to how many places require visits, *e.g.* an *ad hoc* visit to Russia in 1998 took 14 days. Up until the year 2003 the Committee has made over 160 visits and for the reasons mentioned above the Committee's time has not been distributed equally among State Parties, *e.g.* Turkey — 14 visits, Spain — eight visits, UK — eight visits and the Netherlands — six visits, Greece — one visit. In the year 2003, visits have been made to such States as France, Poland, Italy, Turkey and the Russian Federation.

However, before any visit is undertaken, the Committee must notify the State concerned of its intention (Art. 8). The State in turn shall permit: (a) unrestricted access to its territory; (b) provide full information concerning the places to be visited; (c) unlimited access to any place; and (d) any other information which would enable the delegates to carry out their tasks (Art. 8(2)). The Committee, for their part, will inform the State of the specific sites their members will wish to visit. However, once there, delegates may visit other places not stated in the notification.

It is essential that the Committee (represented usually by two or more delegates, experts and advisors), in order to carry out their duties effectively and thoroughly, have unrestricted access to sites where persons are held. Such places include police stations, prisons, detention centres, holding centres (*e.g.* for asylum-seekers, illegal immigrants and the like), military establishments, hospitals and psychiatric institutions; indeed, all places which house persons on the authority of government officials. For example, between May 25–27, 1998 the Committee made an *ad hoc* visit to Germany's Frankfurt am Main Airport where they inspected various detention and holding centres for immigrant detainees and asylum-seekers. Although persons questioned there made no allegations of ill-treatment, the Committee did receive reports of a number of detainees who had suffered severe ill-treatment at the hands of certain officials. Although complaints were made and investigations carried out, the result was that no action was taken on some complaints through lack of evidence, and on others the investigations were on-going. Of paramount importance of any such visit will undoubtedly include gathering information directly from the detainees themselves through questioning and written statements (Art. 8(3)). The answering of such questions is purely voluntary. Although information received by this method is treated in the strictest confidence, some interviewees may feel that it is not in their best interests to answer questions, even where they have undergone some form of ill-treatment. For example, immigrants detainees may be reluctant or frightened to divulge information against officials of a State in which they are seeking asylum status for fear of receiving a less than sympathetic hearing as a result of their co-operation with the Committee.

7–023 Whilst there are no reservations permitted under the Convention (Art. 21), a State Party may attempt to resist access to certain places on the grounds of national defence, public safety, the threat of public disorder, the medical condition of a person or because of the necessity to interrogate a suspect about a serious crime is in progress (Art. 9(1)). In such cases dialogue will commence between the parties concerned in order to reach a compromise without disruption to the every-day duties of the state officials, whilst at the same time attempting not to hinder, where not absolutely necessary, the work of the delegates.

Having concluded their visit, the Committee will then make an interim report. This report will detail its findings, including various comments, recommendations and observations (Art. 10(1)). This is then submitted to the State concerned for its consideration; they will normally respond by giving explanations for its conduct and perhaps clarifying or disputing certain facts in the report. The report itself may not disclose certain data that might subsequently have detrimental effects on those who volunteered such information. For instance, the naming of those detainees questioned about their treatment may be omitted for fear of reprisals by the state against such persons. Under Art. 10(2) if the State does not implement the recommendations made in the report, then the Committee may make public its findings. However, this must be agreed by a majority of at least two-thirds of its members. For instance, in December 1996 the Committee issued a public statement on Turkey (CPT/Inf (96) 34) in which were set out damming comments concerning human rights violations in that State. The statement drew attention to the fact that although some progress had been made, "the translations of words into deeds is proving to be a highly protracted process" (para. 2). The Committee found that the practice of torture and ill-treatment by the Turkish authorities remained widespread. Beatings, suspension by the arms and electric shock equipment was still being used on detainees. Complaints made by detainees of ill-treatment were not being adequately or objectively dealt with. Suspects were being held incommunicado for long periods of time (in some cases up to thirty days). One of the most fundamental rights of access to a lawyer was being denied for up to five days; this, the Committee found to be unacceptable. Despite legislation in place to combat human rights abuses, and the Constitution of the Republic of Turkey (Art. 17(3)) proclaiming that "No one shall be subjected to torture or ill-treatment ...," in practice, implementation of these laws were seriously lacking. Moreover, recommendations by the Committee from previous visits were not being complied with. In spite of the Committee's findings being submitted to the Turkish authorities, the latter's response was not only wholly inadequate but also they refused to acknowledge the gravity of the situation. Since that time the Committee has made a number of return visits to Turkey; the latest being from March 21–27 and September 1–6, 2002, to investigate and make recommendations relating to prison conditions, and in particular, the ill-treatment meted out to detainees by law enforcement officials.

The report by the Committee to the Spanish Government (CPT/Inf (2000))

7–024   Generally, all information accumulated as a result of the Committee's visit is confidential. However, a State may request the Committee to publish its report, although no personal information may be disclosed without the express consent of the person concerned (Art. 11(1)–(3)). Subject to this exception, each year a general report is submitted to the Consultative Assembly and is made public (Art. 12). By the beginning of the year 2000, out of 92 visit reports which had been submitted to the governments of State Parties 62 have been published. By way of example the report on Spain has been selected to illustrate the workings of the Committee in practice.

From the November 22 – December 4, 1998, in accordance with Art. 7 of the Convention, the Committee visited Spain. This was the third periodic visit to that state (there were also three *ad hoc* visits — one in 1994 and two in 1997) and the Spanish Government requested that the subsequent report be published, in line with Art. 11(2). As an intricate part of the visit, the delegates met with various local and government officials as well as NGOs to discuss, *inter alia*, matters relating to the conditions of detainees in that State. Their visit included going to various police stations, prisons and detention and remand centres (eight police stations, four prisons, one psychiatric hospital, and one vessel which transported prisoners between the Canary Islands and mainland Spain). The delegates noted with satisfaction that the 1995 Criminal Code (Art. 174) introduced penalties of up to six-year's imprisonment for those officials convicted of torture offences, and for offences of ill-treatment up to two years (Art. 173). Although no detainees questioned claimed that they had been tortured, they did, nevertheless, allege ill-treatment by the National Police at the time of arrest. Moreover, delegates received information relating to serious ill-treatment of detainees in custody suspected of terrorist offences, including beatings, asphyxiation by placing a bag over the detainee's head and sexual assaults by police officers on female suspects. The Committee requested that the authorities provide information relating to the number of complaints made by detainees of ill-treatment, the outcome of these complaints and any prosecutions which resulted therefrom.

The Committee in its report reiterated its views on the protection of detainees against ill-treatment, which they maintain can be strengthened by permitting the detainee the fundamental rights of: (1) access to legal advice, from the outset; (2) notifying a third party of his detention; and (3) access to a doctor. In (1) the Spanish authorities acknowledged that access should be allowed from the outset, but in practice the Committee did not find this to be the case and recommended rectifying the matter. After consultation with the Committee the authorities agreed to take steps to implement their recommendation. In (2) the Committee found that as much as five days can elapse before a third party is notified of the detainee's custody; this was considered unjustifiable — a maximum of 48 hours in exceptional cases was suggested. The authorities agreed to shorten the notification period. In (3) where access to a doctor was permitted, the record of the examination was found by the Committee to be inadequate. The form (*Protocola*) did not contain any statement by the detainee of ill-treatment, nor the doctor's conclusions, nor details about the origin of the injuries. The Committee recommended that the results of any examination be recorded including allegations of ill-treatment and to what extent those allegations are consistent with the results of the medical examination. The authorities agreed to implement these recommendations. On previous visits the Committee recommended that an independent authority should make regular inspections to detention centres to ensure that the proper legal procedures were being adhered to against those held in custody. Seemingly, this particular recommendation had not been implemented. The Committee also criticised the detention conditions and facilities and the difference between the quality of cells in police stations in some areas compared with others. The Committee recommended that the situation be remedied as a matter of urgency. The Committee also commented on the general state of the prisons they had visited and on reports of ill-treatment to prisoners by prison staff. Such abuses included prisoners being sprayed with tear gas, kicked and beaten with batons. Whilst the Committee recognised that on occasion prison officers may have to use limited force to control violent prisoners, the force used must be no more than is strictly necessary. The Committee recommended that prison staff be reminded of these precepts and noted that a formal investigation by the authorities set up to inquire into ill-treatment of prisoners throughout Spain. The report requested the State authorities to submit an interim and a follow-up report on the steps taken by them on the above recommendations made by the Committee. Since that time the Spanish Government has responded *via* an interim report.

Conclusion

It is not uncommon for certain offending States to employ subterfuge tactics **7–025** in order to hide the true state of affairs from outsiders. This of course makes the job of the delegates and experts all the more difficult in giving a true evaluation of the situation there. This is especially so concerning periodic visits where the State concerned must first be given notification of the impending arrival of the delegates. Suddenly, detention centres and prisons are transformed to look very presentable; detainees are treated in a more humane and dignified manner and their conditions improved, at least for the immediate future. To counteract this false impression delegates may, for instance, decide to deviate from their initial notification list of places to visit and inspect other less obvious sites where they have received reports of human rights abuses. This cat-and-mouse game only serves to hinder the true portrayal of a State's treatment of its detainees. Nevertheless, the Committee has at its disposal many reliable sources of intelligence, other than the visit itself including, but not exclusively, NGOs, reliable informants, official medical, judicial and detention records, statements from interviewees and so forth, all of which contribute to a more accurate evaluation of the conditions in a particular State. As shown by the improvements in many European States *via* the comments and recommendations of the Committee's reports their work is constructive, effective and significant in the fight against torture and the general mistreatment of detainees. However, as more States become parties to the Convention it becomes increasingly more difficult to spend the appropriate time making reports, investigating and visiting places, and there is the danger that the Committee may have to resort to more selective visits. It is therefore vital that in the future more administrative, investigative manpower and financial resources are made available to maintain the momentum of this important work.

INTERNATIONAL COVENANT ON CIVIL AND POLITICAL RIGHTS 1966 ("ICCPR")

7–026   The UDHR, whilst still at the forefront of human rights, has been somewhat overshadowed by other legally enforceable treaties which dictate rather than suggest implementation by States of its provisions, and to that extent have overtaken the UDHR's influence. Nevertheless, it still remains profoundly important when one discusses the obligations of States to respect the principles of international human rights and fundamental freedoms, and is now an generally accepted as being an integral and valuable part of customary international law.

Apart from the UDHR, in 1948 the Commission of Human Rights was given the task of drafting two covenants which would legally ensure protection of human rights by Member States, *i.e.* the ICCPR, dealing primarily with civil and political rights; and the ICESCR, for the protection of economic, social and cultural rights. The ICCPR came into force in 1976 (to date some 144 States have signed up to it) and recognised, *inter alia*, "the ideal of free human beings enjoying civil and political freedom and freedom from fear and want can only be achieved if conditions are created whereby everyone enjoy his civil and political rights, as well as his economic, social and cultural rights". As part of the ICCPR's mandate the Human Rights Committee ("HRC") was created to fulfil the task of overseeing that Member States adhere to their obligations under the Covenant. The rights set out in the ICCPR include Art. 7 which states that "[n]o one shall be subjected to torture or to cruel, inhuman or degrading treatment or punishment. In particular, no one shall be subjected without his free consent to medical or scientific experimentation".

Just how the individual State will implement these articles is decided according to their national laws. Accordingly, by adopting the ICCPR, as with many other treaties, each State undertakes not only to recognise those rights set out in the covenant but also to provide effective remedies, which include judicial, administrative and legislative measures (Art. 2(3)). Thus, under Art. 2(2) where a particular right does not already exist in national law, that State is only under a duty to bring in measures which conform to the Covenant. It is not necessary to incorporate the ICCPR, only to adopt its articles in some form which would entitle a group or individual to have an effective remedy against a violation of one of the articles. For instance, under Art. 7 if no domestic legislation prohibits such an activity, the offending State would be responsible for introducing such a law. However, problems remain even though there are existing national laws against torture. Since there are various degrees of torture and inhuman treatment, the issue may become somewhat complicated where one State considers another State as using tor-turous methods, whereas that State deems their laws sufficient to deal with the situation, *e.g.* does 72-hours detention in a police cell amount to inhuman treatment? Does waiting on death row (if capital punishment exists in the particular Member State) for five years or more constitute inhuman punishment? Is the method of execution, *e.g.* by electrocution, injection, hanging, decapitation and so forth, inhuman? Answers to such questions vary according to the particular legal system prevailing amongst different States. But, above all, State laws must not conflict with their existing international obligations nor be discordant with the norms of international law.

However, under Art. 4(1), in times of national crises or emergency, a coun-   **7–027** try is permitted to derogate from their normal responsibilities and international undertakings provided it is only: to the extent strictly required by the exigencies of the situation; the measures taken are not inconsistent with their other obligations under international law; and they do not involve discrimination solely on the ground race, colour, sex, language, religion or social origin. However, no derogation is permitted which involves arbitrarily depriving someone of their life (Art. 6); or which results in torture or cruel, inhuman treatment or punishment (Art. 7); or slavery (Art. 8); or under Arts 11 (the presumption of innocence) and 15 (the right to a nationality); Art. 16 the right to marry); or Art. 18 (the right to freedom of thought, conscience and religion). Once a legitimate derogation is in place, the period should only be limited to the length of the emergency itself. Once the emergency has subsided, the derogation itself should end.

Human Rights Committee

Unlike the UDHR where there are no direct mechanisms for enforcement   **7–028** to ensure States abide by its obligations, the ICCPR does possess ways and measures to ensure that the principles and aims are adopted by its members.

By Art. 28 of the ICCPR the Human Rights Committee was established to oversee implementation. The Committee consists of 18 members, elected for four years to carry out various functions. Its members consist of an equitable representation of the different States and the principal legal systems (Art. 31(2), and act in their personal capacity and thus are impartial and independent from the views of their governments (see Arts 35 and 38).

Under Art. 40(1) of the ICCPR, State Parties are under a duty to submit reports to the Secretary-General and thereafter sent to the HRC on the methods used by them and to what extent they have adopted the Articles of the ICCPR, *e.g. via* legislation, administration, judicial or other measures. Member States undertake to make these reports within one year of the measures taken by them *vis-à-vis* the implementation, progress and difficulties that have arisen by the adoption of the covenant. This is passed to the Human Rights Committee who will make comments it deems appropriate in the circumstances. Under Art. 40(1)(b) the Committee may request further reports when it so wishes. This is particularly important when a State decides to derogate from its obligations under the covenant or argues that there is an infringement of Art. 2(7) of the United Nations Charter, *i.e.* it is purely a domestic matter. In recent years requests for reports have been made from Iraq, Bosnia, Peru, Angola, Rwanda, Haiti. Problems have, in the past, arisen regarding these reports from various government representatives. In certain cases the issued reports have been extremely biased in favour of the government concerned or the reports have been irrelevant or long overdue or in some instances no reports were issued at all. Where problems of unsatisfactory reporting has arisen, the Committee has turned to indirect means of gathering reliable information about a situation in a particular state, *via* specialised agencies, other international organisations (ILO) or even through NGOs who provide valuable material to the Committee from less than forthcoming governments. Other information may be gathered from individual experts who have made investigations and possess direct knowledge of the true situation in a particular State.

7–029   The HRC will then make reports and general comments to the State Parties (Art. 4(4)). When making comments and recommendations the HRC will evaluate and interpret the feasibility of a State's report according to its General Comments. The General Comments ("GC") are comments on the meaning of most but not all of the various articles. They are guidelines by which Member States can foresee to some degree whether they have conformed to the spirit, practice and intention of the ICCPR. They exist in order to draw attention to inaccuracies, insufficient detail or lack of clarification in the report. But the comments are on the general overall meaning of the ICCPR's specific articles. For instance, with regard to torture, General Comment No.20 (1992) states that, "[i]t is the duty of the State Party to afford everyone protection through legislation and other measures as may be necessary against the acts prohibited by Article 7, whether inflicted by people acting in their capacity, outside their official capacity or in a private capacity" (para. 2 of GC).

Article 7 may be taken in isolation or in conjunction with other Articles which may be considered relevant to allegations of torture. For example, torture may arise from a violation of Art. 10(1), *i.e.* all persons deprived of their liberty shall be treated with humanity and with respect for the inherent dignity of the human person. Also, under Art. 6, where State Parties have retained the death penalty, any execution "must be carried out in such a way as to cause the least possible physical and mental suffering" (para. 6 of GC). In a State's report relating to Art. 7, No.21 of GC recommends that such a report should not only specify the protective measures already in existence against torture under national law but should also, by way of observance of the ICCPR, include:

(a) the legislative, administrative, judicial and other measures to prevent torture (para. 8);

(b) adopt measures which prohibit the transfer of an individual to a state where that individual would be in danger of being subjected to torture (para. 9);

(c) take measures to prohibit medical or scientific experimentation without the free consent of the person concerned (para. 7);

(d) keep under review the interrogation practices and the general treatment of detainees and prisoners (para. 11);

(e) expressly prohibit under national laws the use of confessions in judicial proceedings obtained through torture or other forms of ill-treatment (para. 12);

(f) indicate what provisions and penalties are in place for those individuals who commit torturous acts (para. 13); and

(g) what provisions are available under national law for persons alleging torture to make complaints and obtain legal redress for their suffering, in accordance with Art. 2(3) of the Covenant (para. 14).

One of the HRC's most important remits is to hear complaints made by a Member State against another State for not upholding their responsibilities under the covenant (Art. 41). But first, the State Party must make a declaration that "it recognises the competence of the Committee to receive and consider communications" (Art. 41(1). The procedure for such complaints is set out in Art. 41(1)(a)–(h) and may be summed up as follows: the complainant state communicates to the alleged offending State, stating the particular grievance or violation. Within three months, the offending State must give a reply. If the response (within six months) does not satisfy both parties, and no friendly solution can be found, either State may refer the matter to the Human Rights Committee. After consideration, the HRC shall within 12 months (assuming no friendly solution has been found in the meantime) make a report on the matter. If, thereafter, still no solution can be found, a Conciliation Commission will be set up to examine the problem, and within 12 months give its views and recommendations. Within three months thereafter, the State Parties shall notify the chairman of the HRC whether or not they accept the contents of the report of the Commission. (Art. 41 (7)(d)).

Under certain circumstances, individuals who are victims of violations may submit a written communication to the HRC for consideration provided they have first exhausted all domestic remedies. This procedure is permitted by what is known as the First Optional Protocol (95 States have so far signed up to this). Thereafter the offending State has six months in which to reply to the HRC giving "their side of the story", and stating what recourse or remedy, if any, they have taken. The HRC after examination will then pass its views to the State concerned and to the individual (Art. 40(4)). But it must always be remembered that the HRC is not a court, nor does it possess the powers of a judicial body; more in keeping with a quasi-judicial body, and therefore its views and recommendations cannot be legally enforced. Many states have not, as yet ratified the optional protocol. It must also be born in mind that it can take anything up to four years for a decision to be made. Not all communications by an individual may be considered admissible. For an individual to be allowed, in the first place, to make a complaint, he must satisfy the following criteria: he must be the victim of the alleged violation; he must be a citizen of the alleged offending state; the complaint must come within one of the Articles; all domestic remedies should first be exhausted; the state must be shown not to have a legitimate derogation in force at the time. Under Art. 2 the State Party undertakes to provide an effective and enforceable remedy where the Committee has found a violation of the Covenant. The State authorities must within 90 days submit a report to the Committee detailing the measures taken to express the views given by the Committee in the communication.

7–030   An example of the workings of the HRC may be observed from the case of *Johnson v Jamaica* (Communication 599/1994), B.H.R.C. 37:

Facts.   In 1983 Johnson was convicted of murder and sentenced to death. In 1988, his application for leave to appeal was rejected by the Jamaican Court of Appeal. In 1992 the Judicial Committee of the Privy Council also dismissed his appeal. Therefore all domestic remedies had been exhausted. In 1994 he made a submission to the United Nations Human Rights Committee. He complained that:

(1)   Being on death row for over 10 years amounted to cruel and degrading treatment and/or punishment and was therefore a violation of Art. 7 and Art. 10(1) of the ICCPR.

(2)   He was subjected to beatings in order to extract a confession, in violation of Arts 7, 10(1) and 14(3)(g) (*i.e.* not to be compelled to confess guilt).

(3)   The delay of 51 months between his trial and the dismissal of his appeal (1988–1992) was a violation of Art. 14(3)(c).

Views.   In point (1) above, the Committee considered that the Covenant does not prohibit the death penalty, though it subjects it use to severe restrictions (see Art. 6(1) and (2) of the Convention). Therefore the death penalty itself cannot be considered to be a violation of Arts 7 and 10. No minimum nor maximum period exists such that it automatically becomes a violation of Art. 7 if such a period is exceeded (this had previously been confirmed in *Pratt v A-G of Jamaica* (1993) 4 All E.R. 769). If such a deadline did exist States may be encouraged to carry out an execution too rapidly, perhaps without examining the case thoroughly. Further, it would be inconsistent with the Covenant's object and purpose of reducing the use of the death penalty. However, the length of period on death may be relevant and therefore a violation of Art. 7 where there exist *compelling circumstances* which make the detention unjustifiable, *e.g.* delays, through the fault of the prosecution to make and deliver reports of the case to the appeal courts or *male fides* on the part of the prosecution to expedite the case as soon as is reasonably possible. In this case no compelling circumstances existed which turned the length of detention into a violation of Art. 7.

In point (2), above, there did not exist sufficient evidence to prove that the confession was anything but voluntary. The trial transcript was handed over to the committee which evidenced that the judge had properly considered and examined the whole matter.

In point (3), above, the State authorities had not provided the Committee with any material to show the reasons why there had been a long delay of 51 months between his conviction and the dismissal of his appeal. Counsel for Johnson provided information which showed that the delay was due to the irresponsibility of the State Party. In the Committee's opinion 51 months to hear an appeal was unreasonably long and incompatible with Art. 14(3)(c), unless there were exceptional circumstances — here there were none. Accordingly there was a violation of Art. 14(3)(c).

In 1995, Johnson's death sentence was re-classified as a non-capitol murder and the sentence was commuted to life imprisonment — not, it must be added, as a result of the Committee's views but due to the Jamaican's re-classification of the particular crime. The Committee did recommend that clemency would be appropriate in the circumstances.

Generally, where torture is involved, Art. 7 is not read in isolation but **7–031** rather is examined in conjunction with other relevant Articles which may either be associated with or come under the guise of torture, notably, Art. 6 the right to life; Art. 8 freedom from slavery; Art. 9 freedom from arbitrary arrest and detention; Art. 10(1) deprivation of an individual's liberty and the treatment of prisoners. For example, the case of *Mukong v Cameroon* ((1994) Communication No. 458/1991) illustrates the connection between Art. 7 and arbitrary arrest and detention in Art. 9. In that case, between August 1988 and May 1989 the author, a journalist, was arrested and held in detention after he made remarks about the Cameroon President and made his views known for a pro multi-party democracy. His views were considered subversive under the existing national law. He was held in a small cell with 25 other detainees. Initially, he was refused food, was forced to sleep on the floor and no sanitary facilities were provided. The charges against him were later dropped and he was released. In February 1990 he was again arrested for publicly spouting his opinions for a pro-democracy multi-party State. On this occasion he was held incommunicado and was subjected to death threats. He was later prosecuted but eventually acquitted. The substantive questions were did his detention constitute an infringement of Art. 7 and was his freedom of speech restricted under Art. 19? Was his arrest arbitrary under Art. 9(1)–(5), *i.e.* no one shall be subjected to arbitrary arrest or detention? In relation to Art. 7 the Committee stated that the conditions during the author's detention could, and in fact did, amount to cruel and degrading treatment. Being held incommunicado and being subjected to death threats was in line with General Comment No.20 and was a violation of Art. 7. The State argued that the burden of proof lay with the author to substantiate these allegations of ill-treatment. The Committee said that once the author has provided sufficient information of ill-treatment, it is then up to the State to disprove those allegations.

Despite the arrest and detention being lawful according to national law, nevertheless the Committee had to consider whether his arrest and detention was arbitrary within Art. 9(1). The Committee said that arbitrariness was not the same as "against the law" but "more broadly included such elements as inappropriateness, injustice, lack of predictability and due process of law" (para. 9.8). In other words, an arrest must not only be lawful but reasonable in all the circumstances and remand (detention) must also be necessary, *e.g.* to prevent flight, interference with evidence or the recurrence of crime (para. 9.8). Here, the State had not shown that any of these factors existed. Although the freedom of expression in Art. 19 has lawful restrictions, *e.g.* Art. 19(3)(a) "for respect of the rights or reputation of others" and under para. (3)(b) "for the protection of national security or of public order or of public health or morals", the committee found that none of these exceptions existed in his case and thus his detention was neither reasonable nor necessary in the circumstances. Accordingly, there was a violation of Art. 9(1).

EUROPEAN CONVENTION ON HUMAN RIGHTS (ART. 3)

"No one shall be subjected to torture or to inhuman or degrading treatment or punishment". — Art. 3 of the ECHR

7–032 Article 3 is a doubly unusual provision of the Convention which operates as an especially strong guarantee of the rights which it protects. It places freedom from torture and inhuman treatment as one of the most fundamental rights of a citizen, and in fact puts these rights at a higher priority than the right to life. Article 2 allows States to have the death penalty and also places the right to life in the balance against other lawful interests. By contrast, the rights under Art. 3 are given unqualified protection. Unlike almost all the other Articles, there are no exceptions stated in Art. 3, and derogation from these rights is impossible for a State even in times of war or national emergency. Thus, there is no reason or excuse which will permit torture or inhuman or degrading treatment, no matter how desperate the situation may be at the time, and the UK cannot use the situation relating to terrorism in Northern Ireland or world wide since September 11, 2001, as a justification for derogating from this Article (although it has tried to do so).

While the ECHR was not the first multi-State treaty to prohibit torture and related practices, its absolute, unqualified, non-derogable prohibition in Art. 3 and the breadth of behaviour which has since been held to fall within the Art. 3 prohibition make it worthy of detailed consideration. Unlike the UN Torture Convention, there is no definition of the terms within Art. 3 of the ECHR: the meaning of "torture" and "inhuman or degrading treatment or punishment" must be found within key decisions of the European Court of Human Rights and the former Commission; since the Convention is a living instrument, the definitions will evolve over time to keep pace with societal change and with the discovery of new wrongs. A further difference from the UN Torture Convention is that for the ECHR the motive for the torture, etc. is irrelevant; it is caught by Art. 3 even if carried out for its own sake (see *Tyrer v UK* (1979–1980) 2 EHRR 1, *X and Y v The Netherlands* (1986) 8 EHRR 235). This, together with the State's positive obligation to prevent Art. 3 breaches (discussed below) and the generally high level of enforceability give the ECHR great potential in this field, stretching as far as the creation of State liability for non-State actors (see *Aydin v Turkey* (1997) (1988) 25 EHRR 251, *X and Y v The Netherlands* (1985).

The general language and lack of explanation of Art. 3 has much to do with its history. Nazi atrocities and recent events created a very strong impetus behind the inclusion of a torture prohibition in the Convention by its drafters, but this had to be balanced against the fact that many States signing or likely to sign the Convention still had capital or corporal punishment and some had compulsory sterilisation of rapists. Hence the language used in Art. 3 was general as a result of necessary compromise, and the lack of specific definitions and examples was due to the wide variance in States" criminal law practice and procedure. There have since developed two quite separate levels of infringement of Art. 3: "true" torture and inhuman treatment (rape, violent beatings and so on) and "quality of life" infringements at a more sophisticated level, which are unlikely to leave a lasting physical or psychological mark upon the victim. However, the three terms within Art. 3 have also been treated as distinct, and thus "torture", "inhuman treatments or punishment" and "degrading treatment or punishment" shall be discussed separately.

The definitions were discussed in some detail by the court in *Ireland v UK* **7–033** (1978) 2 EHRR 25, where the court found that the "five techniques" used during interrogation of terrorist suspects caused "at least intense physical and mental suffering to the person subjected thereto . . . They accordingly fell into the category of inhuman treatment (and) . . . were also degrading since they were such as to arouse in their victims feelings of fear, anguish and inferiority capable of humiliating and debasing them and possibly breaking their physical or moral resistance" (para. 167). The object of these techniques was to elicit certain information from the arrestees, *e.g.* to obtain confessions, their affiliation with the IRA, and other secret information about that organisation. Fourteen of the internees were subjected to this treatment which consisted of: (a) wall-standing: standing on their toes with their legs and feet apart for hours against a cell wall; (b) hooding: putting a bag over the internee's head throughout most of their period of imprisonment; (c) noise: subjecting the person to continuous loud and hissing noises; (d) sleep deprivation: depriving the person of continual sleep; and (e) food and drink: depriving the person of sufficient nourishment. The distinction between inhuman/degrading treatment and torture was found to be that the latter causes much more intense suffering; thus it is a question of degree. The Commission examined some eight cases. They ruled that the practices of the "five techniques" constituted, not only inhuman and degrading treatment, but also torture.

The Commission also found that it was probable that physical violence accompanied the five techniques in certain cases, however, they ruled that in only one case (out of a possible 14) was it actually shown. The court then declared such practices to be degrading, and by causing intense physical and psychological suffering during questioning constituted inhuman treatment under Art. 3. They found that although the treatment which the detainees received was of an inhuman and degrading nature, this did not escalate to the intensity required for the treatment to be considered "torture". In the opinion of the court it had been the intention of the drafters of the Convention to attach a special stigma to "deliberate inhuman treatment causing very serious and cruel suffering" by labelling it as torture, even though there is no difference in sanction due to the more serious term. The "five techniques" were found to be inhuman treatment which nevertheless fell short of the level of intensity of suffering required for torture:

> "Although the five techniques, as applied in combination, undoubtedly amounted to inhuman and degrading treatment, although their object was the extraction of confessions, the naming of others and/or information and although they were used systematically, they did not occasion suffering of the particular intensity and cruelty implied by the word torture as so understood."

An interesting dissent was given by Judge Zekia, who thought that torture should incorporate a subjective element and so its effect on the specific victim should be taken into account; thus cruelty to an elderly or frail victim should more readily receive the higher stigma of a finding of torture. Also dissenting, Judge O'Donoghue stated that since torture may be mental as well as physical, the five techniques should have qualified.

7–034   From the *Ireland* case, some tentative definitions of the Art. 3 terms can be found. "Degrading treatment" seems to involve: causing fear, anguish and inferiority; humiliation or debasement; "breaking" a person by overcoming their physical or moral resistance. "Inhuman treatment" may be characterised by: causing intense physical and/or mental suffering; inflicting psychiatric distress; and prolonged duration. "Torture" is the least defined, but is a special finding which signifies the extreme gravity of behaviour which would otherwise qualify as one of the lesser categories, but is especially severe in the case in question. However, it is clear that the categories incorporate some vagueness and frequently overlap.

Before each category is examined, it should be noted that the 1998 reorganisation of the European Court of Human Rights and the disbandment of the Commission have led to a new set of rules and procedures for fact-finding which are of particular use in Art. 3 cases. Few States are willing to be associated with torture, even if their liability is never established; in such cases the facts are almost always hotly disputed. The court may now hear witnesses and experts, request information from the parties, commission reports from any person or institution. Further, a judge or judges may be chosen to carry out an investigation or mount an inquiry, with possible assistance from independent external experts.

In practice, evidence found in any of these ways or supplied by either of the case's parties can be used either directly, to show a violation based on positive actions by a person for whom the State is responsible; or indirectly, *via* a finding that the defendant State has failed to carry out an effective investigation of an arguable violation (see *Akkoc v Turkey*, [2000] Apps. Nos. 22947/93 and 22948/93 (2002) 34 EHRR 51).

There are very few cases in which torture has been found to exist on the **7–035** facts by the court or former Commission. One example of such a case is *Aksoy v Turkey* (1996) 23 EHRR 533.

The applicant was suspected of being a PKK terrorist and during his four-day detention he was blindfolded, stripped, his hands tied behind his back, strung up by his arms and then electrocuted. This was followed by repeated beatings. The court found that this was clearly and incontrovertibly torture.

Inhuman treatment and punishment

A reasonably clear, if not all-inclusive definition was given in *Soering v UK* **7–036** (1989) 11 EHRR 439 at 104, where the court stated that:

> "inhuman treatment covers such acts as intentionally inflicting severe mental or physical suffering or if the treatment inflicted humiliates the person before others or drives him to act against his own will or conscience."

In order for ill-treatment to be established under Art. 3, a minimum level of severity against an applicant must exist, and this may include the court looking to the long-term effects as a result of the actions taken against the applicant. There is no requirement that inhuman treatment or punishment should involve physical contact or proximity. For example, in *Selcuk and Asker v Turkey* (1998) 26 EHRR 477, the applicants had to watch security forces burning down their homes; this was found to be inhuman treatment. Whether this severity of the ill-treatment amounts to a violation depends on all the circumstances of the case, such as the duration of the treatment, its physical and/or mental effects, and in some cases the sex, age and state of health of the victim (para. 76). The applicants were aged 54 and 60 respectively; their homes and property were destroyed; they could only stand by and watch as this was going on. They subsequently had to leave the village where they had lived all their lives; their protests to the security forces were ignored; very little protection from smoke or flames was given to the applicants, and no assistance was provided after the destruction of their property (para. 77). The court concluded that the particular circumstances amounted to inhuman treatment and therefore a violation of Art. 3. Whether each of the events, taken by themselves, would have amounted to such severity so as to constitute inhuman treatment not only depended on the acts done by the security forces, but also on the effect that such acts had on the applicants. In *Selcuk* the catalogue of events which ensued, although they in themselves would normally be considered serious, together established ill-treatment of such a nature so as to constitute a violation of Art. 3. It seems in the above case that the court not only looked at the acts themselves and the immediate results, but also at the long-term consequences, *i.e.* having to leave the village and start their lives afresh elsewhere, in deciding whether or not there had been a violation of Art. 3.

Further, the effect of "disappearances" upon the relatives of the disappeared may also be an Art. 3 violation — *Kurt v Turkey* (1998) 27 EHRR 373.

Degrading treatment and punishment

7–037 Inhuman punishment generally involves some form of legally authorised assault on the victim, but whether or not the particular violence will constitute a breach of Art. 3 may be a question of degree.

Everyone, at some time or other, has suffered some degree of degradation or humiliation by some person in public authority, and no doubt stress, anxiety, despair, etc. has resulted as a consequence. Whether, the court (if it reaches that stage) would entertain a complaint under those circumstances, will depend, *inter alia*, on the level of severity which the complainant has suffered. "Inhuman treatment" covers such acts as intentionally inflicting severe mental or physical suffering or if the treatment inflicted humiliates the person before others or drives him to act against his own will or conscience. What may distinguish this form of treatment from actual severe punishment is that here psychological damage is more likely to result in humiliation, demoralisation, loss of a person's self respect, and free will may have been sapped due to the degrading treatment carried out. If the applicant has suffered injuries while in State custody, the onus is clearly placed upon the State to prove that the injuries were not the result of any ill-treatment. This is an unusual reversed burden of proof, which further requires the State to prove a negative. For instance, in *Tomasi v France* (1992) 15 EHRR 455.

Facts. The applicant claimed that he had been beaten by police during an interrogation. The French courts threw out his case because a *prima facie* case against the police for inflicting the injuries had not been made out. The applicant had been charged and remained in detention for five years and seven months before eventual acquittal. He complained to the Commission that whilst in custody, he had been beaten by the police on a number of occasions, which resulted in not only physical and mental pain, but he had suffered "fear, anguish and inferiority capable of humiliating him and breaking his physical and moral resistance". Medical reports by four doctors indicated that the injuries could only have been sustained during a specified 40-hour interrogation whilst in detention. The Commission was of the opinion that although the injuries themselves were "relatively slight", the assault in combination with the detention element (depriving the person of his freedom) led to a state of inferiority, and therefore constituted both inhuman and degrading treatment.

Decision. The court put great emphasis on the medical reports about the number of blows inflicted and their intensity. Coupled with this was the lack of evidence by the respondents for alternative reasons for the injuries sustained by the applicant. As a result, the court unanimously held that there had been a violation of Art. 3 in this case.

So, where a suspect is detained at a police station and is in good health upon his arrival, and upon his release is found to have sustained injuries, it is up to the police to account for those injuries. Whether or not the police are subsequently prosecuted the State will not be absolved from responsibility under the Convention. In *Selmouni v France* (2000) 29 EHRR 403, the applicant was arrested on suspicion of drug-trafficking and taken to a police station where, he alleged he was beaten repeatedly, hit with objects, urinated upon, threatened with a blowlamp, dragged by the hair and suffered physical and mental injuries as a result of this ill-treatment. Having examined the medical evidence the Commission found these allegations to be established. The court stated that it was "incumbent on the state to provide a plausible explanation on how those injuries were caused, failing which a clear issue arises under Art. 3 of the Convention"(at para. 87). Having considered all the evidence the court found that the pain and suffering undergone by the applicant attained the "severity" necessary for it to constitute torture, not merely inhuman or degrading treatment. The court further noted that, because "the Convention is a living instrument and must be interpreted in the light of present day conditions, certain acts which were classified in the past as "inhuman and degrading treatment" as opposed to "torture" could be classified differently in future. It takes the view that the increasingly high standard being required in the area of the protection of human rights and fundamental liberties correspondingly and inevitably requires greater firmness in assessing breaches of the fundamental values of democratic societies" (at para. 101).

The following series of corporal punishment cases illustrate very well the **7–038** difficulties surrounding what amounts to inhuman or degrading punishment. First, *Tyrer v UK* (1978) 2 EHRR 1:

Facts. The applicant, a boy of 15, pleaded guilty to assault charges and was sentenced to three strokes of the birch, which were administered in the presence of his father and a doctor at a police station.

Decision. The punishment was not severe enough for torture, nor even for inhuman punishment; thus the only question was whether the punishment was "degrading" (Para. 30). Generally, mere legal punishment, although *per se* humiliating, is not to be construed as degrading within Art. 3. The court noted first of all that a person might be humiliated by the mere fact of being criminally convicted. However, what is relevant for the purposes of Art. 3 is that he should be humiliated not simply by his conviction but by the execution of the punishment which is imposed on him. In fact, in most if not in all cases this may be one of the effects of judicial punishment, involving as it does unwilling subjection to the demands of the penal system. But punishment may still be degrading and breach Art. 3 even if it is an effective crime deterrent; it is also no defence to argue that the punishment was administered in private, without causing any permanent injury, and is in keeping with the mores of the society which sanctions it. The court said that the legal inflicting of corporal punishment by those in authority constituted an attack on "a person's dignity and physical integrity", which Art. 3 sought to protect. Added to this, the possible psychological problems from having to wait six weeks before sentence was carried out and the bending over a table with his buttocks naked to receive his punishment from strangers, all contributed to the court's conclusion that "the element of humiliation attained the level inherent in the notion of degrading punishment" under Art. 3. For punishment to be degrading in the sense required by Art. 3, the humiliation must have attained a particular level; however this was again left undefined by the court, who stated that whether that level has been reached depends "on all the circumstances of the case and, in particular, on the nature and context of the punishment itself and the manner and method of its execution." Thus, there had been a violation.

In *Y v United Kingdom* (1994) 17 EHRR 238, a 15-year-old boy was given four strokes of the cane on his trouser-covered bottom by a headmaster at a private school. Having lost a civil claim at the county court for damages for assault, and being advised of no prospects of success on appeal, the parent complained to the Commission alleging a breach of Art. 3. The Government responded that the punishment "was moderate and reasonable and did not attain the high level of severity condemned by the court in the *Tyrer* case (see, above). The Commission considered, however, that the severity of the caning itself, which caused physical injury (four raised streak marks on his buttocks) and the humiliation, amounted to degrading treatment and punishment under Art. 3. The case eventually ended with a friendly settlement (£8,000 plus costs) prior to the court's judgment. However, in *Costello-Roberts v United Kingdom* [1994] 1 F.C.R. 65 where a seven-year-old schoolboy was given three smacks with a slipper on his fully clothed bottom, the Commission in examining the above cases, found that such mild chastisement which caused no injury, did not reach the harshness required for a violation under Art. 3 — but only just (by five votes to four). Two of the dissenting judgments in this case, said that merely because the punishment was mild was not in itself the deciding factor, other issues pointed to the punishment reaching the level of severity, *e.g.* the boy being a seven-year-old who had to wait three days for the punishment — a long time in this instance. Further, the court should have considered the vulnerability, sensitivity and lack of maturity in one so young, and of the effects of any physical force on his being by someone in authority Thus, having considered the full circumstances, the minority concluded that the boy suffered inhuman and degrading punishment in violation of Art. 3.

These two cases illustrate the practical problems involved in interpreting the Convention before incorporation; the stronger case was settled out of court, and the weaker case proceeded to judgment — stronger cases may have fallen at earlier fences. The pressures which discourage applications and encourage settlements result in an arbitrariness which may belie the true state of civil liberties in a country. It is hoped that incorporation of the ECHR has gone some way towards improving this situation. Another factor which was highlighted in the following case, was whether the mere threat of punishment, without it actually being carried through, constituted "degrading" within Art. 3. In *Campbell and Cozans v United Kingdom* (1981) 3 EHRR 531, the court did not rule out the possibility of threats alone reaching the required level of severity in order to amount to a breach. In this case, one of the boys was due to be caned, but he did not suffer the actual physical punishment although he had this threat hanging over him for some four months before it was finally suspended. The court found, on the facts, that he did not suffer any psychological effects from the experience.

This was further developed in the case of *A v UK* (1998) 27 EHRR 611:   **7–039**

Facts. The applicant, aged nine, had been beaten with a cane by his stepfather, who was acquitted of s.47 of the Offences Against the Person Act 1861 (assault occasioning actual bodily harm) after the judge's direction that a parent was entitled to "lawfully chastise" a child in his care.

Decision. The court found that:

(1) the beating was severe enough to violate Art. 3; and (more importantly)

(2) that even though the injuries were inflicted by a private individual, the State was under a positive duty to ensure that individuals within its borders are not subjected to any violation of Art. 3, even one carried out by a non-State actor. Thus the State would be responsible for failing to investigate, punish and possibly even to prevent the harm inflicted by private individuals in violation of Art. 3.

For detailed discussion of the scope and applicability of positive obligations upon a state in relation to Art. 3, see de Than, "Positive obligations under the European Convention on Human Rights: towards the human rights of victims and vulnerable witnesses? J.C.L. 67 (2003) 165.

A SPECIAL CASE: EXTRADITION, EXPULSION AND DEPORTATION

One unexpected and fast-developing field of ECHR jurisprudence on Art. 3   **7–040** related to immigration and asylum law, and allows Art. 3 to be used to prevent the extradition, expulsion or deportation of a person from a contracting State to a non-contracting State; this can be done whenever the applicant successfully argues that he would face torture or inhuman or degrading treatment or punishment after arrival in the non-contracting State. In this way, a contracting State is held indirectly responsible for Art. 3 breaches which may occur outside its jurisdiction and beyond its possible control. *Soering v UK* (1989) 11 EHRR 439 is an early example.

Facts. The UK wished to extradite S to the USA, where he was wanted for homicide; the death penalty was likely if he was convicted. S argued that the whole experience known as the "death row phenomenon", particularly the long periods often spent on death row before execution, were inhuman treatment or punishment and so the UK would breach Art. 3 if it extradited him to face these circumstances.

Decision. The ECtHR found that it would be contrary to the spirit and intendment of Art. 3 to knowingly give up a person to another state where:

> "substantial grounds have been shown for believing that the person concerned, if extradited, faces a real risk of being subjected to torture or to inhuman or degrading treatment or punishment in the requesting country."

Vilvarajah v UK (1991) 14 EHRR 248 further developed this principle:

Facts. The applicants were five Tamils who were in the UK illegally and were removed to Sri Lanka. They had claimed that they would be persecuted there, and in fact three of them were tortured after being returned to Sri Lanka. They appealed successfully under domestic law, but also brought an ECHR action.

Decision. There had been no violation of Art. 3 since, at the time of their removal from the UK, the subsequent torture had not been foreseeable in all the circumstances.

In *Chahal v UK* (1997) 23 EHRR 413, the ECtHR found that the key question (para. 80) was whether "it has been substantiated that there is a real risk that Chahal, if expelled, would be subjected to treatment prohibited by [Art. 3]." Since he had not yet been deported, all facts and circumstances in existence at the time of the ECtHR's decision were to be taken into consideration. But the court confirmed that the applicant's own behaviour, even if a threat to national security, was not relevant since Art. 3 has no limitations or exceptions, whatever the danger posed by the individual claiming its protection. Thus, in *D v UK* (1997) 24 EHRR 423, where it was D's illness which would kill him if he were deported to a State with worse medical facilities than the UK, there was a violation of Art. 3. Further relevant cases argued on this basis are discussed elsewhere in this book.

INTERNATIONAL CRIMINAL COURT

7–041   Under Art. 7(ii)(e) of the ICC, "[T]orture means the intentional infliction of severe pain or suffering, whether physical or mental, upon a person in the custody or under the control of the accused, except that torture shall not include pain or suffering arising only from, inherent in or incidental to lawful sanctions".

In the elements of crime provision for crimes against humanity under the ICC, torture means that:

(1) The perpetrator inflicted severe physical or mental pain or suffering upon one or more persons.

(2) Such person or persons were in the custody or under the control of the perpetrator.

(3) Such pain or suffering did not arise only from, and was not inherent in or identical to, lawful sanctions.

(4) The conduct was committed as part of a widespread or systematic attack directed against a civilian population.

(5) The perpetrator knew that the conduct was part of or intended the conduct to be part of a widespread or systematic attack directed against a civilian population.

Since torture is proscribed absolutely under international criminal law, it is difficult to envisage circumstances whereby it would be permitted, under para. 3 above, in relation to "lawful sanctions". It would appear that such an exception is axiomatic, since if the "pain and suffering arising from, inherent in or incidental to lawful sanctions" were permitted, it would not under such circumstances constitute torture. However, even where a State does not designate certain ill-treatment as torture, if the actions in fact come within the definition, those persons responsible for committing such acts should nevertheless be prosecuted for torture.

Finally, although torture is expressly prohibited in war under Art. 8(2)(a)(ii), the accused may nevertheless be charged cumulatively for torture under crimes against humanity and as a war crime, since the elements of each specific provision differ. For instance, according to the elements of torture as a war crime the victims are limited to those persons who have "protected status" as opposed to "any civilian population" under the ICC, or indeed the ICTY, or the discriminatory grounds under Art. 3 of the ICTR.

CONCLUSION

Torture is practised in some form or another in the majority of States **7–042** throughout the world. Yet, under international criminal law it is still not recognised as a self-standing international crime; rather it is still looked upon as a sub-category offence, enumerated in the other "core" crimes, *e.g.* under crimes against humanity, grave breaches of the Geneva Conventions and Common Art. 3 of the Geneva Conventions. This is despite the offence being well established under customary international law as well as in numerous international treaties, and possessing the status of *jus cogens* and recognised as *ergo omnes*.

The practice of State torture can be stated, metaphorically, to be a human rights disease, which at present appears to continue to spread. Up to now, the treatment, prevention and antidotes for this disease have only met with very limited success. It continues to be one of the most serious offences, and unfortunately, one of the most exploited evils in international criminal law. But as long as State protection from disclosure subsists, and the fear of reprisals against torture victims remains, as well as the absence of the proper political determination to enact legislation to combat torture, and resistance to put on trial offenders prevails, this particular human rights atrocity will continue to spiral upwards. Even where the State does bring the perpetrators of torture to justice, convictions may be difficult to obtain. For various reasons evidence given by victims at trial may be unreliable and will nearly always be uncorroborated. For instance, positive identification may be impossible where the victim was blindfolded during the interrogation, or he may be so traumatised by the whole ordeal that he is unable to recall the identity of the perpetrator. Worst of all, victims may lack confidence in the judicial system of the State concerned and may be reluctant to bring charges for fear of reprisals. In such circumstances their only option may be to flee rather than remain and face being re-tortured, or worse, possibly death.

Chapter 8

TERRORISM

"We thus find ourselves between the threats and the wars of the twentieth century and those of the twenty-first. The war in Afghanistan is not a war against a geographically bounded state, nor is it a war against a religion, a people, or a civilization. It is a new kind of war, a war against stateless, networked individuals. The goal of this war is not economic advantage, territorial gain, or the submission of another state. It is to bring individual terrorists to justice and to punish and deter the states that harbor them." (D. Slaughter and W. Burke-White, "An international constitutional moment", H.I.L.J., Vol.43, 4, 2002.)

INTRODUCTION

International terrorism has grown in profile in recent decades for a combina-   **8–001** tion of reasons. Terrorism itself is certainly not a new form of behaviour: the use of violence against non-war targets to achieve political gains dates back as far as does history. The term itself originates in the State terror instigated during the French Revolution — the arrest and execution of political targets and dissenters in order to secure oneself as the new government. Since the end of the Cold War, the targets have become more disparate, the causes greater in number and the weapons have become more indiscriminate. Somewhat paradoxically, terrorism is often both decentralised and composed of highly organised networks. Democratic States face a real problem in maintaining their security and the safety of their citizens without cutting too far into the human rights of their citizens.

Terrorists now have a wide array of ever more effective weapons at their disposal, and have developed sophisticated techniques of persuasion. Technology such as the internet has facilitated exchange of information and a new form of property to sabotage. Terrorists are more mobile than ever before. Diplomacy has become a tactical requirement for illicit organisations and those who negotiate with them. The international element of terrorism has expanded as barriers between States have been removed and it has become a common tactic for terrorists to take action not only against those with whom they have a grievance, but also against neutral third party States and their citizens, *e.g.* by hijacking an aeroplane in order to create international pressure to accede to their demands or in order to draw media attention to their cause.

As a result, international and European co-operation between States to combat terrorism has been undertaken.

The events of September 11, 2001 have thrown the threat posed by terrorist acts into sharp focus, and highlighted the inefficacy, inefficiency and piecemeal nature of the existing international measures against acts of random or targeted violence. Although State terror has claimed a phenomenally higher number of victims than has its non-State counterpart, it is perhaps the unpredictability of the latter which heightens its perceived threat. The attacks also used a different form of weapon, an unforeseen innovative use of existing tactics (aircraft hijacking), when fears are generally that terrorists will capture sophisticated new purpose-designed weapons of mass destruction. This horrific innovation pointed out the deficiencies of both domestic and international law to deal with such evolutionary developments. Further international legal and co-operative measures are planned to tackle the problem, some of which themselves raise human rights–related concerns. In the author's belief, what is necessary is a single broadly-defined and enforceable offence of terrorism to replace the many specific, narrow Conventions and declarations which have appeared over the years. This would allow consistency of approach and reduce impunity for this serious international crime. However, until such an offence exists, there are a number of basic definitional problems which must be addressed before the relevant international legal materials can be examined.

WHAT IS TERRORISM?

8–002   There is by no means one consistent and enforced definition of "terrorism" or of "terrorist acts". Monumental acts of indiscriminate violence may well fall outside any definition. In criminal law, motivation of the actor is generally irrelevant, but when terrorism is concerned it is the defendant's motive which converts his domestic criminal liability into an international crime. Further, he may be liable for aggravated offences in domestic law on the basis of a terrorist motive and will usually have less protection of his civil liberties and human rights than if he were not suspected of a terrorist offence. For example, under the Terrorism Act 2000 (as under previous legislation) terrorist suspects in the UK may be detained for longer without charge (seven days maximum, instead of four days under ordinary domestic legislation) and were the first category of suspect to receive the new amended definition of the right to silence.

It is also not clear in international law whether an act is terrorist only if it is politically motivated. Since it is such a crucial question, it is unfortunate that one man's terrorist is another's hero or freedom fighter; the boundary between legitimate dissidence or freedom-fighting and terrorist activity is a difficult one which involves a question of perspective and which is vulnerable to changes in judgment over history. There is a further difficulty in assessing whether state violence should fall within the definition of terrorism: states are responsible for far more terror and violence than are individuals or non-State groups.

Attempts to create binding international law principles criminalising terrorism are not new. In 1937 the League of Nations adopted the Convention for the Creation of an International Criminal Court ostensibly as an anti-terrorism measure. But the Convention never came into force, failing to attract sufficient signatures and superseded to a large extent by the events signalling the oncoming World War. Art. 1(2) defined terrorism as:

> "criminal acts directed against a State and intended to or calculated to create a state of terror in the minds of particular persons, or a group of persons or the general public."

A possible problem with such a general and all-inclusive definition is that it could criminalise the legitimate acts of persons struggling against State oppression or to set up a free state, and hence conflict with the right to self determination. But since the events of September 2001 the priorities of the international community have changed, and there are strong arguments for an effective and broad definition. Yet the requirement that the acts be directed "against a State" might exclude some acts of extreme violence which do inflict terror but are either directed against the world in general, a sub-group of a State or undirected in nature.

Cherif Bassiouni defined terrorism in "Legal Responses to International **8–003** Terrorism: United States Procedural Aspects [1988]" as an:

> "ideologically-motivated strategy of internationally proscribed violence designed to inspire terror within a particular segment of a given society in order to achieve a power-outcome or to propagandise a claim or grievance irrespective of whether its perpetrators are acting for and on behalf of themselves or on behalf of a State."

The International Law Commission has defined terrorism to include:

> "(i)   Any act causing death or grievous bodily harm or loss of liberty to a Head of State, persons exercising the prerogatives of the Head of State, their hereditary or designated successors, the spouse of such persons, or persons charged with public functions or holding public positions when the act is directed against them in their public capacity;
>
> (ii)   Acts calculated to destroy or damage public property or property devoted to a public purpose;
>
> (iii) Any act likely to imperil human lives through the creation of a public danger, in particular the seizure of aircraft, the taking of hostages and any form of violence directed against persons who enjoy international protection or diplomatic immunity;
>
> (iv) The manufacture, obtaining, possession or supplying of arms, ammunition, explosives or harmful substances with a view to the commission of a terrorist act."

Until 2000, the UK defined terrorism as "the use of violence for political ends", including "any use of violence for the purpose of putting the public or any section of the public in fear." This limited definition, which applied only in reference to Northern Ireland, was to be found in all anti-terrorism legislation until and including the Prevention of Terrorism (Temporary Provisions) Act 1989. The Terrorism Act 2000 was an attempt to introduce a wider definition to cover, within one regulatory framework, domestic and international terrorism of all forms, whether motivated by politics, religion or ideology. It should also encompass some non-violent forms of actions such as interference with the water and power supplies, since such acts may risk life and health. Further, it was seen as important that violent acts committed for their own sake should be within the definition, regardless of whether there was an ulterior aim of influencing government or intimidating members of the public. The Terrorism Act 2000 provides:

"(1)   In this Act "terrorism" means the use or threat of action where—

    (a)   the action falls within subsection (2),

    (b)   the use or threat is designed to influence the government or to intimidate the public or a section of the public, and

    (c)   the use or threat is made for the purpose of advancing a political, religious or ideological cause.

(2)   Action falls within this subsection if it—

    (a)   involves serious violence against a person,

    (b)   involves serious damage to property

    (c)   endangers a person's life, other than that of the person committing the action

    (d)   creates a serious risk to the health or safety of the public or a section of the public, or

    (e)   Is designed seriously to interfere with or seriously to disrupt an electronic system.

(3)   The use or threat of action falling within subsection (2) which involves the use of firearms or explosives is terrorism whether or not subsection (1)(b) is satisfied.

(4)   In this section—

    (a)   "action" includes action outside the United Kingdom,

    (b)   a reference to any person or to property is a reference to any person, or to property, wherever situated,

    (c)   a reference to the public includes a reference to the public of a country other than the United Kingdom, and

    (d)   "the government" means the government of the United Kingdom, of a part of the United Kingdom or of a country other than the United Kingdom."

It is submitted that the approach of the UK, whilst going much further than the contemporary piecemeal international law definition, is the preferable of the two due to its non-specificity and adaptability to new situations. As recent events have shown, terrorists are becoming more inventive and more effective, and their acts seemingly more unpredictable. The present international crimes which are regarded as terrorism cannot be stretched to cover all acts which the international community would label as terrorist acts and, while more comprehensive than the existing conventions, the ILC definition to some extent shares the latter's defects. Not all terrorist incidents involving planes are adequately labelled as hijacking or hostage taking; and random killing of ordinary citizens without use of explosives or guns should surely be a terrorist act if its motivations are fear-inducing or ideology-related.

An acceptable and workable halfway position would be for the ICC to adopt a new offence of terrorism, with a broad, general definition along the lines of the current UK definition, and a non-exclusive list of examples incorporating the existing terror-related international crimes including hijack, hostage taking, crimes against diplomatically protected persons, financing terrorism and so on. Given the jurisdiction and other strengths of the ICC, this would surely be advantageous. The ICC Statute provides that the court shall have jurisdiction over persons for "the most serious crimes of international concern" (Art.1); an amendment to include terrorism within its jurisdiction may be time-consuming and subject to an initial delay, but is a pressing concern.

The Security Council, the prosecutor or a Member State could refer acts of **8–004** terrorism to the court; the advantages of a neutral trial venue have already been displayed in relation to the Lockerbie situation, and the trials relating to the latter could have been far simpler and speedier if an international court had been available to establish jurisdiction and provide a forum. The unwillingness of certain states to prosecute or extradite terrorist suspects would also be made irrelevant by this process. The court could also work towards providing universal, consistent rules and definitions relating to terrorist crimes and their distinction from "political acts".

There were several attempts to include a crime of terrorism within the ambit of the International Criminal Court. In fact the initiators of the moves towards the ICC, Trinidad and Tobago, were concerned about the terrorism associated with international drug trafficking in making their request to the General Assembly that an international court with criminal jurisdiction should be established. At the Rome Conference in 1998, 12 States argued forcefully in favour of inclusion of the offence in some form, including Libya, Algeria and Israel. While most wanted a free-standing offence, some argued that it should also be a crime against humanity. But a combination of the fear that its inclusion would politicise the ICC and the lack of agreement as to a workable definition of terrorism led to its final elimination from the ICC's ambit.

At the time of writing (mid 2003), the UN Ad Hoc Anti-Terrorism Committee was finalising a draft terrorism Convention, but had reached sticking-points in relation to the definition of terrorism and the question of liability for acts of armed forces. The Convention would have a comprehensive scope if adopted.

The lack of a comprehensive approach to the prevention and prosecution of terrorist activity

8–005   Customary and statutory international law have not developed an all-embracing crime of terrorism. Rather, the approach has been piecemeal and incremental, with new developments occurring as a response to each fresh terrorist attack and the change in perception of threats which attacks provoke. Thus, the prevalence of hijacking of passenger aeroplanes in the 1950s and 1960s led to the introduction of the Tokyo (1963), Hague (1970) and Montreal (1971) Conventions, which have unfortunately proved to be lacking in effective enforcement procedures. The United Nations attempted to draft a Terrorism Convention in 1972 but after its failure a patchwork of treaties became the way forward, each of which dealt with a specific crime or harm such as hostage-taking, hijack or bombing, and urged State Parties to prevent and punish it. The end result is patchy and difficult to enforce, leaving indefensible gaps. The United Nations General Assembly ad hoc Committee on Terrorism (1972) was unable to agree upon one set of recommendations and referred its questions back to the General Assembly, which has since adopted a number of Conventions and resolutions related to international terrorism, but most deal only with single issues such as the kidnapping of diplomats (1973 Convention on the Prevention and Punishment of Crimes against Internationally Protected Persons Including Diplomatic Agents) or the taking of hostages (1979 International Convention against the Taking of Hostages). In fact, comprehensive measures to combat individual terrorism have to some extent been the victim of the deflection of international attention towards State terrorism and the use of force.

There are many general statements against terrorism by both the General Assembly and the Security Council, but these take the form of repeated condemnation of terrorist activity, calls for the ratification of the existing relevant Conventions by those States which remain reluctant to do so, and calls for increased international co-operation to prevent and punish terrorism.

The most recent, the General Assembly Resolution of September 18, 2001, is as follows:

> **"56/1. Condemnation of terrorist attacks in the United States of America**
> *The General Assembly,*
> *Guided* by the purposes and principles of the Charter of the United Nations,
> 1. *Strongly condemns* the heinous acts of terrorism, which have caused enormous loss of human life, destruction and damage in the cities of New York, host city of the United Nations, and Washington, D.C., and in Pennsylvania;
> 2. *Expresses its condolences and solidarity* with the people and Government of the United States of America in these sad and tragic circumstances;
> 3. *Urgently calls* for international co-operation to bring to justice the perpetrators, organizers and sponsors of the outrages of 11 September 2001;
> 4. *Also urgently calls* for international cooperation to prevent and eradicate acts of terrorism, and stresses that those responsible for aiding, supporting or harbouring the perpetrators, organizers and sponsors of such acts will be held accountable."

Enforcement

The specific international conventions related to terrorism do contain some 8–006 enforcement procedures, which are discussed below, but there have been problems in ensuring state compliance with their provisions. Declarations that terrorism is an international crime in all its forms and that those who commit terrorist acts should be extradited to any state in which they are to face trial are of little use unless enforced consistently and promptly. For example, Libya refused for a protracted time to comply with requests for the deportation of the suspected bombers in the *Lockerbie* case, and it was only *via* extended diplomatic measures that an uneasy compromise was reached on the issue to allow a trial in a neutral state. However it appears that the Security Council considers itself to have the power to impose sanctions upon states which carry out or support terrorist activities; Security Council resolution 1060 (1996) states that "the suppression of acts of international terrorism, including those in which states are involved is essential for the maintenance of international peace and security." Thus, even if a State is not the terrorist aggressor, use of force or of self-defence might be possible in international criminal law, although such measures would be extreme and inadvisable unless the terrorist activities posed a grave threat to the security of a State. So, this potential method of enforcement of the relevant international law seems to have little prospect of application to the more usual type of terrorism, where an individual or group uses hijacking, bombing or murder as a political weapon on a relatively small scale.

Originally, the new ICC would have had terrorism and drug trafficking within its scope, but its terms of reference were redefined and limited, to the exclusion of these offences. Thus no new international criminal remedy will exist in respect of these offences, and the opportunity to refine and redefine was missed.

International legal provisions

Many of the international human rights documents are indirectly relevant to 8–007 terrorism, in that they enshrine the right to life, and to security of the person and of physical property. There are however few specific references to terrorist activity in the main documents.

As mentioned above, there is an *ad hoc* Committee which considers how best to improve the anti-terrorism provisions.

UN Resolutions Repeatedly, in fact in almost every session of the General 8–008 Assembly, there is a Resolution adopted concerning measures to eliminate international terrorism. Each such resolution uses very similar strong words urging international co-operation to combat terrorist activity, condemns all such activities and suggests that a more comprehensive international legislative framework may be necessary. However three recent resolutions are noteworthy. In 1994 the annex to resolution 49/60 was the Declaration on Measures to Eliminate International Terrorism, which unequivocally condemns all acts of terrorism as a grave violation of the purposes and principles of the United Nations and incapable of justification on any grounds whatsoever. Resolution 51/210 added to that Declaration and (*inter alia*) urges States to take steps to prevent the funding of terrorists and terrorist organisations. In 1997, after a draft Convention had been prepared by the *ad hoc* Committee, the International Convention for the Suppression of Terrorist Bombings was annexed to resolution 52/164.

8–009 *Conventions* The Tokyo, Hague and Montreal Conventions are discussed below in relation to hijacking. The following also create specific criminal offences which are within the definition of terrorism and related offences.

(i) The International Convention against the Taking of Hostages (New York, 1979)

8–010 Article 1 states that:

> "Any person who seizes or detains and threatens to kill, to injure or to continue to detain another person (hereafter referred to as "the hostage") in order to compel a third party, namely, a State, an international intergovernmental organisation, a natural or juridical person, or a group of persons, to do or abstain from doing any act as an explicit or implicit condition for the release of the hostage commits the offence of taking of hostages ('hostage-taking') within the meaning of this Convention."

Article 2 criminalises attempts and participation in hostage-taking. It is unusual amongst similar offences that here no motivation for the hostage-taking is required or excluded. The definition of hostage-taking is comprehensive but in fact the Convention is usually subsidiary to domestic law; even if a State does not have a specific offence of hostage-taking, it will have comparable criminal offences of false imprisonment or kidnapping.

(ii) The Convention on the Prevention and Punishment of Crimes against Internationally Protected Persons including Diplomatic Agents (New York, 1973)

8–011 Article 2 states that:

> "The intentional commission of:
> a murder, kidnapping, or other attack upon the person or liberty of an internationally protected person;
> a violent attack upon the official premises, the private accommodation or the means of transport of an internationally protected person likely to endanger his person or liberty; and
> a threat to commit any such attack;
> an attempt to commit any such attack;
> an act constituting participation as an accomplice in any such attack; shall be made by each State Party a crime under its internal law."

The crime must carry an appropriately serious range of penalties and these provisions do not reduce any other international law duties to prevent attacks upon internationally protected persons. Again, all such activities would in any case be criminal if committed against a person who was not internationally protected, since they would constitute murder, kidnapping, criminal damage or other similar offences. Therefore the Convention appears to have a declaratory function.

(iii) The Convention for the Suppression of Unlawful Acts against the Safety of Maritime Navigation (Rome, 1988)

Article 3(1) states that: **8–012**

> "Any person commits an offence if that person unlawfully and intentionally:
> seizes or exercises control over a ship by force or threat thereof or any other form of intimidation; or
> performs an act of violence against a person on board a ship if that act is likely to endanger the safe navigation of that ship; or
> destroys a ship or causes damage to a ship or to its cargo which is likely to endanger the safe navigation of that ship; or
> places or causes to be placed on a ship, by any means whatsoever, a device or substance which is likely to destroy that ship, or cause damage to that ship or its cargo which endangers or is likely to endanger the safe navigation of a ship; or
> destroys or seriously damages maritime navigational facilities or seriously interferes with their operation, if any such act is likely to endanger the safe navigation of a ship; or
>
> (a) communicates information which he knows to be false, thereby endangering the safe navigation of a ship;
> (b) injures or kills any person, in connection with the commission or the attempted commission of any of the offences set forth in subparagraphs (a) to (f)."

Threats to commit any of the offences in (b), (c) and (e) above will also be an offence.

(iv) International Convention for the Suppression of Terrorist Bombings (1998)

This Convention, which came into force on May 23, 2001, represents a recog-   **8–013**
nition of the ever-growing international demand for new measures to prevent and prosecute terrorist acts. This is shown in the preamble, which echoes the words of the many preceding Resolutions of the General Assembly, but uses far stronger language, talking of the "urgent need to enhance international co-operation", and the need for an urgent review of the scope of existing international anti-terrorism legislation.

Article 2 states that:

> "Any person commits an offence within the meaning of this Convention if that person unlawfully and intentionally delivers, places, discharges or detonates an explosive or other lethal device in, onto or against a place of public use, a State or government facility, a public transportation system or an infrastructure facility:
> with the intent to cause death or serious bodily injury; or
> with the intent to cause extensive destruction of such a place, facility or system, where such destruction results in or is likely to result in major economic loss."

Attempts, participation or organisation of such activities are also offences. The offences are to be criminal in nature and their penalties are to reflect the severity of such conduct. Article 5 compels States to ensure that there is no justification possible for terrorist bombing offences in domestic law, even from "considerations of a political, philosophical, ideological, racial, ethnic, religious or other similar nature". The offences in Art. 2 are deemed to be included as extraditable in any extradition treaty (Art. 9) and if a State in which a suspected offender is present does not extradite him, then a domestic prosecution must be commenced (Art. 8). The offences in Art. 2 are not capable of classification as "political offences" and so requests for extradition or for mutual legal assistance cannot be refused on that basis. Thus, once the Convention is widely adopted, this famous problem should be avoided and the loophole in the Hague Convention will not occur in relation to bombings. This is especially true in view of Art. 15 and the increased pressure towards international co-operation in the prosecution, prevention, detection and investigation of terrorism. It is unfortunate that a piecemeal approach has been taken to terrorist offences, since the 1998 Convention was an opportunity to iron out the inconsistencies in the preceding international instruments, but this opportunity was not taken therefore and no unified definition of terrorism was created.

The Council of Europe adopted the European Convention for the Suppression of Terrorism in 1977, and almost all Member States have ratified it. Article 1 states that, for the purposes of extradition, the signatory countries agree that they will not consider the following to be "political offences": kidnapping; hijacking; hostage-taking; attacks upon diplomats; endangering life by bombing or the use of automatic weapons. However, the Convention was the result of so much compromise that it is practically ineffective since Art. 13 allows States to evade Art. 1 by refusing to extradite and going through the motions of commencing a domestic prosecution. Thus a Convention which aimed to close the loopholes in the Tokyo, Hague and Montreal Conventions has suffered from the same problem it sought to solve.

(v) The International Convention for the Suppression of the Financing of Terrorism 1999

8–014 This Convention creates an offence if a person (Art. 2)(1):

"by any means, directly or indirectly, unlawfully and wilfully, provides or collects funds with the intention that they should be used or in the knowledge that they are to be used, in full or in part, in order to carry out:

(a) An act which constitutes an offence within the scope of and as defined in one of the treaties listed in the Annex; or

(b) any other act. . . ."

The trio of anti-hijacking conventions are discussed separately, below.

Hijack: an example of complexity of UN Conventions   **8–015**

Aircraft hijacking is a relatively new phenomenon in terms of historical and international criminality. Historically, from the late 1940s until 1967 hijacking was mostly sporadic consisting of, on average, between three and seven successful hijacks per annum. However, in 1968 alone some 30 successful attempts were made, and in 1969 the figure escalated to almost 100. Until fairly recently it had been presumed, wrongly as it turns out, that due to the increase in security controls and domestic legislation as well as international co-operation between States through various anti-hijacking and extradition treaties (see, below) hijacking had been severely curtailed. However, on September 11, 2001, the hijacking of four commercial airliners, which resulted in the implosion of the World Trade Center in New York and the part destruction of the Pentagon in Washington, once again emphasised the dangers of wholly inadequate security measures and laws relating to international and internal flights.

The reasons behind hijacking vary considerably. In the early years it was mainly politically motivated; for the purposes of individuals seeking political asylum in another State or for terrorists publicising a political cause or attempting to force a State to release political prisoners — what the hijackers themselves might call "justified reasons". Other reasons have included purely domestic orientated crime, *e.g.* escapees from justice, military deserters, mentally disturbed persons, robbery, kidnapping and the like (see A.E. Evans "Aircraft Hijacking: Its Cause and Cure" — A.J.I.L. (1969) 695). In the late 1950s and early 1960s there was a common consensus amongst the international community that the then present law was neither adequate nor consistent enough to deal with this new crime wave against civil aviation. One of the main questions which had to be addressed in this area was that of jurisdiction. At present, offence of hijacking is not perceived as establishing universal jurisdiction and in the following treaties discussed below, it is all too apparent that the offence remains municipal-law orientated.

The Tokyo Convention

The Tokyo Convention on Crimes and Certain Other Acts Committed on   **8–016**
Board Aircraft of 1963 ("Tokyo Convention") came into force in 1969 and to date has been ratified by 147 States. The Tokyo Convention was introduced to not only deal with illegal acts on board an aircraft but also any other acts which jeopardizes or may jeopardise the safety of the aircraft, persons or property on board (Art. 1). The most relevant Article for the

purposes of unlawful seizure of an aircraft is contained in Art. 11 which states that:

> "When a person on board has unlawfully committed by force or threat thereof an act of interference, seizure, or other wrongful exercise of control of an aircraft in flight or such an act about to be committed, Contracting States shall take all appropriate measures to restore control of the aircraft to its lawful commander, or to preserve control of the aircraft".

A number of issues arise from the wording of this particular Article. First of all, the meaning of the word "unlawfully" is to be determined by the national laws of the State in which the aircraft is registered (Art. 3). Further, State Parties bear the responsibility of taking "such measures as may be necessary to establish its jurisdiction as the state of registration over offences committed on board aircraft registered in such state" (Art. 3(2)). Ordinarily a State Party which is not the State of registration does not possess the requisite jurisdiction over hijacking offences in flight. However, under Art. 4 there exists a number of exceptions whereby jurisdiction may be exercised, *e.g.* where the offence has effect on the territory of such State; the offence is against the security of the particular State or the offence has been committed by or against a national or permanent resident of such (for the full list see Art. 4(a)–(e)). Secondly, for any offence to be committed it must take place when the aircraft is "in flight". Under Art. 1(3) "in flight" commences from the moment when power is applied for take-off until the moment when the landing run ends. Thirdly, the offence can only be committed by "a person on board". This has the consequence that evidence of any interference with an aircraft by a person (which includes pilot and cabin-crew) who is in an airport lounge awaiting boarding that particular flight will not come within the confines of the Tokyo Convention.

Fourthly, unlawful acts includes acts which are "about to be committed". The exact meaning of these words is somewhat contentious depending on their interpretation. For instance, does the phrase relate solely to time? Thus where the unlawful act has not yet occurred but is about to happen immediately or shortly afterwards, that will constitute a violation of Art. 11. On the other hand does the phrase refer to the intentions of potential offenders to commit an illegal act, but as yet have not even begun to put their plans into operation? At the international Tokyo Conference in 1963 various State representatives put forward diametric views on the specific wording to be included in, what was later to become Art. 11. Some States preferred using such words as "attempt" or "intention". After much debate the Draft Committee adopted the words "an act about to be committed". It would seem that mere intention alone would not suffice to fall within the meaning of an act about to be committed. In M. Shubber's article "Is Hijacking of Aircraft Piracy?" 1968–1969 43 B.Y.I.L. 193 at 198, he took the view that "the phrase may be interpreted to mean that some manifestation of the intention to hijack an aircraft should take place before Art. 11(1), of the Tokyo Convention can be invoked".

The final words of Art. 11(1) state that "Contracting States shall take all appropriate measures to restore control of the aircraft to its lawful commander, or to preserve control of the aircraft". Thus under the Convention contracting States have certain obligations towards the aircraft itself but there is no corresponding duty to prosecute or in appropriate cases to extradite the hijacker(s). It is left up to the individual State to decide according to their own laws what further action, if any, should be taken against the offender(s).

The Hague Convention

Piracy *jure gentium* (see Chapter 9) and hijacking are not identical in conceptual terms or nature, although both offences may overlap in circumstances such that they may appear to originate from similar actions. However, as will be discussed below, under the Hague and Montreal Conventions, the conditions of one offence may necessarily exclude the other.   **8–017**

Due to the widespread increase in international hijacking by the latter part of 1969 and the jurisdictional and criminal enforcement restrictions inherent in the Tokyo Convention, the international community adopted the Hague Convention for the Suppression of Unlawful Seizure of Aircraft 1970, which came into force in 1971. Its principle purpose was to bring about a more effective and efficient means of dealing with hijacking offenders. Thus under Art. 2 "[E]ach Contracting State undertakes to make the offence punishable by severe penalties". Surprisingly enough the Hague Convention itself does not specifically mention the word "hijack" but the term is implied and a description of the circumstances under which the offence may be committed is contained in Art. 1 which states that:

> "Any person who on board an aircraft in flight:
>
> (a) unlawfully, by force or threat thereof, or by any other form of intimidation, seizes, or exercises control of, that aircraft, or attempts to perform any such act, or
> (b) is an accomplice of a person who performs or attempts to perform any such act
>
> commits an offence".

The offences mentioned in Art. 1 constitute an exhaustive list, and therefore not every seizure or control of a civil aircraft automatically amounts to a hijacking. For example, a person, by deceit, may convince an otherwise authorised pilot to dispense with his normal duties and hand over control of the aircraft to him. This scenario would not, it seems, constitute an offence under Art. 1. There has been no force or threat or intimidation involved, only deception.

As with the Tokyo Convention the words "any person who on board" is given like definition. However, "in flight" has an extended meaning under Art. 3, para. 1 which states that:

"... an aircraft is considered to be in flight at any time from the moment when all its external doors are closed following embarkation until the moment when any such door is opened for disembarkation. In the case of a forced landing, the flight shall be deemed to continue until the competent authorities take over the responsibilities for the aircraft and for persons and property abroad".

In Art. 1(b) it is presumed that accomplices include those who aid and abet, counsel and procure others to commit the offence of hijacking, provided that such persons are on board at the commencement of the unlawful act.

8-018   Under the Hague Convention "aircraft" is restricted to civil aircraft and does not include military, customs or police service aircraft (Art. 3(2)). As stated above, the Hague Convention was especially influential in widening a states jurisdictional powers and under Art. 4 states the circumstances whereby a State was entitled to exercise its jurisdiction. They are as follows:

(a)   when the offence is committed on board an aircraft registered in that State;

(b)   when the aircraft on board which the offence is committed lands in its territory with the alleged offender still on board;

(c)   when the offence is committed on board an aircraft leased without crew to a lessee who has his principal place of business or, if the lessee has no such place of business, his permanent residence, in that State.

Thus it is legally permissible for a contracting State to intervene where: (1) the aircraft is registered in that particular State; (2) sets down in that State; (3) the lessee has his principal place of business; or (4) the lessee has no place of business in that State but permanently resides there. With regard to point (1), above, this particular condition is in line with the Tokyo Convention, albeit now the Hague Convention is given additional powers to arrest, prosecute and extradite the offender where the offence has taken place outside a States jurisdiction (see Art. 8, below). The same authorisation is given to a contracting State where the aircraft has landed despite the fact that the hijacking itself may have commenced outside that particular State's borders. This is surely correct, not only for the purposes of international co-operation and in the interest of international justice, but also for the offence of hijacking itself which should be treated as a continuing offence. Thus, when entering the airspace of a contracting State the offence itself is on-going and responsibility rightfully falls on the State where the aircraft has landed to deal with the matter and take the appropriate legal action.

The Hague Convention acknowledges a contracting State's jurisdiction once the offender is "present in its territory" (Art. 4(2)) or "found" in its territory (Art. 7). Does this mean that if an alleged hijacker is brought back non-voluntarily to a State to answer internationally recognised criminal charges, that he can then also be prosecuted for hijacking? Or must the offender have been legally extradited or consented or of his own volition returned to the prosecuting State? In the case of *United States of America v Yunis (No.3)* (1992) I.L.R. Vol 88 at 176:

Facts. The appellant and four others seized control of a Royal Jordanian Airlines aircraft departing from Beirut, Lebanon. They forced the pilot to re-route the aircraft to Tunis. However, on arrival at Tunis, the authorities refused landing permission and blocked the runway. Eventually the hijackers were forced to return to Beirut where they released the passengers, two of whom were American, blew up the aircraft and fled. In 1987, using subterfuge, FBI agents lured the appellant onto a yacht and once in international waters arrested him. He was then flown to the US where he was charged with, hostage taking, aircraft damage and air piracy. He was subsequently convicted and sentenced to 30 years imprisonment. He appealed, *inter alia*, on the grounds that "hostage taking and air piracy statutes do not authorize assertion of federal jurisdiction over him . . . (and) conflict with established principles of international law . . . ".

Decision. Under the Antihijacking Act 1974, persons who hijack aircraft outside the special jurisdiction of the US are liable for criminal punishment provided that the hijacker is later "found in the United States" (This Act was brought in to abide by the United States" ratification of the Hague Convention). The appellant argued that "found in the United States" was not to be equated with "brought to the United States" to stand trial; the latter, he declared, precluded prosecution. The court stated that it made no difference how offenders came to be in the United States, nor that they must have arrived here voluntarily. Accordingly the appellant had been properly indicted. The court further highlighted the universal principle of hijacking in international law by stating that it "may well be one of the few crimes so clearly condemned under the law of nations that states may assert universal jurisdiction to bring offenders to justice, even when the state has no territorial connection to the hijacking and its citizens are not involved" (at p. 182).

Under the Hague Convention hijacking is now an extraditable offence. If the alleged hijacker is discovered in the territory of a contracting State, then that State is under an obligation to either extradite him or prosecute him themselves according to the laws of that State (Art. 7). According to Art. 8(1) there is a presumption that in any existing or future extradition treaty between contracting States the offence of hijacking cannot be excluded from such a treaty. Article 8 cites the offence as being an *extraditable offence*. Do these words make it a condition that the requested State must extradite the alleged offender or is it merely construed as a discretionary election which may or may not be fulfilled? Article 8 does not specifically stipulate that extradition must be adhered to when requested; indeed Art. 8 is couched in terms of non-enforceable language. For example, in Art. 8(2) and (3) extradition "shall be subject to the conditions provided by the law of the requested state", thereby permitting national laws to take precedent over the Convention obligations. The better interpretation, it is suggested, is that the words represent non-imperative action. (For a view on both sides of the argument see S. Shubber "Aircraft Hijacking under Hague Convention 1970 — A New Regime?" Vol. 22 I.C.L.Q. 687–726 (1972–1973)).

There may be circumstances whereby the surrendering State will refuse **8–019** extradition if to do so would be contrary to their own laws or practices. For example, a contracting State may prohibit handing over a hijacker where the alleged offender is seeking political asylum. The convention does not oblige

States to alter its own national laws regarding political offences. Thus, where there already exists laws preventing extradition for political motives, either under an existing extradition treaty, or under national law, then the surrendering State may legitimately resist extradition. However, what precisely constitutes a political crime is not always easy to ascertain and may be used by the offender purely as a ploy to avoid extradition. It is suggested that the question should be decided according to the laws of the requested State, since ultimately it is those laws that will determine the hijacker's fate. The same reasoning would also apply where a state was requested to surrender one of its own nationals.

Finally, where no extradition treaty exists, the surrendering contracting state has the discretion to cite the Convention as a legal ground for permitting extradition (Art. 8(2)).

The Montreal Convention

8–020 The Hague Convention represented a vast improvement over the Tokyo Convention in the area of aircraft hijacking but it did not take long for international incidents in the skies to reveal the inherent weaknesses, gaps and deficiencies in both these Conventions to deal with other forms of crimes perpetrated against civilian aircraft. As a result, in September 1971 in Montreal the Convention for the Suppression of Unlawful Acts against the Safety of Civil Aviation ("Montreal Convention") was adopted, and came into force in 1973. No longer necessarily relevant, under the Montreal Convention, are the hitherto preconditions that the offender had to be "on board" or that it was necessary for the aircraft to be "in flight", before any crime was committed; under certain circumstances it is sufficient if the aircraft is merely "in service". Article 1 of the Montreal Convention cites the *mens rea* required and lists the circumstances that constitute unlawful acts and provides as follows:

1. Any person commits an offence if he unlawfully and intentionally:
   (a) performs an act of violence against a person on board an aircraft in flight if that act is likely to endanger the safety of that aircraft; or
   (b) destroys an aircraft in service or causes damage to such an aircraft which renders it incapable of flight or which is likely to endanger its safety in flight;or
   (c) places or causes to be placed on an aircraft in service, by any means whatsoever, a device or substance which is likely to destroy that aircraft, or to cause damage to it which renders it incapable of flight, or to cause damage to it which is likely to endanger its safety in flight; or
   (d) destroys or damages air navigation facilities or interferes with their operation, if such act is likely to endanger the safety of aircraft in flight; or
   (e) communicates information which he knows to be false, thereby endangering the safety of the aircraft in flight.

As is immediately apparent, the offences that may be committed under Art. 1 are much broader than under the Hague Convention and include for the first time the prerequisite of intention. The definition of intention is not given here, but appears to differ from that used in English criminal law, relating to "purpose"; it is broad enough to encompass recklessness (but not negligence) and requires that any conduct should be deliberate and voluntary. The Montreal Convention extends to circumstances where the aircraft is "in service", and under Art. 2(b) includes from the commencement of the preflight preparation or up until 24 hours after the aircraft has landed. "In service" includes "in flight" as determined by Art. 2(a), which is identical to Art. 3(1) of the Hague Convention. Also Art. 5(1), in relation to measures to be undertaken by State Parties in order to establish jurisdiction, accords with Art. 4 of the Hague Convention with the additional circumstance in Art. 5(1)(a) "that the offence is committed in the territory of that State".

Article 7 (*i.e.* a State's obligation to prosecute or extradite), and Art. 8 (*i.e.* conditions for extraditing), are identical in both the Hague and Montreal Conventions. Problems regarding extradition for criminal offences, where there is no existing extradition treaty between states, is well illustrated in the matter of the *"Lockerbie Bomb Disaster"* in 1988. Pan-Am flight 103 was headed for New York when a bomb exploded on board killing all 259 people (including 172 Americans and 66 British, as well as 11 inhabitants of the village of Lockerbie). In 1991, the US, UK and initially France requested Libya to extradite two of their nationals suspected of committing the crime. No extradition treaty exists between Libya and these other States. Libya refused their request to extradite and instead decided to prosecute the suspects themselves under domestic law. The requesting States found this unacceptable and referred the matter to the United Nations Security Council for consideration. In January 1992 the Security Council adopted Resolution 731 which, *inter alia*, urged Libya "to respond fully and effectively to those requests". When no response was forthcoming, the Security Council, under Resolution 748 ordered that the two suspects be extradited and imposed sanctions on Libya for non-compliance. Under Art. 14 of the Montreal Convention, once a dispute between two or more contracting States cannot be settled by negotiation, the parties involved must bring the matter to arbitration within six months. If the parties cannot agree on arbitration, then the dispute may be referred to the International Court of Justice. The Libyans took the later course. Eventually, in 1999 after considerable diplomatic negotiations the suspects were extradited to the Netherlands where they were tried before a specially constituted Scottish court. One defendant was subsequently found guilty and sentenced to life imprisonment; the other defendant was acquitted.

Emphasis of the Tokyo and Hague Conventions was placed upon and limited to offences against the aircraft, and the crew and passengers on board. Under Art. 1 *bis* of the 1988 Protocol, the Montreal Convention offences extends to incidents which occur at the airport itself, but is restricted to acts which, at the very least, are likely to endanger safety at the airport. These acts include actual or attempted serious violence against persons or serious damage to facilities or aircraft not in service, which are directly connected with serving international civil aviation Art. 1 *bis* (a) and (b).

THE EUROPEAN POSITION ON TERRORISM

8–021   The European stance on terrorism centres on the European Convention for the Suppression of Terrorism (1977) ("ECST"), which came into force in 1978, and the European Convention on Human Rights (1950) ("Convention"), although further and more comprehensive measures are planned in response to recent events. Both treaties have been adopted by most European states and incorporated into their respective municipal laws. For example, the UK enacted the Suppression of Terrorism Act 1978 as a direct result of their ratification of the ECST and, long after most of its European counterparts, finally incorporated the Convention directly into domestic law *via* the Human Rights Act 1998, which came into force on October 2, 2000.

It cannot be stated with any real conviction that the different terrorist groups in Western Europe have seriously challenged the authority of their respective governments. For example, the Baader-Meinhof gang in Germany is now defunct; and in Spain the Euskadi ta Askatasuna, ("Basque Nation and Liberty") is relatively inactive, save for a number of anomalistic incidents. The threat is more one of perception than of reality. However, the position in the UK is not so inert. At present there are in existence a number of terrorist organisations each with their own political agenda who have remained particularly active, especially in the last 30 years; amongst these include, the Irish National Liberation Army ("INLA"), The Ulster Volunteer Force ("UVF") and probably the best known, the Irish Republican Army ("IRA"). In spite of the continuing peace process and repeated cease-fires, the violence has never really stopped.

In the fight against terrorism the UK government has introduced severe, some might call draconian, legislation to deal with the "troubles" in Northern Ireland, *e.g.* the Prevention of Terrorism (Temporary Provisions) Act 1974, which gave the police extended arrest, search and detention powers and created the ability to control movement of persons between Britain and Northern Ireland. Although intended as a temporary measure, this series of statutes, now much extended, was still in existence some 25 years later. Following on from this, the UK introduced further emergency powers legislation specifically for problems in Northern Ireland. The Government in 1998 appeared to be considering abandoning the specific legislation but in fact announced an overhaul of the legislation, with stronger powers for policing and investigation, a new definition of terrorism which would extend beyond political purposes, and a broader, more international focus. This was achieved *via* the Terrorism Act 2000, which remains largely in force, although certain aspects were amended by the Anti-terrorism, Crime and Security Act 2001 in response to the events of September 11, 2001. The amendments increased police powers in respect to the arrest and detention of foreign nationals, leading to a derogation from the ECHR and a consequent outcry from eminent human rights lawyers and academics. It is expected that the legality of both the new Act and the derogation will be challenged, first in the domestic courts and then in the European Court of Human Rights.

With regard to terrorist offences, the UK has been brought before the ECHR on a number of occasions for violations of the Convention and especially on matters related to the treatment of terrorist suspects in their custody under Art. 5 (see *Brannigan and McBride v UK* (1994) 17 EHRR 539 and *Murray v UK* (1994) 19 EHRR 193). As a method of circumventing Art. 5 the UK government has, since 1984, formally recognised that a emergency situation exists in Northern Ireland and taken taking advantage of the derogation provision in Art. 15 of the ECHR. That derogation was removed when the Human Rights Act came into force, but of course the situation has again changed.

8–022

In the past, the IRA has mostly confined its activities to within their own national borders, *i.e.* Northern Ireland and mainland Britain, unlike some international terrorists groups whose exploits and explosions have vibrated around the world. However, in March 1988 three IRA terrorists, suspected of about to carry out a bomb attack were shot dead in Gibraltar by the SAS (Special Air Services). Eventually, the applicants brought proceedings against the UK before the European Court of Human Rights complaining that the UK was in violation of Art. 2 of the ECHR (see *McCann v UK* (1996) 21 EHRR 97). Article 2 states that "Everyone's right to life shall be protected by law". There are a number of defences under this Article which protect a person from causing the intentional death of another. The relevant defence in this case was under Art. 2(2)(a), which permits "the use of force which is no more that absolutely necessary . . . in defence of any person from unlawful violence". The court appreciated the SAS dilemma, *i.e.* the duty to protect the people of Gibraltar, on the one hand, and the confines and restraints of national and international law of using lethal force against the suspects on the other hand. Nevertheless, the court, by 10 votes to nine, having examined all the circumstances, concluded that they were not persuaded that the use of force was no more than absolutely necessary in this instance. Accordingly, the UK was found to be in violation of Art. 2.

UN and EU statements since September 11, 2001 concerning international terrorism: a summary

September 12, 2001: Prodi, the President of the EU Commission, made a statement re the previous day's attacks, stressing the need for closer co-operation between the EU and the USA to combat terrorism. This was later backed up by a joint EU/US statement of partnership. NATO's statement of September 12 made it clear that they regarded the situation as one within Art. 5 of the Washington Treaty, *i.e.* an armed attack against one Ally which was

8–023

to be regarded as an attack against them all. On September 14, a Joint Declaration by the Heads of State and Government of the EU, the Presidents of the European Parliament and the European Commission, and the High Representative for the Common Foreign and Security Policy stated that all countries should make the greatest efforts to fight against terrorism, and that in their view international law made it possible to seek out those involved in or supporting terrorism. The UN Security Council Resolution 1373, made on September 28, urged all states *inter alia* to prevent and suppress the financing of terrorism, refrain from supporting persons or bodies involved in terrorism, and to take necessary steps to prevent the commission of terrorist acts. By a letter dated October 7, 2001, the USA informed the Security Council that it was "exercising its inherent right of individual and collective self defence" on the basis of "clear and compelling information" of the central involvement of Al-Qaeda in the attacks.

How to classify the attacks of September 11, 2001 under international criminal law?

8–024   Obviously, the Hague Convention for the Suppression of Unlawful Seizure of Aircraft would be applicable. The Hague Convention contains international criminal offences of performing or being involved in the hijack of an aircraft, and the offences are extraditable and of universal jurisdiction. But these were not straightforward hijacks; the planes were used as weapons of destruction to murder many hundreds and to cause immense damage to property. Other related Conventions are also of limited help: the 1963 Tokyo Convention on Offences and Certain Other Acts Committed On Board Aircraft and the 1971 Montreal Convention for the Suppression of Unlawful Acts Against the Safety to Civil Aviation again have limited jurisdiction and do not reflect the full horror and effects of the situation. It is not too great a stretch of imagination and law to label them as crimes against humanity on that basis, forming as they did "part of a systematic attack on a civilian population" within the terms of the ICC Statute.

The International Convention for the Suppression of Terrorist Bombings 1997 came into force on May 23, 2001, but has not at the time of writing been ratified by the US and covers only "explosive and other lethal devices". That could be stretched to include the present situation if the motives of the terrorists were given primacy in the definition rather than strict questions of interpretation. The Convention operates on the basis of *aut dedere aut judicare*, with an express denial of any political offence exception, criminalises inchoate offences such as attempts, and creates liability for accomplices and joint enterprise. Thus there is great potential in the Convention to assist prosecution of those involved in other terrorist acts, even if it cannot be stretched to cover the present topic of discussion.

It would be very difficult indeed to classify the attacks as war crimes, although much political and media debate has centred upon the "war against terrorism". Since neither terrorism nor any of those suspected of involvement are a State *per se*, the majority of war crimes under the Geneva Conventions are expressly excluded. Common Art. 3 of the Conventions applies to non-interstate armed conflict, but was designed to deal with internal conflicts, not those with any international element. The attacks were neither fully interstate nor internal, and so the Geneva Conventions are an extremely bad fit. Clearly they were an act of aggression, but the crime of aggression under the jurisdiction of the ICC will not be in force for some time yet, if at all. Crimes against peace face similar enforcement problems in this context. But, somewhat paradoxically, the use of force by the US and allies did have the character of an interstate conflict and so the laws of war applied. It can be suggested that it is time for an overhaul of the UN position regarding the liability and treatment of nonstate actors so that, should any such situation occur again, there would be a framework of legality to govern it and the likely response.

The reaction: self-defence? Were the attacks an "armed attack" or an "act **8–025** of war" against the United States? Article 51 of the UN Charter authorises states to use force to vindicate "the inherent right of collective or individual self-defence if an armed attack occurs against a Member of the United Nations, until the Security Council as taken measures necessary to maintain international peace and security." NATO and the US have so classified them; the former by invoking their Art. 5 to assist the US in using armed force as defence. The Security Council agreed in Resolution 1368 (2001).

One problem is that the State against which armed force was used, Afghanistan, is not the State of nationality of the terrorists and it has not been established that the Taliban government were party to the attacks. However, a strong case has been made that the Taliban government did knowingly shelter at least some of the parties behind the attacks, if not those directly responsible, and so some kind of accessory liability argument can be used to justify the use of force against them. On September 28, 2001, the Security Council adopted Resolution 1373 under its Chapter VII jurisdiction, requiring *all* States (not just UN Member States) to:

- prevent and suppress the financing of terrorist acts;
- criminalise the wilful financing of such acts;
- freeze assets of persons or entities involved in such acts;
- refrain from supporting anyone involved in terrorist acts;
- deny safe haven to those involved in terrorism;
- prevent the use of their territory for terrorist purposes;
- ensure that terrorists are brought to justice;
- assist criminal proceedings and investigations relating to terrorism; and

- prevent the movement of terrorists by maintaining effective border controls.

All States were also urged to become parties to existing anti-terrorism treaties, and the inherent right of individual or collective self-defence against terrorist acts was underlined, although not specifically endorsed until Resolution 1378, which condemned the Taliban for allowing Afghanistan to be used as a base for terrorism and its export.

8–026 Security Council Resolution 1456 (20/1/2003) reaffirmed the severity of the terrorist threat and called on all states to take urgent action to prevent and suppress all active and passive support for terrorism. The attached action plan has three areas: to work with Member States to raise their capacity to defeat terrorism within their borders; to promote assistance programmes to support this; and to create a global network of international and regional organisations.

Until the ICC is fully functional, it would of course fall to any State to prosecute under one of the existing heads of jurisdiction, including universal. Territorial jurisdiction would be an obvious pointer towards the US as venue, and the US has complex anti-terrorism statutes applicable to offences committed on its own ground. But issues related to fairness of trial might cause pressure for a neutral venue, as in the recent *Lockerbie* trials. In any case, there is a seductive argument that criminal prosecution is an ineffective weapon against those terrorists who are willing to use techniques such as suicide bombing, and further that the use of force is a more useful weapon.

TERRORISM AND HUMAN RIGHTS

8–027 There still remains to be discussed the extent to which it is possible or desirable to regard terrorist suspects as having different (or maybe lesser) human rights than other persons. In spite of the lack of a clear, universally agreed definition of "terrorism" in international law, there has developed a reasonably coherent body of ECHR case law in relation to terrorist suspects" human rights under Arts 2, 3, 5, 6 and 10. Further and similar rights of course exist under international law. A key and difficult issue has been the balance to be maintained between such rights and the interests of society in national security. Further, as discussed above, the UK's derogation from Art. 5 has been questioned as to scope and indeed validity.

Two main dangers of the fight against terrorism are:

- that "the delegitimising process will lead to an unjustified denial of the human rights of those suspected to be terrorists and that who support the terrorists' ends, even those who do not positively distance themselves from them, will be identified with the terrorists and treated likewise."

- "that measures justified by reference to terrorism will come to be used against drug-traffickers, organised criminals, ordinary criminals, so that what begin as measures to meet a discrete and confined phenomenon leak out into mainstream law enforcement, putting in jeopardy the human rights of many people." (C. Warbrick, "The Principles of the European Convention on Human Rights and the response of States to terrorism", 3 EHRR 288)

In spite of the lack of consensus as to the definition of terrorism in international law, ECHR case law has brought into being a set of human rights constraints which restrict States' response to terrorist acts. As always, the rights have limitations and are subject to balancing against the competing rights of other such as the victims of crime and the public in general. Neither the Convention nor the Court have a definition of terrorism, and arguably no single definition can encompass the whole range of terrorist acts, from those committed by an individual such as the "Unabomber", to those of cross-national organisations or States. The court's approach has rather been to judge the extent to which interference with a terrorist suspect's rights is justified as a response to the particular threat to the State in each individual case. Thus the focus is upon the real or potential effects of terrorism rather than its nature. Further, the suspicion that a person is a terrorist will not of itself justify the use of lethal force against him, nor will it necessarily justify more emphatic State action than if he had been involved in another form of serious crime.

Under the Convention there are both positive and negative obligations **8–028** upon the State in relation to the human rights of terrorist suspects; in other words, not only must the State itself refrain from violating such rights, but also it must prevent and/or redress violations by third parties of some of the most important rights (see de Than, "Positive Obligations under the European Convention on Human Rights: Towards the Human Rights of Victims and Vulnerable Witnesses?" (2003) 67 J.C.L. 165).

Article 2: right to life

States must protect the right to life of all persons within their territory. The **8–029** fact that a person killed by security forces is suspected of terrorist involvement does not necessarily mean that lethal force against him was justified: see *McCann v UK* (1995) 21 EHRR 97. In every case of lethal force it must be established that such force was "absolutely necessary". In *McCann*, the EctHR found (by a majority of one) that the planning of the operation in which the terrorist suspects in Gibraltar were shot dead was so defective that the State had violated Art. 2.

Positive obligations under Art. 2 include the right to an effective investigation of every death, which is capable of leading to the trial of those responsible. See *McKerr v UK* (2002) 34 EHRR 520 and, *Jordan v UK* (2003) 11 BHRC 1 for the requirements of inquests and investigations into deaths.

Article 3: right not to be tortured or subjected to inhuman or degrading treatment or punishment

8–030   The famous case of *Ireland v UK* (1978) 2 EHRR 25 shows the extent to which interrogation techniques may violated this requirement. The EctHR further requires any injuries suffered by a person in state custody to be explained and justified by the State, with a presumption that they were inflicted unlawfully if no satisfactory plausible explanation is provided (see, *Selmouni v France*, No. 25803/94 (July 28, 1999)).

A second and important impact of Art. 3 has been in relation to immigration, asylum and deportation law, as seen in the case of *Chahal v UK* (1996) 23 EHRR 413. The applicant, a terrorist suspect, had been tortured in India after committing similar offences. He used the decision in *Soering v UK* (1989) 11 EHRR 439 as a basis for arguing that if deported to India there was a real risk that he would be treated in a manner incompatible with Art. 3; whilst the court acknowledged that this was a very sensitive case and involved difficult assessment of evidence, it concluded that his deportation would violate Art. 3 (which is non-derogable and phrased as an absolute right, in spite of recent statements by member of the UK government that they wished somehow to avoid this obligation in future). Far from considering that the applicant's involvement in terrorism should be seen as limiting his rights, the court found rather that it reinforced his need for protection by the State, since it increased the risk of torture in India by security forces there. Thus, to the limited extent that the court took his involvement in terrorism into account, it was a factor in favour of protecting his rights and not a reason to deny them.

The *Chahal* decision hence creates a real dilemma for States in dealing with international terrorism and the balance of rights; if they deport a suspect to a country willing to take him then they may violate Art. 3, and if they deport to a "safe third State" in which there is no risk to his safety then he may be able to continue his activities unchecked.

Article 5: the right to liberty and security of the person

8–031   Almost all anti-terrorism laws created by States involve some form of extended detention for such suspects when compared to those arrested for other offences. The UK has just announced (in May 2003) that it intends to extend detention powers for terrorist suspects even further, potentially to two weeks without charge. The UK currently has a (questionable) derogation in force in relation to Art. 5 for terrorist suspects, whether domestic or international, and previously had a more limited one in relation to Northern Ireland only.

Article 5(3) requires that persons arrested be brought "promptly" before a judge or equivalent to determine whether detention is justified or whether bail should be granted. When no derogation was in force, extended detention powers were the cause of several violations for the UK: see *Brogan v UK*

(1988) 11 EHRR 117. Domestic courts have upheld both the derogation and the detention powers as lawful; see *A v SSHD* [2001].

Article 6: right to a fair trial

Everyone has a right to a fair trial, whatever their offence. Some States   **8–032**
choose to have a separate court procedure for terrorist offences; see *Incal v Turkey* (1998) 4 BHRC 476; in the latter case, Turkey's National Security Courts were found to lack the independence and impartiality required by Art. 6. Other Art. 6 rights which States have attempted to vary, usually unsuccessfully, in relation to terrorism case include:

- the right to a public trial (protection of witnesses being a legitimate reason for restricting access to proceedings);

- the resumption of innocence (shifting the burden of proof in some offences has caused violation, see *R v DPP, Ex p Kebilene* [1999] 3 W.L.R. 972);

- the right to silence/privilege against self-incrimination (one of the earliest rights to be limited in the UK under anti-terrorism legislation; see *Murray v UK* (1994) 99 Cr App R 396; *Condron v UK* [2000] Crim CR 679;

- equality of arms, *i.e.* the prosecution must disclose all material evidence to the defence (see *Edwards v UK* (1992) 15 EHRR 417); and

- right to call and cross-examine witnesses (can be limited to protect witnesses); see *Van Mechelen v Netherlands* (1998) 25 EHRR 647.

Similar rights are to be found in the United Nations human rights conventions and covenants. For example, Art. 14 of the International Covenant on Civil and Political Rights stresses:

> "(1)   All persons shall be equal before the courts and tribunals. In the determination of any criminal charge against him, or of his rights and obligations in a suit at law, everyone shall be entitled to a fair and public hearing by a competent, independent and impartial tribunal established by law . . . .
> (2)   Everyone charged with a criminal offense shall have the right to be presumed innocent until proved guilty according to law.
> (3)   In the determination of any criminal charge against him, everyone shall be entitled to the following minimum guarantees, in full equality. . ."

and further guarantees the right to be informed of the charges brought against him, in a language that he can understand, the right to consult with an attorney of his choice, the right to be present during the trial and the right to cross-examine witnesses.

Article 8: right to respect for private life, etc.

8–033 See *e.g. Klass v Germany* (1978) 2 EHRR 214 — telephone tapping — court found this to be necessary and proportionate in response to the threats posed by ever-more-sophisticated methods of spying and terrorist activity.

Article 10: freedom of expression

8–034 Many States criminalise support for or sympathy with, the views of terrorists or terrorist organisations. To do so does sail close to an infringement of Art. 10, particularly if the law does not distinguish with sufficient precision between a person who has the same views as a terrorist group, and a person who also endorses the methods used by a terrorist group. Only the latter should have the expression of his opinions and beliefs restricted, particularly if a criminal sanction is to be attached; there is a right to give and receive information under Art. 10, even if it is likely to shock, offend or disgust (see *Jersild v Denmark* (1994) 19 EHRR 1; and, *Oberschlick v Austria* ((1998) 25 EHRR 357).

Article 1 of First Protocol; right to property

8–035 This right could be invoked by those who have assets seized or frozen under suspicion of terrorist activity; see *Phillips v UK*, ECHR, July 5, 2001, however, for the wide margin of appreciation in this respect.

Part of the problem in relation to how best to deal with terrorism is really one of the difficult relationship between international criminal law and international human rights, with their competing perspectives; the former seeking to criminalise some of those whom the latter seeks to protect. This can be seen in the United Nations General Assembly Resolution of December 1985, which, while condemning "unequivocally . . .as criminal, all acts, methods and practices of terrorism", reaffirmed every person's right to self-determination and the legitimacy of struggle against oppressive regimes.

Chapter 9

"UNCOMMON CRIMES"

PIRACY *JURE GENTIUM*

The traditional concept of piracy on the high seas may be thought of as a **9–001** remnant leftover from the by-gone days of Bluebeard and swash-buckling buccaneers generally. In reality the problems associated with piracy are as relevant, if not more so, today than they ever were. Piracy still flourishes in many parts of the world including South America (in particular Brazil, Peru and Ecuador); South and South-East Asia (India, Indonesia, Philippines, Bangladesh, Malaysia and especially China where recently 13 people were sentenced to death for hijacking crimes, involving the murder of 23 Chinese seamen); Africa and the Middle East (Nigeria, Angola, Guinea, Sudan and indeed around most of the African coast). In its annual report *"Piracy and Armed Robbery Against Ships"*, the International Maritime Bureau ("IMB") stated that in the year 2000 there were some 469 incidents of attacks on ships either at sea, at anchor or in port. In South East Asia alone there were 119 cases involving hijacking and violent attacks upon ships. Such is the accepted abhorrence of piracy worldwide, that it is now recognised as one of the few international crimes having universal jurisdiction as well as coming under the umbrella of customary international law. Thus, by committing the crime of piracy the offenders have put themselves outside the pale and protection of all states, *i.e.* the pirates have become *hostis humani generis*. As a result, it is now universally acknowledged that all States possess the jurisdiction and responsibility to arrest and prosecute those involved in piratical acts.

The definition of piracy is somewhat obscured, ostensibly due to the difference in interpretation between national laws and those set down by various international treaties. It is often the case that States give a broader meaning as to what constitutes piracy and consequently may be outside the more limited bounds of recognised international law. For example, in *Cameron and Others v HM Advocate* (1971) S.L.T. 333, the defendant crew members were found guilty of unlawfully taking possession of a trawler situated approximately three miles off the coast of Aberdeenshire; threatening the skipper, robbing him of his keys and seizing the stores. Although the charge itself did not mention the word "piracy", the judge directed the jury on its meaning and stated that it was piracy or nothing else. They appealed, *inter alia*, on the grounds that: (1) the charge was irrelevant and that; (2) the court lacked jurisdiction. The High Court of Judiciary stated with regard to

(1) above, that it had to determine whether the facts set out in the charge constituted a crime recognised by the law of Scotland. Section 5 of the Criminal Procedure (Scotland) Act 1887 provides that it shall not be necessary in any indictment to specify by any *nomen juris* the crime which is charged, but it shall be sufficient that the indictment sets forth facts relevant and sufficient to constitute an indictable crime. Since the facts in the charge were subsequently proved, the jury was entitled to find the defendants guilty of piracy. Therefore, even though the acts were committed within territorial waters, the Scottish courts possessed the necessary jurisdiction. As regards (2) above, the appellants argued that piracy could only be committed on the high seas, which was not the case here. The court said that "in effect, the difference relates simply to the basis of jurisdiction and nothing else. The same acts involved the same consequences. If it is committed within territorial waters, there is automatic jurisdiction. If it takes place on the high seas, then jurisdiction is assumed if the qualifying conditions are satisfied." (at p. 335). Accordingly, the appeals were dismissed.

The modern definition of piracy is set out in Art. 101 of the UN Convention on the Law of the Sea 1982 ("CLS") which describes the offence as:

(a) any illegal acts of violence, or detention, or any act of depredation, committed for private ends by the crew or the passenger of a private ship or a private aircraft, and directed:

(i) on the high sea against another ship or aircraft, or against persons or property on board such ship or aircraft;

(ii) against a ship, aircraft, persons or property in a place outside the jurisdiction of any state;

(b) any act of voluntary participation in the operation of a ship or of an aircraft with knowledge of facts making it a pirate ship or aircraft;

(c) any act of inciting or of intentionally facilitating an act described in sub-paragraph (a) or (b).

The above definition in Art. 101 of the CLS, relating to acts of piracy, is also cited in Art. 15 of the Geneva Convention of the High Seas 1958. The piracy offences listed in Art. 101(a) and (b) are restricted to the more serious crimes and therefore other acts such as theft, without more, will not be considered piratical. Since Art. 101 does not refer to "threats" of violence or detention or depredation, it would seem that this is not included in the list of offences. However, it was decided in *In re Piracy Jure Gentium* (1934) AC 586, that an attempt to rob, despite not being a completed substantive offence, would come within the bounds of a piratical act. One of the basic characteristics of any form of piracy is that the ship or aircraft (modern piracy includes acts committed by a private aircraft under Art. 101(a)(i) of the CLS) must be privately owned; it cannot be the property of a state and excludes State involvement of any kind. Further, the words "any illegal acts" refers to acts carried out by a ship whose State, by flying its flag, has not condoned. This flag State element goes back to the practice that vessels on the high seas are only subject to the authority of the State whose flag is shown, *i.e.* no jurisdiction over foreign vessels; although this is a general rule and there are exceptions to this under different treaty and customary law. (see the *Lotus* case at PCIJ, Series A, No.10 (p. 25)).

Under Art. 101(a) of the CLS, the act of piracy must be "committed for **9–002** private ends", which includes looting, murder, robbery, taking control of another ship to escape or for revenge reasons or other acts for personal financial benefit, *e.g.* renaming, repainting and subsequently reselling the captured vessel. Excluded from the definition of piracy and in particular "private ends" are acts involving public ends. The question then becomes which acts constitute "public ends". Most commonly, these words relate to acts committed for political purposes. However, in any prosecution for piracy merely putting forward the defence that the reasons behind such acts were politically motivated will not automatically exculpate the offenders. Proof of legitimate political objectives will need to be demonstrated, for instance, showing that those involved belonged to groups recognised as insurgents, rebels or belligerents. Since piracy lacks State authority, the acts of such groups may come within the meaning of political ends, provided they are against a particular State, and are externally recognised by other States, or control a part of the territory of the State against which they are in conflict. If not, then acts committed by such groups against vessels of other States may be considered piratical (see the American case of *The Ambrose Light* (1885) 25 Fed. 408). For example, in 1877 during a rebellion at Callao in Peru, a ship called the *Huascar*, which was taken over by the insurgents, attacked British steamers, seized supplies of coal from one vessel and took captive two Peruvian officials from another. The British considered such acts as piracy and subsequently attacked the *Huascar*. However, in the case of the *Republic of Bolivia v Indemnity Mutual Marine Insurance Co Ltd.* (1909) 1 K.B. 785, goods were insured *via* a marine policy which included risks attributed to acts of piracy. Brazilian malcontents, who wished to establish an independent State, attacked and seized goods shipped by the Bolivian government from the Amazon bound for a territory which bordered Bolivia and Brazil. The Bolivian authorities sought to claim on the insurance; the attack, they argued, being an act of piracy. Pickford J. having examined the definition of piracy stated, applying the principles put forward in Hall's International Law (5th edition) that "a man who is plundering indiscriminately for his own ends, and not a man who is simply operating against the property of a particular State for a public end of establishing a government, although that act may be illegal and even criminal, and although he may not be acting on behalf of a society which is, to use the expression in Hall on International Law, politically organised" (at p. 791). He further stated that even though the particular State being targeted may consider such acts as piracy "they are for practical purposes not piratical with reference to other States, because they neither interfere with nor menace the safety of those States nor the general good order of the seas" (at p. 792). In this case, since the malcontents were not plundering for their own personal gain, but for a political objective against a particular State, it was held that the loss was not caused by an act of piracy.

However, difficulties arise where there is an overlap between personal and public interests. For example, would attacks by animal rights activists upon ships involved in the lawful killing of whales constitute acts of piracy or would such conduct be considered as being for purely public motives, *i.e.* in the public interest to save the possible future extinction of this particular species? In the case of *Castle John and Another v NV Mabeco and Another* (1986) I.L.R. 77 at p. 537, members of the environmental group "Greenpeace" boarded and damaged two Dutch vessels that were discharging noxious waste into the sea. The operators of the vessels, *via* the Belgium courts, attempted to obtain an injunction against such interference. At first instance, the court held that it had no jurisdiction to consider such matters and that any action was exclusively within the jurisdiction of the flag State, which was in this case the Netherlands. However, the Court of Appeal held that the Belgium courts did possess the necessary jurisdiction over their own nationals in this instance because the acts amounted to piracy for which the law of the flag State could not be claimed. It was noted by the Belgium Court of Cassation that the acts were not committed "in the interest or to the detriment of a State or a State system rather than purely in support of a personal point of view concerning a particular problem, even if they reflected a political perspective" (at p. 540). Accordingly, the acts amounted to piracy within the meaning of Art. 15(1) of the Geneva Convention on the High Seas 1958. This case seems to suggest that acts committed for political motives will be narrowly construed and that offences involving matters relating to personal convictions, no matter how public in reality the objectives are, will nevertheless be interpreted as for "private ends". By omitting "political ends" from the piracy equation, the CLS has allowed various political groups to evade international jurisdiction and must be considered a serious weakness of the Convention overall, and in the light of modern-day terrorist activities ought to be clarified in any future international treaty.

No piracy offence may be committed unless it takes place "on the high seas" or a place outside the jurisdiction of any State, *e.g. terra nullius*. "High seas" includes any area which is outside territorial waters and not within the jurisdiction of any State (Art. 105). A more precise definition is set out in Art. 86 and states that high seas exclude the exclusive economic zone, in the territorial sea or the internal waters of a State, or in the archipelagic waters of an archipelagic State. As far as the UK is concerned under s.26(2) of the Merchant Shipping and Maritime Security Act 1997, "high seas" includes all waters beyond the territorial seas of the UK or of any other State. In such cases, any State may seize the pirate ship or aircraft and arrest the persons and seize the property on board (Art. 105). Any such seizure may only be carried by identifiable government vessels or aircraft authorised to undertake such action (Art. 107).

Under Art. 101(a)(i) any illegal act must be committed "against another 9–003 ship or aircraft". Thus acts committed on a ship or aircraft without the involvement of any other vessel would not constitute a piracy offence; there must be some form of ship-to-ship contact. For instance, terrorists hijacking a plane would not, by itself, be considered as an act of piracy since it would not be against another aircraft. Mutiny on board a government ship *per se* would also not come within the confines of piracy (Art. 102); there being no other ship involved, although it may after be re-defined as a private vessel since the crew are now considered to be in "dominant control" within Art. 103. Any act committed afterwards by the mutineers within Art. 101 against some other ship would then become a piracy offence. The rationale behind including the words "against another ship or aircraft" stems from the danger of unnecessarily expanding the meaning of the offence of piracy. If otherwise, many not-so-serious illegal acts committed aboard a vessel would come within the boundaries of piracy, when in reality they were only minor criminal offences that could adequately be dealt with by the relevant State authorities.

However, by restricting the circumstances whereby an act of piracy may be committed, there exists the inherent danger that many illegal acts committed on the high seas may go either unpunished or be left to the international political machinery to solve. One notorious example of this occurred in 1985 when four members of the Palestinian Liberation Front ("PLO") seized control of an Italian cruise ship, named the *Achille Lauro*, which at the time was docked off the coast of Alexandria, Egypt. On board were some 320 crew members and 80 passengers. The PLO demanded, in exchange for the safety of their hostages, the release of 50 Palestinians held in jails in Israel. The terrorists attempted to set sail for Tartus, Syria, but were refused permission to dock there, so instead sailed for Port Said in Egypt. After intense negotiations it was agreed that the PLO members were to be allowed safe passage from Egypt to another state in return for the safe release of the passengers. It was then discovered that the PLO had shot and killed a wheelchair-bound Jewish passenger and thrown his body overboard. The United States immediately took action to prevent the terrorists evading capture. An Egyptian Boeing 737, carrying the four PLO members, on a flight to Tunisia was intercepted by F-14 aircraft and ordered to land in Sigonella, Italy. The four terrorists were eventually handed over to the Italian authorities where they were subsequently prosecuted for murder. The foregoing events wholly circumvented the CLS and precluded, on a number of grounds, the terrorists being designated as pirates. For example, their actions did not come within Art. 101 since they were already passengers on the cruise itself and therefore their conduct could not be considered "against another ship". Instead, the eventual outcome relied heavily on political and military pressure by the US, and somewhat reluctantly on both Egypt and Italy, to bring the incident to a satisfactory conclusion.

A State ship is recognisable by the flying of the flag of that particular State (Art. 90). Generally warships and other government vessels used for purposes that are not commercial enjoy complete immunity from the jurisdiction of any State other than the flag State (Arts 95 and 96). Where a ship or aircraft has been taken over by pirates, provided it is on the high seas, any State warship, military aircraft or other authorised government vessel used for such purposes may arrest those persons involved in piracy and confiscate any property found (Arts 105 and 107). Under the recognised universal jurisdiction, the arresting State may then prosecute the offending pirates, and deal with any property seized subject to the rights of third parties acting in good faith (Art.105). However, before boarding a ship or aircraft, a State must have reasonable grounds for suspecting various illegal activities, including: (a) that the ship is engaged in piracy; (b) in the slave trade; (c) in unauthorised broadcasting; (d) the ship is without nationality; (e) refusing to fly its flag (Art. 110). Any wrongful seizure of a ship or aircraft by a State will entitle the victim to damages for any loss caused by the intervention.

9–004   The introduction of the CLS cannot be characterised as an overwhelming success. It has done nothing to alleviate the situation; indeed piratical incidents are not waning but increasing worldwide. Since the treaty's inception it has rarely be used by States to bring piratical offenders to justice. Instead it has been the individual national laws of States which have determined legal enforcement and protection in this area. Nevertheless, various interested governments do recognise the importance of effective international legislation against the ever present danger, and in 1988 the Rome Convention on the Suppression of Unlawful Acts Against the Safety of Maritime Navigation was introduced to aid the prosecution of pirates, but as yet only 43 States have ratified the convention.

SLAVERY

9–005   Prior to the latter part of the eighteenth century, slavery and the slave-trade were recognised worldwide as respectable and lucrative businesses and engaged in wholeheartedly by all the major superpowers of that time, notably the Portuguese, French, Dutch, Spanish and British. Indeed, such was the enormous economic importance and profitability of the slave-trade that the British government formally granted "sole distribution rights" to the South Sea Company, whose ships departed from the ports of Bristol and Liverpool laden with their human cargo for sale abroad. Africa was the heartland for the exploitation and exportation of these slaves; their final destination being mainly the colonial plantations of the Americas and West Indies. The most industrious slavery years spanned some 250 years, from the middle of the fifteenth century to the end of the eighteenth century. The actual number of slaves transported during this period is unknown but estimates have ranged from between 12 million–25 million (Britain alone was responsible for sending some two million slaves to the Americas between 1680–1786), excluding the countless number who died on slave ships, from starvation, suicide, disease and torture. Whilst Britain was at the forefront of this trade in human property, they were also the first to recognise its abhorrence and from the middle of the eighteenth century many politicians and anti-slave trade movements were demanding an end to slavery and the slave trade. As a consequence, in 1807 the slave trade was declared illegal as being contrary to the principles of justice and humanity. In 1834 slavery itself was abolished throughout the British Empire and compensation paid to the former slave-owners of some £20m. By the end of 1890 most of Europe had followed suit. For those who flagrantly disregarded the new anti-slave trade laws, the British courts took affirmative action. For instance, in a case headed *The Fortuna* (1811) 165 E.R. 1240, the British navy, in October 1810, intercepted and captured the vessel "Fortuna". There was overwhelming evidence that the ship was to be deployed for the transportation of slaves and was fitted out for just such a purpose. The court stated that "any trade contrary to the general law of nations, although not tending to or accompanied with any infraction of the belligerent rights of that country, whose tribunals are called upon to consider it, may subject the vessel employed in that trade to confiscation". Accordingly, restitution of the ship to its owners was denied as, in this case, the confiscation was deemed lawful.

In 1862 after the American civil war had been concluded, President Lincoln issued the Emancipation Proclamation declaring an end to slavery. This was accompanied by Amendment 13 to the Constitution of the United States of America in 1865 prohibiting slavery in all States. Thus, even before the United Nations Charter and the accompanying Universal Declaration of Human Rights in 1948, slavery was recognised as an international crime, yet unfortunately some States have been slow to officially realise their obligations in this area, *e.g.* Saudi Arabia formally abolished slavery in 1963 followed by Mauritania in 1980. Even today a small number of States still openly engage in the slave trade.

Customary international law recognises that, without freedom of the person, most other human rights are irrelevant, insignificant or unenforceable. Thus in customary law, the slave trade has been illegal for over 100 years. But, there is a discernible difference between theory and practice where slavery is concerned: from the relevant treaty provisions and from the lack of recent case law, it would appear that the abolition of slavery in all its forms was achieved long ago and therefore that this international crime is merely of historical interest. However, it is far more accurate to state that slavery and forced labour continue to be an international problem. Although it is more frequently addressed by diplomacy and political pressure it remains a live issue in international criminal law *via* international treaties and tribunals such as the ICTY, ICTR and the recently formed ICC..

Measures to prevent the transport of slaves: law of the sea

Since the trade in human beings has been outlawed internationally, it is unsurprising that a number of provisions of the international law of the sea

9–006

aim to reinforce this prohibition by the introduction of ancillary rules and sanctions. Slave trading was one of the first international criminal offences to be recognised as being of universal jurisdiction. According to Art. 13 of the Geneva Convention on the High Seas (which is identical to Art. 99 of the UN Convention on the Law of the Sea):

> "Every State shall adopt effective measures to prevent and punish the transport of slaves in ships authorised to fly its flag, and to prevent the unlawful use of its flag for that purpose. Any slave taking refuge on board any ship, whatever its flag, shall *ipso facto* be free."

Further, Art. 22 provides that there is an exception to the normal rules which prevent the hostile boarding of merchant ships:

> "Except where acts of interference derive from powers conferred by treaty, a warship which encounters a foreign merchant ship on the high seas is not justified in boarding her unless there is reasonable ground for suspecting . . . (b) That the ship is engaged in the slave trade . . ."

However, customary international law does not provide any further powers over foreign ships on the high seas in respect of the slave trade, and it is the responsibility of the flag State to institute any proceedings against the ship in question.

Freedom from slavery and forced labour

9–007 Every international human rights document contains a prohibition upon slavery and the use of forced or "unfree" labour, and the domestic law of many States allows prosecution for slavery offences regardless of where committed or of who the wrongdoer may be. The most obvious legal provisions are the Slavery Convention 1926 and the Forced Labour Convention 1930, which are some of the earliest specialised international agreements. There are also many more general applicable provisions. Article 4 of the Universal Declaration of Human Rights states that:

> "No one shall be held in slavery or servitude; slavery and the slave trade shall be prohibited in all their forms".

Article 8 of the International Covenant on Civil and Political Rights goes further: in addition to the prohibition of slavery and servitude, Art. 8(3)(a) states: "No one shall be required to perform forced or compulsory labour".

However there are exceptions from the definition of forced labour which exempt: legal punishment by forced labour; military and national service; compulsory service in times of State emergency; and any work which forms part of a citizen's normal civil obligations.

The 1956 Convention on the Abolition of Slavery, the Slave Trade and Institutions and Practices similar to Slavery (the Supplementary Slavery Convention) was designed to plug several gaps in the provisions of the 1926 Convention, and so does not seek to provide a comprehensive definition of slavery. The 1956 Convention was also the result of much debate and bargaining between the panel of States who drafted it; this process involved many compromises which narrowed the Convention's scope. For example, the UK wished to treat the transport of slaves by sea as an act of piracy, with the concomitant powers of search and seizure, but was unsuccessful in achieving this aim. Further, several States sought the introduction of a minimum age of 14 for marriage in order to prevent the practice of child marriage being used as a property transaction, but agreement could not be reached on this issue. The Convention does not state that all slavery-related practices must cease immediately, but rather that "all practicable and necessary legislative measures to bring about progressively and as soon as possible the complete abandonment" of such practices should be taken. As the UK's representative explained, "practices similar to slavery are deeply rooted in the tradition of many centuries in some parts of the world, and their immediate abolition would cause considerable disorganisation." Unfortunately, it is arguable that this continues to be the case over 40 years later, and perhaps if stronger words and enforcement procedures had been used in the Convention there would not still be so great a trade in human life and the exploitation of unfree labour.

The 1956 Convention has three focuses: (i) institutions and practices simi-   **9–008**
lar to slavery; (ii) the prohibition of the slave trade; and (iii) "certain practices which accompany both slavery and institutions similar to slavery." A few words of explanation of each of these focuses may be useful.

(i)   Institutions and practices similar to slavery include: enslavement as a punishment for, or a method of repaying, debt; adoption of children in order to exploit their labour; child marriage; and the treatment of women as the property of their fathers or husbands.

(ii) The prohibition of slave trading is broadly similar to that under the 1926 Convention and other international instruments, discussed above, but does not contain any enforcement procedure by which one State could use powers of visit, search and seizure against a vessel of another State where that vessel was suspected of being involved in the slave trade.

(iii) Practices accompanying both slavery and institutions similar to slavery include the use of branding or tattooing to indicate servile status or as punishment for attempts to escape, the transport of persons from one state to another for the purposes of slavery, and any attempt to enslave another person, whatever its form.

Thus the 1956 Convention does not redefine slavery or significantly extend the pre-existing Convention's definition, but rather explains that definition and reiterates the hope that all such exploitative practices shall be prohibited. Either it is not yet "practicable" to eliminate all slavery-related practices throughout the world, or more pessimism is required about the ability of legal prohibition to change entrenched attitudes and behaviour, however abhorrent they may be to modern eyes.

The European position

9–009   Article 4(1) and (2) of the European Convention on Human Rights ("ECHR") declares that no one shall be held in slavery or servitude or be required to perform forced or compulsory labour. However, this Article is not unfettered and there are in existence a number of exceptions which permit certain categories of persons to be legitimately "forced" to perform particular tasks. For example, in various States where national military service is still compulsory under domestic law, those eligible are required to serve; if conscientious objectors to substitute military service by undertaking other work. Also, persons sentenced to a term of imprisonment may legitimately be expected to work. Further, a convicted person may be lawfully expected to undertake community service as a means of punishment. In some states where the jury system is in place, a citizen may be required to serve as part of a jury. Finally, in cases of a national emergency which threatens the wellbeing of a State it may be incumbent on an individual to provide assistance during this period (Art. 4(3)(c)).

DRUG TRAFFICKING

9–010   International criminal law is just as concerned about the increasing trade in illegal drugs as is the domestic law of any State (unsurprisingly since the drug trade may well be turning over several hundred billion pounds per year), and international legal bodies continue to search for new and innovative measures to combat the problems related to drug trafficking. Drug trafficking is an offence which rarely travels alone; it is closely connected to terrorism and its financing, to organised crime, computer crime and money laundering, for example. The people who operate at the higher levels of the trade are efficient, organised, professional and often powerful. International measures must therefore attack the problem in all its manifestations if they are to be successful, workable and easily enforceable in a field which by its very nature requires international co-operation between the governments and criminal justice systems of almost every State, whether a State is an exporter or a "victim" of the drug trade. It is difficult to know whether to tackle the problem at the producer or consumer end, since supply and demand are in a somewhat "chicken and egg" situation here. But attempts to tackle the producers have clearly not been successful so far and have indeed resulted in a number of assassinations of the "drug tsars" brought in to implement them, and so attention is focusing upon reducing consumer demand. Legalisation is not a widely favoured method; most States and international organisations prefer the use of heavy punitive sanctions against not only those who traffic in drugs but also those who buy or possess them. These sanctions are usually backed up by treatment programmes for addicts and stringent procedures for the confiscation of assets which either are, or could be, the proceeds of crime. Some such measures, discussed below, fit uneasily against basic civil liberties and human rights.

Resolutions of the General Assembly

Resolution 39/142, passed in 1984 following a series of similar resolutions which began in 1978, adopted the Declaration on the Control of Drug Trafficking and Drug Abuse. The Declaration affirms the seriousness of the international problem and makes its eradication the collective responsibility of all States. "The illegal production of, illicit demand for, abuse of and illicit trafficking in drugs impede economic and social progress, constitute a grave threat to the security and development of many countries and peoples and should be combated by all moral, legal and institutional means, at the national. regional and international levels." Member States are to work together on economic, social and cultural programmes to deal with the problem.

9–011

Conventions

(i) Convention against Illicit Traffic in Narcotic Drugs and Psychotropic Substances (Vienna, 1988)

9–012

The purpose of this Convention is to "promote co-operation among the parties so that they may address more effectively the various aspects of illicit traffic" in these substances in the international field (Art. 2). Article 3 obliges each Party State to establish the following as criminal offences (amongst many others) when they are committed intentionally:

- the production, offering for sale, distribution, sale transport, dispatch, importation or exportation of narcotic drugs or psychotropic substances;

- the cultivation of opium, coca or cannabis in order to produce narcotic drugs;

- possession of narcotics or psychotropics for the purpose of sale or supply; and

- conversion or transfer of property, knowing that it is derived from one of the above offences.

Mere possession of such drugs, their proceeds or equipment used in their production or cultivation are to be criminal offences only insofar as this does not conflict with the constitutional principles of a State and the basic concepts of its legal system. Article 5 provides that States are to adopt measures necessary in order to enable the confiscation of drugs and of the proceeds of drug offences, including procedures which allow assets to be traced, identified, frozen and seized. Financial records should be made available to other States on request, and bank secrecy is no defence. Article 6 contains extradition rules and Art. 7 requires mutual legal assistance between State Parties. In fact, the entire Convention expects and requires a high level of co-operation between governments in order to achieve its aims (Art. 17).

(ii) Schengen Convention (1990): a convention between the Governments of Germany, France and Benelux

9–013   This regional Convention has had a significant, if largely declaratory and symbolic, effect upon international law since Art. 71 adopted the UN Conventions on illicit traffic in narcotics and psychotropics. It strengthens external border controls in order to facilitate enforcement of the UN Conventions, provides for surveillance, and promises heavy penalties for the criminal offences. Much of the remainder of the Convention (which opened up internal borders well in advance of the process in the rest of the EU) has been superseded by the Treaty of the European Union. It is perhaps unfortunate that this Convention did not have a wider application, but in practice its terms and aims are now general throughout Europe.

THE FUTURE?

9–014   Recent press releases from the General Assembly's Third Committee show that drug trafficking has become a priority issue. There is a new Convention against Transnational Organised Crime which should be fully ratified by the end of 2003. There is also a Declaration on Guiding Principles of Drug Demand Reduction which is likely to be adopted in full at around the same time. The Report of the Secretary-General (53/456, 1998) highlights the need for Art. 17 of the UN Convention against Illicit Traffic in Narcotic Drugs and Psychotropic Substances to be implemented effectively and lists current measures which seek to achieve that end. Such measures include improved co-ordination and communications between the various authorities involved in maritime drug law enforcement; the activities of the United Nations Drug Control Programme ("UNDCP"), which has undertaken pilot schemes of regional co-operation in drug law enforcement and runs training schemes for enforcement officials; and the UNDCP has established an Informal Correspondence Group which is assembling a database towards model legislation which would help States to carry out their obligations under Art. 17.

PART THREE: INDIVIDUAL RESPONSIBILITY AND IMPUNITY

Chapter 10

INTERNATIONAL CRIMINAL COURTS FOR THE INDICTMENT OF INDIVIDUALS

INTRODUCTION

The recognition and acceptance of international courts as a means of prose-   **10–001**
cuting individuals for various humanitarian crimes is a relatively new phenomenon. Prior to 1945 prosecutions of high-ranking military officials for
violations of international law and State practices during wartime were
mainly dealt with by either military tribunals, which possessed limited jurisdiction, or in exceptional circumstances, by the domestic courts. In practice
neither forum proved proficient either as a deterrent to potential warmongers
or as a satisfactory solution for punishing those responsible for waging
aggressive wars. After the First World War had ended in 1918 the allies
attempted, *via* the Versailles Treaty (1919), to create a special tribunal to
prosecute war criminals; sadly, this did not come to fruition. A limited and
non-productive attempt was made at that time, in accordance with the
Versailles Treaty, to institute proceedings against the Kaiser, Wilhelm II, for
war crimes. He eventually made his way to Holland where he was granted
political asylum. A request to extradite him was refused and he eventually
died there in 1941; the international community having long since given up
any hope of bringing him to justice. Instead, the German authorities themselves prosecuted their own nationals for various war crimes. However,
despite some 900 individuals being indicted before the national courts, very
few were eventually convicted and even fewer still served prison terms. Reasons for the failure by the international community to prosecute wartime
offenders included the absence of any proper legal enforcement mechanism;
the lack of international co-operation generally; and the well accepted global
policy at that time that disputes between States were precisely that, and such
matters were not of international concern. Moreover, internal State conflicts,
no matter how barbaric, were not, until the conclusion of the Second World
War, considered to be the business of the international community.

Historically, prior to the latter half of the nineteenth century, war was
recognised as a legitimate means of settling disputes between rival States.
However, even then the behaviour of these States during war was not uncon-
strained and through the centuries various rules, regulations and customs,
mostly unwritten, developed which accorded States to recognise certain

international principles which bound a State's conduct in the event of hostilities. These "laws" included responsibilities for humane treatment of prisoners of war, care of the wounded and the restriction and use of particular weapons such as bacteriological and asphyxiating gases. For example, the Hague Convention II (1899) was specifically concerned with the customs of war on land and dealt with the treatment of prisoners of war (Arts 4–20) and with the care for the sick and wounded. The Geneva Conventions of 1864 and 1929 also set about establishing better treatment and conditions for prisoners of war and the war wounded; contracting States also agreed on the prohibition of the use of bacteriological weapons and poison gases in war (Geneva Protocol 1925).

Despite these attempts at bringing about some semblance of international humanitarian law and order to the conduct of war itself, it was not until the Hague Conventions of 1907, particularly the "Convention for Pacific Settlement of International Disputes" that the international community set about tackling ways of preventing armed conflicts arising in the first place and set about establishing regulations for the maintenance of international peace. However, the effectiveness of their impact was weakened by contracting states being permitted to denounce the Convention by notification in writing to the Netherlands government (Art. 8). Despite this "get-out clause" it was generally accepted that these treaties established certain written rules and conduct of war which applied internationally regardless of whether or not States were parties to the various relevant conventions in force. Unfortunately, nowhere in the Hague Conventions was it categorically stated that war constituted a crime; only that a belligerent party, which violated the provisions of the regulations, was liable to pay compensation (Hague Convention IV [1907], "Respecting the Laws and Customs of War on Land", Art. 3). This limited consequence of a violation of the various treaties diluted their overall effectiveness and subsequently did not prevent The Great War befalling Europe in 1914 and nor did it effectively eliminate the use of toxic weapons during those hostilities. Between 1925 and 1939 Germany entered into an era of signing a number of non-aggression pacts with many of its neighbours, notably with Czechoslovakia and Poland agreeing, *inter alia*, to resolve any disputes peaceably through arbitration, and by the Locarno Pact of 1925, Germany agreed to respect the territorial independence of sovereign States. Moreover, even as late as 1939 Germany signed a separate non-aggression pact with Russia and Denmark. But perhaps the most significant and far-reaching of these treaties was the Pact of Paris in 1928 (also known as the Kellogg-Briand Pact). Some 63 states were signatories to this treaty (called "The General Treaty for the Renunciation of War") including Germany, the US, France, Britain, Italy and Japan. Under Art. 1 "The High Contracting Parties solemnly declare in the name of their respective peoples that they condemn recourse to war for the solution of international controversies, and renounce it, as an instrument of national policy in their relations with one another". In 1945, during the Nuremberg trials, the International Military

Tribunal interpreted the Article to mean that war was not only illegal but also constituted a crime under international law. Despite the well-intentioned provisions of the above-mentioned treaties the lack of observance by Germany led to the commencement of its expansionist programme, culminating in the Second World War in late 1939.

THE NUREMBERG MILITARY TRIBUNAL

After the Second World War had ended, the expression "to the victor the spoils" took on a whole new meaning. The Allies sought to punish not only those government and military officials directly connected with the war itself but also all persons involved in humanitarian crimes against civilians including mass murder, persecution, deportation, enslavement, extermination, and in modern parlance "ethnic cleansing", and, of course, the "Final Solution of the Jewish Question". The seeds for such prosecutions were finally sown at the Moscow Conference in 1943, attended by the leaders of Britain, the US and the Soviet Union and in 1945 along with France signed the London Agreement and Charter, under which the International Military Tribunal was established; later to become known as the Nuremberg War Crimes Tribunal. The Charter also established the jurisdiction and procedures of the Tribunal. Its primary objective was to prosecute those individuals responsible for various atrocities committed during the Second World War, irrespective of in which sovereign State the crimes were committed. The composition of the Tribunal comprised of four judges; one member being appointed from each of the London Agreement signatories. The trials commenced in November 1945 with lawyers from all the four major powers conducting the prosecution case against 22 individuals indicted for crimes under three main categories; crimes against peace, war crimes and crimes against humanity. The accused were represented by German counsel.

10–002

Thus, for the first time individuals were held accountable, not only for specific war infringements contrary to international humanitarian law, but also for conduct amounting to crimes against humanity. Also, for the first time precise definitions, in so far as it was possible to do so, were set out in Art. 6 of the Charter stating, the meanings and circumstances by which these offences could be committed. For example, under Art. 6(a) crimes against peace included acts of planning, preparation, initiation or waging of a war of aggression, or a war in violation of international treaties or participation in a common plan or conspiracy for the accomplishment of war crimes or crimes against humanity. Under Art. 6(b) war crimes included "violations of the laws or custom of war", and extended to the murder and ill-treatment of civilians and prisoners of war, as well as the "wanton destruction of cities, towns and villages, or devastation not justified by military necessity". Finally, under Art. 6(c) crimes against humanity were acts directed principally, but not exclusively, against the civilian population before or during the war, and included offences such as, extermination, murder, enslavement or political, racial and religious persecutions. Such crimes made the instigators of and collaborators in war, *e.g.* heads of State, government and high-ranking military officials, ultimately responsible for their actions. The Charter reaffirmed the legal position that even prior to 1945 the laws and customs regarding war were firmly established and universally recognised in international law *via* pre-existing international treaties, State law and practice.

As is immediately apparent, there is a general overlap between the three categories of crime. Crimes against humanity are probably the most extensive and inconclusive offence. Despite the wording of Art. 6(c) that various crimes against humanity could be committed "before" the war, no previous laws existed which permitted prosecution for such a crime prior to the outbreak of the war. The Tribunal declared that "the acts relied on before the outbreak of war must have been in execution of, or in connection with, any crime within the jurisdiction of the Tribunal . . . (and) that revolting and horrible as many of these crimes were, it has not been satisfactory proved that they were done in execution of, or in connection with, any such crime" (see "The Nuremberg Trials" (1947) 41 AJIL 249). This narrow interpretation is somewhat strange since it alters the express language of Art. 6(c), which the Tribunal felt hitherto bound by. Thus, crimes against humanity at that time had to be connected with war crimes in some manner; nowadays this is not generally the case under customary international law. Article 6(c) also includes the words "other inhumane acts committed against any civilian population"; a far-reaching description, which gave the Tribunal wide jurisdictional powers over abuses perhaps not contemplated at the time of drafting the Charter, but which might come to light at some later period. The words could also be interpreted as meaning acts similar to those already enumerated in Art. 6, above.

10–003   There is more than a hint in the above three definitions in Art. 6 that the Allies constructed these offences in such a way so as to protect and exculpate themselves from any action for which they themselves could be technically accused. With regard to war crimes, the devastation that the Allies caused during the war, for instance, the bombing of Dresden, Nagasaki and Heroshima, could be defended, they would argue, on the grounds of being "justified by military necessity" and were conducted legitimately against the "enemy". However, at the time such arguments were considered not to be relevant to the Nuremberg Trials.

During the trials, it was argued by the defendants that, *inter alia*, since a war of aggression under Art. 6(a), *i.e.* crimes against peace, was not a crime under existing international law, any prosecution for such actions was itself retroactive, and therefore unlawful. This statement was countered by the argument that those States which attack another State in contravention of existing treaties (see, for instance the Pact of Paris, Hague Conventions and the Geneva Conventions, above) to which the attacker was a party, must be aware that they were doing wrong and in violation of the agreement, and therefore their conduct was illegal. Besides, the tribunal stated that the

Charter itself was not new law but represented existing international law and thus could not be considered as *ex post facto* law. As a consequence, morally, legally and in the interests of justice they were to be held criminally accountable for their actions (see (1947) 41 AJIL 172). The defendants further argued that international law governs States only and not individuals. This was refuted by the Tribunal which stated that "[c]rimes against international law are committed by men, not by abstract entities, and only by punishing individuals who commit such crimes can the provisions of international law be enforced" (at p. 221).

Further, under Art. 7 it did not avail the head of State or government officials to argue the defence that they were acting under the official policies of the State; such a defence was not recognised. The Tribunal declared that "[h]e who violates the laws of war cannot obtain immunity while acting in pursuance of the authority of the State if the State in authorising action moves outside its competence under international law". Nor under Art. 8 that the defendant was "acting under orders", although the Tribunal were permitted to take this into account as mitigating circumstances when sentencing a defendant upon conviction. The true test, the Tribunal declared, "which is found in varying degrees in the criminal law of most nations is not the existence of the order, but whether moral choice was in fact possible".

In all, 22 individuals were indicted under the offences set out in Art. **10–004** 6(a)–(c). The defendants were also prosecuted for the offence of conspiracy to commit any of the crimes mentioned in Art. 6(a)–(c). The Nazi organisations of the SS, the Gestapo and the Leadership Corps of the Nazi Party were all declared by the Tribunal as criminal under Art. 9 and under Art. 10 an individual may be prosecuted for being a member of such an organisation. Judgment of the trials was handed down on October 1, 1946 and resulted in 12 accused being sentenced to death by hanging (including Martin Bormann who was tried *in absentia*; Hermann Goering committed suicide only a few hours before he was due to be executed). Seven other convicted individuals received long terms of imprisonment ranging from 10 years to life (Rudolph Hess who had been detained since 1941 was sentenced to life imprisonment for crimes against peace; he had been acquitted of war crimes and crimes against humanity); the three remaining accused were found not guilty.

In hindsight could it be said that the defendants received a fair trial? There have been a number of criticisms concerning procedural and evidential matters. Some critics suggested that the mere composition of the court itself did not lend itself to the general legal principles of impartiality and independence required, and thus the whole process suffered from a defect of bias. The trials themselves lasted over nine months, but this must surely be acceptable on account of the unusual and complex legal issues involved, as well as the oral evidence (some 113 witnesses), the enormity of the documentary evidence submitted (approximately 38,000 affidavits were examined) and the number of defendants prosecuted. On the other hand, it may be argued that the commencement date of the trials was too early. Such was the magnitude and importance of the proceedings that the defendants were entitled to more time to properly prepare their defence. The tribunal has also been criticised for hearing both hearsay as well as opinion evidence. Finally, the right to a fair trial was undermined by the fact that the Tribunal's decisions were final; there were no appeal procedures.

10–005   The Nuremberg Tribunal was not the only trial forum in operation at that time; the International Military Tribunal of Tokyo was also established soon after under very similar, but not identical, conditions, where 25 high-ranking officials were eventually convicted. Further, as an addendum to the London Agreement of 1945, the Allied Control Council Law No. 10 established in December 1945 tribunals for the prosecution of war criminals arrested by occupying forces and other offenders who had not been dealt with by the Nuremberg Tribunal. Under Art. II (a)–(d) the Council set out the relevant offences under its authority in similar terms to that of the Charter, with the added offence of membership of a criminal group or organisation, punishable by death (previously recognised by the Nuremberg Tribunal as a crime). Between 1946 and 1949 some 200 individuals were prosecuted under Control Council No.10.

It continues to be debated whether the Allies set up these tribunals for political purposes, or revenge motives, or purely in the interests of international justice, or were they merely "show-trials" to ease the international conscience? Whatever the real reasons were, and it is suggested that the motives behind their decision are immaterial, there is little doubt that these tribunals themselves were highly successful and influential. They focused the world's attention, truly for the first time, not only on the general principles of international law regarding war crimes, but also defined those crimes and founded a proper forum to implement those laws. What was perhaps even more poignant was the credence that the international community gave to matters relating to humanitarian crimes at that time. The Tribunal showed, through these trials, that the international community would no longer tolerate "man's inhumanity to man".

With the dismantling of the Nuremberg Military Tribunals and the other associated forums for the prosecution of individuals for war and human rights violations, the major powers lost both the opportunity and the enthusiasm to create a permanent world criminal court. The general reasons for this would appear to be that all States, both victors and vanquished, wished to concentrate more fully on rebuilding and restructuring their own economies and to finally draw a line under the period 1939–1945. Further, it seemed the general misguided consensus that the taste for international armed conflict had subsided, at least for the foreseeable future, and therefore no imminent need for any further international judicial retribution. However, it was not long before the major powers were again at variance with each other. With the advent of the Cold War era, and in the early 1950s the Korean War and the continuing Middle East conflict, international crises loomed once more. The superpowers concentrated on solving these particular problems and, as a result, the international drive to put war criminals on trial waned as did the momentum and impetus to create any kind of new permanent criminal tribunal. Although at that time the UN Secretary-General assigned to the International Law Commission ("ILC") the task of formulating a draft statute for international crimes, in practice, little headway was made. Instead, post-Second World War, the international community, *via* the United Nations, chose a secondary option by advancing a multitude of treaties relating to war and human rights issues in the form of conventions as well as declarations and resolutions in the hope that signatory states would abide by such documents. Sadly, many of these treaties do not possess the enforcement qualities, potency or effectiveness of a judicial tribunal. Diplomatic pressure, sanctions, embargoes and the like, against those states who have violated their international obligations under various treaties have either not achieved the desired result or have taken too long to work. In the meantime much human suffering will have been inflicted. Besides it is often the case that such measures often result in doing irrefutable harm to an innocent civilian population; the very people the international community is trying to protect. Even on the few occasions where the UN (and NATO), as a last resort, has applied military force, this has not rid the world of recognised tyrants.

In reality, after 1945 few states fervently sought the capture and indictment **10–006** of known wanted war criminals and up until the present day few such offenders have been brought to justice for their horrific crimes. In recent times those who have been tried before national courts in France include Paul Touvier (1975), Klaus Barbie (1983) and Maurice Papon (1996); Erich Priebke (1997) in Italy; and Andrei Sawoniuk (1999) in the UK. However, perhaps the most significant trial to occur in the post-war era by a national court was that of Adolf Eichmann in Israel in 1961. At the time this case highlighted a number of jurisdictional problems likely to be encountered by national courts attempting to bring perpetrators of human rights atrocities to trial in the future. The subsequent trial of Adolf Eichmann concerned for the most part the restricted legal area of the "final solution of the Jewish problem" during the Second World War. Some six million European Jews, along with other minority groups such as gypsies, homosexuals, communists and others who dared to oppose the Nazi regime, perished as a result of Germany's genocidal policies. The trial of Adolf Eichmann commenced on April 11, 1961. It was alleged that the accused, as head of the Gestapo department for Jewish Affairs caused the persecution, extermination, deportation and murder of millions of Jews, as well as their enslavement and torture in concentration camps such as Auschwitz, Dachau and Buchenwald between the periods 1939–1945. He was indicted on 15 counts under the Nazi and Nazi Collaborators (Punishment) Law 1950 for crimes against the Jewish people, war crimes and crimes against humanity and for being a member of a criminal organisation under Art. 9 of the Nuremberg Charter. Although the indictment was brought under the 1950 Act, the substance of the crimes alleged were founded principally under international law. Defence counsel argued on behalf of the accused that the 1950 Act was retrospective and therefore the court lacked the necessary jurisdiction to try the case. This was rejected by the court which declared that the crimes alleged did not create any new offences; such crimes were already established under international law and various treaties. Following the speeches of the Nuremberg Tribunal, the court reiterated that an accused committing such offences could not successfully argue that he did not know or was not aware that what he was doing was a criminal act. It was further argued by the defence that it was the accused's duty to carry out the prevailing laws of that State and since it was the head of State or the government authorities that enacted legislation, it was not the fault of the accused if those laws were contrary to international law. In such cases, it was the politicians who were criminally responsible not the individuals who acted upon those laws. Again, this defence was rejected on the grounds that persons who commit crimes contrary to international law are not alleviated from their responsibilities under such laws.

Since the crimes did not occur in the State of Israel, was this case an exception to the territorial jurisdictional principle or could Israel excuse itself on the grounds that such crimes were permissible as part of the development of international law? The court declared that genocide was generally recognised as a crime of universal jurisdiction and therefore States were obliged to treat it as such, irrespective of their membership of the Genocide Convention. Although Art. IV of the Genocide Convention limits the offence to territorial jurisdiction, the court stated that the laws of Israel did not conflict with international law and had the right to try the accused under the passive and protective principles and hence Israel possessed the necessary jurisdiction in this case. It was argued by the defence that there must be an effective or connecting link between the prosecuting State and the crime itself. Since the State of Israel only came into existence in 1948, after the crimes alleged were committed, it was argued that Israel did not possess the required link and therefore the requisite jurisdiction to prosecute the case. The court declared that the crimes perpetrated against the Jewish people were by their very nature crimes against Israel. The loss of their families by so many of those Jews who had migrated to Israel and the survivors themselves showed that a sufficient link existed between the crimes perpetrated against the Jewish people and the State of Israel. The court declared that "(T)he right of the injured party to punish offenders derives directly . . . from the crime committed against them by the offender, and it is only want of sovereignty that denies it the power to try and punish the offender. If the injured group or people thereafter achieves political sovereignty in any territory, it may exercise such sovereignty for the enforcement of its natural right to punish the offender who injured it" (1961 I.L.R. pp.56–57). Accordingly, Israel possessed the legitimate right to indict those responsible for committing such crimes. Eichmann was eventually found guilty and sentenced to death by hanging.

Initially, because Eichmann had been kidnapped in Argentina and illegally brought to Israel to face charges, it was submitted by the defence that any subsequent trial would be unlawful. The court declared that it was not open to the State authorities to question the methods used to bring Eichmann to Israel. It was sufficient only that the accused was lawfully detained in Israel and that the receiving State had the proper jurisdiction to initiate proceedings. After initial complaints were made by Argentina, that government eventually withdrew its protests.

INTERNATIONAL CRIMINAL TRIBUNAL FOR THE FORMER YUGOSLAVIA

It was not until the early 1990s that the international community again called for a judicial solution to the horrific humanitarian crimes being perpetrated in the Federal Republic of Yugoslavia. In the preceeding years many international humanitarian crimes were being committed which would have justifiably warranted heads of government and high-ranking military officials to be prosecuted for their offences. Prime examples include Pol Pot in Cambodia, Idi Amin in Uganda and Saddam Hussein in Iraq. However, potential despots, as a rule, do not concern themselves with the criminality of their actions nor the possible judicial consequences, at least, within their own borders. Psychologically, they see themselves as somehow being protected and immune from any outside interference. This attitude is no doubt aided by Art. 2(7) of the UN Charter preventing the United Nations from intervening in matters which are essentially within the domestic jurisdiction of the offending State. Indeed pre-1993 such was the apathy and lack of any real constructive headway towards punishing individuals for their violations of international criminal law, that it would not be an exaggeration to state that respect for international humanitarian and human rights laws were being seriously undermined. **10–007**

However, with the break-up of the Soviet Union in 1989 the role of the Security Council became more poignant. Under Art. 29 of the UN Charter the Security Council is given wide powers whereby it "may establish such subsidiary organs as it deems necessary for the performance of its functions". Since the Security Council is charged with the maintenance of international peace and security, this seemingly includes the power to create a judicial tribunal the purpose of which would be to prosecute individuals who pose a threat to peace and security in violation of international law under Chapter VII and in particular Arts 39, 41 and 42 of the Charter.

The establishing of the Tribunal

With the creation of independent Balkan States also came the realisation that this transformation was not going to be a smooth and peaceful process. In particular when Bosnia-Herzegovina, Croatia, Slovenia and Macedonia, declared independence from the Former Republic of Yugoslavia there followed both armed conflict and widespread humanitarian atrocities **10–008** reminiscent of the Second World War. Reports and media film emanating from those territories depicted scenes of horrific human rights violations. Such atrocities included civilians being indiscriminately murdered and thrown into mass graves; the starvation of the civilian population; the establishing of concentration camps; deportation; ethnic cleansing; and widespread and systematic raping. In 1991 and again in 1992 negotiations took place between the various interested parties to reach a peaceful settlement but without success. Eventually in 1993, under the authority of Chapter VII, the Security Council adopted resolution 808 (reaffirming the previous resolution 764 [1992]) which declared:

> "that all parties are bound to comply with the obligations under international humanitarian law and in particular the Geneva Conventions of 12 August 1949, and that persons who commit or order the commission of grave breaches of the Convention are individually responsible in respect of such breaches . . . and to take effective measures to bring to justice the persons who are responsible for them.

> (And) that an international tribunal shall be established for the prosecution of persons responsible for serious violations of international humanitarian law committed in the territory of the former Yugoslavia since 1991".

The establishing of an international tribunal was adopted by Security Council Resolution 827 after the Secretary-General submitted a report on the situation to the Security Council. Thereafter in 1993 the International Criminal Tribunal for the Former Yugoslavia ("ICTY") came into being as well as the Statute of the International Tribunal ("SITY") governing the offences, rules and procedures of the Tribunal. The composition of the Tribunal consists in total of 11 judges overseeing three separate trial courts; this includes five judges sitting in the Appellate Chamber. It should be noted that the establishing of such a tribunal is on an *ad hoc* basis only and has the disadvantage of existing only for the purpose of bringing to justice those nationals who committed serious international crimes in that region. Once that purpose has been fulfilled or is deemed no longer necessary then the Tribunal itself will be dismantled.

Article 1 of the SITY states that the Tribunal has the power to prosecute individuals for serious violations of international humanitarian law. The word "serious" means violations which "constitute a breach of a rule protecting important values, and the breach must involve grave consequences for the victim" (*Tadic* (October 2, 1995) para. 610). Jurisdiction is limited to crimes within the territory of the former Yugoslavia and then only for those crimes that took place after January 1, 1991. When prosecutions take place against individuals for violations of the SITY the question becomes what international/ national laws should the Tribunal consider are within their domain? In *Tadic* ((1995) at para. 143) the Tribunal stated that they would examine: (i) customary international law; (ii) international humanitarian law which includes customary international law; (iii) various other treaties which were either part of customary international law or the State was a signatory to a specific treaty and was part of national law; and (iv) laws prohibited under standard national law.

Under Art. 9(1) although the Tribunal and national courts shall have concurrent jurisdiction to prosecute persons, the Tribunal will have primacy over the national courts; thereby permitting the Tribunal to request a national court to defer the case to their jurisdiction at any stage of the proceedings (Art. 9(2)). Once tried by the Tribunal for crimes under the Statute, the accused may not be tried again by a national court. Conversely, if tried by a national court the accused may still be indicted by the Tribunal if "(a) the act for which he or she was tried was characterised as an ordinary crime; or (b) the national court proceedings were not impartial or independent, were designed to shield the accused from international criminal responsibility, or the case was not diligently prosecuted" (Art. 10).

Within Arts 2–5 there is an exhaustive list of the categories of crimes for **10–009** which individuals may be prosecuted, namely, grave breaches of the Geneva Conventions of 1949 against protected persons and property (Art. 2), violations of the laws or customs of war (Art. 3), genocide (Art. 4) and crimes against humanity (Art. 5).

Grave breaches of the Geneva Conventions 1949 (Art. 2)

Prior to the twentieth century a civilian population caught up in hostilities **10–010** were largely unprotected against the violence meted out by the armed forces to the conflict. No properly formulated rules existed which distinguished between civilians and combatants for the purpose of protection against ill-treatment. It was not until the introduction and adoption of the Geneva Convention in 1864 that victims of war were granted some semblance of protection during armed conflicts, including care for the sick and wounded military personnel. However, the real development and impact of international humanitarian law really began with the adoption, now almost universal, of the four Geneva Conventions of 1949. Of particular importance is the Geneva Convention IV "Relative to the Protection of Civilian Persons in Time of War", which includes safeguarding would-be victims against grave breaches committed during an armed conflict. The other three Geneva Conventions relate to the protection for the sick and wounded of the armed forces on land, as well as those sick, wounded and shipwrecked members of the armed forces at sea, and the treatment of prisoners of war. However, jurisdiction and prosecutions under Art. 2 of the SITY are restricted to "grave breaches" of the Geneva Conventions 1949.

In order for Art. 2 to apply, three essential ingredients are required: (1) grave breaches of the Geneva Conventions; (2) the acts must be committed against protected persons or property; and (3) any alleged offence must be closely related to the armed conflict. Grave breaches include wilful killing, serious injuries and torture or inhuman treatment, unjustifiable destruction of property, unlawful deportation and confinement of a civilian and the taking of hostages (see Art 2(a)–(h) for the complete list). Further, it is now well established that State Parties to the Geneva Conventions possess jurisdiction for such breaches in international armed conflicts. Thus, even in the absence of the existence of an international court, State Parties still possess the power and are under a duty to enact legislation and initiate criminal proceedings against those persons responsible, irrespective of their nationality, for committing grave breaches or alternatively extradite to a foreign State, provided the latter has been able to make out a *prima facie* case against the accused. Such an obligation is contained in all four of the Geneva Conventions 1949 (see Arts 49, 50, 129 and 146 of Geneva Conventions (I)–(IV) respectively). Why "grave breaches" only and not all types of violations? One reason is that the "grave breaches" element is considered so serious that any such violation under Art. 2 constitutes a universal jurisdiction empowering all State Parties to indict or extradite those persons committing such offences (*Tadic* para. 80).

Does Art. 2 relate solely to international armed conflicts, *i.e.* war between two or more States, or can it apply also to armed conflict which are internal in nature, *i.e.* hostilities between two or more existing armed groups within the same State, *e.g.* civil insurrection or rebellion? Those Geneva Conventions which specifically relate to "grave breaches" seemingly refers to international armed conflicts only. Evidence of this interpretation is borne out by common Art. 2 of the Geneva Conventions which state that ". . . the present Convention shall apply to all cases of declared war or of any other armed conflict which may arise between two or more of the High Contracting Parties, even if the state of war is not recognised by one of them". Under customary international law it has been judicially decided that certain rules and principles protecting the civilian population apply to both internal and international conflicts. In the *Tadic* case, the Appeals Chamber stated that ". . . it cannot be denied that customary rules have developed to govern internal strife. These rules . . . cover such areas as protection of civilians from hostilities, in particular from indiscriminate attacks, protection of civilian objects, in particular cultural property, protection of all those who do not (or no longer) take part in hostilities, as well as prohibition of means warfare proscribed in international armed conflicts and ban of certain methods of conducting hostilities" (October 2, 1995 at para. 127). Why, therefore, does Art. 2 of the ICTY not automatically include internal conflicts? Many States would have been reluctant to ratify the Convention if they were also compelled under the universal jurisdiction principle to indict individuals for offences solely related to internal conflicts. On the other hand, a number of judges of the ICTY have expressed their opposition to merely limiting "grave breaches" to international conflicts alone. Another answer is that even though common Art. 3 of the Geneva Conventions 1949 specifically relates to armed conflicts "not of an international character" it does not expressly confer any criminal liability for those in violation of that provision, unlike the criminal sanctions for "grave breaches" in other provisions of the Geneva Conventions. Further, Art. 2 of the ICTY is limited to acts specifically against "persons or property protected" (for the meaning of these words, see *Tadic* judgment, below); unlike common Art. 3 which is wider and refers to non-combatants. Although common Art. 3 does not specifically mention "grave breaches", the development in international humanitarian law in recent years has been such that some States, in particular the US and Germany, regard "grave breaches" as encompassing both situations, whilst other States have not outrightly rejected the possibility that it could come within either international or internal armed conflicts. Notwithstanding this, even if Art. 2 restricts "grave breaches" to international conflicts only, may it still be the case that some internal conflicts possess the true characteristics of an international one and should be treated as such? This was one of a number of important questions facing the Appeals Chamber in the following case of *The Prosecutor v Dusko Tadic* (Judgment of July 15, 1999), the first case to be tried fully before the ICTY.

Facts. On April 26, 1995 the defendant was charged with 31 different counts of grave breaches of the Geneva Conventions of 1949 under Art. 2, as well as other international crimes under Arts 3–5 and pleaded not guilty. He was originally convicted of 11 counts in total and found not guilty on 20 counts. He appealed before the Appeals Chamber, *inter alia*, on the grounds that he had not received a fair trial and in particular that the conduct of the proceedings lacked "equality of arms". He further appealed that the Trial Chamber erred when deciding that it was satisfied beyond a reasonable doubt that he was guilty of two specific murders and he requested that the decision be reversed. The Appeals Chamber rejected these appeals. The prosecutor cross-appealed, *inter alia*, on the grounds that the Trial Chamber erred when it decided that the victims were not "protected persons" under the Geneva Conventions 1949, as recognised by Art. 2 of SITY. The Appeals Chamber thereupon examined in great detail the requirements of Art. 2 of SITY and in particular under what circumstances might a *prima facie* internal conflict, in reality, constitute an international one.

Decision. The Appeals Chamber clarified the legal elements necessary for Art. 2 to apply: (i) The nature of the conflict — the conflict itself must possess the essential element of being international; and (ii) the status of the victim — grave breaches must be perpetrated against "protected persons" or property, as defined by the Geneva Conventions 1949 (at para. 80). Since Art. 2 of the Geneva Conventions applies only to international armed conflicts, could there be circumstances which turn a *prima facie* internal conflict into an international one? The Appeals Chamber stated that an internal conflict may become international if: (a) another State intervenes in that conflict through its troops; or alternatively if (b) some of the participants in the internal conflict act on behalf of that other State (para. 84). The Prosecution argued that it should be classed as an international armed conflict between States, *i.e.* Bosnia-Herzegovina on the one side and the FRY on the other. The Appeals Chamber examined specifically the issue of when a conflict, which is *prima facie* internal, armed forces may be regarded as acting on behalf of a foreign power, thereby rendering the conflict international. The question is how close must the relationship be between a party to the conflict inside the State to that of a foreign power, in order for it not merely to be categorised as a purely internal conflict, but one of international propensity. Further, what is the measure of control required by a foreign "interfering" power over the actual violators of international humanitarian law within the State being violated? Having considered the general principles of international humanitarian law, the Appeals Chamber declared that "humanitarian law holds accountable not only those having formal positions of authority but also those who wield *de facto* power as well as those who exercise control over perpetrators of serious violations of international humanitarian law" (para. 96). Once this proposition was firmly established it was necessary to discover the circumstances in which the illegal acts of a *de facto* group may be attributed to a particular State. The Appeals Chamber examined the *Nicaragua Merits Case* (1986) I.C.J., and in particular the "agency" and "effective control" tests enunciated by the court there (see Chapter 1). However, the Appeals Chamber found such tests to be unconvincing and unpersuasive as well as being at variance with judicial and State practice. Although the effective control test could be applied with regard to individuals or unorganised groups acting on behalf of states, the same test was not applicable where military or paramilitary groups were concerned. The Appeals Chamber preferred instead to use the criteria of "overall control". The question was to what degree of authority or control was required over the fighting on their (the foreign power) behalf in another state in what was *prima facie* an internal conflict. The Appeals Chamber concluded that "given that the Bosnian-Serb armed forces constituted a 'military organisation', the control of the FRY authorities over these armed forces required by international law was overall control going beyond the mere financing and equipping of such forces and involving also participation in the planning and supervision of military operations" (para. 145). However, it was not necessary for a State to go further and issue instructions to the particular group to carry out illegal acts in order to constitute "overall control". On the facts, the Appeals Chamber found that there existed overall control of the Bosnian–Serb army ("VRS") by the Yugoslav army, thereby constituting a *de facto* organ of the State, and found that an international armed conflict existed from the beginning of 1992 and continued thereafter.

Once the conflict was deemed international, the next issue to be decided was, were the victims "protected persons" as required by Art. 2 of SITY, and as defined by Art. 4 of the Geneva Convention IV 1949 entitled "Relative to the Protection of Civilian Persons in Time of War"? "Protected persons" is defined in Art. 4 of the Geneva Convention IV 1949 ". . . are those who, at a given moment and in any manner whatsoever, find themselves, in the case of a conflict or occupation, *in the hands of a party to the conflict or Occupying Power of which they are not nationals* (italics added)". Although the Trial Chamber found that the population of Bosnia were not protected persons, the Appeals Chamber declared otherwise. They stated that "the Convention also intends to protect civilians in occupied territory who, while having the nationality of the party to the conflict in whose hands they find themselves, are refugees and thus no longer owe allegience to this party and no longer enjoy its diplomatic protection" (at para. 164). The Appeals Chamber considered that modern warfare, unlike past conflicts, in many cases centres around ethnicity rather than nationality, and accordingly, "[u]nder these conditions, the requirement of nationality is even less adequate to define protected persons. In such conflicts not only the text and the drafting history of the Convention but also, and more importantly, the Convention's object and purpose suggest that allegiance to a party to the conflict and, correspondingly, control by this party over persons in a given territory, may be regarded as the crucial test" (at para. 166). Once it had been established that the VRS were *de facto* organs of FRY, they (the victims), even if Bosnians themselves, were "protected persons" because "they found themselves in the hands of armed forces of a State of which they were not nationals"(para. 167). Article 4 intends to look to the substance of relations, not to their legal characterisation as such (para. 168). Accordingly, the decision was reversed and the appellant was found guilty of the seven charges under Art. 2.

The above findings in *Tadic*, *i.e.* that nationality itself is not the determining factor, was later confirmed in the case of *Prosecutor v Delalic, Mucic, Delic and Land* (the *Celebici* case (Judgment November 16, 1998)). One of the main legal issues in this later case was whether in international armed conflicts, people, such as refugees, who found themselves captive can be declared as having a different nationality status, despite being in the hands of armed forces of the same nationality; thus falling within the confines of "protected persons" under Art. 2 of the SITY. The appellants in *Celebici* argued before the Appeals Chamber that the Trial Chamber erred in law in finding that the Bosnian-Serbs detained at the Celebici camp in central Bosnia-Herzogovina were not nationals of Bosnia-Herzogovina for the purpose of "protected persons" under Geneva Convention IV. The appellants argued, *inter alia*, that the word "national" should be given its natural and ordinary meaning in Geneva Convention IV (Appeals Chamber — February 20, 2001). In order to ascertain its proper meaning the Appeals Chamber analysed Art. 31 of the Vienna Convention on the Law of Treaties (1969) which states that "[A] treaty shall be interpreted in good faith in accordance with the ordinary meaning to be given to the terms of the treaty in their context and in the light of its object and purpose". The Appeals Chamber considered that such is the changing face of modern armed conflicts it was incumbent upon them to evaluate, where applicable, the ethnic (or indeed religious) status of the populous when determining the nationality of "protected persons"; such an extended interpretation is in line with both the "object and purpose" of the Geneva Convention IV and as set down in Art.31 of the Vienna Convention. Thus, the Appeals Chamber when examining the background to the conflict declared that since the Bosnian-Serbs were acting on behalf of FRY against the authorities of Bosnia-Herzegovina, the former could be classified as possessing a different nationality from that of their captors. Accordingly, the appeal failed.

Apart from the two necessary elements required for a violation of Art. 2, *i.e.* grave breaches and protected persons or property, there must also be in existence an armed conflict. Further, there must also exist the necessary ingredient of a link between the offence and the armed violence. This link need not be limited to the hostilities occurring in a particular area or period, but may also include connected offences which have a bearing on the existing conflict as a whole. In *Tadic* (para. 70) the Appeals Chamber stated that "[I]t is sufficient that the alleged crimes were closely related to the hostilities occurring in other parts of the territories controlled by the parties to the conflict".

10–011

War crimes (Art. 3)

10–012   Wars between States have long been subject to and form an intricate part of
customary international law and treaty obligations. Article 3 of the SITY
refers specifically to violations of the laws or customs of war and includes,
but is not limited to, the use of poisonous weapons; the deliberate destruction of cities and the like, not justified by military necessity; attacks on
undefended towns or buildings; and the plunder, seizure or damage to public or private property. Article 3 deals primarily with war crimes *via* the
Hague Convention IV, "Respecting the Law and Customs of War on Land"
and the early Geneva Conventions of 1864 and 1907 used by the
Nuremberg Trials as a basis for their jurisdiction. As can be observed from
the above discussion regarding Art. 2, that Article is limited to grave
breaches, protected persons or property. Article 3 contains no such restrictions. This Article exists to cover any potential loophole that is not already
filled by Arts 2, 4 or 5; thus preventing a defendant from putting forward a
defence to a crime that was not within the jurisdiction of the Tribunal.
Article 3 is wider than Art. 2 because it involves all violations of the Geneva
Conventions and will include common Art. 3 of all four of the Geneva
Conventions 1949. Accordingly, Art. 3 of the SITY not only covers international armed conflicts, but also internal insurrections and hostilities. It
was stated in *Tadic* (Appeals Chamber, October 2, 1995 at para. 94) that in
order for Art. 3 of the SITY to apply, there must be: (i) a violation which
breaches a rule of international humanitarian law; (ii) the breached rule
must be part of customary or treaty law; (iii) the violation must be of a serious matter (a minor infringement will not be sufficient to constitute the
application of Art. 3); or (iv) individual criminal responsibility must be
ascertained (for a full discussion on War Crimes, see Chapter 6). Whilst
there is ample evidence, *via* treaties and customary law, to show that in
international armed conflicts rules exist for the protection of civilians
caught up in the hostilities, the question then becomes whether it necessarily follows that the same rules will apply for civilian protection in internal
armed conflicts. The Appeals Chamber in *Tadic* examined in great detail the
existing legal stance in relation to civilians in internal conflicts. They concluded that customary rules have developed in this area and that civilians
are indeed protected and "in particular from indiscriminate attacks, protection of civilian objects, in particular cultural property, protection of all
those who do not (or no longer) taking part in hostilities, as well as prohibition of means of warfare prescribed in international armed conflicts and
ban of certain methods of conducting hostilities" (at para. 127).

Genocide (Art. 4)

10–013   On the hierarchy of humanitarian and human rights crimes there can be little doubt that genocide ranks as one of the most serious and heinous of

offences. Genocide is not only recognised as a crime under customary international and treaty law but is also now generally accepted as acquiring *jus cogens* status (for a detailed discussion see Chapter 4). Article 4(2) states that "[G]enocide means any of the following acts committed with intent to destroy, in whole or in part, a national, ethnical, racial or religious group, as such:

(a) killing members of the group;
(b) causing serious bodily or mental harm to members of the group;
(c) deliberately inflicting on the group conditions of life calculated to bring about its physical destruction in whole or in part;
(d) imposing measures intended to prevent births within the group;
(e) forcibly transferring children of the group to another group."

Under Art. 4(3)(a)–(e) complicity in or conspiring to or attempting or inciting others to commit genocide is also punishable.

The meaning of genocide and the above sub-categories of offences are fully examined and discussed in Chapter 4.

Crimes against humanity (Art. 5)

This Article is set out in similar but not identical terms in the Statute of the   **10–014**
International Criminal Court ("SICC") (Art. 7) and the ICTR (Art. 3). Comparable words are also contained in parts of Art. 6(c) in the Charter of the International Military Tribunal of Nuremburg. Article 5 respecting crimes against humanity states that the ICTY has the power to prosecute persons for such offences when committed in either international or internal armed conflict and directed against any civilian population. Crimes against humanity comprise of the separate offences of deportation, imprisonment, enslavement, murder, extermination, torture, rape, persecution and other inhumane acts (Art. 5(a)–(i)).

The above categories of crimes against humanity are fully examined in Chapter 5.

Individual criminal responsibility (Art. 7)

Under Art. 7(1) those individuals who planned, instigated, ordered, commit-   **10–015**
ted or otherwise aided and abetted in the planning, preparation or execution of a crime in the aforementioned offences under Arts 2–5 are to be held criminal responsibile for their actions. The forms of liability were defined in *Akayesu* (Judgment September 2, 1998) (paras 480–484) as follows: "planning" implies that one or several persons contemplate designing the commission of a crime at both the preparatory and execution phases, "instigation" involves prompting another to commit an offence, "ordering" implies a superior or subordinate relationship between the person giving the order and the one receiving it, "aiding" means giving assistance to someone, "abetting"

involves facilitating the commission of an act by being sympathetic thereto. The Trial Chamber also stated that it would suffice if the offence would be committed by either aiding or abetting, *i.e.* attaching a disjunctive meaning to those words. The same is true under Art. 6 of the ICTR for the relevant offences set out in Arts 2–4 of the Rwandan Statute. The test for individual involvement is "(i) participation, that is, that the accused's conduct contributed to the commission of the illegal act, and (ii) knowledge or intent, that is awareness by the actor of his participation in a crime" (see *Prosecution v Kayishema's Ruzindana* Judgment; May 21, 1999 at para. 198). This test is applicable not only to positive actions taken by the accused, but is equally relevant to acts of omission. Thus, under Art. 6(1) of the ICTR and Art. 7(1) of the ICTY liability is limited to actual knowledge of the commission of the offence; constructive knowledge will not suffice to render the perpetrator criminally liable. In order to be criminally responsibile is it sufficient merely to plan or prepare the crime or must those involved actually execute their plans? It is suggested that due to the seriousness of the crimes themselves and the consequences which flow from such crimes, it should suffice that the mere planning of such operations, coupled with the intent to carry out such atrocities be considered more than mere preparatory to the main offence and be punishable under international law.

Apart from military personnel, private individuals acting within the framework of, or in connection with, armed forces, or in collusion with State authorities may be regarded as *de facto* State officials and therefore may be held legally accountable for their actions. Further, the Appeal Chamber in *Tadic* stated that the object and purpose of the Statute is based on the proposition that it intends to extend the jurisdiction of the international tribunal to all those responsible for serious violations of international humanitarian law; not merely to those who actually commit the crime, *i.e.* the principal offenders, but also to those persons who order, participate, conspire, incite, attempt and are involved in the complicity of such crimes. Moreover, even those who form part of a group, but take no part in the actual crimes set out in Arts 2–5 of the Statute, may be found culpable. In other words, such persons are collectively responsible. The Chamber also set out the conditions upon which such persons may be criminally liable: (1) the accused must voluntarily participate in one aspect of the common design, for instance, by inflicting non-fatal violence upon the victim or by providing material assistance to or facilitating the activities of his co-conspirators; and (2) the accused, even if not personally effecting the killing, must nevertheless intend this result.

Ever since World War I it has been recognised both under treaty and customary international law that military commanders may be criminally liable for the illegal acts of their subordinates. Such liability may take the form of positive acts or acts of omission where there exists a legal obligation to take appropriate measures to prevent the illegal conduct. Thus, as was stated by the Trial Chamber in the *Celebici* case that "a superior may be held criminally responsible not only for ordering, instigating or planning criminal acts by his subordinates, but also for failing to take measures to prevent or repress the unlawful conduct of his subordinates" (para. 333).

Article 7(3) concerns the criminal liability of a superior for the actions of **10–016** his subordinates, "if he knew or had reason to know that the subordinate was about to commit such acts or had done so and the superior failed to take necessary and reasonable measures to prevent such acts or to punish the perpetrators thereof". In the *Celebici* case the Trial Chamber identified three essential elements of command responsibility for failure to act: (i) the existence of a superior-subordinate relationship; (ii) the superior knew or had reason to know that the criminal act was about to be or had been committed; and (iii) the superior failed to take the necessary and reasonable measures to prevent the criminal act or punish the perpetrator thereof (para. 346).

Article 7 applies to both military and civilian superiors, *i.e.* Heads of State, government officials, civilians in non-military positions, private businessmen and so forth (see Art. 7(2)). Thus, the military commander who possesses legal authority over his subordinates may be held accountable for the latter's conduct if he knew or had reason to know of the illegal acts committed. But there may also be instances where a military commander, although not legally empowered to issue orders, does nevertheless in practice exercise control over his subordinates. The higher up the chain of command the person giving the orders is, the more likely it is that this will occur. For example, the rules of command of the particular armed forces may be ambiguous, the boundaries of power uncertain, or he may assume *de facto* power over an area or armed group not originally under his *de jure* command. In such circumstances, will he still be responsible for the illegal acts of his subordinates? It will be a question of fact in each case whether the commander, in reality, had sufficient control over his subordinates such that he will be unable to absolve himself from criminal liability for offences committed by those persons (see also Art. 28(a) of the SICC where a commander may be held criminally liable for acts committed by his forces where he exercises "effective authority and control"). The meaning of effective control was stated in *Prosecutor v Krnojelac* as "the material ability to prevent offences or punish the principal offenders" (para. 93). It was stated in *The Prosecution v Zejnil Delalic, Zdravko Mucic, Hazim Delic and Esad Landzo ("The Celebici Judgment")* (IT-96-21-T November 16, 1998) at para. 377 that "the doctrine of command responsibility is ultimately predicated upon the power of the superior to control the acts of his subordinates", and therefore is not restricted to merely legal control. The converse is also true in that there are cases where persons of high rank who possess authority but do not command. For example, the functions of certain staff officers may be limited to carrying out office duties which do not entail issuing orders to be carried out by subordinates, or at least not orders which might involve criminal activities. Such a ranking officer, if he does not possess the requisite control over his subordinates, or is not in a position to prevent or punish those responsible for committing criminal acts, is not himself criminally responsible for their actions. The Trial Chamber in *Celebici* opined that "a position of command is indeed a necessary precondition for the imposition of command responsibility. However, this statement must be qualified by the recognition that the existence of such a position cannot be determined by reference to formal statute alone. Instead, the factor that determines liability for this type of criminal responsibility is the actual possession, or non-possession, of powers of control over the actions of subordinates. Accordingly, formal designation as a commander should not be considered to be a necessary prerequisite for command responsibility to attach, as such responsibility may be imposed by virtue of a person's *de facto*, as well as *de jure*, position as a commander" (para. 370). Thus it would appear that a commander may be criminally liable for the actions not only of his subordinates but also for other persons for whom he has *de facto* control. However, where the powers of control are non-existent or barely present then criminal responsibility will not lie with that particular commander. According to the Trial Chamber in *Celebici* "in order for the principle of superior responsibility to be applicable, it is necessary that the superior have effective control over the persons committing the underlying violations of international humanitarian law, in the sense of having the material ability to prevent and punish the commissin of these offences" (para. 378).

Regarding the mental element of knowledge for criminal responsibility, it is no longer the case that a superior is presumed to know all the activities of his subordinates. It was stated in *Celebici* that "a superior may possess the *mens rea* required to incur criminal liability where: (1) he had actual knowledge, established through direct or circumstantial evidence, that his subordinates were committing or about to commit crimes referred to Arts 2 to 5 of the Statute, or (2) where he had in his possession information of a nature, which at the least, would put him on notice of the risk of such offences by indicating the need for additional investigation in order to ascertain whether such crimes were committed or were about to be committed by his subordinates"(at para. 383). In point (1) above, the meaning of the words "actual knowledge" can be ascertained through being aware of or possessing direct knowledge of the atrocities being carried out under his command or *via* circumstantial evidence. As with all circumstantial evidence it is generally made up of individual different facts which together point to the conclusion that the particular commander had knowledge of the crimes committed, and therefore was himself criminally liable for his subordinate's actions. Examples of such circumstantial evidence include knowledge of the type and scope of the illegal acts; the geographical location of the acts; the *modus operandi* of similar illegal acts; the widespread occurrence of the acts and so forth (see the *Celebici* case at para. 386 where the Trial Chamber quoted the above examples listed by the Commission of Experts in its Final Report). In point (2) above, once he has received information which gives him "reason to know" that his subordinates are involved in the recognised prohibited acts stated in the Statute, then he is under a positive duty to investigate and take some form of preventative action or punish those responsible. If he ignores the information then he himself may be criminally liable for his subordinates present or future illegal conduct. The question then arises is whether a commander is always under a duty of strict liability to know the conduct of his subordinates or is he only criminally liable if he is put on actual notice that his subordinates are or about to commit illegal acts? In order to answer this question the Trial Chamber in the *Celebici* case after having considered Arts 86 and 87 of Additional Protocol I concluded "that a superior cannot be held criminally responsible only if some specific information was in fact available to him which would provide notice of offences committed by his subordinates. This information need not be such that it by itself was sufficient to compel the conclusion of the existence of such crimes. It is sufficient that the superior was put on further inquiry by the information, or, in other words, that it indicated the need for additional investigation in order to ascertain whether offences were being committed or about to be committed by his subordinates. This standard, which must be considered to reflect the position of customary law at the time of the offences alleged in the Indictment, is accordingly controlling for the construction of the *mens rea* standard established in Art. 7(3)" (para. 393).

Although national courts may also prosecute individuals for international **10–017** humanitarian crimes, under Art. 9, the ICTY has the power to relieve the court of this function and request that the case be referred to the tribunal for hearing, circumstances permitting, *e.g.* the trial before the national court was biased towards the accused, or because the case was conducted neither impartially nor independently, or because the proceedings were not diligently prosecuted (Art. 10).

To date some 80 individuals have been indicted by the Tribunal, 33 of which are at present in detention awaiting trial or are at the trial stage. Many of those indicted have still not been apprehended and remain living in the now independent states of the FRY. Top of the list are Radavan Karadzic and Ratko Mladic whose whereabouts appear to be known to the Bosnian-Serb authorities but have not as yet been handed-over for trial to the Tribunal. In May 1999 the former president of the FRY, Slobodan Milosevic was charged (along with four others) with crimes against humanity and war crimes in Bosnia and Croatia between 1991 and 1995 and in Kosovo in 1999. In June 2001 the Serb authorities surrendered Milosovic to the Hague where on February 12, 2002 his trial commenced relating to the events that took place in Kosovo only. In relation to those charges, on September 11, 2002 the prosecution completed their case. As regards the indictments concerning Bosnia and Croatia, those proceedings commenced on September 26, 2002. The whole trial is expected to last approximately two years.

10–018   The initial indictments have all been amended. At present, as regards Bosnia, the charges against the accused are as follows:

10–019   *Bosnia (case no. IT-01-51-I)*

    (a)   genocide or complicity in genocide under Art. 4 of the SITY;

    (b)   crimes against humanity involving persecution, extermination, murder, imprisonment, torture, deportation and inhumane acts (forcible transfers) under Art. 5 of the Statute;

    (c)   grave breaches of the Geneva Conventions 1949 involving wilful killing, unlawful confinement, wilfully causing great suffering, unlawful deportation or transfer, and extensive destruction and appropriation of property under Art. 2 of the Statute; and

    (d)   violations of the laws or customs of war involving, *inter alia,* attacks on civilians, unlawful destruction, plunder of property, and cruel treatment under Art. 3 of the Statute. (See *Prosecutor v Slobodan Milosevic* before a judge of the Tribunal relating to "Decision on Review of Indictment" November 22, 2001)

The above indictment (29 counts in all) deals with atrocities that occurred in Bosnia and Herzegovina between 1992 and 1995 including the torture, killings and genocidal acts committed against thousands of Bosnian-Muslims civilians, as well as the destruction and plundering of many towns, villages and cultural and religious properties, belonging to those people. Hundreds of thousands of people were forced to leave their homes and deported to neighbouring States. In relation to genocide, as set out in the second amended indictment, the accused was charged with: (a) the widespread killing of thousands of Bosnian Croats in 25 towns and villages within Bosnia and Herzegovina including Sokolac, Brcko and Srebrenica where some 7,000 men and boys had been brutally murdered. In many other places leading members of these targeted groups were singled out for execution; (b) the killing of thousands of Bosnian Muslims and Bosnian Croats in detention facilities within Bosnia and Herzegovina, including those situated within the territories of Prijedor, Sanki Most and Sokolac; (c) the causing of serious bodily and mental harm to those groups within the detention facilities by continuously subjecting them to, or forcing them to witness, inhumane acts, including murder, sexual violence, torture and beatings; and (d) subjecting those targeted groups to conditions of life calculated to bring about their partial physical destruction, namely through starvation, contaminated water, forced labour, inadequate medical care and constant physical and psychological assault. The accused was also charged under Art. 7(1) of the Statute in that it was alleged that he planned, instigated, ordered, committed or otherwise aided and abetted the crimes set out above.

Kosovo (Case No. IT-99-37-PT)

Violations of the laws or customs of war (Art. 3 — murder), crimes against **10–020**
humanity (Art. 5 — deportation; murder; persecutions on political, racial or
religious grounds; other inhumane acts (forcible transfer)).

The above charges (counts 1–5) as set out in the second amended indictment (October 29, 2001) deal with the atrocities carried out from approximately January 1, 1999 — June 20, 1999 by the armed forces of the FRY and
Serbia against the Kosovo-Albanians living in Kosovo. These violations
included forcibly removing some 800,000 Kosovan-Albanians from their
homes and transferring them to other areas within Kosovo; attacking and
destroying towns and villages; carrying out murders, mass killings and sexually assaulting Kosovan-Albanian women. The accused was also charged
under Art. 7(1) and in particular with the expulsion of a substantial part of
the Kosovan-Albanian population from Kosovo.

Croatia (Case No. IT-02-54-T)

Grave breaches of the 1949 Geneva Conventions (Art. 2 thereof — wilful **10–021**
killing; unlawful confinement; torture; wilfully causing great suffering;
unlawful deportation or transfer; and extensive destruction and appropriation of property, not justified by military necessity and carried out unlawfully
and wantonly),

Violations of the laws or customs of war (Art. 3 thereof — murder; torture; cruel treatment; wanton destruciton of villages, or devastation not justified by military necessity; destruction or wilful damage done to institutions
dedicated to education or religion; plunder of public or private property;
attacks on civilians; destruction or wilful damage done to historic monuments and institutions dedicated to education or religion; unlawful attacks on
civilian objects); and crimes against humanity (Art. 5 thereof — persecutions
on political, racial or religious grounds; extermination; murder; imprisonment; torture; inhumane acts; deportation; and inhumane acts (forcible
transfers)).

The above charges (32 counts in total) relate to the period from or about
August, 1991–June 1992 when Serb forces along with other police and paramilitary units attacked and destroyed various villages and towns in Croatia
and subjected the Croatians and non-Serb population there to violations
which included persecution, extermination, imprisonment, inhumane living
conditions, torture and mass killings, and the forcible transfer and
deportation of some 200,000 people to other areas and territories.

Apart from the accused being charged under Art. 7(1) he was also held **10–022**
individually criminally responsible under Art. 7(3) for the acts of his subordinates in that as President of the FRY he was the supreme commander and
exercised *de jure* authority and control over the JNA and VJ. It was also
alleged that he exercised *de facto* power over numerous institutions involved
in the conduct alleged in the indictment, namely the Serbian police force,

military and paramilitary units, various political and economical institutions and the media.

The ICTY has developed significantly since the time of the Nuremberg Trials. For instance, the composition of the respective courts has changed dramatically — the Nuremberg judges represented the four major powers; ICTY judges comprise of 11 judges from various States. Unlike Nuremberg, there is no death penalty for international crimes under the ICTY. The ICTY does not permit trials *"in absentia"*; nor allow criminalisation of organisations and whereas the *ratione loci* for crimes at the Nuremberg Trials was in theory unlimited the jurisdiction of the ICTY is restricted to the geographical territory of the FRY. Finally, under the ICTY there is an appeal process, unlike that at Nuremberg. .

THE INTERNATIONAL CRIMINAL TRIBUNAL FOR RWANDA

10–023 The establishment of the International Criminal Tribunal for Rwanda ("ICTR") came about as a result of the genocidal policies, mass murders and other inhumane and grave violations of international humanitarian and human rights law of the then Hutu government in that State in 1994. Even prior to its independence in 1962, armed insurrection between the two main ethnic groups, the Tutsis (Rwandan Patriotic Front) and the Hutu Rwandan government forces (Forces Armees Rwandandaises) for political domination in Rwanda continued unabated. After independence the policies of the first Hutu government only exacerbated the situation and many Tutsis were forced to either take refuge in neighbouring States or suffer severe reprisals if they remained. Over the next 10 years there followed a period of fierce cross-border fighting between the groups, and despite a military coup in 1973, little was achieved in alleviating an already volatile situation. Civil war broke out in 1990 between the Hutu extremists and the Tutsis. On the April 6, 1994 President Habyarimana was killed in a plane crash after returning from Tanzania where a tentative peace agreement had been reached. Immediately after this episode, all-out civil war began, and in the short period, April to July 1994, it is estimated that approximately one million people were slaughtered, the vast majority of which were Tutsis. Originally there were some 2,700 UN personnel (United Nations Assistance Mission for Rwanda) stationed in the area, but soon after 10 Belgium soldiers were killed, the vast majority of those remaining observers were recalled. The United Nations was very slow to acknowledge or take any positive action to prevent what was to become the worst genocidal tragedy of the second half of the twentieth century. The peace-keeping force already there were wholly inadequate to prevent further bloodshed. As a judicial response, on November 8, 1994, the Security Council (Resolution 955) established the International Criminal Tribunal for Rwanda for the prosecution of those persons responsible for serious violations of international humanitarian law in Rwanda and its neighbouring states.

The Statute of the International Tribunal for Rwanda ("the Rwandan Statute") sets out three separate categories of crime which comes within the Tribunal's jurisdiction; genocide (Art. 2), crimes against humanity (Art. 3) and serious violations of Art. 3 common to the Geneva Conventions 1949 and Additional Protocol II of 1977 (Art. 4). Overall, the Rwandan Statute is set out in comparable terms to that of the Yugoslav Tribunal, but with many marked elementary and essential differences. The following discussion will not reiterate features common to the above-stated analysis on the ICTY, but instead will mainly concentrate on the salient distinctions between the two Tribunals.

Article 1 of the Rwandan Statute grants the Tribunal the power to prosecute persons for serious violations of international humanitarian law. However, unlike the territorial restriction of Art. 1 of the Yugoslav Statute, *i.e.* relating only to crimes within the territory of the former Yugoslavia, the Rwandan Tribunal's powers extend to "violations committed in the territory of neighbouring states". Moreover, under the Rwandan Statute prosecutions are limited to those crimes which took place between the period January 1 and December 31, 1994, whilst under the Yugoslav Statute the period commences from January 1, 1991 and continues thereafter.

The Tribunal is made up of three Trial Chambers and an Appeals Chamber. The Tribunal consists of 14 independent judges in total (three judges per Trial Chamber and five judges in the Appeals Chamber), elected by the United Nations General Assembly (Arts 10–12). They are elected for four years and are eligible for re-election. There is an independent prosecutor whose task it is to investigate, gather evidence and prosecute those persons responsible for serious violations of international humanitarian law (Arts 15 and 17). The Tribunal sits in Arusha, Tanzania. However, the Appeals Chamber and the Office of the Prosecutor reside in The Hague. Although the legal right remains for national courts to prosecute those persons responsible for serious violations of international humanitarian law, if they so wish, the Rwandan Tribunal may relieve a state of that responsibility and order the matter be deferred to their jurisdiction, by making a formal request to that effect (Arts 8 and 9, equivalent to Arts 9 and 10 of the Yugoslav Statute). **10–024**

Article 2 of the Rwandan Statute, relating to genocide, is extracted from Arts II and III of the Genocide Convention 1948, and is identical to Art. 4 of the Yugoslav Statute (for a full discussion on genocide see Chapter 4):

Article 3 of the Rwandan Statute, relating to crimes against humanity, is similar to Art. 5 of the Yugoslav Statute, save in three important respects. First, under the Rwandan Statute the crimes mentioned, *e.g.* murder, extermination, torture, rape and so forth (the same in both Statutes), must be "committed as part of a widespread or systematic attack". These words are not contained in the Yugoslav Statute (for their meaning, see Art. 5 of the SITY), although recognised as an essential ingredient by the Tribunal in any potential prosecution. Secondly, Art. 3 of the Rwandan Statute restricts prosecutions for crimes committed against any civilian population on "national, political, ethnic, racial or religious grounds". These words are not included in the equivalent Art. 5 of the Yugoslav Statute nor in Art. 7 of the ICC. Thus, Art. 3 deals with the mental element of the offence on a discriminatory intent basis. This limitation has not, to date, caused too much consternation when it comes to issuing indictments against the various individuals under this Article. Thirdly, Art. 5 of the Yugoslav Statute, in relation to armed conflict, includes the words "whether international or internal in character"; these words are not contained in Art. 3 of the Rwandan Statute. Despite the Yugoslav situation being judicially recognised as an international conflict and the Rwandan as primarily an internal one, the principles surrounding crimes against humanity are perceived as applying to either international or internal armed conflicts. For a full discussion on crimes against humanity, see Chapter 5.

10–025   Common Art. 3 of the Geneva Conventions (Art. 4)

Whilst the war in the former Yugoslavia was looked upon as international, the hostilities in Rwanda were considered to be more akin to an internal conflict. To accommodate this difference, Art. 4 of the Rwandan Statute specifically relates to internal armed conflict in that the Tribunal has "the power to prosecute persons committing or ordering to be committed serious violations of Article 3 common to the Geneva Conventions of 12 August 1949 for the Protection of War Victims, and of Additional Protocol II thereto of 8 June 1977". It might be assumed that a treaty to protect war victims from human rights violations would be universally welcomed and readily adopted by the international community. Sadly, historically, this was not the case. In 1949, at the Conference for the Establishment of International Conventions for the Protection of Victims of War, in Geneva, the International Committee of the Red Cross ("ICRC") forcibly argued that the future four Geneva Conventions should not only apply to armed conflicts of an international character, but to internal conflicts also. This was overwhelmingly opposed to by the other States; outside encroachment on what these States viewed as purely internal matters was regarded as unacceptable, and an infringement of state sovereignty. Notwithstanding this, it was recognised that some form of protection ought to be given to the ordinary civilian population caught up in an internal armed conflict. Eventually, after much debate, Common Art. 3 was agreed upon and incorporated in all four Geneva Conventions for this purpose. In 1977 the situation was further improved upon by the introduction of Additional Protocols I (relating to international conflicts) and II, which supplemented the protection already given to civilians from internal armed conflict. Common Art. 3 states:

> "In the case of armed conflict not of an international character occurring in the territory of one of the High contracting Parties, each Party to the conflict shall be bound to apply, as a minimum, the following provisions:

(1) Persons taking no active part in the hostilities, including members of armed forces who have laid down their arms and those placed hors de combat by sickness, wounds, detention, or any other cause, shall in all circumstances be treated humanely, without any adverse distinction founded on race, colour, religion, or faith, sex, birth, or wealth, or any other similar criteria.

To this end, the following acts are and shall remain prohibited at any time and in any place whatsoever with respect to the above-mentioned persons: . . .".

The list of prohibited acts enumerated in Art. 4(a)–(h) of the Rwandan Statute are a combination of offences described in common Art. 3(1)(a)–(d)) and Additional Protocol II (Art. 4(2) and include, but are not limited to, serious violence, *e.g.* murder, cruel inhuman and degrading treatment and torture; the taking of hostages; the passing of sentences and executions outside the due process of law, acts of terrorism, rape, enforced prostitution, collective punishments, pillage, and threats to commit any of those acts. It is universally recognised that Common Art. 3 is now part of customary international law. Initially Additional Protocol II ("AP II") was not viewed with the same legal importance. However, it has now been widely accepted that many of its provisions, especially Art. 4(2) of AP II, are to be treated as such.

Does Art. 4 of the ICTR restrict the category of persons criminally liable for such offences to those individuals who are public officials or government representatives or *de facto* officials, or may ordinary individuals wholly unconnected to a government office be held responsible for their illegal actions under this provision? In *Akayesu* (Judgment September 2, 1998) the defendant was acquitted on five counts under Art. 4 including murder, cruel treatment and outrages upon public dignity. The Trial Chamber stated that offences under Art. 4 may only be committed by either public agents or government representatives. They stated that "[T]he duties and responsibilities of the Geneva Conventions and the Additional Protocol, hence, will normally apply only to individuals of all ranks belonging to the armed forces under the military command of either of the belligerent parties, or to individuals who were legitimately mandated and expected, as public officials or agents or persons otherwise holding public authority or *de facto* representing the government to support or fulfil the war effort" (para. 631). Since it was not proved that the defendant came within any of these categories, he was acquitted on these charges. The prosecution appealed against the verdict (Appeals Chamber, June 1, 2001) on the grounds that the Trial Chamber erred when applying the public agent or government representative test. Alternatively, if that test was deemed correct, the prosecution alleged that the defendant was in fact a public official for the purposes of Art. 4. The prosecution argued that humanitarian law imposes obligations on all persons whatever their rank or service, "indeed on the entire civilian population". The Appeals Chamber noted that Art. 4 refers to "the power to prosecute persons" for violations of

Common Art. 3, without identifying whether or not those persons must be members of the armed forces or public officials or even *de facto* representatives of the government. Thus, the Appeals Chamber continued, there was no explicit provision in the Statute that restricted criminal liability to a particular class of persons. They stated that "[T]he primary purpose of this provision (Common Art. 3) is to highlight the 'unconditional' character of the duty imposed on each party to afford minimum protection to persons covered under Common Article 3. In the opinion of the Appeals Chamber, it does not follow that the perpetrator of a violation of Article 3 must of necessity have a specific link with one of the aforementioned Parties" (para. 437). This point was emphasised later on in the judgement when the Appeals Chamber considered one of the essential elements of Common Art. 3, *i.e.* that there must be a link between the violations and the armed conflict. The Appeals Chamber stated that "[T]his nexus between violation and the armed conflict implies, in most cases, the perpetrator of the crime will probably have a special relationship with one party to the conflict. However, such a special relationship is not a condition precedent to the application Article 3 and, hence of Article 4 of the Statute" (para. 444).

The essential elements of Art. 4

10–026   In order for Art. 4 to apply the Trial Chamber in *Prosecutor v Kayishema and Ruzindana* (at para. 169) stated that the presence of the following four elements were necessary;

   (i)   It must be established that the armed conflict in Rwanda in this period of time was of a non-international character;

   (ii)   There must also be a link between the accused and the armed forces;

   (iii) Further, the crimes must be committed *ratione loci* and *ratione personae*;

   (iv)   Finally, there must be a nexus between the crime and the armed conflict. (Numbers added)

In relation to element (i) above, there must first be in existence: (a) an armed conflict; and (b) the nature of the armed conflict must be non-international. Not all violence or hostilities within a state constitute an armed conflict. For instance, under Art. 1(2) of Additional Protocol II "situations of internal disturbances and tensions, such as riots, isolated and sporadic acts of violence and other acts of a similar nature" would not amount to an armed conflict. More specifically, Art. 1 of Additional Protocol II is applied to armed conflicts which "take place in the territory of a High Contracting Party between its armed forces and dissident armed forces or other organised armed groups which, under responsible command, exercise such control over a part of its territory as to enable them to carry out sustained and concerted military operations and to implement this Protocol". Although not formulated to be a definition as such, the Article does in fact contain the majority of criteria which would constitute a general meaning of an armed conflict. Whether or not an armed conflict does in fact exist is decided upon objectively. In recent years the distinction between international and internal armed conflicts has become obscure and somewhat muddled. One of the main reasons behind this uncertainty lies in the financial, military and advisory assistance given to various dissident armed groups by interested foreign powers, *eg.* the US in Nicaragua; the Serbs in Bosnia; the Zimbabweans in the Congo, and so forth. Whether such assistance will turn an otherwise internal conflict into an international one will depend on such matters as the extent of aid received by the armed group plus the level of participation of the foreign State in the control of the internal war. It was held recently in the *Tadic* judgment that what is regarded as a *prima facie* internal conflict may become international if a foreign power exerts "overall control" over the military operation of an armed group.

Although Common Art. 3 refers to armed conflicts "not of an international character", it would appear that it could also be committed in international conflicts. The Appeals Chamber in *Celebici* declared that "[I]t is both legally and morally untenable that the rules contained in Common Article 3, which constitute mandatory minimum rules applicable to internal conflicts, in which rules are less developed than in respect of international conflicts, would not be applicable to conflicts of an international character. The rules of Common Article 3 are encompassed and further developed in the body of rules applicable to international conflicts. It is logical that this minimum be applicable to international conflicts as the substance of these core rules is identical. In the Appeals Chamber's view, something which is prohibited in internal conflicts is necessarily outlawed in an international conflict where the scope of the rules is broader" (para. 150). Further, according to the Appeals Chamber in *Akayesu* "Common Art. 3 seeks to extend to non international armed conflicts, the protection contained in the provisions which apply to international armed conflicts. Its object and purpose is to broaden the application of the international humanitarian law by defining what constitutes minimum humane treatment and the rules applicable under all circumstances" (para. 442).

In element (ii) above, the nexus of the accused and the armed forces need not necessarily be a formal or *de jure* connection, *eg.* a military commander or government official; the nexus condition will equally apply to civilian personnel who are *de facto* acting on behalf of, or supporting the government or other armed forces. Thus, civilians could also be held criminally accountable for their unlawful actions. The Trial Chamber in *Kayishema* gave the example of captured members of the dissident armed forces, the RPF, (Rwandese Patriotic Front) being brought to any location within Rwanda and kept there and under the control of persons who were not members of the FAR (Forces Armees Rwandaises). Such persons have a responsibility to their captives and if seriously mistreated may be held criminally liable. Whether the accused does in fact come within this nexus will depend on all the circumstances of the particular case, viewed in an objective manner.

10–027 In relation to element (iii) above, *i.e.* the persons (*ratione personae*) against and by whom the crimes were committed and the areas (*rationae loci*) where the events took place, it is an essential ingredient for any prosecution under Art. 4 to establish against whom and where the offence occurred. The *ratione personae* in this instance refers to: (a) the class of victims, *i.e.* the civilian population; and (b) the class of perpetrators, *i.e.* government officials or *de facto* officials. The civilian population are those persons who are not at the time of the armed conflict members of the armed forces. Although the civilian population is entirely made up of civilians, the converse is not always true, *i.e.* it is not always the case that civilians always form part of the civilian population. In some cases civilians may not be victims. Indeed, they may aid and support an armed group and even fight on their behalf. It would be wrong to state that merely because they are termed "civilians" that they should be allowed to escape prosecution for any serious illegal acts that they may commit. On the other hand, the "civilian population" do not involve themselves in armed hostilities and as such are always entitled to be considered as victims when directly affected by the armed conflict under Art. 4. As regards the *ratione loci* of the armed conflict it is not the case that the perpetrator must have been involved in some illegal act in the same place where the hostilities themselves occurred.

Finally, in relation to element (iv) above, for any successful prosecution under Art. 4 it must be proved that there existed a direct link between the offence and the armed conflict. The link between the crime and the armed conflict must be more than tenuous; it should be either direct or at least closely related to the hostilities. It is not the closeness between the offence and the actual area of combat that determines whether or not there has been a violation of Art. 4 but rather that there is a connection between the act and the armed conflict, taken as a whole. Thus, on this broad basis, what is of the upmost importance in internal conflicts, as stated in *Tadic* (Interlocutory Appeals on Jurisdiction October 2, 1995, para. 70), is "[T]he nexus required is only a relationship between the conflict and the deprivation of liberty, not that the deprivation occurred in the midst of battle". In *Kunarac* (Judgment June 12, 2002) the Appeals Chamber stated that: "[I]n determining whether or not the act in question is sufficiently related to the armed conflict, the Trial Chamber may take into acount, *inter alia*, the following factors: the fact that the perpetrator is a combatant; the fact that the victim is a non-combatant; the fact that the victim is a member of the opposing party; the fact that the act may be said to serve the ultimate goal of a military campaign; and the fact that the crime is committed as part of or in the context of the perpetrator's official duties".Thus, from all the above conditions it can be observed that

Common Art. 3 and Additional Protocol II do not apply to violations during peacetime nor to purely domestic troubles, *eg.* civil disturbances and demonstrations, minor skirmishes, criminal gang warfare and the like.

In recent decisions of the ICTR the scope of the application of Common Art. 3 has considerably broadened. In *Akayesu* the Appeals Chamber developed a number of other elements, some of which are an extension to the elements already stated. In summary the latest tests include the following:

(i)　"The offence (serious violation) must be committed within the context of an armed conflict;

(ii)　The armed conflict can be internal or international;

(iii)　The offence must be against persons who are not taking any active part in the hostilities;

(iv)　There must be a nexus between the violations and the armed conflict" (para. 438).

Omitted from the above elements intentionally is the class of individuals that may be held responsible under Art. 4. It had been previously recognised that only public or government officials could be held criminally liable for serious violations of common Art. 3 and Additional Protocol II. It now appears from the dictum of the Appeal Chamber in *Akayesu* that any individual, irrespective of their status, *i.e.* government or otherwise, may be criminally responsible for violations of this particular Article.

Judicial co-operation and assistance

Under Art. 28 (equivalent to Art. 29 of the ICTY) States are under a manda-　**10–028** tory obligation to cooperate with the Tribunal in the areas of investigation, prosecution and other assistance of persons accused of crimes against international humanitarian law. This includes arresting such persons, and if requested, surrendering and transferring them to the Tribunal for trials as well as other matters such as, identification and location of persons and taking statements from witnesses, etc. (Art. 28(2)(a)–(e)). If a State refuses, the matter is reported to the Security Council *via* the President of the Tribunal. To date, co-operation in this area has proved very successful. Accused persons have been transferred from various States to which they fled, namely, Kenya, Zambia, South Africa, and other African States, as well as Switzerland, France, Cameroon, Belgium, Denmark, the UK and the US.

As of April 2003, 65 suspects have been arrested and detained. Eight suspects have already been tried and sentenced from 12 years to life imprisonment. Three of these are awaiting appeal and the remaining 31 are either at the trial stage or awaiting trial. Three have been released and one has died. The accused have included high-ranking military personnel, businessmen and various ministers of the former Rwandan government, most notably the former Prime Minister who pleaded guilty to various international humanitarian crimes, including genocide, and was sentenced to life imprisonment.

CUMULATIVE OFFENCES AND CONVICTIONS

10–029   The "core crimes" of the ICTY and the ICTR provide a multitude of offences, although the statutory provisions themselves are contained in a relatively few Articles. Many of these offences may be committed in the same or similar way and indeed possess similar elements. There are even a number of different Articles containing the same or similar named offence, *e.g.* torture, murder, rape persecution and so forth. Where the accused has been charged and convicted with such offences stated as separate counts in the indictment, should he be convicted with just one offence or should the Trial Chamber be permitted to convict the accused for all the crimes in the indictment irrespective of their similarity?

To date, the standard practice in cases brought before the ICTY and ICTR has been for the prosecution to charge the accused in the indictment with numerous counts relating to different offences under a single or several Articles of the relevant Statute. In those circumstances such cumulative charging creates few difficulties and the accused may be convicted for each separate offence. However, problems do arise where the indictment contains multiple counts of the same or similar offence, based on the same set of facts, yet classified under the same or different Articles. In such cases, is it fair to convict the accused for all such offences separately when committed within one criminal act? For example, may the accused be convicted for torture as a crime against humanity and then again in the same indictment be separately convicted for torture as a war crime. It is generally accepted under differing national legal systems and international law that an accused should not be convicted for the same crime twice, based on the same set of facts. The reasons behind such a policy originates from the courts showing fairness to the accused in those circumstances in not being sentenced for the same crime twice, and stems from the legal principles of double jeopardy and *non bis in idem*.

Cumulative charging

10–030   A wide degree of flexibility is granted to the prosecution when charging the accused with multiple offences. Indeed, it has become common practice for the accused to be indicted on numerous counts, based on the same or similar set of facts. Initially, the Tribunals were more concerned with the consequences of sentencing than specific charging requirements. In the *Tadic* case the Trial Chamber stated: "In any event, since this is a matter that will only be at all relevant in so far as it might affect penalty, it can best be dealt with if and when matters of penalty fall for consideration. What can, however, be said with certainty, is that penalty cannot be made to depend upon whether offences arising from the same conduct are alleged cumulatively or in the alternative. What is to be punished by penalty is proven criminal conduct and that will not depend upon technicalities of pleading" (*Prosecutor v Dusko*

Tadic, Decision on the Defence Motion on the Form of the Indictment, Case No IT-94-1-T, November 14, 1995, p. 10). This position was re-emphasised in the *Celebici* case where the Appeals Chamber (February 20, 2001) stated that "Cumulative charging is to be allowed in the light of the fact that, prior to the presentation of all the evidence it is not possible to determine to a certainty which of the charges brought against the accused will be proven. The Trial Chamber is better poised, after the parties" presentation of the evidence, to evaluate, which of the charges may be retained, based upon the sufficiency of the evidence. In addition, cumulative charging constitutes the usual practice of both this tribunal and the ICTR" (para. 400).

Whether or not cumulative offences may be legitimately charged in the same indictment will depend on whether the crimes charged can be regarded as the same offence. Such a circumstance is termed *concur d"infraction* or concurrence of violations. In order to unravel this dilemma two main questions require examination: (1) do the crimes charged contain the same elements; and (2) do the laws in question protect the same social interests? In order to answer these questions it is necessary to address the charges themselves and determine whether those crimes do possess or could possess, under the circumstances, the same elements. If the answers are affirmative then the Trial Chamber will consider the different counts unsustainable; thereafter those particular offences should only be classified and charged as one. An example of this is discussed below.

Prosecutor v Kayishema (Judgment, May 21, 1999)

Facts. The accused was charged with, *inter alia,* genocide, crimes against humanity (extermination) and crimes against humanity (murder) in four different "crime sites" in Rwanda where thousands of Tutsis were massacred. In respect of these particular offences there were in total 12 counts (three multiplied by four).

Decision. The first issue to be considered is whether the elements are the same for both genocide and crimes against humanity. The answer is clearly in the negative. There are numerous differences between the two crimes. For example, crimes against humanity do not require the destruction of a particular group in whole or in part, nor necessarily the destruction of any group at all. Also, whilst genocide involves actions against a racial, religious, ethnic of national group, crimes against humanity under the ICTR is wider and under the ICTY is indiscriminate, *i.e.* any civilian population — genocide being more specific. Further, the element of a widespread or systematic attack is not a necessary ingredient in genocide. The *mens rea* for genocide is one of specific intent; the same is not necessarily so for crimes against humanity. Yet, despite genocide and crimes against humanity constituting different elements *per se* there may be situations where legally and factually one crime may be enveloped in the other. In the instant case common to both types of crimes was the element that the victims were part of the Tutsi ethnic civilian population. Evidence showed that the policy of genocide in Kibuya also proved the policy element for crimes against humanity. The elements of the crimes of extermination and murder are not, by any means, necessarily enveloped within genocide and may be limited to crimes against humanity alone. Indeed, the elements for extermination differ from those of murder. For instance, murder does not necessarily require the element of a mass killing policy, an essential

303

ingredient for extermination. Also, whilst genocide must be committed against a specific group, extermination may be conducted against any group, and is therefore indiscriminate. However, in this case the Trial Chamber found that the elements and evidence used to prove these offences were the same for genocide as for crimes of extermination and murder. They found that "[A]ll the killings were premeditated and were part of the overall plan to exterminate or destroy the Tutsi population. The killings go to prove the charges of Crimes Against Humanity for murder as well as extermination and genocide. None of the killings were presented to the Trial Chamber as a separate or detached incident from the massacres that occurred in the four crime sites in question" (para. 644). Thus, once the Prosecution put forward the same evidence to prove genocide, extermination and murder, the Trial Chamber declared that, under these particular circumstances the accused should not be charged with all three offences. Since genocide had already been proved against the accused, he could not also be convicted for murder and/or extermination. Accordingly, in this case the counts of extermination and murder were fully enveloped by the counts of genocide.

The next issue concerned whether the laws in relation to the particular offences protected different social interests. Since the victims were part of the same group, *i.e.* Tutsi civilians, for genocide as well as for murder and extermination, and based on the same evidence, the social interest protected was the same for the three crimes. Hence no difference lay in relation to this specific test.

Cumulative convictions

10–031   The legal principles for determining whether a conviction for multiple offences is sustainable will depend on whether the same act, based on the same facts, violates at least two rules of the provision of the relevant Statute, or in reality only one provision has been violated. In *Akayesu*, the Trial Chamber concluded on the basis of national and international law and jurisprudence that "it is acceptable to convict the accused of two offences in relation to the same set of facts in the following circumstances: (1) where the offences have different elements; or (2) where the provisions creating the offences protect different interests; or (3) where it is necessary to record a conviction for both offences in order fully to describe what the accused did. However, the Chamber finds that it is not justifiable to convict an accused of two offences in relation to the same set of facts where; (a) one offence is a lesser included offence of the other, for example, murder and grievous bodily harm, robbery and theft, or rape and indecent assault; or (b) where one offence charges accomplice liability and the other offence charges liability as a principle, *e.g.* genocide and complicity in genocide" (para. 468).

In relation to point (2) above, *i.e.* the protection of different interests, the Trial Chamber stated "that the offences under the statute — genocide, crimes against humanity and violation of article 3 common to the Geneva Convention and of additional protocol II — have different elements and, moreover, are intended to protect different interests. The crime of genocide exists to protect certain groups from extermination or attempted extermination. The concept of crimes against humanity exists to protect civilian populations against persecution. The idea of violation of Art. 3 common to the Geneva Conventions and of Additional Protocol II is to protect non-combatants from war crimes in civil war. These crimes have different purposes and are therefore never co-extensive. Thus, it is legitimate to charge these crimes in relation to the same set of facts. It may additionally depending on the case, be necessary to record a conviction for more than one of these offences in order to reflect what crimes an accused committed" (para. 469). In *Akayesu* the test appears to be disjunctive, whereas in the later case of *Kupreskic* the Trial Chamber there appears to regard the test as conjunctive. In that case the Trial Chamber gave the example of resorting "to prohibited weapons with genocidal intent. This would be contrary to both Art. 3 and Art. 4 of the Statute. Art. 3 intends to impose upon belligerents the obligation to behave in a fair manner in the choice of arms and targets, thereby (i) sparing the enemy combatants unnecessary suffering and (ii) protecting the population from the use of inhumane weapons. By contrast, Art. 4 primarily intends to protect groups from extermination. A breach of both provisions with a single act would then entail a double conviction" (para. 694). However, it is submitted that, in practice, it is not really a test at all. Indeed, in some decided cases no references had been made to this "test" when discussing specific multiple offences. Where it has been cited it has been found to corroborate other principles already laid down in the *Blockburger* case and those of reciprocal speciality (see, below).

The "*Blockburger*" test

In attempting to unravel the circumstances in which it may be possible to successfully indict the accused for more than one offence for the same act, but under different provisions, the Trial Chamber in *Prosecutor v Kupreskic* (judgment, January 14, 2000), examined existing national and international criminal law. One method the Trial Chamber used in answering this problem was to consider certain criteria laid down in the case of *Blockburger v USA* (1932) 284 U.S. 299, 304, 52 S. Ct. 180, where the court stated that "the applicable rule is that where the same act or transaction constitutes a violation of two distinct statutory provisions, the test to be applied to determine whether there are two offences or only one, is whether each provision requires proof of an additional fact which the other does not" (the *Blockburger* test). The Trial Chamber continued, "the test then lies in determining whether each offence contains an element not required by the other. If so, the criminal act in question fulfils the extra requirement of each offence, the same act will constitute an offence under each provision. If the *Blockburger* test is not met, then it follows that one of the offences falls entirely within the ambit of the other offence (since it does not possess any element which the other lacks)" (paras 682 and 683). Accordingly, the accused may only be indicted for one offence in those circumstances.

10–032

In *Kupreskic* the accused was charged, *inter alia*, with: (1) murder as a crime against humanity under Art. 5 and murder as war crime under Art. 3 of the Statute; and (2) murder as a crime against humanity (Art. 5(a)) and persecution as a crime against humanity (Art. 5(h)). Applying the criteria to point (1) above, the relevant questions are: (i) whether murder as a war crime requires proof of facts which murder as a crime against humanity does not require and *vice versa* (the *Blockburger* test); and (ii) whether the prohibition of murder as a war crime protects different values from those safeguarded by the prohibition of murder as a crime against humanity. In relation to point (i) above, whilst one of the essential elements of murder as a crime against humanity requires that there be a systematic or widespread attack on the civilian population, murder as a war crime contains no prerequisite. Thus, according to the Trial Chamber, in this instance, since the *Blockburger* test had not been met, *i.e.* no reciprocal speciality, then the prosecution should indict the accused for murder as a crime against humanity only. However, on Appeal by the prosecutor, this decision was reversed. The Appeal Chamber (October 23, 2001) referred to the *Celebici* case where the Appeal Chamber (February 20, 2001) there held that "for reasons of fairness to the accused and the consideration that only distinct crimes may justify multiple convictions, lead to the conclusion that multiple criminal convictions entered under different statutory provisions but based on the same conduct are permissible only if each statutory provision involved has a materially distinct element not contained in the other. An element is materially distinct from another if it requires proof of a fact not required by the other" (para. 412). Thus, in relation to where the accused is charged with murder as a war crime under Art. 3 of the ICTY and murder under Art. 5 as a crime against humanity, the elements for murder under Art. 3 consist of: (i) death of the victim by the accused; (ii) committed with the intention to cause the illegal act; and (iii) committed within the context of an armed conflict. Murder under Art. 5 includes the element that the act must be committed as part of a widespread or systematic attack upon a civilian population. Murder under Art. 3 requires a materially distinct element to be proved, *i.e.* the nexus between the act of the accused and the armed conflict; Art. 5 requires no such necessary element. Further, Art. 5 entails the distinct element of a widespread or systematic attack; Art. 3 requires no such element. Since each offence requires proof of elements not required by the other the test is satisfied and therefore convictions for murder may be entered separately under Art. 3 and Art. 5.

In relation to point (2) above, *i.e.* murder and persecution charged separately as crimes against humanity, may or may not fall within the *Blockburger* test. Not all crimes of persecution are crimes of murder and *vice versa*. Persecution may involve the destruction of property and/or injuries to people, short of killing. Murder may be committed without a discriminatory intent. In other words, each offence may possess unique elements and therefore in each case they may be charged cumulatively. However, there may be cases where the crimes of murder and persecution, involving murder, contain similar elements. As the Trial Chamber in *Kupreskic* stated "the same acts of murder may be material to both crimes. This is so if it is proved that (i) murder as a form of persecution meets both the requirement of discriminatory intent and that of the widespread or systematic practice of persecution, and (ii) murder as a crime against humanity fulfils the requirement for the wilful taking of life of innocent civilians and that of a widespread or systematic practice of murder of civilians. If these requirements are met, we are clearly faced with a case of reciprocal speciality or in other words the requirements of the *Blockburger* are fulfilled. Consequently, murder will constitute an offence under both provisions of the Statute (Art. 5(h) and (a))" (para. 708).

The principle of "speciality"

Under this principle, where the accused has been charged with two offences, based on the same facts, and one contains an additionally material distinct element not contained in the other, then the accused should only be convicted of one offence. Thus, where one offence is completely enveloped within another, the question then becomes for which crime ought the accused be prosecuted? In deciding this question, the Trial Chamber noted that "the choice between the two provisions is dictated by the maxim *in tot iure generi per speciem derogatur* (or *lex specialis derogat generali*), whereby the more specific or less sweeping should be chosen" (para. 683). This is often referred to as the "principle of speciality". The phrase means that where there are two provisions, one of which requires proof of a fact which the other does not, then the former, *i.e.* the more specific provision is the offence for which the accused ought to be charged. For example, in the *Celebici* case two of the accused had been convicted, *inter alia*, under Art. 2 (grave breaches of the Geneva Convention) for: (1) wilful killing; (2) wilfully causing great suffering or serious injury to body or health; (3) torture; and (4) inhuman treatment. They were also convicted under Art. 3 (violations of the law or customs of war) with murder, cruel treatment, torture, and cruel treatment. The main question then became whether one provision contained a materially distinct legal element not present in the other. One distinct characteristic of Art. 2 is the essential ingredient that all offences under that provision required that the action be taken against protected persons, unlike Art. 3 which involves offences against persons taking no active part in the hostilities — a much broader concept. Therefore, Art. 2 requires proof of a materially distinct element not present in Art. 3. Conversely, Art. 3 does not contain any additional element requiring proof not already present in Art. 2. Accordingly, all the convictions under Art. 2 were upheld and those under Art. 3 were dismissed.

The above case dealt with speciality in relation to different Articles. The same criteria holds true for offences under the same Article. For example, where the accused was charged with persecutions (forcible transfer) and other inhumane acts (forcible transfer). Although the offence of persecution requires an additional distinct material element not contained in other

10–033

307

inhumane acts, namely discriminatory intent, there is no counterbalancing element in the offence of other inhumane acts required for persecution. Therefore, the accused cannot be indicted for both offences. Since persecution is the more specific provision by requiring the "additional distinct element", the accused can be convicted of that offence only.

Where the prosecution is not permitted, or would encounter difficulties if, charging the accused with multiple offences, for the reasons set out above, other options are available which may be utilised in such circumstances. For instance, the accused may be charged with a "lesser included offence", *e.g.* in the case of indecent assault and rape, the accused would only be charged with rape — the more grave offence. Another option, circumstances permitting, would be to charge the accused "in the alternative", *e.g.* genocide or in the alternative crimes against humanity. This may result in giving the prosecutor "two bites of the cherry", where the evidence is somewhat uncertain as regards the main offence. For instance, under Art. 4 of the ICTY (genocide) the prosecutor must prove, as one of the essential elements, the destruction of a specific group on either racial, religious, ethnic or national grounds. No such discriminatory grounds exist in crimes against humanity under Art. 5, which refers merely to "any civilian population".

10–034   In the course of a trial it may appear to the prosecution, from the evidence submitted, that a different charge against the accused and not the one charged in the indictment, would have been more apt in the circumstances. Or, as the charges stand there is a strong likelihood that the accused will be found not guilty, whereas he would have been convicted on another offence not listed in the indictment. In such circumstances, the prosecutor may request leave from the Trial Chamber to amend the indictment.

SENTENCING

10–035   The overall purpose and objective of the Tribunals in imposing sentences of imprisonment was summed up in *Prosecutor v Kambanda* (Judgment, September 4, 1998) as "on the one hand, at *retribution* of the said accused, who must see their crimes punished, and over and above that, on the other hand, at *deterrence*, namely dissuading for good those who will attempt in future to perpetrate such atrocities by showing them that the international community was not ready to tolerate the serious violations of international humanitarian law and human rights" (para. 28). (italics added)

Restitution is but one element to be considered by the relevant Trial Chamber in apportioning sentence. It exists more to appease the victim or the victim's family and to show society's contempt for the accused's conduct than as a part of the "justice" in sentencing. In reality, the State is taking revenge in the name of the victim. Nevertheless, the sentence should not be disproportionate to the crime and many important determinants, as well as retribution, will be considered by the Trial Chamber, before sentence is finally passed.

Deterrence is seen by many States as one of the most important reasons for any imprisonment term. Whether in reality deterrence works as a preventative measure or cure is debatable and it has its opponents as well as its proponents. It is used to dissuade not only the individual concerned from committing future criminal acts, but also as a type of warning to other would-be offenders that a similar fate befalls those who commit such crimes.

What factors should a Tribunal consider in relation to penalties prior to sentencing the accused to a term of imprisonment? Since there are no practice directions, tariffs or sentencing lists available for guidance in this matter, it is incumbent on the Trial Chamber to look to other sources with regard to the questioning of sentencing. Both the Statutes and Rules of Procedures and Evidence of the ICTY and ICTR do contain broad provisions to determine the nature of the penalty to be imposed. For instance Art. 24 of the ICTY states that: **10–036**

1. The penalty imposed by the Trial Chamber shall be limited to imprisonment. In determining the terms of imprisonment, the Trial Chambers shall have recourse to the general practice regarding prison sentencing in the courts of the former Yugoslavia.

2. In imposing the sentences, the Trial Chamber should take into account such factors as the gravity of the offence and the individual circumstances of the convicted person.

3. In addition to imprisonment, the Trial Chambers may order the return of any property and proceeds acquired by criminal conduct, including by means of duress, to their rightful owners.

Under Art. 24(1) the Trial Chamber "shall have recourse to the general practice regarding prison sentences in the courts". The word "recourse here means that the Trial Chamber should consider the national sentencing provisions of the particular State, as well as the sentencing practices of the courts themselves. But the national laws or court decisions are not binding on the Trial Chamber — they are more a means of interpretational assistance and there is no legal obligation to follow such laws. For example, the SFRY Penal Code allows for the death penalty to be imposed under certain circumstances, whereas the maximum penalty under the Statute and Rules of the International Tribunal is life imprisonment.

Gravity of the crime

Under Art. 24(2) in determining the length of the sentence to be imposed the Trial Chamber will take into account the "gravity of the offence", for which the accused has been convicted. They will analyse "the particular circumstances of the case, as well as, the form and degree of the participation of the   **10–037** crime" (*Kupreskic* judgment, January 14, 2000, para. 852). It is not the classification given to a particular crime that determines its gravity, *e.g.* crimes against human is not categorised as a more serious crime that war crimes, or *vice versa*. Rather it is the severity of the acts themselves that will be one of the deciding factors when it comes time for sentencing. Were the acts committed or authorised by the accused particularly vicious? How many people were killed as a result of the accused's actions? What was the scale of the attack? When considering these types of questions the Trial Chamber decisions are restricted to the harm and suffering caused by the accused against his victims and their families only, as opposed to the overall harm to others in a particular area where the conflict took place.

Apart from the "gravity" factor, under Rule 101(B) of the Procedures and Evidence the Trial Chamber must also consider other factors such as:

(i)   any aggravating circumstances;

(ii)   any mitigating circumstances including the substantial co-operation with the prosecutor by the convicted person before or after conviction;

(iii)   the general practice regarding prison sentences in the courts of the former Yugoslavia; and

(iv)   the extent to which any penalty imposed by a court of any State on the convicted person for the same act has already been served, as referred to in Art. 10, para. 3 of the Statute.

(C) The Trial Chamber shall indicate whether multiple sentences shall be served consecutively or concurrently.

(D) Credit shall be given to the convicted person for the period, if any, during which the convicted person was detained in custody pending surrender to the Tribunal or pending trial or appeal.

In deciding whether or not mitigating or aggravating factors exist, Art. 41(1) of the SFRY (Socialist Federal Republic of Yugoslavia) Code looks at the personal attributes of the accused and should also be considered for guidance purposes. That Article states that ". . . all the circumstances bearing on the magnitude of the punishment (extenuating and aggravating circumstances), and in particular, the degree of criminal responsibility, the motives from which the act was committed, the past conduct of the offender, his personal situation and his conduct after the commission of the criminal act, as well as other circumstances relating to the personality of the offender". When considering aggravating factors, the Trial Chamber will only take account of those matters which were proved beyond reasonable doubt. Whereas mitigating factors to be considered will be those which were proven by the accused on a balance of probabilities.

Aggravating factors

In relation to *"aggravating circumstances"* in Rule 101(B)(i), the Trial will **10–038** consider such factors as the voluntary participation of the accused in the criminal conduct for which he has been found guilty, as well as the methods and nature of the cruelty used against the victims and the resulting mental and physical effects suffered therefrom. The more vicious and cruel the particular acts the more likelihood the Trial Chamber will decide such conduct as an aggravating circumstance. It is difficult to lay down hard and fast rules in this area of sentencing and although the Trial Chamber will take into account the circumstances of each individual case, certain crimes are in themselves almost always viewed as an aggravating circumstance, *e.g.* torture and rape. Thus, the more prominent the role the accused played in the interrogation of a victim, which ultimately results in torture, the more likely that this will be seen as an aggravating factor, despite the accused not actually inflicting the pain and suffering on the person. Also, merely aiding and abetting another to commit rape may well by itself be considered an aggravating factor despite that person not being the principle offender. The enormity of the crime itself will also be a relevant factor. Thus, the greater the scale of the event and the greater the number of victims who suffered as a result of the accused's actions, the more probable it will be that the Trial Chamber will categorise such conduct as an aggravating circumstance. For instance, in the case of the *Prosecutor v Jean Kambanda* (Judgment September 4, 1998), the accused, as the former Prime Minister of the Interim Government of Rwanda from April 8 to July 17, 1994 pleaded guilty to six counts of genocide, conspiracy to commit, direct and public incitement to commit genocide, complicity in genocide and crimes against humanity. In relation to the specific acts of genocide, he was found guilty by his acts or omissions surrounding the horrific events that occurred during the "100 day" period of his leadership, including causing serious bodily or mental harm against members of the Tutsi population as well as publicly inciting others and conspiring with others to kill the Tutsi people and was complicit in the killing of that group. Despite his guilty plea and fully co-operating with the office of the prosecutor, the Chamber rejected his plea in mitigation. This rejection was based on the fact that due to the gravity of the crime; that the accused committed the crimes knowingly and with premeditation and that as Prime Minister he was entrusted with the protection of the population, which he abused. Consequently, he was sentenced to life imprisonment.

Mitigating factors

In reaching a decision on the appropriate sentence, the Trial Chamber will **10–039** also take into account mitigating circumstances, under Rule 101(B)(ii), which may result in reducing the term of imprisonment. As stated in the sub-rule, such factors will include the co-operation given by the accused to the prosecutor before or after conviction. Other factors for consideration will include how major a role did the accused take in the specific events? How high up the chain of command was he during that particular period? How significant was his role in the broader context of the whole conflict taking place in the affected region? Was he the one issuing the orders or was he merely carrying the orders of his superiors? All of these questions are to be determined on a case-by-case analysis. Whether or not the answers to these questions might constitute mitigating circumstances lies with the discretion of the Trial Chamber.

Although defences, such as duress and diminished mental responsibility are not considered defences to charges for crimes against humanity or war crimes, they may nevertheless be considered for the purposes of mitigation. Remorse, which is genuine and sincere, will also be taken into account as a mitigating factor. In *Blaskic* (Judgment, March 3, 2000) the Trial Chamber noted that "the feeling of remorse must be analysed in the light of not only the accused's statements but also of his behaviour (voluntary surrender, guilty plea)" (para. 775). The Trial Chamber must be convinced that the accused is truly expressing remorse and that his sentiments are not, in reality, false. Finally, the motives behind the acts of the convicted person may, depending on the circumstances, also be considered as either an aggravating or a mitigating factor. In the *Celebici* case (Judgment, November 16, 1998) the Trial Chamber opined that "where the accused is found to have committed the offence charged with cold, calculated premeditation, suggestive of revenge against the individual victim or group to which the victim belongs, such circumstances necessitate the imposition of aggravated punishment. On the other hand, if the accused is found to have committed the offence charged reluctantly and under the influence of group pressure and, in addition, demonstrated compassion towards the victim or the group to which the victim belongs, these are certainly mitigating factors which the Trial Chamber will take into consideration in the determination of the appropriate sentence" (para. 1235). Ultimately, as with aggravating circumstances, the weight to be applied as to whether there are mitigating circumstances, is at the discretion of the Trial Chamber. Thus, for example, even though it is usual for the Trial Chamber to reduce a sentence after the accused has entered a guilty plea, the actual weight, if any, will be at the discretion of the Trial Chamber. There may even be cases where no credit is given to the accused for his guilty plea (see *Prosecutor v Jelisic*, Appeals Chamber, July 5, 2001).

10–040   The case of *Prosecutor v Vasiljevic* (November 29, 2002) case provides a good example of the relevant matters a Trial Chamber should take into account prior to sentencing the accused:

Facts. The accused was found guilty on the following charges: (1) Persecution, under Art. 5 (crimes against humanity) for the murder of five Muslim men and the inhumane acts inflicted on two other Muslim men; and (2) Murder, under Art. 3 (laws or customs of war) of five Muslim men. These events took place beside the Drina River. The accused was sentenced to 20 years imprisonment to run concurrently.

Reasons for Sentence. The prosecution argued that there were a number of aggravating factors in the circumstances which went against the accused. They included the following: (i) there were multiple victims involved; (ii) they were killed by the side of the river to avoid the problem of having to bury them; (iii) the victims were verbally abused before being killed; (iv) the trauma still being suffered by the survivors of the shooting; (v) the pleas by the men for their lives were ignored by the accused; (vi) the cold-blooded nature of the killing; and (vii) the victims were selected because of their ethnic background (see paras 276, 277 and 279). The Trial Chamber stated that factor (vii) above would only be taken into account where the offence does not include a discriminatory state of mind element. Since persecution, by definition, requires a discriminatory state of mind as an essential ingredient, it can not also be considered as an aggravating factor. On the other hand, Art. 3 requires no such element and therefore may be considered by the Trial Chamber as an aggravating circumstance. As for mitigating factors the accused, during the trial, put forward the defence of diminished mental responsibility. However, even if such a defence were proved then the accused would not be acquitted; the defence is only relevant to the issue of sentencing as a mitigating circumstance. In this instance, on the evidence submitted by the accused the Trial Chamber rejected the defence. The Prosecution further argued that "(a) the Accused had shown no remorse towards his victims, that (b) he did not plead guilty and that (c) he did not surrender voluntarily to the Tribunal" (para. 296). The Trial Chamber did not attach any importance to (b) and (c), above, since the indictment itself remained confidential up until the day he was arrested and therefore the accused had no knowledge of its contents. Accordingly, his conduct could not be adjudged as aggravating in the circumstances.

The fact that the accused co-operated by making a statement may be given some weight as a mitigating factor, despite the statement being exculpatory. In this case the co-operation given by the accused was "indeed modest", and very little consideration was attached to it. The fact that the accused was married and has two children is considered a mitigating factor and should be taken into account. Although the accused was not a high ranking officer, the Trial Chamber found that "his crimes were particularly serious in terms of the protected interests which he violated — the life as well as the physical and mental integrity of the victims, the consequences for the victims (death for five of them and great suffering for the other two), and the reasons for which these crimes were committed (that is, no reason other than sheer ethnic hatred)" (para. 303). On the other hand, the Trial Chamber stated there are "degrees of culpability within the concept of intention". The fact that the accused did not appear to be involved in the actual planning of the executions but only took an active part a short time before they were killed, was taken into account. Accordingly, the Trial Chamber, having considered all the relevant evidence and arguments sentenced the accused to 20 years imprisonment for the two counts on which he was found guilty.

Other factors

Other factors to be considered by the Trial Chamber include: (i) protecting society against persons who because of their actions are seen to be, for the foreseeable future at least, a threat or danger if long terms of imprisonment are not handed down; and (ii) rehabilitation of the offender is considered an

10–041

important component when sentencing the accused. In the *Celebici* case (November 16, 1998) the Trial Chamber stated that: "[T]he age of the accused, his circumstances, his ability to be rehabilitated and availability of facilities in the confinement facility can, and should, be relevant considerations in this regard" (para. 1233).

Sentencing for multiple offences

10–042   As a general rule, sentences are served either consecutively or concurrently. It is not the objective of the respective Trial Chamber to impose a prison sentence that is disproportionate to the criminal acts committed. When the accused is finally sentenced, the length of that sentence should reflect the full consequences of the crimes committee, or, as was stated by the Appeals Chamber in the *Celebici* case (February 20, 2001) "it should reflect the gravity of the offences and the culpability of the offender so that it is both just and appropriate" (para. 429). They continued "[T]his can be achieved through either the imposition of one sentence in respect of all offences, or several sentences ordered to run concurrently, consecutively or both. The decision as to how this should be achieved lies within the discretion of the Trial Chamber" (para. 430). Accordingly, as regards sentencing for multiple offences, the principles acceptable to both Tribunals appear to be those established by the ICTY under Art. 24(1) in that the Trial Chamber must have recourse to the general practices of the courts of the former Yugoslavia, and in particular Art. 48 of the SFRY, which includes that "if the perpetrator by one deed has committed several criminal offences or by several deeds has committed several criminal offences none of which has yet been adjudicated, the court shall first assess the punishment for each criminal offence and then proceed with the determination of the principal punishment in the following way . . . If the punishments of imprisonment were assessed by the court for the concurring criminal offences, it shall impose one punishment consisting of an aggravation of the most severe punishment, but the aggravated punishment may not be as high as the total of all incurred punishments . . .". In reality it does not matter whether the accused is sentenced for each individual offence or merely imposing upon him a sentence for the gravest crime. In *Furundzija* the accused was found guilty of torture under Art. 3 and sentenced to 10 years imprisonment. He was also convicted of outrages upon personal dignity, including rape, under Art. 3 and sentenced to eight years imprisonment — both sentences to run concurrently.

The accused may appeal against convictions and/or sentence. Article 25 of the ICTY states that "[T]he Appeals Chamber shall hear appeals from persons convicted by the Trial Chambers or from the Prosecutor on the following grounds:

(a) an error on a question of law invalidating the decision; or
(b) an error of fact which has occasioned a miscarriage of justice.

2.   The Appeals Chamber may affirm, reverse or revise the decision taken by the Trial Chambers".

In relation to appeal against sentencing, since there are no specific tariffs in existence to formulate proper sentencing provisions, it is, for the most part, up to the discretion of the Trial Chamber judges to decide on the proper penalty to be imposed. That exercise of discretion is not unfettered and of course it is possible for mistakes to be made. In deciding whether or not errors have occurred it was held by the Appeals Chamber in the *Celebici* case (February 20, 2001) that it will not substitute its sentence for that of a Trial Chamber unless "it believes that the Trial Chamber has committed an error in exercising its discretion, or has failed to follow applicable law" (quotation taken from, amongst other decisions, *Aleksovski* Appeal judgment, para. 187). The Appeals Chamber will only intervene if it finds that the error was "discernible". As long as the Trial Chamber does not venture outside its "discretionary framework" in imposing sentence, the Appeals Chamber will not intervene. The burden of proof lies on the appellant or prosecutor to show that the Trial Chamber did indeed breach that discretionary framework. For example, if it can be shown that certain factors when considering sentence the Trial Chamber did not properly consider the gravity of the offence and the individual circumstances of the convicted person, as required by Art. 24 of the ICTY, then the Appeals Chamber must review the sentence in order to discover whether or not the proper sentence had originally been imposed.

Finally, in accordance with most national legal systems the accused is entitled to a reduction in his sentence for any time served in detention, prior to the final sentence. Also, he will be given credit for the time spent in custody awaiting the determination by the President in accordance with Rule 103(1) as to which State the accused is to serve his sentence.

THE INTERNATIONAL CRIMINAL COURT: A HISTORICAL BACKGROUND

Individuals who committed human rights violations were, until fairly recently, not held accountable for their crimes *via* an international forum. Apart from the Nuremberg and Tokyo trials 1945–1948 (see above), individuals, whether government officials, high-ranking military officers or ordinary civilian officials were never brought to justice at an international level for humanitarian crimes and very rarely by their own national courts. From 1948–1993 lacklustre attempts were made *via* various international conventions to encourage the establishment of an international court. For example, in 1948 the vast majority of States adopted The Prevention and Punishment of the Crime of

10–043

Genocide ("the Genocide Convention"). Article VI stipulates that genocide constitutes an international crime and those responsible "shall be tried by a competent tribunal of the State in the territory of which the act was committed or by such international penal tribunal as may have jurisdiction . . .". Sadly, no international *forum conveniens* was afterwards established for the perpetrators of such a crime. In 1951 and again in 1953 the General Assembly assigned to the International Law Commission ("ILC") the task of preparing a draft statute for the possible setting up of an international court, but even these efforts largely resulted in stagnation over the following 40 years.

It was not until the dramatic human rights violations perpetrated in the Former Yugoslavia and Rwanda in the early 1990's that the international community decided once more to put on trial those persons responsible for committing such atrocities. Accordingly, in 1993 the International Criminal Tribunal for The Former Yugoslavia (Security Council Resolution 827) and shortly after a similar tribunal for Rwanda (1994) (see above) were set up to hold accountable those individuals accused of committing international humanitarian crimes. Their primary function was the prosecution of individuals for the main international "core crimes", *i.e.* grave breaches of the Geneva Conventions 1949, genocide, war crimes and crimes against humanity. Unfortunately, from their inception, these tribunals lacked the essential ingredient of permanency; a fundamental element for any future international court. The idea of a permanent criminal court really only gathered momentum after 1989 when at the request of the General Assembly, the ILC were again invited to prepare a draft statute for the setting up of such a court. Eventually in 1994 a draft statute was submitted to the General Assembly for consideration. Subsequently, the Preparatory Committee on the Establishment of an ICC was created in late 1995 to examine the draft statute and met in session on six occasions from 1996–1998 to debate the whole issue, culminating with the UN Diplomatic Conference held on the July 17, 1998 in Rome. This conference was attended by some 160 States as well as human rights representatives from 14 specialised agencies, 17 intergovernmental and 124 non-governmental organisations. At its conclusion the Rome Statute of the International Criminal Court ("ICC") was adopted overwhelmingly in a non-recorded vote by 120 States, with seven against (including US, China and India) and with 21 abstentions (including Turkey, Singapore, Sri Lanka and Mexico). However, negotiations were often rombustuous and intense with many states vehemently voicing their concerns. For instance, India and Mexico protested against the non-inclusion of the prohibition of nuclear weapons as a war crime. Turkey and Sri-Lanka objected to terrorism not being included as a crime. The US refused to support the Statute. Apart from recommending various amendments, which were overwhelmingly rejected by the other participating members, the US felt that as the Statute stands it was possible that individuals, especially from its armed forces abroad could be prosecuted for various criminal acts committed, even in a State that had not ratified the Statute. They felt that there was an inherent danger that non-friendly states might either through revenge or malice instigate prosecutions against American citizens.

A minimum of 60 ratifications were required before the court could formally become fully operational. The pace for ratification gathered momentum in recent years and the required quota was finally reached in April 11, 2002; the court being set up in July of that year. The period for signing the Statute ended December 31, 2000. After that date those who had not signed will not be entitled to be part of the Assembly of State Parties. When the court is fully up-and-running it will possess wide jurisdictional powers and not be bound by the constraints of existing international tribunals. At the very outset it must be pointed out that the ICC is the first international court to be established by, and with the co-operation of, the world community; unlike previous and existing international tribunals, *e.g.* Nuremberg and Tokyo War Crimes Tribunals (created by the major Allied Powers) or the ICTY and ICTR (set up under different resolutions of the Security Council). The Statute itself, with all its ambiguities and unresolved questions, must still be respected and admired in its entirety for its comprehensiveness and its expediency to be completed by the conclusion of the Rome Conference. To amass representatives of the majority of the world's nations under one roof to negotiate, debate and make positive contributions to the formulation of the Statute, is in itself no mean feat.

A brief comparison at this early stage between the ICC and other existing **10–044** forums is important to appreciate the developments made at the Rome Conference. For example, some of the differences between the ICC and the other tribunals are as follows:

(a) Permanence, unlike the International Tribunals of former Yugoslavia and Rwanda which were set up for the specific purposes of human rights atrocities of those States and will eventually be disbanded at some time in the future, *i.e.* they remain merely *ad hoc* tribunals.

(b) For the prosecution of individuals only; unlike the existing ICJ which is for the hearing of complaints by States against other States.

(c) For the prosecution of grave humanitarian and human rights crimes globally; they are not geographically confined, as is the Yugoslavia Tribunal.

(d) Complementary to national criminal jurisdictions; so that foremost it is the responsibility of Party States to bring those individuals to justice *via* their own national courts.

(e) Concerned with internal armed conflict crimes as well as international humanitarian crimes. Indeed, no nexus to an armed conflict will be necessary, if other conditions are met.

(f) Ratified by States which will thereafter accept the binding jurisdiction of the court; and not established *via* Security Council resolutions.

(g) Granting to the Prosecutor powers to initiate his investigations by *proprio motu* (of his own motion).

(h) The jurisdiction of the court will not be confined to territorial and/or nationality conditions.

(i) Only possessing jurisdiction over crimes committed after the establishment of the ICC; unlike the Yugoslav and Rwandan Tribunals, which has the power to prosecute individuals for crimes prior to the setting up of those tribunals.

(j) The Statute of the ICC is much more detailed than either the ICTY or the ICTR and incorporates "elements of crimes" provisions which will be used by the court as interpretational aids.

(k) State Parties are obligated to incorporate relevant Articles of the ICC into their own national laws.

BASIS OF THE ICC

10–045   The laws, rules and procedures are set out in the Statute of the International Court ("the Statute") and must be applied in accordance with international law. Included in the Preamble to the Statute are the aims and objectives of the court "[A]ffirming that the most serious crimes of concern to international community as a whole must not go unpunished and that their effective prosecution must be ensured by taking measures at the national level and by enhancing international co-operation, and "determined to put an end to impunity for the perpetrators of these crimes" and "reaffirming the Purposes and Principles of the Charter of the United Nations . . . ".

Part 1 "The Court" (Arts 1–4)

10–046   The composition of the court itself is made up of 18 judges; elected by secret ballot by the Assembly of State Parties. After the first election judges shall serve for a period of nine years and not be eligible for re-election (Art. 36(9)(a)–(c)). No two judges may be nationals of the same State (Art. 36(7)). The court will consist of various Chambers namely, the Pre-Trial Chamber, the Trial Chamber and Appeals Chamber. The various officials concerned include the President, the prosecutor and registrar. The President and the First and Second Vice-Presidents shall be elected by an absolute majority of the judges, and serve for a term of three years and be eligible for re-election once (Art. 38(1). An independent prosecutor shall be elected by an absolute majority of the Assembly of State Parties and shall serve for a term of nine years and not be eligible for re-election (Art. 42(4)).

Under Art. 1 of the Statute "the Court shall have the power to exercise its jurisdictions over persons for the most serious crimes of international concern." Further, the court shall be "complementary to national criminal jurisdiction". Thus, it is hoped that its services will only by called upon as a last resort and only then under very specific circumstances. Initially, it is the obligation of the particular State to bring to justice the responsible individual or individuals. If they cannot or are unwilling to sanction justice against those particular perpetrators of international crime, it is only then that the functions and powers of the ICC will be called upon to fulfil that role. The purpose of "complementarity" is twofold. First, State Parties would have been more reluctant to ratify the Statute if it meant soley divesting the power to prosecute their own nationals in the ICC, without the right to first has the option of putting on trial such persons before the national courts. In some respects it would have been seen as surrendering their judicial sovereignty. Secondly, trials of this nature have to be carried out fairly and expeditiously. In many instances, it will be easier to gather evidence and reports if the trial is held in the same territory where the crimes were carried out. Moreover, as may be observed from the present international tribunals, the time between arrest and trial are often very lengthy and this may alleviated where national courts take over the investigation and ultimate trial of a person prosecuted for international crimes.

The court will normally sit in The Hague, but may function elsewhere, when it is convenient to do so (Art. 3). Further, under Art. 4(2) of the Statute the court may exercise its functions and powers on the territory of contracting states but also, "by special agreement", on the territory of non-Party States.

Part 2– "Crimes and Jurisdiction" (Arts 5–21)

Under Art. 5 there is an exhaustive list of serious crimes that will come within the jurisdiction of the court. They are: **10–047**

- (a)   the crime of genocide;

- (b)   crimes against humanity;

- (c)   war crimes; and

- (d)   the crime of aggression.

The most intense discussions that took place during the Rome Conference concerned the categories of crimes that would eventually come within the jurisdiction of the court. If the selection of serious crimes was too wide this would undoubtedly have inhibited States signing up to the Statute. Eventually, agreement was reached on the existing core crimes under customary international law, *i.e.* genocide, crimes against humanity and war crimes. Although the crime of aggression is listed as a serious crime under the Statute, no consensus was reached as to its definition. Further debate on this particular offence will only be considered at some future date by a Review Conference. Accordingly, at present, this is not an active offence.

(a) The crime of genocide (Art. 6)

10–048   Genocide, as an international crime, has been universally recognised both under customary international law and by the Genocide Convention of 1948, but unfortunately, until recently, had been completely ineffectual in bringing those individuals responsible to international justice. On the hierarchy of humanitarian and human rights crimes there can be little doubt that genocide ranks as one of the most serious and heinous of offences. Genocide is not only recognised as a crime under customary international and treaty law but is also now generally accepted as acquiring *jus cogens* status (for a detailed discussion see Chapter 4).

Genocide is defined in Art. 6 of the Statute (adopting the exact definition of the Genocide Convention) and is concerned with the intended annihilation of a protected group, be it national, ethnical, racial or religious. Acts of genocide may only be committed "with intent to destroy, in whole or in part", a particular group (see above, Art. II of Genocide Convention, Chapter 4).

(b) Crimes against humanity (Art. 7)

10–049   Prosecutions for crimes against humanity really came to the fore as a result of the London Agreement and Charter in 1945 and consequently became a major indictable offence during the Nuremberg and Tokyo trials and other tribunals at that time, and the recent Yugoslavian and Rwandan Tribunals. This particular offence is not limited to internal and international conflicts but also may occur in peacetime. The enumerated list of offences under the ICC has been extended and the meanings of these crimes have been set out separately in Art. 7(2). Although under Art. 3 of the ICTR the victims of this offence are limited to those attacks against the civilian population on national, political, ethnic, racial or religious grounds, the ICC extends the grounds (save for the offence of persecution) to *any* civilian population; in line with Art. 5 of the ICTY (for a full discussion of this offence see Chapter 5).

(c) War crimes (Art. 8)

10–050   For the 100 years war crimes have been recognised as an offence under customary international law and various international treaties, *e.g.* Hague

Convention IV (1907), Geneva Conventions, the Pact of Paris (1928) and the London Charter of 1945. The extended definition of war crimes is stated under Art. 8 of the Statute and includes under Art. 8(2)(a), grave breaches of the Geneva Conventions 1949, namely: (i) wilful killing; (ii) torture or inhuman treatment, including biological experiments; (iii) wilfully causing great suffering, or serious injury to body or health; and (iv) extensive destruction and appropriation of property, not justified by military necessity and carried out unlawfully and wantonly. Also included in this category are other serious violations of the laws and customs applicable in international armed conflict (Art. 8(2)(a)(b)); namely, intentionally directing attacks against the civilian population or non-military objectives, *e.g.* hospitals, religious temples, schools and villages; or against those persons or property involved in a humanitarian capacity in accordance with the UN Charter, *e.g.* UN peace keeping forces and the International Red Cross. War crimes also include killing or wounding treacherously individuals belonging to the hostile nations army or declaring that no quarter will be given; pillaging, rape, enforced prostitution, sexual slavery and other forms of sexual violence which constitute a grave breach of the Geneva Conventions; the bombing of non-military targets or using asphyxiating and poison weapons or gases. Surprisingly enough, the use of biological and chemical materials has not been prohibited. Also excluded from this list is the prohibition of nuclear weapons and in general weapons of mass destruction, the existence and use of which are not considered a crime under international law. At the Rome Conference many nuclear and non-nuclear States (including India, Cuba, the Arab States and Egypt) requested for it to be included in the Statute (for a full list see Art. 8(2)(a)(i)–(xxvi)).

Under Art. 8(2)(c)–(f) where the armed conflict is *not* of an international nature, Art. 3 common to all of the four Geneva Conventions (1949) (for a full discussion see Chapter 6) will apply, *i.e.* those persons who form part of the civilian population, or prisoners of the armed conflict, or those persons who have been detained, injured or sick as a result of the hostilities. Such persons are to be protected against torture, cruel treatment, violence, humiliating or degrading treatment, hostage taking, conscripting children under the age of 15 into the armed forces and execution without a fair trial. In general, any of the series of serious violations which are attributable to armed conflicts and which are not of an international nature but which come within the confines of customary international law, *e.g.* attacks on civilians and non-participants, sexual offences (see specifically Art. 8(2)(e)(i)–(xii)). However, domestic situations such as riots, isolated and sporadic acts of violence, *e.g.* civil disorder, violent demonstrations and the like, do not apply to the war crimes protections. Notwithstanding, internal conflicts do come within the meaning of war crimes where there exists a long-term armed conflict between the state and organised armed groups or between such groups (Art. 8(2)(f)). Despite the acknowledgement that acts of terrorism *per se* are not presently within the jurisdiction of the ICC (at the Rome Conference certain States argued for the incorporation of terrorism as a war crime, including Turkey and Sri Lanka), this particular Article would suggest exactly the opposite interpretation, unless it refers to only non-political groups of the purely domestic criminal kind.

Under Art. 8(1) war crimes jurisdiction will only apply where the actions are "part of a plan or policy or as part of a large scale commission of such crimes". Therefore, the ICC may have jurisdiction over armed conflicts which are not only of an international nature, but may include serious violation during domestic conflicts, and civilians and prisoners have certain rights which are applicable to both international and international war conflicts.

(d) Acts of aggression

10–051   At present, there is no definition in the statute itself on the meaning of the term "acts of aggression". The expression may include the description *"with the object of establishing a military occupation of, or annexing, the territory"* (UNGA resolution 3314 of 1974 adapted from the Nuremberg principles). The court will only have jurisdiction on this particular crime once a definition has been formulated. This is expressly provided for by Art. 5(2). The reason for this omission was simply that during the Rome conference, the participating members could not reach an agreement concerning the meaning of the words. Indeed some States argued whether such acts should be included as a crime at all. It is interesting to note that those who voiced their concerns the loudest, *e.g.* India, China, Pakistan and Russia, have unsettled territorial problems outside of their own immediate borders. The whole issue has long been a very sensitive area in international law, although at Nuremburg aggression was included as a crime. Chapter VII of the UN Charter (Art. 39) does mention the consequences of an act of aggression (in conjunction with "threat to the peace and breach of the peace") but does not define thereafter the words. A definition was given by the General Assembly in 1974 by Resolution 3314 (69 A.J.I.L. 480) as ". . . the use of force by a state against the sovereignty, territorial integrity or political independence of another state, or in any other manner inconsistent with the Charter of the UN..."(Art. 1) and therefore would include such actions as invasion by armed forces, bombardment, sending mercenaries into another state, using another state from which to attack a third State or using blockades against a neighbouring State (Art. 3), but excludes economic aggression. This is neither a precise nor proper definition since it seems to exclude internal aggression. However the words "or in any manner inconsistent with the Charter of the UN" would probably include certain internal matters. But, as against this it may be argued that a State would invoke Art. 2(7) as such types of aggression being purely an internal dispute, and not one for consideration by outside interference.

The Elements of Crimes provisions (Art. 9)

Unlike the ICTY and ICTR the elements of these crimes are set out in **10–052** detail under the present Statute. Article 9 states that "[T]he Elements of Crimes shall assist the Court in the interpretation and application of the articles 6,7 and 8". The words "shall assist the Court" mean that the elements are used as an interpretational aid as opposed to being binding on the court. The elements themselves are not necessarily permanent. Amendments may be be proposed by any State Party; judges acting by an absolute majority; or by the prosecutor, and adopted by a two-thirds majority of the members of the Assembly of State Parties (Art. 9(2)). The elements of crimes provisions were eventually decided upon in the finalised draft text of the Report of the Preparatory Commission for the International Criminal Court (PCNICC) on June 30, 2000. The actual workings of the elements of crimes can best be illustrated by way of example. In relation to genocide (PCNICC/2000/INF/33/Add.2) each category of crime comprises its own individual elements. For example, in Art. 6(c) relating specifically to "deliberately inflicting on the group conditions of life calculated to bring about its physical destruction in whole or in part", the Elements consist of the following:

1. The perpetrator inflicted certain conditions of life upon one or more persons.

2. Such person or persons belonged to a particular national, ethnical, racial or religious group.

3. The perpetrator intended to destroy, in whole or in part, that national, ethnical, racial or religious group, as such.

4. The conditions of life were calculated to bring about the physical destruction of that group, in whole or in part.

5. The conduct took place in the context of a manifest pattern of similar conduct directed against that group or was conduct that could itself effect such destruction.

The words stated in paras 2, 3 and 5 above are common throughout all of enumerated offences in Art. 6(a)–(e). (see Appendix 9 for full citation of the offences)

The status of the perpetrator is immaterial, *i.e.* acts of genocide may be carried out by either government officials or private individuals. Finally, although not expressly stipulated in Art. 6, in accordance with Art. 1 of the Genocide Convention, acts of genocide may take place during war or peacetime and in circumstances of an armed conflict which is either of an international or internal nature.

he extent of the jurisdiction of the ICC

10–053 The court has jurisdiction only with respect to crimes committed after the entry into force of this statute (Art. 11). Once a State has ratified this statute, then that State automatically submits to its jurisdiction. However, there is an exception to this under Art. 124. This Article allows a State Party the option of declaring that it will not be bound by the jurisdiction of the court for a period of seven years for war crimes committed in its territory or by one of its nationals from the date of ratification by that State. This declaration is limited to war crimes and excludes all other offences in Arts 6 and 7 and whether or not it also applies to acts of aggression is still to be decided.

Arts 13–15 refer to the special circumstances by which the court may exercise its jurisdiction for the prosecution of the international crimes set out in Art. 5. They are, as follows, under Art. 13:

(a) A State Party may refer a situation to the prosecutor in accordance with Art. 14.

(b) The Security Council may, under Chapter VII, refer a situation to the prosecutor for investigation.

(c) The Prosecutor may initiate an investigation *proprio motu* (on his own initiative) on the basis of information received of crimes within the jurisdiction of the court in accordance with Art. 15.

It is of the utmost importance that the ICC should be fair, effective, independent, impartial and free from encumbrances and pressure from outside influences. Likewise, the office of the investigating Prosecutor should expound those same attributes. Under Art. 15(2), the Prosecutor is to be given a free hand in analysing the seriousness of the particular international crime, including receiving reports and information from various sources, *e.g.* states, the United Nations, inter-governmental and NGOs or indeed any reliable sources where information may be gathered, including individuals. Under Art. 15(3), once the Prosecutor is convinced that an investigation is warranted, he will then submit a request to the Pre-Trial Chamber for authorisation to commence investigations. Once the Pre-Trial Chamber considers that "there is a reasonable basis to proceed with an investigation", then it will authorise the commencement of a full investigation. As part of this investigation, victims are permitted to make representations to the Pre-Trial Chamber along with legally admissible supporting material. If the Pre-Trial Chamber refuses the Prosecutor's request, the latter may at some future date resubmit his application should new facts or evidence come to his notice. It is immediately recognisable that the Pre-Trial Chamber plays a vital role throughout the stages of any investigation and possesses the power to curtail the Prosecutor's so-called independent authority. The functions of the Pre-Trial Chamber are set out in Art. 57 and include being permitted to rule on a number of issues contained in Arts 15, 18, 19, 54(2), 61(7), and 72. In the aforementioned Articles a majority ruling, at least, by the judges is required before any of their decisions may be implemented. However, under Art. 57(1)(b) "in all other cases, a single judge of the Pre-Trial Chamber may exercise the functions provided for in this Statute, unless otherwise provided for in the Rules of Procedure and Evidence or by a majority of the Pre-Trial Chamber".

According to Art s 12(2)(a) and (b) (see, below) when a situation is referred to the prosecutor by a State Party or the Prosecutor has used his *proprio motu* powers (see Art. 13(a) and (c)), the court may exercise its jurisdiction if one or more of the following States are parties to the Statute:

(a) The State on the territory of which the conduct in question occurred or, if the crime was committed on board a vessel or aircraft, the state or registration of that vessel or aircraft.

(b) The State of which the person accused of the crime is a national.

According to Art. 12(2) in connection with Art. 12(3), the court may also exercise its jurisdiction over States who, although are not parties to the Statute, have accepted its jurisdiction, *via* a declaration lodged with the Registrar to that effect. It is therefore possible that even though a State is not a member, its nationals might still fall under the jurisdiction of the ICC if they commit a crime abroad, *i.e.* in a State that is not a party to the Statute. By way of explanation, there are three main separate situations which will now be considered and are referred to as the principles of territorial, national and consensual jurisdiction. For example, with regard to the following:

(a) *Territorial jurisdiction:* A commits a crime within the territory of State X. A is not a national of State X, but of State Y. Y is not a party to the ICC. X is a member of the ICC. Therefore A comes within the jurisdiction of the ICC.

(b) *National jurisdiction:* A commits a crime in State X. A is not a national of X, but of State Y. Y is a party to the ICC. But X is not a member of the ICC. Nevertheless, A comes within the jurisdiction of the ICC.

(c) *Consensual jurisdiction:* A commits a crime in State X. A is not a national of X, but of State Y. X and Y are not parties to the ICC. X does not prosecute A (because, for instance, State X is unable or unwilling to do so) in its national courts. Neither X nor Y make a declaration accepting the jurisdiction of the ICC under Art. 12(3). In this case, the ICC has no jurisdiction. However, if Y for example, does makes a declaration accepting jurisdiction, then A falls under the ICC's jurisdiction.

10–054   However, according to Art. 13(b), where the Security Council, under Chapter VII, refers a situation to the Prosecutor for investigation, the above examples of jurisdictional principles do not apply. Here, the Prosecutor may investigate and prosecute *any* person irrespective of the territory, national or consensual rules set out above.

Under Art. 16 the Security Council has the power, by a resolution adopted under Chapter VII, to defer a potential or on-going investigation or prosecution for a period of 12 months, if it requests the court to do so. This request may be renewed. It is conceivable that such a request, could in theory, be renewed indefinitely. This particular Article may have serious negative consequences, not only on the independence of the Prosecutor, but on the whole of the ICC. The words of Art. 16 refer to a "request" as opposed to an order. Thus, it is submitted that the court may refuse such a request where it believes that it would be in the interests of justice to do so. However, taking such a path may cause problems and conflict between the ICC and the Security Council.

The purpose of the deferral is to permit the Security Council to persue its own negotiations for peace in a given situation without the possible infringement of an on-going investigation or prosecution. The requested deferral may not only delay, but may ultimately stifle the Prosecutor's investigation. Such interference by the Security Council may result in weakening the potency of the role of the Prosecutor. Article 16 may be used as "a bargaining chip". "In-house" diplomatic deals may be negotiated between various Permanent Members of the Security Council which, in exchange for halting an existing investigation, may result in a particular offender not being tried, let alone investigated. This may result in the individual concerned having the time to make investigations himself and to destroy or "bury" incriminating evidence, or "persuade" potential witnesses not to testify and so forth. The net result would be that such a permissible interference would defeat the whole principle and purpose of an independent, impartial and non-political process. The saving grace of this particular Article is that any deferral is subject under Chapter VII to a veto. Moreover, the Security Council is not given unlimited powers over referrals. This exercise is restricted to Chapter VII, *i.e.* such as threat to the peace, breach of the peace or acts of aggression. Article 16 appears to have been side-stepped to some degree by Resolution 1422 adopted by the Security Council in July 2002, which states in para. 1 that:

> " . . . if a case arises involving current or former officials or personnel from a contributing State not a Party to the Rome Statute over acts or omissions relating to a United Nations established or authorized operation, shall for a twelve-month period starting 1 July 2002 not commence or proceed with investigation or prosecution of any such case, unless the Security Council decides otherwise".

This could result in Non-Party State officials, such as US military personnel and civilians on United Nations business, being deferred from investigation or prosecution before the ICC for any violations of the crimes stated in

Art. 5. Paragraph 2 of the Resolution reiterates the "renewal" request in Art. 16 but adding that such a request, although initially lasting for 12 months, may continue for *as long as may be necessary*. In practice such a deferral may last indefinitely. Since Russia, China and the United States are not Parties to the ICC Statute, this Resolution may prove to be of special benefit to those and other Non-Party States whose nationals could, in theory, be free from any prosecution for an indeterminate period.

Issues of admissibility

As already stated in the Preamble and Art. 1 the ICC shall be complementary to national criminal jurisdictions. First and foremost, it is the responsibility of the respective national court to prosecute violators of the crimes stated in Art. 5. Under Art. 17(1)(a)–(d) it is up to the court to decide whether to proceed with the trial and shall determine that a case is inadmissible where: **10–055**

(a) The case is being investigated or prosecuted by a State which has jurisdiction over it, unless the State is unwilling or unable genuinely to carry out the investigation or prosecution;

(b) The case has been investigated by a State which has jurisdiction over it and the State has decided not to prosecute the person concerned, unless the decision resulted from the unwillingness or inability of the State genuinely to prosecute;

(c) The person concerned has already been tried for conduct which is the subject of the complaint, and a trial by the court is not permitted under Art. 20, para. 3;

(d) The case is not of sufficient gravity to justify further action by the court.

Thus, primarily State Parties are not only encouraged, but are seen as preferable, to prosecute the accused in their own courts. However, under Arts 17(2)(a)–(c) and 17(3), the court's jurisdiction may be re-established in circumstances where the national court has been unwilling or unable to prosecute an individual, namely, shielding the individual through, for instance: internal political pressure not to prosecute or granting amnesty to the individual from any further prosecutions; the proceeding not being conducted expeditiously; the proceedings not being independent or impartial; the proceedings being conducted inconsistently with an intent to prosecute; or due to a total or substantial collapse of the national judicial system or otherwise unable to carry out its proceedings. Under Art. 17(3) the court will also decide on a State's inability to prosecute by examining such factors as a State being "unable to obtain the accused or the necessary evidence and testimony". The danger here lies in that some States judicial systems may be more developed than others or a State may genuinely believe that there are insufficient grounds for a prosecution. In such circumstances, the court may decide to override that State's decision; a prospect which could damage the relationship between that State and the court. This particular Article may also cause future problems for the ICC in relation to sentencing by allowing states a wider independence than was originally envisaged. For instance, even where the accused has been prosecuted and convicted by a national court, the sentence may not correspond to the seriousness of the offence and indirectly allow the accused to effectively evade the proper punishment for his crimes.

Once a State Party has requested the Prosecutor to investigate a situation and the prosecutor has decided that there is a reasonable basis to commence such an investigation, or to initiate an investigation *proprio motu,* he is under an obligation to inform all State Parties and those States directly concerned of his decision (Art. 18(1)). But he may, in the interests of justice limit his notification if he believes that to do otherwise would lead to the investigation being obstructed by evidence being destroyed or the suspect fleeing or in order to protect persons, such as witnesses from being threatened, harmed or intimidated. The State concerned will then, within one month, inform the court that it is undertaking the investigation into the criminal conduct alleged. Unless the Pre-Trial Chamber objects, the Prosecutor will then leave it up to that state's authorities to investigate and request interim progress reports. However, within six months or in certain circumstances before, if the Prosecutor is dissatisfied with the investigating State's progress, he may apply to the Pre-Trial Chamber to take over the case. If the Prosecutor or investigating state are unhappy with a decision of the Pre-Trial Chamber either may then appeal to the Appeal Chamber for a ruling (Art. 18(4).

Under Art. 19 it is up to the court itself to decide whether it possesses the required jurisdiction and whether the case is admissible under Art. 17. These decisions may be challenged by the accused, a suspect, a member or another State who has a legitimate interest in the overall proceedings or investigation. Normally this may only be done once and then only prior to the trial itself. Although in exceptional circumstances challenges may be instigated after the trial has begun, with leave of the court, and then only under Art. 17(1)(c) (see Art. 19(4)). Prior to a valid indictment all challenges regarding jurisdiction and admissibility are to go before the Pre-Trial Chamber; once a valid indictment has been secured all such challenges are to be taken up by the Trial Chamber. Appeals to these challenges go before the Appeals Chamber (Art. 19(6)).

10–056   Article 20 provides for the rule of *ne bis in idem* and relates to "double jeopardy" principles, in that an accused may not be tried twice for the same offence. The Article states that an accused cannot be tried by another court for a crime referred to in Art. 5 for which he has been convicted or acquitted by the court. The converse also appears to be the case. However, despite being tried once by a national court the defendant may be re-tried by the court where the proceedings in the national court were conducted in a manner which either shielded the accused, were not administered independently or impartially or were inconsistent with an intent to bring the person to justice (Art. 20(3)(a) and (b)). Article 20(1) uses the expression "conduct which formed the basis of crimes", which may be interpreted to mean that once the conduct comes within the Art. 5 crimes generally, then the defendant is ultimately absolved from any further prosecution. Indictments should therefore be framed widely so as to discount the possibility of a defendant escaping the net by claiming that despite the indictment not mentioning a particular count he cannot be tried again only because the offence came within the basis of crimes stated in Art. 5. Similar provisions of the ICTY (Art. 10) and ICTR (Art. 9) set out the same principles. However, under Art. 10(2) (and Art. 9(2)) it is stated that, apart from the exceptions set out in Art. 20 of the ICC, "[A] person who has been tried by a national court for acts constituting serious violations of international humanitarian law may be subsequently tried by the International Tribunal only if: (a) the act for which he or she was tried was characterized as an ordinary crime. What constitutes an 'ordinary crime'? Is it merely a minor offence, or can it be a serious offence by national standards, but not one to be considered as such under international law? It would appear that an ordinary crime is more apt to come within the boundaries of the latter, *i.e.* not so serious as, for example, crimes against humanity or genocide, but nevertheless serious enough to be tried subsequently by the ICC. Finally, any future charges and convictions will also have to consider the problematic area of multiple offences and the consequences arising therefrom."

Article 21(1) refers to the particular law to be applied by the court in any proceedings, namely, the Statute itself, Elements of Crimes and its Rules of Procedure and Evidence; applicable treaties; principles and rules of international law, including those of armed conflict; general principles of national law, provided such laws are not inconsistent with this Statute, international law or international recognised means and standards; or previous court decisions. All the above-mentioned laws are to be based on near non-discriminatory grounds, *i.e.* gender as defined in Art. 7(3) concerning age, race, colour, language, religion or belief, political or other opinion, national, ethnic or social origin, wealth birth or other status (Art. 21(3)).

Part 3–"Principles of International Criminal Law" (Arts 22–33)

Under Articles 22 and 23 the internationally recognised principles of *nullem crimen sine lege* and *nulla poena sine lege* are maintained, *i.e.* there is no crime nor punishment except in accordance with the law, in this case, the jurisdiction of the court. Where the definition of a crime is ambiguous, it shall be interpreted in favour of the person being investigated, prosecuted or convicted (Art. 22(2)). Under Art. 24 the long-standing legal principle of non-retroactivity is included and thus no individual may be prosecuted for illegal conduct prior to the entry into force of the Statute (Art. 24(1)). This, of

10–057

course, does not prevent established laws from progressing or evolving. Indeed, in common law systems especially, it is not at all uncommon for precedents to develop in this way.

Under Art. 25 the jurisdiction of the court is not restricted to the actual perpetrators of crimes under Art. 5 but extends to those persons responsible for ordering, soliciting, attempting, aiding and abetting, inducing the commission or attempted commission of a crime, or otherwise assisting in its commission or attempted commission by a group with a common purpose, or inciting others to commit genocide (Art. 25(3)(a)–(f). "Incitement" only refers to genocide, but not the other inchoate or full offences. The reason for this appears to be due to the language problems when interpreting this word in different national legal systems. However, it is suggested that this should not cause difficulties in any future prosecutions since the different variations to commit the other offences appear to be aptly covered. Article 25 refers to "natural persons". Thus, organisations and companies, as separate legal entities, cannot be indicted. Nevertheless, directors, agents and employees of these companies may still, under certain circumstances, be held accountable for their crimes.

No prosecutions may be brought against persons who at the time when the alleged offences were committed were under the age of 18 (Art. 26). Nowadays, it is not uncommon for "child soldiers" to attain a high ranking position of responsibility and command in an armed force, especially where internal armed conflicts are concerned. To automatically exempt such persons for their inhumane actions in such circumstances may well turn out to be detrimental in future prosecutions coming before the ICC. Nevertheless, apart from that exception, the Statute applies to all persons regardless of their official position and title. Thus, it includes State leaders and all government officials and civilians, as well as those persons claiming diplomatic or other immunity (Art. 27). In particular, under Art. 28 military or *de facto* commanders and civilian superiors shall be held criminally responsible for the acts of their forces or subordinates under their "command and control or effective authority and control" (for the precise meanings of these words see Art. 7(3) of SITY). In the case of military or *de facto* commanders such persons shall be held accountable where that person: (i) "either knew or, owing to the circumstances at the time, should have known that the forces were committing or about to commit such crimes; and (ii) that person failed to take all necessary and reasonable measures within his or her power to prevent or repress their commission or to submit the matter to the competent authorities for investigation and prosecution" (Art. 28(a)). The test here is cumulative. Article 28(b) also refers, in similar language, to civilian leaders who may also be held criminally liable for the crimes of their subordinates where: (i) they knew or should have known about such crimes; (ii) the crimes concerned activities that were within the effective responsibility and control of the superior; and (iii) he failed to take all necessary and reasonable steps to prevent their commission or report the matter to the proper authorities.

Regarding the criminal liability for military and non-military superiors, **10–058** the former requires either direct knowledge or that he "should have known" of his subordinates involvement in any illegal activities. The *mens rea* requirement here suggests a higher level of responsibility than that of a non-military superior, where the latter must either know or "consciously disregarded information which clearly indicated" his subordinates present or future illegal conduct. Thus, a non-military superior may well have a defence by stating that the information he received did not, on its face, clearly indicate any danger of his subordinates committing or about to commit a crime. On the other hand, the same information in the hands of a military superior may produce a different result if it can be proved that he "should have known" of his subordinates illegal conduct and failed to take any action against those responsible.

Article 30 defines the *mens rea* for the offences under the Statute and states that "unless otherwise provided, a person shall be criminally responsible and liable for punishment for a crime within the jurisdiction of the Court only if the material mental elements are committed with intent and knowledge" (Art. 30(1). Therefore, in common with international law generally, the essential ingredients for any successful criminal prosecution within this Statute are intention and knowledge. Under Art. 30(2) a person has intent where: (a) in relation to conduct, that person means to engage in the conduct; and (b) in relation to a consequence, that person means to cause that consequence or is aware that it will occur in the ordinary course of events. And under Art. 30(3) "knowledge" means awareness that a circumstance exists or a consequence will occur in the ordinary course of events. The words "unless otherwise provided" are an added complication to Art. 30. There are a number of provisions in the Statute that require either intent or knowledge, but not necessarily both. For example, under Art. 8(b)(i) in relation to war crimes the words "[I]ntentionally directing attacks against the civilian population . . . " would appear to mean that knowledge is also a necessary requirement for the purposes of establishing guilt. Conversely, under Art. 28(a)(i) it is sufficient for a commander to be held criminally liable for the acts of his subordinates where he "either knew or, . . . should have known that the forces were committing or about to commit such crimes".

In common with many existing national legal systems a defendant will have a number of defences at his disposal when indicted which may absolve him fully from criminal liability for the offences contained in Art. 5, *e.g.* insanity; involuntary intoxication; self-defence or defence of another; or in certain circumstances defence of property, but only in the case of war crimes; duress; or at trial where the proceedings were not in accordance with the applicable law as laid down by Art. 21 (Art. 31(1)(a)–(d) and para. 3). Further, under Art. 32(1) and (2) a mistake of fact will only be considered as a proper defence if it negates the mental element required by the crime. Under Art. 32(2) a mistake of law as to whether a particular type of conduct is a crime shall not be a ground for excluding criminal responsibility, unless it negates the mental element required by such a crime, or as provided for in Art. 33.

10–059 It has never been the case under international criminal law that the accused has been permitted to raise the defence that he was merely obeying the law of the State or that he was only carrying out the orders of his superiors, although the latter excuse has been used in the past, in certain circumstances, for mitigating purposes when it came to sentencing. These principles have been reinforced in Art. 33 but omitting any assistance for mitigating circumstances. Article 33(1) states that where crimes were committed by an individual on the orders of a government or a superior, that person shall not be relieved of criminal responsibility unless:

(a) the person was under a legal obligation to obey orders of the government or the superior in question;

(b) the person did not know that the order was unlawful; and

(c) the order was not manifestly unlawful.

For the purposes of this article, orders to commit genocide or crimes against humanity are manifestly unlawful.

In order for the accused to exculpate himself from criminal responsibility in these circumstances he must pass over all three hurdles stipulated in Art. 33(1)(a)–(c), *i.e.* the test is cumulative. However, with regard to genocide and crimes against humanity, since these crimes are always manifestly unlawful, the accused may be successful in proving points (a) and (b) but he will never be able to prove (c), above, *i.e.* that the order was manifestly lawful. Thus, it is only with war crimes that the defendant will have any chance of success in proving (a)–(c) above. This is made all the harder to do by the wording of this particular Article which appears to make (a) and (c) objective tests and only (b) subjective.

Part 4–"Composition and Workings of the Court" (Arts 34–52)

10–060 The composition of the court has already been discussed briefly at the beginning of this particular section. For the complete explanation and details on the different functions, elections, regulations and so forth, relating to the officers and staff of the court, as well as the judicial qualifications, see Arts 34–52 of the Statute. With respect to the Rules of Procedure and Evidence ("RPE"), under Art. 51(1), the existing RPE may be amended by any State Party; the judge acting by an absolute majority; or the Prosecutor. Under Art. 51(3) where, in exceptional cases the Rules do not provide for a specific situation "the judges may, by a two-thirds majority, drawn up provisional Rules to be applied until adopted, amended or rejected at the next ordinary or special session of the Assembly of State Parties".

Part 5–"Investigation, Arrest and Commencement of Proceedings" (Arts 53–61)

Inherent in any criminal enquiry carried out by an investigating Prosecutor is **10–061** the pre-requisite that it should be impartial and independent. The Prosecutor's task will undeniably be a difficult one. He will have to deal with uncommon and serious situations and crimes not ordinarily found at the domestic level. Investigations in certain States may prove troublesome, if not impossible. Insurmountable barriers may be put up by the individual State being investigated in order to protect a particular individual. Getting witnesses to make statements and to testify presents its own inherent problems. Although the Prosecutor's powers under the ICC are wide and varied, they are not unfettered. Any investigative action that the Prosecutor may decide to take must first be approved by the Pre-Trial Chamber. For example, under Art. 53(1), once the Prosecutor determines that there is a reasonable basis to commence the investigation and that the case would be admissible under Art. 17, he must inform the Pre-Trial Chamber of his decision. He must also inform the Pre-Trial Chamber should he declare that he is not proceeding with the investigation, stating the reasons under Art. 53(2)(a)–(c), *i.e.* insufficient evidence for an arrest warrant; the case does not fall under Art. 17 or a prosecution would not be within the interests of justice. What constitutes a case being withdrawn "in the interests of justice" is difficult to determine. However, under Art. 53(2)(c) the Prosecutor will consider all the circumstances, including the gravity of the crime, the interests of the victims and the age or infirmity of the alleged perpetrator, and his or her role in the alleged crime. At the request of a State or the Security Council making a referral, the Pre-Trial Chamber may review the Prosecutor's decision not to proceed and request him to reconsider his decision (Art. 53(3)(a). Where the Prosecutor has decided not to investigate in the interests of justice the Pre-Trial Chamber, may on its own initiative request him to reconsider his decision. The duties and powers of the Prosecutor are set out in Art. 54 and include collecting and examining evidence, questioning suspects, victims and witnesses, request the co-operation of any State or intergovernmental organisation and take appropriate action, where necessary, to protect the confidentiality of information and persons concerned in the investigation.

The rights of any individual being investigated are contained in Art. 55(1)(a)–(d) and include not being compelled to incriminate himself; or being exposed to coercion, duress or threats, to torture or any other form of cruel, inhuman or degrading treatment or punishment; or being subjected to arbitrary arrest or detention. Further, prior to questioning the individual concerned must be informed of the grounds for such questioning; and that he has a right to remain silent; and the right to legal advice unless he has waived that right (Art. 55(2)(a)–(d).

It is the responsibility of the Pre-Trial Chamber to issue the arrest warrant, but only after it has been satisfied by the Prosecutor that there are reasonable grounds to believe that the crime comes within the jurisdiction of the court; and that the arrest appears necessary to ensure the suspects attendance at trial or to prevent obstruction to the investigation or the court proceedings or to prevent the accused from committing further crimes (Art. 58(1)(a) and (b)). If the prosecutor fails to satisfy the Pre-Trial Chamber of the above detention criteria, then the suspect must be released with or without conditions (Art. 60(2)).

Parts 6 and 8–"Criminal Trial and Appeal" (Arts 62–76 and 81–85)

10–062   Once the trial has commenced, the Statute sets out various provisions which must be complied with in order to ensure a fair hearing. This is emphasised under Art. 64(2) which states that the Trial Chamber shall ensure that a trial is fair and expeditious and is conducted with full respect for the rights of the accused and due regard for the protection of victims and witnesses. Under Art. 67 the accused is entitled to a fair trial which includes: (a) being informed promptly and in detail the content of the charges; (b) being permitted adequate time to prepare his defence; (c) being tried without undue delay; (d) being granted legal assistance, if requested; (e) being allowed to examine and cross-examine witnesses; (f) being given the assistance of an interpretor; (g) not being compelled to testify or confess guilt and to remain silent; (h) being permitted to make unsworn defence statements; and (i) not to have imposed upon him the burden of proof. Generally, the trial will be held in public but may, under special circumstances, be held in closed session in order to protect victims and witnesses (see Art. 68) or to protect confidential or sensitive information to be given in evidence (Art. 64(7)). Whether evidence is considered relevant and admissible is determined broadly by the court. Article 69(4) states that in such circumstances the court will take into account, *inter alia*, "the probative value of the evidence and any prejudice that such evidence may cause to a fair trial or to a fair evaluation of the testimony of a witness, in accordance with the Rules of Procedure and Evidence". But what the court will not do is determine the admissibility or relevance of the evidence by the application of the State's national law (Art. 69(8)).

Under Art. 74 the decision of the court should be unanimous. However, failing that a majority decision will suffice. Under Art. 81 an appeal against the decision may be proffered by the Prosecutor or the convicted person. In relation to the Prosecutor, the grounds of appeal are limited to: (i) procedural error, (ii) error of fact, or (iii) error of law. As regards the convicted person (or the Prosecutor on his behalf) the grounds of appeal are as above but also include any other ground that affects the fairness or reliability of the proceedings or decision (Art. 81(1)(a) and (b)). Under Art. 82(2)(a) a sentence may be appealed in accordance with the Rules of Procedure and Evidence by the Prosecutor or the convicted person on the ground of disproportion between the crime and the sentence.

Part 7–"Judicial Decisions, Punishment and other Penalties" (Articles 77–80)

Any decisions of the court must be reached by at least a majority of the judges. Article 77 determines the range of different punishments and penalties that the court may impose against a convicted individual. These include a term of imprisonment not exceeding 30 years or imprisonment for life, if warranted, according to the seriousness of the crime. In line with the provisions set out under the ICTY and ICTR the court must take into account such factors as the gravity of the offence and the individual circumstances of the individual (Art. 78(1)). Again, since there are no tariff provisions it appears that the court exercises a broad discretion when imposing sentences. In addition to sentencing, the court may impose a fine and/or forfeiture of proceeds, property and assets accumulated from the crime itself (Art. 77(1) and (2)). Moreover, the court may award compensation to victims who have suffered loss, damage or injury (Art. 75). Not surprisingly, the death penalty is omitted from the ICC's sentencing provisions.

10–063

During the negotiation stage of the Statute it was argued that potential Member States which possess the death penalty may find its exclusion unacceptable as undermining their own national laws and as a consequence be reluctant to ratify the Statute. As a satisfactory compromise Art. 80 was introduced which states that "Nothing in this Part affects the application by states of penalties prescribed by their national law, nor the law of States which do not provide for penalties prescribed in this Part". Therefore, as far as Art. 80 is concerned, States are expressly left to their own national devises when sentencing and imposing penalties; once again reaffirming the complementary qualities of the Statute. However, Art. 80 is restricted to penalties. The question of when a prisoner is to be released or a sentence reduced is determined by the court in line with Art. 110 and is mandatory on all Member States. This Article states that once the prisoner has served two-thirds of his sentence, or if life, 25 years, only then shall the court review the sentence for the purposes of reduction. The court shall take into account such matters as the willingness to co-operate and assist the court in its investigations and where applicable disclosing the whereabouts of assets subject to fines and/or payment orders to victims, and other considerations which establish "a clear and significant change of circumstances sufficient to justify a reduction of sentence" (Art. 110 (4)(a)–(c). However, even if some or all of the above factors are present, judging from past cases, it will not automatically result in a reduction of sentence. No doubt the court will also examine the accused's position of authority, the seriousness of the crime, his culpability and so forth.

The State in which the prisoner is serving his time may not grant an early release to that person prior to a decision of the review court, even if permissible under their own national laws. This may be viewed as a curtailment of a State's national powers but, such a requirement is essential to demonstrate consistency and equality when dealing with prisoners generally, irrespective of the State where the sentence is being carried out.

Part 9-"State Co-operation with Investigation, Prosecution and Arrest" (Arts 86–102)

10–064   Fundamental to the effective workings of the ICC is the co-operation and collaboration not only between Member States but also between the court and the State or States concerned. Articles 86–102 deal with the co-operation between the court and the State or States involved which directly relate to investigation and prosecution matters. In this respect Member States are under a mandatory obligation to co-operate fully with requests made by the court. Even non-Member States may be called upon to provide assistance, either through some form of *ad hoc* agreement or arrangement. If they refuse the court may inform the Assembly of State Parties or, where the Security Council referred the matter to the court, the Security Council (Art. 87(5)(a) and (b)). The same repercussions will befall those State Parties which refuse to assist the court (Art. 87(7)). Generally the requested State is under an obligation to maintain secrecy in co-operation matters, unless through necessity the carrying out of the request may only be performed publicly. (Art. 87(3). Whatever method is chosen by the court to obtain information and receive assistance it is vital that those persons involved directly in the investigation, *e.g.* victims, potential witnesses and their families, be protected against any harm coming to them as a result of their co-operation.

The court may call upon State Parties as well as Non-State Parties to arrest and surrender an individual suspected of committing crimes under Art. 5 (Art. 89). State Parties must comply with any such requests (see Arts 58(1) and 59). The suspect may appeal against the surrender request on double jeopardy grounds. In such a case the surrendering State will ask the court for a ruling on admissibility and the suspect will not be surrendered until a final ruling has been made on the issue. Apart from this limited exception there are no other grounds or circumstances preventing the requested State from complying with the court's order. The word "surrender" does not, under the Statute, have the same meaning as "extradition". The former is described in Art. 102 as meaning "the delivering up by a state to the Court", whilst the latter means "the delivering up of a person by one state to another as provided by treaty, convention or national legislation".

Circumstances may arise where a State Party not only receives a request from the ICC for the handing-over of a suspect but also another State may request extradition of that same person. The question then becomes who gets priority, the court or the requesting State? Surprisingly enough, the answer is not inevitably the court. Under Art. 90(2) where the requesting State is an ICC Party, the court will get priority under certain circumstances which include, the court determining that the case is admissible under Arts 18 and 19, as well as considering the investigation or prosecution conducted by the requesting State in the extradition matters (Art. 90(2)(a) and (b)). Where the court has not abided by Art. 90(2)(a) or (b) the requested State may, at its discretion, subject to certain conditions, extradite to the requesting State (see

Art. 90(3)). Where the requesting State is a non-ICC Party and has no extradition obligations with the requested State, then provided the court has determined that the case is admissible, the court gets priority in this situation (Art.
90(4)). If inadmissible, the requested State has a discretion and may give priority to the requesting State (Art. 90(5)). However, where the requested State
has extradition obligations to the requesting State, the former will consider
whether to surrender the accused to the court or requesting State by examining all relevant factors, including "whether the crime was committed in its
territory and the nationality of the victims and of the person sought" (Art.
90(6)(b)) (for other factors see (Art. 90(6)(a) and (c)).

The court may also seek co-operation from other States in respect of inves-   **10–065**
tigations or prosecutions of a correlative nature. For instance, the court may
ask a State to furnish it with various types of documents and evidence relating to the investigation, *e.g.* expert and witness statements, exhumation and
examination of grave sites, the service of documents, the tracing and freezing
of assets and so forth (for a full list see Art. 93(1)(a)–(l)). It is not in the
court's interest to alienate State Parties by making unreasonable requests.
Friendly and voluntary co-operation is to be preferred by all the parties concerned. However, even though States are generally bound to co-operate fully
with the court's requests, problems may arise which prevent compliance
where it would be contrary to the national laws of that State to do otherwise.
There are only two reasons why a State may legitimately refuse compliance of
a request. Firstly, where disclosure involves issues of national security (Art.
93(4)). In such cases reference should be made to Art. 72 which details the
procedures and solutions by stating that all reasonable steps must be taken in
order to resolve such a dilemma, including: (i) modifying or clarifying the
request; (ii) efforts should be made to obtain the particular information from
another source; (iii) providing summaries; (iv) the use of in camera or *ex
parte* proceedings; (v) using other protective measures under the Statute and
the Rules of Procedures and Evidence; or (vi) using other reasonable steps to
resolve the matter (Art. 72(4) and (5)). Secondly, a State may refuse compliance with the list under Art. 93(1) on the grounds that disclosure is prohibited under the national law of the requested state (Art. 93(3). In such cases
Art. 93(3) allows for consultation between the court and the requested State
to resolve the matter. If still no agreement can be reached, alterations to the
original request may be necessary to avoid complete non-compliance. The
final wording suggests an obligation, if all else fails, to modify the request. If
the court refuses to do so, the requested State may, it seems, legitimately
refuse to comply with the court's original request. If the information
requested does not come within the list in Art. 93(a)–(i) and is prohibited by
a State's own domestic laws, although voluntary assistance is expected, the
requested State may be within its rights to refuse to comply with the court's
request.

One of the main objectives behind the ICC is to do away with the hitherto
impunity protection granted to international criminals. In other words, there

should be no escape or immunity for perpetrators of international crimes. Indeed, Art. 27(2) reinforces this position by stating that "[I]mmunities or special procedural rules which may attach to the official capacity of a person, whether under national or international law, shall not bar the Court from exercising its jurisdiction over such a person". Yet Art. 98 goes some way in retaining the immunity of a suspected international criminal. Art. 98 states that:

1. The court may not proceed with a request for surrender or assistance which would require the requested State to act inconsistently with its obligations under international law with respect to the State or diplomatic immunity of a person or property of a third State, unless the court can first obtain the co-operation of that third State for the waiver of the immunity.

2. The court may not proceed with a request for surrender which would require the requested State to act inconsistently with its obligations under international agreements pursuant to which the consent of a sending State is required to surrender a person of that State to the court, unless the court can first obtain the co-operation of the sending State for the giving of consent for the surrender.

Article 98(2) is a much wider concept than Art. 98(1). There appears to be a contradiction between Art. 98(1) and Art. 27(2) in relation to the barring of immunity under the Statute. Although the court is not prevented from exercising its jurisdiction over any person, regardless of their status, problems may arise under Art. 98 where the ICC requests the surrendering of that person in contravention of an existing agreement between those States. For example, since States already have multilateral as well as bilateral agreements relating to matters involving extradition, nationality and so forth, it is foreseeable that, depending on the wording of these individual treaties, surrendering a suspect to the ICC may involve complicated diplomatic negotiations. It is possible for two or more States to enter into reciprocal agreements whereby they agree not to surrender a suspect to the ICC without the others consent or alternatively return the suspect to his national home. For instance, under "Status of Forces Agreements" and "Status of Mission Agreements" States agree that where crimes have been committed in one State by a national of another, that State will send such a person back to his own State. There is no obligation upon the receiving State to prosecute or even investigate the criminal allegations. For instance, Art. 98(1) deals with the situation where a national of State X, who is not a State Party commits a crime in State Y, who is a State Party and who has the suspect in custody. There is a reciprocal bilateral agreement between State X and State Y whereby each State returns nationals accused of crimes to their own State. This particular national has diplomatic immunity. The court requests that that person be handed over from State Y to the ICC. State X requests that that person be returned home. Which request takes precedent, State X or the ICC? It may be the case that if State Y delivers that person up to the ICC they might well be in contravention of their agreement with State X, unless they can obtain cooperation from State X for the waiver of the immunity. If such agreements were allowed to be used to take priority in order to circumvent the provisions of Art. 98 then this may amount to a regressive step in the overall effectiveness of the ICC. Moreover, those States that decide to enter into such agreements may possibly be considered to be in violation of the Statute itself as not "co-operating" with the court under Arts 86 and 87. Non-Party States such as the United States, which has recently "unsigned" its signature to the Rome Statute, has long fought to safeguard its citizens from being surrendered up to the ICC, or being tried before another State's national court. Indeed, the United States has in recent years sought to enter into new "non-surrendering" agreements with State Parties which is contrary to the spirit of Art. 98. The intention of the original drafters was that this specific Article was only meant to avoid situations where a confrontation might arise under existing agreements between States; not to be used for the purposes of future agreements. It is suggested that even if such reciprocal agreements are entered into, it is, under international law, the ICC Statute that should take precedence over that which conflicts or is incompatible with a State's obligations and responsibilities under the Statute.

Part 10–"Enforcement of Sentences" (Arts 103–111)

Articles 103–111 deal principally with enforcement provisions in relation to **10–066** sentencing. Under Art. 103(1)(a) a sentence of imprisonment shall be served in a State designated by the court from a list of States which have indicated to the court their willingness to accept sentenced persons. The respective State may not alter that sentence, unless first agreed upon by the court. In determining where the accused will serve his imprisonment, the court will consider such factors as the views of the sentenced person, his nationality, the circumstances of the crime or the person sentenced, or the effective enforcement of the sentence, as may be appropriate in the circumstances (Art. 103(3)(a)–(e)). If no State is designated by the court, then the host State will undertake to imprison the accused for the term of the sentence.

Article 110 concerns the review provisions by the court. Under Art. 110(3), where the person has served two thirds of the sentence, or 25 years in the case of life imprisonment, the court shall review the sentence to determine whether it should be reduced. The court may reduce the sentence if it finds either that: (a) the person was willing to co-operate with the court in its investigations and prosecutions; (b) voluntarily assisted the court *via* enforcement of the judgments and orders, *e.g.* locating assets subject to orders of fines, forfeiture or reparations for the benefit of victims; or (c) other factors which justify a reduction of sentence (Art. 110(4)(a)–(c)).

ASSEMBLY OF STATE PARTIES

10–067 Article 112 concerns the establishment and obligation of the Assembly of State Parties. Among its most important responsibilities are to consider and adopt as appropriate, recommendations of the Preparatory Commission; consider and decide the budget of the court and consider the question of non-co-operation under Art. 87(5) and (7).

Unlike most other treaties, this Statute contains no reservations or derogations. Either Member States fully accept all its articles or none at all. A State may withdraw from the Statute, but this will not take immediate effect; it will only be considered a lawful withdrawal after one year after the date of receipt of the notification (Art. 127).

CONCLUSION

10–068 At the time of writing the ICC has been established for just under a year. It has been ratified by 90 States, (Lithuania became the 90th State Party on May 15, 2003) and its membership will no doubt go on increasing. Once the ICC has been firmly and fully established it will possess the unique feature of being the first international court to be created to specifically deal with serious humanitarian and human rights crimes which have not yet occurred; unlike the tribunals of the ICTY, ICTR and Nuremberg which were established to try those responsible for offences that had already taken place. Consequently, potential perpetrators should now think twice before embarking on exploits contrary to international criminal law.

Although it will be interesting to observe how the ICC will conduct itself when confronted with its first actual trial, the success or failure of the Statute will be determined more on how a State Party will proceed when faced with its obligations of prosecuting a individual for a serious "core crime" offence. Past experience has shown that the vast majority of States are not overly concerned with prosecuting its own citizens for human rights atrocities, unless it is politically expedient to do so. Where some States lack the political will to legislate against international crimes or where existing laws need modification and developing, the creation of the international court is a necessary implement to fill the *lacunae* which may be absent under national laws. But even where adequate laws exist at the national level there is always the ever-present danger that a trial will not take place for fear that evidence might come to light which would be potentially damaging to the authorities, or worse still, show that the government itself has been involved in human rights atrocities. Further, some national courts may show bias, either for or against the accused, or lack the required independence and impartiality necessary for a fair trial. In such cases another forum is essential to counteract these imbalances. It is hoped that State members will abide by the Preamble of the Statute which provides that ". . . *Recalling* that it is the duty of every State to exercise its criminal jurisdiction over those responsible for international crimes, . . . *Resolved* to guarantee lasting respect for and the enforcement of international justice". This Statute will actually put friendly pressure on State Parties to bring those responsible to justice or at least shame that state into taking the required action.

The success of the ICC will be greatly determined by the number of States which eventually ratify the Statute; the greater the number the fewer hiding places for potential perpetrators of international crimes. A number of powerful States have decided not to ratify the Statute, including three permanent members of the Security Council (United States, China and Russia). It will be interesting in the coming years to see how their absence affects, politically and otherwise, the implementation and strength of the ICC.

Proponents of the ICC would no doubt argue that the existence of such a **10–069** forum would act, not only as a deterrent for such crimes in the future, but also those individuals presently responsible would be brought to account for their actions. The deterrence factor may in fact turn out to be an illusion. Where attrocities occur within the confines of a State's borders, the more powerful the perpetrator and the more popular the policies of that State are, the more difficult and politically awkward it will be for that State to prosecute its offenders and even less probable that they would hand over those people to the ICC, short of threatened military action against that state or bestowing some incentive to surrender the suspects. The history of some States shows that protracted internal wars between rival factions are the norm with only intermittent periods of peace. In such cases, it is doubtful whether the prosecution of a few of its leaders will in reality diffuse a persistent volatile situation which is embedded in the political and social culture of such a State.

In reality, the vast majority of those responsible for committing international attrocities will never be arrested, let alone prosecuted. A regime is made up of its supporters, but even when that regime has ended, many of those people who remain still retain the same or similar ideological philosophies as before, but lacking only the means and power to carry out their plans. Indeed, many of its survivors remain in power, or at least in subordinate positions of authority, but their convictions remain the same. National courts or the ICC will only be effective where collective responsibility is recognised and criminal class actions are taken against the perpetrators. It is only then that an ordinary soldier will come to realise that if he initiates or obeys an order to commit a serious international crime, he will, as part of a military group suffer the consequences of his deeds. Such a proposal is not unrealistic. For instance, although some 200,000 men of the Serb forces could, in theory, be accused of humanitarian crimes, in reality less than 0.1 per cent of those responsible will ever be tried at the national level or before the ICTY.

Although the formation of the ICC will not in reality prevent future human rights abuses, the existence of such a forum sends out a powerful message to those aggressive States that individuals responsible for human rights atrocities will be tried and punished for their crimes should the domestic courts themselves not take the appropriate judicial action in such cases.

PART FOUR:
INDIVIDUAL HUMAN RIGHTS IN INTERNATIONAL CRIMINAL LAW

Chapter 11

WOMEN, SEXUAL VIOLENCE AND INTERNATIONAL CRIME: A UNIFYING EXAMPLE

"Women are raped in all forms of armed conflict, international and internal, whether the conflict is fought primarily on religious, ethnic, political or nationalist grounds, or a combination of all these. They are raped by men from all sides — both enemy and "friendly" forces. There have been reports of rapes and other forms of sexual abuse committed by members of United Nations peacekeeping forces; women are not free from interference even from those who are in the territory with an international mandate to restore peace and security. International media attention has been directed towards the widespread rapes, torture and forced pregnancies in the former Yugoslavia. The "mobilisation of shame" which has been identified as the primary means of enforcing international humanitarian law has to some extent been activated in this instance. Nonetheless, the international response in itself carries the risk that violent offences against women will be perceived as something exceptional, peculiar to this particular conflict. The reality is that rape and violent sexual abuse of women in armed conflict has a long history . . . Rape in war is not merely a matter of chance, of women victims being in the wrong place at the wrong time. Nor is it a question of sex. It is rather a question of power and control which is structured by male soldiers" notions of their masculine privilege, by the strength of the military's lines of command and by class and ethnic inequalities among women." (C. Chinkin, "Rape And Sexual Abuse Of Women In International Law", 1994, 5 E.J.I.L. 326)

"Throughout the world, sexual violence is routinely directed against females during situations of armed conflict. This violence may take gender-specific forms, like sexual mutilation, forced pregnancy, rape or sexual slavery. Being female is a risk-factor; women and girls are often targeted for sexual abuse on the basis of their gender, irrespective of their age, ethnicity or political affiliation . . . Rape in conflict is also used as a weapon to terrorize and degrade a particular community and to achieve a specific political end. In these situations, gender intersects with other aspects of a woman's identity such as ethnicity, religion, social class or political affiliation. The humiliation, pain and terror inflicted by the rapist is meant to degrade not just the individual woman but also to strip the humanity from the larger group of which he is a part. The rape of one person is translated into an assault upon the community through the emphasis laced in every culture on women's sexual virtue: the shame of the rape humiliates the family and all those associated with the survivor. Combatants who rape in war often explicitly link their acts of sexual violence to this broader social degradation. In the aftermath of such abuse, the harm done to the individual woman is often obscured or even compounded by the perceived harm to the community."

("Shattered Lives: Sexual Violence during the Rwandan Genocide and its Aftermath" (B. Nowrojee, New York Human Rights Watch, 1996))

INTRODUCTION

11–001   Context is also important. We are at a time in which there is an unprecedented degree of cross-pollination and harmonisation of international criminal law, human rights and humanitarian law. International criminal law and
international human rights are inextricably linked. The same harms form
many international crimes and fundamental human rights violations, *e.g.* torture, slavery and unlawful killing. Once an international human rights-based
duty binds a person, its violation may be pursued in multiple venues: international criminal law, international humanitarian law and international
human rights. The three disciplines are converging and exchanging principles
at an increasing rate, although of course some actions entail state rather than
individual responsibility. Also of note is the primarily US development of
tort-based liability for human rights violations, particularly torture.

> "[there has been] explosive development of international criminal law in the post
> World War II era. Accordingly, international humanitarian law (the law regulat-
> ing armed conflict) has had a formidable impact on the development of interna-
> tional criminal law. In addition, attempts to seek and promote accountability for
> gross violations of human rights have had a direct and substantial impact on the
> elaboration of what constitutes international crimes and demonstrates how a cul-
> ture of impunity for acts of violence destroys societies, prevents healing and
> impedes progress." (D. Koenig and K. Askin, "International Criminal Law and
> the International Criminal Court Statute: Crimes against Women" in *Women and
> International Human Rights Law*, 2000, Vol. 2, D. Koenig and L. Askin, Eds).

For many centuries, women were viewed as victor's spoils. In recent
decades, concern has grown for the victims of such war crimes, and so has
publicity. However, the publicity tends to wane once the fighting ends, and
the women fade from the picture. It is only with the discovery of the scale of
sexual atrocities committed during the war in the former Yugoslavia that the
issue of wartime sex crime has truly become a priority concern for the international community. In late 1992, shock newspaper headlines such as 'serbs
Rape on the Highest Orders" and "Rape Camp Evil" brought to the world's
attention that rape and sexual violence were being used as an intentional, systematic tool for war victory. The discovery that, in Europe in the late twentieth century, detention centres had been set up for the explicit purpose of
raping and violating women (with sanction from the highest levels of the military command structure) led to understandable outrage. These graphic
images brought a new focus for the United Nations, and an unprecedented
formal attempt to redress wartime sex crime. However, the partial and piecemeal nature of the United Nations framework for dealing with international
crimes committed during armed conflict had led to serious defects in its
ability to provide justice for rape victims, and to prevent impunity for their
attackers. As will be seen from cases discussed in this chapter, rape charges
have been few and far between on ICTY and, to a lesser extent, ICTR,

indictments of that tiny proportion of suspects against whom charges are ever brought.

Although wartime sexual violence affects both men and women, women are by far the more likely target, and also face additional risks such as pregnancy. The implications of being a rape victim for women in many societies are extreme, including ostracism and loss of "marriageable" status. Sexual violence is only one of the ways in which war affects women, although the focus upon that aspect detracts from the visibility of other factors. Not only men, but women and children too, take part in wars as active combatants. Women are more likely than men to become displaced or refugees. Women's traditional roles mean that they are more often injured by landmines, because it is they who will be expected to go out in search of water and to grow food. When many societies are undergoing strictures, it is the women who suffer most since they occupy a position at the bottom of the pyramid of advantage. Without the ceaseless campaigning of women's NGOs, many such concerns would go unraised, and little can be done to address them without concerted planned effort and a huge injection of funding.

WHAT IS WARTIME SEXUAL VIOLENCE?

Although rape is understandably given the most attention, it is only one of **11–002** the types of sexual violence inflicted during wars. Equally devastating and dangerous to health are sexual mutilation, forced prostitution and forced pregnancy. Throughout history, women's status as property led to them being seen as part of the spoils of war, a bonus for the victor. Perhaps more significantly, women became a means of keeping troops happy and weakening the enemy by inflicting terror, destroying community values and pride. Often widespread and planned, sexual violence may be part of a genocidal strategy with the aim of weakening and then ultimately destroying a whole people.

Rape and sexual violence have an extremely long history as wartime tactics. In ancient Greece, as in many other societies, the victor in war gained the "right to rape"; in the First World War the German army used sexual violence as a means of domination; and the extent of the mass rapes and sexual enslavements by Japanese soldiers in the Second World War is only now being acknowledged. Brothels were long maintained at military camps in the belief that this would improve morale, and with varying levels of free choice for the women who worked there. War glorifies violence of various kinds, but sexual violence in wartime has been a highly effective method of dehumanisation, domination, humiliation and, ironically, attacking the masculinity of the men who were proved "unable to protect their women". If societies cannot prevent or curtail sexual atrocities in peacetime, what hope is there of doing so during war? It is true that of course many domestic criminal proceedings have been commenced, and jurisdictions such as the US now recognise torture as a tort; but is it even enough to recognise wartime and obviously State-sanctioned sexual violence as international crimes? Is it not time to abandon the public/private divide and national/international schism? If international criminal law and international human rights are to develop harmoniously and to complement each other, then arguably it is time to make much braver attempts to criminalise sexual violence as an international crime, regardless of venue or perpetrator.

History

11–003   The 1990s saw the beginning of the end of the historical silence concerning crimes committed against women, whether in war or in the private sphere, but contrary to public belief, rape has been a war crime since at least the fifteenth century.

Sexual violence was clearly an issue in the Second World War, but not one that is visible in the relevant historical records. It was not spoken about or highlighted for a number of reasons. It was committed by all "sides" at a time when society was not comfortable speaking about even consensual sexual matters. Further, there was no effective women's rights lobby to get the talking going. Now, however, research has shown the plight of (for example) the thousands of Asian women and girls who were forced to become "comfort women" for the Japanese army, sexual slaves who were raped many times a day. Licence to rape has regularly been an employment term for mercenaries.

Neither the Nuremberg nor Tokyo tribunals made any mention of sexual violence in their Charters, even though rape had clearly been a crime in war for hundreds of years. Not one charge of rape was brought at Nuremberg, despite references to it in the evidence presented. Some of the Tokyo trials did involve rape charges. For example, General Matsui was convicted of crimes against humanity and war crimes, partly on the basis that the troops under his command had committed rape. However, not one rape victim was called as a witness. Rape was merely an additional, sidelined aspect of the trial, almost an afterthought.

11–004   In the war crimes trials of Nazis after Nuremberg, held under Control Council Order No. 10, no rape charges were brought, although rape was specifically listed as one of the crimes within the Control Council's jurisdiction *via* Art. II(I)(c);

> "Atrocities and offences, including but not limited to murder, extermination, enslavement, deportation, imprisonment, torture, rape, or other inhumane acts committed against any civilian population, or persecutions on political, racial or religious grounds whether or not in violation of the domestic laws of the country where perpetrated."

The absence of women from the drafting of United Nations instruments and from participation in international bodies until recently, together with the decision not to prosecute wartime acts of sexual violence as such but to hide them behind generic charges of violence, downplayed both the occurrence and the gravity of the true situation. Further, labels have often been applied to wartime sexual violence to "decriminalise" it. "Comfort women" were called prostitutes, not the victims of sexual slavery that they were. The camps in which they were forcibly held were referred to as "brothels", not rape camps. It was only after the full horror of the situation in the former Yugoslavia began to emerge that relabelling of wartime rape occurred. It was finally perceived as the part of ethnic cleansing that it truly was, rather than an unfortunate, unavoidable and private matter. It should not be forgotten, however, that there was nothing new about this treatment of women as spoils of war or as property. It is simply that the reality of women's experience of many wars was beginning to be recognised for what it was. Any rape is a serious crime and the circumstances of conflict, whether international or internal, cannot lessen its nature or effects.

THE PRESENT LAW ON WARTIME SEXUAL VIOLENCE

The Geneva Conventions: sexual violence as a war crime

The Geneva Conventions of 1949, brought about by the International Committee of the Red Cross as specific measures to help war victims, do contain provisions which apply specifically to women and/or children. Some provisions of the four Conventions and their Additional Protocols do deal expressly with sexual violence, while others look to women in their capacity as mothers or 'special needs' prisoners. Even when the Conventions are explicitly addressing sexual violence as a crime, they do not seem to give it the priority it deserves. Sexual violence is not listed among the "grave breaches" of the Conventions and Additional Protocol I and so, *prima facie*, it is not among the crimes for which States have a duty to seek out and try or extradite suspects. Most experts now agree that sexual violence is a grave breach of the Conventions by implication within explicit categories such as "torture or inhuman treatment" or "willfully causing great suffering or injury to body or health". However, the need to do this by implication is telling; the international community was slow indeed to recognise and address the seriousness of wartime sexual violence, and to apply a label that reflects its significance for victims.

    11–005

Perhaps more telling than the absence of express designation as a grave breach is the language itself used in the Conventions and Protocols. Rape and sexual violence fall within the classification of "attacks against the honour of women" or "outrages upon human dignity". The belief that a raped woman is dishonoured or loses her dignity is a persistent one in many societies, but should have no place in international humanitarian or criminal law. Men do not give women their honour, and so cannot take it away. Rape, as with all crimes of sexual violence, is a crime of *violence*, an attack upon the body. It is a violation of basic human rights, of personal self-determination and much else besides. To view it as an attack upon honour both trivialises it and focuses upon depicting women as passive and in need of protection, rather than upon the attacker as in need of punishment.

Article 27 of the Geneva Convention IV Relative to the Protection of Civilian Persons provides:

"Women shall be especially protected against any attack on their honour, in particular against rape, enforced prostitution, or any form of indecent assault."

Article 76(1) of the Additional Protocol I of 1977 provides:

"Women shall be the object of special respect and shall be protected in particular against rape, forced prostitution, and any other form of indecent assault."

Article 4(2)(e) of the Additional Protocol II of 1977 prohibits:

"Outrages upon personal dignity, in particular humiliating and degrading treatment, rape, enforced prostitution and any form of indecent assault."

Some specific measures towards the protection of women

11–006 *UN 1993 Vienna Conference on Human Rights*

"The 1993 UN World Conference on Human Rights, held in Vienna, was a watershed for women's human rights. Of particular significance was the recognition that violence against women, such as domestic abuse, mutilation, burning and rape, is a human rights issue. Previously, these acts had been regarded as private matters, and therefore not appropriate for government or international action." (Women 2000 Report, United Nations, 1998).

At the Conference, the Vienna Declaration and Programme of Action was drafted. Article 38 of the Declaration states:

"Violations of the human rights of women in situations of armed conflict are violations of the fundamental principles of international human rights and humanitarian law. All violations of this kind, including in particular murder, systematic rape, sexual slavery and forced pregnancy, require a particularly effective response."

11–007 *UN 1995 Beijing Declaration and Platform for Action*

These paired documents identified armed conflict and its effect on women as one of the 12 crucial areas of concern to be addressed by States and by the international community. Paragraph 135 of the Declaration states:

"While entire communities suffer the consequences of armed conflict and terrorism, women and girls are particularly affected because of their status in society

350

and their sex. Parties to the conflict often rape women with impunity, sometimes using systematic rape as a tactic of war and terrorism. The impact of violence against women and violations of the human rights of women in such situations is experienced by women of all ages, who suffer displacement, loss of home and property, loss or involuntary disappearance of close relatives, poverty and family separation and disintegration, and who are victims of acts of murder, terrorism, torture, involuntary disappearance, sexual slavery, rape, sexual abuse and forced pregnancy in situations of armed conflict, especially as a result of policies of ethnic cleansing and other new and emerging forms of violence. This is compounded by the life-long social, economic and psychologically traumatic consequences of armed conflict and foreign occupation and alien domination."

Strategic objectives identified within the Platform for Action include:

"D. Violence Against Women

D.1. Take integrated measures to prevent and eliminate violence against women

D.2. Study the causes and consequences of violence against women and the effectiveness of preventive measures

D.3. Eliminate trafficking in women and assist victims of violence due to prostitution and trafficking

E. Women and Armed Conflict

E.1. Increase the participation of women in conflict resolution at decision-making levels and protect women living in situations of armed and other conflicts or under foreign occupation

E.2. Reduce excessive military expenditures and control the availability of armaments

E.3. Promote non-violent forms of conflict resolution and reduce the incidence of human rights abuse in conflict situations

E.4. Promote women's contribution to fostering a culture of peace

E.5. Provide protection, assistance and training to refugee women, other displaced women in need of international protection and internally displaced women

E.6. Provide assistance to the women of the colonies and non-self-governing territories . . ."

But, although a positive step and the source of much publicity, of course no such declarations can be effective without immense resources and international co-operation.

The United Nations response to wartime sexual violence

11–008 Various United Nations bodies and representatives have expressed concern about women's plight during war, including the Commission on the Status of Women 1969, the General Assembly's Declaration on the Protection of Women and Children in Emergency and Armed Conflict 1974, and ECOSOC's resolutions on the situation of women and children living in the occupied Arab territories, under apartheid, and in Namibia (1980s). Not one of these statements referred expressly to sexual violence. Even the Forward-Looking Strategies for the Advancement of Women (Nairobi Conference, 1985) did not refer to sexual violence in the context of armed conflict. Rape of Kuwaiti women by Iraqi troops during the invasion of Kuwait in 1990 was documented in UN reports, and the resultant UN Compensation Committee for Kuwait dealt with claims by rape victims. However, the real change began with Security Council Resolution 798 of December 18, 1992, which denounced the "massive, organized and systematic detention and rape of women, in particular Muslim women, in Bosnia and Herzegovina". The Yugoslav Commission of Experts, which investigated violations of international humanitarian law, gave priority to sexual assaults and documented over 1000 cases. It found that, although all armies involved had committed acts of sexual violence, the overwhelming majority of perpetrators were Bosnian Serbs. Further, the overwhelming majority of victims were Bosnian Muslims, and most of the rape camps were run by Serbs. A Special Rapporteur on the Situation of Human Rights in the Territory of the Former Yugoslavia was appointed, and in 1993 he sent in a task force charged with investigating the occurrence of rape. The team found evidence of the use of rape as a tool for ethnic cleansing, with either the express or implied consent of military and other leaders. The landmark was the creation of the Ad Hoc War Crimes Tribunal in 1993, at the behest of the Security Council, with the task of prosecuting suspects for international humanitarian law violations during the war in the former Yugoslavia. Sexual violence was clearly within its remit from the beginning, as can be seen from its Statute's classification of rape as one of the crimes against humanity.

> "Numerous legal, social, political, financial and logistical obstacles are posed by the international prosecution of rape and other sexual assaults. Some of these have been previously confronted in domestic jurisdictions with varying degrees of success. Others are unique because of the international nature of the Tribunal and the specific subject matter of its jurisdiction. There is no doubt that the Statute and Rules of the Tribunal represent a progressive legislative framework. However, many of the problems will not find their solution rooted in legislative enactment . . . Ultimately, success can only be measured by the prosecution and adjudication of these crimes, which in turn will only occur when women trust the international criminal justice system as an effective and secure avenue of redress."
> (K. Fitzgerald, "Problems of Prosecution and Adjudication of Rape and other Sexual Assaults under International Law", 1998, 8 E.J.I.L. 638)

The international community's response to Rwanda

The sheer scale of the sexual violence inflicted upon Rwandan women during the genocide of 1994 was enormous. Many thousands of women were raped, brutalised with sharp objects, forced into sexual slavery or mutilated. Often this was the penultimate act after the woman had been forced to watch the torture and murder of her family, her own murder following the rape. **11–009**

One of the major positive developments between Nuremberg and Rwanda was the emergence of a strong and effective feminist movement with a powerful NGO base for lobbying and publicity. It was primarily due to lobbying from NGOs that the war in Rwanda became an item on the international agenda after an arguably embarrassingly long delay in UN response. Conservative estimates of the number of women who suffered sexual violence during the war reach many thousands. By 1996, the Special Rapporteur for Rwanda had reported that sexual violence was both systematic and employed as a weapon:

> "Rape was the rule and its absence the exception . . . Under-age children and elderly women were not spared . . . Pregnant women were not spared. Women about to give birth or who had just given birth were also the victims of rape in hospitals . . . Women who were 'untouchable' according to custom (*e.g.* nuns) were also involved and even corpses, in the case of women who were raped just after being killed." (report of January 29, 1996).

Tutsi women were specifically targeted for rape on account of ethnic and gender stereotypes. Perceived as more desirable and more conceited than Hutu women, rape was a method by which they could be humiliated and undermined. Further, violence against women was already very much a factor in Rwandan society, with government estimates of domestic violence stating that one in five women was beaten by her partner. The rapes and other sexual violence during the conflict were therefore not just the "usual" wartime rapes, but also partly born from long-held prejudices and from the mob mentality of mass violence which over-ran the country.

Rwanda is now a predominantly female country, and women from both Tutsi and Hutu families have been profoundly affected by the war and its aftermath. It is possible that the majority of women and girls who survived the massacres are rape victims, that rape was the norm. Even those who have been fortunate enough not to have to endure the loss of their families or personal harm still have to deal with social and health problems and, increasingly, poverty. For those who have survived sexual attacks, sexually transmitted diseases, including HIV, are a serious threat. Many were faced with the choice between an illegal abortion and forced pregnancy with the child of a rapist. Although trials for war crimes committed in Rwanda continue to take place, particularly in other African states asserting universal jurisdiction, hundreds of thousands are suspected of involvement in the violence and so the likely eventual scale of impunity is vast. Rape victims have to overcome additional obstacles at every stage of seeking redress, and so their chances of vindication of their human rights are very small indeed. Initially, the Rwanda Tribunal did little to investigate allegations of rape. The majority of the investigators were male and hence unlikely to be told of rape by the victim due to cultural reasons. In July 1996, a Sexual Assault Committee for the Rwanda Tribunal began to operate and attempted to rebalance the scales by adopting new investigative procedures. However, the number of convictions for crimes of sexual violence to date speaks for itself.

> "Women simply conclude that reporting their cases to the Rwandan judiciary or to the International Criminal Tribunal is not worth the potential risk [of ostracism or violence, since often it was people they knew who raped them]. Rwandan women have also expressed either no knowledge or little confidence in the International Criminal Tribunal to address the issue of rape . . . According to the United Nations Special Rapporteur on Violence Against Women, rape remains the least condemned war crime; throughout history, the rape of hundreds of thousands of women and children in all regions of the world has been a bitter reality . . . Rape has long been mischaracterized and dismissed by military and political leaders as a private crime or the unfortunate behaviour of a renegade soldier. Worse still, it has been accepted precisely because it is so commonplace. The fact that rape often functions in ways similar to other human rights abuses makes all the more striking the fact that, until recently, it has not been exposed and condemned like any other violation. The differential treatment of gender-based violence makes clear that the problem, for the most part, lies not in the absence of adequate legal prohibitions, but in the international community's willingness to tolerate sexual abuse against women."
> (B. Nowrojee, "Shattered Lives: Sexual Violence during the Rwandan Genocide and its Aftermath", Human Rights Watch, New York, 1996)

In the two years following the violence, local police inspectors appear to have turned away women who came to them to report rape. Some of them were unaware that rape was a crime even though it was a crime under Rwandan law. It was also mainly due to the efforts of NGOs that official documentation of the scale of the rapes in Rwanda took place. In spite of overwhelming evidence of rapes in the *Akayesu* case, it appears that the prosecutors were not planning to amend the indictments to include any charges related to sexual violence, until an *amicus curiae* brief was filed by various women's and human rights groups. Two weeks later, the prosecutor changed his mind to include rape charges on the indictment. Remarkably, there is no mention of the brief in the case documentation.

But the creation of ICTR, the Rwanda Tribunal, was not a panacea. Very little investigation of sexual violence was carried out in the first two years of the Tribunal's existence, and consequently the first indictment to charge rape as a crime was in 1997. This is all the more surprising when compared to the advances made on paper by the Rwanda Tribunal's Statute, which not only followed ICTY's example by listing rape as a crime against humanity, but also expressly declared rape, enforced prostitution and indecent assault to be violations of Common Art. 3 of the Geneva Conventions and Additional Protocol II.

One of the problems in adequately labeling crimes of sexual violence com- **11–010**
mitted on a vast scale is that genocide requires proof of an ulterior, or specific, intent. The acts of rape must be committed with the intent of
destroying, in whole or in part, a national, ethnic, racial or religious group.
Just because the rapes occur contemporaneously to, or within the general
environment of, genocide does not mean that it will fit that crime's definition.
There must be clear evidence that the rapes had such an intention behind
them. This has proved very difficult indeed to show, although it may be
inferred from all the surrounding circumstances. To most observers, there is
no doubt that the vast majority of the rapes were part of a genocidal intent,
or that many of the rapists at least expected that the physical and psychological damage their acts would inflict would be a step towards the grand plan
of the destruction of the Tutsi people. Many victims of rape were killed or
left for dead, which is further evidence of relevant specific intent.

Sexual violence in the ICTY and ICTR Statutes and the Rules of Procedure   **11–011**
and Evidence

Under the ICTY Statute, sexual violence is only included explicitly as follows:

> "Article 5. Crimes against humanity.
>
> The International Tribunal shall have the power to prosecute persons responsible
> for the following crimes when committed in armed conflict, whether international
> or internal in character, and directed against any civilian population:
>
> . . . (g) rape . . . "

Similarly under the ICTR Statute (the differences between the wording of the
Articles is largely due to the different nature of each conflict, and have been
discussed in detail elsewhere in this book):

> "Article 3. Crimes against humanity.
>
> The International Tribunal for Rwanda shall have the power to prosecute persons
> responsible for the following crimes when commtted as part of a widespread or
> systematic attack against any civilian population on national, political, ethnic,
> racial or religious grounds:
>
> . . . (g) rape . . . "

Although both Tribunals have jurisdiction over grave breaches of the Geneva
Conventions including Common Art. 3, Art. 4 as the relevant provisions of
the ICTR Statute makes sexual violence explicit:

"VIOLATIONS OF ARTICLE 3 COMMON TO THE GENEVA CONVENTIONS AND OF ADDITIONAL PROTOCOL II

The International Tribunal for Rwanda shall have the power to prosecute persons committing or ordering to be committed serious violations of Article 3 common to the Geneva Conventions of 12 August 1949 for the Protection of War Victims, and of Additional Protocol II thereto of 8 June 1977. These violations shall include, but shall not be limited to:

. . . (e) Outrages upon personal dignity humiliating and degrading treatment, rape, enforced prostitution and any form of indecent assault . . . "

Thus, although there has been a general if slow expansion in the scope of sexual violence in the statutory measures, there remains a strong and largely unwelcome link between sexual violence and honour or dignity. Further, until the ICC Statute it has been through cases of the two tribunals that the real progress in the potential punishment of sexual violence in international criminal law has occurred, with each court interpreting the other offences under its Statute to include sexual violence by implication.

Under the Nuremberg Charter, although rape was a crime against humanity, crimes against humanity as a whole were only punishable if they occurred in the context of war. Under the ICTY Statute, that category of crimes was punishable whether committed in an internal or international armed conflict. By Rwanda, the relevant Statute provision had progressed to cover crimes committed "as part of a widespread or systematic attack". Can crimes against humanity now be prosecuted even when committed in peacetime?

The Rules of Procedure and Evidence of ICTY were drafted by its judges. Since there was so little pre-existing statutory or international law, they employed tools and rules from many national jurisdictions, yet had to maintain their focus on the situation in the former Yugoslavia. The resultant rules represent a compromise between the rights of the accused, those of the victims and witnesses, and the international community's need for crimes to be punished.

11–012 One strength of ICTY has been the extent to which its rules of procedure and evidence in the context of sexual violence cases far outstrip those of most domestic legal systems. Due to the wartime nature of the rapes dealt with by the Tribunal, many of the factors that result in the extraordinarily high acquittal rate in national courts are deemed to be simply irrelevant or inadmissible. Further, the measures for the protection of witnesses and victims are both a sensible precaution and extensive, on paper at least. Pseudonyms are used, voices and photo images electronically disguised and transcripts are edited to remove any reference to the victim's identity. Evidence can be given *in camera* or *via* one-way CCTV, a Victims and Witnesses Unit has been operational since 1995, and (most controversially) in certain cases the identity of the victim and some witnesses may be kept secret from the accused even at trial. Similar provisions apply under the ICTR Rules of Procedure and Evidence (see Rules 69 and 75).

But do such measures go far enough? When trying cases involving allegations of rape and sexual assault, an awareness of the specific social, customary and cultural factors which affect witnesses and victims is paramount, in addition to an understanding of the devastating effect which trauma resulting from sexual assault may have upon every aspect of a person's life and being, including her memory.

Rule 34A of ICTY established the Victims and Witnesses Unit with the remit to:

(i) recommend protective measures for victims and witnesses in accordance with Article 22 of the Statute; and

(ii) provide counseling and support for them, in particular in cases of rape and sexual assault

The definition of "victim" (under Rule 2[A]) is "a person against whom a crime over which the Tribunal has jurisdiction has allegedly been committed."

The Unit is independent and provides its services to both defence and prosecution witnesses. Similar services on a greater scale are provided for by the ICC Statute, see below.

Rule 34A of ICTR similarly but more expansively provides: **11–013**

"VICTIMS AND WITNESSES SUPPORT UNIT

There shall be set up under the authority of the Registrar a Victims and Witnesses Support Unit consisting of qualified staff to:

(i) recommended the adoption of protective measures for victims and witnesses in accordance with Article 21 of the Statute;

(ii) ensure that they receive relevant support, including physical and psychological rehabilitation, especially counseling in cases of rape and sexual assault; and

(iii) develop short term and long term plans for the protection of witnesses who have testified before the Tribunal and who fear a threat to their life, property or family.

B. A gender sensitive approach to victims and witnesses protective and support measures should be adopted and due consideration given, in the appointment of staff within this Unit, to the employment of qualified women."

Rule 96

Rule 96 of the ICTY Rules deals with corroboration, consent as a defence, **11–014** and evidence of prior sexual history of the complainant. There have been three versions of Rule 96. It started as a blanket denial of the need for certain well established, common and traditional rules of criminal evidence that have a large negative impact on the rights of complainants of sexual offences. It went far beyond previous international criminal law (to the extent that such rules existed therein), and far outstripped most domestic legal systems in protection of victims" rights. The first version (February 11, 1994) provided:

"In cases of sexual assault:

    (i)   no corroboration of the victim's testimony shall be required;
    (ii)   consent shall not be allowed as a defence;
    (iii) prior sexual conduct of the victim shall not be admitted in evidence."

The driving force behind the blanket prohibition on any consent-based defence was due to a stand that consent is irrelevant in the context of war, when the victim is one of a subjugated people under attack. It is true that, on the facts of any of the cases so far prosecuted as sex crimes in either ICTY or ICTR, the idea of a consent defence beggars belief. However, the fact that no borderline case has been prosecuted does not mean that the Tribunal, which is at least strongly persuasive in the formation and formulation of international criminal law and procedures, should ignore the defendant's human/due process rights altogether. A false or mistaken allegation is perfectly possible, even in the context of war crimes.

As regards the prohibition of questioning the victim as to her previous sexual experiences, this is a powerful provision that saves victims from undergoing the distress and humiliation such examination and cross-examination has so commonly caused in domestic cases. When the factual situation is as extreme as that of war or internal armed conflict, behaviour of any party before the conflict is hardly relevant. In Rwanda, previously civil and even happy neighbours tortured and murdered each other. When the victims have undergone such great torment and pain, to allow further attacks on their dignity within the court room would be very difficult to justify.

The second version (May 5,1994) was introduced to allow a limited defence of consent in accordance with the rights of the defendant in international law, and to judge the defendant on the basis of his own actions and beliefs, rather than on the existence of widespread violence in wartime:

"In cases of sexual assault:

    (i)   no corroboration of the victim's testimony shall be required;
    (ii)   consent shall not be allowed as a defence if the victim

        (a)   has been subjected to or threatened with or has reason to fear violence, duress, detention or psychological oppression, or
        (b)   reasonably believed that if she did not submit, another might be so subjected, threatened or put in fear;

    (iii) prior sexual conduct of the victim shall not be admitted in evidence."

There was an outcry against this amendment, and on January 30, 1995 a third version was adopted, which falls (in terms of balance of victim's and defendant's rights) between Versions 1 and 2:

"In cases of sexual assault:

   (i)   no corroboration of the victim's testimony shall be required;

   (ii)   consent shall not be allowed as a defence if the victim

        (a)   has been subjected to or threatened with or has had reason to fear violence, duress, detention, or psychological oppression, or

        (b)   reasonably believed that if the victim did not submit, another might be so subjected, threatened or put in fear;

   (iv)   prior sexual conduct of the victim shall not be admitted in evidence."

There was an outcry against this amendment, and on January 30, 1995 a third version was adopted, which falls (in terms of balance of victim's and defendant's rights) between the first two versions:

"In cases of sexual assault:

   (i)   no corroboration of the victim's testimony shall be required;

   (ii)   consent shall not be allowed as a defence if the victim

        (a)   has been subjected to or threatened with or has had reason to fear violence, duress, detention, or psychological oppression, or

        (b)   reasonably believed that if the victim did not submit, another might be so subjected, threatened or put in fear;

   (iii)   before evidence of the victim's consent is admitted, the accused shall satisfy the Trial Chamber in camera that the evidence is relevant and credible;

   (iv)   prior sexual conduct of the victim shall not be admitted in evidence."

This third version appears to reach an acceptable compromise between the rights of the defendant and victim. The limited consent defence remains, but must be backed by "relevant and credible" evidence before it can be argued in court. Thus, judges act as a filter to prevent outrageous consent allegations. Would not such a test conceivably work in national courts?

It remains unclear, however, whether the test for belief in consent is an **11–015** objective or subjective one. All three versions of the Rule made a significant statement in denying outright the need for corroboration of the victim's testimony. Women are not to be doubted just because they have made a complaint of a sexual offence. However, all three suffer from one major defect, as far as consent is concerned: the lack of a rule that a child below a stipulated age, preferably 16, cannot give a consent that would form any defence. This is a serious defect when many reports exist from both the former Yugoslavia and Rwanda of the rape and sexual mutilation of very young children.

"... the exclusion of the corroboration requirement confirms the formal international standards of equality between the sexes. In other words, the decisions by the ICTR and the ICTY simply bring women into an equal position as men under international law, vis — à-vis their status as innocent civilians. In short, rather than reinforcing tired stereotypes about women and their weakness and vulnerability during war, the decisions by the tribunals, especially the Kunarac decision by the ICTY, actually make women more fully members of the international community and subject to the same protections as men." (J.R. McHenry III, "The Prosecution of Rape under International Law: Justice that is Long Overdue", (2002) Vanderbilt Journal of Transnational Law Vol. 35, no. 4.)

Collection of evidence has been a major problem for the Tribunals, never more so than when the charges are related to sexual assault. How can evidence be collected and evaluated successfully without the co-operation of those in power in the territory? After the Second World War, the Nuremberg trials were possible only because the Allies had control over the territory where the investigations centred, and had physical custody of many of those whom they wanted to send for trial. This was not the case in either the former Yugoslavia or Rwanda. It does not help that many potential witnesses have fled, become refugees or otherwise disappeared. Medical evidence is not always available, and even when the victim received prompt medical treatment and samples, evidence and records were kept, many have since been destroyed.

The Office of the Prosecutor for the Yugoslavia Tribunal was intended to function in a form that recognised wartime violence against women and charged offences correspondingly. For that purpose, a legal adviser for gender issues was appointed and specific investigatory teams were created for sexual violence. The impact of gender integration and attention to cases of sexual violence has not been as great as might have been hoped. As will be seen, the wait for a conviction for rape in ICTY was a long one, and the most significant case development came from the younger Rwanda Tribunal.

Recognition of the importance of actually including rape and sexual assault charges on indictments alongside more "tried and tested" charges came not from the prosecutors but first from judges. In a number of cases before ICTY, judges have urged the prosecutor to think again and amend the charge list, having heard clear testimony from witnesses about the events in rape camps. The *Dragan Nikolic* Decision (Trial Chamber I, 20/11/1995) is one example of this:

> "From multiple testimony and the witness statements submitted by the Prosecutor to this Trial Chamber, it appears that women (and girls) were subjected to rape and other forms of sexual assault during their detention as Susica camp. Dragan Nikolic and other persons connected with the camp are alleged to have been directly involved in some of these rapes or sexual assaults. These allegations do not seem to relate solely to isolated instances . . . The Trial Chamber feels that the prosecutor may be well advised to review these statements carefully with a view to ascertaining whether to charge Dragan Nikolic with rape and other forms of sexual assault, either as a crime against humanity or as grave breaches or war crimes."

Although it is, in the main, a good thing that the indictments in several high-profile ICTY and ICTR cases have been amended to add charges related to sexual violence, why were such charges not brought originally? The possibility of amendment itself shows that sufficient evidence was already available to support those charges.

The evidence of rape and sexual assaults in the above case, as in several **11–016** others, was obvious and strong. The Tribunal's Rules of Procedure and Evidence contain a list of provisions with the specific aim of protecting vulnerable witnesses and testifying victims, because it was expected from the outset that prosecutions for sexual violence would be taking place. In the light of this, why were sex-related charges so noticeably absent in so many trials? Even before the Tribunal was created, such charges were anticipated, *per* the Secretary-General's Report on Aspects of Establishing an International Tribunal for the Prosecution of Persons Responsible for Serious Violations of International Humanitarian Law Committed in the Territory of the Former Yugoslavia, S/25704, 1993:

> "In the light of the particular nature of the crimes committed in the former Yugoslavia, it will be necessary for the International Tribunal to ensure the protection of victims and witnesses. Necessary protection measures should therefore be provided in the rules of procedure and evidence for victims and witnesses, especially in cases of rape or sexual assault."

In relation to the importance of protection for witnesses and victims of sexual assault:

> "It is important not to underrate the extent to which a variety of measures may be necessary to protect the witnesses, and their families, before, during and after testifying. Continuing, if not open, hostilities, an uncooperative government and a firmly entrenched international mafia all constitute justification for a comprehensive witness protection scheme able to respond to varying threat levels. This service should include relocation of witnesses, which is recognized internationally as the most effective form of protection. Incidental to the provision of protection is the responsibility to inform every witness, but particularly those for whom adequate protection cannot be provided, of the risks they may encounter by testifying. The availability of adequate procedural safeguards may be a decisive factor in a woman's decision to testify before the Tribunal. Without guarantees that her identity will be protected a witness may face reprisals, not only from those against whom she testifies but from her husband, family and society. In communities where a woman's value is defined according to her virginity and chastity, raped women suffer rejection. For male victims, the sexual assault challenges notions of manhood and virility. The additional stigma that many cultures attach to homosexuality will undoubtedly influence a decision to testify." (K. Fitzgerald, "Problems of Prosecution and Adjudication of Rape and other Sexual Assaults under International Law", (1998) 8 E.J.I.L. 638.)

Support may have to continue in the long-term, and will require cultural sensitivity and working with local communities to develop a trust-based relationship. A remaining problem is that to undertake this all properly requires an enormous amount of funding. Will even the ICC be able to raise it, given the problems there have been in reaching agreement on even the most basic issues?

11–017   *Tadic guidelines on protection of witnesses*

Cases have taken further initiatives towards witness protection in the Tribunals. In *Tadic* the Trial Chamber found that, under both the Statute and the Rules of the Tribunal, it was possible to protect the identity of witnesses from the public, and even from the accused. The majority of the judges, acknowledging the balancing act involved between the rights of the accused and the victim, found the following factors to be relevant in determining on the facts of each individual case whether to protect identity: whether the witness's testimony is vital to the prosecution, whether they have support available within their family and/or community, the perceived fears of the witness and whether these are merely of future reprisals or based in existing threats. Also relevant are the availability of resources to the Tribunal, the persisting tensions in the geographical region and, above all, the Tribunal's key purpose of administering justice and punishing the persons responsible for grave violations of human rights.

KEY FURTHER DEVELOPMENTS IN CASE LAW

11–018   Female judges in both ICTY and ICTR played a crucial role in the formulation of rules of evidence and procedure such as Rule 96 and have had an impact upon several key case decisions. Selected significant decisions from each Tribunal so far will be examined in detail below, but the fact that it is possible to refer to all cases so far decided demonstrates just how few trials have actually taken place.

The presence of women in significant positions in both the ICTY and the ICTR is far superior to the traditional minimal and invisible role of women in international organisations and bodies and in the previous criminal tribunals. Many of the crimes charged in the cases which have appeared so far in front of ICTY and ICTR were those committed disproportionately against women and girls, so there is a greater visibility of women in the decisions. It is hoped that the case law will have great impact on the law's future treatment of victims of sexual violence and other forms of violence.

Ironically, the general failures of the two tribunals to adequately prosecute and punish sexual violence have actually been useful. They have identified the express and unseen discriminatory practices in international criminal law and procedures and have, by trial and error, developed some gender-sensitive mechanisms to protect victims and witnesses.

Selected landmarks

11–019   The main impact of the case law of the two Tribunals has been upon the definitions of rape and sexual violence which they have provided and incrementally expanded, and which are becoming part of international criminal law. However, other significant changes have been introduced to rules and procedure as well as to law.

Tadic, ICTY 1996

The Tadic indictments at first did not recognise the significance of the evidence of the rapes at Omarska, focusing rather upon the physical violence endured by male prisoners. It was an amicus brief that spurred on the judges to question the lack of charges of sexual violence, and the indictment was amended to include rape. However, the rape charges were then dropped because a witness, lacking effective protection, would not testify. The Tribunal took the opportunity to develop guidelines for giving witnesses/victims confidentiality and sometimes anonymity even from the defence.   **11–020**

Tadic was a Bosnian Serb café owner, karate instructor and part-time traffic policeman, who was tried for 31 counts of grave breaches, war crimes, and crimes against humanity relating to the torture and murder of Muslims at three Serb prison camps. With 125 witnesses and 400 exhibits, this was a big trial for a comparatively small fish. He was convicted of 11 counts. The 301 page judgment is very detailed, full of insights into international criminal law and procedure and the workings of ICTY/ what it sees as its role.

The Tadic Trial Chamber heard the first ever testimony given of rape as a war crime. Although the rape charges in that case were withdrawn before the trial began, witness testimony about rapes was used as part of the evidence against Tadic in relation to the other charges he faced. This was the first time in history that an international tribunal had heard direct evidence of rape. The Tribunal stated:

> "It has been noted that rape and sexual assault often have particularly devastating consequences which, in certain instances, may have a detrimental effect upon the victim . . . It has been noted further that testifying about the event is often difficult, particularly in public, and can result in rejection by the victim's family and community . . . In addition, traditional court practice and procedures have been known to exacerbate the victim's ordeal during trial. Women who have been raped and have sought justice in the legal system commonly compare this experience to being raped a second time."

The ICTY Trial Chamber convicted him of sex crimes (although not those originally charged) and specifically referred to sexual violence against both men and women, citing in great detail the pain and suffering of the victims. It was expected to be the first international war crimes tribunal ever to prosecute rape separately as a war crime but the prosecutor had to withdraw the rape charges in counts 2–4 of the indictment because a witness was too frightened to testify. But amongst the convictions were "inhumane acts" including sexual mutilation as both a crime against humanity and a war crime; and of persecution including rape and other forms of sexual violence. It includes an important statement by the Tribunal that corroboration is not necessary due to Rule 96(I): this "accords to the testimony of a victim of sexual assault the same presumption of reliability as the testimony of victims of other crimes, something long denied to victims of sexual assault by the common law" (para. 536), concluding that corroboration is not part of customary international law and need not be required by the ICTY (para. 539). Although there was not sufficient admissible evidence that Tadic himself had committed rape, the tribunal did state that rape and other forms of sexual violence were pervasive and had devastating effects on the victims and the community; thus even a nonstate actor or a minor official may be convicted as an accomplice to or knowing participant in sexual violence, including by tacit encouragement.

Furundzija, ICTY, 1998

11–021 The Tribunal rejected the idea that Post Traumatic Stress Disorder necessarily makes a victim an unreliable witness. He was a military commander, Croatian, and charged in relation to the rape and assault of one Muslim victim. It should have been a simple trial but false memory syndrome of the victim was alleged and later discounted; he was found guilty on both counts of war crimes. The Tribunal looked at many countries" definitions of rape to make theirs, conducting the first of several exercises in comparative law, and the resulting expansive definition was welcome. The war crimes conviction is important because it recognised rape as a war crime; this has been adopted by the ICC Statute. The Tribunal gave definitions of rape and of aiding and abetting, the Trial Chamber attempting to give an "accurate definition of rape based on the criminal law principle of specificity."

Celebici Camp (Delalic), ICTY, 1998

11–022 The court removed from the record questioning about a witness" previous abortion, hence reasserting the importance of Rule 96's ban on questioning and evidence relating to the prior sexual history of the victim of a sex offence.

The *Delalic/Celebici* camp case is important, in that it recognises rape as torture even when it occurs outside circumstances of interrogation. Further, the court saw the extent to which rape causes both physical and psychological suffering to the victim and to others, and found that rape which occurs in armed conflict almost automatically has the purposes required for a finding of torture, *i.e.* punishment, coercion, intimidation or discrimination. The four defendants were three Bosnian Muslims and one Bosnian Croat who were at different levels (up to commander) of the prison camp at Celebici. The Commander was found guilty under principle of command responsibility for various acts of torture and ill-treatment. Two others were also found guilty of grave breaches of Geneva Conventions and violations of laws/customs of war. The Tribunal dealt with both rape as torture and as a war crime (grave breach of Geneva Conventions). It examined torture by means of rape, adopting the expansive and considered ICTR *Akayesu* definition of rape, which is discussed further below. Command responsibility was defined and used as a method of creating liability: D need not be a military commander, just someone with *de facto* authority over those who commit the crime, and must know or have constructive knowledge that there is a risk of such crimes being committed. This was the first decision since Nuremberg and Tokyo to apply the principle, it was thought to have fallen into disuse but could be of great use in international criminal law in the punishment of wartime sexual violence. The Tribunal further found that the definition of torture under the Torture Convention has become customary international law and gave it a very broad meaning. The definition given to rape was also very broad — physical invasion of a sexual nature, committed on a person under circumstances which are coercive. Although, as the sentencing was concurrent not consecutive, sentences served will be surprisingly short, *e.g.* seven years for Mucic after conviction of 11 counts (seven years each).

Kvocka

Rape, threat of rape and other forms of sexual violence can amount to torture.   **11–023**
This is important because it is broader than *Aydin* as it includes sexual harassment, intimidation and humiliation as being capable of amounting to torture.

Musema

The Appeals Chamber quashed conviction for rape as a crime against   **11–024**
humanity due to presentation of new evidence, but some useful statements were made at the trial.

Kunarac, Kovac and Vukovic, ICTY, 2001

The court expressly recognised the victim's right to sexual autonomy.   **11–025**
Although, the concentration is still almost entirely on sexual violence not on women's experiences of armed conflict. The trial was of three Serbs involved in running the rape camp at Foca, which was found to be part of systematic attack against Muslim civilians. It was held that there is no defence of superior orders. The case was a significant advance in international law regarding the treatment of sexual violence in wartime: rape will not be accepted as part of war; and there were no other charges in this case. It is also a landmark decision on sexual violence and enslavement: the first conviction for enslavement as a crime against humanity. Rape was recognised as a weapon of war. The Tribunal further seems to be trying to broaden the definition of torture beyond that of the Convention by claiming that no state official needs to be present or involved here. There was an immediate positive response from human rights organisations across the world regarding the expanded definition of sexual slavery as a crime against humanity and the clear definition of rape camps as both a war crime and a crime against humanity. It can thus be seen as a strong endorsement of the human rights of women in war or armed conflict and distances the Tribunal from international law's regular identification of women with questions of honour. It is also possible to read the decision as containing or supporting questionable views of women as weak

and defenseless creatures, with almost automatic "victim status" in war particularly in relation to crimes against humanity. The Tribunal used the decision of ICTR in *Akayesu* as a foundation from which to close pre-existing gaps in international criminal law regarding torture, rape, sexual slavery, war crimes, genocide and crimes against humanity.

Todorovic indictment

11–026   Here, rape and other forms of sexual violence were charged for forcing two prisoners to perform sexual acts upon each other. The individual directly responsible for the sexual violence and the superior who failed to prevent, stop, or punish him were charged under exactly the same articles and subarticles.

Akayesu, ICTR, 1998

11–027   The defendant was Burgomaster of Taba commune (*i.e.* controller of public order); Tutsis sought refuge there, and A incited their rape and murder. This historic case was the first ever conviction in an international tribunal for genocide. The Tribunal found that sexual violence including rape can be genocide. The landmark definition given of rape is that of "a physical invasion of a sexual nature, committed on a person under circumstances which are coercive."

It is recognised as a remarkable judgment due to its detailed legal analysis of issues, especially sexual violence. The court was very sensitive to the victims, and very flexible in in its procedures to help them. It also invented a crime of sexual violence falling short of rape, but unfortunately did not give this a clear definition.

This case became the first ever international criminal tribunal conviction for genocide and a historic decision on sexual violence, but did not start out as a sexual violence trial. Evidence of rape was heard during the trial and the indictment was amended accordingly. Witness testimony went on to establish that sexual violence was an integral and a fundamental element of the Rwandan genocide. The indictment defined acts of sexual violence to "include forcible sexual penetration of the vagina, anus or oral cavity by a penis and/or of the vagina or anus by some other object, and sexual abuse, such as forced nudity" (para. 10A). The inclusion of forced nudity as an offence in the indictment supports the view that violence need not result solely from physical violence, but also includes mental violence of this nature. He was found guilty *inter alia* of knowing that crimes of sexual violence were being committed, facilitating and indeed ordering their commission and on some occasions being present. The main points of significance of the decision for international criminal law include: the trial chamber recognising sexual violence as an integral part of the genocide in Rwanda, and finding the accused guilty of genocide for crimes that included sexual violence; the chamber recognising rape and other forms of sexual violence as independent crimes constituting crimes against humanity; and the chamber enunciating a broad, progressive international definition of both rape and sexual violence. The tribunal defined rape as "a physical invasion of a sexual nature, committed on a person under circumstances which are coercive." The tribunal also showed sensitivity to the needs, dignity and suffering of victims of sexual violence. *Akayesu* highlights the extent to which sexual violence was an integral part of the Rwandan genocide and is also the most progressive decision in any international case concerning sexual violence:

> "*Akayesu* was a landmark: the first international conviction for genocide, the first judgment to recognize rape and sexual violence as constitutive acts of genocide, and the first to advance a broad definition of rape as a physical invasion of a sexual nature, freeing it from mechanical descriptions and required penetration of the vagina by the penis. The judgment also held that forced nudity is a form of inhumane treatment, and it recognized that rape is a form of torture and noted the failure to charge it as such under the rubric of war crimes." (R. Copelon, "Gender Crimes as War Crimes: Integrating Crimes Against Women into International Criminal Law" ((2000) 46 McGill L.J. 217.)

As Copelon points out, some of the clearest evidence of genocide in the Akayesu case was that concerning the rapes and other sexual violence. This seems somewhat paradoxical when considering the difficulties in getting that evidence to court in the first place, and appears to indicate that many other cases could, in fact, be supported rather than weakened by including sexual violence on indictments, and thereby getting such evidence into the tribunals.

Nyiramusuhuko and Ntahobali, ICTR, 2001

These cases are notable since they include a woman defendant for charges **11–028** including sexual violence. The mother and son defendants were guilty of a crime against humanity where they used a roadblock to commit offences including murder, inciting murder, and systematic rapes. Nyiramasuhuko is the first woman to be convicted of rape as an international crime by an international tribunal, and was an accomplice by omission, in that she knew that her subordinates were raping Tutsi women and failed to take measures to either prevent it or to punish the perpetrators.

In spite of these quite remarkable developments in the ICTY and ICTR cases, as pointed out by Copelon there is still no room for complacency and much for improvement:

> " ... notwithstanding the landmark *Akayesu* judgment, the ICTR prosecutor has been slow to incorporate charges of sexual violence consistently and in accordance with their deserved gravity. There is an apparent absence of both a clear policy that gender is a priority concern and of a gender expert, with oversight authority, on-site. Issues of witness protection, the gender — sensitivity of investigations, and community relations have been equally significant. Perhaps someday the integration of and respect for gender expertise will become routine, dispensing with the need for continued monitoring by feminist attorneys and activists. That day is still far off."

SELECTED DECISIONS IN GREATER DETAIL

Trial of Jean-Paul Akayesu, ICTR September 2, 1998

11–029   **Facts**: Jean-Paul Akayesu was the bourgmestre (mayor) of the Taba commune at the time the crimes alleged were committed. In that capacity he was in charge of public order and various administrative functions in the commune, including controlling the local police and the administration of justice. He was responsible only to the prefect. It was argued that the crimes committed in the commune were so open and so widespread that Akayesu must have known about them. Between April and July 1994, hundreds of displaced civilians sought refuge on bureau communal premises. Many of them were women who were subjected to repeated acts of sexual violence on the communal premises, and concurrent threats of death. Others were murdered or tortured. It was not argued that he himself committed any substantive offences, rather that he incited, facilitated and failed to prevent those committed by others or gave his implicit support. Akayesu, a man previously considered by the community to be possessed of high morals, intelligence and integrity, was charged with genocide, crimes against humanity, and violations of Common Art. 3 of the Geneva Conventions:

> Genocide; complicity in genocide; the crime against humanity of extermination; incitement to commit genocide; direct and public incitement to commit genocide; the crime against humanity of murder; the Geneva Convention violation of murder; torture as a crime against humanity; cruel treatment as a Geneva Convention violation; rape as a crime against humanity; other inhumane acts as a crime against humanity; outrages upon personal dignity (rape and sexual violence) as a Geneva Convention violation.

The last three counts (those relating to sexual violence and rape) were added more than a year after the initial charges. Akayesu pleaded not guilty to all charges, running a defence of straightforward denial of any involvement in wrongdoing: in relation to the murder charges he denied that he could have prevented the killings; and in relation to the sexual violence charges, he denied that any such acts were committed at all, arguing that the charges had been added only due to the pressure of public opinion and that some witnesses were fantasists (a variant of the familiar "women lie about rape" story).

Decision.   As a finding of fact, the Chamber held that there was sufficient credible evidence to establish beyond a reasonable doubt that the rapes had occurred and that the Accused "had reason to know and in fact knew that sexual violence was taking place on or near the premises of the bureau communal. . . .[t]here is no evidence that the Accused took any measures to prevent acts of sexual violence or to punish the perpetrators of sexual violence. In fact there is evidence that the Accused ordered, instigated and otherwise aided and abetted sexual violence." Finding that rape falls within the scope of genocidal measures, they convicted Akayesu (*inter alia*) of genocide and crimes against humanity. One interesting aspect of the decision is the scope of the definition given to rape as a crime against humanity:

> "687. The Tribunal considers that rape is a form of aggression and that the central elements of the crime of rape cannot be captured in a mechanical description of objects and body parts. The Tribunal also notes the cultural sensitivities involved in public discussion of intimate matters and recalls the painful reluctance and inability of witnesses to disclose graphic anatomical details of sexual

violence they endured. The United Nations Convention Against Torture and Other Cruel, Inhuman and Degrading Treatment or Punishment does not catalogue specific acts in its definition of torture, focusing rather on the conceptual framework of State-sanctioned violence. The Tribunal finds this approach more useful in the context of international law. Like torture, rape is used for such pruposes as intimidation, degradation, humiliation, discrimination, punishment, control or destruction of a person. Like torture, rape is a violation of personal dignity, and rape in fact constitutes torture when it is inflicted by or at the instigation of or with the consent or acquiescence of a public official or other person acting in an official capacity.

688. The Tribunal defines rape as a physical invasion of a sexual nature, committed on a person under circumstances which are coercive. The Tribunal considers sexual violence, which includes rape, as any act of a sexual nature which is committed on a person under circumstances which are coercive. Sexual violence is not limited to physical invasion of the human body and may include acts which do not involve penetration or even physical contact. . . .''

Trial of Anto Furundzija

Furundzija is a very difficult case from which to draw conclusions since it was **11–030** both conducted largely *in camera* and the transcript was redacted. The essence of the indictment was that F was present while acts of sexual violence were committed, including rape, and that he did nothing to prevent them and/or implicitly encouraged their occurrence (*i.e.* aided or abetted rape). One particular problem with the case was the trial chamber's order that the prosecution should disclose all documents in their possession relating to the material and relevant to the issue of any medical, psychological or psychiatric treatment or counseling received by Witness A after May 1993. This order is extremely invasive of privacy, allowing access to irrelevant documents as well as those relevant, without any sifting process by the court.

- The prohibition against torture was found to have achieved the status of *jus cogens*, *i.e.* a peremptory norm of international law from which no derogation can be permitted.

- Rape and other serious sexual assaults in armed conflict indisputably entail individual responsibility for their perpetrators.

- Agreeing with the *Celebici* verdict, the Tribunal found that rape may amount to torture under international law, and widened the definition of rape beyond that in the *Akayesu* decision. Rape under international law now comprises "the sexual penetration, however slight, either of the vagina or anus of the victim by the penis of the perpetrator, or any other object used by the perpetrator, or of the mouth of the victim by the penis of the perpetrator, where such penetration is effected by coercion or force or threat of force against the victim or a third person."

- An accused who participates in an integral part of torture and is a party to the prohibited purpose behind the torture (*i.e.* intent to obtain information or a confession, to punish or intimidate, humiliate, coerce or discriminate against the victim or a third person) is responsible as a *co-perpetrator.*

Facts. The accused was charged with a grave breach of the Geneva Conventions and violations of the laws or customs of war. The individual charges were: torture and inhumane treatment, and torture and outrages upon personal dignity including rape. The charges related to acts that took place at the headquarters of the Jokers, a special unit within the Croatian Defence Council (HVO). He pleaded not guilty to all charges. The grave breach charge was withdrawn and the prosecution filed a motion seeking protection measures for victims and witnesses, which was granted. Pseudonyms were used, two of the witnesses testified in closed session and image distortion was used for two others. The first trial ended with a finding of serious misconduct by the prosecution, in that they had failed to disclose facts concerning the principal witness" medical treatment and counseling. A new trial began and found that post traumatic stress disorder did not necessarily affect the credibility of a witness, stating that:

> "there is no reason why a person with PTSD cannot be a perfectly reliable witness. The Trial Chamber is of the view that survivors of such traumatic experiences cannot reasonably be expected to recall the precise minutiae of events, such as exact dates or times. Neither can they reasonably be expected to recall every single element of a complicated and traumatic sequence of events. In fact, inconsistencies may, in certain circumstances, indicate truthfulness and the absence of interference with witnesses."

At the full trial, the defendant was charged with two counts of violations of the laws or customs of war under Art. 3 of the Statute of the International Tribunal: torture and outrages upon personal dignity, including rape. The defendant was present while the victim was threatened and raped by another soldier.

> "There is no doubt that the accused and Accused B, as commanders, divided the process of interrogation by performing different functions. The role of the accused was to question, while Accused B's role was to assault and threaten in order to elicit the required information from Witness A and Witness D."

Decision of the Appeal Chamber July 21, 2000

(i)   *False memory syndrome*

The appellant alleged that Witness A's memory was unreliable because she suffered from PTSD. The Appeal Chamber agreed with the Trial Chamber that "even when a person is suffering from PTSD, this does not mean that he or she is necessarily inaccurate in the evidence given. There is no reason why a person with PTSD cannot be a perfectly reliable witness." [para. 109]

(ii)   *Accomplice to rape*

The appellant argued that there was no evidence that his actions had contributed to the rape directly, or that the rape would not have happened in this manner had he not aided it willingly. Additionally, he claimed that failing to endeavour to prevent the rape of Witness A was not enough to create accomplice liability for him, as there was no evidence that his mere presence was calculated to give additional confidence to the perpetrator of the rape, and there was no allegation of a common purpose behind the rape. Thus, he argued, there was no basis in existing case law on which he could be held responsible as an accomplice to rape.

The prosecutor argued that the appellant had misunderstood the relevant case law. A "knowing presence" which has a direct and substantial effect on the commission of the illegal act is sufficient "to base a finding of participation and assign the criminal culpability that accompanies it." [*Delalic*, 16/11/1998, paras 327–8]

(iii) *Torture*

The Appeal Chamber found it "inconceivable that it could ever be argued that the acts charged ... namely, the rubbing of a knife against a woman's thighs and stomach, coupled with a threat to insert the knife into her vagina, once proven, are not serious enough to amount to torture."

(iv) *Judge Mumba's human rights involvement*

Furundzija attempted to question Judge Mumba's impartiality by referring to her former involvement with the UN Commission on the Status of Women (UNCSW). UNCSW was involved in the preparations for the Beijing Women's Conference in 1995 and participated in drafting the "Platform for Action", which identified 12 key areas of concern for women's rights and contained a five-year plan to achieve gender equality by the year 2000. Referring to relevant ECHR cases on the impartiality of judges, the Appeal Chamber found that "even if it were established that Judge Mumba expressly shared the goals and objectives of the UNCSW and the Platform for Action, in promoting and protecting the human rights of women, that inclination, being of a general nature, is distinguishable from an inclination to implement those goals and objectives as a judge in a particular case. It follows that she could sit on a case and impartially decide upon issues affecting women. Indeed, even if Judge Mumba sought to implement the relevant objectives of the UNCSW, those goals merely reflected the objectives of the United Nations, and were contemplated by the Security Council resolutions leading to the establishment of this Tribunal. These resolutions condemned the systematic rape and detention of women in the former Yugoslavia and expressed a determination "to put an end to such crimes and to take effective measures to bring to justice the persons who are responsible for them." ... To endorse the view that rape as a crime is abhorrent and that those responsible for it should be prosecuted within the constraints of the law cannot in itself constitute grounds for disqualification."

One interesting aspect of the above case is an *amicus curiae* brief from a group of women's human rights legal scholars and NGOs, requesting that the tribunal should reconsider its original decision in the case and should have greater regard to the rights of Witness A to equality, privacy and security of the person, and to representation of victims by legal counsel. The brief contained the following points and statements:

- On 16/7/1998 the Trial Chamber had ordered the production of potentially highly discriminatory, intimate and prejudicial confidential information about Witness A's medical treatment and counselling:

  "The effort by Defence counsel to obtain confidential information is historically one tactic in a long line of tactics based upon discriminatory attitudes towards women and rejected by this Tribunal in Rule 96"

- The Trial Chamber did not take account of "the harm to victims which would result from the disclosure of intensely personal records and the broad cross-examination of witnesses in respect of their medical, psychological and psychiatric records."

- "In accordance with the above concerns, this Brief will submit that:

  (1) gender discrimination fundamentally informs requests for disclosure of confidential records in cases of sexual violence;
  (2) requests for disclosure are most often founded upon irrelevant and prejudicial rape myths and discriminatory attitudes towards women who are victims of sexual assault;
  (3) the cross-examination of survivors of sexual violence risks unwarranted and severe intimidation and revictimisation of these witnesses, thus jeopardising both their mental and physical integrity;
  (4) the disclosure of counseling records profoundly affects (a) women's equal rights to access to justice; and (b) the goal of bringing perpetrators of sexual violence in armed conflict before the two International Criminal Tribunals."

"sexual violence is a crime which is predominantly committed against women, including during times of armed conflict. Moreover, the violence is committed against these women because of their gender, in addition to their ethnic origin or religion. Although sexual violence in armed conflict is often a tool used to subordinate a group of people, it is in every case a means of subjugating, objectifying and dehumanising women. For this reason, the Amici have argued before the ICTY and ICTR that a failure by the Tribunals to respect the dignity and autonomy of victims of sexual violence amounts to a denial of equal justice to women. Such a failure deprives women, in this case women from the former Yugoslavia, of the recognition and vindication of their suffering that is an essential component of their ability to rebuild their lives and their self-esteem on a foundation of equality and dignity." [*Amicus* brief, *Furundzija*]

Rule 96 of ICTY prevents defence counsel from attacking rape victims by raising rape myths about sexual history, but requests for victims counselling records feed exactly the set of beliefs that Rule 96 was designed to prevent. By contrast, the defence did not seek the counseling records of one of the other prosecution witnesses, who had had medical treatment for 20 days because he had "mental problems."

11–031   Thus, we have a paradox: the United Nations General Assembly and the Tribunal's Rules encourage women who have been victims of sexual violence to undergo counselling. An example would be General Assembly Resolution 50/192 of December 1995, which urged all States and concerned organisations to facilitate "necessary medical and psychological care to victims of rape within the framework of programmes to rehabilitate women and children traumatised by war, as well as the provision of protection, counseling and support to victims and witnesses."

"The conflict in the former Yugoslavia was the catalyst that brought the issue of sexual violence during armed conflict squarely onto the international agenda, but much more remains to be done. Formal recognition of the problem is an important first step, but this must now be translated into a positive outcome for women and girls affected by sexual violence in all armed conflicts." (Women 2000 Report, United Nations, 1998)

It is not known exactly how much effect the above *amicus* brief had upon the eventual decision in the case.

Kunarac, Kovac And Vukovic, Appeal Chamber Of ICTY, June 12, 2002

Facts. During 1992 and early 1993, there was an armed conflict between Bosnian **11–032** Serbs and Bosnian Muslims in Foca. The appellants were Bosnian Serb soldiers who were charged in relation to the systematic abuse of Muslims, particularly women. Kunarac was the leader of a reconnaissance unit and was found guilty of eleven counts of crimes under Arts 3 and 5 of the Statute: torture and rape as crimes against humanity, torture and rape as violations of the laws or customs of war and enslavement as a crime against humanity. The rape charges were both as a principal and as an aider and abettor. The victims had been brought to his headquarters and gang-raped, and some were kept in a house as sexual slaves for up to six months. Kovac was found guilty of four counts of crimes under Arts 3 and 5 of the Statute: rape and outrages upon personal dignity as violations of the laws or customs of war and rape, and enslavement as crimes against humanity, again both as a principal and as an accomplice. He and another man kept four girls prisoner in his apartment, raping, humiliating and degrading them repeatedly. Vukovic was found guilty of four counts under Arts 3 and 5 of the Statute: torture and rape as violations of the laws or customs of war, and torture and rape as crimes against humanity. He had abducted a teenage girl and raped her. Each man appealed on a variety of grounds, ranging from impotence to procedural technicalities and the length of sentences given. All appeals were rejected, and the Appeals Chamber made several important statements and clarifications as to the status and definition of rape and other forms of sexual violence as crimes in international law.

Two days after the *Foca* indictment was issued, a headline on the front page of the New York Times declared, "For First Time, Court Defines Rape as War Crime," and asserted:

"This is a landmark indictment because it focuses exclusively on sexual assaults, without including any other charges . . . There is no precedent for this. It is of major legal significance because it illustrates the court's strategy to focus on gender-related crimes and give them their proper place in the prosecution of war crimes." (M. Simons, New York Times, June 28, 1996)

The case has the potential to be a far-reaching new precedent in international law; it is a shame there were no genocide charges though on the facts there was a horrific catalogue of rape and related charges. There appears to have been intent to destroy a protected group but it was not charged as genocide; almost every other possible crime variant was among the charges however. Finally, this was the first time enslavement had been charged for crimes of sexual violence.

Decision. Kunarac and Kovac had both disagreed with the Trial Chamber's definition of the crime of enslavement, arguing that it required prolonged "ownership" of the victim and, in addition, the clear and constant lack of consent by the victim. The Appeals Chamber found that the traditional concept of slavery had evolved to encompass contemporary forms of slavery, which are less extreme but are clearly part of the crime of enslavement within customary international law. It was only required that the accused exercised any or all of the powers attaching to the right of ownership over the victim. The indicia of enslavement, as identified by the Trial Chamber, include "control of someone's movement, control of physical environment, psychological control, measures taken to prevent or deter escape, force, threat of force or coercion, duration, assertion of exclusivity, subjection to cruel treatment and abuse, control of sexuality and forced labour." Lack of consent is not a definitional element of the crime, although it may be relevant as evidence. The *mens rea* is the "intentional exercise of a power attaching to the right of ownership"; it is not necessary to prove that the accused intended to detain the victims in order to use them for sexual acts.

The appellants had also challenged the Trial Chamber's definition of rape, proposing instead that force or threat of force and the victim's continuous or genuine resistance were required. The Trial Chamber had concluded that:

> "the *actus reus* of the crime of rape in international law is constituted by: the sexual penetration, however slight: (a) of the vagina or anus of the victim by the penis of the perpetrator or any other object used by the perpetrator; or (b) the mouth of the victim by the penis of the perpetrator; where such sexual penetration occurs without the consent of the victim. Consent for this purpose must be consent given voluntarily, as a result of the victim's free will, assessed in the context of the surrounding circumstances. The *mens rea* is the intention to effect this sexual penetration, and the knowledge that it occurs without the consent of the victim."

The Appeals Chamber agreed with the Trial Chamber's definition of rape, but chose to emphasise two points. First, that there was no basis whatsoever in customary international law for any requirement of resistance by the victim, and that it was an absurd suggestion that continuous resistance was the only way in which a perpetrator could receive notice from the victim that there was no consent. Secondly, although the Trial Chamber had appeared to differ from earlier cases, definitions of rape, by stressing that rape was a crime of sex without consent, the Trial Chamber had been seeking to explain the relationship between force and consent: "force or threat of force provides clear evidence of non-consent, but force is not an element *per se* of rape . . . A narrow focus on force or threat of force could permit perpetrators to evade liability for sexual activity to which the other party had not consented by taking advantage of coercive circumstances without relying on physical force."

The Appeals Chamber looked at the definitions of rape in various domestic jurisdictions as an aid, finding that some States have offences which penalise sexual acts with prisoners, and that consent is not an element of these offences. The Chamber stated in addition that true consent is not possible in the circumstances of the present cases (and in most other cases charged as either war crimes or crimes against humanity), since those circumstances are almost universally coercive:

> "For the most part, the Appellants in this case were convicted of raping women held in *de facto* military headquarters, detention centres and apartments maintained as soldiers" residences. As the most egregious aspect of the conditions, the victims were considered the legitimate sexual prey of their captors. Typically, the women were raped by more than one perpetrator and with a regularity that is nearly inconceivable. (Those who initially sought help or resisted were treated to an extra level of brutality). Such detentions amount to circumstances that were so coercive as to negate any possibility of consent."

Inter alia in relation to their torture convictions, the appellants had argued that they did not intend to inflict pain or suffering by the rapes, their motives being purely sexual in nature. They also denied having any of the prohibited purposes listed in the definition of the crime of torture — to obtain information or a confession or to punish, intimidate or coerce the victim or a third person, or to discriminate on any ground whatsoever. The Appeal Chamber rebutted these assertions, finding that rape is an act which *per se* inflicts severe pain or suffering (whether physical or mental) upon its victim and so no further evidence as to that matter needs to be established beyond the fact of a rape. Further, there is an important distinction between intent and motivation; "even if the perpetrator's motivation is entirely sexual, it does not follow that the perpetrator does not have the intent to commit an act of torture or that his conduct does not cause severe pain or suffering, whether physical or mental, since such pain or suffering is a likely and logical consequence of his conduct. In view of the definition, it is important to establish whether a perpetrator intended to act in a way which, in the normal course of events, would cause severe pain or suffering, whether physical or mental, to his victims." Nor need an act be carried out solely for one of the listed purposes; even if the primary purpose was one of sexual gratification, if "one prohibited purpose is fulfilled by the conduct, the fact that such conduct was also intended to achieve a non-listed purpose (even one of a sexual nature) is immaterial."

As so often, the accused were charged with outrages upon personal dignity in relation to sexual violence. The Appeals Chamber found that there is no necessity to define specific acts committed by the accused that may constitute outrages upon personal dignity. Rather, it is sufficient that the humiliation of the victim be so intense that any reasonable person would be outraged, and that the accused committed any act or omission which would be generally considered to cause serious humiliation, degradation or otherwise be a serious attack on human dignity. The *mens rea* is that the accused knew that his act or omission *could* cause serous humiliation, degradation or otherwise be a serious attack on human dignity. In other words, only knowledge of the *possible* consequences of his act or omission is required, and not any specific intent to humiliate, degrade or otherwise seriously to attack human dignity. It is hence clearly a crime that can be assessed on the basis of subjective knowledge and objective potential harm.

Each appellant argued that the double charging of rape and torture was unlawful, but the Appeals Chamber disagreed on the basis that rape and torture each contain one materially different element not contained in the other (penetration and prohibited purpose, respectively), and so convictions for both on the same facts are possible. Most significantly, the reasoning in *Akayesu* and *Kunarac* leaves little room for argument against the proposition that the prohibition of rape is a *jus cogens* principle.

Kvocka/Kos/Radic/Zigic/Prcac, ICTY, November 2, 2001

Facts. The defendants were charged in relation to events at Omarska camp. In addition to many others, some of the charges concerned multiple rapes and other forms of sexual violence. All defendants were charged with crimes against humanity of persecution and inhumane acts, and with violations of the laws or customs of war of outrages upon personal dignity. The persecution charges included sexual assault and rape. Radic was charged separately with rape and torture as crimes against humanity, and with torture and outrages upon personal dignity for crimes of sexual violence committed against detainees at Omarska camp.

Decision. The Trial Chamber agreed with the Trial Chamber in *Kunarac*'s wider formulation of the definition of rape, *i.e.* "where sexual penetration occurs without the consent of the victim", and consent only exists where it is "given voluntarily, as a

11–033

result of the victim's free will assessed in the context of the surrounding circumstances". The principal focus should be on whether there were serious violations of sexual autonomy. "sexual penetration" retains its *Furundzija* definition of "the sexual penetration, however slight: of the vagina or anus of the victim by the penis of the perpetrator or any other object used by the perpetrator; or of the mouth of the victim by the penis of the perpetrator".

In its fullest range of possibilities, for sexual activity to be classified as rape:

"(i)   the sexual activity must be accompanied by force or threat of force to the victim or a third party; or

(ii)   the sexual activity must be accompanied by force *or* a variety of other specified circumstances which made the victim particularly vulnerable or negated her ability to make an informed refusal; or
the sexual activity must occur without the consent of the victim."

The *mens rea* of rape is intent to effect a sexual penetration and the knowledge that it occurs without the consent of the victim.

So, ICTY and ICTR have been responsible for the most significant developments in criminalisation of sexual violence in international law. Sexual violence has been charged as violations of the laws or customs of war, genocide, crimes against humanity, grave breaches of the 1949 Geneva Conventions, and violations of common Art. 3 of the 1949 Geneva Conventions and of the 1977 Additional Protocols. Key and often revolutionary decisions of both tribunals provided blueprints for the new ICC rules on helping victims of crime — see *Furundzija* and *Celebici*, and contributed greatly towards the definitions of the ICC crimes encompassing or constituting sexual violence.

What still needs to be done:

- sentencing needs to reflect the gravity of the crimes charged;

- sexual content in charges should always be made explicit, not hidden within vague language;

- language in treaties must be specific; and

- arguably a treaty is needed which specifically deals with and criminalises in its own right, gender-based violence in any armed conflict.

SEXUAL VIOLENCE IN THE ICC STATUTE

11–034   "Historically, international humanitarian law treaties omitted, trivialized or mischaracterized gender and sexual violence. This was due to a myriad of reasons, such as sexist beliefs that rape is a natural part of every war or that these crimes are of secondary importance to other crimes. As a result, the mass rapes and other forms of sexual and gender violence which have been a pervasive part of almost every war have been historically underinvestigated and underprosecuted. The Statute adopted in Rome for the establishment of an International Criminal Court (ICC) goes a long way to redressing this imbalance by recognizing a broad spectrum of sexual and gender violence crimes of the most serious nature." (B. Bedont, "Gender-Specific Provisions in the Statute of the ICC", in F. Lattanzi and W. Schabs eds, *Essays on the Rome Statute of the International Criminal Court*, Naples: Editorials Scientifica, 1999.)

During PrepCom, the Women's Caucus for Gender Justice lobbied hard and effectively for provisions to be included in the ICC Statute which would make it possible to investigate and prosecute gender crimes. One major problem was that the primary focus of the Statute was to be the codification of existing international law rather than its development. Since existing international law was seriously deficient in respect of violence against women, the Women's Caucus had both to show the inadequacy of existing treaty laws and (somewhat contradictorily) that customary international law already contained the tools that could be used to remedy these deficiencies. Thus the eventual provisions of the Rome Statute bear the marks of this compromise and show both the expansion of customary international law and the abandonment of some out-of-date treaty provisions.

But some major problems were more difficult to resolve. When the ICC statute was being drafted, the US objected to the use of the *Akayesu* definition of rape, insisting that both force and penetration had to be included as elements. The US position was a serious attempt to undermine one of the major strengths of the ICC, *i.e.* a forward-thinking, broad-brush codification of existing customary international law. It further ignored the reality of rape in wartime: physical force is rarely necessary to achieve a rape when the entire situation is frightening and coercive, and there are acts which are just as degrading and harmful to the victim as physical penetration by a penis.

The Rome Statute, however, remains a significant landmark in the development of international law's response to gender and violence. It in effect also codifies many of women's international human rights.

The gender-specific provisions of the ICC Statute

The crimes The ICC Prosecutor is under a duty to investigate crimes of sexual and gender violence (Art. 54(1)(b)). **11–035**

Sexual Violence as War Crimes

Article 8 of the Rome Statute specifically includes the following in the list of war crimes over which the ICC has jurisdiction in either international or internal conflict: **11–036**

> "(xxii) . . . rape, sexual slavery, enforced prostitution, forced pregnancy . . . enforced sterilization or any other form of sexual violence also constituting" either a grave breach or a violation of Common Article 3 of the Geneva Conventions.

This is an expansion on previous lists and, most positively, rejects the classification of sexual violence as being anything to do with humiliation or attacks on dignity. The war crime of rape is defined in the 'Elements of Crimes' as requiring that:

1. The perpetrator invaded the body of a person by conduct resulting in penetration, however slight, of any part of the body of the victim or the perpetrator with a sexual organ, or of the anal or genital opening of the victim with any object or any other part of the body.
2. the invasion was committed by force, or by threat of force or coercion, such as that caused by fear of violence, duress, detention, psychological oppression or abuse of power, against such person or another person, or by taking advantage of a coercive environment, or the invasion was committed against a person incapable of giving genuine consent.
3. the conduct took place in the context of and was associated with an international armed conflict.
4. The perpetrator was aware of factual circumstances that established the existence of an armed conflict."

This is narrower than some of the decisions of ICTY and ICTR examined above in relation to consent.

Sexual violence as crimes against humanity

Article 7 of the Rome Statute provides:

11–037   "For the purpose of this Statute, 'crime against humanity' means any of the following acts when committed as part of a widespread or systematic attack directed against any civilian population, with knowledge of the attack:

. . . (g) Rape, sexual slavery, enforced prostitution, forced pregnancy, enforced sterilization, or any other form of sexual violence of comparable gravity;"

The crime against humanity of rape is defined in the Elements of Crime as for the war crime, except that the third element is replaced by "The conduct was committed as part of a widespread or systematic attack directed against a civilian population" and the fourth element is amended accordingly.

The crime of persecution was one difficult issue to resolve, since it now includes persecution on gender grounds as well as on grounds of race, ethnicity, nationality, religion or politics. However, the US managed to limit the offence by requiring an act of violence to be proved, eg torture, killing, or a war crime.

Crimes against humanity are within the jurisdiction of the ICC, whether committed during war or peace and whether committed by State or Non-State actors. This is broader than the widely accepted view of the corresponding customary international law. However, there is a limitation that is narrower than under customary international law, since a policy to commit a widespread or systematic attack must be related to a state or organisational policy and to multiple acts.

The categorisation of sexual violence as serious crimes

Part 2 of the Rome Statute explicitly lists crimes of sexual and gender vio-   **11–038**
lence under separate paras in the definitions of both crimes against humanity (Art. 7) and war crimes (Art. 8), whether in an international or
non-international armed conflict. The following are the relevant crimes:

- rape, sexual slavery, enforced prostitution, forced pregnancy, enforced
  sterilization, other forms of sexual violence constituting a grave
  breach of the Geneva Conventions (re war crimes), other forms of
  sexual violence of comparable gravity (re crimes against humanity).

Gender is also relevant in two further crimes against humanity:

- Persecution, where gender is one of the grounds upon which the
  identified group or collectivity is selected.
- Enslavement, which is defined as the exercise of any power attaching
  to the right of ownership over a person, including in the course of
  trafficking in persons, in particular women and children.

Interpretation

According to Art. 21(3), the application and interpretation of international   **11–039**
law must be consistent with internationally-recognised human rights, and
without gender bias. Judges will therefore be able to refer to CEDAW, the
Vienna and Beijing Declarations and international human rights documents
in general whenever interpreting the provisions of the ICC Statute.

Rules of procedure and evidence

The ICC Statute builds upon the developments made in this regard by ICTY   **11–040**
and ICTR. Of particular note are the following Rules:

> "Rule 70. PRINCIPLES OF EVIDENCE IN CASES OF SEXUAL
> VIOLENCE
>
> In cases of sexual violence, the Court shall be guided by and, where appropriate,
> apply the following principles:
>
> (a) Consent cannot be inferred by reason of any words or conduct of a vic-
>   tim where force, threat of force, coercion or taking advantage of a coer-
>   cive environment undermined the victim's ability to give voluntary and
>   informed consent;
> (b) Consent cannot be inferred by reason of any words or conduct of a
>   victim where the victim is incapable of giving genuine consent;

(c) Consent cannot be inferred by reason of the silence of, or lack of resistance by, a victim to the alleged sexual violence;

(d) Credibility, character or predisposition to sexual availability of a victim or witness cannot be inferred by reason of the sexual nature of the prior or subsequent conduct of a victim or witness"

"Rule 72. IN CAMERA PROCEDURE TO CONSIDER RELEVANCE OR ADMISSIBILITY OF EVIDENCE

1. Where there is an intention to introduce or elicit, including by means of the questioning of a victim or witness, evidence that the victim consented to an alleged crime of sexual violence, or evidence of the words, conduct, silence or lack of resistance of a victim or witness. . . . notification shall be provided to the Court which shall describe the substance of the evidence intended to be introduced or elicited and the relevance of the evidence to the issues of the case.

2. In deciding whether the evidence . . . is relevant or admissible, a Chamber shall hear in camera the views of the Prosecutor, the defence, the witness and the victim or his or her legal representative, if any, and shall take into account whether that evidence has a sufficient degree of probative value to an issue in the case and the prejudice that such evidence may cause . . ."

Rules 85–98 also provide detailed measures for the protection of victims and witnesses going far beyond those guaranteed by the two prior Tribunals.

Equality in staffing

11–041 According to Art. 36, when States are selecting judges, they must have regard to the need for a fair representation of men and women, and must remember the need for judges to have legal expertise in the field of violence against women and children. The same factors must be taken into account when appointing staff for the Offices of the Prosecutor and the Registry and legal advisors. It should be noted that unfortunately some States strongly resisted the introduction of such provisions, and that the final version is a compromise.

The definition of gender and gender crimes in the Statute

11–042 These terms were used rather than "sex" and "sexual violence" because "It is understood that the term "gender" refers to the two sexes, male and female, within the context of society. The term 'gender' does not indicate any meaning different from the above" (Art. 7(3)). This reflects language-based concerns at Beijing.

The importance of the gender-specific ICC provisions

11–043 Some general points:

- Earlier drafts hardly mentioned sexual violence, and maintained existing international law's unhelpful categorisation within war crimes of sexual violence as "outrages upon personal dignity". Obviously the final version is a great improvement in that respect.

- The ICC Statute fills in the gaps in customary and treaty-based international criminal law regarding sexual violence other than rape, and underlines that such crimes are of the most serious nature. Listing crimes of sexual violence as a separate category does not merely have symbolic importance; it also recognises that victims of such crimes suffer a special type of additional or aggravated harm. The previous trend of fitting such crimes into the definitions of existing crimes such as torture, whilst an important step towards reducing impunity, ignored the true significance and effects of the crimes. But, as noted elsewhere in this chapter, a separate crime of sexual violence would have been a stronger and more useful advance.

- There are advances in the forms of sexual violence punishable in international criminal law under the Statute: the crime of sexual slavery receives its first treaty recognition, and trafficking in persons is recognised as a form of enslavement for the first time.

- Having learned from the experiences of ICTY and ICTR, the Rome Statute's procedural provisions should make the experience of victims and other vulnerable witnesses far more comfortable. Hopefully, unhelpful previous practices like the use of male interpreters when questioning victims of sexual violence and the mindset of viewing rape as "less important" than the genocide within which it was taking place, will now be eliminated. The ICC's power to order compensation will be a major improvement over its predecessors, in terms of recognition of the victim's plight and rights. Specific provisions include: Art. 57 (the pre-trial Chamber has powers to provide for the protection of victims and witnesses), and Article 64; the Trial Chamber shall ensure that trials are conducted with due regard to the protection of victims and witnesses; a Victims and Witnesses unit, staffed by trauma experts, is to be created (Arts 43(6) and 68); it is recognised that a fair trial must be fair to the rights of both defendants AND VICTIMS (Arts 64(2) and 68(1)); victims have a right to participate in the proceedings and to have a legal representative (Art. 68(3)); further, they may be awarded remedies, including compensation and rehabilitation (Art. 75). Article 68 meris further examination.

"PROTECTION OF THE VICTIMS AND WITNESSES AND THEIR PARTICIPATION IN THE PROCEEDINGS

1. The Court shall take appropriate measures to protect the safety, physical and psychological well-being, dignity and privacy of victims and witnesses. In so doing, the Court shall have regard to all relevant factors,

including age, gender . . . . and health, and the nature of the crime, in particular, but not limited to, where the crime involves sexual or gender violence or violence against children. The Prosecutor shall take such measures particularly during the investigation and prosecution of crimes. These measures shall not be prejudicial to or inconsistent with the rights of the accused and a fair and impartial trial.

2. As an exception to the principle of public hearings provided for in Article 67, the Chambers of this Court may, to protect victims and witnesses or an accused, conduct any part of the proceedings in camera or allow the presentation of evidence by electronic or other special means. In particular, such measures shall be implemented in the case of a victim of sexual violence or a child who is a victim or a witness, unless otherwise ordered by the Court, having regard to all the circumstances, particularly the views of the victim or witness.

3. Where the personal interests of the victims are affected, the Court shall permit their views and concerns to be presented and considered at stages of the proceedings determined to be appropriate by the Court and in a manner which is not prejudicial to or inconsistent with the rights of the accused and a fair and impartial trial. . . .

4. The Victims and Witnesses Unit may advise the Prosecutor and the Court on appropriate protective measures, security arrangements, counselling and assistance . . .

5. Where the disclosure of evidence or information pursuant to this Statute may lead to the grave endangerment of the security of a witness or his or her family, the Prosecutor may . . . withhold such evidence or information and instead submit a summary thereof. Such measures shall be exercised in a manner which is not prejudicial to or inconsistent with the rights of the accused and a fair and impartial trial. . . ."

- One problem is that intention is required for all ICC crimes, and intention is particularly difficult to establish in relation to sexual violence. Another problem is that, for the sex crimes which are within the ICC's definitions of crimes against humanity, they must be part of a systematic or widespread attack. Rape and sexual torture in war are not always so. But it was most expedient to "push" sex crimes into the category of crimes against humanity since there is no single governing treaty/convention which would require stretching or amendment.

Potentially the ICC could be an accountability mechanism for crimes of sexual violence in the context of armed conflict, but it is hoped that the effect will be more far-reaching by establishing basic rules of gender equality in international criminal law, and that eventually these will be incorporated into national legal systems. Even if this does not happen or takes a long time, the process of creation and preparation of the ICC Statute provided a real opportunity for re-examination and re-evaluation of the definitions of the crimes within the Court's jurisdiction. As part of this process there has been, arguably, a recognition that sexual or gender-based violence is in every way as serious as violence motivated by ethnic origin, race or religion. One way forward is that, in relation to complementarity, the decision whether the ICC has jurisdiction due to another State's failure to adequately prosecute should be informed by the willingness or otherwise of that State to genuinely address gender-based crimes.

"One of the greatest accomplishments made at the conference was placing gender issues at the forefront of international concern. However, as suggested by the High Commission on Human Rights in their Position Paper, sexual assaults should have been given their own article under the Rome Statute. Neither the false dichotomy between sexual assaults as international crimes and human rights violations nor the continuing fallacy that prosecution depends on numbers or detailed policies can continue . . . The international community must realize that the focus should not be on establishing that such an act was committed in a certain context which is forbidden, but that there is no acceptable context for the commission of rape by an authority or someone act acting under the color of authority. These crimes cannot go unpunished. Where the national courts are unable or unwilling to do so, the international community must rise to the responsibility . . . Omission of a separate article in the Rome Statute requires that the articles that do explicitly prohibit rape and other forms of sexual assault, especially crimes against humanity, must be interpreted as broadly as possible." (S. Ryan, "From the Furies of Nanking to the Eumenides of the International Criminal Court; the Evolution of Sexual Assaults as International Crimes", (1999) PACE International Law Review, Vol. XI, No. 2).

But, while recognising the huge changes which have occurred in recent years, does the repeated recognition of rape as various types of international crime really change anything for even those victims whose attackers are sentenced, let alone those whose attackers have never been caught? Sexual violence continues to be used in wars, and even life sentences are arguably too lenient for the thousands of rapes committed by, at the instigation of, or for the motives of state officials. In Furundzija's appeal, the prosecutor argued that the sentencing of ICTY and ICTR for international crimes including genocide, crimes against humanity and war crime indicated that these crimes were "less serious" than domestic crimes, and that this erroneous appearance needed to be redressed. Protection and prevention are underused tactics for women's rights and the redress of sexual violence in wartime. NGOs cannot do it all alone, particularly without realistic funding. The United Nations has a role to play and the funds and power available to make a difference, but still can do little on the ground when faced with armed fighting forces who show contempt for the rules and customs of international law, and of war itself. However, they can do something about the under-reporting of wartime sexual violence, the identification of existing victims and the relocation of those in danger zones. The resources and support made available when the International Criminal Court handles its first cases of sexual violence will be telling.

APPENDICES:
TREATIES AND DOCUMENTS IN
INTERNATIONAL
CRIMINAL LAW

Appendix 1

CONVENTION ON THE PREVENTION AND PUNISHMENT OF THE CRIME OF GENOCIDE

The Contracting Parties, Having considered the declaration made by the General Assembly of the United Nations in its resolution 96 (I) dated 11 December 1946 that genocide is a crime under international law, contrary to the spirit and aims of the United Nations and condemned by the civilized world,   **App1–001**

Recognizing that at all periods of history genocide has inflicted great losses on humanity, and

Being convinced that, in order to liberate mankind from such an odious scourge, international co-operation is required,

Hereby agree as hereinafter provided:

Article 1   **App1–002**

The Contracting Parties confirm that genocide, whether committed in time of peace or in time of war, is a crime under international law which they undertake to prevent and to punish.

Article 2   **App1–003**

In the present Convention, genocide means any of the following acts committed with intent to destroy, in whole or in part, a national, ethnical, racial or religious group, as such:

    (a) Killing members of the group;

    (b) Causing serious bodily or mental harm to members of the group;

    (c) Deliberately inflicting on the group conditions of life calculated to bring about its physical destruction in whole or in part;

    (d) Imposing measures intended to prevent births within the group;

    (e) Forcibly transferring children of the group to another group.

Article 3   **App1–004**

The following acts shall be punishable:

    (a) Genocide;

    (b) Conspiracy to commit genocide;

    (c) Direct and public incitement to commit genocide;

    (d) Attempt to commit genocide;

    (e) Complicity in genocide.

App1–005 **Article 4**

Persons committing genocide or any of the other acts enumerated in article III shall be punished, whether they are constitutionally responsible rulers, public officials or private individuals.

App1–006 **Article 5**

The Contracting Parties undertake to enact, in accordance with their respective Constitutions, the necessary legislation to give effect to the provisions of the present Convention, and, in particular, to provide effective penalties for persons guilty of genocide or any of the other acts enumerated in article III.

App1–007 **Article 6**

Persons charged with genocide or any of the other acts enumerated in article III shall be tried by a competent tribunal of the State in the territory of which the act was committed, or by such international penal tribunal as may have jurisdiction with respect to those Contracting Parties which shall have accepted its jurisdiction.

App1–008 **Article 7**

Genocide and the other acts enumerated in article III shall not be considered as political crimes for the purpose of extradition.

The Contracting Parties pledge themselves in such cases to grant extradition in accordance with their laws and treaties in force.

App1–009 **Article 8**

Any Contracting Party may call upon the competent organs of the United Nations to take such action under the Charter of the United Nations as they consider appropriate for the prevention and suppression of acts of genocide or any of the other acts enumerated in article III.

App1–010 **Article 9**

Disputes between the Contracting Parties relating to the interpretation, application or fulfilment of the present Convention, including those relating to the responsibility of a State for genocide or for any of the other acts enumerated in article III, shall be submitted to the International Court of Justice at the request of any of the parties to the dispute.

App1–011 **Article 10**

The present Convention, of which the Chinese, English, French, Russian and Spanish texts are equally authentic, shall bear the date of 9 December 1948.

App1–012 **Article 11**

The present Convention shall be open until 31 December 1949 for signature on behalf of any Member of the United Nations and of any nonmember State to which an invitation to sign has been addressed by the General Assembly.

The present Convention shall be ratified, and the instruments of ratification shall be deposited with the Secretary-General of the United Nations.

After 1 January 1950, the present Convention may be acceded to on behalf of any Member of the United Nations and of any non-member State which has received an invitation as aforesaid. Instruments of accession shall be deposited with the Secretary-General of the United Nations.

Article 12 **App1–013**

Any Contracting Party may at any time, by notification addressed to the Secretary-General of the United Nations, extend the application of the present Convention to all or any of the territories for the conduct of whose foreign relations that Contracting Party is responsible.

Article 13 **App1–014**

On the day when the first twenty instruments of ratification or accession have been deposited, the Secretary-General shall draw up a proces-verbal and transmit a copy thereof to each Member of the United Nations and to each of the non-member States contemplated in article 11.

The present Convention shall come into force on the ninetieth day following the date of deposit of the twentieth instrument of ratification or accession.

Any ratification or accession effected, subsequent to the latter date shall become effective on the ninetieth day following the deposit of the instrument of ratification or accession.

Article 14 **App1–015**

The present Convention shall remain in effect for a period of ten years as from the date of its coming into force.

It shall thereafter remain in force for successive periods of five years for such Contracting Parties as have not denounced it at least six months before the expiration of the current period.

Denunciation shall be effected by a written notification addressed to the Secretary-General of the United Nations.

Article 15 **App1–016**

If, as a result of denunciations, the number of Parties to the present Convention should become less than sixteen, the Convention shall cease to be in force as from the date on which the last of these denunciations shall become effective.

Article 16 **App1–017**

A request for the revision of the present Convention may be made at any time by any Contracting Party by means of a notification in writing addressed to the Secretary-General.

The General Assembly shall decide upon the steps, if any, to be taken in respect of such request.

Article 17 **Appl–018**

The Secretary-General of the United Nations shall notify all Members of the United Nations and the non-member States contemplated in article XI of the following:

(a) Signatures, ratifications and accessions received in accordance with article 11;

(b) Notifications received in accordance with article 12;

(c) The date upon which the present Convention comes into force in accordance with article 13;

(d) Denunciations received in accordance with article 14;

(e)   The abrogation of the Convention in accordance with article 15;

(f)   Notifications received in accordance with article 16.

App1–019   **Article 18**

The original of the present Convention shall be deposited in the archives of the United Nations.

A certified copy of the Convention shall be transmitted to each Member of the United Nations and to each of the non-member States contemplated in article XI.

App1–020   **Article 19**

The present Convention shall be registered by the Secretary-General of the United Nations on the date of its coming into force.

CONVENTION FOR THE SUPPRESSION OF UNLAWFUL ACTS AGAINST THE SAFETY OF CIVIL AVIATION

The States Parties to this Convention

CONSIDERING that unlawful acts against the safety of civil aviation jeopardize the safety of persons and property, seriously affect the operation of air services, and undermine the confidence of the peoples of the world in the safety of civil aviation;

CONSIDERING that the occurrence of such acts is a matter of grave concern;

CONSIDERING that, for the purpose of deterring such acts, there is an urgent need to provide appropriate measures for punishment of offenders;

HAVE AGREED AS FOLLOWS:

Article 1   App2–001

1. Any person commits an offence if he unlawfully and intentionally:

   (a) performs an act of violence against a person on board an aircraft in flight if that act is likely to endanger the safety of that aircraft; or

   (b) destroys an aircraft in service or causes damage to such an aircraft which renders it incapable of flight or which is likely to endanger its safety in flight; or

   (c) places or causes to be placed on an aircraft in service, by any means whatsoever, a device or substance which is likely to destroy that aircraft, or to cause damage to it which renders it incapable of flight, or to cause damage to it which is likely to endanger its safety in flight; or

   (d) destroys or damages air navigation facilities or interferes with their operation, if any such act is likely to endanger the safety of aircraft in flight; or

   (e) communicates information which he knows to be false, thereby endangering the safety of an aircraft in flight.

2. Any person also commits an offence if he:

   (a) attempts to commit any of the offences mentioned in paragraph 1 of this Article; or

   (b) is an accomplice of a person who commits or attempts to commit any such offence.

Article 2   App2–002

For the purposes of this Convention:

    (a)   an aircraft is considered to be in flight at any time from the moment when all its external doors are closed following embarkation until the moment when any such door is opened for disembarkation; in the case of a forced landing, the flight shall be deemed to continue until the competent authorities take over the responsibility for the aircraft and for persons and property on board;

    (b)   an aircraft is considered to be in service from the beginning of the preflight preparation of the aircraft by ground personnel or by the crew for a specific flight until twenty-four hours after any landing; the period of service shall, in any event, extend for the entire period during which the aircraft is in flight as defined in paragraph (a) of this Article.

App2–003   **Article 3**

Each Contracting State undertakes to make the offences mentioned in Article 1 punishable by severe penalties.

App2–004   **Article 4**

1. This Convention shall not apply to aircraft used in military, customs or police services.

2. In the cases contemplated in subparagraphs (a), (b), (c) and (e) of paragraph 1 of Article 1, this Convention shall apply, irrespective of whether the aircraft is engaged in an international or domestic flight, only if:

    (a)   the place of take-off or landing, actual or intended, of the aircraft is situated outside the territory of the State of registration of that aircraft; or

    (b)   the offence is committed in the territory of a State other than the State of registration of the aircraft.

3. Notwithstanding paragraph 2 of this Article, in the cases contemplated in subparagraphs (a), (b), (c) and (e) of paragraph 1 of Article 1, this Convention shall also apply if the offender or the alleged offender is found in the territory of a State other than the State of registration of the aircraft.

4. With respect to the States mentioned in Article 9 and in the cases mentioned in subparagraphs (a), (b), (c) and (e) of paragraph 1 of Article 1, this Convention shall not apply if the places referred to in subparagraph (a) of paragraph 2 of this Article are situated within the territory of the same State where that State is one of those referred to in Article 9, unless the offence is committed or the offender or alleged offender is found in the territory of a State other than that State.

5. In the cases contemplated in subparagraph (d) of paragraph 1 of Article 1, this Convention shall apply only if the air navigation facilities are used in international air navigation.

6. The provisions of paragraphs 2, 3, 4 and 5 of this Article shall also apply in the cases contemplated in paragraph 2 of Article 1.

App2–005   **Article 5**

1. Each Contracting State shall take such measures as may be necessary to establish its jurisdiction over the offences in the following cases:

    (a)   when the offence is committed in the territory of that State;

    (b)   when the offence is committed against or on board an aircraft registered in that State;

(c) when the aircraft on board which the offence is committed lands in its territory with the alleged offender still on board;

(d) when the offence is committed against or on board an aircraft leased without crew to a lessee who has his principal place of business or, if the lessee has no such place of business, his permanent residence, in that State.

2. Each Contracting State shall likewise take such measures as may be necessary to establish its jurisdiction over the offences mentioned in Article 1, paragraph 1(a), (b) and (c), and in Article 1, paragraph 2, in so far as that paragraph relates to those offences, in the case where the alleged offender is present in its territory and it does not extradite him pursuant to Article 8 to any of the States mentioned in paragraph 1 of this Article.

3. This Convention does not exclude any criminal jurisdiction exercised in accordance with national law.

Article 6 App2–006

1. Upon being satisfied that the circumstances so warrant, any Contracting State in the territory of which the offender or the alleged offender is present, shall take him into custody or take other measures to ensure his presence. The custody and other measures shall be as provided in the law of that State but may only be continued for such time as is necessary to enable any criminal or extradition proceedings to be instituted.

2. Such State shall immediately make a preliminary enquiry into the facts.

3. Any person in custody pursuant to paragraph 1 of this Article shall be assisted in communicating immediately with the nearest appropriate representative of the State of which he is a national.

4. When a State, pursuant to this Article, has taken a person into custody, it shall immediately notify the States mentioned in Article 5, paragraph 1, the State of nationality of the detained person and, if it considers it advisable, any other interested States of the fact that such person is in custody and of the circumstances which warrant his detention. The State which makes the preliminary enquiry contemplated in paragraph 2 of this Article shall promptly report its findings to the said States and shall indicate whether it intends to exercise jurisdiction.

Article 7 App2–007

The Contracting State in the territory of which the alleged offender is found shall, if it does not extradite him, be obliged, without exception whatsoever and whether or not the offence was committed in its territory, to submit the case to its competent authorities for the purpose of prosecution. Those authorities shall take their decision in the same manner as in the case of any ordinary offence of a serious nature under the law of that State.

Article 8 App2–008

1. The offences shall be deemed to be included as extraditable offences in any extradition treaty existing between Contracting States. Contracting States undertake to include the offences as extraditable offences in every extradition treaty to be concluded between them.

2. If a Contracting State which makes extradition conditional on the existence of a treaty receives a request for extradition from another Contracting State with which it has no extradition treaty, it may at its option consider this Convention as the legal basis for extradition in respect of the offences. Extradition shall be subject to the other conditions provided by the law of the requested State.

3. Contracting States which do not make extradition conditional on the existence of a treaty shall recognize the offences as extraditable offences between themselves subject to the conditions provided by the law of the requested State.

4. Each of the offences shall be treated, for the purpose of extradition between Contracting States, as if it had been committed not only in the place in which it occurred but also in the territories of the States required to establish their jurisdiction in accordance with Article 5, paragraph 1(b), (c) and (d).

App2–009   **Article 9**

The Contracting States which establish joint air transport operating organisations or international operating agencies, which operate aircraft which are subject to joint or international registration shall, by appropriate means, designate for each aircraft the State among them which shall exercise the jurisdiction and have the attributes of the State of registration for the purpose of this Convention and shall give notice thereof to the International Civil Aviation Organization which shall communicate the notice to all States Parties to this Convention.

App2–010   **Article 10**

1. Contracting States shall, in accordance with international and national law, endeavour to take all practicable measures for the purpose of preventing the offences mentioned in Article 1.

2. When, due to the commission of one of the offences mentioned in Article 1, a flight has been delayed or interrupted, any Contracting State in whose territory the aircraft or passengers or crew are present shall facilitate the continuation of the journey of the passengers and crew as soon as practicable, and shall without delay return the aircraft and its cargo to the persons lawfully entitled to possession.

App2–011   **Article 11**

1. Contracting States shall afford one another the greatest measure of assistance in connection with criminal proceedings brought in respect of the offences. The law of the State requested shall apply in all cases.

2. The provisions of paragraph 1 of this Article shall not affect obligations under any other treaty, bilateral or multilateral, which governs or will govern, in whole or in part, mutual assistance in criminal matters.

App2–012   **Article 12**

Any Contracting State having reason to believe that one of the offences mentioned in Article 1 will be committed shall, in accordance with its national law, furnish any relevant information in its possession to those States which it believes would be the States mentioned in Article 5, paragraph 1.

ENDNOTES

[1] Came into force on 26 January 1973 in respect of the following States, on behalf of which an instrument of ratification or accession had been deposited with the Governments of the Union of Soviet Socialist Republics, the United Kingdom of Great Britain and Northern Ireland or the United States of America, i.e. 30 days following the date (27 December 1972) of deposit of the instruments of ratification of ten signatory States having participated in the Montreal Conference, in accordance with article 15(3):

State	Date of deposit of instrument of ratification or accession (a) at London (L), Moscow (M) or Washington (W)	
Brazil*	24 July	1972 (L,M,W)
Canada	19 June	1972 (L)
	20 June	1972 (W)
	23 July	1972 (M)
Chad	12 July	1972 (L,W)
	17 August	1972 (M)
German Democratic Republic*	9 July	1972 (M)
Guyana	21 December	1972 a (W)
Hungary*	27 December	1972 (L,M,W)
Israel	30 June	1972 (L)
	6 July	1972 (W)
	10 July	1972 (M)
Malawi*	21 December	1972 a (W)
Mali	24 August	1972 a (W)
Mongolia*	5 September	1972 (W)
	14 September	1972 (L)
	20 October	1972 (M)
Niger	1 September	1972 (W)
Panama	24 April	1972 (W)
Republic of China	27 December	1972 (W)
South Africa*	30 May	1972 (W)
Spain	30 October	1972 (W)
Trinidad and Tobago	9 February	1972 (W)
United States of America	1 November	1972 (W)
	15 November	1972 (L)
	22 November	1972 (M)
Yugoslavia	2 October	1972 (L,M,W)

Subsequently, the Convention came into force for the States listed below 30 days after the date of deposit of their instrument of ratification or accession with the Governments of the Union of Soviet Socialist Republics, the United Kingdom of Great Britain and Northern Ireland or the United States of America, in accordance with article 15 (4):

State	Date of deposit of instrument of ratification or accession (a) at London (L), Moscow (M) or Washington (W)	
Argentina	26 November	1973 (L,M,W)
(With effect from 25 December 1973)		
Australia	12 July	1973 (L,M,W)
(With effect from 11 August 1973)		
Austria	11 February	1973 (L,M,W)
(With effect from 13 March 1974)		
Bulgaria*	22 February	1973 (L)
(With effect from 24 March 1973)	28 March	1973 (W)
	20 March	1974 (M)
Byelorussian Soviet Socialist Republic*	31 January	1973 (M)
(With effect from 2 March 1973)		
Chile	28 February	1974 a (W)
(With effect from 30 March 1974)		
Costa Rica	21 September	1973 (W)
(With effect from 21 October 1973)		
Cyprus	27 July	1973 (L)
(With effect from 14 September 1973)	30 July	1973 (M)
	15 August	1973 (W)

State	Date of deposit of instrument of ratification or accession (a) at London (L), Moscow (M) or Washington (W)	
Czechoslovakia* .... (With effect from 9 September 1973)	10 August	1973 (L,M,W)
Denmark .... (With effect from 16 February 1973. Decision reserved as regards the application of the Convention to the Faroe Islands and Greenland)	17 January	1973 (L,M,W)
Dominic Republic .... (With effect from 28 December 1973)	28 November	1973 (W)
Fiji .... (With effect from 4 April 1973)	5 March	1973 (W)
	18 April	1973 (L)
	28 April	1973 (M)
Finland .... (With effect from 12 August 1973)	13 July	1973 a (L,M,W)
Ghana .... (With effect from 11 January 1974)	12 December	1973 a (W)
Greece .... (With effect from 14 February 1974)	15 January	1974 (W)
Iceland .... (With effect from 29 July 1973)	29 June	1973 (M)
	29 June	1973 a (L,W)
Iran .... (With effect from 9 August 1973)	10 July	1973 a (L,M,W)
Iraq* .... (With effect from 10 October 1974)	10 September	1974 a (M)
Italy .... (With effect from 21 March 1974)	19 February	1974 (L,M,W)
Ivory Coast .... (With effect from 8 February 1973)	9 January	1973 a (W)
Japan .... (With effect from 12 July 1974)	12 June	1974 a (L,W)
Jordan .... (With effect from 15 March 1973)	13 February	1973 (L)
	19 February	1973 (M)
	25 April	1973 (W)
Libyan Arab Republic .... (With effect from 21 March 1974)	19 February	1974 a (W)
Mexico .... (With effect from 12 October 1974)	12 September	1974 (L,M,W)
Netherlands .... (With effect from 26 September 1973 for the Kingdom in Europe and Surinam, and with a declaration to the effect that the Convention shall apply to the Netherlands Antilles from 11 June 1974)	27 August	1973 (L,M,W)
New Zealand .... (With effect from 14 March 1974)	12 February	1974 (L,M,W)
Nicaragua .... (With effect from 6 December 1973)	6 November	1973 (W)
Nigeria .... (With effect from 2 August 1973)	3 July	1973 a (W)
	9 July	1973 a (L)
	20 July	1973 a (M)
Norway .... (With effect from 31 August 1973)	1 August	1973 a (L,M,W)
Pakistan .... (With effect from 15 February 1974)	16 January	1974 a (M)
	25 January	1974 a (L,W)

State	Date of deposit of instrument of ratification or accession (a) at London (L), Moscow (M) or Washington (W)	
Paraguay .... (With effect from 4 April 1974)	5 March	1974 (W)
Phillippines .... (With effect from 25 April 1973)	26 March	1973 (W)
Poland* .... (With effect from 27 February 1975)	26 January	1975 (L,M)
Portugal .... (With effect from 14 February 1973)	15 January	1973 (L)
Republic of Korea* .... (With effect from 1 September 1973)	2 August	1973 a (W)
Saudi Arabia* .... (With effect from 14 July 1974)	14 June	1974 a (W)
Sweden .... (With effect from 9 August 1973)	10 July	1973 a (L,M,W)
Ukrainian Soviet Socialist Republic* .... (With effect from 28 March 1973)	26 February	1973 (M)
Union of Soviet Socialist Republics* .... (With effect from 21 March 1973)	19 February	1973 (L,M,W)
United Kingdom of Great Britain and Northern Ireland* .... (With effect from 24 November 1973. In respect of the United Kingdom of Great Britain and Northern Ireland and Territories under the territorial sovereignty of the United Kingdom as well as the British Solomon Islands Protectorate)	25 October	1973 (L,M,W)
United Republic of Cameroon* .... (With effect from 10 August 1973)	11 July	1973 a (W)

* See p. 223 of this volume for the text of the reservations and declarations made upon ratification or accession.

UNITED NATIONS CONVENTION ON
THE LAW OF THE SEA

PREAMBLE

Prompted by the desire to settle, in a spirit of mutual understanding and cooperation, all issues relating to the law of the sea and aware of the historic significance of this Convention as an important contribution to the maintenance of peace, justice and progress for all peoples of the world. **App3–001**

Noting that developments since the United Nations Conferences on the Law of the Sea held at Geneva in 1958 and 1960 have accentuated the need for a new and generally acceptable Convention on the law of the sea, **App3–002**

Conscious that the problems of ocean space are closely interrelated and need to be considered as a whole, **App3–003**

Recognizing the desirability of establishing through this Convention, with due regard for the sovereignty of all States, a legal order for the seas and oceans which will facilitate international communication, and will promote the peaceful uses of the seas and oceans, the equitable and efficient utilization of their resources, the conservation of their living resources, and the study, protection and preservation of the marine environment, **App3–004**

Bearing in mind that the achievement of these goals will contribute to the realization of a just and equitable international economic order which takes into account the interests and needs of mankind as a whole and, in particular, the special interests and needs of developing countries, whether coastal or land-locked, **App3–005**

Desiring by this Convention to develop the principles embodied in resolution 2749 (XXV) of 17 December 1970 in which the General Assembly of the United Nations solemnly declared *inter alia* that the area of the seabed and ocean floor and the subsoil thereof, beyond the limits of national jurisdiction, as well as its resources, are the common heritage of mankind, the exploration and exploitation of which shall be carried out for the benefit of mankind as a whole, irrespective of the geographical location of States, **App3–006**

Believing that the codification and progressive development of the law of the sea achieved in this Convention will contribute to the strengthening of peace, security, cooperation and friendly relations among all nations in conformity with the principles of justice and equal rights and will promote the economic and social advancement of all peoples of the world, in accordance with the Purposes and Principles of the United Nations as set forth in the Charter, **App3–007**

Affirming that matters not regulated by this Convention continue to be governed by the rules and principles of general international law, **App3–008**

Have agreed as follows: **App3–009**

PART VII HIGH SEAS

SECTION 1. GENERAL PROVISIONS

App3–010 **Article 100 Duty to cooperate in the repression of piracy**

All States shall cooperate to the fullest possible extent in the repression of piracy on the high seas or in any other place outside the jurisdiction of any State.

App3–011 **Article 101 Definition of piracy**

Piracy consists of any of the following acts:

(a) any illegal acts of violence or detention, or any act of depredation, committed for private ends by the crew or the passengers of a private ship or a private aircraft, and directed:

(i) on the high seas, against another ship or aircraft, or against persons or property on board such ship or aircraft;

(ii) against a ship, aircraft, persons or property in a place outside the jurisdiction of any State;

(b) any act of voluntary participation in the operation of a ship or of an aircraft with knowledge of facts making it a pirate ship or aircraft;

(c) any act of inciting or of intentionally facilitating an act described in subparagraph (a) or (b).

App3–012 **Article 102 Piracy by a warship, government ship or government aircraft whose crew has mutinied**

The acts of piracy, as defined in article 101, committed by a warship, government ship or government aircraft whose crew has mutinied and taken control of the ship or aircraft are assimilated to acts committed by a private ship or aircraft.

App3–013 **Article 103 Definition of a pirate ship or aircraft**

A ship or aircraft is considered a pirate ship or aircraft if it is intended by the persons in dominant control to be used for the purpose of committing one of the acts referred to in article 101. The same applies if the ship or aircraft has been used to commit any such act, so long as it remains under the control of the persons guilty of that act.

App3–014 **Article 104 Retention or loss of the nationality of a pirate ship or aircraft**

A ship or aircraft may retain its nationality although it has become a pirate ship or aircraft. The retention or loss of nationality is determined by the law of the State from which such nationality was derived.

App3–015 **Article 105 Seizure of a pirate ship or aircraft**

On the high seas, or in any other place outside the jurisdiction of any State, every State may seize a pirate ship or aircraft, or a ship or aircraft taken by piracy and under the control of pirates, and arrest the persons and seize the property on board. The courts of the State which carried out the seizure may decide upon the penalties to be imposed, and may also determine the action to be taken with regard to the ships, aircraft or property, subject to the rights of third parties acting in good faith.

Article 106 Liability for seizure without adequate grounds   App3–016

Where the seizure of a ship or aircraft on suspicion of piracy has been effected without adequate grounds, the State making the seizure shall be liable to the State the nationality of which is possessed by the ship or aircraft for any loss or damage caused by the seizure.

Article 107 Ships and aircraft which are entitled to seize on account of piracy   App3–017

A seizure on account of piracy may be carried out only by warships or military aircraft, or other ships or aircraft clearly marked and identifiable as being on government service and authorized to that effect.

Article 108 Illicit traffic in narcotic drugs or psychotropic substances   App3–018

1. All States shall cooperate in the suppression of illicit traffic in narcotic drugs and psychotropic substances engaged in by ships on the high seas contrary to international conventions.
2. Any State which has reasonable grounds for believing that a ship flying its flag is engaged in illicit traffic in narcotic drugs or psychotropic substances may request the cooperation of other States to suppress such traffic.

CONVENTION AGAINST TORTURE AND OTHER CRUEL, INHUMAN OR DEGRADING TREATMENT OR PUNISHMENT

The States Parties to this Convention, Considering that, in accordance with the principles proclaimed in the Charter of the United Nations, recognition of the equal and inalienable rights of all members of the human family is the foundation of freedom, justice and peace in the world, **App4–001**

Recognizing that those rights derive from the inherent dignity of the human person,

Considering the obligation of States under the Charter, in particular Article 55, to promote universal respect for, and observance of, human rights and fundamental freedoms,

Having regard to article 5 of the Universal Declaration of Human Rights and article 7 of the International Covenant on Civil and Political Rights, both of which provide that no one shall be subjected to torture or to cruel, inhuman or degrading treatment or punishment,

Having regard also to the Declaration on the Protection of All Persons from Being Subjected to Torture and Other Cruel, Inhuman or Degrading Treatment or Punishment, adopted by the General Assembly on 9 December 1975,

Desiring to make more effective the struggle against torture and other cruel, inhuman or degrading treatment or punishment throughout the world,

Have agreed as follows:

PART I

Article 1 **App4–002**

1. For the purposes of this Convention, the term "torture" means any act by which severe pain or suffering, whether physical or mental, is intentionally inflicted on a person for such purposes as obtaining from him or a third person information or a confession, punishing him for an act he or a third person has committed or is suspected of having committed, or intimidating or coercing him or a third person, or for any reason based on discrimination of any kind, when such pain or suffering is inflicted by or at the instigation of or with the consent or acquiescence of a public official or other person acting in an official capacity. It does not include pain or suffering arising only from, inherent in or incidental to lawful sanctions.

2. This article is without prejudice to any international instrument or national legislation which does or may contain provisions of wider application.

Article 2 **App4–003**

1. Each State Party shall take effective legislative, administrative, judicial or other measures to prevent acts of torture in any territory under its jurisdiction.

2. No exceptional circumstances whatsoever, whether a state of war or a threat of war, internal political in stability or any other public emergency, may be invoked as a justification of torture.

3. An order from a superior officer or a public authority may not be invoked as a justification of torture.

App4–004   **Article 3 General comment on its implementation**

1. No State Party shall expel, return ("refouler") or extradite a person to another State where there are substantial grounds for believing that he would be in danger of being subjected to torture.

2. For the purpose of determining whether there are such grounds, the competent authorities shall take into account all relevant considerations including, where applicable, the existence in the State concerned of a consistent pattern of gross, flagrant or mass violations of human rights.

App4–005   **Article 4**

1. Each State Party shall ensure that all acts of torture are offences under its criminal law. The same shall apply to an attempt to commit torture and to an act by any person which constitutes complicity or participation in torture.

2. Each State Party shall make these offences punishable by appropriate penalties which take into account their grave nature.

App4–006   **Article 5**

1. Each State Party shall take such measures as may be necessary to establish its jurisdiction over the offences referred to in article 4 in the following cases:

    (a) When the offences are committed in any territory under its jurisdiction or on board a ship or aircraft registered in that State;

    (b) When the alleged offender is a national of that State;

    (c) When the victim is a national of that State if that State considers it appropriate.

2. Each State Party shall likewise take such measures as may be necessary to establish its jurisdiction over such offences in cases where the alleged offender is present in any territory under its jurisdiction and it does not extradite him pursuant to article 8 to any of the States mentioned in paragraph I of this article.

3. This Convention does not exclude any criminal jurisdiction exercised in accordance with internal law.

App4–007   **Article 6**

1. Upon being satisfied, after an examination of information available to it, that the circumstances so warrant, any State Party in whose territory a person alleged to have committed any offence referred to in article 4 is present shall take him into custody or take other legal measures to ensure his presence. The custody and other legal measures shall be as provided in the law of that State but may be continued only for such time as is necessary to enable any criminal or extradition proceedings to be instituted.

2. Such State shall immediately make a preliminary inquiry into the facts.

3. Any person in custody pursuant to paragraph I of this article shall be assisted in communicating immediately with the nearest appropriate representative of the State of which he is a national, or, if he is a stateless person, with the representative of the State where he usually resides.

4. When a State, pursuant to this article, has taken a person into custody, it shall immediately notify the States referred to in article 5, paragraph 1, of the fact that such person is in custody and of the circumstances which warrant his detention. The State which makes the preliminary inquiry contemplated in paragraph 2 of this article shall promptly report its findings to the said States and shall indicate whether it intends to exercise jurisdiction.

Article 7

App4–008

1. The State Party in the territory under whose jurisdiction a person alleged to have committed any offence referred to in article 4 is found shall in the cases contemplated in article 5, if it does not extradite him, submit the case to its competent authorities for the purpose of prosecution.

2. These authorities shall take their decision in the same manner as in the case of any ordinary offence of a serious nature under the law of that State. In the cases referred to in article 5, paragraph 2, the standards of evidence required for prosecution and conviction shall in no way be less stringent than those which apply in the cases referred to in article 5, paragraph 1.

3. Any person regarding whom proceedings are brought in connection with any of the offences referred to in article 4 shall be guaranteed fair treatment at all stages of the proceedings.

Article 8

App4–009

1. The offences referred to in article 4 shall be deemed to be included as extraditable offences in any extradition treaty existing between States Parties. States Parties undertake to include such offences as extraditable offences in every extradition treaty to be concluded between them.

2. If a State Party which makes extradition conditional on the existence of a treaty receives a request for extradition from another State Party with which it has no extradition treaty, it may consider this Convention as the legal basis for extradition in respect of such offences. Extradition shall be subject to the other conditions provided by the law of the requested State.

3. States Parties which do not make extradition conditional on the existence of a treaty shall recognize such offences as extraditable offences between themselves subject to the conditions provided by the law of the requested State.

4. Such offences shall be treated, for the purpose of extradition between States Parties, as if they had been committed not only in the place in which they occurred but also in the territories of the States required to establish their jurisdiction in accordance with article 5, paragraph 1.

Article 9

App4–010

1. States Parties shall afford one another the greatest measure of assistance in connection with criminal proceedings brought in respect of any of the offences referred to in article 4, including the supply of all evidence at their disposal necessary for the proceedings.

2. States Parties shall carry out their obligations under paragraph I of this article in conformity with any treaties on mutual judicial assistance that may exist between them.

Article 10

App4–011

1. Each State Party shall ensure that education and information regarding the prohibition against torture are fully included in the training of law enforcement personnel, civil or military, medical personnel, public officials and other persons who may be

involved in the custody, interrogation or treatment of any individual subjected to any form of arrest, detention or imprisonment.

2. Each State Party shall include this prohibition in the rules or instructions issued in regard to the duties and functions of any such person.

App4–012   Article 11

Each State Party shall keep under systematic review interrogation rules, instructions, methods and practices as well as arrangements for the custody and treatment of persons subjected to any form of arrest, detention or imprisonment in any territory under its jurisdiction, with a view to preventing any cases of torture.

App4–013   Article 12

Each State Party shall ensure that its competent authorities proceed to a prompt and impartial investigation, wherever there is reasonable ground to believe that an act of torture has been committed in any territory under its jurisdiction.

App4–014   Article 13

Each State Party shall ensure that any individual who alleges he has been subjected to torture in any territory under its jurisdiction has the right to complain to, and to have his case promptly and impartially examined by, its competent authorities. Steps shall be taken to ensure that the complainant and witnesses are protected against all ill-treatment or intimidation as a consequence of his complaint or any evidence given.

App4–015   Article 14

1. Each State Party shall ensure in its legal system that the victim of an act of torture obtains redress and has an enforceable right to fair and adequate compensation, including the means for as full rehabilitation as possible. In the event of the death of the victim as a result of an act of torture, his dependants shall be entitled to compensation.

2. Nothing in this article shall affect any right of the victim or other persons to compensation which may exist under national law.

App4–016   Article 15

Each State Party shall ensure that any statement which is established to have been made as a result of torture shall not be invoked as evidence in any proceedings, except against a person accused of torture as evidence that the statement was made.

App4–017   Article 16

1. Each State Party shall undertake to prevent in any territory under its jurisdiction other acts of cruel, inhuman or degrading treatment or punishment which do not amount to torture as defined in article I, when such acts are committed by or at the instigation of or with the consent or acquiescence of a public official or other person acting in an official capacity. In particular, the obligations contained in articles 10, 11, 12 and 13 shall apply with the substitution for references to torture of references to other forms of cruel, inhuman or degrading treatment or punishment.

2. The provisions of this Convention are without prejudice to the provisions of any other international instrument or national law which prohibits cruel, inhuman or degrading treatment or punishment or which relates to extradition or expulsion.

PART II

Article 17 App4–018

1. There shall be established a Committee against Torture (hereinafter referred to as the Committee) which shall carry out the functions hereinafter provided. The Committee shall consist of ten experts of high moral standing and recognized competence in the field of human rights, who shall serve in their personal capacity. The experts shall be elected by the States Parties, consideration being given to equitable geographical distribution and to the usefulness of the participation of some persons having legal experience.

2. The members of the Committee shall be elected by secret ballot from a list of persons nominated by States Parties. Each State Party may nominate one person from among its own nationals. States Parties shall bear in mind the usefulness of nominating persons who are also members of the Human Rights Committee established under the International Covenant on Civil and Political Rights and who are willing to serve on the Committee against Torture.

3. Elections of the members of the Committee shall be held at biennial meetings of States Parties convened by the Secretary-General of the United Nations. At those meetings, for which two thirds of the States Parties shall constitute a quorum, the persons elected to the Committee shall be those who obtain the largest number of votes and an absolute majority of the votes of the representatives of States Parties present and voting.

4. The initial election shall be held no later than six months after the date of the entry into force of this Convention. At. least four months before the date of each election, the Secretary-General of the United Nations shall address a letter to the States Parties inviting them to submit their nominations within three months. The Secretary-General shall prepare a list in alphabetical order of all persons thus nominated, indicating the States Parties which have nominated them, and shall submit it to the States Parties.

5. The members of the Committee shall be elected for a term of four years. They shall be eligible for re-election if renominated. However, the term of five of the members elected at the first election shall expire at the end of two years; immediately after the first election the names of these five members shall be chosen by lot by the chairman of the meeting referred to in paragraph 3 of this article.

6. If a member of the Committee dies or resigns or for any other cause can no longer perform his Committee duties, the State Party which nominated him shall appoint another expert from among its nationals to serve for the remainder of his term, subject to the approval of the majority of the States Parties. The approval shall be considered given unless half or more of the States Parties respond negatively within six weeks after having been informed by the Secretary-General of the United Nations of the proposed appointment.

7. States Parties shall be responsible for the expenses of the members of the Committee while they are in performance of Committee duties. (amendment (see General Assembly resolution 47/111 of 16 December 1992); status of ratification)

Article 22 App4–019

1. A State Party to this Convention may at any time declare under this article that it recognizes the competence of the Committee to receive and consider communications from or on behalf of individuals subject to its jurisdiction who claim to be victims of a violation by a State Party of the provisions of the Convention. No communication shall be received by the Committee if it concerns a State Party which has not made such a declaration.

2. The Committee shall consider inadmissible any communication under this article which is anonymous or which it considers to be an abuse of the right of

submission of such communications or to be incompatible with the provisions of this Convention.

3. Subject to the provisions of paragraph 2, the Committee shall bring any communications submitted to it under this article to the attention of the State Party to this Convention which has made a declaration under paragraph I and is alleged to be violating any provisions of the Convention. Within six months, the receiving State shall submit to the Committee written explanations or statements clarifying the matter and the remedy, if any, that may have been taken by that State.

4. The Committee shall consider communications received under this article in the light of all information made available to it by or on behalf of the individual and by the State Party concerned.

5. The Committee shall not consider any communications from an individual under this article unless it has ascertained that:

    (a)   The same matter has not been, and is not being, examined under another procedure of international investigation or settlement;

    (b)   The individual has exhausted all available domestic remedies; this shall not be the rule where the application of the remedies is unreasonably prolonged or is unlikely to bring effective reliefto the person who is the victim of the violation of this Convention.

6. The Committee shall hold closed meetings when examining communications under this article.

7. The Committee shall forward its views to the State Party concerned and to the individual.

8. The provisions of this article shall come into force when five States Parties to this Convention have made declarations under paragraph 1 of this article. Such declarations shall be deposited by the States Parties with the Secretary-General of the United Nations, who shall transmit copies thereof to the other States Parties. A declaration may be withdrawn at any time by notification to the Secretary-General. Such a withdrawal shall not prejudice the consideration of any matter which is the subject of a communication already transmitted under this article; no further communication by or on behalf of an individual shall be received under this article after the notification of withdrawal of the declaration has been received by the SecretaryGeneral, unless the State Party has made a new declaration.

App4–020   **Article 23**

The members of the Committee and of the ad hoc conciliation commissions which may be appointed under article 21, paragraph I (e), shall be entitled to the facilities, privileges and immunities of experts on mission for the United Nations as laid down in the relevant sections of the Convention on the Privileges and Immunities of the United Nations.

App4–021   **Article 24**

The Committee shall submit an annual report on its activities under this Convention to the States Parties and to the General Assembly of the United Nations.

EUROPEAN CONVENTION FOR THE PREVENTION OF TORTURE AND INHUMAN OR DEGRADING TREATMENT OR PUNISHMENT STRASBOURG, 26.XI.1987

The member States of the Council of Europe, signatory hereto,
 Having regard to the provisions of the Convention for the Protection of Human Rights and Fundamental Freedoms,
 Recalling that, under Article 3 of the same Convention, "no one shall be subjected to torture or to inhuman or degrading treatment or punishment";
 Noting that the machinery provided for in that Convention operates in relation to persons who allege that they are victims of violations of Article 3;
 Convinced that the protection of persons deprived of their liberty against torture and inhuman or degrading treatment or punishment could be strengthened by non-judicial means of a preventive character based on visits,
 Have agreed as follows:

App5–001

CHAPTER I

Article 1

App5–002

There shall be established a European Committee for the Prevention of Torture and Inhuman or Degrading Treatment or Punishment (hereinafter referred to as "the Committee"). The Committee shall, by means of visits, examine the treatment of persons deprived of their liberty with a view to strengthening, if necessary, the protection of such persons from torture and from inhuman or degrading treatment or punishment.

Article 2

App5–003

Each Party shall permit visits, in accordance with this Convention, to any place within its jurisdiction where persons are deprived of their liberty by a public authority.

Article 3

App5–004

In the application of this Convention, the Committee and the competent national authorities of the Party concerned shall co-operate with each other.

CHAPTER II

Article 4

App5–005

1 The Committee shall consist of a number of members equal to that of the Parties.

2 The members of the Committee shall be chosen from among persons of high moral character, known for their competence in the field of human rights or having professional experience in the areas covered by this Convention.

3 No two members of the Committee may be nationals of the same State.

4 The members shall serve in their individual capacity, shall be independent and impartial, and shall be available to serve the Committee effectively.

App5–006 **Article 5[1]**

1 The members of the Committee shall be elected by the Committee of Ministers of the Council of Europe by an absolute majority of votes, from a list of names drawn up by the Bureau of the Consultative Assembly of the Council of Europe; each national delegation of the Parties in the Consultative Assembly shall put forward three candidates, of whom two at least shall be its nationals.

Where a member is to be elected to the Committee in respect of a non-member State of the Council of Europe, the Bureau of the Consultative Assembly shall invite the Parliament of that State to put forward three candidates, of whom two at least shall be its nationals. The election by the Committee of Ministers shall take place after consultation with the Party concerned.

2 The same procedure shall be followed in filling casual vacancies.

3 The members of the Committee shall be elected for a period of four years. They may be re-elected twice. However, among the members elected at the first election, the terms of three members shall expire at the end of two years. The members whose terms are to expire at the end of the initial period of two years shall be chosen by lot by the Secretary General of the Council of Europe immediately after the first election has been completed.

4 In order to ensure that, as far as possible, one half of the membership of the Committee shall be renewed every two years, the Committee of Ministers may decide, before proceeding to any subsequent election, that the term or terms of office of one or more members to be elected shall be for a period other than four years but not more than six and not less than two years.

5 In cases where more than one term of office is involved and the Committee of Ministers applies the preceding paragraph, the allocation of the terms of office shall be effected by the drawing of lots by the Secretary General, immediately after the election.

App5–007 **Article 6**

1 The Committee shall meet in camera. A quorum shall be equal to the majority of its members. The decisions of the Committee shall be taken by a majority of the members present, subject to the provisions of Article 10, paragraph 2.

2 The Committee shall draw up its own rules of procedure.

3 The Secretariat of the Committee shall be provided by the Secretary General of the Council of Europe.

CHAPTER III

App5–008 **Article 7**

1 The Committee shall organise visits to places referred to in Article 2. Apart from periodic visits, the Committee may organise such other visits as appear to it to be required in the circumstances.

2 As a general rule, the visits shall be carried out by at least two members of the Committee. The Committee may, if it considers it necessary, be assisted by experts and interpreters.

Article 8

1 The Committee shall notify the Government of the Party concerned of its intention to carry out a visit. After such notification, it may at any time visit any place referred to in Article 2.

2 A Party shall provide the Committee with the following facilities to carry out its task:

   a   access to its territory and the right to travel without restriction;

   b   full information on the places where persons deprived of their liberty are being held;

   c   unlimited access to any place where persons are deprived of their liberty, including the right to move inside such places without restriction;

   d   other information available to the Party which is necessary for the Committee to carry out its task.

In seeking such information, the Committee shall have regard to applicable rules of national law and professional ethics.

3 The Committee may interview in private persons deprived of their liberty.

4 The Committee may communicate freely with any person whom it believes can supply relevant information.

5 If necessary, the Committee may immediately communicate observations to the competent authorities of the Party concerned.

Article 9

1 In exceptional circumstances, the competent authorities of the Party concerned may make representations to the Committee against a visit at the time or to the particular place proposed by the Committee. Such representations may only be made on grounds of national defence, public safety, serious disorder in places where persons are deprived of their liberty, the medical condition of a person or that an urgent interrogation relating to a serious crime is in progress.

2 Following such representations, the Committee and the Party shall immediately enter into consultations in order to clarify the situation and seek agreement on arrangements to enable the Committee to exercise its functions expeditiously. Such arrangements may include the transfer to another place of any person whom the Committee proposed to visit. Until the visit takes place, the Party shall provide information to the Committee about any person concerned.

Article 10

1 After each visit, the Committee shall draw up a report on the facts found during the visit, taking account of any observations which may have been submitted by the Party concerned. It shall transmit to the latter its report containing any recommendations it considers necessary. The Committee may consult with the Party with a view to suggesting, if necessary, improvements in the protection of persons deprived of their liberty.

2 If the Party fails to co-operate or refuses to improve the situation in the light of the Committee's recommendations, the Committee may decide, after the Party has had an opportunity to make known its views, by a majority of two-thirds of its members to make a public statement on the matter.

App5–012   **Article 11**

1 The information gathered by the Committee in relation to a visit, its report and its consultations with the Party concerned shall be confidential.

2 The Committee shall publish its report, together with any comments of the Party concerned, whenever requested to do so by that Party.

3 However, no personal data shall be published without the express consent of the person concerned.

App5–013   **Article 12[2]**

Subject to the rules of confidentiality in Article 11, the Committee shall every year submit to the Committee of Ministers a general report on its activities which shall be transmitted to the Consultative Assembly and to any non-member State of the Council of Europe which is a party to the Convention, and made public.

App5–014   **Article 13**

The members of the Committee, experts and other persons assisting the Committee are required, during and after their terms of office, to maintain the confidentiality of the facts or information of which they have become aware during the discharge of their functions

App5–015   **Article 14**

1 The names of persons assisting the Committee shall be specified in the notification under Article 8, paragraph 1.

2 Experts shall act on the instructions and under the authority of the Committee. They shall have particular knowledge and experience in the areas covered by this Convention and shall be bound by the same duties of independence, impartiality and availability as the members of the Committee.

3 A Party may exceptionally declare that an expert or other person assisting the Committee may not be allowed to take part in a visit to a place within its jurisdiction.

CHAPTER IV

App5–016   **Article 15**

Each Party shall inform the Committee of the name and address of the authority competent to receive notifications to its Government, and of any liaison officer it may appoint.

App5–017   **Article 16**

The Committee, its members and experts referred to in Article 7, paragraph 2 shall enjoy the privileges and immunities set out in the annex to this Convention.

App5–018   **Article 17**

1 This Convention shall not prejudice the provisions of domestic law or any international agreement which provide greater protection for persons deprived of their liberty.

2 Nothing in this Convention shall be construed as limiting or derogating from the competence of the organs of the European Convention on Human Rights or from the obligations assumed by the Parties under that Convention.

3 The Committee shall not visit places which representatives or delegates of Protecting Powers or the International Committee of the Red Cross effectively visit on a regular basis by virtue of the Geneva Conventions of 12 August 1949 and the Additional Protocols of 8 June 1977 thereto.

ENDNOTE

[1] Text amended according to the provisions of Protocols No. 1 (ETS No. 151) and No. 2 (ETS No. 152).
[2] Text amended according to the provisions of Protocol No. 1 (ETS No. 151).

THE TRIBUNAL FOR THE FORMER YUGOSLAVIA

Having been established by the Security Council acting under Chapter VII of the Charter of the United Nations, the International Tribunal for the Prosecution of Persons Responsible for Serious Violations of International Humanitarian Law Committed in the Territory of the Former Yugoslavia since 1991 (hereinafter referred to as "the International Tribunal") shall function in accordance with the provisions of the present Statute.

App6–001

Article 1 Competence of the International Tribunal

App6–002

The International Tribunal shall have the power to prosecute persons responsible for serious violations of international humanitarian law committed in the territory of the former Yugoslavia since 1991 in accordance with the provisions of the present Statute.

Article 2 Grave breaches of the Geneva Conventions of 1949

App6–003

The International Tribunal shall have the power to prosecute persons committing or ordering to be committed grave breaches of the Geneva Conventions of 12 August 1949, namely the following acts against persons or property protected under the provisions of the relevant Geneva Convention:

(a) wilful killing;

(b) torture or inhuman treatment, including biological experiments;

(c) wilfully causing great suffering or serious injury to body or health;

(d) extensive destruction and appropriation of property, not justified by military necessity and carried out unlawfully and wantonly;

(e) compelling a prisoner of war or a civilian to serve in the forces of a hostile power;

(f) wilfully depriving a prisoner of war or a civilian of the rights of fair and regular trial;

(g) unlawful deportation or transfer or unlawful confinement of a civilian;

(h) taking civilians as hostages.

Article 3 Violations of the laws or customs of war

App6–004

The International Tribunal shall have the power to prosecute persons violating the laws or customs of war. Such violations shall include, but not be limited to:

(a) employment of poisonous weapons or other weapons calculated to cause unnecessary suffering;

(b) wanton destruction of cities, towns or villages, or devastation not justified by military necessity;

(c) attack, or bombardment, by whatever means, of undefended towns, villages, dwellings, or buildings;

(d) seizure of, destruction or wilful damage done to institutions dedicated to religion, charity and education, the arts and sciences, historic monuments and works of art and science;

(e) plunder of public or private property.

App6–005 **Article 4 Genocide**

1. The International Tribunal shall have the power to prosecute persons committing genocide as defined in paragraph 2 of this article or of committing any of the other acts enumerated in paragraph 3 of this article.

2. Genocide means any of the following acts committed with intent to destroy, in whole or in part, a national, ethnical, racial or religious group, as such:

(a) killing members of the group;

(b) causing serious bodily or mental harm to members of the group;

(c) deliberately inflicting on the group conditions of life calculated to bring about its physical destruction in whole or in part;

(d) imposing measures intended to prevent births within the group;

(e) forcibly transferring children of the group to another group.

3. The following acts shall be punishable:

(a) genocide;

(b) conspiracy to commit genocide;

(c) direct and public incitement to commit genocide;

(d) attempt to commit genocide;

(e) complicity in genocide.

App6–006 **Article 5 Crimes against humanity**

The International Tribunal shall have the power to prosecute persons responsible for the following crimes when committed in armed conflict, whether international or internal in character, and directed against any civilian population:

(a) murder;

(b) extermination;

(c) enslavement;

(d) deportation;

(e) imprisonment;

(f) torture;

(g) rape;

(h)   persecutions on political, racial and religious grounds;

(i)   other inhumane acts.

Article 6 Personal jurisdiction

App6–007

The International Tribunal shall have jurisdiction over natural persons pursuant to the provisions of the present Statute.

Article 7 Individual criminal responsibility

App6–008

1. A person who planned, instigated, ordered, committed or otherwise aided and abetted in the planning, preparation or execution of a crime referred to in articles 2 to 5 of the present Statute, shall be individually responsible for the crime.

2. The official position of any accused person, whether as Head of State or Government or as a responsible Government official, shall not relieve such person of criminal responsibility nor mitigate punishment.

3. The fact that any of the acts referred to in articles 2 to 5 of the present Statute was committed by a subordinate does not relieve his superior of criminal responsibility if he knew or had reason to know that the subordinate was about to commit such acts or had done so and the superior failed to take the necessary and reasonable measures to prevent such acts or to punish the perpetrators thereof.

4. The fact that an accused person acted pursuant to an order of a Government or of a superior shall not relieve him of criminal responsibility, but may be considered in mitigation of punishment if the International Tribunal determines that justice so requires.

Article 8 Territorial and temporal jurisdiction

App6–009

The territorial jurisdiction of the International Tribunal shall extend to the territory of the former Socialist Federal Republic of Yugoslavia, including its land surface, airspace and territorial waters. The temporal jurisdiction of the International Tribunal shall extend to a period beginning on 1 January 1991.

Article 9 Concurrent jurisdiction

App6–010

1. The International Tribunal and national courts shall have concurrent jurisdiction to prosecute persons for serious violations of international humanitarian law committed in the territory of the former Yugoslavia since 1 January 1991.

2. The International Tribunal shall have primacy over national courts. At any stage of the procedure, the International Tribunal may formally request national courts to defer to the competence of the International Tribunal in accordance with the present Statute and the Rules of Procedure and Evidence of the International Tribunal.

Article 10 *Non-bis-in-idem*

App6–011

1. No person shall be tried before a national court for acts constituting serious violations of international humanitarian law under the present Statute, for which he or she has already been tried by the International Tribunal.

2. A person who has been tried by a national court for acts constituting serious violations of international humanitarian law may be subsequently tried by the International Tribunal only if:

(a)   the act for which he or she was tried was characterized as an ordinary crime; or

(b) the national court proceedings were not impartial or independent, were designed to shield the accused from international criminal responsibility, or the case was not diligently prosecuted.

3. In considering the penalty to be imposed on a person convicted of a crime under the present Statute, the International Tribunal shall take into account the extent to which any penalty imposed by a national court on the same person for the same act has already been served.

App6–012   **Article 16 The Prosecutor**

1. The Prosecutor shall be responsible for the investigation and prosecution of persons responsible for serious violations of international humanitarian law committed in the territory of the former Yugoslavia since 1 January 1991.

2. The Prosecutor shall act independently as a separate organ of the International Tribunal. He or she shall not seek or receive instructions from any Government or from any other source.

3. The Office of the Prosecutor shall be composed of a Prosecutor and such other qualified staff as may be required.

4. The Prosecutor shall be appointed by the Security Council on nomination by the Secretary-General. He or she shall be of high moral character and possess the highest level of competence and experience in the conduct of investigations and prosecutions of criminal cases. The Prosecutor shall serve for a four-year term and be eligible for reappointment. The terms and conditions of service of the Prosecutor shall be those of an Under-Secretary-General of the United Nations.

5. The staff of the Office of the Prosecutor shall be appointed by the Secretary-General on the recommendation of the Prosecutor.

App6–013   **Article 17 The Registry**

1. The Registry shall be responsible for the administration and servicing of the International Tribunal.

2. The Registry shall consist of a Registrar and such other staff as may be required.

3. The Registrar shall be appointed by the Secretary-General after consultation with the President of the International Tribunal. He or she shall serve for a four-year term and be eligible for reappointment. The terms and conditions of service of the Registrar shall be those of an Assistant Secretary-General of the United Nations.

4. The staff of the Registry shall be appointed by the Secretary-General on the recommendation of the Registrar.

App6–014   **Article 18 Investigation and preparation of indictment**

1. The Prosecutor shall initiate investigations *ex-officio* or on the basis of information obtained from any source, particularly from Governments, United Nations organs, intergovernmental and non-governmental organizations. The Prosecutor shall assess the information received or obtained and decide whether there is sufficient basis to proceed.

2. The Prosecutor shall have the power to question suspects, victims and witnesses, to collect evidence and to conduct on-site investigations. In carrying out these tasks, the Prosecutor may, as appropriate, seek the assistance of the State authorities concerned.

3. If questioned, the suspect shall be entitled to be assisted by counsel of his own choice, including the right to have legal assistance assigned to him without payment by him in any such case if he does not have sufficient means to pay for it, as well as to necessary translation into and from a language he speaks and understands.

4. Upon a determination that a *prima facie* case exists, the Prosecutor shall prepare an indictment containing a concise statement of the facts and the crime or crimes with which the accused is charged under the Statute. The indictment shall be transmitted to a judge of the Trial Chamber.

STATUTE OF THE INTERNATIONAL TRIBUNAL FOR RWANDA
(As amended)

As amended by the Security Council acting under Chapter VII of the Charter of the **App7–001** United Nations, the International Criminal Tribunal for the Prosecution of Persons Responsible for Genocide and Other Serious Violations of International Hunanitarina Law Committed in the Territory of Rwanda and Rwandan Citizens responsible for genocide and other such violations committed in the territory of neighbouring States, between 1 January 1994 and 31 December 1994 (hereinafter referred to as "The International Tribunal for Rwanda") shall function in accordance with the provisions of the present Statute.

Article 1: Competence of the International Tribunal for Rwanda   App7–002

The International Tribunal for Rwanda shall have the power to prosecute persons responsible for serious violations of international humanitarian law committed in the territory of Rwanda and Rwandan citizens responsible for such violations committed in the territory of neighbouring States between 1 January 1994 and 31 December 1994, in accordance with the provisions of the present Statute.

Article 2: Genocide   App7–003

1. The International Tribunal for Rwanda shall have the power to prosecute persons committing genocide as defined in paragraph 2 of this Article or of committing any of the other acts enumerated in paragraph 3 of this Article.

2. Genocide means any of the following acts committed with intent to destroy, in whole or in part, a national, ethnical, racial or religious group, such as:

(a) Killing members of the group;

(b) Causing serious bodily or mental harm to members of the group;

(c) Deliberately inflicting on the group conditions of life calculated to bring about its physical destruction in whole or in part;

(d) Imposing measures intended to prevent births within the group;

(e) Forcibly transferring children of the group to another group.

3. The following acts shall be punishable:

(a) Genocide;

(b) Conspiracy to commit genocide;

(c) Direct and public incitement to commit genocide;

(d) Attempt to commit genocide;

(e) Complicity in genocide.

App7–004 **Article 3: Crimes against Humanity**

The International Tribunal for Rwanda shall have the power to prosecute persons responsible for the following crimes when committed as part of a widespread or systematic attack against any civilian population on national, political, ethnic, racial or religious grounds:

    (a) Murder;

    (b) Extermination;

    (c) Enslavement;

    (d) Deportation;

    (e) Imprisonment;

    (f) Torture;

    (g) Rape;

    (h) Persecutions on political, racial and religious grounds;

    (i) Other inhumane acts.

App7–005 **Article 4: Violations of Article 3 Common to the Geneva Conventions and of Additional Protocol II**

The International Tribunal for Rwanda shall have the power to prosecute persons committing or ordering to be committed serious violations of Article 3 common to the Geneva Conventions of 12 August 1949 for the Protection of War Victims, and of Additional Protocol II thereto of 8 June 1977. These violations shall include, but shall not be limited to:

    (a) Violence to life, health and physical or mental well-being of persons, in particular murder as well as cruel treatment such as torture, mutilation or any form of corporal punishment;

    (b) Collective punishments;

    (c) Taking of hostages;

    (d) Acts of terrorism;

    (e) Outrages upon personal dignity, in particular humiliating and degrading treatment, rape, enforced prostitution and any form of indecent assault;

    (f) Pillage;

    (g) The passing of sentences and the carrying out of executions without previous judgement pronounced by a regularly constituted court, affording all the judicial guarantees which are recognized as indispensable by civilised peoples;

    (h) Threats to commit any of the foregoing acts.

Article 5: Personal Jurisdiction

App7–006

The International Tribunal for Rwanda shall have jurisdiction over natural persons pursuant to the provisions of the present Statute.

Article 6: Individual Criminal Responsibility

App7–007

1. A person who planned, instigated, ordered, committed or otherwise aided and abetted in the planning, preparation or execution of a crime referred to in Articles 2 to 4 of the present Statute, shall be individually responsible for the crime.

2. The official position of any accused person, whether as Head of state or government or as a responsible government official, shall not relieve such person of criminal responsibility nor mitigate punishment.

3. The fact that any of the acts referred to in Articles 2 to 4 of the present Statute was committed by a subordinate does not relieve his or her superior of criminal responsibility if he or she knew or had reason to know that the subordinate was about to commit such acts or had done so and the superior failed to take the necessary and reasonable measures to prevent such acts or to punish the perpetrators thereof.

4. The fact that an accused person acted pursuant to an order of a government or of a superior shall not relieve him or her of criminal responsibility, but may be considered in mitigation of punishment if the International Tribunal for Rwanda determines that justice so requires.

Article 7: Territorial and Temporal Jurisdiction

App7–008

The territorial jurisdiction of the International Tribunal for Rwanda shall extend to the territory of Rwanda including its land surface and airspace as well as to the territory of neighbouring States in respect of serious violations of international humanitarian law committed by Rwandan citizens. The temporal jurisdiction of the International Tribunal for Rwanda shall extend to a period beginning on 1 January 1994 and ending on 31 December 1994.

Article 8: Concurrent Jurisdiction

App7–009

1. The International Tribunal for Rwanda and national courts shall have concurrent jurisdiction to prosecute persons for serious violations of international humanitarian law committed in the territory of Rwanda and Rwandan citizens for such violations committed in the territory of the neighbouring States, between 1 January 1994 and 31 December 1994.

2. The International Tribunal for Rwanda shall have the primacy over the national courts of all States. At any stage of the procedure, the International Tribunal for Rwanda may formally request national courts to defer to its competence in accordance with the present Statute and the Rules of Procedure and Evidence of the - International Tribunal for Rwanda.

Article 9: *Non Bis in Idem*

App7–010

1. No person shall be tried before a national court for acts constituting serious violations of international humanitarian law under the present Statute, for which he or she has already been tried by the International Tribunal for Rwanda.

2. A person who has been tried before a national court for acts constituting serious violations of international humanitarian law may be subsequently tried by the International Tribunal for Rwanda only if:

(a) The act for which he or she was tried was characterised as an ordinary crime; or

(b)   The national court proceedings were not impartial or independent, were designed to shield the accused from international criminal responsibility, or the case was not diligently prosecuted.

3. In considering the penalty to be imposed on a person convicted of a crime under the present Statute, the International Tribunal for Rwanda shall take into account the extent to which any penalty imposed by a national court on the same person for the same act has already been served.

App7–011   **Article 10: Organisation of the International Tribunal for Rwanda**

The International Tribunal for Rwanda shall consist of the following organs:

(a)   The Chambers, comprising three Trial Chambers and an Appeals Chamber;

(b)   The Prosecutor;

(c)   A Registry.

App7–012   **Article 11: Composition of the Chambers**

1. The Chambers shall be composed of 16 permanent independent judges, no two of whom may be nationals of the same State, and a maximum at any one time of four *ad litem* independent judges appointed in accordance with article 12 *ter*, paragraph 2, of the present Statute, no two of whom may be nationals of the same State.

2. Three permanent judges and a maximum at any one time of four *ad litem* judges shall be members of each Trial Chamber. Each Trial Chamber to which *ad litem* judges are assigned may be divided into sections of three judges each, composed of both permanent and *ad litem* judges. A section of a Trial Chamber shall have the same powers and responsibilities as a Trial Chamber under the present Statute and shall render judgement in accordance with the same rules.

3. Seven of the permanent judges shall be members of the Appeals Chamber. The Appeals Chamber shall, for each appeal, be composed of five of its members.

4. A person who for the purposes of membership of the Chambers of the International Tribunal for Rwanda could be regarded as a national of more than one State shall be deemed to be a national of the State in which that person ordinarily exercises civil and political rights.

Appendix 8

ROME STATUTE OF THE INTERNATIONAL CRIMINAL COURT

PREAMBLE

The States Parties to this Statute,

Conscious that all peoples are united by common bonds, their cultures pieced together in a shared heritage, and concerned that this delicate mosaic may be shattered at any time,

Mindful that during this century millions of children, women and men have been victims of unimaginable atrocities that deeply shock the conscience of humanity,

Recognizing that such grave crimes threaten the peace, security and well-being of the world,

Affirming that the most serious crimes of concern to the international community as a whole must not go unpunished and that their effective prosecution must be ensured by taking measures at the national level and by enhancing international cooperation,

Determined to put an end to impunity for the perpetrators of these crimes and thus to contribute to the prevention of such crimes,

Recalling that it is the duty of every State to exercise its criminal jurisdiction over those responsible for international crimes,

Reaffirming the Purposes and Principles of the Charter of the United Nations, and in particular that all States shall refrain from the threat or use of force against the territorial integrity or political independence of any State, or in any other manner inconsistent with the Purposes of the United Nations,

Emphasizing in this connection that nothing in this Statute shall be taken as authorizing any State Party to intervene in an armed conflict or in the internal affairs of any State,

Determined to these ends and for the sake of present and future generations, to establish an independent permanent International Criminal Court in relationship with the United Nations system, with jurisdiction over the most serious crimes of concern to the international community as a whole,

Emphasizing that the International Criminal Court established under this Statute shall be complementary to national criminal jurisdictions,

Resolved to guarantee lasting respect for and the enforcement of international justice,

Have agreed as follows:

PART 1. ESTABLISHMENT OF THE COURT

Article 1 The Court

An International Criminal Court ("the Court") is hereby established. It shall be a permanent institution and shall have the power to exercise its jurisdiction over persons

App8–001

App8–002

425

for the most serious crimes of international concern, as referred to in this Statute, and shall be complementary to national criminal jurisdictions. The jurisdiction and functioning of the Court shall be governed by the provisions of this Statute.

App8–003 **Article 2 Relationship of the Court with the United Nations**

The Court shall be brought into relationship with the United Nations through an agreement to be approved by the Assembly of States Parties to this Statute and thereafter concluded by the President of the Court on its behalf.

App8–004 **Article 3 Seat of the Court**

1. The seat of the Court shall be established at The Hague in the Netherlands ("the host State").
2. The Court shall enter into a headquarters agreement with the host State, to be approved by the Assembly of States Parties and thereafter concluded by the President of the Court on its behalf.
3. The Court may sit elsewhere, whenever it considers it desirable, as provided in this Statute.

App8–005 **Article 4 Legal status and powers of the Court**

The Court shall have international legal personality. It shall also have such legal capacity as may be necessary for the exercise of its functions and the fulfilment of its purposes.
2. The Court may exercise its functions and powers, as provided in this Statute, on the territory of any State Party and, by special agreement, on the territory of any other State.

PART 2. JURISDICTION, ADMISSIBILITY AND APPLICABLE LAW

App8–006 **Article 5 Crimes within the jurisdiction of the Court**

The jurisdiction of the Court shall be limited to the most serious crimes of concern to the international community as a whole. The Court has jurisdiction in accordance with this Statute with respect to the following crimes:

    (a)   The crime of genocide;

    (b)   Crimes against humanity;

    (c)   War crimes;

    (d)   The crime of aggression.

2. The Court shall exercise jurisdiction over the crime of aggression once a provision is adopted in accordance with articles 121 and 123 defining the crime and setting out the conditions under which the Court shall exercise jurisdiction with respect to this crime. Such a provision shall be consistent with the relevant provisions of the Charter of the United Nations.

App8–007 **Article 6 Genocide**

For the purpose of this Statute, "genocide" means any of the following acts committed with intent to destroy, in whole or in part, a national, ethnical, racial or religious group, as such:

    (a)   Killing members of the group;

    (b)   Causing serious bodily or mental harm to members of the group;

    (c)   Deliberately inflicting on the group conditions of life calculated to bring about its physical destruction in whole or in part;

    (d)   Imposing measures intended to prevent births within the group;

    (e)   Forcibly transferring children of the group to another group.

Article 7 Crimes against humanity   **App8–008**

1. For the purpose of this Statute, "crime against humanity" means any of the following acts when committed as part of a widespread or systematic attack directed against any civilian population, with knowledge of the attack:

    (a)   Murder;

    (b)   Extermination;

    (c)   Enslavement;

    (d)   Deportation or forcible transfer of population;

    (e)   Imprisonment or other severe deprivation of physical liberty in violation of fundamental rules of international law;

    (f)   Torture;

    (g)   Rape, sexual slavery, enforced prostitution, forced pregnancy, enforced sterilization, or any other form of sexual violence of comparable gravity;

    (h)   Persecution against any identifiable group or collectivity on political, racial, national, ethnic, cultural, religious, gender as defined in paragraph 3, or other grounds that are universally recognized as impermissible under international law, in connection with any act referred to in this paragraph or any crime within the jurisdiction of the Court;

    (i)   Enforced disappearance of persons;

    (j)   The crime of apartheid;

    (k)   Other inhumane acts of a similar character intentionally causing great suffering, or serious injury to body or to mental or physical health.

2. For the purpose of paragraph 1:

    (a)   "Attack directed against any civilian population" means a course of conduct involving the multiple commission of acts referred to in paragraph 1 against any civilian population, pursuant to or in furtherance of a State or organizational policy to commit such attack;

    (b)   "Extermination" includes the intentional infliction of conditions of life, inter alia the deprivation of access to food and medicine, calculated to bring about the destruction of part of a population;

    (c)   "Enslavement" means the exercise of any or all of the powers attaching to the right of ownership over a person and includes the exercise of such power in the course of trafficking in persons, in particular women and children;

    (d)   "Deportation or forcible transfer of population" means forced displacement of the persons concerned by expulsion or other coercive acts from the area in which they are lawfully present, without grounds permitted under international law;

(e) "Torture" means the intentional infliction of severe pain or suffering, whether physical or mental, upon a person in the custody or under the control of the accused; except that torture shall not include pain or suffering arising only from, inherent in or incidental to, lawful sanctions;

(f) "Forced pregnancy" means the unlawful confinement of a woman forcibly made pregnant, with the intent of affecting the ethnic composition of any population or carrying out other grave violations of international law. This definition shall not in any way be interpreted as affecting national laws relating to pregnancy;

(g) "Persecution" means the intentional and severe deprivation of fundamental rights contrary to international law by reason of the identity of the group or collectivity;

(h) "The crime of apartheid" means inhumane acts of a character similar to those referred to in paragraph 1, committed in the context of an institutionalized regime of systematic oppression and domination by one racial group over any other racial group or groups and committed with the intention of maintaining that regime;

(i) "Enforced disappearance of persons" means the arrest, detention or abduction of persons by, or with the authorization, support or acquiescence of, a State or a political organization, followed by a refusal to acknowledge that deprivation of freedom or to give information on the fate or whereabouts of those persons, with the intention of removing them from the protection of the law for a prolonged period of time.

3. For the purpose of this Statute, it is understood that the term "gender" refers to the two sexes, male and female, within the context of society. The term "gender" does not indicate any meaning different from the above.

App8–009 **Article 8 War crimes**

1. The Court shall have jurisdiction in respect of war crimes in particular when committed as part of a plan or policy or as part of a large-scale commission of such crimes.

2. For the purpose of this Statute, "war crimes" means:

(a) Grave breaches of the Geneva Conventions of 12 August 1949, namely, any of the following acts against persons or property protected under the provisions of the relevant Geneva Convention:

(i) Wilful killing;
(ii) Torture or inhuman treatment, including biological experiments;
(iii) Wilfully causing great suffering, or serious injury to body or health;
(iv) Extensive destruction and appropriation of property, not justified by military necessity and carried out unlawfully and wantonly;
(v) Compelling a prisoner of war or other protected person to serve in the forces of a hostile Power;
(vi) Wilfully depriving a prisoner of war or other protected person of the rights of fair and regular trial;
(vii) Unlawful deportation or transfer or unlawful confinement;
(viii) Taking of hostages.

(b) Other serious violations of the laws and customs applicable in international armed conflict, within the established framework of international law, namely, any of the following acts:

(i) Intentionally directing attacks against the civilian population as such or against individual civilians not taking direct part in hostilities;

(ii) Intentionally directing attacks against civilian objects, that is, objects which are not military objectives;

(iii) Intentionally directing attacks against personnel, installations, material, units or vehicles involved in a humanitarian assistance or peacekeeping mission in accordance with the Charter of the United Nations, as long as they are entitled to the protection given to civilians or civilian objects under the international law of armed conflict;

(iv) Intentionally launching an attack in the knowledge that such attack will cause incidental loss of life or injury to civilians or damage to civilian objects or widespread, long-term and severe damage to the natural environment which would be clearly excessive in relation to the concrete and direct overall military advantage anticipated;

(v) Attacking or bombarding, by whatever means, towns, villages, dwellings or buildings which are undefended and which are not military objectives;

(vi) Killing or wounding a combatant who, having laid down his arms or having no longer means of defence, has surrendered at discretion;

(vii) Making improper use of a flag of truce, of the flag or of the military insignia and uniform of the enemy or of the United Nations, as well as of the distinctive emblems of the Geneva Conventions, resulting in death or serious personal injury;

(viii) The transfer, directly or indirectly, by the Occupying Power of parts of its own civilian population into the territory it occupies, or the deportation or transfer of all or parts of the population of the occupied territory within or outside this territory;

(ix) Intentionally directing attacks against buildings dedicated to religion, education, art, science or charitable purposes, historic monuments, hospitals and places where the sick and wounded are collected, provided they are not military objectives;

(x) Subjecting persons who are in the power of an adverse party to physical mutilation or to medical or scientific experiments of any kind which are neither justified by the medical, dental or hospital treatment of the person concerned nor carried out in his or her interest, and which cause death to or seriously endanger the health of such person or persons;

(xi) Killing or wounding treacherously individuals belonging to the hostile nation or army;

(xii) Declaring that no quarter will be given;

(xiii) Destroying or seizing the enemy's property unless such destruction or seizure be imperatively demanded by the necessities of war;

(xiv) Declaring abolished, suspended or inadmissible in a court of law the rights and actions of the nationals of the hostile party;

(xv) Compelling the nationals of the hostile party to take part in the operations of war directed against their own country, even if they were in the belligerent's service before the commencement of the war;

(xvi) Pillaging a town or place, even when taken by assault;

(xvii) Employing poison or poisoned weapons;

(xviii) Employing asphyxiating, poisonous or other gases, and all analogous liquids, materials or devices;

(xix) Employing bullets which expand or flatten easily in the human body, such as bullets with a hard envelope which does not entirely cover the core or is pierced with incisions;

(xx) Employing weapons, projectiles and material and methods of warfare which are of a nature to cause superfluous injury or unnecessary suffering or which are inherently indiscriminate in violation of the international law of armed conflict, provided that such weapons, projectiles and material and methods of warfare are the subject of a comprehensive prohibition and are included in an annex to this Statute, by an amendment in accordance with the relevant provisions set forth in articles 121 and 123;

(xxi) Committing outrages upon personal dignity, in particular humiliating and degrading treatment;

(xxii) Committing rape, sexual slavery, enforced prostitution, forced pregnancy, as defined in article 7, paragraph 2 (f), enforced sterilization, or any other form of sexual violence also constituting a grave breach of the Geneva Conventions;

(xxiii) Utilizing the presence of a civilian or other protected person to render certain points, areas or military forces immune from military operations;

(xxiv) Intentionally directing attacks against buildings, material, medical units and transport, and personnel using the distinctive emblems of the Geneva Conventions in conformity with international law;

(xxv) Intentionally using starvation of civilians as a method of warfare by depriving them of objects indispensable to their survival, including wilfully impeding relief supplies as provided for under the Geneva Conventions;

(xxvi) Conscripting or enlisting children under the age of fifteen years into the national armed forces or using them to participate actively in hostilities.

(c) In the case of an armed conflict not of an international character, serious violations of article 3 common to the four Geneva Conventions of 12 August 1949, namely, any of the following acts committed against persons taking no active part in the hostilities, including members of armed forces who have laid down their arms and those placed hors de combat by sickness, wounds, detention or any other cause:

(i) Violence to life and person, in particular murder of all kinds, mutilation, cruel treatment and torture;

(ii) Committing outrages upon personal dignity, in particular humiliating and degrading treatment;

(iii) Taking of hostages;

(iv) The passing of sentences and the carrying out of executions without previous judgement pronounced by a regularly constituted court, affording all judicial guarantees which are generally recognized as indispensable.

(d) Paragraph 2 (c) applies to armed conflicts not of an international character and thus does not apply to situations of internal disturbances and tensions, such as riots, isolated and sporadic acts of violence or other acts of a similar nature.

(e) Other serious violations of the laws and customs applicable in armed conflicts not of an international character, within the established framework of international law, namely, any of the following acts:

    (i)   Intentionally directing attacks against the civilian population as such or against individual civilians not taking direct part in hostilities;

    (ii)   Intentionally directing attacks against buildings, material, medical units and transport, and personnel using the distinctive emblems of the Geneva Conventions in conformity with international law;

    (iii)   Intentionally directing attacks against personnel, installations, material, units or vehicles involved in a humanitarian assistance or peacekeeping mission in accordance with the Charter of the United Nations, as long as they are entitled to the protection given to civilians or civilian objects under the international law of armed conflict;

    (iv)   Intentionally directing attacks against buildings dedicated to religion, education, art, science or charitable purposes, historic monuments, hospitals and places where the sick and wounded are collected, provided they are not military objectives;

    (v)   Pillaging a town or place, even when taken by assault;

    (vi)   Committing rape, sexual slavery, enforced prostitution, forced pregnancy, as defined in article 7, paragraph 2 (f), enforced sterilization, and any other form of sexual violence also constituting a serious violation of article 3 common to the four Geneva Conventions;

    (vii)   Conscripting or enlisting children under the age of fifteen years into armed forces or groups or using them to participate actively in hostilities;

    (viii)   Ordering the displacement of the civilian population for reasons related to the conflict, unless the security of the civilians involved or imperative military reasons so demand;

    (x)   Killing or wounding treacherously a combatant adversary;

    (x)   Declaring that no quarter will be given;

    (xi)   Subjecting persons who are in the power of another party to the conflict to physical mutilation or to medical or scientific experiments of any kind which are neither justified by the medical, dental or hospital treatment of the person concerned nor carried out in his or her interest, and which cause death to or seriously endanger the health of such person or persons;

    (xii)   Destroying or seizing the property of an adversary unless such destruction or seizure be imperatively demanded by the necessities of the conflict;

(f) Paragraph 2 (e) applies to armed conflicts not of an international character and thus does not apply to situations of internal disturbances and tensions, such as riots, isolated and sporadic acts of violence or other acts of a similar nature. It applies to armed conflicts that take place in the territory of a State when there is protracted armed conflict between governmental authorities and organized armed groups or between such groups.

3. Nothing in paragraph 2 (c) and (e) shall affect the responsibility of a Government to maintain or re-establish law and order in the State or to defend the unity and territorial integrity of the State, by all legitimate means.

App8–010   **Article 9 Elements of Crimes**

1. Elements of Crimes shall assist the Court in the interpretation and application of articles 6, 7 and 8. They shall be adopted by a two-thirds majority of the members of the Assembly of States Parties.

2. Amendments to the Elements of Crimes may be proposed by:

(a)   Any State Party;

(b)   The judges acting by an absolute majority;

(c)   The Prosecutor.

Such amendments shall be adopted by a two-thirds majority of the members of the Assembly of States Parties.

3. The Elements of Crimes and amendments thereto shall be consistent with this Statute.

App8–011   **Article 10**

Nothing in this Part shall be interpreted as limiting or prejudicing in any way existing or developing rules of international law for purposes other than this Statute.

App8–012   **Article 11 Jurisdiction ratione temporis**

1. The Court has jurisdiction only with respect to crimes committed after the entry into force of this Statute.

2. If a State becomes a Party to this Statute after its entry into force, the Court may exercise its jurisdiction only with respect to crimes committed after the entry into force of this Statute for that State, unless that State has made a declaration under article 12, paragraph 3.

App8–013   **Article 12 Preconditions to the exercise of jurisdiction**

1. A State which becomes a Party to this Statute thereby accepts the jurisdiction of the Court with respect to the crimes referred to in article 5.

2. In the case of article 13, paragraph (a) or (c), the Court may exercise its jurisdiction if one or more of the following States are Parties to this Statute or have accepted the jurisdiction of the Court in accordance with paragraph 3:

(a)   The State on the territory of which the conduct in question occurred or, if the crime was committed on board a vessel or aircraft, the State of registration of that vessel or aircraft;

(b)   The State of which the person accused of the crime is a national.

3. If the acceptance of a State which is not a Party to this Statute is required under paragraph 2, that State may, by declaration lodged with the Registrar, accept the exercise of jurisdiction by the Court with respect to the crime in question. The accepting State shall cooperate with the Court without any delay or exception in accordance with Part 9.

App8–014   **Article 13 Exercise of jurisdiction**

The Court may exercise its jurisdiction with respect to a crime referred to in article 5 in accordance with the provisions of this Statute if:

(a) A situation in which one or more of such crimes appears to have been committed is referred to the Prosecutor by a State Party in accordance with article 14;

(b) A situation in which one or more of such crimes appears to have been committed is referred to the Prosecutor by the Security Council acting under Chapter VII of the Charter of the United Nations; or

(c) The Prosecutor has initiated an investigation in respect of such a crime in accordance with article 15.

Article 14 Referral of a situation by a State Party App8–015

1. A State Party may refer to the Prosecutor a situation in which one or more crimes within the jurisdiction of the Court appear to have been committed requesting the Prosecutor to investigate the situation for the purpose of determining whether one or more specific persons should be charged with the commission of such crimes.

2. As far as possible, a referral shall specify the relevant circumstances and be accompanied by such supporting documentation as is available to the State referring the situation.

Article 15 Prosecutor App8–016

1. The Prosecutor may initiate investigations *proprio motu* on the basis of information on crimes within the jurisdiction of the Court.

2. The Prosecutor shall analyse the seriousness of the information received. For this purpose, he or she may seek additional information from States, organs of the United Nations, intergovernmental or non-governmental organizations, or other reliable sources that he or she deems appropriate, and may receive written or oral testimony at the seat of the Court.

3. If the Prosecutor concludes that there is a reasonable basis to proceed with an investigation, he or she shall submit to the Pre-Trial Chamber a request for authorization of an investigation, together with any supporting material collected. Victims may make representations to the Pre-Trial Chamber, in accordance with the Rules of Procedure and Evidence.

4. If the Pre-Trial Chamber, upon examination of the request and the supporting material, considers that there is a reasonable basis to proceed with an investigation, and that the case appears to fall within the jurisdiction of the Court, it shall authorize the commencement of the investigation, without prejudice to subsequent determinations by the Court with regard to the jurisdiction and admissibility of a case.

5. The refusal of the Pre-Trial Chamber to authorize the investigation shall not preclude the presentation of a subsequent request by the Prosecutor based on new facts or evidence regarding the same situation.

6. If, after the preliminary examination referred to in paragraphs 1 and 2, the Prosecutor concludes that the information provided does not constitute a reasonable basis for an investigation, he or she shall inform those who provided the information. This shall not preclude the Prosecutor from considering further information submitted to him or her regarding the same situation in the light of new facts or evidence.

Article 16 Deferral of investigation or prosecution App8–017

No investigation or prosecution may be commenced or proceeded with under this Statute for a period of 12 months after the Security Council, in a resolution adopted under Chapter VII of the Charter of the United Nations, has requested the Court to that effect; that request may be renewed by the Council under the same conditions.

App8–018 **Article 17 Issues of admissibility**

1. Having regard to paragraph 10 of the Preamble and article 1, the Court shall determine that a case is inadmissable where:

    (a) The case is being investigated or prosecuted by a State which has jurisdiction over it, unless the State is unwilling or unable genuinely to carry out the investigation or prosecution;

    (b) The case has been investigated by a State which has jurisdiction over it and the State has decided not to prosecute the person concerned, unless the decision resulted from the unwillingness or inability of the State genuinely to prosecute;

    (c) The person concerned has already been tried for conduct which is the subject of the complaint, and a trial by the Court is not permitted under article 20, paragraph 3;

    (d) The case is not of sufficient gravity to justify further action by the Court.

2. In order to determine unwillingness in a particular case, the Court shall consider, having regard to the principles of due process recognized by international law, whether one or more of the following exist, as applicable:

    (a) The proceedings were or are being undertaken or the national decision was made for the purpose of shielding the person concerned from criminal responsibility for crimes within the jurisdiction of the Court referred to in article 5;

    (b) There has been an unjustified delay in the proceedings which in the circumstances is inconsistent with an intent to bring the person concerned to justice;

    (c) The proceedings were not or are not being conducted independently or impartially, and they were or are being conducted in a manner which, in the circumstances, is inconsistent with an intent to bring the person concerned to justice.

3. In order to determine inability in a particular case, the Court shall consider whether, due to a total or substantial collapse or unavailability of its national judicial system, the State is unable to obtain the accused or the necessary evidence and testimony or otherwise unable to carry out its proceedings.

App8–019 **Article 18 Preliminary rulings regarding admissibility**

1. When a situation has been referred to the Court pursuant to article 13 (a) and the Prosecutor has determined that there would be a reasonable basis to commence an investigation, or the Prosecutor initiates an investigation pursuant to articles 13 (c) and 15, the Prosecutor shall notify all States Parties and those States which, taking into account the information available, would normally exercise jurisdiction over the crimes concerned. The Prosecutor may notify such States on a confidential basis and, where the Prosecutor believes it necessary to protect persons, prevent destruction of evidence or prevent the absconding of persons, may limit the scope of the information provided to States.

2. Within one month of receipt of that notification, a State may inform the Court that it is investigating or has investigated its nationals or others within its jurisdic-

tion with respect to criminal acts which may constitute crimes referred to in article 5 and which relate to the information provided in the notification to States. At the request of that State, the Prosecutor shall defer to the State's investigation of those persons unless the Pre-Trial Chamber, on the application of the Prosecutor, decides to authorize the investigation.

3. The Prosecutor's deferral to a State's investigation shall be open to review by the Prosecutor six months after the date of deferral or at any time when there has been a significant change of circumstances based on the State's unwillingness or inability genuinely to carry out the investigation.

4. The State concerned or the Prosecutor may appeal to the Appeals Chamber against a ruling of the Pre-Trial Chamber, in accordance with article 82. The appeal may be heard on an expedited basis.

5. When the Prosecutor has deferred an investigation in accordance with paragraph 2, the Prosecutor may request that the State concerned periodically inform the Prosecutor of the progress of its investigations and any subsequent prosecutions. States Parties shall respond to such requests without undue delay.

6. Pending a ruling by the Pre-Trial Chamber, or at any time when the Prosecutor has deferred an investigation under this article, the Prosecutor may, on an exceptional basis, seek authority from the Pre-Trial Chamber to pursue necessary investigative steps for the purpose of preserving evidence where there is a unique opportunity to obtain important evidence or there is a significant risk that such evidence may not be subsequently available.

7. A State which has challenged a ruling of the Pre-Trial Chamber under this article may challenge the admissibility of a case under article 19 on the grounds of additional significant facts or significant change of circumstances.

Article 19 Challenges to the jurisdiction of the Court or the admissibility of a case

App8–020

1. The Court shall satisfy itself that it has jurisdiction in any case brought before it. The Court may, on its own motion, determine the admissibility of a case in accordance with article 17.

2. Challenges to the admissibility of a case on the grounds referred to in article 17 or challenges to the jurisdiction of the Court may be made by:

(a) An accused or a person for whom a warrant of arrest or a summons to appear has been issued under article 58;

(b) A State which has jurisdiction over a case, on the ground that it is investigating or prosecuting the case or has investigated or prosecuted; or

(c) A State from which acceptance of jurisdiction is required under article 12.

3. The Prosecutor may seek a ruling from the Court regarding a question of jurisdiction or admissibility. In proceedings with respect to jurisdiction or admissibility, those who have referred the situation under article 13, as well as victims, may also submit observations to the Court.

4. The admissibility of a case or the jurisdiction of the Court may be challenged only once by any person or State referred to in paragraph 2. The challenge shall take place prior to or at the commencement of the trial. In exceptional circumstances, the Court may grant leave for a challenge to be brought more than once or at a time later than the commencement of the trial. Challenges to the admissibility of a case, at the commencement of a trial, or subsequently with the leave of the Court, may be based only on article 17, paragraph 1 (c).

5. A State referred to in paragraph 2 (b) and (c) shall make a challenge at the earliest opportunity .

6. Prior to the confirmation of the charges, challenges to the admissibility of a case or challenges to the jurisdiction of the Court shall be referred to the Pre-Trial Chamber. After confirmation of the charges, they shall be referred to the Trial Chamber. Decisions with respect to jurisdiction or admissibility may be appealed to the Appeals Chamber in accordance with article 82.

7. If a challenge is made by a State referred to in paragraph 2 (b) or (c), the Prosecutor shall suspend the investigation until such time as the Court makes a determination in accordance with article 17.

8. Pending a ruling by the Court, the Prosecutor may seek authority from the Court:

(a) To pursue necessary investigative steps of the kind referred to in article 18, paragraph 6;

(b) To take a statement or testimony from a witness or complete the collection and examination of evidence which had begun prior to the making of the challenge; and

(c) In cooperation with the relevant States, to prevent the absconding of persons in respect of whom the Prosecutor has already requested a warrant of arrest under article 58.

9. The making of a challenge shall not affect the validity of any act performed by the Prosecutor or any order or warrant issued by the Court prior to the making of the challenge.

10. If the Court has decided that a case is inadmissible under article 17, the Prosecutor may submit a request for a review of the decision when he or she is fully satisfied that new facts have arisen which negate the basis on which the case had previously been found inadmissible under article 17.

11. If the Prosecutor, having regard to the matters referred to in article 17, defers an investigation, the Prosecutor may request that the relevant State make available to the Prosecutor information on the proceedings. That information shall, at the request of the State concerned, be confidential. If the Prosecutor thereafter decides to proceed with an investigation, he or she shall notify the State to which deferral of the proceedings has taken place.

App8–021   **Article 20** *Ne bis in idem*

1. Except as provided in this Statute, no person shall be tried before the Court with respect to conduct which formed the basis of crimes for which the person has been convicted or acquitted by the Court.

2. No person shall be tried by another court for a crime referred to in article 5 for which that person has already been convicted or acquitted by the Court.

3. No person who has been tried by another court for conduct also proscribed under article 6, 7 or 8 shall be tried by the Court with respect to the same conduct unless the proceedings in the other court:

(a) Were for the purpose of shielding the person concerned from criminal responsibility for crimes within the jurisdiction of the Court; or

(b) Otherwise were not conducted independently or impartially in accordance with the norms of due process recognized by international law and were conducted in a manner which, in the circumstances, was inconsistent with an intent to bring the person concerned to justice.

Article 21 Applicable law   App8–022

1. The Court shall apply:

(a) In the first place, this Statute, Elements of Crimes and its Rules of Procedure and Evidence;

(b) In the second place, where appropriate, applicable treaties and the principles and rules of international law, including the established principles of the international law of armed conflict;

(c) Failing that, general principles of law derived by the Court from national laws of legal systems of the world including, as appropriate, the national laws of States that would normally exercise jurisdiction over the crime, provided that those principles are not inconsistent with this Statute and with international law and internationally recognized norms and standards.

2. The Court may apply principles and rules of law as interpreted in its previous decisions.

3. The application and interpretation of law pursuant to this article must be consistent with internationally recognized human rights, and be without any adverse distinction founded on grounds such as gender as defined in article 7, paragraph 3, age, race, colour, language, religion or belief, political or other opinion, national, ethnic or social origin, wealth, birth or other status.

PART 3. GENERAL PRINCIPLES OF CRIMINAL LAW

Article 22 *Nullum crimen sine lege*   App8–023

1. A person shall not be criminally responsible under this Statute unless the conduct in question constitutes, at the time it takes place, a crime within the jurisdiction of the Court.

2. The definition of a crime shall be strictly construed and shall not be extended by analogy. In case of ambiguity, the definition shall be interpreted in favour of the person being investigated, prosecuted or convicted.

3. This article shall not affect the characterization of any conduct as criminal under international law independently of this Statute.

Article 23 *Nulla poena sine lege*   App8–024

A person convicted by the Court may be punished only in accordance with this Statute.

Article 24 Non-retroactivity ratione personae   App8–025

1. No person shall be criminally responsible under this Statute for conduct prior to the entry into force of the Statute.

2. In the event of a change in the law applicable to a given case prior to a final judgement, the law more favourable to the person being investigated, prosecuted or convicted shall apply.

Article 25 Individual criminal responsibility   App8–026

1. The Court shall have jurisdiction over natural persons pursuant to this Statute.

2. A person who commits a crime within the jurisdiction of the Court shall be individually responsible and liable for punishment in accordance with this Statute.

3. In accordance with this Statute, a person shall be criminally responsible and liable for punishment for a crime within the jurisdiction of the Court if that person:

(a) Commits such a crime, whether as an individual, jointly with another or through another person, regardless of whether that other person is criminally responsible;

(b) Orders, solicits or induces the commission of such a crime which in fact occurs or is attempted;

(c) For the purpose of facilitating the commission of such a crime, aids, abets or otherwise assists in its commission or its attempted commission, including providing the means for its commission;

(d) In any other way contributes to the commission or attempted commission of such a crime by a group of persons acting with a common purpose. Such contribution shall be intentional and shall either:

    (i) Be made with the aim of furthering the criminal activity or criminal purpose of the group, where such activity or purpose involves the commission of a crime within the jurisdiction of the Court; or

    (ii) Be made in the knowledge of the intention of the group to commit the crime;

(e) In respect of the crime of genocide, directly and publicly incites others to commit genocide;

(f) Attempts to commit such a crime by taking action that commences its execution by means of a substantial step, but the crime does not occur because of circumstances independent of the person's intentions. However, a person who abandons the effort to commit the crime or otherwise prevents the completion of the crime shall not be liable for punishment under this Statute for the attempt to commit that crime if that person completely and voluntarily gave up the criminal purpose.

4. No provision in this Statute relating to individual criminal responsibility shall affect the responsibility of States under international law.

App8–027   **Article 26 Exclusion of jurisdiction over persons under eighteen**

The Court shall have no jurisdiction over any person who was under the age of 18 at the time of the alleged commission of a crime.

App8–028   **Article 27 Irrelevance of official capacity**

1. This Statute shall apply equally to all persons without any distinction based on official capacity. In particular, official capacity as a Head of State or Government, a member of a Government or parliament, an elected representative or a government official shall in no case exempt a person from criminal responsibility under this Statute, nor shall it, in and of itself, constitute a ground for reduction of sentence.

2. Immunities or special procedural rules which may attach to the official capacity of a person, whether under national or international law, shall not bar the Court from exercising its jurisdiction over such a person.

App8–029   **Article 28 Responsibility of commanders and other superiors**

In addition to other grounds of criminal responsibility under this Statute for crimes within the jurisdiction of the Court:

(a) A military commander or person effectively acting as a military commander shall be criminally responsible for crimes within the jurisdiction of the Court committed by forces under his or her effective command and control, or effective authority and control as the case may be, as a result of his or her failure to exercise control properly over such forces, where:

    (i) That military commander or person either knew or, owing to the circumstances at the time, should have known that the forces were committing or about to commit such crimes; and

    (ii) That military commander or person failed to take all necessary and reasonable measures within his or her power to prevent or repress their commission or to submit the matter to the competent authorities for investigation and prosecution.

(b) With respect to superior and subordinate relationships not described in paragraph (a), a superior shall be criminally responsible for crimes within the jurisdiction of the Court committed by subordinates under his or her effective authority and control, as a result of his or her failure to exercise control properly over such subordinates, where:

    (i) The superior either knew, or consciously disregarded information which clearly indicated, that the subordinates were committing or about to commit such crimes;

    (ii) The crimes concerned activities that were within the effective responsibility and control of the superior; and

    (iii) The superior failed to take all necessary and reasonable measures within his or her power to prevent or repress their commission or to submit the matter to the competent authorities for investigation and prosecution.

Article 29 Non-applicability of statute of limitations   App8–030

The crimes within the jurisdiction of the Court shall not be subject to any statute of limitations.

Article 30 Mental element   App8–031

1. Unless otherwise provided, a person shall be criminally responsible and liable for punishment for a crime within the jurisdiction of the Court only if the material elements are committed with intent and knowledge.

2. For the purposes of this article, a person has intent where:

(a) In relation to conduct, that person means to engage in the conduct;

(b) In relation to a consequence, that person means to cause that consequence or is aware that it will occur in the ordinary course of events.

3. For the purposes of this article, "knowledge" means awareness that a circumstance exists or a consequence will occur in the ordinary course of events. "Know" and "knowingly" shall be construed accordingly.

Article 31 Grounds for excluding criminal responsibility   App8–032

1. In addition to other grounds for excluding criminal responsibility provided for in this Statute, a person shall not be criminally responsible if, at the time of that person's conduct:

(a) The person suffers from a mental disease or defect that destroys that person's capacity to appreciate the unlawfulness or nature of his or her conduct, or capacity to control his or her conduct to conform to the requirements of law;

(b) The person is in a state of intoxication that destroys that person's capacity to appreciate the unlawfulness or nature of his or her conduct, or capacity to control his or her conduct to conform to the requirements of law, unless the person has become voluntarily intoxicated under such circumstances that the person knew, or disregarded the risk, that, as a result of the intoxication, he or she was likely to engage in conduct constituting a crime within the jurisdiction of the Court;

(c) The person acts reasonably to defend himself or herself or another person or, in the case of war crimes, property which is essential for the survival of the person or another person or property which is essential for accomplishing a military mission, against an imminent and unlawful use of force in a manner proportionate to the degree of danger to the person or the other person or property protected. The fact that the person was involved in a defensive operation conducted by forces shall not in itself constitute a ground for excluding criminal responsibility under this subparagraph;

(d) The conduct which is alleged to constitute a crime within the jurisdiction of the Court has been caused by duress resulting from a threat of imminent death or of continuing or imminent serious bodily harm against that person or another person, and the person acts necessarily and reasonably to avoid this threat, provided that the person does not intend to cause a greater harm than the one sought to be avoided. Such a threat may either be:

(i) Made by other persons; or
(ii) Constituted by other circumstances beyond that person's control.

2. The Court shall determine the applicability of the grounds for excluding criminal responsibility provided for in this Statute to the case before it.

3. At trial, the Court may consider a ground for excluding criminal responsibility other than those referred to in paragraph 1 where such a ground is derived from applicable law as set forth in article 21. The procedures relating to the consideration of such a ground shall be provided for in the Rules of Procedure and Evidence.

App8–033 **Article 32 Mistake of fact or mistake of law**

1. A mistake of fact shall be a ground for excluding criminal responsibility only if it negates the mental element required by the crime.

2. A mistake of law as to whether a particular type of conduct is a crime within the jurisdiction of the Court shall not be a ground for excluding criminal responsibility. A mistake of law may, however, be a ground for excluding criminal responsibility if it negates the mental element required by such a crime, or as provided for in article 33.

App8–034 **Article 33 Superior orders and prescription of law**

1. The fact that a crime within the jurisdiction of the Court has been committed by a person pursuant to an order of a Government or of a superior, whether military or civilian, shall not relieve that person of criminal responsibility unless:

(a) The person was under a legal obligation to obey orders of the Government or the superior in question;

(b)   The person did not know that the order was unlawful; and

(c)   The order was not manifestly unlawful.

For the purposes of this article, orders to commit genocide or crimes against humanity are manifestly unlawful.

PART 4. COMPOSITION AND ADMINISTRATION OF THE COURT

Article 34 Organs of the Court   App8–035

The Court shall be composed of the following organs:

(a)   The Presidency;

(b)   An Appeals Division, a Trial Division and a Pre-Trial Division;

(c)   The Office of the Prosecutor;

(d)   The Registry.

Article 35 Service of judges   App8–036

1. All judges shall be elected as full-time members of the Court and shall be available to serve on that basis from the commencement of their terms of office.

2. The judges composing the Presidency shall serve on a full-time basis as soon as they are elected.

3. The Presidency may, on the basis of the workload of the Court and in consultation with its members, decide from time to time to what extent the remaining judges shall be required to serve on a full-time basis. Any such arrangement shall be without prejudice to the provisions of article 40.

4. The financial arrangements for judges not required to serve on a full-time basis shall be made in accordance with article 49.

Article 36 Qualifications, nomination and election of judges   App8–037

1. Subject to the provisions of paragraph 2, there shall be 18 judges of the Court.

2. (a)   The Presidency, acting on behalf of the Court, may propose an increase in the number of judges specified in paragraph 1, indicating the reasons why this is considered necessary and appropriate. The Registrar shall promptly circulate any such proposal to all States Parties.

(b)   Any such proposal shall then be considered at a meeting of the Assembly of States Parties to be convened in accordance with article 112. The proposal shall be considered adopted if approved at the meeting by a vote of two thirds of the members of the Assembly of States Parties and shall enter into force at such time as decided by the Assembly of States Parties.

(c)   (i)   Once a proposal for an increase in the number of judges has been adopted under subparagraph (b), the election of the additional judges shall take place at the next session of the Assembly of States Parties in accordance with paragraphs 3 to 8, and article 37, paragraph 2;

(ii)   Once a proposal for an increase in the number of judges has been adopted and brought into effect under subparagraphs (b) and (c) (i), it shall be open to the Presidency at any time thereafter, if the workload of the Court justifies it, to propose a reduction in the number of judges, provided that the number of judges shall not be reduced below that specified in paragraph 1. The proposal shall be dealt with in accordance with the procedure laid down in subparagraphs (a) and (b). In the event that the proposal is adopted, the number of judges shall be progressively decreased as the terms of office of serving judges expire, until the necessary number has been reached.

3. (a) The judges shall be chosen from among persons of high moral character, impartiality and integrity who possess the qualifications required in their respective States for appointment to the highest judicial offices.

(b) Every candidate for election to the Court shall:

   (i)   Have established competence in criminal law and procedure, and the necessary relevant experience, whether as judge, prosecutor, advocate or in other similar capacity, in criminal proceedings; or
   (ii) Have established competence in relevant areas of international law such as international humanitarian law and the law of human rights, and extensive experience in a professional legal capacity which is of relevance to the judicial work of the Court;

(c) Every candidate for election to the Court shall have an excellent knowledge of and be fluent in at least one of the working languages of the Court.

4. (a) Nominations of candidates for election to the Court may be made by any State Party to this Statute, and shall be made either:

   (i)   By the procedure for the nomination of candidates for appointment to the highest judicial offices in the State in question; or
   (ii) By the procedure provided for the nomination of candidates for the International Court of Justice in the Statute of that Court.

Nominations shall be accompanied by a statement in the necessary detail specifying how the candidate fulfils the requirements of paragraph 3.

(b) Each State Party may put forward one candidate for any given election who need not necessarily be a national of that State Party but shall in any case be a national of a State Party.

(c) The Assembly of States Parties may decide to establish, if appropriate, an Advisory Committee on nominations. In that event, the Committee's composition and mandate shall be established by the Assembly of States Parties.

5. For the purposes of the election, there shall be two lists of candidates:

List A containing the names of candidates with the qualifications specified in paragraph 3 (b) (i); and

List B containing the names of candidates with the qualifications specified in paragraph 3 (b) (ii).

A candidate with sufficient qualifications for both lists may choose on which list to appear. At the first election to the Court, at least nine judges shall be elected from list A and at least five judges from list B. Subsequent elections shall be so organized as to maintain the equivalent proportion on the Court of judges qualified on the two lists.

6. (a) The judges shall be elected by secret ballot at a meeting of the Assembly of States Parties convened for that purpose under article 112. Subject to paragraph 7, the persons elected to the Court shall be the 18 candidates who obtain the highest number of votes and a two-thirds majority of the States Parties present and voting.

(b) In the event that a sufficient number of judges is not elected on the first ballot, successive ballots shall be held in accordance with the procedures laid down in subparagraph (a) until the remaining places have been filled.

7. No two judges may be nationals of the same State. A person who, for the purposes of membership of the Court, could be regarded as a national of more than one State shall be deemed to be a national of the State in which that person ordinarily exercises civil and political rights.

8. (a) The States Parties shall, in the selection of judges, take into account the need, within the membership of the Court, for:

(i) The representation of the principal legal systems of the world;
(ii) Equitable geographical representation; and
(iii) A fair representation of female and male judges.

(b) States Parties shall also take into account the need to include judges with legal expertise on specific issues, including, but not limited to, violence against women or children.

9. (a) Subject to subparagraph (b), judges shall hold office for a term of nine years and, subject to subparagraph (c) and to article 37, paragraph 2, shall not be eligible for re-election.

(b) At the first election, one third of the judges elected shall be selected by lot to serve for a term of three years; one third of the judges elected shall be selected by lot to serve for a term of six years; and the remainder shall serve for a term of nine years.

(c) A judge who is selected to serve for a term of three years under subparagraph (b) shall be eligible for re-election for a full term.

10. Notwithstanding paragraph 9, a judge assigned to a Trial or Appeals Chamber in accordance with article 39 shall continue in office to complete any trial or appeal the hearing of which has already commenced before that Chamber.

Article 37 Judicial vacancies   App8–038

1. In the event of a vacancy, an election shall be held in accordance with article 36 to fill the vacancy.

2. A judge elected to fill a vacancy shall serve for the remainder of the predecessor's term and, if that period is three years or less, shall be eligible for re-election for a full term under article 36.

Article 38 The Presidency   App8–039

1. The President and the First and Second Vice-Presidents shall be elected by an absolute majority of the judges. They shall each serve for a term of three years or until the end of their respective terms of office as judges, whichever expires earlier. They shall be eligible for re-election once.

2. The First Vice-President shall act in place of the President in the event that the President is unavailable or disqualified. The Second Vice-President shall act in place of the President in the event that both the President and the First Vice-President are unavailable or disqualified.

3. The President, together with the First and Second Vice-Presidents, shall constitute the Presidency, which shall be responsible for:

    (a) The proper administration of the Court, with the exception of the Office of the Prosecutor; and

    (b) The other functions conferred upon it in accordance with this Statute.

4. In discharging its responsibility under paragraph 3 (a), the Presidency shall coordinate with and seek the concurrence of the Prosecutor on all matters of mutual concern.

App8–040   **Article 39 Chambers**

1. As soon as possible after the election of the judges, the Court shall organize itself into the divisions specified in article 34, paragraph (b). The Appeals Division shall be composed of the President and four other judges, the Trial Division of not less than six judges and the Pre-Trial Division of not less than six judges. The assignment of judges to divisions shall be based on the nature of the functions to be performed by each division and the qualifications and experience of the judges elected to the Court, in such a way that each division shall contain an appropriate combination of expertise in criminal law and procedure and in international law. The Trial and Pre-Trial Divisions shall be composed predominantly of judges with criminal trial experience.

    2. (a) The judicial functions of the Court shall be carried out in each division by Chambers.

    (b) (i)   The Appeals Chamber shall be composed of all the judges of the Appeals

        (ii)   The functions of the Trial Chamber shall be carried out by three judges of the Trial Division;

        (iii) The functions of the Pre-Trial Chamber shall be carried out either by three judges of the Pre-Trial Division or by a single judge of that division in accordance with this Statute and the Rules of Procedure and Evidence;

    (c) Nothing in this paragraph shall preclude the simultaneous constitution of more than one Trial Chamber or Pre-Trial Chamber when the efficient management of the Court's workload so requires.

    3. (a) Judges assigned to the Trial and Pre-Trial Divisions shall serve in those divisions for a period of three years, and thereafter until the completion of any case the hearing of which has already commenced in the division concerned.

    (b) Judges assigned to the Appeals Division shall serve in that division for their entire term of office.

4. Judges assigned to the Appeals Division shall serve only in that division. Nothing in this article shall, however, preclude the temporary attachment of judges from the Trial Division to the Pre-Trial Division or vice versa, if the Presidency considers

that the efficient management of the Court's workload so requires, provided that under no circumstances shall a judge who has participated in the pre-trial phase of a case be eligible to sit on the Trial Chamber hearing that case.

Article 40 Independence of the judges

App8–041

1. The judges shall be independent in the performance of their functions.

2. Judges shall not engage in any activity which is likely to interfere with their judicial functions or to affect confidence in their independence.

3. Judges required to serve on a full-time basis at the seat of the Court shall not engage in any other occupation of a professional nature.

4. Any question regarding the application of paragraphs 2 and 3 shall be decided by an absolute majority of the judges. Where any such question concerns an individual judge, that judge shall not take part in the decision.

Article 41 Excusing and disqualification of judges

App8–042

The Presidency may, at the request of a judge, excuse that judge from the exercise of a function under this Statute, in accordance with the Rules of Procedure and Evidence.

2. (a) A judge shall not participate in any case in which his or her impartiality might reasonably be doubted on any ground. A judge shall be disqualified from a case in accordance with this paragraph if, *inter alia*, that judge has previously been involved in any capacity in that case before the Court or in a related criminal case at the national level involving the person being investigated or prosecuted. A judge shall also be disqualified on such other grounds as may be provided for in the Rules of Procedure and Evidence.

(b) The Prosecutor or the person being investigated or prosecuted may request the disqualification of a judge under this paragraph.

(c) Any question as to the disqualification of a judge shall be decided by an absolute majority of the judges. The challenged judge shall be entitled to present his or her comments on the matter, but shall not take part in the decision.

Article 42 The Office of the Prosecutor

App8–043

1. The Office of the Prosecutor shall act independently as a separate organ of the Court. It shall be responsible for receiving referrals and any substantiated information on crimes within the jurisdiction of the Court, for examining them and for conducting investigations and prosecutions before the Court. A member of the Office shall not seek or act on instructions from any external source.

2. The Office shall be headed by the Prosecutor. The Prosecutor shall have full authority over the management and administration of the Office, including the staff, facilities and other resources thereof. The Prosecutor shall be assisted by one or more Deputy Prosecutors, who shall be entitled to carry out any of the acts required of the Prosecutor under this Statute. The Prosecutor and the Deputy Prosecutors shall be of different nationalities. They shall serve on a full-time basis.

3. The Prosecutor and the Deputy Prosecutors shall be persons of high moral character, be highly competent in and have extensive practical experience in the prosecution or trial of criminal cases. They shall have an excellent knowledge of and be fluent in at least one of the working languages of the Court.

4. The Prosecutor shall be elected by secret ballot by an absolute majority of the members of the Assembly of States Parties. The Deputy Prosecutors shall be elected in the same way from a list of candidates provided by the Prosecutor. The Prosecutor

shall nominate three candidates for each position of Deputy Prosecutor to be filled. Unless a shorter term is decided upon at the time of their election, the Prosecutor and the Deputy Prosecutors shall hold office for a term of nine years and shall not be eligible for re-election.

5. Neither the Prosecutor nor a Deputy Prosecutor shall engage in any activity which is likely to interfere with his or her prosecutorial functions or to affect confidence in his or her independence. They shall not engage in any other occupation of a professional nature.

6. The Presidency may excuse the Prosecutor or a Deputy Prosecutor, at his or her request, from acting in a particular case.

7. Neither the Prosecutor nor a Deputy Prosecutor shall participate in any matter in which their impartiality might reasonably be doubted on any ground. They shall be disqualified from a case in accordance with this paragraph if, *inter alia*, they have previously been involved in any capacity in that case before the Court or in a related criminal case at the national level involving the person being investigated or prosecuted.

8. Any question as to the disqualification of the Prosecutor or a Deputy Prosecutor shall be decided by the Appeals Chamber.

(a) The person being investigated or prosecuted may at any time request the disqualification of the Prosecutor or a Deputy Prosecutor on the grounds set out in this article;

(b) The Prosecutor or the Deputy Prosecutor, as appropriate, shall be entitled to present his or her comments on the matter;

9. The Prosecutor shall appoint advisers with legal expertise on specific issues, including, but not limited to, sexual and gender violence and violence against children.

App8–044   **Article 43 The Registry**

1. The Registry shall be responsible for the non-judicial aspects of the administration and servicing of the Court, without prejudice to the functions and powers of the Prosecutor in accordance with article 42.

2. The Registry shall be headed by the Registrar, who shall be the principal administrative officer of the Court. The Registrar shall exercise his or her functions under the authority of the President of the Court.

3. The Registrar and the Deputy Registrar shall be persons of high moral character, be highly competent and have an excellent knowledge of and be fluent in at least one of the working languages of the Court.

4. The judges shall elect the Registrar by an absolute majority by secret ballot, taking into account any recommendation by the Assembly of States Parties. If the need arises and upon the recommendation of the Registrar, the judges shall elect, in the same manner, a Deputy Registrar.

5. The Registrar shall hold office for a term of five years, shall be eligible for re-election once and shall serve on a full-time basis. The Deputy Registrar shall hold office for a term of five years or such shorter term as may be decided upon by an absolute majority of the judges, and may be elected on the basis that the Deputy Registrar shall be called upon to serve as required.

6. The Registrar shall set up a Victims and Witnesses Unit within the Registry. This Unit shall provide, in consultation with the Office of the Prosecutor, protective measures and security arrangements, counselling and other appropriate assistance for witnesses, victims who appear before the Court, and others who are at risk on account of testimony given by such witnesses. The Unit shall include staff with expertise in trauma, including trauma related to crimes of sexual violence.

Article 44 Staff App8–045

1. The Prosecutor and the Registrar shall appoint such qualified staff as may be required to their respective offices. In the case of the Prosecutor, this shall include the appointment of investigators.

2. In the employment of staff, the Prosecutor and the Registrar shall ensure the highest standards of efficiency, competency and integrity, and shall have regard, mutatis mutandis, to the criteria set forth in article 36, paragraph 8.

3. The Registrar, with the agreement of the Presidency and the Prosecutor, shall propose Staff Regulations which include the terms and conditions upon which the staff of the Court shall be appointed, remunerated and dismissed. The Staff Regulations shall be approved by the Assembly of States Parties.

4. The Court may, in exceptional circumstances, employ the expertise of gratis personnel offered by States Parties, intergovernmental organizations or non-governmental organizations to assist with the work of any of the organs of the Court. The Prosecutor may accept any such offer on behalf of the Office of the Prosecutor. Such gratis personnel shall be employed in accordance with guidelines to be established by the Assembly of States Parties.

Article 45 Solemn undertaking App8–046

Before taking up their respective duties under this Statute, the judges, the Prosecutor, the Deputy Prosecutors, the Registrar and the Deputy Registrar shall each make a solemn undertaking in open court to exercise his or her respective functions impartially and conscientiously.

Article 46 Removal from office App8–047

1. A judge, the Prosecutor, a Deputy Prosecutor, the Registrar or the Deputy Registrar shall be removed from office if a decision to this effect is made in accordance with paragraph 2, in cases where that person:

(a) Is found to have committed serious misconduct or a serious breach of his or her duties under this Statute, as provided for in the Rules of Procedure and Evidence; or

(b) Is unable to exercise the functions required by this Statute.

2. A decision as to the removal from office of a judge, the Prosecutor or a Deputy Prosecutor under paragraph 1 shall be made by the Assembly of States Parties, by secret ballot:

(a) In the case of a judge, by a two-thirds majority of the States Parties upon a recommendation adopted by a two-thirds majority of the other judges;

(b) In the case of the Prosecutor, by an absolute majority of the States Parties;

(c) In the case of a Deputy Prosecutor, by an absolute majority of the States Parties upon the recommendation of the Prosecutor.

3. A decision as to the removal from office of the Registrar or Deputy Registrar shall be made by an absolute majority of the judges.

4. A judge, Prosecutor, Deputy Prosecutor, Registrar or Deputy Registrar whose conduct or ability to exercise the functions of the office as required by this Statute is challenged under this article shall have full opportunity to present and receive evidence and to make submissions in accordance with the Rules of Procedure and

Evidence. The person in question shall not otherwise participate in the consideration of the matter.

App8–048　**Article 47 Disciplinary measures**

A judge, Prosecutor, Deputy Prosecutor, Registrar or Deputy Registrar who has committed misconduct of a less serious nature than that set out in article 46, paragraph 1, shall be subject to disciplinary measures, in accordance with the Rules of Procedure and Evidence.

App8–049　**Article 48 Privileges and immunities**

1. The Court shall enjoy in the territory of each State Party such privileges and immunities as are necessary for the fulfilment of its purposes.

2. The judges, the Prosecutor, the Deputy Prosecutors and the Registrar shall, when engaged on or with respect to the business of the Court, enjoy the same privileges and immunities as are accorded to heads of diplomatic missions and shall, after the expiry of their terms of office, continue to be accorded immunity from legal process of every kind in respect of words spoken or written and acts performed by them in their official capacity.

3. The Deputy Registrar, the staff of the Office of the Prosecutor and the staff of the Registry shall enjoy the privileges and immunities and facilities necessary for the performance of their functions, in accordance with the agreement on the privileges and immunities of the Court.

4. Counsel, experts, witnesses or any other person required to be present at the seat of the Court shall be accorded such treatment as is necessary for the proper functioning of the Court, in accordance with the agreement on the privileges and immunities of the Court.

5. The privileges and immunities of:

    (a)　A judge or the Prosecutor may be waived by an absolute majority of the judges;

    (b)　The Registrar may be waived by the Presidency;

    (c)　The Deputy Prosecutors and staff of the Office of the Prosecutor may be waived by the Prosecutor;

    (d)　The Deputy Registrar and staff of the Registry may be waived by the Registrar.

App8–050　**Article 49 Salaries, allowances and expenses**

The judges, the Prosecutor, the Deputy Prosecutors, the Registrar and the Deputy Registrar shall receive such salaries, allowances and expenses as may be decided upon by the Assembly of States Parties. These salaries and allowances shall not be reduced during their terms of office.

App8–051　**Article 50 Official and working languages**

1. The official languages of the Court shall be Arabic, Chinese, English, French, Russian and Spanish. The judgements of the Court, as well as other decisions resolving fundamental issues before the Court, shall be published in the official languages. The Presidency shall, in accordance with the criteria established by the Rules of Procedure and Evidence, determine which decisions may be considered as resolving fundamental issues for the purposes of this paragraph.

2. The working languages of the Court shall be English and French. The Rules of Procedure and Evidence shall determine the cases in which other official languages may be used as working languages.

3. At the request of any party to a proceeding or a State allowed to intervene in a proceeding, the Court shall authorize a language other than English or French to be used by such a party or State, provided that the Court considers such authorization to be adequately justified.

Article 51 Rules of Procedure and Evidence   App8–052

1. The Rules of Procedure and Evidence shall enter into force upon adoption by a two-thirds majority of the members of the Assembly of States Parties.

2. Amendments to the Rules of Procedure and Evidence may be proposed by:

(a)   Any State Party;

(b)   The judges acting by an absolute majority; or

(c)   The Prosecutor.

Such amendments shall enter into force upon adoption by a two-thirds majority of the members of the Assembly of States Parties.

3. After the adoption of the Rules of Procedure and Evidence, in urgent cases where the Rules do not provide for a specific situation before the Court, the judges may, by a two-thirds majority, draw up provisional Rules to be applied until adopted, amended or rejected at the next ordinary or special session of the Assembly of States Parties.

4. The Rules of Procedure and Evidence, amendments thereto and any provisional Rule shall be consistent with this Statute. Amendments to the Rules of Procedure and Evidence as well as provisional Rules shall not be applied retroactively to the detriment of the person who is being investigated or prosecuted or who has been convicted.

5. In the event of conflict between the Statute and the Rules of Procedure and Evidence, the Statute shall prevail.

Article 52 Regulations of the Court   App8–053

1. The judges shall, in accordance with this Statute and the Rules of Procedure and Evidence, adopt, by an absolute majority, the Regulations of the Court necessary for its routine functioning.

2. The Prosecutor and the Registrar shall be consulted in the elaboration of the Regulations and any amendments thereto.

3. The Regulations and any amendments thereto shall take effect upon adoption unless otherwise decided by the judges. Immediately upon adoption, they shall be circulated to States Parties for comments. If within six months there are no objections from a majority of States Parties, they shall remain in force.

PART 5. INVESTIGATION AND PROSECUTION

Article 53 Initiation of an investigation   App8–054

1. The Prosecutor shall, having evaluated the information made available to him or her, initiate an investigation unless he or she determines that there is no reasonable basis to proceed under this Statute. In deciding whether to initiate an investigation, the Prosecutor shall consider whether:

(a)   The information available to the Prosecutor provides a reasonable basis to believe that a crime within the jurisdiction of the Court has been or is being committed;

(b)   The case is or would be admissible under article 17; and

(c)   Taking into account the gravity of the crime and the interests of victims, there are nonetheless substantial reasons to believe that an investigation would not serve the interests of justice.

If the Prosecutor determines that there is no reasonable basis to proceed and his or her determination is based solely on subparagraph (c) above, he or she shall inform the Pre-Trial Chamber.

2. If, upon investigation, the Prosecutor concludes that there is not a sufficient basis for a prosecution because:

(a)   There is not a sufficient legal or factual basis to seek a warrant or summons under article 58;

(b)   The case is inadmissible under article 17; or

(c)   A prosecution is not in the interests of justice, taking into account all the circumstances, including the gravity of the crime, the interests of victims and the age or infirmity of the alleged perpetrator, and his or her role in the alleged crime;

the Prosecutor shall inform the Pre-Trial Chamber and the State making a referral under article 14 or the Security Council in a case under article 13, paragraph (b), of his or her conclusion and the reasons for the conclusion.

3. (a)   At the request of the State making a referral under article 14 or the Security Council under article 13, paragraph (b), the Pre-Trial Chamber may review a decision of the Prosecutor under paragraph 1 or 2 not to proceed and may request the Prosecutor to reconsider that decision.

(b)   In addition, the Pre-Trial Chamber may, on its own initiative, review a decision of the Prosecutor not to proceed if it is based solely on paragraph 1 (c) or 2 (c). In such a case, the decision of the Prosecutor shall be effective only if confirmed by the Pre-Trial Chamber.

4. The Prosecutor may, at any time, reconsider a decision whether to initiate an investigation or prosecution based on new facts or information.

App8–055   **Article 54 Duties and powers of the Prosecutor with respect to investigations**

1. The Prosecutor shall:

(a)   In order to establish the truth, extend the investigation to cover all facts and evidence relevant to an assessment of whether there is criminal responsibility under this Statute, and, in doing so, investigate incriminating and exonerating circumstances equally;

(b)   Take appropriate measures to ensure the effective investigation and prosecution of crimes within the jurisdiction of the Court, and in doing so, respect the interests and personal circumstances of victims and witnesses, including age, gender as defined in article 7, paragraph 3, and health, and take into account the nature of the crime, in particular where it involves sexual violence, gender violence or violence against children; and

    (c)   Fully respect the rights of persons arising under this Statute.

2. The Prosecutor may conduct investigations on the territory of a State:

    (a)   In accordance with the provisions of Part 9; or

    (b)   As authorized by the Pre-Trial Chamber under article 57, paragraph 3 (d).

3. The Prosecutor may:

    (a)   Collect and examine evidence;

    (b)   Request the presence of and question persons being investigated, victims and witnesses;

    (c)   Seek the cooperation of any State or intergovernmental organization or arrangement in accordance with its respective competence and/or mandate;

    (d)   Enter into such arrangements or agreements, not inconsistent with this Statute, as may be necessary to facilitate the cooperation of a State, intergovernmental organization or person;

    (e)   Agree not to disclose, at any stage of the proceedings, documents or information that the Prosecutor obtains on the condition of confidentiality and solely for the purpose of generating new evidence, unless the provider of the information consents; and

    (f)   Take necessary measures, or request that necessary measures be taken, to ensure the confidentiality of information, the protection of any person or the preservation of evidence.

Article 55 Rights of persons during an investigation   **App8–056**

1. In respect of an investigation under this Statute, a person:

    (a)   Shall not be compelled to incriminate himself or herself or to confess guilt;

    (b)   Shall not be subjected to any form of coercion, duress or threat, to torture or to any other form of cruel, inhuman or degrading treatment or punishment;

    (c)   Shall, if questioned in a language other than a language the person fully understands and speaks, have, free of any cost, the assistance of a competent interpreter and such translations as are necessary to meet the requirements of fairness; and

    (d)   Shall not be subjected to arbitrary arrest or detention, and shall not be deprived of his or her liberty except on such grounds and in accordance with such procedures as are established in this Statute.

2. Where there are grounds to believe that a person has committed a crime within the jurisdiction of the Court and that person is about to be questioned either by the Prosecutor, or by national authorities pursuant to a request made under Part 9, that person shall also have the following rights of which he or she shall be informed prior to being questioned:

    (a)   To be informed, prior to being questioned, that there are grounds to believe that he or she has committed a crime within the jurisdiction of the Court;

(b)   To remain silent, without such silence being a consideration in the determination of guilt or innocence;

(c)   To have legal assistance of the person's choosing, or, if the person does not have legal assistance, to have legal assistance assigned to him or her, in any case where the interests of justice so require, and without payment by the person in any such case if the person does not have sufficient means to pay for it; and

(d)   To be questioned in the presence of counsel unless the person has voluntarily waived his or her right to counsel.

App8–057   **Article 56 Role of the Pre-Trial Chamber in relation to a unique investigative opportunity**

1.   (a)   Where the Prosecutor considers an investigation to present a unique opportunity to take testimony or a statement from a witness or to examine, collect or test evidence, which may not be available subsequently for the purposes of a trial, the Prosecutor shall so inform the Pre-Trial Chamber.

(b)   In that case, the Pre-Trial Chamber may, upon request of the Prosecutor, take such measures as may be necessary to ensure the efficiency and integrity of the proceedings and, in particular, to protect the rights of the defence.

(c)   Unless the Pre-Trial Chamber orders otherwise, the Prosecutor shall provide the relevant information to the person who has been arrested or appeared in response to a summons in connection with the investigation referred to in subparagraph (a), in order that he or she may be heard on the matter.

2. The measures referred to in paragraph 1 (b) may include:

(a)   Making recommendations or orders regarding procedures to be followed;

(b)   Directing that a record be made of the proceedings;

(c)   Appointing an expert to assist;

(d)   Authorizing counsel for a person who has been arrested, or appeared before the Court in response to a summons, to participate, or where there has not yet been such an arrest or appearance or counsel has not been designated, appointing another counsel to attend and represent the interests of the defence;

(e)   Naming one of its members or, if necessary, another available judge of the Pre-Trial or Trial Division to observe and make recommendations or orders regarding the collection and preservation of evidence and the questioning of persons;

(f)   Taking such other action as may be necessary to collect or preserve evidence.

3. (a)   Where the Prosecutor has not sought measures pursuant to this article but the Pre-Trial Chamber considers that such measures are required to preserve evidence that it deems would be essential for the defence at trial, it shall consult with the Prosecutor as to whether there is good reason for the Prosecutor's failure to request the measures. If upon consultation, the

Pre-Trial Chamber concludes that the Prosecutor's failure to request such measures is unjustified, the Pre-Trial Chamber may take such measures on its own initiative.

(b) A decision of the Pre-Trial Chamber to act on its own initiative under this paragraph may be appealed by the Prosecutor. The appeal shall be heard on an expedited basis.

4. The admissibility of evidence preserved or collected for trial pursuant to this article, or the record thereof, shall be governed at trial by article 69, and given such weight as determined by the Trial Chamber.

Article 57 Functions and powers of the Pre-Trial Chamber App8–058

1. Unless otherwise provided in this Statute, the Pre-Trial Chamber shall exercise its functions in accordance with the provisions of this article.

2. (a) Orders or rulings of the Pre-Trial Chamber issued under articles 15, 18, 19, 54, paragraph 2, 61, paragraph 7, and 72 must be concurred in by a majority of its judges.

(b) In all other cases, a single judge of the Pre-Trial Chamber may exercise the functions provided for in this Statute, unless otherwise provided for in the Rules of Procedure and Evidence or by a majority of the Pre-Trial Chamber.

3. In addition to its other functions under this Statute, the Pre-Trial Chamber may:

(a) At the request of the Prosecutor, issue such orders and warrants as may be required for the purpose of an investigation;

(b) Upon the request of a person who has been arrested or has appeared pursuant to a summons under article 58, issue such orders, including measures such as those described in article 56, or seek such cooperation pursuant to Part 9 as may be necessary to assist the person in the preparation of his or her defence;

(c) Where necessary, provide for the protection and privacy of victims and witnesses, the preservation of evidence, the protection of persons who have been arrested or appeared in response to a summons, and the protection of national security information;

(d) Authorize the Prosecutor to take specific investigative steps within the territory of a State Party without having secured the cooperation of that State under Part 9 if, whenever possible having regard to the views of the State concerned, the Pre-Trial Chamber has determined in that case that the State is clearly unable to execute a request for cooperation due to the unavailability of any authority or any component of its judicial system competent to execute the request for cooperation under Part 9.

(e) Where a warrant of arrest or a summons has been issued under article 58, and having due regard to the strength of the evidence and the rights of the parties concerned, as provided for in this Statute and the Rules of Procedure and Evidence, seek the cooperation of States pursuant to article 93, paragraph 1 (k), to take protective measures for the purpose of forfeiture, in particular for the ultimate benefit of victims.

App8–059 **Article 58 Issuance by the Pre-Trial Chamber of a warrant of arrest or a summons to appear**

1. At any time after the initiation of an investigation, the Pre-Trial Chamber shall, on the application of the Prosecutor, issue a warrant of arrest of a person if, having examined the application and the evidence or other information submitted by the Prosecutor, it is satisfied that:

    (a)   There are reasonable grounds to believe that the person has committed a crime within the jurisdiction of the Court; and

    (b)   The arrest of the person appears necessary:

        (i)   To ensure the person's appearance at trial,
        (ii) To ensure that the person does not obstruct or endanger the investigation or the court proceedings, or
        (iii) Where applicable, to prevent the person from continuing with the commission of that crime or a related crime which is within the jurisdiction of the Court and which arises out of the same circumstances.

2. The application of the Prosecutor shall contain:

    (a)   The name of the person and any other relevant identifying information;

    (b)   A specific reference to the crimes within the jurisdiction of the Court which the person is alleged to have committed;

    (c)   A concise statement of the facts which are alleged to constitute those crimes;

    (d)   A summary of the evidence and any other information which establish reasonable grounds to believe that the person committed those crimes; and

    (e)   The reason why the Prosecutor believes that the arrest of the person is necessary.

3. The warrant of arrest shall contain:

    (a)   The name of the person and any other relevant identifying information;

    (b)   A specific reference to the crimes within the jurisdiction of the Court for which the person's arrest is sought; and

    (c)   A concise statement of the facts which are alleged to constitute those crimes.

4. The warrant of arrest shall remain in effect until otherwise ordered by the Court.

5. On the basis of the warrant of arrest, the Court may request the provisional arrest or the arrest and surrender of ther person under Part 9.

6. The Prosecutor may request the Pre-Trial Chamber to amend the warrant of arrest by modifying or adding to the crimes specified therein. The Pre-Trial Chamber shall so amend the warrant if it is satisfied that there are reasonable grounds to believe that the person committed the modified or additional crimes.

7. As an alternative to seeking a warrant of arrest, the Prosecutor may submit an application requesting that the Pre-Trial Chamber issue a summons for the person to appear. If the Pre-Trial Chamber is satisfied that there are reasonable grounds to believe that the person committed the crime alleged and that a summons is sufficient to ensure the person's appearance, it shall issue the summons, with or without condi-

tions restricting liberty (other than detention) if provided for by national law, for the person to appear. The summons shall contain:

(a) The name of the person and any other relevant identifying information;

(b) The specified date on which the person is to appear;

(c) A specific reference to the crimes within the jurisdiction of the Court which the person is alleged to have committed; and

(d) A concise statement of the facts which are alleged to constitute the crime.

The summons shall be served on the person.

Article 59 Arrest proceedings in the custodial State   App8–060

1. A State Party which has received a request for provisional arrest or for arrest and surrender shall immediately take steps to arrest the person in question in accordance with its laws and the provisions of Part 9.
2. A person arrested shall be brought promptly before the competent judicial authority in the custodial State which shall determine, in accordance with the law of that State, that:

(a) The warrant applies to that person;

(b) The person has been arrested in accordance with the proper process; and

(c) The person's rights have been respected.

3. The person arrested shall have the right to apply to the competent authority in the custodial State for interim release pending surrender.
4. In reaching a decision on any such application, the competent authority in the custodial State shall consider whether, given the gravity of the alleged crimes, there are urgent and exceptional circumstances to justify interim release and whether necessary safeguards exist to ensure that the custodial State can fulfil its duty to surrender the person to the Court. It shall not be open to the competent authority of the custodial State to consider whether the warrant of arrest was properly issued in accordance with article 58, paragraph 1 (a) and (b).
5. The Pre-Trial Chamber shall be notified of any request for interim release and shall make recommendations to the competent authority in the custodial State. The competent authority in the custodial State shall give full consideration to such recommendations, including any recommendations on measures to prevent the escape of the person, before rendering its decision.
6. If the person is granted interim release, the Pre-Trial Chamber may request periodic reports on the status of the interim release.
7. Once ordered to be surrendered by the custodial State, the person shall be delivered to the Court as soon as possible.

Article 60 Initial proceedings before the Court   App8–061

1. Upon the surrender of the person to the Court, or the person's appearance before the Court voluntarily or pursuant to a summons, the Pre-Trial Chamber shall satisfy itself that the person has been informed of the crimes which he or she is alleged to have committed, and of his or her rights under this Statute, including the right to apply for interim release pending trial.
2. A person subject to a warrant of arrest may apply for interim release pending trial. If the Pre-Trial Chamber is satisfied that the conditions set forth in article 58,

paragraph 1, are met, the person shall continue to be detained. If it is not so satisfied, the Pre-Trial Chamber shall release the person, with or without conditions.

3. The Pre-Trial Chamber shall periodically review its ruling on the release or detention of the person, and may do so at any time on the request of the Prosecutor or the person. Upon such review, it may modify its ruling as to detention, release or conditions of release, if it is satisfied that changed circumstances so require.

4. The Pre-Trial Chamber shall ensure that a person is not detained for an unreasonable period prior to trial due to inexcusable delay by the Prosecutor. If such delay occurs, the Court shall consider releasing the person, with or without conditions.

5. If necessary, the Pre-Trial Chamber may issue a warrant of arrest to secure the presence of a person who has been released.

App8–062 **Article 61 Confirmation of the charges before trial**

1. Subject to the provisions of paragraph 2, within a reasonable time after the person's surrender or voluntary appearance before the Court, the Pre-Trial Chamber shall hold a hearing to confirm the charges on which the Prosecutor intends to seek trial. The hearing shall be held in the presence of the Prosecutor and the person charged, as well as his or her counsel.

2. The Pre-Trial Chamber may, upon request of the Prosecutor or on its own motion, hold a hearing in the absence of the person charged to confirm the charges on which the Prosecutor intends to seek trial when the person has:

    (a)   Waived his or her right to be present; or

    (b)   Fled or cannot be found and all reasonable steps have been taken to secure his or her appearance before the Court and to inform the person of the charges and that a hearing to confirm those charges will be held.

In that case, the person shall be represented by counsel where the Pre-Trial Chamber determines that it is in the interests of justice.

3. Within a reasonable time before the hearing, the person shall:

    (a)   Be provided with a copy of the document containing the charges on which the Prosecutor intends to bring the person to trial; and

    (b)   Be informed of the evidence on which the Prosecutor intends to rely at the hearing.

The Pre-Trial Chamber may issue orders regarding the disclosure of information for the purposes of the hearing.

4. Before the hearing, the Prosecutor may continue the investigation and may amend or withdraw any charges. The person shall be given reasonable notice before the hearing of any amendment to or withdrawal of charges. In case of a withdrawal of charges, the Prosecutor shall notify the Pre-Trial Chamber of the reasons for the withdrawal.

5. At the hearing, the Prosecutor shall support each charge with sufficient evidence to establish substantial grounds to believe that the person committed the crime charged. The Prosecutor may rely on documentary or summary evidence and need not call the witnesses expected to testify at the trial.

6. At the hearing, the person may:

    (a)   Object to the charges;

    (b)   Challenge the evidence presented by the Prosecutor; and

    (c)   Present evidence.

7. The Pre-Trial Chamber shall, on the basis of the hearing, determine whether there is sufficient evidence to establish substantial grounds to believe that the person committed each of the crimes charged. Based on its determination, the Pre-Trial Chamber shall:

(a) Confirm those charges in relation to which it has determined that there is sufficient evidence, and commit the person to a Trial Chamber for trial on the charges as confirmed;

(b) Decline to confirm those charges in relation to which it has determined that there is insufficient evidence;

(c) Adjourn the hearing and request the Prosecutor to consider:

   (i)   Providing further evidence or conducting further investigation with respect to a particular charge; or

   (ii) Amending a charge because the evidence submitted appears to establish a different crime within the jurisdiction of the Court.

8. Where the Pre-Trial Chamber declines to confirm a charge, the Prosecutor shall not be precluded from subsequently requesting its confirmation if the request is supported by additional evidence.

9. After the charges are confirmed and before the trial has begun, the Prosecutor may, with the permission of the Pre-Trial Chamber and after notice to the accused, amend the charges. If the Prosecutor seeks to add additional charges or to substitute more serious charges, a hearing under this article to confirm those charges must be held. After commencement of the trial, the Prosecutor may, with the permission of the Trial Chamber, withdraw the charges.

10. Any warrant previously issued shall cease to have effect with respect to any charges which have not been confirmed by the Pre-Trial Chamber or which have been withdrawn by the Prosecutor.

11. Once the charges have been confirmed in accordance with this article, the Presidency shall constitute a Trial Chamber which, subject to paragraph 9 and to article 64, paragraph 4, shall be responsible for the conduct of subsequent proceedings and may exercise any function of the Pre-Trial Chamber that is relevant and capable of application in those proceedings.

PART 6. THE TRIAL

Article 62 Place of trial   App8–063

Unless otherwise decided, the place of the trial shall be the seat of the Court.

Article 63 Trial in the presence of the accused   App8–064

1. The accused shall be present during the trial.

2. If the accused, being present before the Court, continues to disrupt the trial, the Trial Chamber may remove the accused and shall make provision for him or her to observe the trial and instruct counsel from outside the courtroom, through the use of communications technology, if required. Such measures shall be taken only in exceptional circumstances after other reasonable alternatives have proved inadequate, and only for such duration as is strictly required.

Article 64 Functions and powers of the Trial Chamber

1. The functions and powers of the Trial Chamber set out in this article shall be exercised in accordance with this Statute and the Rules of Procedure and Evidence.

2. The Trial Chamber shall ensure that a trial is fair and expeditious and is conducted with full respect for the rights of the accused and due regard for the protection of victims and witnesses.

3. Upon assignment of a case for trial in accordance with this Statute, the Trial Chamber assigned to deal with the case shall:

(a) Confer with the parties and adopt such procedures as are necessary to facilitate the fair and expeditious conduct of the proceedings;

(b) Determine the language or languages to be used at trial; and

(c) Subject to any other relevant provisions of this Statute, provide for disclosure of documents or information not previously disclosed, sufficiently in advance of the commencement of the trial to enable adequate preparation for trial.

4. The Trial Chamber may, if necessary for its effective and fair functioning, refer preliminary issues to the Pre-Trial Chamber or, if necessary, to another available judge of the Pre-Trial Division.

5. Upon notice to the parties, the Trial Chamber may, as appropriate, direct that there be joinder or severance in respect of charges against more than one accused.

6. In performing its functions prior to trial or during the course of a trial, the Trial Chamber may, as necessary:

(a) Exercise any functions of the Pre-Trial Chamber referred to in article 61, paragraph 11;

(b) Require the attendance and testimony of witnesses and production of documents and other evidence by obtaining, if necessary, the assistance of States as provided in this Statute;

(c) Provide for the protection of confidential information;

(d) Order the production of evidence in addition to that already collected prior to the trial or presented during the trial by the parties;

(e) Provide for the protection of the accused, witnesses and victims; and

(f) Rule on any other relevant matters.

7. The trial shall be held in public. The Trial Chamber may, however, determine that special circumstances require that certain proceedings be in closed session for the purposes set forth in article 68, or to protect confidential or sensitive information to be given in evidence.

8. (a) At the commencement of the trial, the Trial Chamber shall have read to the accused the charges previously confirmed by the Pre-Trial Chamber. The Trial Chamber shall satisfy itself that the accused understands the nature of the charges. It shall afford him or her the opportunity to make an admission of guilt in accordance with article 65 or to plead not guilty.

(b) At the trial, the presiding judge may give directions for the conduct of proceedings, including to ensure that they are conducted in a fair and impartial manner. Subject to any directions of the presiding judge, the parties may submit evidence in accordance with the provisions of this Statute.

9. The Trial Chamber shall have, inter alia, the power on application of a party or on its own motion to:

(a) Rule on the admissibility or relevance of evidence; and

(b) Take all necessary steps to maintain order in the course of a hearing.

10. The Trial Chamber shall ensure that a complete record of the trial, which accurately reflects the proceedings, is made and that it is maintained and preserved by the Registrar.

Article 65 Proceedings on an admission of guilt   App8–066

1. Where the accused makes an admission of guilt pursuant to article 64, paragraph 8 (a), the Trial Chamber shal determine whether:

(a) The accused understands the nature and consequences of the admission of guilt;

(b) The admission is voluntarily made by the accused after sufficient consultation with defence counsel; and

(c) The admission of guilt is supported by the facts of the case that are contained in:

    (i) The charges brought by the Prosecutor and admitted by the accused;
    (ii) Any materials presented by the Prosecutor which supplement the charges and which the accused accepts; and
    (iii) Any other evidence, such as the testimony of witnesses, presented by the Prosecutor or the accused.

2. Where the Trial Chamber is satisfied that the matters referred to in paragraph 1 are established, it shall consider the admission of guilt, together with any additional evidence presented, as establishing all the essential facts that are required to prove the crime to which the admission of guilt relates, and may convict the accused of that crime.

3. Where the Trial Chamber is not satisfied that the matters referred to in paragraph 1 are established, it shall consider the admission of guilt as not having been made, in which case it shall order that the trial be continued under the ordinary trial procedures provided by this Statute and may remit the case to another Trial Chamber.

4. Where the Trial Chamber is of the opinion that a more complete presentation of the facts of the case is required in the interests of justice, in particular the interests of the victims, the Trial Chamber may:

(a) Request the Prosecutor to present additional evidence, including the testimony of witnesses; or

(b) Order that the trial be continued under the ordinary trial procedures provided by this Statute, in which case it shall consider the admission of guilt as not having been made and may remit the case to another Trial Chamber.

5. Any discussions between the Prosecutor and the defence regarding modification of the charges, the admission of guilt or the penalty to be imposed shall not be binding on the Court.

App8–067   **Article 66 Presumption of innocence**

1. Everyone shall be presumed innocent until proved guilty before the Court in accordance with the applicable law.

2. The onus is on the Prosecutor to prove the guilt of the accused.

3. In order to convict the accused, the Court must be convinced of the guilt of the accused beyond reasonable doubt.

App8–068   **Article 67 Rights of the accused**

1. In the determination of any charge, the accused shall be entitled to a public hearing, having regard to the provisions of this Statute, to a fair hearing conducted impartially, and to the following minimum guarantees, in full equality:

   (a)   To be informed promptly and in detail of the nature, cause and content of the charge, in a language which the accused fully understands and speaks;

   (b)   To have adequate time and facilities for the preparation of the defence and to communicate freely with counsel of the accused's choosing in confidence;

   (c)   To be tried without undue delay;

   (d)   Subject to article 63, paragraph 2, to be present at the trial, to conduct the defence in person or through legal assistance of the accused's choosing, to be informed, if the accused does not have legal assistance, of this right and to have legal assistance assigned by the Court in any case where the interests of justice so require, and without payment if the accused lacks sufficient means to pay for it;

   (e)   To examine, or have examined, the witnesses against him or her and to obtain the attendance and examination of witnesses on his or her behalf under the same conditions as witnesses against him or her. The accused shall also be entitled to raise defences and to present other evidence admissible under this Statute;

   (f)   To have, free of any cost, the assistance of a competent interpreter and such translations as are necessary to meet the requirements of fairness, if any of the proceedings of or documents presented to the Court are not in a language which the accused fully understands and speaks;

   (g)   Not to be compelled to testify or to confess guilt and to remain silent, without such silence being a consideration in the determination of guilt or innocence;

   (h)   To make an unsworn oral or written statement in his or her defence; and

   (i)   Not to have imposed on him or her any reversal of the burden of proof or any onus of rebuttal.

2. In addition to any other disclosure provided for in this Statute, the Prosecutor shall, as soon as practicable, disclose to the defence evidence in the Prosecutor's possession or control which he or she believes shows or tends to show the innocence of the accused, or to mitigate the guilt of the accused, or which may affect the credibility of prosecution evidence. In case of doubt as to the application of this paragraph, the Court shall decide.

Article 68 Protection of the victims and witnesses and their participation in the proceedings

1. The Court shall take appropriate measures to protect the safety, physical and psychological well-being, dignity and privacy of victims and witnesses. In so doing, the Court shall have regard to all relevant factors, including age, gender as defined in article 7, paragraph 3, and health, and the nature of the crime, in particular, but not limited to, where the crime involves sexual or gender violence or violence against children. The Prosecutor shall take such measures particularly during the investigation and prosecution of such crimes. These measures shall not be prejudicial to or inconsistent with the rights of the accused and a fair and impartial trial.

2. As an exception to the principle of public hearings provided for in article 67, the Chambers of the Court may, to protect victims and witnesses or an accused, conduct any part of the proceedings *in camera* or allow the presentation of evidence by electronic or other special means. In particular, such measures shall be implemented in the case of a victim of sexual violence or a child who is a victim or a witness, unless otherwise ordered by the Court, having regard to all the circumstances, particularly the views of the victim or witness.

3. Where the personal interests of the victims are affected, the Court shall permit their views and concerns to be presented and considered at stages of the proceedings determined to be appropriate by the Court and in a manner which is not prejudicial to or inconsistent with the rights of the accused and a fair and impartial trial. Such views and concerns may be presented by the legal representatives of the victims where the Court considers it appropriate, in accordance with the Rules of Procedure and Evidence.

4. The Victims and Witnesses Unit may advise the Prosecutor and the Court on appropriate protective measures, security arrangements, counselling and assistance as referred to in article 43, paragraph 6.

5. Where the disclosure of evidence or information pursuant to this Statute may lead to the grave endangerment of the security of a witness or his or her family, the Prosecutor may, for the purposes of any proceedings conducted prior to the commencement of the trial, withhold such evidence or information and instead submit a summary thereof. Such measures shall be exercised in a manner which is not prejudicial to or inconsistent with the rights of the accused and a fair and impartial trial.

6. A State may make an application for necessary measures to be taken in respect of the protection of its servants or agents and the protection of confidential or sensitive information.

Article 69 Evidence

1. Before testifying, each witness shall, in accordance with the Rules of Procedure and Evidence, give an undertaking as to the truthfulness of the evidence to be given by that witness.

2. The testimony of a witness at trial shall be given in person, except to the extent provided by the measures set forth in article 68 or in the Rules of Procedure and Evidence. The Court may also permit the giving of *viva voce* (oral) or recorded testimony of a witness by means of video or audio technology, as well as the introduction of documents or written transcripts, subject to this Statute and in accordance with the Rules of Procedure and Evidence. These measures shall not be prejudicial to or inconsistent with the rights of the accused.

3. The parties may submit evidence relevant to the case, in accordance with article 64. The Court shall have the authority to request the submission of all evidence that it considers necessary for the determination of the truth.

4. The Court may rule on the relevance or admissibility of any evidence, taking into account, *inter alia*, the probative value of the evidence and any prejudice that such evidence may cause to a fair trial or to a fair evaluation of the testimony of a witness, in accordance with the Rules of Procedure and Evidence.

5. The Court shall respect and observe privileges on confidentiality as provided for in the Rules of Procedure and Evidence.

6. The Court shall not require proof of facts of common knowledge but may take judicial notice of them.

7. Evidence obtained by means of a violation of this Statute or internationally recognized human rights shall not be admissible if:

    (a)   The violation casts substantial doubt on the reliability of the evidence; or

    (b)   The admission of the evidence would be antithetical to and would seriously damage the integrity of the proceedings.

8. When deciding on the relevance or admissibility of evidence collected by a State, the Court shall not rule on the application of the State's national law.

App8–071   **Article 70 Offences against the administration of justice**

1. The Court shall have jurisdiction over the following offences against its administration of justice when committed intentionally:

    (a)   Giving false testimony when under an obligation pursuant to article 69, paragraph 1, to tell the truth;

    (b)   Presenting evidence that the party knows is false or forged;

    (c)   Corruptly influencing a witness, obstructing or interfering with the attendance or testimony of a witness, retaliating against a witness for giving testimony or destroying, tampering with or interfering with the collection of evidence;

    (d)   Impeding, intimidating or corruptly influencing an official of the Court for the purpose of forcing or persuading the official not to perform, or to perform improperly, his or her duties;

    (e)   Retaliating against an official of the Court on account of duties performed by that or another official;

    (f)   Soliciting or accepting a bribe as an official of the Court in connection with his or her official duties.

2. The principles and procedures governing the Court's exercise of jurisdiction over offences under this article shall be those provided for in the Rules of Procedure and Evidence. The conditions for providing international cooperation to the Court with respect to its proceedings under this article shall be governed by the domestic laws of the requested State.

3. In the event of conviction, the Court may impose a term of imprisonment not exceeding five years, or a fine in accordance with the Rules of Procedure and Evidence, or both.

4. (a)   Each State Party shall extend its criminal laws penalizing offences against the integrity of its own investigative or judicial process to offences against the administration of justice referred to in this article, committed on its territory, or by one of its nationals;

(b) Upon request by the Court, whenever it deems it proper, the State Party shall submit the case to its competent authorities for the purpose of prosecution. Those authorities shall treat such cases with diligence and devote sufficient resources to enable them to be conducted effectively.

Article 71 Sanctions for misconduct before the Court

App8–072

1. The Court may sanction persons present before it who commit misconduct, including disruption of its proceedings or deliberate refusal to comply with its directions, by administrative measures other than imprisonment, such as temporary or permanent removal from the courtroom, a fine or other similar measures provided for in the Rules of Procedure and Evidence.

2. The procedures governing the imposition of the measures set forth in paragraph 1 shall be those provided for in the Rules of Procedure and Evidence.

Article 72 Protection of national security information

App8–073

1. This article applies in any case where the disclosure of the information or documents of a State would, in the opinion of that State, prejudice its national security interests. Such cases include those falling within the scope of article 56, paragraphs 2 and 3, article 61, paragraph 3, article 64, paragraph 3, article 67, paragraph 2, article 68, paragraph 6, article 87, paragraph 6 and article 93, as well as cases arising at any other stage of the proceedings where such disclosure may be at issue.

2. This article shall also apply when a person who has been requested to give information or evidence has refused to do so or has referred the matter to the State on the ground that disclosure would prejudice the national security interests of a State and the State concerned confirms that it is of the opinion that disclosure would prejudice its national security interests.

3. Nothing in this article shall prejudice the requirements of confidentiality applicable under article 54, paragraph 3 (e) and (f), or the application of article 73.

4. If a State learns that information or documents of the State are being, or are likely to be, disclosed at any stage of the proceedings, and it is of the opinion that disclosure would prejudice its national security interests, that State shall have the right to intervene in order to obtain resolution of the issue in accordance with this article.

5. If, in the opinion of a State, disclosure of information would prejudice its national security interests, all reasonable steps will be taken by the State, acting in conjunction with the Prosecutor, the defence or the Pre-Trial Chamber or Trial Chamber, as the case may be, to seek to resolve the matter by cooperative means. Such steps may include:

(a) Modification or clarification of the request;

(b) A determination by the Court regarding the relevance of the information or evidence sought, or a determination as to whether the evidence, though relevant, could be or has been obtained from a source other than the requested State;

(c) Obtaining the information or evidence from a different source or in a different form; or

(d) Agreement on conditions under which the assistance could be provided including, among other things, providing summaries or redactions, limitations on disclosure, use of *in camera* or *ex parte* proceedings, or other protective measures permissible under the Statute and the Rules of Procedure and Evidence.

6. Once all reasonable steps have been taken to resolve the matter through cooperative means, and if the State considers that there are no means or conditions under which the information or documents could be provided or disclosed without prejudice to its national security interests, it shall so notify the Prosecutor or the Court of the specific reasons for its decision, unless a specific description of the reasons would itself necessarily result in such prejudice to the State's national security interests.

7. Thereafter, if the Court determines that the evidence is relevant and necessary for the establishment of the guilt or innocence of the accused, the Court may undertake the following actions:

(a) Where disclosure of the information or document is sought pursuant to a request for cooperation under Part 9 or the circumstances described in paragraph 2, and the State has invoked the ground for refusal referred to in article 93, paragraph 4:

(i) The Court may, before making any conclusion referred to in subparagraph 7 (a) (ii), request further consultations for the purpose of considering the State's representations, which may include, as appropriate, hearings *in camera* and *ex parte*;

(ii) If the Court concludes that, by invoking the ground for refusal under article 93, paragraph 4, in the circumstances of the case, the requested State is not acting in accordance with its obligations under this Statute, the Court may refer the matter in accordance with article 87, paragraph 7, specifying the reasons for its conclusion; and

(iii) The Court may make such inference in the trial of the accused as to the existence or non-existence of a fact, as may be appropriate in the circumstances; or

(b) In all other circumstances:

(i) Order disclosure; or

(ii) To the extent it does not order disclosure, make such inference in the trial of the accused as to the existence or non-existence of a fact, as may be appropriate in the circumstances.

App8–074 **Article 73 Third-party information or documents**

If a State Party is requested by the Court to provide a document or information in its custody, possession or control, which was disclosed to it in confidence by a State, intergovernmental organization or international organization, it shall seek the consent of the originator to disclose that document or information. If the originator is a State Party, it shall either consent to disclosure of the information or document or undertake to resolve the issue of disclosure with the Court, subject to the provisions of article 72. If the originator is not a State Party and refuses to consent to disclosure, the requested State shall inform the Court that it is unable to provide the document or information because of a pre-existing obligation of confidentiality to the originator.

App8–075 **Article 74 Requirements for the decision**

1. All the judges of the Trial Chamber shall be present at each stage of the trial and throughout their deliberations. The Presidency may, on a case-by-case basis, designate, as available, one or more alternate judges to be present at each stage of the trial and to replace a member of the Trial Chamber if that member is unable to continue attending.

2. The Trial Chamber's decision shall be based on its evaluation of the evidence and the entire proceedings. The decision shall not exceed the facts and circumstances described in the charges and any amendments to the charges. The Court may base its decision only on evidence submitted and discussed before it at the trial.

3. The judges shall attempt to achieve unanimity in their decision, failing which the decision shall be taken by a majority of the judges.

4. The deliberations of the Trial Chamber shall remain secret.

5. The decision shall be in writing and shall contain a full and reasoned statement of the Trial Chamber's findings on the evidence and conclusions. The Trial Chamber shall issue one decision. When there is no unanimity, the Trial Chamber's decision shall contain the views of the majority and the minority. The decision or a summary thereof shall be delivered in open court.

Article 75 Reparations to victims   App8–076

1. The Court shall establish principles relating to reparations to, or in respect of, victims, including restitution, compensation and rehabilitation. On this basis, in its decision the Court may, either upon request or on its own motion in exceptional circumstances, determine the scope and extent of any damage, loss and injury to, or in respect of, victims and will state the principles on which it is acting.

2. The Court may make an order directly against a convicted person specifying appropriate reparations to, or in respect of, victims, including restitution, compensation and rehabilitation.

Where appropriate, the Court may order that the award for reparations be made through the Trust Fund provided for in article 79.

3. Before making an order under this article, the Court may invite and shall take account of representations from or on behalf of the convicted person, victims, other interested persons or interested States.

4. In exercising its power under this article, the Court may, after a person is convicted of a crime within the jurisdiction of the Court, determine whether, in order to give effect to an order which it may make under this article, it is necessary to seek measures under article 93, paragraph 1.

5. A State Party shall give effect to a decision under this article as if the provisions of article 109 were applicable to this article.

6. Nothing in this article shall be interpreted as prejudicing the rights of victims under national or international law.

Article 76 Sentencing   App8–077

1. In the event of a conviction, the Trial Chamber shall consider the appropriate sentence to be imposed and shall take into account the evidence presented and submissions made during the trial that are relevant to the sentence.

2. Except where article 65 applies and before the completion of the trial, the Trial Chamber may on its own motion and shall, at the request of the Prosecutor or the accused, hold a further hearing to hear any additional evidence or submissions relevant to the sentence, in accordance with the Rules of Procedure and Evidence.

3. Where paragraph 2 applies, any representations under article 75 shall be heard during the further hearing referred to in paragraph 2 and, if necessary, during any additional hearing.

4. The sentence shall be pronounced in public and, wherever possible, in the presence of the accused.

PART 7. PENALTIES

App8–078   **Article 77 Applicable penalties**

1. Subject to article 110, the Court may impose one of the following penalties on a person convicted of a crime referred to in article 5 of this Statute:

    (a)   Imprisonment for a specified number of years, which may not exceed a maximum of 30 years; or

    (b)   A term of life imprisonment when justified by the extreme gravity of the crime and the individual circumstances of the convicted person.

2. In addition to imprisonment, the Court may order:

    (a)   A fine under the criteria provided for in the Rules of Procedure and Evidence;

    (b)   A forfeiture of proceeds, property and assets derived directly or indirectly from that crime, without prejudice to the rights of bona fide third parties.

App8–079   **Article 78 Determination of the sentence**

1. In determining the sentence, the Court shall, in accordance with the Rules of Procedure and Evidence, take into account such factors as the gravity of the crime and the individual circumstances of the convicted person.

2. In imposing a sentence of imprisonment, the Court shall deduct the time, if any, previously spent in detention in accordance with an order of the Court. The Court may deduct any time otherwise spent in detention in connection with conduct underlying the crime.

3. When a person has been convicted of more than one crime, the Court shall pronounce a sentence for each crime and a joint sentence specifying the total period of imprisonment. This period shall be no less than the highest individual sentence pronounced and shall not exceed 30 years imprisonment or a sentence of life imprisonment in conformity with article 77, paragraph 1 (b).

App8–080   **Article 79 Trust Fund**

1. A Trust Fund shall be established by decision of the Assembly of States Parties for the benefit of victims of crimes within the jurisdiction of the Court, and of the families of such victims.

2. The Court may order money and other property collected through fines or forfeiture to be transferred, by order of the Court, to the Trust Fund.

3. The Trust Fund shall be managed according to criteria to be determined by the Assembly of States Parties.

App8–081   **Article 80 Non-prejudice to national application of penalties and national laws**

Nothing in this Part affects the application by States of penalties prescribed by their national law, nor the law of States which do not provide for penalties prescribed in this Part.

PART 8. APPEAL AND REVISION

App8–082   **Article 81 Appeal against decision of acquittal or conviction or against sentence**

1. A decision under article 74 may be appealed in accordance with the Rules of Procedure and Evidence as follows:

(a) The Prosecutor may make an appeal on any of the following grounds:

    (i)   Procedural error,

    (ii)   Error of fact,

    (iii) Error of law, or

(b) The convicted person, or the Prosecutor on that person's behalf, may make an appeal on any of the following grounds:

    (i)   Procedural error,

    (ii)   Error of fact,

    (iii) Error of law, or

    (iv) Any other ground that affects the fairness or reliability of the proceedings or decision.

2. (a) A sentence may be appealed, in accordance with the Rules of Procedure and Evidence, by the Prosecutor or the convicted person on the ground of disproportion between the crime and the sentence;

(b) If on an appeal against sentence the Court considers that there are grounds on which the conviction might be set aside, wholly or in part, it may invite the Prosecutor and the convicted person to submit grounds under article 81, paragraph 1 (a) or (b), and may render a decision on conviction in accordance with article 83;

(c) The same procedure applies when the Court, on an appeal against conviction only, considers that there are grounds to reduce the sentence under paragraph 2 (a).

3. (a) Unless the Trial Chamber orders otherwise, a convicted person shall remain in custody pending an appeal;

(b) When a convicted person's time in custody exceeds the sentence of imprisonment imposed, that person shall be released, except that if the Prosecutor is also appealing, the release may be subject to the conditions under subparagraph (c) below;

(c) In case of an acquittal, the accused shall be released immediately, subject to the following:

    (i)   Under exceptional circumstances, and having regard, inter alia, to the concrete risk of flight, the seriousness of the offence charged and the probability of success on appeal, the Trial Chamber, at the request of the Prosecutor, may maintain the detention of the person pending appeal;

    (ii)   A decision by the Trial Chamber under subparagraph (c) (i) may be appealed in accordance with the Rules of Procedure and Evidence.

4. Subject to the provisions of paragraph 3 (a) and (b), execution of the decision or sentence shall be suspended during the period allowed for appeal and for the duration of the appeal proceedings.

Article 82 Appeal against other decisions

App8–083

1. Either party may appeal any of the following decisions in accordance with the Rules of Procedures and Evidence:

(a) A decision with respect to jurisdiction or admissibility;

(b) A decision granting or denying release of the person being investigated or prosecuted;

(c) A decision of the Pre-Trial Chamber to act on its own initiative under article 56, paragraph 3;

(d) A decision that involves an issue that would significantly affect the fair and expeditious conduct of the proceedings or the outcome of the trial, and for which, in the opinion of the Pre-Trial or Trial Chamber, an immediate resolution by the Appeals Chamber may materially advance the proceedings.

2. A decision of the Pre-Trial Chamber under article 57, paragraph 3 (d), may be appealed against by the State concerned or by the Prosecutor, with the leave of the Pre-Trial Chamber. The appeal shall be heard on an expedited basis.

3. An appeal shall not of itself have suspensive effect unless the Appeals Chamber so orders, upon request, in accordance with the Rules of Procedure and Evidence.

4. A legal representative of the victims, the convicted person or a bona fide owner of property adversely affected by an order under article 75 may appeal against the order for reparations, as provided in the Rules of Procedure and Evidence.

App8–084 **Article 83 Proceedings on appeal**

1. For the purposes of proceedings under article 81 and this article, the Appeals Chamber shall have all the powers of the Trial Chamber.

2. If the Appeals Chamber finds that the proceedings appealed from were unfair in a way that affected the reliability of the decision or sentence, or that the decision or sentence appealed from was materially affected by error of fact or law or procedural error, it may:

(a) Reverse or amend the decision or sentence; or

(b) Order a new trial before a different Trial Chamber.

For these purposes, the Appeals Chamber may remand a factual issue to the original Trial Chamber for it to determine the issue and to report back accordingly, or may itself call evidence to determine the issue. When the decision or sentence has been appealed only by the person convicted, or the Prosecutor on that person's behalf, it cannot be amended to his or her detriment.

3. If in an appeal against sentence the Appeals Chamber finds that the sentence is disproportionate to the crime, it may vary the sentence in accordance with Part 7.

4. The judgement of the Appeals Chamber shall be taken by a majority of the judges and shall be delivered in open court. The judgement shall state the reasons on which it is based. When there is no unanimity, the judgement of the Appeals Chamber shall contain the views of the majority and the minority, but a judge may deliver a separate or dissenting opinion on a question of law.

5. The Appeals Chamber may deliver its judgement in the absence of the person acquitted or convicted.

App8–085 **Article 84 Revision of conviction or sentence**

1. The convicted person or, after death, spouses, children, parents or one person alive at the time of the accused's death who has been given express written instructions from the accused to bring such a claim, or the Prosecutor on the person's behalf, may

apply to the Appeals Chamber to revise the final judgement of conviction or sentence on the grounds that:

(a) New evidence has been discovered that:

    (i) Was not available at the time of trial, and such unavailability was not wholly or partially attributable to the party making application; and

    (ii) Is sufficiently important that had it been proved at trial it would have been likely to have resulted in a different verdict;

(b) It has been newly discovered that decisive evidence, taken into account at trial and upon which the conviction depends, was false, forged or falsified;

(c) One or more of the judges who participated in conviction or confirmation of the charges has committed, in that case, an act of serious misconduct or serious breach of duty of sufficient gravity to justify the removal of that judge or those judges from office under article 46.

2. The Appeals Chamber shall reject the application if it considers it to be unfounded. If it determines that the application is meritorious, it may, as appropriate:

(a) Reconvene the original Trial Chamber;

(b) Constitute a new Trial Chamber; or

(c) Retain jurisdiction over the matter,

with a view to, after hearing the parties in the manner set forth in the Rules of Procedure and Evidence, arriving at a determination on whether the judgement should be revised.

Article 85 Compensation to an arrested or convicted person   App8–086

1. Anyone who has been the victim of unlawful arrest or detention shall have an enforceable right to compensation.

2. When a person has by a final decision been convicted of a criminal offence, and when subsequently his or her conviction has been reversed on the ground that a new or newly discovered fact shows conclusively that there has been a miscarriage of justice, the person who has suffered punishment as a result of such conviction shall be compensated according to law, unless it is proved that the non-disclosure of the unknown fact in time is wholly or partly attributable to him or her.

3. In exceptional circumstances, where the Court finds conclusive facts showing that there has been a grave and manifest miscarriage of justice, it may in its discretion award compensation, according to the criteria provided in the Rules of Procedure and Evidence, to a person who has been released from detention following a final decision of acquittal or a termination of the proceedings for that reason.

PART 9. INTERNATIONAL COOPERATION AND JUDICIAL ASSISTANCE

Article 86 General obligation to cooperate   App8–087

States Parties shall, in accordance with the provisions of this Statute, cooperate fully with the Court in its investigation and prosecution of crimes within the jurisdiction of the Court.

App8–088 **Article 87 Requests for cooperation: general provisions**

1.   (a)   The Court shall have the authority to make requests to States Parties for cooperation. The requests shall be transmitted through the diplomatic channel or any other appropriate channel as may be designated by each State Party upon ratification, acceptance, approval or accession.

Subsequent changes to the designation shall be made by each State Party in accordance with the Rules of Procedure and Evidence.

   (b)   When appropriate, without prejudice to the provisions of subparagraph (a), requests may also be transmitted through the International Criminal Police Organization or any appropriate regional organization.

2. Requests for cooperation and any documents supporting the request shall either be in or be accompanied by a translation into an official language of the requested State or one of the working languages of the Court, in accordance with the choice made by that State upon ratification, acceptance, approval or accession.

Subsequent changes to this choice shall be made in accordance with the Rules of Procedure and Evidence.

3. The requested State shall keep confidential a request for cooperation and any documents supporting the request, except to the extent that the disclosure is necessary for execution of the request.

4. In relation to any request for assistance presented under this Part, the Court may take such measures, including measures related to the protection of information, as may be necessary to ensure the safety or physical or psychological well-being of any victims, potential witnesses and their families. The Court may request that any information that is made available under this Part shall be provided and handled in a manner that protects the safety and physical or psychological well-being of any victims, potential witnesses and their families.

5. (a)   The Court may invite any State not party to this Statute to provide assistance under this Part on the basis of an ad hoc arrangement, an agreement with such State or any other appropriate basis.

   (b)   Where a State not party to this Statute, which has entered into an ad hoc arrangement or an agreement with the Court, fails to cooperate with requests pursuant to any such arrangement or agreement, the Court may so inform the Assembly of States Parties or, where the Security Council referred the matter to the Court, the Security Council.

6. The Court may ask any intergovernmental organization to provide information or documents. The Court may also ask for other forms of cooperation and assistance which may be agreed upon with such an organization and which are in accordance with its competence or mandate.

7. Where a State Party fails to comply with a request to cooperate by the Court contrary to the provisions of this Statute, thereby preventing the Court from exercising its functions and powers under this Statute, the Court may make a finding to that effect and refer the matter to the Assembly of States Parties or, where the Security Council referred the matter to the Court, to the Security Council.

App8–089 **Article 88 Availability of procedures under national law**

States Parties shall ensure that there are procedures available under their national law for all of the forms of cooperation which are specified under this Part.

Article 89 Surrender of persons to the Court **App8–090**

1. The Court may transmit a request for the arrest and surrender of a person, together with the material supporting the request outlined in article 91, to any State on the territory of which that person may be found and shall request the cooperation of that State in the arrest and surrender of such a person. States Parties shall, in accordance with the provisions of this Part and the procedure under their national law, comply with requests for arrest and surrender.

2. Where the person sought for surrender brings a challenge before a national court on the basis of the principle of *ne bis in idem* as provided in article 20, the requested State shall immediately consult with the Court to determine if there has been a relevant ruling on admissibility. If the case is admissible, the requested State shall proceed with the execution of the request. If an admissibility ruling is pending, the requested State may postpone the execution of the request for surrender of the person until the Court makes a determination on admissibility.

3. (a) A State Party shall authorize, in accordance with its national procedural law, transportation through its territory of a person being surrendered to the Court by another State, except where transit through that State would impede or delay the surrender.

   (b) A request by the Court for transit shall be transmitted in accordance with article 87. The request for transit shall contain:

   (i) A description of the person being transported;

   (ii) A brief statement of the facts of the case and their legal characterization; and

   (iii) The warrant for arrest and surrender;

   (c) A person being transported shall be detained in custody during the period of transit;

   (d) No authorization is required if the person is transported by air and no landing is scheduled on the territory of the transit State;

   (e) If an unscheduled landing occurs on the territory of the transit State, that State may require a request for transit from the Court as provided for in subparagraph (b). The transit State shall detain the person being transported until the request for transit is received and the transit is effected, provided that detention for purposes of this subparagraph may not be extended beyond 96 hours from the unscheduled landing unless the request is received within that time.

4. If the person sought is being proceeded against or is serving a sentence in the requested State for a crime different from that for which surrender to the Court is sought, the requested State, after making its decision to grant the request, shall consult with the Court.

Article 90 Competing requests **App8–091**

1. A State Party which receives a request from the Court for the surrender of a person under article 89 shall, if it also receives a request from any other State for the extradition of the same person for the same conduct which forms the basis of the crime for which the Court seeks the person's surrender, notify the Court and the requesting State of that fact.

2. Where the requesting State is a State Party, the requested State shall give priority to the request from the Court if:

    (a)   The Court has, pursuant to article 18 or 19, made a determination that the case in respect of which surrender is sought is admissible and that determination takes into account the investigation or prosecution conducted by the requesting State in respect of its request for extradition; or

    (b)   The Court makes the determination described in subparagraph (a) pursuant to the requested State's notification under paragraph 1.

3. Where a determination under paragraph 2 (a) has not been made, the requested State may, at its discretion, pending the determination of the Court under paragraph 2 (b), proceed to deal with the request for extradition from the requesting State but shall not extradite the person until the Court has determined that the case is inadmissible. The Court's determination shall be made on an expedited basis.

4. If the requesting State is a State not Party to this Statute the requested State, if it is not under an international obligation to extradite the person to the requesting State, shall give priority to the request for surrender from the Court, if the Court has determined that the case is admissible.

5. Where a case under paragraph 4 has not been determined to be admissible by the Curt, the requested State may, at its discretion, proceed to deal with the request for extradition from the requesting State.

6. In cases where paragraph 4 applies except that the requested State is under an existing international obligation to extradite the person to the requesting State not Party to this Statute, the requested State shall determine whether to surrender the person to the Court or extradite the person to the requesting State. In making its decision, the requested State shall consider all the relevant factors, including but not limited to:

    (a)   The respective dates of the requests;

    (b)   The interests of the requesting State including, where relevant, whether the crime was committed in its territory and the nationality of the victims and of the person sought; and

    (c)   The possibility of subsequent surrender between the Court and the requesting State.

7. Where a State Party which receives a request from the Court for the surrender of a person also receives a request from any State for the extradition of the same person for conduct other than that which constitutes the crime for which the Court seeks the person's surrender:

    (a)   The requested State shall, if it is not under an existing international obligation to extradite the person to the requesting State, give priority to the request from the Court;

    (b)   The requested State shall, if it is under an existing international obligation to extradite the person to the requesting State, determine whether to surrender the person to the Court or to extradite the person to the requesting State. In making its decision, the requested State shall consider all the relevant factors, including but not limited to those set out in paragraph 6, but shall give special consideration to the relative nature and gravity of the conduct in question.

8. Where pursuant to a notification under this article, the Court has determined a case to be inadmissible, and subsequently extradition to the requesting State is refused, the requested State shall notify the Court of this decision.

Article 91 Contents of request for arrest and surrender

1. A request for arrest and surrender shall be made in writing. In urgent cases, a request may be made by any medium capable of delivering a written record, provided that the request shall be confirmed through the channel provided for in article 87, paragraph 1 (a).

2. In the case of a request for the arrest and surrender of a person for whom a warrant of arrest has been issued by the Pre-Trial Chamber under article 58, the request shall contain or be supported by:

(a) Information describing the person sought, sufficient to identify the person, and information as to that person's probable location;

(b) A copy of any warrant of arrest for that person;

(c) Such documents, statements or information as may be necessary to meet the requirements for the surrender process in the requested State, except that those requirements should not be more burdensome than those applicable to requests for extradition pursuant to treaties or arrangements between the requested State and other States and should, if possible, be less burdensome, taking into account the distinct nature of the Court.

3. In the case of a request for the arrest and surrender of a person already convicted, the request shall contain or be supported by:

(a) A copy of the warrant of arrest; and

(b) A copy of the judgement of conviction;

(c) Information to demonstrate that the person sought is the one referred to in the judgement of conviction; and

(d) If the person sought has been sentenced, a copy of the sentence imposed and, in the case of a sentence for imprisonment, a statement of any time already served and the time remaining to be served.

4. Upon the request of the Court, a State Party shall consult with the Court, either generally or with respect to a specific matter, regarding any requirements under its national law that may apply under paragraph 2 (c). During the consultations, the State Party shall advise the Court of the specific requirements of its national law.

Article 92 Provisional arrest

1. In urgent cases, the Court may request the provisional arrest of the person sought, pending presentation of the request for surrender and the documents supporting the request as specified in article 91.

2. The request for provisional arrest shall be made by any medium capable of delivering a written record and shall contain:

(a) Information describing the person sought, sufficient to identify the person, and information as to that person's probable location;

(b) A concise statement of the crimes for which the person's arrest is sought and of the facts which are alleged to constitute those crimes, including, where possible, the date and location of the crime;

(c) A statement of the existence of a warrant of arrest or a judgement of conviction against the person sought; and

(d) A statement that a request for surrender of the person sought will follow.

3. A person who is provisionally arrested may be released from custody if the requested State has not received the request for surrender and the documents supporting the request as specified in article 91 within the time limits specified in the Rules of Procedure and Evidence. However, the person may consent to surrender before the expiration of this period if permitted by the law of the requested State. In such a case, the requested State shall proceed to surrender the person to the Court as soon as possible.

4. The fact that the person sought has been released from custody pursuant to paragraph 3 shall not prejudice the subsequent arrest and surrender of that person if the request for surrender and the documents supporting the request are delivered at a later date.

App8–094   **Article 93 Other forms of cooperation**

1. States Parties shall, in accordance with the provisions of this Part and under procedures of national law, comply with requests by the Court to provide the following assistance in relation to investigations or prosecutions:

(a) The identification and whereabouts of persons or the location of items;

(b) The taking of evidence, including testimony under oath, and the production of evidence, including expert opinions and reports necessary to the Court;

(c) The questioning of any person being investigated or prosecuted;

(d) The service of documents, including judicial documents;

(e) Facilitating the voluntary appearance of persons as witnesses or experts before the Court;

(f) The temporary transfer of persons as provided in paragraph 7;

(g) The examination of places or sites, including the exhumation and examination of grave sites;

(h) The execution of searches and seizures;

(i) The provision of records and documents, including official records and documents;

(j) The protection of victims and witnesses and the preservation of evidence;

(k) The identification, tracing and freezing or seizure of proceeds, property and assets and instrumentalities of crimes for the purpose of eventual forfeiture, without prejudice to the rights of bona fide third parties; and

(l) Any other type of assistance which is not prohibited by the law of the requested State, with a view to facilitating the investigation and prosecution of crimes within the jurisdiction of the Court.

2. The Court shall have the authority to provide an assurance to a witness or an expert appearing before the Court that he or she will not be prosecuted, detained or subjected to any restriction of personal freedom by the Court in respect of any act or omission that preceded the departure of that person from the requested State.

3. Where execution of a particular measure of assistance detailed in a request presented under paragraph 1, is prohibited in the requested State on the basis of an existing fundamental legal principle of general application, the requested State shall

promptly consult with the Court to try to resolve the matter. In the consultations, consideration should be given to whether the assistance can be rendered in another manner or subject to conditions. If after consultations the matter cannot be resolved, the Court shall modify the request as necessary.

4. In accordance with article 72, a State Party may deny a request for assistance, in whole or in part, only if the request concerns the production of any documents or disclosure of evidence which relates to its national security.

5. Before denying a request for assistance under paragraph 1 (l), the requested State shall consider whether the assistance can be provided subject to specified conditions, or whether the assistance can be provided at a later date or in an alternative manner, provided that if the Court or the Prosecutor accepts the assistance subject to conditions, the Court or the Prosecutor shall abide by them.

6. If a request for assistance is denied, the requested State Party shall promptly inform the Court or the Prosecutor of the reasons for such denial.

7. (a) The Court may request the temporary transfer of a person in custody for purposes of identification or for obtaining testimony or other assistance. The person may be transferred if the following conditions are fulfilled:

  (i) The person freely gives his or her informed consent to the transfer; and
  (ii) The requested State agrees to the transfer, subject to such conditions as that State and the Court may agree.

 (b) The person being transferred shall remain in custody. When the purposes of the transfer have been fulfilled, the Court shall return the person without delay to the requested State.

8. (a) The Court shall ensure the confidentiality of documents and information, except as required for the investigation and proceedings described in the request.

 (b) The requested State may, when necessary, transmit documents or information to the Prosecutor on a confidential basis. The Prosecutor may then use them solely for the purpose of generating new evidence.

 (c) The requested State may, on its own motion or at the request of the Prosecutor, subsequently consent to the disclosure of such documents or information. They may then be used as evidence pursuant to the provisions of Parts 5 and 6 and in accordance with the Rules of Procedure and Evidence.

9. (a) (i) In the event that a State Party receives competing requests, other than for surrender or extradition, from the Court and from another State pursuant to an international obligation, the State Party shall endeavour, in consultation with the Court and the other State, to meet both requests, if necessary by postponing or attaching conditions to one or the other request.

  (ii) Failing that, competing requests shall be resolved in accordance with the principles established in article 90.

 (b) Where, however, the request from the Court concerns information, property or persons which are subject to the control of a third State or an international organization by virtue of an international agreement, the requested States shall so inform the Court and the Court shall direct its request to the third State or international organization.

10. (a) The Court may, upon request, cooperate with and provide assistance to a State Party conducting an investigation into or trial in respect of conduct which constitutes a crime within the jurisdiction of the Court or which constitutes a serious crime under the national law of the requesting State.

(b) (i) The assistance provided under subparagraph (a) shall include, *inter alia*:

      a. The transmission of statements, documents or other types of evidence obtained in the course of an investigation or a trial conducted by the Court; and

      b. The questioning of any person detained by order of the Court;

    (ii) In the case of assistance under subparagraph (b) (i) a:

      a. If the documents or other types of evidence have been obtained with the assistance of a State, such transmission shall require the consent of that State;

      b. If the statements, documents or other types of evidence have been provided by a witness or expert, such transmission shall be subject to the provisions of article 68.

(c) The Court may, under the conditions set out in this paragraph, grant a request for assistance under this paragraph from a State which is not a Party to this Statute.

App8–095 Article 94 Postponement of execution of a request in respect of ongoing investigation or prosecution

1. If the immediate execution of a request would interfere with an ongoing investigation or prosecution of a case different from that to which the request relates, the requested State may postpone the execution of the request for a period of time agreed upon with the Court. However, the postponement shall be no longer than is necessary to complete the relevant investigation or prosecution in the requested State. Before making a decision to postpone, the requested State should consider whether the assistance may be immediately provided subject to certain conditions.

2. If a decision to postpone is taken pursuant to paragraph 1, the Prosecutor may, however, seek measures to preserve evidence, pursuant to article 93, paragraph 1 (j).

App8–096 Article 95 Postponement of execution of a request in respect of an admissibility challenge

Where there is an admissibility challenge under consideration by the Court pursuant to article 18 or 19, the requested State may postpone the execution of a request under this Part pending a determination by the Court, unless the Court has specifically ordered that the Prosecutor may pursue the collection of such evidence pursuant to article 18 or 19.

App8–097 Article 96 Contents of request for other forms of assistance under article 93

1. A request for other forms of assistance referred to in article 93 shall be made in writing. In urgent cases, a request may be made by any medium capable of delivering a written record, provided that the request shall be confirmed through the channel provided for in article 87, paragraph 1 (a).

2. The request shall, as applicable, contain or be supported by the following:

(a) A concise statement of the purpose of the request and the assistance sought, including the legal basis and the grounds for the request;

(b) As much detailed information as possible about the location or identification of any person or place that must be found or identified in order for the assistance sought to be provided;

(c) The reasons for and details of any procedure or requirement to be followed;

(d) A concise statement of the essential facts underlying the request;

(e) Such information as may be required under the law of the requested State in order to execute the request; and

(f) Any other information relevant in order for the assistance sought to be provided.

3. Upon the request of the Court, a State Party shall consult with the Court, either generally or with respect to a specific matter, regarding any requirements under its national law that may apply under paragraph 2 (e). During the consultations, the State Party shall advise the Court of the specific requirements of its national law.

4. The provisions of this article shall, where applicable, also apply in respect of a request for assistance made to the Court.

Article 97 Consultations   App8–098

Where a State Party receives a request under this Part in relation to which it identifies problems which may impede or prevent the execution of the request, that State shall consult with the Court without delay in order to resolve the matter. Such problems may include, *inter alia*:

(a) Insufficient information to execute the request;

(b) In the case of a request for surrender, the fact that despite best efforts, the person sought cannot be located or that the investigation conducted has determined that the person in the requested State is clearly not the person named in the warrant; or

(c) The fact that execution of the request in its current form would require the requested State to breach a pre-existing treaty obligation undertaken with respect to another State.

Article 98 Cooperation with respect to waiver of immunity and consent to surrender   App8–099

1. The Court may not proceed with a request for surrender or assistance which would require the requested State to act inconsistently with its obligations under international law with respect to the State or diplomatic immunity of a person or property of a third State, unless the Court can first obtain the cooperation of that third State for the waiver of the immunity.

2. The Court may not proceed with a request for surrender which would require the requested State to act inconsistently with its obligations under international agreements pursuant to which the consent of a sending State is required to surrender a person of that State to the Court, unless the Court can first obtain the cooperation of the sending State for the giving of consent for the surrender.

Article 99 Execution of requests under articles 93 and 96   App8–100

1. Requests for assistance shall be executed in accordance with the relevant procedure under the law of the requested State and, unless prohibited by such law, in the manner

specified in the request, including following any procedure outlined therein or permitting persons specified in the request to be present at and assist in the execution process.

2. In the case of an urgent request, the documents or evidence produced in response shall, at the request of the Court, be sent urgently.

3. Replies from the requested State shall be transmitted in their original language and form.

4. Without prejudice to other articles in this Part, where it is necessary for the successful execution of a request which can be executed without any compulsory measures, including specifically the interview of or taking evidence from a person on a voluntary basis, including doing so without the presence of the authorities of the requested State Party if it is essential for the request to be executed, and the examination without modification of a public site or other public place, the Prosecutor may execute such request directly on the territory of a State as follows:

(a) When the State Party requested is a State on the territory of which the crime is alleged to have been committed, and there has been a determination of admissibility pursuant to article 18 or 19, the Prosecutor may directly execute such request following all possible consultations with the requested State Party;

(b) In other cases, the Prosecutor may execute such request following consultations with the requested State Party and subject to any reasonable conditions or concerns raised by that State Party. Where the requested State Party identifies problems with the execution of a request pursuant to this subparagraph it shall, without delay, consult with the Court to resolve the matter.

5. Provisions allowing a person heard or examined by the Court under article 72 to invoke restrictions designed to prevent disclosure of confidential information connected with national security shall also apply to the execution of requests for assistance under this article.

App8–101   **Article 100 Costs**

1. The ordinary costs for execution of requests in the territory of the requested State shall be borne by that State, except for the following, which shall be borne by the Court:

(a) Costs associated with the travel and security of witnesses and experts or the transfer under article 93 of persons in custody;

(b) Costs of translation, interpretation and transcription;

(c) Travel and subsistence costs of the judges, the Prosecutor, the Deputy Prosecutors, the Registrar, the Deputy Registrar and staff of any organ of the Court;

(d) Costs of any expert opinion or report requested by the Court;

(e) Costs associated with the transport of a person being surrendered to the Court by a custodial State; and

(f) Following consultations, any extraordinary costs that may result from the execution of a request.

2. The provisions of paragraph 1 shall, as appropriate, apply to requests from States Parties to the Court. In that case, the Court shall bear the ordinary costs of execution.

Article 101 Rule of speciality

1. A person surrendered to the Court under this Statute shall not be proceeded against, punished or detained for any conduct committed prior to surrender, other than the conduct or course of conduct which forms the basis of the crimes for which that person has been surrendered.

2. The Court may request a waiver of the requirements of paragraph 1 from the State which surrendered the person to the Court and, if necessary, the Court shall provide additional information in accordance with article 91. States Parties shall have the authority to provide a waiver to the Court and should endeavour to do so.

Article 102 Use of terms

For the purposes of this Statute:

    (a) "surrender" means the delivering up of a person by a State to the Court, pursuant

    (b) "extradition" means the delivering up of a person by one State to another as provided by treaty, convention or national legislation.

PART 10. ENFORCEMENT

Article 103 Role of States in enforcement of sentences of imprisonment

1. (a) A sentence of imprisonment shall be served in a State designated by the Court from a list of States which have indicated to the Court their willingness to accept sentenced persons.

    (b) At the time of declaring its willingness to accept sentenced persons, a State may attach conditions to its acceptance as agreed by the Court and in accordance with this Part.

2. (c) The State of enforcement shall notify the Court of any circumstances, including the exercise of any conditions agreed under paragraph 1, which could materially affect the terms or extent of the imprisonment. The Court shall be given at least 45 days" notice of any such known or foreseeable circumstances. During this period, the State of enforcement shall take no action that might prejudice its obligations under article 110.

    (b) Where the Court cannot agree to the circumstances referred to in subparagraph (a), it shall notify the State of enforcement and proceed in accordance with article 104, paragraph 1.

    (c) A State designated in a particular case shall promptly inform the Court whether it accepts the Court's designation.

3. In exercising its discretion to make a designation under paragraph 1, the Court shall take into account the following:

    (a) The principle that States Parties should share the responsibility for enforcing sentences of imprisonment, in accordance with principles of equitable distribution, as provided in the Rules of Procedure and Evidence;

    (b) The application of widely accepted international treaty standards governing the treatment of prisoners;

(c) The views of the sentenced person;

(d) The nationality of the sentenced person;

(e) Such other factors regarding the circumstances of the crime or the person sentenced, or the effective enforcement of the sentence, as may be appropriate in designating the State of enforcement.

4. If no State is designated under paragraph 1, the sentence of imprisonment shall be served in a prison facility made available by the host State, in accordance with the conditions set out in the headquarters agreement referred to in article 3, paragraph 2. In such a case, the costs arising out of the enforcement of a sentence of imprisonment shall be borne by the Court.

App8–105   **Article 104 Change in designation of State of enforcement**

1. The Court may, at any time, decide to transfer a sentenced person to a prison of another State.

2. A sentenced person may, at any time, apply to the Court to be transferred from the State of enforcement.

App8–106   **Article 105 Enforcement of the sentence**

1. Subject to conditions which a State may have specified in accordance with article 103, paragraph 1 (b), the sentence of imprisonment shall be binding on the States Parties, which shall in no case modify it.

2. The Court alone shall have the right to decide any application for appeal and revision. The State of enforcement shall not impede the making of any such application by a sentenced person.

App8–107   **Article 106 Supervision of enforcement of sentences and conditions of imprisonment**

1. The enforcement of a sentence of imprisonment shall be subject to the supervision of the Court and shall be consistent with widely accepted international treaty standards governing treatment of prisoners.

2. The conditions of imprisonment shall be governed by the law of the State of enforcement and shall be consistent with widely accepted international treaty standards governing treatment of prisoners; in no case shall such conditions be more or less favourable than those available to prisoners convicted of similar offences in the State of enforcement.

3. Communications between a sentenced person and the Court shall be unimpeded and confidential.

App8–108   **Article 107 Transfer of the person upon completion of sentence**

1. Following completion of the sentence, a person who is not a national of the State of enforcement may, in accordance with the law of the State of enforcement, be transferred to a State which is obliged to receive him or her, or to another State which agrees to receive him or her, taking into account any wishes of the person to be transferred to that State, unless the State of enforcement authorizes the person to remain in its territory.

2. If no State bears the costs arising out of transferring the person to another State pursuant to paragraph 1, such costs shall be borne by the Court.

3. Subject to the provisions of article 108, the State of enforcement may also, in accordance with its national law, extradite or otherwise surrender the person to a

State which has requested the extradition or surrender of the person for purposes of trial or enforcement of a sentence.

Article 108 Limitation on the prosecution or punishment of other offences

App8–109

1. A sentenced person in the custody of the State of enforcement shall not be subject to prosecution or punishment or to extradition to a third State for any conduct engaged in prior to that person's delivery to the State of enforcement, unless such prosecution, punishment or extradition has been approved by the Court at the request of the State of enforcement.

2. The Court shall decide the matter after having heard the views of the sentenced person.

3. Paragraph 1 shall cease to apply if the sentenced person remains voluntarily for more than 30 days in the territory of the State of enforcement after having served the full sentence imposed by the Court, or returns to the territory of that State after having left it.

Article 109 Enforcement of fines and forfeiture measures

App8–110

1. States Parties shall give effect to fines or forfeitures ordered by the Court under Part 7, without prejudice to the rights of bona fide third parties, and in accordance with the procedure of their national law.

2. If a State Party is unable to give effect to an order for forfeiture, it shall take measures to recover the value of the proceeds, property or assets ordered by the Court to be forfeited, without prejudice to the rights of bona fide third parties.

3. Property, or the proceeds of the sale of real property or, where appropriate, the sale of other property, which is obtained by a State Party as a result of its enforcement of a judgement of the Court shall be transferred to the Court.

Article 110 Review by the Court concerning reduction of sentence

App8–111

1. The State of enforcement shall not release the person before expiry of the sentence pronounced by the Court.

2. The Court alone shall have the right to decide any reduction of sentence, and shall rule on the matter after having heard the person.

3. When the person has served two thirds of the sentence, or 25 years in the case of life imprisonment, the Court shall review the sentence to determine whether it should be reduced. Such a review shall not be conducted before that time.

4. In its review under paragraph 3, the Court may reduce the sentence if it finds that one or more of the following factors are present:

(a) The early and continuing willingness of the person to cooperate with the Court in its investigations and prosecutions;

(b) The voluntary assistance of the person in enabling the enforcement of the judgements and orders of the Court in other cases, and in particular providing assistance in locating assets subject to orders of fine, forfeiture or reparation which may be used for the benefit of victims; or

(c) Other factors establishing a clear and significant change of circumstances sufficient to justify the reduction of sentence, as provided in the Rules of Procedure and Evidence.

5. If the Court determines in its initial review under paragraph 3 that it is not appropriate to reduce the sentence, it shall thereafter review the question of reduction

of sentence at such intervals and applying such criteria as provided for in the Rules of Procedure and Evidence.

App8–112 **Article 111 Escape**

If a convicted person escapes from custody and flees the State of enforcement, that State may, after consultation with the Court, request the person's surrender from the State in which the person is located pursuant to existing bilateral or multilateral arrangements, or may request that the Court seek the person's surrender, in accordance with Part 9. It may direct that the person be delivered to the State in which he or she was serving the sentence or to another State designated by the Court.

PART 11. ASSEMBLY OF STATES PARTIES

App8–113 **Article 112 Assembly of States Parties**

1. An Assembly of States Parties to this Statute is hereby established. Each State Party shall have one representative in the Assembly who may be accompanied by alternates and advisers. Other States which have signed this Statute or the Final Act may be observers in the Assembly.
   2. The Assembly shall:

    (a) Consider and adopt, as appropriate, recommendations of the Preparatory Commission;

    (b) Provide management oversight to the Presidency, the Prosecutor and the Registrar regarding the administration of the Court;

    (c) Consider the reports and activities of the Bureau established under paragraph 3 and take appropriate action in regard thereto;

    (d) Consider and decide the budget for the Court;

    (e) Decide whether to alter, in accordance with article 36, the number of judges;

    (f) Consider pursuant to article 87, paragraphs 5 and 7, any question relating to non-cooperation;

    (g) Perform any other function consistent with this Statute or the Rules of Procedure and Evidence.

    3. (a) The Assembly shall have a Bureau consisting of a President, two Vice-Presidents and 18 members elected by the Assembly for three-year terms.

    (b) The Bureau shall have a representative character, taking into account, in particular, equitable geographical distribution and the adequate representation of the principal legal systems of the world.

    (c) The Bureau shall meet as often as necessary, but at least once a year. It shall assist the Assembly in the discharge of its responsibilities.

4. The Assembly may establish such subsidiary bodies as may be necessary, including an independent oversight mechanism for inspection, evaluation and investigation of the Court, in order to enhance its efficiency and economy.
5. The President of the Court, the Prosecutor and the Registrar or their representatives may participate, as appropriate, in meetings of the Assembly and of the Bureau.

6. The Assembly shall meet at the seat of the Court or at the Headquarters of the United Nations once a year and, when circumstances so require, hold special sessions. Except as otherwise specified in this Statute, special sessions shall be convened by the Bureau on its own initiative or at the request of one third of the States Parties.

7. Each State Party shall have one vote. Every effort shall be made to reach decisions by consensus in the Assembly and in the Bureau. If consensus cannot be reached, except as otherwise provided in the Statute:

  (a) Decisions on matters of substance must be approved by a two-thirds majority of those present and voting provided that an absolute majority of States Parties constitutes the quorum for voting;

  (b) Decisions on matters of procedure shall be taken by a simple majority of States Parties present and voting.

8. A State Party which is in arrears in the payment of its financial contributions towards the costs of the Court shall have no vote in the Assembly and in the Bureau if the amount of its arrears equals or exceeds the amount of the contributions due from it for the preceding two full years. The Assembly may, nevertheless, permit such a State Party to vote in the Assembly and in the Bureau if it is satisfied that the failure to pay is due to conditions beyond the control of the State Party.

9. The Assembly shall adopt its own rules of procedure.

10. The official and working languages of the Assembly shall be those of the General Assembly of the United Nations.

PART 12. FINANCING

Article 113 Financial Regulations

App8–114

Except as otherwise specifically provided, all financial matters related to the Court and the meetings of the Assembly of States Parties, including its Bureau and subsidiary bodies, shall be governed by this Statute and the Financial Regulations and Rules adopted by the Assembly of States Parties.

Article 114 Payment of expenses

App8–115

Expenses of the Court and the Assembly of States Parties, including its Bureau and subsidiary bodies, shall be paid from the funds of the Court.

Article 115 Funds of the Court and of the Assembly of States Parties

App8–116

The expenses of the Court and the Assembly of States Parties, including its Bureau and subsidiary bodies, as provided for in the budget decided by the Assembly of States Parties, shall be provided by the following sources:

  (a) Assessed contributions made by States Parties;

  (b) Funds provided by the United Nations, subject to the approval of the General Assembly, in particular in relation to the expenses incurred due to referrals by the Security Council.

Article 116 Voluntary contributions

App8–117

Without prejudice to article 115, the Court may receive and utilize, as additional funds, voluntary contributions from Governments, international organizations, individuals, corporations and other entities, in accordance with relevant criteria adopted by the Assembly of States Parties.

App8–118   **Article 117 Assessment of contributions**

The contributions of States Parties shall be assessed in accordance with an agreed scale of assessment, based on the scale adopted by the United Nations for its regular budget and adjusted in accordance with the principles on which that scale is based.

App8–119   **Article 118 Annual audit**

The records, books and accounts of the Court, including its annual financial statements, shall be audited annually by an independent auditor.

PART 13. FINAL CLAUSES

App8–120   **Article 119 Settlement of disputes**

1. Any dispute concerning the judicial functions of the Court shall be settled by the decision of the Court.

2. Any other dispute between two or more States Parties relating to the interpretation or application of this Statute which is not settled through negotiations within three months of their commencement shall be referred to the Assembly of States Parties. The Assembly may itself seek to settle the dispute or may make recommendations on further means of settlement of the dispute, including referral to the International Court of Justice in conformity with the Statute of that Court.

App8–121   **Article 120 Reservations**

No reservations may be made to this Statute.

App8–122   **Article 121 Amendments**

1. After the expiry of seven years from the entry into force of this Statute, any State Party may propose amendments thereto. The text of any proposed amendment shall be submitted to the Secretary-General of the United Nations, who shall promptly circulate it to all States Parties.

2. No sooner than three months from the date of notification, the Assembly of States Parties, at its next meeting, shall, by a majority of those present and voting, decide whether to take up the proposal. The Assembly may deal with the proposal directly or convene a Review Conference if the issue involved so warrants.

3. The adoption of an amendment at a meeting of the Assembly of States Parties or at a Review Conference on which consensus cannot be reached shall require a two-thirds majority of States Parties.

4. Except as provided in paragraph 5, an amendment shall enter into force for all States Parties one year after instruments of ratification or acceptance have been deposited with the Secretary-General of the United Nations by seven-eighths of them.

5. Any amendment to articles 5, 6, 7 and 8 of this Statute shall enter into force for those States Parties which have accepted the amendment one year after the deposit of their instruments of ratification or acceptance. In respect of a State Party which has not accepted the amendment, the Court shall not exercise its jurisdiction regarding a crime covered by the amendment when committed by that State Party's nationals or on its territory.

6. If an amendment has been accepted by seven-eighths of States Parties in accordance with paragraph 4, any State Party which has not accepted the amendment may withdraw from this Statute with immediate effect, notwithstanding article 127, paragraph 1, but subject to article 127, paragraph 2, by giving notice no later than one year after the entry into force of such amendment.

7. The Secretary-General of the United Nations shall circulate to all States Parties any amendment adopted at a meeting of the Assembly of States Parties or at a Review Conference.

Article 122 Amendments to provisions of an institutional nature App8–123

1. Amendments to provisions of this Statute which are of an exclusively institutional nature, namely, article 35, article 36, paragraphs 8 and 9, article 37, article 38, article 39, paragraphs 1 (first two sentences), 2 and 4, article 42, paragraphs 4 to 9, article 43, paragraphs 2 and 3, and articles 44, 46, 47 and 49, may be proposed at any time, notwithstanding article 121, paragraph 1, by any State Party. The text of any proposed amendment shall be submitted to the Secretary-General of the United Nations or such other person designated by the Assembly of States Parties who shall promptly circulate it to all States Parties and to others participating in the Assembly.

2. Amendments under this article on which consensus cannot be reached shall be adopted by the Assembly of States Parties or by a Review Conference, by a two-thirds majority of States Parties. Such amendments shall enter into force for all States Parties six months after their adoption by the Assembly or, as the case may be, by the Conference.

Article 123 Review of the Statute App8–124

1. Seven years after the entry into force of this Statute the Secretary-General of the United Nations shall convene a Review Conference to consider any amendments to this Statute. Such review may include, but is not limited to, the list of crimes contained in article 5. The Conference shall be open to those participating in the Assembly of States Parties and on the same conditions.

2. At any time thereafter, at the request of a State Party and for the purposes set out in paragraph 1, the Secretary-General of the United Nations shall, upon approval by a majority of States Parties, convene a Review Conference.

3. The provisions of article 121, paragraphs 3 to 7, shall apply to the adoption and entry into force of any amendment to the Statute considered at a Review Conference.

Article 124 Transitional Provision App8–125

Notwithstanding article 12, paragraphs 1 and 2, a State, on becoming a party to this Statute, may declare that, for a period of seven years after the entry into force of this Statute for the State concerned, it does not accept the jurisdiction of the Court with respect to the category of crimes referred to in article 8 when a crime is alleged to have been committed by its nationals or on its territory. A declaration under this article may be withdrawn at any time. The provisions of this article shall be reviewed at the Review Conference convened in accordance with article 123, paragraph 1.

Article 125 Signature, ratification, acceptance, approval or accession App8–126

1. This Statute shall be open for signature by all States in Rome, at the headquarters of the Food and Agriculture Organization of the United Nations, on 17 July 1998. Thereafter, it shall remain open for signature in Rome at the Ministry of Foreign Affairs of Italy until 17 October 1998. After that date, the Statute shall remain open for signature in New York, at United Nations Headquarters, until 31 December 2000.

2. This Statute is subject to ratification, acceptance or approval by signatory States. Instruments of ratification, acceptance or approval shall be deposited with the Secretary-General of the United Nations.

3. This Statute shall be open to accession by all States. Instruments of accession shall be deposited with the Secretary-General of the United Nations.

App8–127 **Article 126 Entry into force**

1. This Statute shall enter into force on the first day of the month after the 60th day following the date of the deposit of the 60th instrument of ratification, acceptance, approval or accession with the Secretary-General of the United Nations.

2. For each State ratifying, accepting, approving or acceding to this Statute after the deposit of the 60th instrument of ratification, acceptance, approval or accession, the Statute shall enter into force on the first day of the month after the 60th day following the deposit by such State of its instrument of ratification, acceptance, approval or accession.

App8–128 **Article 127 Withdrawal**

1. A State Party may, by written notification addressed to the Secretary-General of the United Nations, withdraw from this Statute. The withdrawal shall take effect one year after the date of receipt of the notification, unless the notification specifies a later date.

2. A State shall not be discharged, by reason of its withdrawal, from the obligations arising from this Statute while it was a Party to the Statute, including any financial obligations which may have accrued. Its withdrawal shall not affect any cooperation with the Court in connection with criminal investigations and proceedings in relation to which the withdrawing State had a duty to cooperate and which were commenced prior to the date on which the withdrawal became effective, nor shall it prejudice in any way the continued consideration of any matter which was already under consideration by the Court prior to the date on which the withdrawal became effective.

App8–129 **Article 128 Authentic texts**

The original of this Statute, of which the Arabic, Chinese, English, French, Russian and Spanish texts are equally authentic, shall be deposited with the Secretary-General of the United Nations, who shall send certified copies thereof to all States.

IN WITNESS WHEREOF, the undersigned, being duly authorized thereto by their respective Governments, have signed this Statute.

DONE at Rome, this 17th day of July 1998.

ELEMENTS OF CRIMES

GENERAL INTRODUCTION

1. Pursuant to article 9, the following Elements of Crimes shall assist the Court in the interpretation and application of articles 6, 7 and 8, consistent with the Statute. The provisions of the Statute, including article 21 and the general principles set out in Part 3, are applicable to the Elements of Crimes.

App9–001

2. As stated in article 30, unless otherwise provided, a person shall be criminally responsible and liable for punishment for a crime within the jurisdiction of the Court only if the material elements are committed with intent and knowledge. Where no reference is made in the Elements of Crimes to a mental element for any particular conduct, consequence or circumstance listed, it is understood that the relevant mental element, *i.e.*, intent, knowledge or both, set out in article 30 applies.

Exceptions to the article 30 standard, based on the Statute, including applicable law under its relevant provisions, are indicated below.

3. Existence of intent and knowledge can be inferred from relevant facts and circumstances.

4. With respect to mental elements associated with elements involving value judgement, such as those using the terms "inhumane" or "severe", it is not necessary that the perpetrator personally completed a particular value judgement, unless otherwise indicated.

5. Grounds for excluding criminal responsibility or the absence thereof are generally not specified in the elements of crimes listed under each crime.[1]

6. The requirement of "unlawfulness" found in the Statute or in other parts of international law, in particular international humanitarian law, is generally not specified in the elements of crimes.

7. The elements of crimes are generally structured in accordance with the following principles:

- As the elements of crimes focus on the conduct, consequences and circumstances associated with each crime, they are generally listed in that order;

- When required, a particular mental element is listed after the affected conduct, consequence or circumstance;

- Contextual circumstances are listed last.

8. As used in the Elements of Crimes, the term "perpetrator" is neutral as to guilt or innocence. The elements, including the appropriate mental elements, apply, *mutatis mutandis,* to all those whose criminal responsibility may fall under articles 25 and 28 of the Statute.

9. A particular conduct may constitute one or more crimes.

10. The use of short titles for the crimes has no legal effect.

App9–002 **Article 6 Genocide**

Introduction

With respect to the last element listed for each crime:

- The term "in the context of" would include the initial acts in an emerging pattern;

- The term "manifest" is an objective qualification;

- Notwithstanding the normal requirement for a mental element provided for in article 30, and recognizing that knowledge of the circumstances will usually be

addressed in proving genocidal intent, the appropriate requirement, if any, for a mental element regarding this circumstance will need to be decided by the Court on a case-by-case basis.

App9–003 **Article 6(a) Genocide by killing**

Elements

1. The perpetrator killed[2] one or more persons.
2. Such person or persons belonged to a particular national, ethnical, racial or religious group.
3. The perpetrator intended to destroy, in whole or in part, that national, ethnical, racial or religious group, as such.
4. The conduct took place in the context of a manifest pattern of similar conduct directed against that group or was conduct that could itself effect such destruction.

App9–004 **Article 6(b) Genocide by causing serious bodily or mental harm**

Elements

1. The perpetrator caused serious bodily or mental harm to one or more persons.[3]
2. Such person or persons belonged to a particular national, ethnical, racial or religious group.
3. The perpetrator intended to destroy, in whole or in part, that national, ethnical, racial or religious group, as such.
4. The conduct took place in the context of a manifest pattern of similar conduct directed against that group or was conduct that could itself effect such destruction.

App9–005 **Article 6(c) Genocide by deliberately inflicting conditions of life calculated to bring about physical destruction**

Elements

1. The perpetrator inflicted certain conditions of life upon one or more persons.
2. Such person or persons belonged to a particular national, ethnical, racial or religious group.
3. The perpetrator intended to destroy, in whole or in part, that national, ethnical, racial or religious group, as such.
4. The conditions of life were calculated to bring about the physical destruction of that group, in whole or in part.[4]
5. The conduct took place in the context of a manifest pattern of similar conduct directed against that group or was conduct that could itself effect such destruction.

Article 6(d) Genocide by imposing measures intended to prevent births

App9–006

Elements

1. The perpetrator imposed certain measures upon one or more persons.
2. Such person or persons belonged to a particular national, ethnical, racial or religious group.
3. The perpetrator intended to destroy, in whole or in part, that national, ethnical, racial or religious group, as such.
4. The measures imposed were intended to prevent births within that group.
5. The conduct took place in the context of a manifest pattern of similar conduct directed against that group or was conduct that could itself effect such destruction.

Article 6(e) Genocide by forcibly transferring children

App9–007

Elements

1. The perpetrator forcibly transferred one or more persons.[5]
2. Such person or persons belonged to a particular national, ethnical, racial or religious group.
3. The perpetrator intended to destroy, in whole or in part, that national, ethnical, racial or religious group, as such.
4. The transfer was from that group to another group.
5. The person or persons were under the age of 18 years.
6. The perpetrator knew, or should have known, that the person or persons were under the age of 18 years.
7. The conduct took place in the context of a manifest pattern of similar conduct directed against that group or was conduct that could itself effect such destruction. 8

Article 7 Crimes against humanity

App9–008

Introduction

1. Since article 7 pertains to international criminal law, its provisions, consistent with article 22, must be strictly construed, taking into account that crimes against humanity as defined in article 7 are among the most serious crimes of concern to the international community as a whole, warrant and entail individual criminal responsibility, and require conduct which is impermissible under generally applicable international law, as recognized by the principal legal systems of the world.

2. The last two elements for each crime against humanity describe the context in which the conduct must take place. These elements clarify the requisite participation in and knowledge of a widespread or systematic attack against a civilian population. However, the last element should not be interpreted as requiring proof that the perpetrator had knowledge of all characteristics of the attack or the precise details of the plan or policy of the State or organization. In the case of an emerging widespread or systematic attack against a civilian population, the intent clause of the last element indicates that this mental element is satisfied if the perpetrator intended to further such an attack.

3. "Attack directed against a civilian population" in these context elements is understood to mean a course of conduct involving the multiple commission of acts referred to in article 7, paragraph 1, of the Statute against any civilian population, pursuant to or in furtherance of a State or organizational policy to commit such attack. The acts need not constitute a military attack. It is understood that "policy to commit such attack" requires that the State or organization actively promote or encourage such an attack against a civilian population.[6]

App9–009 **Article 7 (1)(a) Crime against humanity of murder**

Elements

1. The perpetrator killed[7] one or more persons.
2. The conduct was committed as part of a widespread or systematic attack directed against a civilian population.
3. The perpetrator knew that the conduct was part of or intended the conduct to be part of a widespread or systematic attack against a civilian population.

App9–010 **Article 7 (1)(b) Crime against humanity of extermination**

Elements

1. The perpetrator killed[8] one or more persons, including by inflicting conditions of life calculated to bring about the destruction of part of a population.[9]
2. The conduct constituted, or took place as part of,[10] a mass killing of members of a civilian population.
3. The conduct was committed as part of a widespread or systematic attack directed against a civilian population.
4. The perpetrator knew that the conduct was part of or intended the conduct to be part of a widespread or systematic attack directed against a civilian population.

App9–011 **Article 7 (1)(c) Crime against humanity of enslavement**

Elements

1. The perpetrator exercised any or all of the powers attaching to the right of ownership over one or more persons, such as by purchasing, selling, lending or bartering such a person or persons, or by imposing on them a similar deprivation of liberty.[11]
2. The conduct was committed as part of a widespread or systematic attack directed against a civilian population.
3. The perpetrator knew that the conduct was part of or intended the conduct to be part of a widespread or systematic attack directed against a civilian population.

App9–012 **Article 7 (1)(d) Crime against humanity of deportation or forcible transfer of population**

Elements

1. The perpetrator deported or forcibly[12] transferred,[13] without grounds permitted under international law, one or more persons to another State or location, by expulsion or other coercive acts.
2. Such person or persons were lawfully present in the area from which they were so deported or transferred.
3. The perpetrator was aware of the factual circumstances that established the lawfulness of such presence.
4. The conduct was committed as part of a widespread or systematic attack directed against a civilian population.
5. The perpetrator knew that the conduct was part of or intended the conduct to be part of a widespread or systematic attack directed against a civilian population.

Article 7 (1)(e) Crime against humanity of imprisonment or other severe deprivation of physical liberty   App9–013

Elements

1. The perpetrator imprisoned one or more persons or otherwise severely deprived one or more persons of physical liberty.

2. The gravity of the conduct was such that it was in violation of fundamental rules of international law.

3. The perpetrator was aware of the factual circumstances that established the gravity of the conduct.

4. The conduct was committed as part of a widespread or systematic attack directed against a civilian population.

5. The perpetrator knew that the conduct was part of or intended the conduct to be part of a widespread or systematic attack directed against a civilian population.

Article 7 (1)(f) Crime against humanity of torture[14]   App9–014

Elements

1. The perpetrator inflicted severe physical or mental pain or suffering upon one or more persons.

2. Such person or persons were in the custody or under the control of the perpetrator.

3. Such pain or suffering did not arise only from, and was not inherent in or incidental to, lawful sanctions.

4. The conduct was committed as part of a widespread or systematic attack directed against a civilian population.

5. The perpetrator knew that the conduct was part of or intended the conduct to be part of a widespread or systematic attack directed against a civilian population.

Article 7 (1)(g)–1 Crime against humanity of rape   App9–015

Elements

1. The perpetrator invaded[15] the body of a person by conduct resulting in penetration, however slight, of any part of the body of the victim or of the perpetrator with a sexual organ, or of the anal or genital opening of the victim with any object or any other part of the body.

2. The invasion was committed by force, or by threat of force or coercion, such as that caused by fear of violence, duress, detention, psychological oppression or abuse of power, against such person or another person, or by taking advantage of a coercive environment, or the invasion was committed against a person incapable of giving genuine consent.[16]

3. The conduct was committed as part of a widespread or systematic attack directed against a civilian population.

4. The perpetrator knew that the conduct was part of or intended the conduct to be part of a widespread or systematic attack directed against a civilian population.

Article 7 (1)(g)–2 Crime against humanity of sexual slavery[17]   App9–016

Elements

1. The perpetrator exercised any or all of the powers attaching to the right of ownership over one or more persons, such as by purchasing, selling, lending or bartering such a person or persons, or by imposing on them a similar deprivation of liberty.[18]

2. The perpetrator caused such person or persons to engage in one or more acts of a sexual nature.

3. The conduct was committed as part of a widespread or systematic attack directed against a civilian population.

4. The perpetrator knew that the conduct was part of or intended the conduct to be part of a widespread or systematic attack directed against a civilian population.

App9–017   **Article 7 (1)(g)–3 Crime against humanity of enforced prostitution**

Elements

1. The perpetrator caused one or more persons to engage in one or more acts of a sexual nature by force, or by threat of force or coercion, such as that caused by fear of violence, duress, detention, psychological oppression or abuse of power, against such person or persons or another person, or by taking advantage of a coercive environment or such person's or persons" incapacity to give genuine consent.

2. The perpetrator or another person obtained or expected to obtain pecuniary or other advantage in exchange for or in connection with the acts of a sexual nature.

3. The conduct was committed as part of a widespread or systematic attack directed against a civilian population.

4. The perpetrator knew that the conduct was part of or intended the conduct to be part of a widespread or systematic attack directed against a civilian population.

App9–018   **Article 7 (1)(g)–4 Crime against humanity of forced pregnancy**

Elements

1. The perpetrator confined one or more women forcibly made pregnant, with the intent of affecting the ethnic composition of any population or carrying out other grave violations of international law.

2. The conduct was committed as part of a widespread or systematic attack directed against a civilian population.

3. The perpetrator knew that the conduct was part of or intended the conduct to be part of a widespread or systematic attack directed against a civilian population.

App9–019   **Article 7 (1)(g)–5 Crime against humanity of enforced sterilization**

Elements

1. The perpetrator deprived one or more persons of biological reproductive capacity.[19]

2. The conduct was neither justified by the medical or hospital treatment of the person or persons concerned nor carried out with their genuine consent.[20]

3. The conduct was committed as part of a widespread or systematic attack directed against a civilian population.

4. The perpetrator knew that the conduct was part of or intended the conduct to be part of a widespread or systematic attack directed against a civilian population.

App9–020   **Article 7 (1)(g)–6 Crime against humanity of sexual violence**

Elements

1. The perpetrator committed an act of a sexual nature against one or more persons or caused such person or persons to engage in an act of a sexual nature by force, or by threat of force or coercion, such as that caused by fear of violence, duress, deten-tion, psychological oppression or abuse of power, against such person or persons or

another person, or by taking advantage of a coercive environment or such person's or persons" incapacity to give genuine consent.

2. Such conduct was of a gravity comparable to the other offences in article 7, paragraph 1 (g), of the Statute.

3. The perpetrator was aware of the factual circumstances that established the gravity of the conduct.

4. The conduct was committed as part of a widespread or systematic attack directed against a civilian population.

5. The perpetrator knew that the conduct was part of or intended the conduct to be part of a widespread or systematic attack directed against a civilian population.

Article 7 (1)(h) Crime against humanity of persecution

App9–021

Elements

1. The perpetrator severely deprived, contrary to international law,[21] one or more persons of fundamental rights.

2. The perpetrator targeted such person or persons by reason of the identity of a group or collectivity or targeted the group or collectivity as such.

3. Such targeting was based on political, racial, national, ethnic, cultural, religious, gender as defined in article 7, paragraph 3, of the Statute, or other grounds that are universally recognized as impermissible under international law.

4. The conduct was committed in connection with any act referred to in article 7, paragraph 1, of the Statute or any crime within the jurisdiction of the Court.[22]

5. The conduct was committed as part of a widespread or systematic attack directed against a civilian population.

6. The perpetrator knew that the conduct was part of or intended the conduct to be part of a widespread or systematic attack directed against a civilian population.

Article 7 (1)(i) Crime against humanity of enforced disappearance of persons[23,24]

App9–022

Elements

1. The perpetrator:

    (a)   Arrested, detained[25,26] or abducted one or more persons; or

    (b)   Refused to acknowledge the arrest, detention or abduction, or to give information on the fate or whereabouts of such person or persons.

2. (a)   Such arrest, detention or abduction was followed or accompanied by a refusal to acknowledge that deprivation of freedom or to give information on the fate or whereabouts of such person or persons; or

    (b)   Such refusal was preceded or accompanied by that deprivation of freedom.

3. The perpetrator was aware that:[27]

    (a)   Such arrest, detention or abduction would be followed in the ordinary course of events by a refusal to acknowledge that deprivation of freedom or to give information on the fate or whereabouts of such person or persons;[28] or

    (b)   Such refusal was preceded or accompanied by that deprivation of freedom.

4. Such arrest, detention or abduction was carried out by, or with the authorization, support or acquiescence of, a State or a political organization.

5. Such refusal to acknowledge that deprivation of freedom or to give information on the fate or whereabouts of such person or persons was carried out by, or with the authorization or support of, such State or political organization.

6. The perpetrator intended to remove such person or persons from the protection of the law for a prolonged period of time.

7. The conduct was committed as part of a widespread or systematic attack directed against a civilian population.

8. The perpetrator knew that the conduct was part of or intended the conduct to be part of a widespread or systematic attack directed against a civilian population.

App9–023   **Article 7 (1)(j) Crime against humanity of apartheid**

Elements

1. The perpetrator committed an inhumane act against one or more persons.

2. Such act was an act referred to in article 7, paragraph 1, of the Statute, or was an act of a character similar to any of those acts.[29]

3. The perpetrator was aware of the factual circumstances that established the character of the act.

4. The conduct was committed in the context of an institutionalized regime of systematic oppression and domination by one racial group over any other racial group or groups.

5. The perpetrator intended to maintain such regime by that conduct.

6. The conduct was committed as part of a widespread or systematic attack directed against a civilian population.

7. The perpetrator knew that the conduct was part of or intended the conduct to be part of a widespread or systematic attack directed against a civilian population.

App9–024   **Article 7 (1)(k) Crime against humanity of other inhumane acts**

Elements

1. The perpetrator inflicted great suffering, or serious injury to body or to mental or physical health, by means of an inhumane act.

2. Such act was of a character similar to any other act referred to in article 7, paragraph 1, of the Statute.[30]

3. The perpetrator was aware of the factual circumstances that established the character of the act.

4. The conduct was committed as part of a widespread or systematic attack directed against a civilian population.

5. The perpetrator knew that the conduct was part of or intended the conduct to be part of a widespread or systematic attack directed against a civilian population.

App9–025   **Article 8 War crimes**

INTRODUCTION

The elements for war crimes under article 8, paragraph 2 (c) and (e), are subject to the limitations addressed in article 8, paragraph 2 (d) and (f), which are not elements of crimes.

The elements for war crimes under article 8, paragraph 2, of the Statute shall be interpreted within the established framework of the international law of armed conflict including, as appropriate, the international law of armed conflict applicable to armed conflict at sea.

With respect to the last two elements listed for each crime:

- There is no requirement for a legal evaluation by the perpetrator as to the existence of an armed conflict or its character as international or non-international;

- In that context there is no requirement for awareness by the perpetrator of the facts that established the character of the conflict as international or non-international;

- There is only a requirement for the awareness of the factual circumstances that established the existence of an armed conflict that is implicit in the terms "took place in the context of and was associated with".

Article 8 (2)(a)

Article 8 (2)(a)(i) War crime of wilful killing

App9–026

Elements

1. The perpetrator killed one or more persons.[31]

2. Such person or persons were protected under one or more of the Geneva Conventions of 1949.

3. The perpetrator was aware of the factual circumstances that established that protected status.[32,33]

4. The conduct took place in the context of and was associated with an international armed conflict.[34]

5. The perpetrator was aware of factual circumstances that established the existence of an armed conflict.

Article 8 (2)(a)(ii)-1 War crime of torture

App9–027

Elements[35]

1. The perpetrator inflicted severe physical or mental pain or suffering upon one or more persons.

2. The perpetrator inflicted the pain or suffering for such purposes as: obtaining information or a confession, punishment, intimidation or coercion or for any reason based on discrimination of any kind.

3. Such person or persons were protected under one or more of the Geneva Conventions of 1949.

4. The perpetrator was aware of the factual circumstances that established that protected status.

5. The conduct took place in the context of and was associated with an international armed conflict.

6. The perpetrator was aware of factual circumstances that established the existence of an armed conflict.

Article 8 (2)(a)(ii)-2 War crime of inhuman treatment

App9–028

Elements

1. The perpetrator inflicted severe physical or mental pain or suffering upon one or more persons.

2. Such person or persons were protected under one or more of the Geneva Conventions of 1949.

3. The perpetrator was aware of the factual circumstances that established that protected status.

4. The conduct took place in the context of and was associated with an international armed conflict.

5. The perpetrator was aware of factual circumstances that established the existence of an armed conflict.

App9–029 **Article 8 (2)(a)(ii)-3 War crime of biological experiments**

Elements

1. The perpetrator subjected one or more persons to a particular biological experiment.

2. The experiment seriously endangered the physical or mental health or integrity of such person or persons.

3. The intent of the experiment was non-therapeutic and it was neither justified by medical reasons nor carried out in such person's or persons" interest.

4. Such person or persons were protected under one or more of the Geneva Conventions of 1949.

5. The perpetrator was aware of the factual circumstances that established that protected status.

6. The conduct took place in the context of and was associated with an international armed conflict.

7. The perpetrator was aware of factual circumstances that established the existence of an armed conflict.

App9–030 **Article 8 (2)(a)(iii) War crime of wilfully causing great suffering**

Elements

1. The perpetrator caused great physical or mental pain or suffering to, or serious injury to body or health of, one or more persons.

2. Such person or persons were protected under one or more of the Geneva Conventions of 1949.

3. The perpetrator was aware of the factual circumstances that established that protected status.

4. The conduct took place in the context of and was associated with an international armed conflict.

5. The perpetrator was aware of factual circumstances that established the existence of an armed conflict.

App9–031 **Article 8 (2)(a)(iv) War crime of destruction and appropriation of property**

Elements

1. The perpetrator destroyed or appropriated certain property.

2. The destruction or appropriation was not justified by military necessity.

3. The destruction or appropriation was extensive and carried out wantonly. 20

4. Such property was protected under one or more of the Geneva Conventions of 1949.

5. The perpetrator was aware of the factual circumstances that established that protected status.

6. The conduct took place in the context of and was associated with an international armed conflict.

7. The perpetrator was aware of factual circumstances that established the existence of an armed conflict.

Article 8 (2)(a)(v) War crime of compelling service in hostile forces   App9–032

Elements

1. The perpetrator coerced one or more persons, by act or threat, to take part in military operations against that person's own country or forces or otherwise serve in the forces of a hostile power.

2. Such person or persons were protected under one or more of the Geneva Conventions of 1949.

3. The perpetrator was aware of the factual circumstances that established that protected status.

4. The conduct took place in the context of and was associated with an international armed conflict.

5. The perpetrator was aware of factual circumstances that established the existence of an armed conflict.

Article 8 (2)(a)(vi) War crime of denying a fair trial   App9–033

Elements

1. The perpetrator deprived one or more persons of a fair and regular trial by denying judicial guarantees as defined, in particular, in the third and the fourth Geneva Conventions of 1949.

2. Such person or persons were protected under one or more of the Geneva Conventions of 1949.

3. The perpetrator was aware of the factual circumstances that established that protected status.

4. The conduct took place in the context of and was associated with an international armed conflict.

5. The perpetrator was aware of factual circumstances that established the existence of an armed conflict. 21

Article 8 (2)(a)(vii)–1 War crime of unlawful deportation and transfer   App9–034

Elements

1. The perpetrator deported or transferred one or more persons to another State or to another location.

2. Such person or persons were protected under one or more of the Geneva Conventions of 1949.

3. The perpetrator was aware of the factual circumstances that established that protected status.

4. The conduct took place in the context of and was associated with an international armed conflict.

5. The perpetrator was aware of factual circumstances that established the existence of an armed conflict.

Article 8 (2)(a)(vii)–2 War crime of unlawful confinement   App9–035

Elements

1. The perpetrator confined or continued to confine one or more persons to a certain location.

2. Such person or persons were protected under one or more of the Geneva Conventions of 1949.

3. The perpetrator was aware of the factual circumstances that established that protected status.

4. The conduct took place in the context of and was associated with an international armed conflict.

5. The perpetrator was aware of factual circumstances that established the existence of an armed conflict.

App9–036 **Article 8 (2)(a)(viii) War crime of taking hostages**

Elements

1. The perpetrator seized, detained or otherwise held hostage one or more persons.

2. The perpetrator threatened to kill, injure or continue to detain such person or persons.

3. The perpetrator intended to compel a State, an international organization, a natural or legal person or a group of persons to act or refrain from acting as an explicit or implicit condition for the safety or the release of such person or persons.

4. Such person or persons were protected under one or more of the Geneva Conventions of 1949.

5. The perpetrator was aware of the factual circumstances that established that protected status.

6. The conduct took place in the context of and was associated with an international armed conflict.

7. The perpetrator was aware of factual circumstances that established the existence of an armed conflict.

Article 8 (2)(b)

App9–037 **Article 8 (2)(b)(i) War crime of attacking civilians**

Elements

1. The perpetrator directed an attack.

2. The object of the attack was a civilian population as such or individual civilians not taking direct part in hostilities.

3. The perpetrator intended the civilian population as such or individual civilians not taking direct part in hostilities to be the object of the attack.

4. The conduct took place in the context of and was associated with an international armed conflict.

5. The perpetrator was aware of factual circumstances that established the existence of an armed conflict.

App9–038 **Article 8 (2)(b)(ii) War crime of attacking civilian objects**

Elements

1. The perpetrator directed an attack.

2. The object of the attack was civilian objects, that is, objects which are not military objectives.

3. The perpetrator intended such civilian objects to be the object of the attack.

4. The conduct took place in the context of and was associated with an international armed conflict.

5. The perpetrator was aware of factual circumstances that established the existence of an armed conflict.

Article 8 (2)(b)(iii) War crime of attacking personnel or objects involved in a humanitarian assistance or peacekeeping mission   App9–039

Elements

1. The perpetrator directed an attack.

2. The object of the attack was personnel, installations, material, units or vehicles involved in a humanitarian assistance or peacekeeping mission in accordance with the Charter of the United Nations.

3. The perpetrator intended such personnel, installations, material, units or vehicles so involved to be the object of the attack.

4. Such personnel, installations, material, units or vehicles were entitled to that protection given to civilians or civilian objects under the international law of armed conflict.

5. The perpetrator was aware of the factual circumstances that established that protection.

6. The conduct took place in the context of and was associated with an international armed conflict.

7. The perpetrator was aware of factual circumstances that established the existence of an armed conflict.

Article 8 (2)(b)(iv) War crime of excessive incidental death, injury, or damage   App9–040

Elements

1. The perpetrator launched an attack.

2. The attack was such that it would cause incidental death or injury to civilians or damage to civilian objects or widespread, long-term and severe damage to the natural environment and that such death, injury or damage would be of such an extent as to be clearly excessive in relation to the concrete and direct overall military advantage anticipated.[36]

3. The perpetrator knew that the attack would cause incidental death or injury to civilians or damage to civilian objects or widespread, long-term and severe damage to the natural environment and that such death, injury or damage would be of such an extent as to be clearly excessive in relation to the concrete and direct overall military advantage anticipated.[37]

4. The conduct took place in the context of and was associated with an international armed conflict.

5. The perpetrator was aware of factual circumstances that established the existence of an armed conflict.

Article 8 (2)(b)(v) War crime of attacking undefended places[38]   App9–041

Elements

1. The perpetrator attacked one or more towns, villages, dwellings or buildings.

2. Such towns, villages, dwellings or buildings were open for unresisted occupation.

3. Such towns, villages, dwellings or buildings did not constitute military objectives.

4. The conduct took place in the context of and was associated with an international armed conflict.

5. The perpetrator was aware of factual circumstances that established the existence of an armed conflict.

App9–042   **Article 8 (2)(b)(vi) War crime of killing or wounding a person *hors de combat***

Elements

1. The perpetrator killed or injured one or more persons.
2. Such person or persons were *hors de combat.*
3. The perpetrator was aware of the factual circumstances that established this status.
4. The conduct took place in the context of and was associated with an international armed conflict.
5. The perpetrator was aware of factual circumstances that established the existence of an armed conflict.

App9–043   **Article 8 (2)(b)(vii)-1 War crime of improper use of a flag of truce**

Elements

1. The perpetrator used a flag of truce.
2. The perpetrator made such use in order to feign an intention to negotiate when there was no such intention on the part of the perpetrator.
3. The perpetrator knew or should have known of the prohibited nature of such use.[39]
4. The conduct resulted in death or serious personal injury.
5. The perpetrator knew that the conduct could result in death or serious personal injury.
6. The conduct took place in the context of and was associated with an international armed conflict.
7. The perpetrator was aware of factual circumstances that established the existence of an armed conflict.

App9–044   **Article 8 (2)(b)(vii)–2 War crime of improper use of a flag, insignia or uniform of the hostile party**

Elements

1. The perpetrator used a flag, insignia or uniform of the hostile party.
2. The perpetrator made such use in a manner prohibited under the international law of armed conflict while engaged in an attack.
3. The perpetrator knew or should have known of the prohibited nature of such use.[40]
4. The conduct resulted in death or serious personal injury.
5. The perpetrator knew that the conduct could result in death or serious personal injury.
6. The conduct took place in the context of and was associated with an international armed conflict.
7. The perpetrator was aware of factual circumstances that established the existence of an armed conflict.

App9–045   **Article 8 (2)(b)(vii)-3 War crime of improper use of a flag, insignia or uniform of the United Nations**

Elements

1. The perpetrator used a flag, insignia or uniform of the United Nations.
2. The perpetrator made such use in a manner prohibited under the international law of armed conflict.

3. The perpetrator knew of the prohibited nature of such use.[41]

4. The conduct resulted in death or serious personal injury.

5. The perpetrator knew that the conduct could result in death or serious personal injury.

6. The conduct took place in the context of and was associated with an international armed conflict.

7. The perpetrator was aware of factual circumstances that established the existence of an armed conflict.

Article 8 (2) b)(vii)-4 War crime of improper use of the distinctive emblems of the Geneva Conventions

App9–046

Elements

1. The perpetrator used the distinctive emblems of the Geneva Conventions.

2. The perpetrator made such use for combatant purposes[42] in a manner prohibited under the international law of armed conflict.

3. The perpetrator knew or should have known of the prohibited nature of such use.[43]

4. The conduct resulted in death or serious personal injury.

5. The perpetrator knew that the conduct could result in death or serious personal injury.

6. The conduct took place in the context of and was associated with an international armed conflict.

7. The perpetrator was aware of factual circumstances that established the existence of an armed conflict.

Article 8 (2)(b)(viii) The transfer, directly or indirectly, by the Occupying Power of parts of its own civilian population into the territory it occupies, or the deportation or transfer of all or parts of the population of the occupied territory within or outside this territory

App9–047

Elements

1. The perpetrator:

    (a) Transferred,[44] directly or indirectly, parts of its own population into the territory it occupies; or

    (b) Deported or transferred all or parts of the population of the occupied territory within or outside this territory.

2. The conduct took place in the context of and was associated with an international armed conflict.

3. The perpetrator was aware of factual circumstances that established the existence of an armed conflict.

Article 8 (2)(b)(ix) War crime of attacking protected objects[45]

App9–048

Elements

1. The perpetrator directed an attack.

2. The object of the attack was one or more buildings dedicated to religion, education, art, science or charitable purposes, historic monuments, hospitals or places where the sick and wounded are collected, which were not military objectives.

3. The perpetrator intended such building or buildings dedicated to religion, education, art, science or charitable purposes, historic monuments, hospitals or places

where the sick and wounded are collected, which were not military objectives, to be the object of the attack.

4. The conduct took place in the context of and was associated with an international armed conflict.

5. The perpetrator was aware of factual circumstances that established the existence of an armed conflict.

App9–049   **Article 8 (2)(b)(x)–1 War crime of mutilation**

Elements

1. The perpetrator subjected one or more persons to mutilation, in particular by permanently disfiguring the person or persons, or by permanently disabling or removing an organ or appendage.

2. The conduct caused death or seriously endangered the physical or mental health of such person or persons.

3. The conduct was neither justified by the medical, dental or hospital treatment of the person or persons concerned nor carried out in such person's or persons" interest.[46]

4. Such person or persons were in the power of an adverse party.

5. The conduct took place in the context of and was associated with an international armed conflict.

6. The perpetrator was aware of factual circumstances that established the existence of an armed conflict.

App9–050   **Article 8 (2)(b)(x)–2 War crime of medical or scientific experiments**

Elements

1. The perpetrator subjected one or more persons to a medical or scientific experiment.

2. The experiment caused death or seriously endangered the physical or mental health or integrity of such person or persons.

3. The conduct was neither justified by the medical, dental or hospital treatment of such person or persons concerned nor carried out in such person's or persons" interest.

4. Such person or persons were in the power of an adverse party.

5. The conduct took place in the context of and was associated with an international armed conflict.

6. The perpetrator was aware of factual circumstances that established the existence of an armed conflict.

App9–051   **Article 8 (2)(b)(xi) War crime of treacherously killing or wounding**

Elements

1. The perpetrator invited the confidence or belief of one or more persons that they were entitled to, or were obliged to accord, protection under rules of international law applicable in armed conflict.

2. The perpetrator intended to betray that confidence or belief.

3. The perpetrator killed or injured such person or persons.

4. The perpetrator made use of that confidence or belief in killing or injuring such person or persons.

5. Such person or persons belonged to an adverse party.

6. The conduct took place in the context of and was associated with an international armed conflict.

7. The perpetrator was aware of factual circumstances that established the existence of an armed conflict.

Article 8 (2)(b)(xii) War crime of denying quarter | App9–052

Elements

1. The perpetrator declared or ordered that there shall be no survivors.

2. Such declaration or order was given in order to threaten an adversary or to conduct hostilities on the basis that there shall be no survivors.

3. The perpetrator was in a position of effective command or control over the subordinate forces to which the declaration or order was directed.

4. The conduct took place in the context of and was associated with an international armed conflict.

5. The perpetrator was aware of factual circumstances that established the existence of an armed conflict.

Article 8 (2)(b)(xiii) War crime of destroying or seizing the enemy's property | App9–053

Elements

1. The perpetrator destroyed or seized certain property.

2. Such property was property of a hostile party.

3. Such property was protected from that destruction or seizure under the international law of armed conflict.

4. The perpetrator was aware of the factual circumstances that established the status of the property.

5. The destruction or seizure was not justified by military necessity.

6. The conduct took place in the context of and was associated with an international armed conflict.

7. The perpetrator was aware of factual circumstances that established the existence of an armed conflict.

Article 8 (2)(b)(xiv) War crime of depriving the nationals of the hostile power of rights or actions | App9–054

Elements

1. The perpetrator effected the abolition, suspension or termination of admissibility in a court of law of certain rights or actions.

2. The abolition, suspension or termination was directed at the nationals of a hostile party.

3. The perpetrator intended the abolition, suspension or termination to be directed at the nationals of a hostile party.

4. The conduct took place in the context of and was associated with an international armed conflict.

5. The perpetrator was aware of factual circumstances that established the existence of an armed conflict.

Article 8 (2)(b)(xv) War crime of compelling participation in military operations | App9–055

Elements

1. The perpetrator coerced one or more persons by act or threat to take part in military operations against that person's own country or forces.

2. Such person or persons were nationals of a hostile party.

3. The conduct took place in the context of and was associated with an international armed conflict.

4. The perpetrator was aware of factual circumstances that established the existence of an armed conflict.

App9–056   **Article 8 (2)(b)(xvi) War crime of pillaging**

Elements

1. The perpetrator appropriated certain property.

2. The perpetrator intended to deprive the owner of the property and to appropriate it for private or personal use.[47]

3. The appropriation was without the consent of the owner.

4. The conduct took place in the context of and was associated with an international armed conflict.

5. The perpetrator was aware of factual circumstances that established the existence of an armed conflict.

App9–057   **Article 8 (2)(b)(xvii) War crime of employing poison or poisoned weapons**

Elements

1. The perpetrator employed a substance or a weapon that releases a substance as a result of its employment.

2. The substance was such that it causes death or serious damage to health in the ordinary course of events, through its toxic properties.

3. The conduct took place in the context of and was associated with an international armed conflict.

4. The perpetrator was aware of factual circumstances that established the existence of an armed conflict.

App9–058   **Article 8 (2)(b)(xviii) War crime of employing prohibited gases, liquids, materials or devices**

Elements

1. The perpetrator employed a gas or other analogous substance or device.

2. The gas, substance or device was such that it causes death or serious damage to health in the ordinary course of events, through its asphyxiating or toxic properties.[48]

3. The conduct took place in the context of and was associated with an international armed conflict.

4. The perpetrator was aware of factual circumstances that established the existence of an armed conflict.

App9–059   **Article 8 (2)(b)(xix) War crime of employing prohibited bullets**

Elements

1. The perpetrator employed certain bullets.

2. The bullets were such that their use violates the international law of armed conflict because they expand or flatten easily in the human body.

3. The perpetrator was aware that the nature of the bullets was such that their employment would uselessly aggravate suffering or the wounding effect.

4. The conduct took place in the context of and was associated with an international armed conflict.

5. The perpetrator was aware of factual circumstances that established the existence of an armed conflict.

Article 8 (2)(b)(xx) War crime of employing weapons, projectiles or materials or methods of warfare listed in the Annex to the Statute

App9–060

Elements

[Elements will have to be drafted once weapons, projectiles or material or methods of warfare have been included in an annex to the Statute.]

Article 8 (2)(b)(xxi) War crime of outrages upon personal dignity

App9–061

Elements

1. The perpetrator humiliated, degraded or otherwise violated the dignity of one or more persons.[49]
2. The severity of the humiliation, degradation or other violation was of such degree as to be generally recognized as an outrage upon personal dignity.
3. The conduct took place in the context of and was associated with an international armed conflict.
4. The perpetrator was aware of factual circumstances that established the existence of an armed conflict.

Article 8 (2)(b)(xxii)–1 War crime of rape

App9–062

Elements

1. The perpetrator invaded[50] the body of a person by conduct resulting in penetration, however slight, of any part of the body of the victim or of the
   perpetrator with a sexual organ, or of the anal or genital opening of the victim with any object or any other part of the body.
2. The invasion was committed by force, or by threat of force or coercion, such as that caused by fear of violence, duress, detention, psychological oppression or
   abuse of power, against such person or another person, or by taking advantage of a coercive environment, or the invasion was committed against a person incapable of giving genuine consent.[51]
3. The conduct took place in the context of and was associated with an international armed conflict.
4. The perpetrator was aware of factual circumstances that established the existence of an armed conflict.

Article 8 (2)(b)(xxii)–2 War crime of sexual slavery[52]

App9–063

Elements

1. The perpetrator exercised any or all of the powers attaching to the right of ownership over one or more persons, such as by purchasing, selling, lending or bartering such a person or persons, or by imposing on them a similar deprivation of liberty.[53]
2. The perpetrator caused such person or persons to engage in one or more acts of a sexual nature.
3. The conduct took place in the context of and was associated with an international armed conflict.
4. The perpetrator was aware of factual circumstances that established the existence of an armed conflict.

App9–064   **Article 8 (2)(b)(xxii)–3 War crime of enforced prostitution**

Elements

1. The perpetrator caused one or more persons to engage in one or more acts of a sexual nature by force, or by threat of force or coercion, such as that caused by fear of violence, duress, detention, psychological oppression or abuse of power, against such person or persons or another person, or by taking advantage of a coercive environment or such person's or persons" incapacity to give genuine consent.

2. The perpetrator or another person obtained or expected to obtain pecuniary or other advantage in exchange for or in connection with the acts of a sexual nature.

3. The conduct took place in the context of and was associated with an international armed conflict.

4. The perpetrator was aware of factual circumstances that established the existence of an armed conflict.

App9–065   **Article 8 (2)(b)(xxii)–4 War crime of forced pregnancy**

Elements

1. The perpetrator confined one or more women forcibly made pregnant, with the intent of affecting the ethnic composition of any population or carrying out other grave violations of international law.

2. The conduct took place in the context of and was associated with an international armed conflict.

3. The perpetrator was aware of factual circumstances that established the existence of an armed conflict.

App9–066   **Article 8 (2)(b)(xxii)–5 War crime of enforced sterilization**

Elements

1. The perpetrator deprived one or more persons of biological reproductive capacity.[54]

2. The conduct was neither justified by the medical or hospital treatment of the person or persons concerned nor carried out with their genuine consent.[55]

3. The conduct took place in the context of and was associated with an international armed conflict.

4. The perpetrator was aware of factual circumstances that established the existence of an armed conflict.

App9–067   **Article 8 (2)(b)(xxii)–6 War crime of sexual violence**

Elements

1. The perpetrator committed an act of a sexual nature against one or more persons or caused such person or persons to engage in an act of a sexual nature by force, or by threat of force or coercion, such as that caused by fear of violence, duress, detention, psychological oppression or abuse of power, against such person or persons or another person, or by taking advantage of a coercive environment or such person's or persons" incapacity to give genuine consent.

2. The conduct was of a gravity comparable to that of a grave breach of the Geneva Conventions.

3. The perpetrator was aware of the factual circumstances that established the gravity of the conduct.

4. The conduct took place in the context of and was associated with an international armed conflict.

5. The perpetrator was aware of factual circumstances that established the existence of an armed conflict.

Article 8 (2)(b)(xxiii) War crime of using protected persons as shields

Elements

1. The perpetrator moved or otherwise took advantage of the location of one or more civilians or other persons protected under the international law of armed conflict.

2. The perpetrator intended to shield a military objective from attack or shield, favour or impede military operations.

3. The conduct took place in the context of and was associated with an international armed conflict.

4. The perpetrator was aware of factual circumstances that established the existence of an armed conflict.

Article 8 (2)(b)(xxiv) War crime of attacking objects or persons using the distinctive emblems of the Geneva Conventions

Elements

1. The perpetrator attacked one or more persons, buildings, medical units or transports or other objects using, in conformity with international law, a distinctive emblem or other method of identification indicating protection under the Geneva Conventions.

2. The perpetrator intended such persons, buildings, units or transports or other objects so using such identification to be the object of the attack.

3. The conduct took place in the context of and was associated with an international armed conflict.

4. The perpetrator was aware of factual circumstances that established the existence of an armed conflict.

Article 8 (2)(b)(xxv) War crime of starvation as a method of warfare

Elements

1. The perpetrator deprived civilians of objects indispensable to their survival.

2. The perpetrator intended to starve civilians as a method of warfare.

3. The conduct took place in the context of and was associated with an international armed conflict.

4. The perpetrator was aware of factual circumstances that established the existence of an armed conflict.

Article 8 (2)(b)(xxvi) War crime of using, conscripting or enlisting children

Elements

1. The perpetrator conscripted or enlisted one or more persons into the national armed forces or used one or more persons to participate actively in hostilities.

2. Such person or persons were under the age of 15 years.

3. The perpetrator knew or should have known that such person or persons were under the age of 15 years.

4. The conduct took place in the context of and was associated with an international armed conflict.

5. The perpetrator was aware of factual circumstances that established the existence of an armed conflict.

Article 8 (2)(c)

App9–072   **Article 8 (2)(c)(i)–1 War crime of murder**

Elements

1. The perpetrator killed one or more persons.
2. Such person or persons were either *hors de combat,* or were civilians, medical personnel, or religious personnel[56] taking no active part in the hostilities.
3. The perpetrator was aware of the factual circumstances that established this status.
4. The conduct took place in the context of and was associated with an armed conflict not of an international character.
5. The perpetrator was aware of factual circumstances that established the existence of an armed conflict.

App9–073   **Article 8 (2)(c)(i)-2 War crime of mutilation**

Elements

1. The perpetrator subjected one or more persons to mutilation, in particular by permanently disfiguring the person or persons, or by permanently disabling or removing an organ or appendage.
2. The conduct was neither justified by the medical, dental or hospital treatment of the person or persons concerned nor carried out in such person's or persons" interests.
3. Such person or persons were either *hors de combat,* or were civilians, medical personnel or religious personnel taking no active part in the hostilities.
4. The perpetrator was aware of the factual circumstances that established this status.
5. The conduct took place in the context of and was associated with an armed conflict not of an international character.
6. The perpetrator was aware of factual circumstances that established the existence of an armed conflict.

App9–074   **Article 8 (2)(c)(i)–3 War crime of cruel treatment**

Elements

1. The perpetrator inflicted severe physical or mental pain or suffering upon one or more persons.
2. Such person or persons were either *hors de combat,* or were civilians, medical personnel, or religious personnel taking no active part in the hostilities.
3. The perpetrator was aware of the factual circumstances that established this status.
4. The conduct took place in the context of and was associated with an armed conflict not of an international character.
5. The perpetrator was aware of factual circumstances that established the existence of an armed conflict.

App9–075   **Article 8 (2)(c)(i)–4 War crime of torture**

Elements

1. The perpetrator inflicted severe physical or mental pain or suffering upon one or more persons.

2. The perpetrator inflicted the pain or suffering for such purposes as: obtaining information or a confession, punishment, intimidation or coercion or for any reason based on discrimination of any kind.

3. Such person or persons were either *hors de combat,* or were civilians, medical personnel or religious personnel taking no active part in the hostilities.

4. The perpetrator was aware of the factual circumstances that established this status.

5. The conduct took place in the context of and was associated with an armed conflict not of an international character.

6. The perpetrator was aware of factual circumstances that established the existence of an armed conflict.

Article 8(2)(c)(ii) War crime of outrages upon personal dignity

App9–076

Elements

1. The perpetrator humiliated, degraded or otherwise violated the dignity of one or more persons.[57]

2. The severity of the humiliation, degradation or other violation was of such degree as to be generally recognized as an outrage upon personal dignity.

3. Such person or persons were either *hors de combat,* or were civilians, medical personnel or religious personnel taking no active part in the hostilities.

4. The perpetrator was aware of the factual circumstances that established this status.

5. The conduct took place in the context of and was associated with an armed conflict not of an international character.

6. The perpetrator was aware of factual circumstances that established the existence of an armed conflict.

Article 8 (2)(c)(iii) War crime of taking hostages

App9–077

Elements

1. The perpetrator seized, detained or otherwise held hostage one or more persons.

2. The perpetrator threatened to kill, injure or continue to detain such person or persons.

3. The perpetrator intended to compel a State, an international organization, a natural or legal person or a group of persons to act or refrain from acting as an explicit or implicit condition for the safety or the release of such person or persons.

4. Such person or persons were either *hors de combat,* or were civilians, medical personnel or religious personnel taking no active part in the hostilities.

5. The perpetrator was aware of the factual circumstances that established this status.

6. The conduct took place in the context of and was associated with an armed conflict not of an international character.

7. The perpetrator was aware of factual circumstances that established the existence of an armed conflict.

Article 8 (2)(c)(iv) War crime of sentencing or execution without due process

App9–078

Elements

1. The perpetrator passed sentence or executed one or more persons.[58]

2. Such person or persons were either *hors de combat,* or were civilians, medical personnel or religious personnel taking no active part in the hostilities.

3. The perpetrator was aware of the factual circumstances that established this status.

4. There was no previous judgement pronounced by a court, or the court that rendered judgement was not "regularly constituted", that is, it did not afford the essential guarantees of independence and impartiality, or the court that rendered judgement did not afford all other judicial guarantees generally recognized as indispensable under international law.[59]

5. The perpetrator was aware of the absence of a previous judgement or of the denial of relevant guarantees and the fact that they are essential or indispensable to a fair trial.

6. The conduct took place in the context of and was associated with an armed not of an international character.

7. The perpetrator was aware of factual circumstances that established the existence of an armed conflict.

Article 8 (2)(e)

App9–079
Article 8 (2)(e)(i) War crime of attacking civilians

Elements

1. The perpetrator directed an attack.
2. The object of the attack was a civilian population as such or individual civilians not taking direct part in hostilities.
3. The perpetrator intended the civilian population as such or individual civilians not taking direct part in hostilities to be the object of the attack.
4. The conduct took place in the context of and was associated with an armed conflict not of an international character.
5. The perpetrator was aware of factual circumstances that established the existence of an armed conflict.

App9–080
Article 8 (2)(e)(ii) War crime of attacking objects or persons using the distinctive emblems of the Geneva Conventions

Elements

1. The perpetrator attacked one or more persons, buildings, medical units or transports or other objects using, in conformity with international law, a distinctive emblem or other method of identification indicating protection under the Geneva Conventions.
2. The perpetrator intended such persons, buildings, units or transports or other objects so using such identification to be the object of the attack.
3. The conduct took place in the context of and was associated with an armed conflict not of an international character.
4. The perpetrator was aware of factual circumstances that established the existence of an armed conflict.

App9–081
Article 8 (2)(e)(iii) War crime of attacking personnel or objects involved in a humanitarian assistance or peacekeeping mission

Elements

1. The perpetrator directed an attack.
2. The object of the attack was personnel, installations, material, units or vehicles involved in a humanitarian assistance or peacekeeping mission in accordance with the Charter of the United Nations.

3. The perpetrator intended such personnel, installations, material, units or vehicles so involved to be the object of the attack.

4. Such personnel, installations, material, units or vehicles were entitled to that protection given to civilians or civilian objects under the international law of armed conflict.

5. The perpetrator was aware of the factual circumstances that established that protection.

6. The conduct took place in the context of and was associated with an armed conflict not of an international character.

7. The perpetrator was aware of factual circumstances that established the existence of an armed conflict.

Article 8 (2)(e)(iv) War crime of attacking protected objects[60]   App9–082

Elements

1. The perpetrator directed an attack.

2. The object of the attack was one or more buildings dedicated to religion, education, art, science or charitable purposes, historic monuments, hospitals or places where the sick and wounded are collected, which were not military objectives.

3. The perpetrator intended such building or buildings dedicated to religion, education, art, science or charitable purposes, historic monuments, hospitals or places where the sick and wounded are collected, which were not military objectives, to be the object of the attack.

4. The conduct took place in the context of and was associated with an armed conflict not of an international character.

5. The perpetrator was aware of factual circumstances that established the existence of an armed conflict.

Article 8 (2)(e)(v) War crime of pillaging   App9–083

Elements

1. The perpetrator appropriated certain property.

2. The perpetrator intended to deprive the owner of the property and to appropriate it for private or personal use.[61]

3. The appropriation was without the consent of the owner.

4. The conduct took place in the context of and was associated with an armed conflict not of an international character.

5. The perpetrator was aware of factual circumstances that established the existence of an armed conflict.

Article 8 (2)(e)(vi)–1 War crime of rape   App9–084

Elements

1. The perpetrator invaded[62] the body of a person by conduct resulting in penetration, however slight, of any part of the body of the victim or of the perpetrator with a sexual organ, or of the anal or genital opening of the victim with any object or any other part of the body.

2. The invasion was committed by force, or by threat of force or coercion, such as that caused by fear of violence, duress, detention, psychological oppression or abuse of power, against such person or another person, or by taking advantage of a coercive environment, or the invasion was committed against a person incapable of giving genuine consent.[63]

3. The conduct took place in the context of and was associated with an armed conflict not of an international character.

4. The perpetrator was aware of factual circumstances that established the existence of an armed conflict.

App9–085   **Article 8 (2)(e)(vi)–2 War crime of sexual slavery**[64]

Elements

1. The perpetrator exercised any or all of the powers attaching to the right of ownership over one or more persons, such as by purchasing, selling, lending or bartering such a person or persons, or by imposing on them a similar deprivation of liberty.[65]

2. The perpetrator caused such person or persons to engage in one or more acts of a sexual nature.

3. The conduct took place in the context of and was associated with an armed conflict not of an international character.

4. The perpetrator was aware of factual circumstances that established the existence of an armed conflict.

App9–086   **Article 8 (2)(e)(vi)–3 War crime of enforced prostitution**

Elements

1. The perpetrator caused one or more persons to engage in one or more acts of a sexual nature by force, or by threat of force or coercion, such as that caused by fear

of violence, duress, detention, psychological oppression or abuse of power, against such person or persons or another person, or by taking advantage of a coercive environment or such person's or persons" incapacity to give genuine consent.

2. The perpetrator or another person obtained or expected to obtain pecuniary or other advantage in exchange for or in connection with the acts of a sexual nature.

3. The conduct took place in the context of and was associated with an armed conflict not of an international character.

4. The perpetrator was aware of factual circumstances that established the existence of an armed conflict.

App9–087   **Article 8 (2)(e)(vi)-4 War crime of forced pregnancy**

Elements

1. The perpetrator confined one or more women forcibly made pregnant, with the intent of affecting the ethnic composition of any population or carrying out other grave violations of international law.

2. The conduct took place in the context of and was associated with an armed conflict not of an international character.

3. The perpetrator was aware of factual circumstances that established the existence of an armed conflict.

App9–088   **Article 8 (2)(e)(vi)–5 War crime of enforced sterilization**

Elements

1. The perpetrator deprived one or more persons of biological reproductive capacity.[66]

2. The conduct was neither justified by the medical or hospital treatment of the person or persons concerned nor carried out with their genuine consent.[67]

3. The conduct took place in the context of and was associated with an armed conflict not of an international character.

4. The perpetrator was aware of factual circumstances that established the existence of an armed conflict.

Article 8 (2)(e)(vi)-6 War crime of sexual violence

App9–089

Elements

1. The perpetrator committed an act of a sexual nature against one or more persons or caused such person or persons to engage in an act of a sexual nature by force, or by threat of force or coercion, such as that caused by fear of violence, duress, detention, psychological oppression or abuse of power, against such person or persons or another person, or by taking advantage of a coercive environment or such person's or persons" incapacity to give genuine consent.

2. The conduct was of a gravity comparable to that of a serious violation of article 3 common to the four Geneva Conventions.

3. The perpetrator was aware of the factual circumstances that established the gravity of the conduct.

4. The conduct took place in the context of and was associated with an armed conflict not of an international character.

5. The perpetrator was aware of factual circumstances that established the existence of an armed conflict.

Article 8 (2)(e)(vii) War crime of using, conscripting and enlisting children

App9–090

Elements

1. The perpetrator conscripted or enlisted one or more persons into an armed force or group or used one or more persons to participate actively in hostilities.

2. Such person or persons were under the age of 15 years.

3. The perpetrator knew or should have known that such person or persons were under the age of 15 years.

4. The conduct took place in the context of and was associated with an armed conflict not of an international character.

5. The perpetrator was aware of factual circumstances that established the existence of an armed conflict.

Article 8 (2)(e)(viii) War crime of displacing civilians

App9–091

Elements

1. The perpetrator ordered a displacement of a civilian population.

2. Such order was not justified by the security of the civilians involved or by military necessity.

3. The perpetrator was in a position to effect such displacement by giving such order.

4. The conduct took place in the context of and was associated with an armed conflict not of an international character.

5. The perpetrator was aware of factual circumstances that established the existence of an armed conflict.

Article 8 (2)(e)(ix) War crime of treacherously killing or wounding

App9–092

Elements

1. The perpetrator invited the confidence or belief of one or more combatant adversaries that they were entitled to, or were obliged to accord, protection under rules of international law applicable in armed conflict.

2. The perpetrator intended to betray that confidence or belief.

3. The perpetrator killed or injured such person or persons.

4. The perpetrator made use of that confidence or belief in killing or injuring such person or persons.

5. Such person or persons belonged to an adverse party.

6. The conduct took place in the context of and was associated with an armed conflict not of an international character.

7. The perpetrator was aware of factual circumstances that established the existence of an armed conflict.

App9–093   **Article 8 (2)(e)(x) War crime of denying quarter**

Elements

1. The perpetrator declared or ordered that there shall be no survivors.

2. Such declaration or order was given in order to threaten an adversary or to conduct hostilities on the basis that there shall be no survivors.

3. The perpetrator was in a position of effective command or control over the subordinate forces to which the declaration or order was directed.

4. The conduct took place in the context of and was associated with an armed conflict not of an international character.

5. The perpetrator was aware of factual circumstances that established the existence of an armed conflict.

App9–094   **Article 8 (2)(e)(xi)–1 War crime of mutilation**

Elements

1. The perpetrator subjected one or more persons to mutilation, in particular by permanently disfiguring the person or persons, or by permanently disabling or removing an organ or appendage.

2. The conduct caused death or seriously endangered the physical or mental health of such person or persons.

3. The conduct was neither justified by the medical, dental or hospital treatment of the person or persons concerned nor carried out in such person's or persons" interest.[68]

4. Such person or persons were in the power of another party to the conflict.

5. The conduct took place in the context of and was associated with an armed conflict not of an international character.

6. The perpetrator was aware of factual circumstances that established the existence of an armed conflict.

App9–095   **Article 8 (2)(e)(xi)-2 War crime of medical or scientific experiments**

Elements

1. The perpetrator subjected one or more persons to a medical or scientific experiment.

2. The experiment caused the death or seriously endangered the physical or mental health or integrity of such person or persons.

3. The conduct was neither justified by the medical, dental or hospital treatment of such person or persons concerned nor carried out in such person's or persons" interest.

4. Such person or persons were in the power of another party to the conflict.

5. The conduct took place in the context of and was associated with an armed conflict not of an international character.

6. The perpetrator was aware of factual circumstances that established the existence of an armed conflict.

Article 8 (2)(e)(xii) War crime of destroying or seizing the enemy's property

Elements

1. The perpetrator destroyed or seized certain property.

2. Such property was property of an adversary.

3. Such property was protected from that destruction or seizure under the international law of armed conflict.

4. The perpetrator was aware of the factual circumstances that established the status of the property.

5. The destruction or seizure was not required by military necessity.

6. The conduct took place in the context of and was associated with an armed conflict not of an international character.

7. The perpetrator was aware of factual circumstances that established the existence of an armed conflict. 48

---

[1] This paragraph is without prejudice to the obligation of the Prosecutor under article 54, paragraph 1, of the Statute. 5

[2] The term "killed" is interchangeable with the term "caused death".

[3] This conduct may include, but is not necessarily restricted to, acts of torture, rape, sexual violence or inhuman or degrading treatment. 6

[4] The term "conditions of life" may include, but is not necessarily restricted to, deliberate deprivation of resources indispensable for survival, such as food or medical services, or systematic expulsion from homes.

[5] The term "forcibly" is not restricted to physical force, but may include threat of force or coercion, such as that caused by fear of violence, duress, detention, psychological oppression or abuse of power, against such person or persons or another person, or by taking advantage of a coercive environment.

[6] A policy which has a civilian population as the object of the attack would be implemented by State or organizational action. Such a policy may, in exceptional circumstances, be implemented by a deliberate failure to take action, which is consciously aimed at encouraging such attack. The existence of such a policy cannot be inferred solely from the absence of governmental or organizational action.

[7] The term "killed" is interchangeable with the term "caused death". This footnote applies to all elements which use either of these concepts.

[8] The conduct could be committed by different methods of killing, either directly or indirectly.

[9] The infliction of such conditions could include the deprivation of access to food and medicine.

[10] The term "as part of" would include the initial conduct in a mass killing.

[11] It is understood that such deprivation of liberty may, in some circumstances, include exacting forced labour or otherwise reducing a person to a servile status as defined in the Supplementary Convention on the Abolition of Slavery, the Slave Trade, and Institutions and Practices Similar to Slavery of 1956. It is also understood that the conduct described in this element includes trafficking in persons, in particular women and children.

[12] The term "forcibly" is not restricted to physical force, but may include threat of force or coercion, such as that caused by fear of violence, duress, detention, psychological oppression or abuse of power against such person or persons or another person, or by taking advantage of a coercive environment.

[13] "Deported or forcibly transferred" is interchangeable with "forcibly displaced".

[14] It is understood that no specific purpose need be proved for this crime.

[15] The concept of "invasion" is intended to be broad enough to be gender-neutral.

[16] It is understood that a person may be incapable of giving genuine consent if affected by natural, induced or age-related incapacity. This footnote also applies to the corresponding elements of article 7 (1) (g)-3, 5 and 6.

[17] Given the complex nature of this crime, it is recognized that its commission could involve more than one perpetrator as a part of a common criminal purpose.

[18] It is understood that such deprivation of liberty may, in some circumstances, include exacting forced labour or otherwise reducing a person to a servile status as defined in the Supplementary Convention on the Abolition of Slavery, the Slave Trade, and Institutions and Practices Similar to Slavery of 1956. It is also understood that the conduct described in this element includes trafficking in persons, in particular women and children.

[19] The deprivation is not intended to include birth-control measures which have a non-permanent effect in practice.

[20] It is understood that "genuine consent" does not include consent obtained through deception.

[21] This requirement is without prejudice to paragraph 6 of the General Introduction to the Elements of Crimes.

[22] It is understood that no additional mental element is necessary for this element other than that inherent in element 6.

[23] Given the complex nature of this crime, it is recognized that its commission will normally involve more than one perpetrator as a part of a common criminal purpose.

[24] This crime falls under the jurisdiction of the Court only if the attack referred to in elements 7 and 8 occurs after the entry into force of the Statute.

[25] The word "detained" would include a perpetrator who maintained an existing detention.

[26] It is understood that under certain circumstances an arrest or detention may have been lawful.

[27] This element, inserted because of the complexity of this crime, is without prejudice to the General Introduction to the Elements of Crimes.

[28] It is understood that, in the case of a perpetrator who maintained an existing detention, this element would be satisfied if the perpetrator was aware that such a refusal had already taken place.

[29] It is understood that "character" refers to the nature and gravity of the act.

[30] It is understood that "character" refers to the nature and gravity of the act.

[31] The term "killed" is interchangeable with the term "caused death". This footnote applies to all elements which use either of these concepts.

[32] This mental element recognizes the interplay between articles 30 and 32. This footnote also applies to the corresponding element in each crime under article 8 (2) (a), and to the element in other crimes in article 8 (2) concerning the awareness of factual circumstances that establish the status of persons or property protected under the relevant international law of armed conflict.

[33] With respect to nationality, it is understood that the perpetrator needs only to know that the victim belonged to an adverse party to the conflict. This footnote also applies to the corresponding element in each crime under article 8 (2) (a).

[34] The term "international armed conflict" includes military occupation. This footnote also applies to the corresponding element in each crime under article 8 (2) (a).

[35] As element 3 requires that all victims must be "protected persons" under one or more of the Geneva Conventions of 1949, these elements do not include the custody or control requirement found in the elements of article 7 (1) (e).

[36] The expression "concrete and direct overall military advantage" refers to a military advantage that is foreseeable by the perpetrator at the relevant time. Such advantage may or may not be temporally or geographically related to the object of the attack. The fact that this crime admits the possibility of lawful incidental injury and collateral damage does not in any way justify any violation of the law applicable in armed conflict. It does not address justifications for war or other rules related to *jus ad bellum*. It reflects the proportionality requirement inherent in determining the legality of any military activity undertaken in the context of an armed conflict.

[37] As opposed to the general rule set forth in paragraph 4 of the General Introduction, this knowledge element requires that the perpetrator make the value judgement as described therein. An evaluation of that value judgement must be based on the requisite information available to the perpetrator at the time.

[38] The presence in the locality of persons specially protected under the Geneva Conventions of 1949 or of police forces retained for the sole purpose of maintaining law and order does not by itself render the locality a military objective.

[39] This mental element recognizes the interplay between article 30 and article 32. The term "prohibited nature" denotes illegality.

[40] This mental element recognizes the interplay between article 30 and article 32. The term "prohibited nature" denotes illegality.

[41] This mental element recognizes the interplay between article 30 and article 32. The "should have known" test required in the other offences found in article 8 (2) (b) (vii) is not applicable here because of the variable and regulatory nature of the relevant prohibitions.

[42] "Combatant purposes" in these circumstances means purposes directly related to hostilities and not including medical, religious or similar activities.

[43] This mental element recognizes the interplay between article 30 and article 32. The term "prohibited nature" denotes illegality.

[44] The term "transfer" needs to be interpreted in accordance with the relevant provisions of international humanitarian law.

[45] The presence in the locality of persons specially protected under the Geneva Conventions of 1949 or of police forces retained for the sole purpose of maintaining law and order does not by itself render the locality a military objective.

[46] Consent is not a defence to this crime. The crime prohibits any medical procedure which is not indicated by the state of health of the person concerned and which is not consistent with generally accepted medical standards which would be applied under similar medical circumstances to persons who are nationals of the party conducting the procedure and who are in no way deprived of liberty. This footnote also applies to the same element for article 8 (2) (b) (x)-2.

[47] As indicated by the use of the term "private or personal use", appropriations justified by military necessity cannot constitute the crime of pillaging.

[48] Nothing in this element shall be interpreted as limiting or prejudicing in any way existing or developing rules of international law with respect to the development, production, stockpiling and use of chemical weapons.

[49] For this crime, "persons" can include dead persons. It is understood that the victim need not personally be aware of the existence of the humiliation or degradation or other violation. This element takes into account relevant aspects of the cultural background of the victim.

[50] The concept of "invasion" is intended to be broad enough to be gender-neutral.

[51] It is understood that a person may be incapable of giving genuine consent if affected by natural, induced or age-related incapacity. This footnote also applies to the corresponding elements of article 8 (2) (b) (xxii)-3, 5 and 6.

[52] Given the complex nature of this crime, it is recognized that its commission could involve more than one perpetrator as a part of a common criminal purpose.

[53] It is understood that such deprivation of liberty may, in some circumstances, include exacting forced labour or otherwise reducing a person to servile status as defined in the Supplementary Convention on the Abolition of Slavery, the Slave Trade, and Institutions and Practices Similar to Slavery of 1956. It is also understood that the conduct described in this element includes trafficking in persons, in particular women and children.

[54] The deprivation is not intended to include birth-control measures which have a non-permanent effect in practice.

[55] It is understood that "genuine consent" does not include consent obtained through deception.

[56] The term "religious personnel" includes those non-confessional non-combatant military personnel carrying out a similar function.

[57] For this crime, "persons" can include dead persons. It is understood that the victim need not personally be aware of the existence of the humiliation or degradation or other violation. This element takes into account relevant aspects of the cultural background of the victim.

[58] The elements laid down in these documents do not address the different forms of individual criminal responsibility, as enunciated in articles 25 and 28 of the Statute.

[59] With respect to elements 4 and 5, the Court should consider whether, in the light of all relevant circumstances, the cumulative effect of factors with respect to guarantees deprived the person or persons of a fair trial.

[60] The presence in the locality of persons specially protected under the Geneva Conventions of 1949 or of police forces retained for the sole purpose of maintaining law and order does not by itself render the locality a military objective.

[61] As indicated by the use of the term "private or personal use", appropriations justified by military necessity cannot constitute the crime of pillaging.

[62] The concept of "invasion" is intended to be broad enough to be gender-neutral.

[63] It is understood that a person may be incapable of giving genuine consent if affected by natural, induced or age-related incapacity. This footnote also applies to the corresponding elements in article 8 (2) (e) (vi)-3, 5 and 6.

[64] Given the complex nature of this crime, it is recognized that its commission could involve more than one perpetrator as a part of a common criminal purpose.

[65] It is understood that such deprivation of liberty may, in some circumstances, include exacting forced labour or otherwise reducing a person to servile status as defined in the Supplementary Convention on the Abolition of Slavery, the Slave Trade, and Institutions and Practices Similar to Slavery of 1956. It is also understood that the conduct described in this element includes trafficking in persons, in particular women and children.

[66] The deprivation is not intended to include birth-control measures which have a non-permanent effect in practice.

[67] It is understood that "genuine consent" does not include consent obtained through deception.

[68] Consent is not a defence to this crime. The crime prohibits any medical procedure which is not indicated by the state of health of the person concerned and which is not consistent with generally accepted medical standards which would be applied under similar medical circumstances to persons who are nationals of the party conducting the procedure and who are in no way deprived of liberty. This footnote also applies to the similar element in article 8 (2)(e)(xi)–2.

INTERNATIONAL CONVENTION FOR THE
SUPPRESSION OF TERRORIST BOMBINGS

The States Parties to this Convention,   **App10–001**

Having in mind the purposes and principles of the Charter of the United Nations concerning the maintenance of international peace and security and the promotion of good-neighbourliness and friendly relations and cooperation among States,

Deeply concerned about the worldwide escalation of acts of terrorism in all its forms and manifestations,

Recalling the Declaration on the Occasion of the Fiftieth Anniversary of the United Nations of 24 October 1995,

Recalling also the Declaration on Measures to Eliminate International Terrorism, annexed to General Assembly resolution 49/60 of 9 December 1994, in which, *inter alia*, "the States Members of the United Nations solemnly reaffirm their unequivocal condemnation of all acts, methods and practices of terrorism as criminal and unjustifiable, wherever and by whomever committed, including those which jeopardize the friendly relations among States and peoples and threaten the territorial integrity and security of States",

Noting that the Declaration also encouraged States "to review urgently the scope of the existing international legal provisions on the prevention, repression and elimination of terrorism in all its forms and manifestations, with the aim of ensuring that there is a comprehensive legal framework covering all aspects of the matter",

Recalling General Assembly resolution 51/210 of 17 December 1996 and the Declaration to Supplement the 1994 Declaration on Measures to Eliminate International Terrorism annexed thereto,

Noting that terrorist attacks by means of explosives or other lethal devices have become increasingly widespread,

Noting also that existing multilateral legal provisions do not adequately address these attacks,

Being convinced of the urgent need to enhance international cooperation between States in devising and adopting effective and practical measures for the prevention of such acts of terrorism and for the prosecution and punishment of their perpetrators,

Considering that the occurrence of such acts is a matter of grave concern to the international community as a whole,

Noting that the activities of military forces of States are governed by rules of international law outside the framework of this Convention and that the exclusion of certain actions from the coverage of this Convention does not condone or make lawful otherwise unlawful acts, or preclude prosecution under other laws,

Have agreed as follows:

Article 1   **App10–002**

For the purposes of this Convention

1. 'state or government facility" includes any permanent or temporary facility or conveyance that is used or occupied by representatives of a State, members of

Government, the legislature or the judiciary or by officials or employees of a State or any other public authority or entity or by employees or officials of an intergovernmental organization in connection with their official duties.

2. "Infrastructure facility" means any publicly or privately owned facility providing or distributing services for the benefit of the public, such as water, sewage, energy, fuel or communications.

3. "Explosive or other lethal device" means:

(a) An explosive or incendiary weapon or device that is designed, or has the capability, to cause death, serious bodily injury or substantial material damage; or

(b) A weapon or device that is designed, or has the capability, to cause death, serious bodily injury or substantial material damage through the release, dissemination or impact of toxic chemicals, biological agents or toxins or similar substances or radiation or radioactive material.

4. "Military forces of a State" means the armed forces of a State which are organized, trained and equipped under its internal law for the primary purpose of national defence or security and persons acting in support of those armed forces who are under their formal command, control and responsibility.

5. "Place of public use" means those parts of any building, land, street, waterway or other location that are accessible or open to members of the public, whether continuously, periodically or occasionally, and encompasses any commercial, business, cultural, historical, educational, religious, governmental, entertainment, recreational or similar place that is so accessible or open to the public.

6. "Public transportation system" means all facilities, conveyances and instrumentalities, whether publicly or privately owned, that are used in or for publicly available services for the transportation of persons or cargo.

App10–003 **Article 2**

1. Any person commits an offence within the meaning of this Convention if that person unlawfully and intentionally delivers, places, discharges or detonates an explosive or other lethal device in, into or against a place of public use, a State or government facility, a public transportation system or an infrastructure facility:

(a) With the intent to cause death or serious bodily injury; or

(b) With the intent to cause extensive destruction of such a place, facility or system, where such destruction results in or is likely to result in major economic loss.

2. Any person also commits an offence if that person attempts to commit an offence as set forth in paragraph 1 of the present article.

3. Any person also commits an offence if that person:

(a) Participates as an accomplice in an offence as set forth in paragraph 1 or 2 of the present article; or

(b) Organizes or directs others to commit an offence as set forth in paragraph 1 or 2 of the present article; or

(c) In any other way contributes to the commission of one or more offences as set forth in paragraph 1 or 2 of the present article by a group of persons acting with a common purpose; such contribution shall be intentional and either be made with the aim of furthering the general criminal activity or purpose of the group or be made in the knowledge of the intention of the group to commit the offence or offences concerned.

Article 3

App10–004

This Convention shall not apply where the offence is committed within a single State, the alleged offender and the victims are nationals of that State, the alleged offender is found in the territory of that State and no other State has a basis under article 6, paragraph 1 or paragraph 2, of this Convention to exercise jurisdiction, except that the provisions of articles 10 to 15 shall, as appropriate, apply in those cases.

Article 4

App10–005

Each State Party shall adopt such measures as may be necessary:

(a) To establish as criminal offences under its domestic law the offences set forth in article 2 of this Convention;

(b) To make those offences punishable by appropriate penalties which take into account the grave nature of those offences.

Article 5

App10–006

Each State Party shall adopt such measures as may be necessary, including, where appropriate, domestic legislation, to ensure that criminal acts within the scope of this Convention, in particular where they are intended or calculated to provoke a state of terror in the general public or in a group of persons or particular persons, are under no circumstances justifiable by considerations of a political, philosophical, ideological, racial, ethnic, religious or other similar nature and are punished by penalties consistent with their grave nature.

Article 6

App10–007

1. Each State Party shall take such measures as may be necessary to establish its jurisdiction over the offences set forth in article 2 when:

(a) The offence is committed in the territory of that State; or

(b) The offence is committed on board a vessel flying the flag of that State or an aircraft which is registered under the laws of that State at the time the offence is committed; or

(c) The offence is committed by a national of that State.

2. A State Party may also establish its jurisdiction over any such offence when:

(a) The offence is committed against a national of that State; or

(b) The offence is committed against a State or government facility of that State abroad, including an embassy or other diplomatic or consular premises of that State; or

(c) The offence is committed by a stateless person who has his or her habitual residence in the territory of that State; or

(d) The offence is committed in an attempt to compel that State to do or abstain from doing any act; or

(e) The offence is committed on board an aircraft which is operated by the Government of that State.

3. Upon ratifying, accepting, approving or acceding to this Convention, each State Party shall notify the Secretary-General of the United Nations of the jurisdiction it has established under its domestic law in accordance with paragraph 2 of the present article. Should any change take place, the State Party concerned shall immediately notify the Secretary-General.

4. Each State Party shall likewise take such measures as may be necessary to establish its jurisdiction over the offences set forth in article 2 in cases where the alleged offender is present in its territory and it does not extradite that person to any of the States Parties which have established their jurisdiction in accordance with paragraph 1 or 2 of the present article.

5. This Convention does not exclude the exercise of any criminal jurisdiction established by a State Party in accordance with its domestic law.

App10–008 **Article 7**

1. Upon receiving information that a person who has committed or who is alleged to have committed an offence as set forth in article 2 may be present in its territory, the State Party concerned shall take such measures as may be necessary under its domestic law to investigate the facts contained in the information.

2. Upon being satisfied that the circumstances so warrant, the State Party in whose territory the offender or alleged offender is present shall take the appropriate measures under its domestic law so as to ensure that person's presence for the purpose of prosecution or extradition.

3. Any person regarding whom the measures referred to in paragraph 2 of the present article are being taken shall be entitled to:

(a) Communicate without delay with the nearest appropriate representative of the State of which that person is a national or which is otherwise entitled to protect that person's rights or, if that person is a stateless person, the State in the territory of which that person habitually resides;

(b) Be visited by a representative of that State;

(c) Be informed of that person's rights under subparagraphs (a) and (b).

4. The rights referred to in paragraph 3 of the present article shall be exercised in conformity with the laws and regulations of the State in the territory of which the offender or alleged offender is present, subject to the provision that the said laws and regulations must enable full effect to be given to the purposes for which the rights accorded under paragraph 3 are intended.

5. The provisions of paragraphs 3 and 4 of the present article shall be without prejudice to the right of any State Party having a claim to jurisdiction in accordance with article 6, subparagraph 1 (c) or 2 (c), to invite the International Committee of the Red Cross to communicate with and visit the alleged offender.

6. When a State Party, pursuant to the present article, has taken a person into custody, it shall immediately notify, directly or through the Secretary-General of the

United Nations, the States Parties which have established jurisdiction in accordance with article 6, paragraphs 1 and 2, and, if it considers it advisable, any other interested States Parties, of the fact that that person is in custody and of the circumstances which warrant that person's detention. The State which makes the investigation contemplated in paragraph 1 of the present article shall promptly inform the said States Parties of its findings and shall indicate whether it intends to exercise jurisdiction.

Article 8 App10–009

1. The State Party in the territory of which the alleged offender is present shall, in cases to which article 6 applies, if it does not extradite that person, be obliged, without exception whatsoever and whether or not the offence was committed in its territory, to submit the case without undue delay to its competent authorities for the purpose of prosecution, through proceedings in accordance with the laws of that State. Those authorities shall take their decision in the same manner as in the case of any other offence of a grave nature under the law of that State.

2. Whenever a State Party is permitted under its domestic law to extradite or otherwise surrender one of its nationals only upon the condition that the person will be returned to that State to serve the sentence imposed as a result of the trial or proceeding for which the extradition or surrender of the person was sought, and this State and the State seeking the extradition of the person agree with this option and other terms they may deem appropriate, such a conditional extradition or surrender shall be sufficient to discharge the obligation set forth in paragraph 1 of the present article.

Article 9 App10–010

1. The offences set forth in article 2 shall be deemed to be included as extraditable offences in any extradition treaty existing between any of the States Parties before the entry into force of this Convention. States Parties undertake to include such offences as extraditable offences in every extradition treaty to be subsequently concluded between them.

2. When a State Party which makes extradition conditional on the existence of a treaty receives a request for extradition from another State Party with which it has no extradition treaty, the requested State Party may, at its option, consider this Convention as a legal basis for extradition in respect of the offences set forth in article 2. Extradition shall be subject to the other conditions provided by the law of the requested State.

3. States Parties which do not make extradition conditional on the existence of a treaty shall recognize the offences set forth in article 2 as extraditable offences between themselves, subject to the conditions provided by the law of the requested State.

4. If necessary, the offences set forth in article 2 shall be treated, for the purposes of extradition between States Parties, as if they had been committed not only in the place in which they occurred but also in the territory of the States that have established jurisdiction in accordance with article 6, paragraphs 1 and 2.

5. The provisions of all extradition treaties and arrangements between States Parties with regard to offences set forth in article 2 shall be deemed to be modified as between State Parties to the extent that they are incompatible with this Convention.

Article 10 App10–011

1. States Parties shall afford one another the greatest measure of assistance in connection with investigations or criminal or extradition proceedings brought in respect of the offences set forth in article 2, including assistance in obtaining evidence at their disposal necessary for the proceedings.

2. States Parties shall carry out their obligations under paragraph 1 of the present article in conformity with any treaties or other arrangements on mutual legal assistance that may exist between them. In the absence of such treaties or arrangements, States Parties shall afford one another assistance in accordance with their domestic law.

App10–012 **Article 11**

None of the offences set forth in article 2 shall be regarded, for the purposes of extradition or mutual legal assistance, as a political offence or as an offence connected with a political offence or as an offence inspired by political motives. Accordingly, a request for extradition or for mutual legal assistance based on such an offence may not be refused on the sole ground that it concerns a political offence or an offence connected with a political offence or an offence inspired by political motives.

App10–013 **Article 12**

Nothing in this Convention shall be interpreted as imposing an obligation to extradite or to afford mutual legal assistance, if the requested State Party has substantial grounds for believing that the request for extradition for offences set forth in article 2 or for mutual legal assistance with respect to such offences has been made for the purpose of prosecuting or punishing a person on account of that person's race, religion, nationality, ethnic origin or political opinion or that compliance with the request would cause prejudice to that person's position for any of these reasons.

App10–014 **Article 13**

1. A person who is being detained or is serving a sentence in the territory of one State Party whose presence in another State Party is requested for purposes of testimony, identification or otherwise providing assistance in obtaining evidence for the investigation or prosecution of offences under this Convention may be transferred if the following conditions are met:

(a)   The person freely gives his or her informed consent; and

(b)   The competent authorities of both States agree, subject to such conditions as those States may deem appropriate.

2. For the purposes of the present article:

(a)   The State to which the person is transferred shall have the authority and obligation to keep the person transferred in custody, unless otherwise requested or authorized by the State from which the person was transferred;

(b)   The State to which the person is transferred shall without delay implement its obligation to return the person to the custody of the State from which the person was transferred as agreed beforehand, or as otherwise agreed, by the competent authorities of both States;

(c)   The State to which the person is transferred shall not require the State from which the person was transferred to initiate extradition proceedings for the return of the person;

(d)   The person transferred shall receive credit for service of the sentence being served in the State from which he was transferred for time spent in the custody of the State to which he was transferred.

3. Unless the State Party from which a person is to be transferred in accordance with the present article so agrees, that person, whatever his or her nationality, shall not be prosecuted or detained or subjected to any other restriction of his or her personal liberty in the territory of the State to which that person is transferred in respect of acts or convictions anterior to his or her departure from the territory of the State from which such person was transferred.

Article 14   App10–015

Any person who is taken into custody or regarding whom any other measures are taken or proceedings are carried out pursuant to this Convention shall be guaranteed fair treatment, including enjoyment of all rights and guarantees in conformity with the law of the State in the territory of which that person is present and applicable provisions of international law, including international law of human rights.

Article 15   App10–016

States Parties shall cooperate in the prevention of the offences set forth in article 2, particularly:

(a) By taking all practicable measures, including, if necessary, adapting their domestic legislation, to prevent and counter preparations in their respective territories for the commission of those offences within or outside their territories, including measures to prohibit in their territories illegal activities of persons, groups and organizations that encourage, instigate, organize, knowingly finance or engage in the perpetration of offences as set forth in article 2;

(b) By exchanging accurate and verified information in accordance with their national law, and coordinating administrative and other measures taken as appropriate to prevent the commission of offences as set forth in article 2;

(c) Where appropriate, through research and development regarding methods of detection of explosives and other harmful substances that can cause death or bodily injury, consultations on the development of standards for marking explosives in order to identify their origin in post-blast investigations, exchange of information on preventive measures, cooperation and transfer of technology, equipment and related materials.

Article 16   App10–017

The State Party where the alleged offender is prosecuted shall, in accordance with its domestic law or applicable procedures, communicate the final outcome of the proceedings to the Secretary-General of the United Nations, who shall transmit the information to the other States Parties.

Article 17   App10–018

The States Parties shall carry out their obligations under this Convention in a manner consistent with the principles of sovereign equality and territorial integrity of States and that of non-intervention in the domestic affairs of other States.

Article 18   App10–019

Nothing in this Convention entitles a State Party to undertake in the territory of another State Party the exercise of jurisdiction and performance of functions which are exclusively reserved for the authorities of that other State Party by its domestic law.

App10–020   Article 19

1. Nothing in this Convention shall affect other rights, obligations and responsibilities of States and individuals under international law, in particular the purposes and principles of the Charter of the United Nations and international humanitarian law.

2. The activities of armed forces during an armed conflict, as those terms are understood under international humanitarian law, which are governed by that law, are not governed by this Convention, and the activities undertaken by military forces of a State in the exercise of their official duties, inasmuch as they are governed by other rules of international law, are not governed by this Convention.

App10–021   Article 20

1. Any dispute between two or more States Parties concerning the interpretation or application of this Convention which cannot be settled through negotiation within a reasonable time shall, at the request of one of them, be submitted to arbitration. If, within six months from the date of the request for arbitration, the parties are unable to agree on the organization of the arbitration, any one of those parties may refer the dispute to the International Court of Justice, by application, in conformity with the Statute of the Court.

2. Each State may at the time of signature, ratification, acceptance or approval of this Convention or accession thereto declare that it does not consider itself bound by paragraph 1 of the present article. The other States Parties shall not be bound by paragraph 1 with respect to any State Party which has made such a reservation.

3. Any State which has made a reservation in accordance with paragraph 2 of the present article may at any time withdraw that reservation by notification to the Secretary-General of the United Nations.

App10–022   Article 21

1. This Convention shall be open for signature by all States from 12 January 1998 until 31 December 1999 at United Nations Headquarters in New York.

2. This Convention is subject to ratification, acceptance or approval. The instruments of ratification, acceptance or approval shall be deposited with the Secretary-General of the United Nations.

3. This Convention shall be open to accession by any State. The instruments of accession shall be deposited with the Secretary-General of the United Nations.

App10–023   Article 22

1. This Convention shall enter into force on the thirtieth day following the date of the deposit of the twenty-second instrument of ratification, acceptance, approval or accession with the Secretary-General of the United Nations.

2. For each State ratifying, accepting, approving or acceding to the Convention after the deposit of the twenty-second instrument of ratification, acceptance, approval or accession, the Convention shall enter into force on the thirtieth day after deposit by such State of its instrument of ratification, acceptance, approval or accession.

App10–024   Article 23

1. Any State Party may denounce this Convention by written notification to the Secretary-General of the United Nations.

2. Denunciation shall take effect one year following the date on which notification is received by the Secretary-General of the United Nations.

Article 24

The original of this Convention, of which the Arabic, Chinese, English, French, Russian and Spanish texts are equally authentic, shall be deposited with the Secretary-General of the United Nations, who shall send certified copies thereof to all States.

INTERNATIONAL CONVENTION FOR THE SUPPRESSION OF THE FINANCING OF TERRORISM

PREAMBLE

The States Parties to this Convention,   **App11–001**
Bearing in mind the purposes and principles of the Charter of the United Nations concerning the maintenance of international peace and security and the promotion of good-neighbourliness and friendly relations and cooperation among States,

Deeply concerned about the worldwide escalation of acts of terrorism in all its forms and manifestations,

Recalling the Declaration on the Occasion of the Fiftieth Anniversary of the United Nations, contained in General Assembly resolution 50/6 of 24 October 1995,

Recalling also all the relevant General Assembly resolutions on the matter, including resolution 49/60 of 9 December 1994 and its annex on the Declaration on Measures to Eliminate International Terrorism, in which the States Members of the United Nations solemnly reaffirmed their unequivocal condemnation of all acts, methods and practices of terrorism as criminal and unjustifiable, wherever and by whomever committed, including those which jeopardize the friendly relations among States and peoples and threaten the territorial integrity and security of States,

Noting that the Declaration on Measures to Eliminate International Terrorism also encouraged States to review urgently the scope of the existing international legal provisions on the prevention, repression and elimination of terrorism in all its forms and manifestations, with the aim of ensuring that there is a comprehensive legal framework covering all aspects of the matter,

Recalling General Assembly resolution 51/210 of 17 December 1996, paragraph 3, subparagraph (f), in which the Assembly called upon all States to take steps to prevent and counteract, through appropriate domestic measures, the financing of terrorists and terrorist organizations, whether such financing is direct or indirect through organizations which also have or claim to have charitable, social or cultural goals or which are also engaged in unlawful activities such as illicit arms trafficking, drug dealing and racketeering, including the exploitation of persons for purposes of funding terrorist activities, and in particular to consider, where appropriate, adopting regulatory measures to prevent and counteract movements of funds suspected to be intended for terrorist purposes without impeding in any way the freedom of legitimate capital movements and to intensify the exchange of information concerning international movements of such funds,

Recalling also General Assembly resolution 52/165 of 15 December 1997, in which the Assembly called upon States to consider, in particular, the implementation of the measures set out in paragraphs 3 (a) to (f) of its resolution 51/210 of 17 December 1996,

Recalling further General Assembly resolution 53/108 of 8 December 1998, in which the Assembly decided that the Ad Hoc Committee established by General Assembly resolution 51/210 of 17 December 1996 should elaborate a draft international convention for the suppression of terrorist financing to supplement related existing international instruments,

Considering that the financing of terrorism is a matter of grave concern to the international community as a whole,

Noting that the number and seriousness of acts of international terrorism depend on the financing that terrorists may obtain,

Noting also that existing multilateral legal instruments do not expressly address such financing,

Being convinced of the urgent need to enhance international cooperation among States in devising and adopting effective measures for the prevention of the financing of terrorism, as well as for its suppression through the prosecution and punishment of its perpetrators,

Have agreed as follows:

App1–002   **Article 1**

For the purposes of this Convention:

1. "Funds" means assets of every kind, whether tangible or intangible, movable or immovable, however acquired, and legal documents or instruments in any form, including electronic or digital, evidencing title to, or interest in, such assets, including, but not limited to, bank credits, travellers cheques, bank cheques, money orders, shares, securities, bonds, drafts, letters of credit.

2. "A State or governmental facility" means any permanent or temporary facility or conveyance that is used or occupied by representatives of a State, members of Government, the legislature or the judiciary or by officials or employees of a State or any other public authority or entity or by employees or officials of an intergovernmental organization in connection with their official duties.

3. "Proceeds" means any funds derived from or obtained, directly or indirectly, through the commission of an offence set forth in article 2.

App1–003   **Article 2**

1. Any person commits an offence within the meaning of this Convention if that person by any means, directly or indirectly, unlawfully and wilfully, provides or collects funds with the intention that they should be used or in the knowledge that they are to be used, in full or in part, in order to carry out:

(a)   An act which constitutes an offence within the scope of and as defined in one of the treaties listed in the annex; or

(b)   Any other act intended to cause death or serious bodily injury to a civilian, or to any other person not taking an active part in the hostilities in a situation of armed conflict, when the purpose of such act, by its nature or context, is to intimidate a population, or to compel a government or an international organization to do or to abstain from doing any act.

2. (a)   On depositing its instrument of ratification, acceptance, approval or accession, a State Party which is not a party to a treaty listed in the annex may declare that, in the application of this Convention to the State Party, the treaty shall be deemed not to be included in the annex referred to in paragraph 1, subparagraph (a). The declaration shall cease to have effect as soon as the treaty enters into force for the State Party, which shall notify the depositary of this fact;

(b)   When a State Party ceases to be a party to a treaty listed in the annex, it may make a declaration as provided for in this article, with respect to that treaty.

3. For an act to constitute an offence set forth in paragraph 1, it shall not be necessary that the funds were actually used to carry out an offence referred to in paragraph 1, subparagraphs (a) or (b).

4. Any person also commits an offence if that person attempts to commit an offence as set forth in paragraph 1 of this article.

5. Any person also commits an offence if that person:

    (a) Participates as an accomplice in an offence as set forth in paragraph 1 or 4 of this article;

    (b) Organizes or directs others to commit an offence as set forth in paragraph 1 or 4 of this article;

    (c) Contributes to the commission of one or more offences as set forth in paragraphs 1 or 4 of this article by a group of persons acting with a common purpose. Such contribution shall be intentional and shall either:

        (i) Be made with the aim of furthering the criminal activity or criminal purpose of the group, where such activity or purpose involves the commission of an offence as set forth in paragraph 1 of this article; or

        (ii) Be made in the knowledge of the intention of the group to commit an offence as set forth in paragraph 1 of this article.

Article 3
App11–004

This Convention shall not apply where the offence is committed within a single State, the alleged offender is a national of that State and is present in the territory of that State and no other State has a basis under article 7, paragraph 1, or article 7, paragraph 2, to exercise jurisdiction, except that the provisions of articles 12 to 18 shall, as appropriate, apply in those cases.

Article 4
App11–005

Each State Party shall adopt such measures as may be necessary:

    (a) To establish as criminal offences under its domestic law the offences set forth in article 2;

    (b) To make those offences punishable by appropriate penalties which take into account the grave nature of the offences.

Article 5
App11–006

1. Each State Party, in accordance with its domestic legal principles, shall take the necessary measures to enable a legal entity located in its territory or organized under its laws to be held liable when a person responsible for the management or control of that legal entity has, in that capacity, committed an offence set forth in article 2. Such liability may be criminal, civil or administrative.

2. Such liability is incurred without prejudice to the criminal liability of individuals having committed the offences.

3. Each State Party shall ensure, in particular, that legal entities liable in accordance with paragraph 1 above are subject to effective, proportionate and dissuasive criminal, civil or administrative sanctions. Such sanctions may include monetary sanctions.

App11–007 Article 6

Each State Party shall adopt such measures as may be necessary, including, where appropriate, domestic legislation, to ensure that criminal acts within the scope of this Convention are under no circumstances justifiable by considerations of a political, philosophical, ideological, racial, ethnic, religious or other similar nature.

App11–008 Article 7

1. Each State Party shall take such measures as may be necessary to establish its jurisdiction over the offences set forth in article 2 when:

    (a) The offence is committed in the territory of that State;

    (b) The offence is committed on board a vessel flying the flag of that State or an aircraft registered under the laws of that State at the time the offence is committed;

    (c) The offence is committed by a national of that State.

2. A State Party may also establish its jurisdiction over any such offence when:

    (a) The offence was directed towards or resulted in the carrying out of an offence referred to in article 2, paragraph 1, subparagraph (a) or (b), in the territory of or against a national of that State;

    (b) The offence was directed towards or resulted in the carrying out of an offence referred to in article 2, paragraph 1, subparagraph (a) or (b), against a State or government facility of that State abroad, including diplomatic or consular premises of that State;

    (c) The offence was directed towards or resulted in an offence referred to in article 2, paragraph 1, subparagraph (a) or (b), committed in an attempt to compel that State to do or abstain from doing any act;

    (d) The offence is committed by a stateless person who has his or her habitual residence in the territory of that State;

    (e) The offence is committed on board an aircraft which is operated by the Government of that State.

3. Upon ratifying, accepting, approving or acceding to this Convention, each State Party shall notify the Secretary-General of the United Nations of the jurisdiction it has established in accordance with paragraph 2. Should any change take place, the State Party concerned shall immediately notify the Secretary-General.

4. Each State Party shall likewise take such measures as may be necessary to establish its jurisdiction over the offences set forth in article 2 in cases where the alleged offender is present in its territory and it does not extradite that person to any of the States Parties that have established their jurisdiction in accordance with paragraphs 1 or 2.

5. When more than one State Party claims jurisdiction over the offences set forth in article 2, the relevant States Parties shall strive to coordinate their actions appropriately, in particular concerning the conditions for prosecution and the modalities for mutual legal assistance.

6. Without prejudice to the norms of general international law, this Convention does not exclude the exercise of any criminal jurisdiction established by a State Party in accordance with its domestic law.

Article 8

1. Each State Party shall take appropriate measures, in accordance with its domestic legal principles, for the identification, detection and freezing or seizure of any funds used or allocated for the purpose of committing the offences set forth in article 2 as well as the proceeds derived from such offences, for purposes of possible forfeiture.

2. Each State Party shall take appropriate measures, in accordance with its domestic legal principles, for the forfeiture of funds used or allocated for the purpose of committing the offences set forth in article 2 and the proceeds derived from such offences.

3. Each State Party concerned may give consideration to concluding agreements on the sharing with other States Parties, on a regular or case-by-case basis, of the funds derived from the forfeitures referred to in this article.

4. Each State Party shall consider establishing mechanisms whereby the funds derived from the forfeitures referred to in this article are utilized to compensate the victims of offences referred to in article 2, paragraph 1, subparagraph (a) or (b), or their families.

5. The provisions of this article shall be implemented without prejudice to the rights of third parties acting in good faith.

Article 9

1. Upon receiving information that a person who has committed or who is alleged to have committed an offence set forth in article 2 may be present in its territory, the State Party concerned shall take such measures as may be necessary under its domestic law to investigate the facts contained in the information.

2. Upon being satisfied that the circumstances so warrant, the State Party in whose territory the offender or alleged offender is present shall take the appropriate measures under its domestic law so as to ensure that person=s presence for the purpose of prosecution or extradition.

3. Any person regarding whom the measures referred to in paragraph 2 are being taken shall be entitled to:

(a) Communicate without delay with the nearest appropriate representative of the State of which that person is a national or which is otherwise entitled to protect that person=s rights or, if that person is a stateless person, the State in the territory of which that person habitually resides;

(b) Be visited by a representative of that State;

(c) Be informed of that person=s rights under subparagraphs (a) and (b).

4. The rights referred to in paragraph 3 shall be exercised in conformity with the laws and regulations of the State in the territory of which the offender or alleged offender is present, subject to the provision that the said laws and regulations must enable full effect to be given to the purposes for which the rights accorded under paragraph 3 are intended.

5. The provisions of paragraphs 3 and 4 shall be without prejudice to the right of any State Party having a claim to jurisdiction in accordance with article 7, paragraph 1, subparagraph (b), or paragraph 2, subparagraph (b), to invite the International Committee of the Red Cross to communicate with and visit the alleged offender.

6. When a State Party, pursuant to the present article, has taken a person into custody, it shall immediately notify, directly or through the Secretary-General of the United Nations, the States Parties which have established jurisdiction in accordance

with article 7, paragraph 1 or 2, and, if it considers it advisable, any other interested States Parties, of the fact that such person is in custody and of the circumstances which warrant that person=s detention. The State which makes the investigation contemplated in paragraph 1 shall promptly inform the said States Parties of its findings and shall indicate whether it intends to exercise jurisdiction.

App11–011   **Article 10**

1. The State Party in the territory of which the alleged offender is present shall, in cases to which article 7 applies, if it does not extradite that person, be obliged, without exception whatsoever and whether or not the offence was committed in its territory, to submit the case without undue delay to its competent authorities for the purpose of prosecution, through proceedings in accordance with the laws of that State. Those authorities shall take their decision in the same manner as in the case of any other offence of a grave nature under the law of that State.

2. Whenever a State Party is permitted under its domestic law to extradite or otherwise surrender one of its nationals only upon the condition that the person will be returned to that State to serve the sentence imposed as a result of the trial or proceeding for which the extradition or surrender of the person was sought, and this State and the State seeking the extradition of the person agree with this option and other terms they may deem appropriate, such a conditional extradition or surrender shall be sufficient to discharge the obligation set forth in paragraph 1.

App11–012   **Article 11**

1. The offences set forth in article 2 shall be deemed to be included as extraditable offences in any extradition treaty existing between any of the States Parties before the entry into force of this Convention. States Parties undertake to include such offences as extraditable offences in every extradition treaty to be subsequently concluded between them.

2. When a State Party which makes extradition conditional on the existence of a treaty receives a request for extradition from another State Party with which it has no extradition treaty, the requested State Party may, at its option, consider this Convention as a legal basis for extradition in respect of the offences set forth in article 2. Extradition shall be subject to the other conditions provided by the law of the requested State.

3. States Parties which do not make extradition conditional on the existence of a treaty shall recognize the offences set forth in article 2 as extraditable offences between themselves, subject to the conditions provided by the law of the requested State.

4. If necessary, the offences set forth in article 2 shall be treated, for the purposes of extradition between States Parties, as if they had been committed not only in the place in which they occurred but also in the territory of the States that have established jurisdiction in accordance with article 7, paragraphs 1 and 2.

5. The provisions of all extradition treaties and arrangements between States Parties with regard to offences set forth in article 2 shall be deemed to be modified as between States Parties to the extent that they are incompatible with this Convention.

App11–013   **Article 12**

1. States Parties shall afford one another the greatest measure of assistance in connection with criminal investigations or criminal or extradition proceedings in respect of the offences set forth in article 2, including assistance in obtaining evidence in their possession necessary for the proceedings.

2. States Parties may not refuse a request for mutual legal assistance on the ground of bank secrecy.

3. The requesting Party shall not transmit nor use information or evidence furnished by the requested Party for investigations, prosecutions or proceedings other than those stated in the request without the prior consent of the requested Party.

4. Each State Party may give consideration to establishing mechanisms to share with other States Parties information or evidence needed to establish criminal, civil or administrative liability pursuant to article 5.

5. States Parties shall carry out their obligations under paragraphs 1 and 2 in conformity with any treaties or other arrangements on mutual legal assistance or information exchange that may exist between them. In the absence of such treaties or arrangements, States Parties shall afford one another assistance in accordance with their domestic law.

Article 13
App11–014

None of the offences set forth in article 2 shall be regarded, for the purposes of extradition or mutual legal assistance, as a fiscal offence. Accordingly, States Parties may not refuse a request for extradition or for mutual legal assistance on the sole ground that it concerns a fiscal offence.

Article 14
App11–015

None of the offences set forth in article 2 shall be regarded for the purposes of extradition or mutual legal assistance as a political offence or as an offence connected with a political offence or as an offence inspired by political motives. Accordingly, a request for extradition or for mutual legal assistance based on such an offence may not be refused on the sole ground that it concerns a political offence or an offence connected with a political offence or an offence inspired by political motives.

Article 15
App11–016

Nothing in this Convention shall be interpreted as imposing an obligation to extradite or to afford mutual legal assistance, if the requested State Party has substantial grounds for believing that the request for extradition for offences set forth in article 2 or for mutual legal assistance with respect to such offences has been made for the purpose of prosecuting or punishing a person on account of that person=s race, religion, nationality, ethnic origin or political opinion or that compliance with the request would cause prejudice to that person=s position for any of these reasons.

Article 16
App11–017

1. A person who is being detained or is serving a sentence in the territory of one State Party whose presence in another State Party is requested for purposes of identification, testimony or otherwise providing assistance in obtaining evidence for the investigation or prosecution of offences set forth in article 2 may be transferred if the following conditions are met:

    (a)   The person freely gives his or her informed consent;

    (b)   The competent authorities of both States agree, subject to such conditions as those States may deem appropriate.

2. For the purposes of the present article:

    (a)   The State to which the person is transferred shall have the authority and obligation to keep the person transferred in custody, unless otherwise requested or authorized by the State from which the person was transferred;

(b)   The State to which the person is transferred shall without delay implement its obligation to return the person to the custody of the State from which the person was transferred as agreed beforehand, or as otherwise agreed, by the competent authorities of both States;

(c)   The State to which the person is transferred shall not require the State from which the person was transferred to initiate extradition proceedings for the return of the person;

(d)   The person transferred shall receive credit for service of the sentence being served in the State from which he or she was transferred for time spent in the custody of the State to which he or she was transferred.

3. Unless the State Party from which a person is to be transferred in accordance with the present article so agrees, that person, whatever his or her nationality, shall not be prosecuted or detained or subjected to any other restriction of his or her personal liberty in the territory of the State to which that person is transferred in respect of acts or convictions anterior to his or her departure from the territory of the State from which such person was transferred.

App11–018   Article 17

Any person who is taken into custody or regarding whom any other measures are taken or proceedings are carried out pursuant to this Convention shall be guaranteed fair treatment, including enjoyment of all rights and guarantees in conformity with the law of the State in the territory of which that person is present and applicable provisions of international law, including international human rights law.

App11–019   Article 18

1. States Parties shall cooperate in the prevention of the offences set forth in article 2 by taking all practicable measures, *inter alia*, by adapting their domestic legislation, if necessary, to prevent and counter preparations in their respective territories for the commission of those offences within or outside their territories, including:

(a)   Measures to prohibit in their territories illegal activities of persons and organizations that knowingly encourage, instigate, organize or engage in the commission of offences set forth in article 2;

(b)   Measures requiring financial institutions and other professions involved in financial transactions to utilize the most efficient measures available for the identification of their usual or occasional customers, as well as customers in whose interest accounts are opened, and to pay special attention to unusual or suspicious transactions and report transactions suspected of stemming from a criminal activity. For this purpose, States Parties shall consider:

(i)   Adopting regulations prohibiting the opening of accounts the holders or beneficiaries of which are unidentified or unidentifiable, and measures to ensure that such institutions verify the identity of the real owners of such transactions;

(ii)   With respect to the identification of legal entities, requiring financial institutions, when necessary, to take measures to verify the legal existence and the structure of the customer by obtaining, either from a public register or from the customer or both, proof of incorporation, including information concerning the customer=s name, legal form, address, directors and provisions regulating the power to bind the entity;

(iii) Adopting regulations imposing on financial institutions the obligation to report promptly to the competent authorities all complex, unusual large transactions and unusual patterns of transactions, which have no apparent economic or obviously lawful purpose, without fear of assuming criminal or civil liability for breach of any restriction on disclosure of information if they report their suspicions in good faith;

(iv) Requiring financial institutions to maintain, for at least five years, all necessary records on transactions, both domestic or international.

2. States Parties shall further cooperate in the prevention of offences set forth in article 2 by considering:

(a) Measures for the supervision, including, for example, the licensing, of all money-transmission agencies;

(b) Feasible measures to detect or monitor the physical cross-border transportation of cash and bearer negotiable instruments, subject to strict safeguards to ensure proper use of information and without impeding in any way the freedom of capital movements.

3. States Parties shall further cooperate in the prevention of the offences set forth in article 2 by exchanging accurate and verified information in accordance with their domestic law and coordinating administrative and other measures taken, as appropriate, to prevent the commission of offences set forth in article 2, in particular by:

(a) Establishing and maintaining channels of communication between their competent agencies and services to facilitate the secure and rapid exchange of information concerning all aspects of offences set forth in article 2;

(b) Cooperating with one another in conducting inquiries, with respect to the offences set forth in article 2, concerning:

(i) The identity, whereabouts and activities of persons in respect of whom reasonable suspicion exists that they are involved in such offences;

(ii) The movement of funds relating to the commission of such offences.

4. States Parties may exchange information through the International Criminal Police Organization (Interpol).

Article 19   App11–020

The State Party where the alleged offender is prosecuted shall, in accordance with its domestic law or applicable procedures, communicate the final outcome of the proceedings to the Secretary-General of the United Nations, who shall transmit the information to the other States Parties.

Article 20   App11–021

The States Parties shall carry out their obligations under this Convention in a manner consistent with the principles of sovereign equality and territorial integrity of States and that of non-intervention in the domestic affairs of other States.

App11–022 **Article 21**

Nothing in this Convention shall affect other rights, obligations and responsibilities of States and individuals under international law, in particular the purposes of the Charter of the United Nations, international humanitarian law and other relevant conventions.

App11–023 **Article 22**

Nothing in this Convention entitles a State Party to undertake in the territory of another State Party the exercise of jurisdiction or performance of functions which are exclusively reserved for the authorities of that other State Party by its domestic law.

App11–024 **Article 23**

1. The annex may be amended by the addition of relevant treaties that:

    (a) Are open to the participation of all States;

    (b) Have entered into force;

    (c) Have been ratified, accepted, approved or acceded to by at least twenty-two States Parties to the present Convention.

2. After the entry into force of this Convention, any State Party may propose such an amendment. Any proposal for an amendment shall be communicated to the depositary in written form. The depositary shall notify proposals that meet the requirements of paragraph 1 to all States Parties and seek their views on whether the proposed amendment should be adopted.

3. The proposed amendment shall be deemed adopted unless one third of the States Parties object to it by a written notification not later than 180 days after its circulation.

4. The adopted amendment to the annex shall enter into force 30 days after the deposit of the twenty-second instrument of ratification, acceptance or approval of such amendment for all those States Parties having deposited such an instrument. For each State Party ratifying, accepting or approving the amendment after the deposit of the twenty-second instrument, the amendment shall enter into force on the thirtieth day after deposit by such State Party of its instrument of ratification, acceptance or approval.

App11–025 **Article 24**

1. Any dispute between two or more States Parties concerning the interpretation or application of this Convention which cannot be settled through negotiation within a reasonable time shall, at the request of one of them, be submitted to arbitration. If, within six months from the date of the request for arbitration, the parties are unable to agree on the organization of the arbitration, any one of those parties may refer the dispute to the International Court of Justice, by application, in conformity with the Statute of the Court.

2. Each State may at the time of signature, ratification, acceptance or approval of this Convention or accession thereto declare that it does not consider itself bound by paragraph 1. The other States Parties shall not be bound by paragraph 1 with respect to any State Party which has made such a reservation.

3. Any State which has made a reservation in accordance with paragraph 2 may at any time withdraw that reservation by notification to the Secretary-General of the United Nations.

Article 25

1. This Convention shall be open for signature by all States from 10 January 2000 to 31 December 2001 at United Nations Headquarters in New York.

2. This Convention is subject to ratification, acceptance or approval. The instruments of ratification, acceptance or approval shall be deposited with the Secretary-General of the United Nations.

3. This Convention shall be open to accession by any State. The instruments of accession shall be deposited with the Secretary-General of the United Nations.

Article 26

1. This Convention shall enter into force on the thirtieth day following the date of the deposit of the twenty-second instrument of ratification, acceptance, approval or accession with the Secretary-General of the United Nations.

2. For each State ratifying, accepting, approving or acceding to the Convention after the deposit of the twenty-second instrument of ratification, acceptance, approval or accession, the Convention shall enter into force on the thirtieth day after deposit by such State of its instrument of ratification, acceptance, approval or accession.

Article 27

1. Any State Party may denounce this Convention by written notification to the Secretary-General of the United Nations.

2. Denunciation shall take effect one year following the date on which notification is received by the Secretary-General of the United Nations.

Article 28

The original of this Convention, of which the Arabic, Chinese, English, French, Russian and Spanish texts are equally authentic, shall be deposited with the Secretary-General of the United Nations who shall send certified copies thereof to all States.

IN WITNESS WHEREOF, the undersigned, being duly authorized thereto by their respective Governments, have signed this Convention, opened for signature at United Nations Headquarters in New York on 10 January 2000.

Annex

1. Convention for the Suppression of Unlawful Seizure of Aircraft, done at The Hague on 16 December 1970.

2. Convention for the Suppression of Unlawful Acts against the Safety of Civil Aviation, done at Montreal on 23 September 1971.

3. Convention on the Prevention and Punishment of Crimes against Internationally Protected Persons, including Diplomatic Agents, adopted by the General Assembly of the United Nations on 14 December 1973.

4. International Convention against the Taking of Hostages, adopted by the General Assembly of the United Nations on 17 December 1979.

5. Convention on the Physical Protection of Nuclear Material, adopted at Vienna on 3 March 1980.

6. Protocol for the Suppression of Unlawful Acts of Violence at Airports Serving International Civil Aviation, supplementary to the Convention for the Suppression of Unlawful Acts against the Safety of Civil Aviation, done at Montreal on 24 February 1988.

7. Convention for the Suppression of Unlawful Acts against the Safety of Maritime Navigation, done at Rome on 10 March 1988.

8. Protocol for the Suppression of Unlawful Acts against the Safety of Fixed Platforms located on the Continental Shelf, done at Rome on 10 March 1988.

9. International Convention for the Suppression of Terrorist Bombings, adopted by the General Assembly of the United Nations on 15 December 1997.

INDEX